B.F. SKINNER

Consensus and Controversy

EDITED BY

Sohan Modgil, PhD

Reader in Educational Research and Development
Brighton Polytechnic

AND

Celia Modgil, PhD

Senior Lecturer in Educational Psychology
London University

REFLECTIONS

BY

B.F. Skinner

Harvard University

Falmer Press

(A member of the Taylor & Francis Group)
(New York, Philadelphia and London)

USA   The Falmer Press, Taylor & Francis Inc., 242 Cherry Street, Philadelphia, PA 19106-1906

UK   The Falmer Press, Falmer House, Barcombe, Lewes, East Sussex, BN8 5DL

First published in 1987
Reprinted 1988

Library of Congress Cataloging in Publication Data

Main entry under title:

B. F. Skinner: consensus and controversy.

(Falmer international masterminds challenge)
1. Behaviorism (Psychology). 2. Human behavior.
3. Skinner, B. F. (Burrhus Frederic), 1904– .
I. Modgil, Sohan. II. Modgil, Celia. III. Series.
BF199.B2 1986   150.19′434   86-13518
ISBN 1-85000-026-3

Jacket design by Caroline Archer

Typeset in 10/12 Times
by Imago Publishing Ltd., Thame, Oxon.

Printed in Great Britain by Taylor & Francis (Printers) Ltd, Rankine Road, Basingstoke, Hants.

Contributors

Dr Sohan Modgil   and   Dr Celia Modgil
Brighton Polytechnic   University of London

Professor B.F. Skinner
Harvard University

Professor Willard Day
University of Nevada, Reno

Professor Roger Schnaitter
Illinois Wesleyan University

Dr James Wright
University of Leeds

Professor Richard Creel
Ithaca College, USA

Professor Marc Richelle
Université de Liège

Professor Howard Rachlin
State University of New York
  at Stony Brook

Professor John Hinson
Washington State University

Professor Steven Hayes
Professor Aaron Brownstein
University of Nevada-Reno

Dr Ullin Place
University of Leeds

Dr Geoffrey Hall
University of York

Professor J. Jacques Vonèche
University of Geneva

Dr Douglas Bethlehem
University of Leeds

Professor Michael Wessells
Randolph-Macon College, USA

Dr Henry Plotkin
University College London

Professor Hugh Lacey
Professor Barry Schwartz
Swarthmore College

Professor John Malone Jr
University of Tennessee

Professor Peter Killeen
Arizona State University

Professor Daniel Dennett
Tufts University

v

Dr Margaret Vaughan
Salem State College, Massachusetts

Professor Terry Knapp
University of Nevada, Las Vegas

Professor Gerald Zuriff
Wheaton College, USA

Dr Robert Epstein
Boston University and
 Cambridge Centre for Behavioral
 Studies, Massachusetts

Professor Linda Parrott
Saint Mary's University in
 Halifax, Canada

Dr Lynn Robertson
University of California, Davis

Professor Richard Garrett
Bentley College, USA

Professor W. Miller Brown
Trinity College Connecticut

Drs Sohan and Celia Modgil
Brighton Polytechnic and
University of London

Acknowledgments

The undertaking of this volume in the *Falmer International Master-Minds Challenged* Psychology Series was only possible in collaboration with the numerous distinguished contributors herein. We are greatly indebted to them for demonstrating their trust by accepting our invitation to join forces to provide statements of how Skinner's theory is seen in relation to particular disciplines.

The volume has been greatly enhanced by the recognition given to it by B.F. Skinner, who increased our confidence in the project by kindly agreeing to contribute. We thank Professor Skinner for his very kind and generous support and for his edifying contribution to the content.

We are further grateful to Falmer Press, a member of the Taylor and Francis group. We express our very sincere gratitude to Malcolm Clarkson, Managing Director, Falmer Press.

Sohan and Celia Modgil
February 1986

Contents

To
Gita, Ramayana, Kush-Luv, Radha and Krishan Arjuan
with love

Part I: Introduction

1.   B.F. Skinner:
Consensus and Controversy

SOHAN AND CELIA MODGIL

INTRODUCTION

During the last fifty years, B.F. Skinner's brilliant contribution to knowledge has been well-known world-wide. From the early transmission, his work has not been without its critics. Naturally, criticisms persist, although his work continues to be frequently acknowledged with great admiration in the channels of psychology. With such prolific work, it would seem justified to consider the discrepancies, the omissions, together with the various interpretations which have been and are currently being highlighted.

The recent issue (1984) of *The Behavioural and Brain Sciences: An International Journal of Current Research and Theory with Open Peer Commentary* has provided an excellent forerunner to a wider directed analysis of Skinner's work and its place in the evolution of psychology.

Catania (1984), who co-edited the particular issue of *The Behavioural and Brain Sciences*, maintains:

> Of all contemporary psychologists, B.F. Skinner is perhaps the most honoured and the most maligned, the most widely recognised and the most misrepresented, the most cited and the most misunderstood. Some still say that he is a stimulus-response psychologist (he is not); some still say that stimulus-response chains play a central role in his treatment of verbal behaviour (they do not); some still say that he disavows evolutionary determinants of behaviour (he does not). These and other misconceptions are common and sometimes even appear in psychology texts (e.g. Todd and Morris 1983). How did they come about, and why do they continue? Although the present *Behavioural and Brain Sciences* treatments will probably not provide an answer, they may help to clarify some of the misunderstandings. (p. 473)

The *Behavioural and Brain Sciences* journal is arranged in sections according to the reproduction of key papers by Skinner, each followed by an open peer commentary, concluding with a response by Skinner to the various commentaries in the section.

1

The first but most recent, 'Selection by Consequences' ('Consequences', Skinner 1981), relates operant theory to other disciplines, and in particular to biology and anthropology. The second, 'Methods and Theories in the Experimental Analysis of Behaviour' ('Methods'), outlines some of the basic concepts of operant theory in the context of a discussion of methodological and theoretical issues; it is an amalgamation of revised versions of 'The Flight from the Laboratory' (Skinner 1961) and 'Are Theories of Learning Necessary?' (Skinner 1950) and a portion of the preface to *Contingencies of Reinforcement* (Skinner 1969). 'The Operational Analysis of Psychological Terms' ('Terms', Skinner 1945) is the earliest work treated; its special concern is with the language of private events, and many features of Skinner's analysis of verbal behaviour are implicit in it. 'An Operant Analysis of Problem Solving' ('Problem Solving', Skinner 1966a), continues the interpretation of verbal behaviour in distinguishing between rule-governed and contingency-shaped behaviour. 'Behaviourism at Fifty' ('Behaviourism — 50', Skinner 1963) addresses the status of behaviourism as a philosophy of science, and points out some of the difficulties that must be overcome by any science of behaviour. 'The Phylogeny and Ontogeny of Behaviour' ('Phylogeny', Skinner 1966b) ... considers how evolutionary variables combine with those operating within an organism's lifetime to determine its behaviour. (Catania, *op. cit.*, p. 473)

CONTINUING THE DEBATE: THE STRATEGY OF THE BOOK

This book continues the evaluation of elements of Skinner's work from the perspectives of a range of areas: radical behaviourism; the epistemology of radical behaviourism; a psychological analysis with political, social and moral implications; philosophy of science and psychology; variation and selection; the explanatory power of Skinnerian principles; the unit of behaviour; Skinner's position against theory and against mentalism; the 'Virtus Dormitiva' argument; rule-governed behaviour; perception/cognition; and naturalistic ethics. It aims to provide in a single source the most recent 'crosscurrents and crossfire', to begin to clarify the contribution of Skinner to the evolution of the understanding of human behaviour.

The volume attempts to provide theoretical analysis supported by research of aspects of Skinner's work, presented predominantly either positively or negatively by *pairs* of distinguished academics representing particular areas of knowledge. The *paired* contributions have been exchanged, through the editors, to provide an opportunity for both parties to refute the 'heart' of the opposing paper. This would perhaps go some way towards the prescription that what the study of human behaviour needs at this stage of its own development is a wide-ranging approach to the facts, furthering the hope that this growth will continue so as to include an openness to the evidence outside Skinner's own framework.

Although axiomatic, it would be expedient to emphasize that the labelling 'predominantly positive' or 'predominantly negative' implies that the writer of the predominantly 'positive' chapter agrees in the *main* with the theory but is not in *entire* agreement, therefore being allowed some latitude towards disagreement. Likewise, 'negative' chapters mean that contributors *predominantly* but not *entirely* disagree, with the theory, therefore permitting some latitude towards agreement. The interchange of chapters therefore produce points of consensus and points of controversy.

The difficulties in this ambitious debate project are not minimized. Although every attempt has been made to achieve precision matching of pairs, in exceptional cases one of the contributors within a matched pair has followed a 'middle

course'. This established itself as a 'contrasting' enough pair to lend itself to the debate format of the book.

Although the editors dictated the generic topics to be debated, the contributors were free to focus on any inherent aspect or specialization of their own. Again, however, the consequent interchange of the chapters allows formulation of points of consensus and of controversy, therefore retaining the thrust of the debate.

The choice of the contributors was restricted to those who are objectively critical and who are knowledgeable about the theory. Some of the most publicized critics tend to have non-scientific axes to grind and their views and their polemics are well-known. The scholarly value of the book could be seriously damaged unless the contributors have the desire and the capacity for the kind of intellectual honesty needed to come to grips seriously with the scientific, psychological and social issues raised by the theory.

CONTENTS OF EACH CONTRIBUTION

The opening chapter by Skinner provides further initiation and his comments stimulate and provoke the reader to engage in the debate. Skinner states, 'In what sense is my work controversial? When I am asked what I regard as my most important contribution, I always say "the original experimental analysis of operant behaviour and its subsequent extension to more and more complex cases." I see nothing controversial about that. Either my results have been confirmed or they have not. At times I have made mistakes and no doubt other flaws will be found in my work, but for the most part I think it stands.'

Radical Behaviourism

An answer to the question 'What is Radical Behaviourism?' is approached by looking at examples of professional writing in which the expression 'radical behaviourism' is used. Willard Day examines three examples of professional philosophical usage. Professional psychological usage was sampled by the following method: subject-matter indexes for *Psychological Abstracts* were searched for topic descriptions actually containing 'radical behaviourism.' In this way 28 publications were identified, and it was their usage of 'radical behaviourism' that Day illustrates here. A classification of seven non-mutually-exclusive categories was devised. These categories involved conceptions of radical behaviourism as (1) basically a theory of learning; (2) bearing similarities to phenomenology; (3) an original formulation derived from earlier work; (4) encompassing an analysis of private events; (5) intrinsically connected with the experimental analysis of behaviour; (6) manifesting the applied aspects of Skinner's work: and (7) the philosophical dimensions of Skinner's thought.

Two major claims have been made for Skinner's radical behaviourism: first that it has generated an effective science of behaviour based on experimental work with non-human animals; second that this science can be used to predict, control, and interpret the everyday behaviour of our own species. Geoffrey Hall asserts that a critical examination of these claims reveals grounds for scepticism.

With respect to the first, it is argued that Skinner's notion of operant conditioning is much less powerful than might be supposed in that it ignores or undervalues the importance of other determinants of behaviour. With respect to the second, it is argued that Skinner's analysis of human behaviour consists, for the most part, not of the application of science as it is usually understood, but in the reinterpretation of human facts in the terminology of determinism and antimentalism. The case for such a reinterpretation is weakened by the extent to which it relies upon the inadequate science of operant behaviour.

The Epistemology of Radical Behaviourism

With particular reference to the epistemology of radical behaviourism, Roger Schnaitter states that Skinner's naturalistic psychology focuses on the adaptation of organisms to their world. According to such a view, knowledge consists of the capacities of the knowing organism to act with regard to the world. Schnaitter maintains that actions themselves are categories whose most basic feature is a relation between the external effects of what the acting organism does and certain reciprocal causal consequences of these external effects on the actor. If these premises of Skinner's are correct, then knowledge must consist, not of certain internal mental possessions of the knower, but of a set of causal inter-relationships through which the knower stands to its world. In another sense, however, the inner states of the knower are fundamental to the behavioural analysis of knowledge, for such inner states provide the material means of sustaining any causal relationship in which the organism stands. J. Jacques Vonèche argues that the classical criticisms levelled against Skinner's position miss the point of Skinner's epistemology, and Vonèche formulates criticisms of a strictly epistemological nature: following Piaget (1942), Vonèche's arguments are both logical *and* sociological. Vonèche concludes that the most pathetic error of behaviourism is that it wants to get rid of the most fundamental principle of any science: the world is not well-known and our relation to it is not primary.

A Psychological Analysis: Political, Social and Moral Implications

Skinner has advocated an all-embracing behavioural technology that has relevance to all aspects of our everyday existence. By eschewing a reductionist philosophy, argues James Wright, Skinner has been able to encourage and contribute to legitimizing the study of behaviour at its own level — the proper study of behaviour is *behaviour*. The value of the insistence on this course is fully appreciated when we consider the current pervasiveness of applied operant work. As Skinner's ideas and philosophy become more widely known his overall system receives more intense scrutiny, especially in terms of ethical and socio-political ramifications. Acknowledging the important contributions of Skinner to scientific psychology, particularly the research and thought that went into his work on operant conditioning and schedules of reinforcement, and, to a lesser extent, in his *Verbal Behaviour*, Douglas Bethlehem argues that unhappily he [Skinner] has always been superficial philosophically, and that shortcoming somewhat limits the value of his scientific contribution, and with his lack of artistic insight, almost

entirely vitiates his extensive writing on politics, ethics, philosophy and art. Bethlehem further considers that Skinner's epistemology is confused, and because he has not grappled sufficiently with the philosophy of science, he is unable to see the shortcomings of his own theorizing or the merits of others'. His appreciation of political philosophy is scanty enough for him to put forward ideas which are superficially benign, but which have totalitarian implications which he himself does not see.

Philosophy of Science and Psychology

Skinner insists that the study of the nature of science should be empirical rather than conceptual. Richard Creel states that our most adequate understanding of the nature of science will be achieved by studying the behaviour distinctive of scientists and identifying the reinforcers that bring it about. The most distinctive reinforcer of scientific behaviour is the newly discovered causal relation. Creel argues that because the larger community depends so heavily on scientific activity for its welfare, it seeks to identify those individuals who are most responsive to newly discovered causal relations, to strengthen and shape their behaviour toward making such discoveries, and to monitor the integrity and safety of their behaviour. This understanding of science provides an illuminating framework within which to expound the nature of explanation, theory, interpretation, technology, and the laboratory. In concluding his contribution, Creel states reasons as to why science has eclipsed so quickly the other approaches to the acquisition of knowledge and why it will continue to do so. Michael Wessells recognizes that Skinner's philosophy of science consists of conceptual imperatives regarding the proper way to analyze behaviour. Wessells argues that while he advocates the functional analysis of the external variables that control behaviour, he rejects mentalistic theories, statistical analysis, hypothesis-testing and inferred theoretical constructs. His philosophy also views philosophical and scientific verbal behaviour as phenomena to be explained via a functional analysis of verbal behaviour. Unfortunately, Skinner's functional analysis of verbal behaviour lacks the extensive empirical base required for his sweeping revision of philosophy. Wessells, in continuation, considers that Skinner's psychological analysis of philosophy stands on philosophical assumptions regarding explanation which cannot be justified from within his system. Being highly pragmatic, he overemphasizes the study of accessible variables, and this leads him to confuse explanation with prediction and control and to reject inferred processes, which have played an important explanatory role in other sciences.

Variation and Selection

With particular reference to variation and selection: the evolutionary analogy in Skinner's theory, Marc Richelle discusses the misrepresentations of Skinner's position towards biology — the 'black box' psychology, the extreme environmentalism and the neglect of species-specific behaviour. Richelle argues that reference to Darwin in Skinner's work is crucial both in suggesting an alternative to intentionality in explaining behaviour and in offering a model of individual behavioural

changes in terms of *variation* and *selection*. Richelle proposes reasons as to why the *variation* aspect of the learning process has been neglected, together with some arguments in favour of the evolutionary analogy, be it only for its heuristic merits. The relevance of Skinner's model with respect to the evolution of learning capacities is compared with the relevance of other current views, and some convergences are noted between Skinner on one hand and Piaget and Lorenz on the other. While recognizing that Skinner is one of a distinguished line of psychologists who have used what is known of the process of evolution as a model to guide thinking about the problems of learning, Henry Plotkin, however, argues that unlike other exponents of the analogy Skinner was never able to use it to real effect, either analytically or empirically. The main reason for this is the refusal of a radical behaviourist to entertain the importance of postulating the existence of unobservable determinants of learned behaviour. This deprived him both of a theoretical position of any significance and also of one which might have generated interesting experimental questions.

The Explanatory Power of Skinnerian Principles

Howard Rachlin maintains that as judged against three other psychological viewpoints, mentalism, cognitivism and physiologism, Skinner's radical behaviourism has great explanatory power: it is internally coherent and, especially in its recent development, expressible in quantitative terms; it has a firm laboratory base in which its principles clearly apply; it is not grossly implausible; most importantly, it has meaningful application both in relatively simple real-world situations (such as prisons, factories and armies) where control of human behaviour has been largely unidirectional and in relatively complex real-world situations (such as families) where control of human behaviour has been multidirectional. In both simple and complex real-world situations the explanatory power of radical behaviourism is much greater than that of the other three viewpoints. However, when considering whether principles generated in Skinner's radical behaviourist research programme eventually, in principle, provide explanations of all human behaviour, Hugh Lacey and Barry Schwartz believe that their answer is negative. They demonstrate why a provisional answer to this question is important. Second, they argue that an appropriate argument for the inherently limited explanatory power of behaviourist principles derives from the positive achievements of an alternative explanatory scheme. Lacey and Schwartz detail what the relevant achievements are, and argue that they are met by the scheme of ordinary teleological explanation. They demonstrate how their argument is associated with a coherent account of the nature of the human person, which conflicts with that which is at the foundation of the radical behaviourist research programme.

The Unit of Behaviour

John Hinson points out that Skinner's operant theory is often mistakenly identified as the commonsense application of the principles of reward and punishment to the study of behaviour. Hinson further considers that Skinner's philosophy of

radical behaviourism is generally either dismissed or believed to be irrelevant to the application of the technical innovations of operant conditioning. In reality, Skinner's operant theory follows directly from his philosophy of radical behaviourism. This philosophy has helped Skinner to avoid the conceptual errors of the alternative theories of his predecessors and contemporaries. The best illustration of Skinner's conceptual analysis is in his treatment of the problem of determining behavioural units of analysis, which appeared in the early works laying the foundation for modern operant theory. Comparison of Skinner's position with the once dominant position of Hull, shows why operant theory, based on radical behaviourism, ultimately achieved superiority. While acknowledging that Skinner provided a promising alternative to associationist and cognitive theories in his analysis of the behavioural unit, published in the thirties, John Malone argues that Skinner seemed to fail to grasp the important aspects of his own analysis and, paradoxically, he emphasized molecular interpretations over many years. Malone considers that this was incompatible with his early analysis and with the defining characteristics of the research programme that has developed under his guidance. One consequence has been the tendency of recent critics, including those expert in the field, to see no difference of substance between his views and those of S-R associationism. Several crucial considerations suggest that the basic terminology used in the analysis of behaviour may contribute to this misunderstanding. Despite obvious dangers, the use of behavioural terms other than those used in basic conditioning research could have great advantages. Chief among these would be the decreased likelihood that the analysis of behaviour will be confused with discredited S-R theory.

Skinner's Position against Theory and against Mentalism

The purpose of the paper by Steven Hayes and Aaron Brownstein is to examine critical issues in psychological analysis in view of recent criticisms of the behavioural approach which seem to suggest a more rapid path to the 'as-yet-unexplained'. Hayes and Brownstein examine the purposes of science, the nature of explanation, the role of private events, and the objection to mentalism. Their main thrust is that behaviour analysis is a powerful and viable approach to psychology when evaluated against its own goals. Peter Killeen examines Skinner's objections to mentalism and concludes that his only valid objections concern the 'specious explanations' that mentalism might afford — explanations that are incomplete, circular, or faulty in other ways. Unfortunately, the mere adoption of behaviouristic terminology does not solve that problem. It camouflages the nature of 'private events', while providing no protection from specious explanations. Killeen argues that covert states and events *are* causally effective, and may be sufficiently different in their nature to deserve a name other than 'behaviour'. To call such events 'mental' does not force a dualistic metaphysics; such a distinction can be easily assimilated by an 'emergent behaviourism'. Emergent behaviourism would make explicit use of theories; it would be inductive and pragmatic, and would evaluate hypothetical constructs in terms of their utility in identifying and solving the outstanding problems of the discipline.

The 'Virtus Dormitiva' Argument

In 'Skinner Skinned', Dennett (1978, Ch. 4) discusses two arguments, the *virtus dormitiva* and intentionality arguments, which he sees as the only solid ground underlying the various arguments which Skinner gives for repudiating the use of mentalistic explanations in a scientific psychology; and of these he endorses only the intentionality argument. Ullin Place argues, (1) that what Skinner finds objectionable in mentalistic idioms is their dispositional character, (2) that both the *virtus dormitiva* and intentionality arguments are arguments against the use of dispositional property ascriptions in scientific explanation, and (3) that, since dispositional property ascriptions are essential to any causal explanation, Dennett has failed to provide any good reason for endorsing Skinner's repudiation of mentalism. It is suggested that mentalism is objectionable only insofar as it involves the use of idioms which presuppose what Skinner (1969) calls 'rule-governed' behaviour to explain behaviour that is 'contingency-shaped'. Daniel Dennett formulates a reply entitled 'Skinner Placed', in which he suggests that his previous writings have been misinterpreted by Place. Dennett therefore attempts to set out more straightforwardly what he takes the issues to be as they arise in Place's paper. This permits a summary of the joint and several objections he and Place have raised to Skinner's work. It is agreed that Skinner has not given a good reason to shun dispositional properties; that mentalistic explanations can have their place in science; and superficially agreed that mentalistic explanations pre-suppose rationality and this is what creates the problems about their status in psychology. Dennett considers that the question for Skinner in his opinion is that of all the criticisms he has levelled against 'mentalism', which strikes him (Skinner) as most important, most telling?

Rule-Governed Behaviour

Rule-governed behaviour was first discussed by Skinner in 1947 when he gave the distinguished William James Lectures at Harvard University. At this time he talked about such behaviour in terms of conditioning the behaviour of the listener — to explain the behaviour of the speaker. It was not until 1965 that Skinner first referred to this behaviour as rule-governed. Margaret Vaughan maintains that in doing so he opened up a new area of investigation. 'Now, twenty years later, rule-governed behaviour is emerging as a critical class of behaviour in analyzing complex human behaviour. The descriptive power of the concept is especially revealing when one is analyzing ... higher mental processes' — such as thinking and problem-solving. As a result of such an analysis, much of the behaviour actually studied by cognitive psychologists as higher mental activity is brought within the realm of a science of behaviour, subject to measurement in physical dimensions. However, Linda Parrott argues that in order to account for the control exerted by rules, rule-governed behaviour must be conceptualized as contingency-shaped behaviour. As such, the only distinction between rule-governed behaviour and contingency-shaped behaviour is that the antecedent stimuli in the former case are always verbal. The significance of this distinction is not fully appreciated by Skinner, however, owing to problems in his analysis of verbal behaviour. Specifically, while verbal episodes are not assumed to exemplify

relations of references, a referential interpretation of rules is made, despite the fact that rules are simply products of verbal behaviour. One result of this confusion is the absence of a satisfactory account of rule-following activity. Parrott further argues that this contradiction may be resolved by adopting a non-mentalistic concept of reference applicable to both verbal behaviour and rule governance. By this means an important distinction between rule-governed and contingency-shaped behaviour may be sustained, and the events of rule following may be explained.

Perception/Cognition

Skinner's analysis of perceptual processes and the problems of perception has been, unlike his many other contributions, largely ignored by the psychology community. Terry Knapp states that Skinner has published relevant papers and research on both visual and auditory 'perception', has articulated a critical analysis of a widely accepted theory of perception, and has offered an analysis of perception as stimulus control through differential reinforcement of discriminative responding. Skinner has suggested an analysis of 'seeing' as behaviour, and traced the implications of respondent and operant conditioning when applied to seeing as a response. Operant psychology's objections to a science of cognition are evaluated with reference to recent evidence showing that 'insightful' behaviour in pigeons can be predicted from an animal's reinforcement history (Epstein, Kirshnit, Lanza and Rubin, 1984). Lynn Robertson argues, with reference to [Epstein *et al.*] data, that the previous history may activate perceptual mechanisms which allow relationships to take place where no relationships previously existed, and that relation formation requires an internal process. These mechanisms are best described at a cognitive level of analysis when cognitive issues are involved and need not be reduced to neurophysiology as is often suggested by operant psychologists. To support this contention, Robertson discusses the rationale for a cognitive psychology.

Naturalistic Ethics

Skinner's system of ethics is naturalistic in the sense that he proposes to derive ethical statements from scientific statements of facts about contingencies of reinforcement and survival. However, Gerry Zuriff argues that it is not naturalistic in the stronger sense of giving a naturalistic justification for these derivations. Attempts at such a justification based on the current practices of our verbal community fail because they do not provide resolutions of conflicts among value communities, among individuals, or among reinforcements. Zuriff therefore debates that Skinner's ethical system is either a prediction about the future deduced from his science of behaviour, or it is a recommendation not logically derived from that science. A suggested behavioural analysis of ethical judgments conceptualizes them as 'generalized contingency establishing verbal responses' and reveals the relationship between ethics and a science of behaviour. Richard Garrett's paper defends Skinner's contention that his principles of psychology permit us to bridge the is/ought gap. The paper seeks to demonstrate how it is possible to

reason legitimately from the psychological-is of Skinner's principles to the moral-ought of practical reason. Garrett argues that in order to do this, however, it was first necessary to show that Skinner himself has not done this. Garrett's paper is divided into two parts. In the first it is argued that Skinner has not disarmed Karl Popper's version of what is sometimes called the 'open-question argument' and that indeed the open-question argument, when turned on Skinner's own analysis, really does expose an inadequate grounding of his genuinely moral claim. In the second part it is argued that Skinner's confidence in the use of his principles as a means of bridging the is/ought gap is nonetheless warranted. In particular, it is argued that his psychological principles, if true, offer us excellent reasons for saying that the moral act, norm or culture (or community) is the one that regards everyone as an end and which, therefore, everyone has a reason to support (viz. is universalizable). These are approximations to Kant's principles, which no one doubts are genuine moral-oughts. But if so, then to the extent that such principles can be derived from Skinner's psychology, Skinner is right in thinking the is/ought gap can be bridged by his psychology after all.

Robert Epstein and W. Miller Brown add further general remarks to the various topics under debate.

A tabulated summary of the various debates, arranged in accordance with the areas of knowledge which the debators represent, has been provided at the end of the book.

REFERENCES

Behavioural and Brain Sciences (1984) *An International Journal of Current Research and Theory with Open Peer Commentary*, 7, 4, pp. 473–701.

Catania, A.C. (1984) 'The operant behaviourism of B.F. Skinner', *Behavioural and Brain Sciences*, 7, 4, p. 473.

Dennett, D. (1978) *Brainstorms*, MIT Press and Harvester, Chs. 1 'Intentional Systems' and 4 'Skinner Skinned'.

Epstein, R., Kirshnit, C.E., Lanza, R.P., and Rubin, L.C. (1984) 'Insights in the pigeon: Antecedents and determinants of an intelligent performance', *Nature*, pp. 61–2.

Piaget, J. (1942) *La Psychologie de l'Intelligence*, Paris, Armand Colin.

Skinner, B.F. (1945) 'The operational analysis of psychological terms', *Psychological Review*, 42, pp. 270–7, 291–4.

Skinner, B.F. (1950) 'Are theories of learning necessary?' *Psychological Review*, 57, pp. 193–216.

Skinner, B.F. (1961) 'The flight from the laboratory', in Dennis, W. *et al.* (Ed.), *Current Trends in Psychological Theory*, University of Pittsburgh Press.

Skinner, B.F. (1963) 'Behaviourism at fifty', *Science*, 140, pp. 951–8.

Skinner, B.F. (1966a) 'An operant analysis of problem solving', in Kleinmuntz, B. (Ed.). *Problem Solving: Research, Methods and Theory*, Chichester, John Wiley and Sons.

Skinner, B.F. (1966b) 'Phylogeny and ontogeny of behaviour', *Science*, 153, pp. 1205–13.

Skinner, B.F. (1969) *Contingencies of Reinforcement: A Theoretical Analysis*, London, Prentice-Hall

Skinner, B.F. (1981) 'Selection by consequences', *Science*, 213, pp. 501–4.

Todd, J.T., and Morris, E.K. (1983) 'Misconception and miseducation: Presentations of radical behaviourism in psychology textbooks', *Behaviour Analyst*, 6, pp. 153–60.

Part II: Reflections

2. Controversy?

B.F. SKINNER

In what sense is my work controversial? When I am asked what I regard as my most important contribution, I always say, 'the original experimental analysis of operant behavior and its subsequent extension to more and more complex cases.' I see nothing controversial about that. Either my results have been confirmed or they have not. At times I have made mistakes and no doubt other flaws will be found in my work, but for the most part I think it stands.

My *Verbal Behavior* has been called controversial, and in one accepted sense of the word perhaps it is, but most of the argumentation is due to a misunderstanding. The book is not about language. A language is a verbal environment, which shapes and maintains verbal behavior. As an environment, it is composed of listeners. Linguists have usually studied listening rather than speaking (a typical question is why a sentence makes sense), but *Verbal Behavior* is an interpretation of the behavior of the *speaker*, given the contingencies of reinforcement maintained by the community. It uses principles drawn from the experimental analysis of non-verbal behavior — and nothing else. So far as I am concerned, the only question is whether the interpretation is adequate, but that is not the question raised in the supposed controversy. Those who want to analyze language as the expression of ideas, the transmission of information, or the communication of meaning naturally employ different concepts. Whether they work better is a question, but is it a controversy?

I would make the same point about *Walden Two*, *Science and Human Behavior*, and *Beyond Freedom and Dignity*, in which principles drawn from the experimental analysis are used to interpret other facts of daily life. The differences between my interpretations and those to be found in political science, economics, theology, philosophy, and so on, may be argued, as one argues differences between one political theory and another, one religious principle and another, or one philosophy and another, but so far as I am concerned, the only useful question is whether I have successfully done the job I set out to do. Whether it can be done better in a different way is a question worth raising, but it is not a matter of controversy about my work.

I am not trying to place my work above criticism. On the contrary, as in all sciences, both laboratory practices and concepts and principles need to be constantly examined, but I see no point in *arguing* with those who want to do things in a different way.

Part III: Radical Behaviorism

3.   What Is Radical Behaviorism?

WILLARD F. DAY

I still like my own definition of 'radical behaviorism' better than any other I have seen yet: 'radical behaviorism is the effect that Skinner's thought happens to have on the behavior of people' (Day, 1983, p. 101). What I really like about this definition is that it is *behavioral*: in essence it is a general, or shorthand, description of a particular set of contingencies. I shall return to this definition at the end of this chapter.

Throughout this chapter I will be primarily concerned with illustrating how professional people use the expression 'radical behaviorism' in their published work. I will first consider some writing by philosophers in which the expression 'radical behaviorism' is contained. Then I will turn to professional psychological writing over the past thirty years. In order to distill this enormous amount of relevant material down to manageable size, I will make use of a method of sampling the literature which generated twenty-eight particular articles that I needed to examine. In studying these selected articles I will be trying to find representative examples of the author(s) usage of 'radical behaviorism' and of the context in which it occurs. Thus most of the discussion of a particular article will consist of more or less lengthy quotations from the article. In this way the reader will be able to respond differentially to usage of the different authors. The articles are classified in seven categories of discriminably different concepts of 'radical behaviorism'. There are a lot of relatively lengthy quotations in what follows, and differential responding on the part of the reader to the articles classified in a particular category is encouraged.

Many more psychologists whose professional work bears a conspicuously behaviorist stamp now speak of their professional orientation as 'radical behaviorist'. How did this come about? To my knowledge, the first significant use of the expression 'radical behaviorism' that is related to the increasing frequency of usage among professional psychologists occurs in Skinner's revolutionary paper (1945), 'On the Operational Analysis of Psychological Terms'. I will examine this historically significant usage of 'radical behaviorism' later in this chapter.

USAGE OF 'RADICAL BEHAVIORISM' BY THREE PHILOSOPHERS

The historical trend we are dealing with here is the increased use of the expression 'radical behaviorism' primarily among professional *psychologists* and among other persons speaking of psychologists identified as radical behaviorists. However, the reader should be aware that the expression 'radical behaviorism' has been used among professional *philosophers*. In general, philosophical usage of 'radical behaviorism' has meant a form of behaviorism that is extreme in some way. For example, psychological views whereby consciousness was said not even to *exist* might be regarded as 'radical behaviorism' in some sense. It is difficult for psychologists to feel comfortable with the intra-verbal, professional, and intellectual context within which philosophical discussions of behaviorism take place. However, consider the following excerpts from the (1958) paper on 'The "Mental" and the "Physical"' by the distinguished philosopher, Herbert Feigl:

(A) No wonder then that after a period of acquiescence with epiphenominalism during the last century ..., the behaviorist movement in psychology took hold, and exercised an unprecedented influence in so many quarters. Behaviorists, in *their* way, repressed the problem in that they either denied the existence of raw feels (materialism); or in that they *defined* them in physical-observation terms (logical behaviorism); or they maintained that the subject matter of scientific and experimental psychology can be nothing but behavior (methodological behaviorism), which leaves the existence of raw feels an open question, but as of no relevance to science. Our previous discussions have, I trust, clearly indicated that behaviorism in the first sense is absurdly false, in second sense it is inadequate as a logical analysis of the meaning of phenomenal terms; and in the third sense, it is an admittedly fruitful but limited program of research, but it entails no conclusion directly relevant to the central philosophical issue.

  The repudiation of radical behaviorism and of logical behaviorism entails the acceptance of some sort of parallelistic doctrine .... (Feigl, 1958, pp. 428–9)

(B) The last epistemological requirement, to be briefly discussed here, is that of a realistic, rather than phenomenalistic or operationalistic, reconstruction of knowledge. With the current liberalization of the criterion of empirical meaningfulness the narrower positivism of the Vienna Circle has been definitively repudiated, and is being replaced by a ('hypercritical') realism. No longer do we identify the meaning of a statement with its method of verification. Nor do we consider the meaning of a concept as equivalent with the set of operations which in test situations enable us to determine its (more or less likely) applicability. Instead we distinguish the evidential (or confirmatory) basis from the factual context or reference of a knowledge claim. Early and crude forms of behaviorism identified mental states with their [*sic*!] observable symptoms. Embarrassment might then mean *nothing but* blushing. [*Note by Day*: the preceding two sentences illustrate what Feigl means in this paper by radical behaviorism or operationism.] But refinements and corrections were introduced in due course. Mental states were considered 'logical' constructions based on observable behavior; and statements about mental states were considered logically translatable into statements about actual or possible behavior, or into statements (or sets of statements) about test conditions and ensuing test results concerning behavior. Mental traits were considered as correlation clusters of their [*sic*!] [These *sics*! are by Feigl.] symptoms and manifestations, and so forth.

  But even such a refined or 'logical' behaviorism is now rejected as an inadequate reconstruction ....

  After the recovery from radical behaviorism and operationism, we need no longer hesitate to distinguish between *evidence* and *reference*, i.e., between manifestations or symptoms on the one hand, and central states on the other .... (Feigl, 1958, pp. 393–5)

(C) ... A physical object or process as perceived in common life, or as conceived in science, is the referent of certain symbolic representations. I submit that it is the preoccupation with the confirmatory evidence which has misled positivists and some pragmatists (all of them phenomenalists, radical empiricists, or operationists) to identify the meaning of

physical object statements with the actual and/or possible data which, according to our view, merely constitute their evidential bases. (Feigl, 1958, pp. 453–4)

(D) *That* pleasure or satisfaction reinforces certain forms of adient behavior can be formulated in the manner of the law of effect (cf. Meehl [1950]). But in the ultimate neurophysiological derivation of this empirical law of behavior, the correlation of pleasure or gratification with certain cerebral states is not required. Behaviorists, especially 'logical behaviorists,' have taken too easy a way out here in simply *defining* the pleasurable as the behaviorally attractive and the painful as the behaviorally repellent. The 'illumination' of certain physically described processes by raw feels is plainly something a radical behaviorist cannot even being to discuss. (Feigl, 1958, p. 476)

What do I want the reader to see in the above four blocks of quoted material from Feigl's paper? First, I have wanted to demonstrate that the expression 'radical behaviorism' does indeed have technical usage in professional philosophy. But, second, this particular usage as illustrated by Feigl is likely to have absolutely zero interest-value to all but an exceedingly small proportion of professional psychologists. Third, whatever 'radical behaviorism' might mean in contemporary psychology, it most surely is not what Feigl is talking about. I added quotation (D) because it deals with the concept of reinforcement. Quotation (C) is an excellent and succinct statement of the basic place Feigl has been trying to reach in that portion of his article that has involved his usage of 'radical behaviorism'. Quotation (B) provides not only an example of Feigl's usage of 'radical behaviorism'; it also provides good clarification of the point stated in (C). In setting up the lengthy case Feigl attempts to make in his paper for a realistic, monist, identity-theoretical account of how mental states can be made sense of in physical terms, the philosophical concerns associated with the concepts of radical behaviorism, operationism, pragmatism, positivism, and phenomenalism have common properties, largely reductionistic, which vitiate their effectiveness as useful concepts in constructing philosophy of science.

However, it is quotation (A) which primarily interests me. I take what Feigl means by 'materialism' in the first paragraph of (A) to be essentially the same cluster of concerns he refers to as 'radical behaviorism' in the second paragraph of quotation (A). In this light, consider the following material quoted from the eleven-volume *International Encyclopedia of Psychiatry*, *Psychology*, *Psychoanalysis, and Neurology*, edited by the psychiatrist, historian, and scholar, Benjamin B. Wolman (1977).[1] Published in 1977, the encyclopedia is reasonably recent. The following material constitutes the only reference to 'radical behaviorism' in the Index to the *Encyclopaedia*.[2] It comes from the entry, not for 'Behaviorism', but for 'Association'.

If one assumes the possibility that the experience of persons ultimately consists of elementary sensations (simples), but is given to the individuals in terms of unified objects (composites) and their relations, then the problem is to explain the classical phenomena of the unity of consciousness .... There have been three general proposals to account for the unity of experience:

   1. Mind is passive and both the relations of simultaneous elementary sensations and the sequential association of elementary sensations or images are explained by a power of the individual or by a principle of association.

   2. Mind is passive but the images and objects and their sequences are presented in relational terms. The notion of a sensory simple, or an instance of a sensation from the stream of experience, is an abstraction.

   3. Mind is both passive and active ....

   The first position appealed to those who defend a philosophic materialism, and in psychology, a radical behaviorism. The strength of this position is that no principle of uniquely mental

processing is introduced into the explanation of physical phenomena, such as the behavior of persons. Its weakness is the restriction of possible physical processes to classical Greek or eighteenth-century Newtonian models.

The second position can be called, in philosophy, phenomenological positivism, as in Mach's *Analysis of Sensations*, and in psychology, a general Gestalt position .... (Wolman, 1977, p. 159)

Here, again, we find a contrast drawn, as in quotation (A) above, between the way in which a particular conception is expressed between philosophical and psychological professional verbal communities. Once again, as in quotation (A), a connection is drawn between radical behaviorism and *materialism*. Yet I would argue that it is not the first position claimed by Wolman to be associated with radical behaviorism that is connected primarily with the work of Skinner. Instead it is the second position described by Wolman above that bears epistemological connections with Skinner's work. The penultimate chapter in Skinner's *The Behavior of Organisms* closes with a substantial quotation from Mach's *The Analysis of Sensations* (Skinner, 1938, p. 432). I have pointed out at length the intellectual importance of Mach's views to the epistemological character of Skinner's work (see, e.g., Day, 1981, pp. 227–32).

Now let me ask the reader to consider a quite different conceptualization of radical behaviorism, even though we remain within the verbal community of professional philosophy. In 1956 the philosopher Michael Scriven published an article entitled 'A Study of Radical Behaviorism', two years prior to Feigl's paper. Both Feigl's paper and Scriven's paper were published in volumes of the ongoing series, *Minnesota Studies in the Philosophy of Science*. Scriven's paper was published in Volume I, edited by Feigl and Scriven; Feigl's paper was published in Volume II, edited by Feigl, Scriven and Grover Maxwell. In the 1950s both Feigl and Scriven were highly respected among psychologists, although for somewhat different reasons. Dr Boring puts the matter succinctly in the case of Feigl.

A Viennese, [Feigl] took his Ph.D. in philosophy at the University of Vienna in 1927, the year that the Vienna circle was getting formed, and he stayed in Vienna teaching until 1930. He knew what was going on in the new positivism, and he also knew Bridgman's book [*The Logic of Modern Physics*] which had been published in 1927. In 1930 he came to Harvard on a fellowship to find out what Bridgman was thinking and to work in philosophy of science in general. It was he who introduced the Harvard psychologists to the ideas of their own colleague, Bridgman, to the work of the Vienna circle, to logical positivism and to operational procedures in general. (Boring, 1950, p. 656)

Scriven was co-editor of the first two volumes of the *Minnesota Studies* just two years after receiving his MA from the University of Melbourne, and he received his DPhil from Oxford University in 1956. I was a graduate student in psychology at approximately this period, and Scriven was perceived, at least among those I knew, as a vigorous young philosopher of science who was seriously interested in what psychologists actually *do*. He became known as psychology's own philosopher: as a philosopher who was interested in bringing philosophical skills to bear on the realities of the professional functioning of psychologists.

In any case, in Scriven we have the author of a paper, published in 1956, which contains our key expression, 'radical behaviorism', in the title of the paper: 'A Study of Radical Behaviorism'. Scriven states his purpose as follows:

(E) In this paper, I want to examine the views of a man who has recommended the abolition of theories: Professor B.F. Skinner. I shall not be trying to show that Skinner's theories are bad: I wish to show only that he does employ them, and that his general arguments against the adoption of theories (or at least certain kinds of theory) are not altogether satisfactory. (Scriven, 1956, p. 88)

Scriven does not clarify what he means by 'radical behaviorism' in the paper; in some forty pages the expression 'radical behaviorism' occurs only five or six times. Scriven develops his argument against 'Skinner's position', 'Skinner's views', 'Skinner's critique', 'Skinner's practice', 'Skinner's system', 'Skinner', etc. It is clear that in some sense Scriven wants to identify Skinner's position with radical behaviorism. The general sense is that if Skinner were not to make so many philosophical errors, his radical behaviorism would be much improved. Here are some relevant quotations:

Yet, there hangs above us the pall of smoke from the battle over introspection. 'How can one deny that "purpose" and "belief" are words with an inner reference, and sometimes with no external manifestations?' say the introspectionists, while the radical behaviorists fidget at this metaphysics . . . . Here I wish only to argue that Skinner's analysis is unsound, *even for a behaviorist*, and does not achieve what he thinks it will achieve. It is not a special feature of *mentalistic concepts* that they cannot be given an explicit unambiguous definition in basic observation language ('the left hand was raised three inches, the head turned to the right about 45°, eye fixation remained constant, etc.'); but it is a feature of *all useful scientific concepts*, including Skinner's own. (Scriven, 1956, p. 112)

The first point made, is that, on a radical behaviorist analysis of inner states, explanations in such terms are vital and legitimate. I did not say 'on Skinner's analysis' because we have already made a number of improvements on that without abandoning radical behaviorism. To uncover some more of the very serious difficulties in Skinner's own analysis, I am going to examine one or two further instances of it, still on his own standard. Then I shall consider the results of our suggested changes in the radical behaviorist analysis of mental-state terminology, in an attempt to show that one can produce a fully scientific account that is much closer to being an analysis of the actual mental concepts we ordinarily employ, which Skinner views with such suspicion. (Scriven, 1956, p. 120)

Scriven states the aims of the paper as follows:

Specifically, I wish to suggest that
(F) 1. Skinner's idea of the relationship between the 'pure' molar behavior approach and neurological, mentalistic, or conceptual theories is seriously oversimplified in a way that, if corrected, renders untenable most of his objections to the latter.
2. Skinner's analysis of causation, explanation, and classification is subject to correction in the same way. (Scriven, 1956, pp. 88–9)

Point 1 in quotation (F) is a more explicit statement of the aim of the paper as more simply expressed in quotation (E): 'I wish to show only that [Skinner] does employ [theories], and that his general arguments against the adoption of theories (or at least certain kinds of theory) are not altogether satisfactory.' If one substitutes 'in particular, theories which attribute causal and explanatory status to mental concepts' for the parenthetical element '(or at least certain kinds of theory)' in quotation (E), then one has a straightforward statement of what Scriven is doing in his paper.

However, what *I* am getting at is that Scriven is speaking at a time, and in an intellectual climate, where if one is going to talk about radical behaviorism, then one has largely 'Skinner's position' to deal with. Yet the characteristic of Skinner's position that is 'too extreme' for Scriven is Skinner's antipathy to theories,

and to mentalistic theories in particular. The upshot of Scriven's paper is to argue that if the objection to theories were to be dropped, including the emphasized objection to mentalistic theories, then we would have a purer, more intellectually coherent radical behaviorism. But what is radical behaviorism, if it is not to be straightforwardly and simply identified with 'Skinner's position'?

As I have said above, Scriven does not clarify what he takes the expression 'radical behaviorism' to mean (such that without Skinner's anti-theory stance and his objection to the use of mental terms in theory, radical behaviorism would be improved). Thus I shall formulate in my own words, out of bits and pieces picked up here and there throughout his paper, roughly what Scriven must have meant by the expression. (It would be nice also to know which environmental factors led Scriven to have the particular conception of radical behaviorism that he had.) My best shot is that by 'radical behaviorism' Scriven must have meant something like this: radical behaviorism is the attempt to describe lawful patterns in the observable relationship between 'molar' behavior and the environment; characteristically such investigations are carried out under controlled conditions in the laboratory, and they have as their ultimate aim the prediction and control of behavior.

I now ask the reader to consider some material concerning radical behaviorism from *The Encyclopedia of Philosophy*, edited by Paul Edwards and published in 1967. The entry is for 'Behaviorism', and it is the work of the philosopher Arnold Kaufman. These considerations have presumably been shaped by the professional *philosophical* verbal community.

> Some behaviorists (for example, B.F. Skinner) claim that whether or not [processes that intervene between the terminal behaviors predicted and the antecedents used as the basis for the prediction] occur, nothing scientifically useful can be said about them .... But it is generally recognized that the fact that a scientific theory can be eliminated does not render it irrelevant. In particular, it may be scientifically fruitful because it provides a means of simplifying complex relationships without which limited human intelligence could not function effectively. Hence, *radical* behaviorists like Skinner are forced to ... show that theories are, from the point of view of prediction (and control), either absolutely pernicious or *relatively* unfruitful. One of the ironies of this position is that although part of the inspiration for behaviorism is the enormous success of the physical sciences, it tends to ignore the undoubted fruitfulness of theorizing in those sciences. Radical behaviorists are willing to use terms that are ordinarily thought to denote mental states or processes — for example, such terms as 'motive' and 'purpose.' But to the extent that they are willing to use such expressions, they require that the expressions be behaviorally *defined* in terms of functional relationships.
>
> It would be unfortunate if readers were to infer that most behaviorists are *radical* behaviorists. We have dwelt on this form of behaviorism at length only because it is convenient to formulate the family of views under consideration by complicating the radical position. In fact, most other behaviorists reject radical behaviorism either on the grounds that intervening variables for which behavioral (or physiological) criteria ... can be given are permissible, or on the grounds that the radical behaviorists' skepticism about the unfruitfulness of theories is unjustified. The second group understand by 'theory' a set of statements that contain constructs for which it is not even possible to provide behavioral criteria of application ....
>
> Among the permissible theoretical constructs [permissible according to a criterion set by Hempel (1952) that is outlined by Kaufman] one might find terms that denote 'unobservable' mental states and processes. It seems clear that anyone who accepts a behaviorism of this kind is participating in a methodological milieu far removed from radical behaviorism. (Kaufman, 1967, pp. 271–2)

It seems to me that Kaufman's views, as expressed in the *Encyclopedia*, are very close to the upshot of Scriven's arguments in 'A Study of Radical Behavior-

ism'. Radical behaviorism must be regarded as being linked very closely to the 'position' ascribed to Skinner, and the difficulties with this position center on the inadequacies of Skinner's assessment of the ways in which theories function effectively in science. Such difficulties with Skinner's analysis of theory in science play havoc with psychology because they would appear to prevent mentalistic language from having any effective role in psychological analysis.

USAGE AMONG PSYCHOLOGISTS

Now I turn to what *psychologists* have had to say about this question. If we are concerned primarily, as we are here, with contemporary professional psychological usage of the expression 'radical behaviorism', then we are clearly talking about something related to the way in which Skinner has used the term. To my knowledge the earliest printed usage of 'radical behaviorism' by Skinner was in the 'Rejoinders and Second Thoughts' section of his contribution to the Symposium on Operationism, published in 1945 by the *Psychological Review*:

> The distinction between public and private is by no means the same as that between physical and mental. That is why methodological behaviorism (which adopts the first) is very different from radical behaviorism (which lops off the latter term in the second). The result is that while the radical behaviorist may in some cases consider private events (inferentially, perhaps, but none the less meaningfully), the methodological operationist has maneuvered himself into a position where he cannot. (Skinner, 1945, p. 294)

This is a well-known passage, in part because it has had some effect on the way people have tended to conceptualize what is meant by 'radical behaviorism'. I think it is safe to say that throughout Skinner's Rejoinder he is concerned with placing his own view of operationism at odds with 'the operationism of Boring and Stevens', with the views of 'current psychological operationists', with 'methodological behaviorists', etc. Yet the effort to make a sharp contrast between 'methodological' and 'radical behaviorism', first made in the material quoted above, can still be found made with much emotion even today, forty-five years later (see Day, 1983). Yet regardless of the implications concerning methodological behaviorism, what the material has to say about radical behaviorism is really quite simple: radical behaviorism argues that there are no such things as *mental* events. What we have here is a simple materialism: events which we have been taught to regard as 'mental' by our culture are actually physical. 'But I contend that my toothache is just as physical as my typewriter . . .' (Skinner, 1945, p. 294).

Even better evidence that such an uncomplicated interpretation is appropriate for this kind of claim about radical behaviorism is found in the exchange between Skinner and Michael Scriven at the Rice Symposium on Behaviorism and Phenomenology.

> *Scriven:* 'Where have we got with a behaviorism that allows us on the one hand a legitimate interpretation of mentalistic language and [on the other] a direct access to "mental" states, with "mental" here meaning . . . a state of the organism which can be directly perceived and which . . . is an indicator of subsequent changes in behavior? . . . Why do you feel that you are, in fact, still in some sense a radical behaviorist rather than someone who is making an extremely useful recommendation about the way in which we should prune the surplus out of mentalistic language?'

Skinner: 'I am a radical behaviorist simply in the sense that I find no place in the formulation for anything which is mental.' ... If 'behaviorism' means 'simply the issue of the stuff of which the mental event is composed' then he [Skinner] is a radical behaviorist. Otherwise he is a 'methodological one, arguing [that] there are better ways of formulating relations than by setting up so-called intervening variables.' (Wann, 1964, p. 106)

This exchange took place in the discussion period following presentation of Skinner's paper, 'Behaviorism at Fifty'. Skinner's use of the expression 'radical behaviorist' in this circumstance might be taken to show merely intra-verbal control from Scriven's question. But that 'radical behaviorism' existed in some strength in Skinner's verbal·repertoire in 1964 is evidenced by the following sentence in the body of the paper itself: 'During this period, however, an effective experimental science of behavior has emerged. Much of what it has discovered bears on the basic issue. A restatement of radical behaviorism would therefore seem to be in order' (Skinner, 1964, p. 80). Ten years later, in *About Behaviorism*, Skinner uses the same contrast between radical and methodological behaviorism as a vehicle for developing what he has to say:

Radical behaviorism restores some kind of balance. It does not insist upon truth by agreement and can therefore consider events taking place within the skin. It does not call these events unobservable, and it does not dismiss them as subjective. It simply questions the nature of the object observed and the reliability of the observations.

The position can be stated as follows: What is felt or introspectively observed is not some nonphysical world of consciousness, mind, or mental life but the observer's own body. (Skinner, 1974, p. 17)

What people mean by 'radical behaviorism' varies widely from psychologist to psychologist, and considerable professional investment is made by the particular authors when they speak of radical behaviorism. Yet Skinner's usage is not so complex. He is likely to use the expression largely in the context of discussions where a possible dualism between the 'mental' and the 'physical' is at issue. Here Skinner will not admit to the existence of anything which is not physical, and he takes this stance under the banner of 'radical behaviorism'. Yet the expression 'radical behaviorism' is not used frequently by Skinner himself. In speaking of his own professional views and interests, Skinner is much more likely to use such expressions as 'the analysis of behavior', or 'operant analysis', or 'a science of behavior'.

I used a particular strategy to help me sift through the enormous amount of professional material that undoubtedly bears on professional psychological usage of the expression 'radical behaviorism' over the past thirty years. I think the strategy turned out to be a good one. I thought of making use of *Psychological Abstracts* in some way. At the end of each year *Psychological Abstracts* puts together two indexes covering the abstracts published during that year: an author index and a subject matter index. Entries in the subject matter indexes are first ordered alphabetically by reasonably crude categories, e.g.:

Behavior Modification
Behavior Problems
Behavior Therapy
Behavioral Assessment
Behaviorism, etc.

Under these headings are listed relevant abstracts contained in that volume, with the major topic(s) dealt with by the abstract material identified by short phrases.

For example, under the heading 'Behaviorism' for Volume 71, one will find the following among the topics pertaining to particular abstracts identified by number:

> analysis of N. Chomsky's cognitivism from B.F. Skinner's behavioral perspective, 9562 ...
> behavior theory, linguistic descriptions of private events, 19277
> ... critique of epistemology by R. Rorty, implications for radical behaviorism, 13776 ... historical relationships between B.F. Skinner's radical behaviorism and J.R. Kantor's interbehavioral psychology, 39 ...

My method was to restrict my survey to those articles whose topic description in the subject matter index for *Psychological Abstracts* contained the expression 'radical behaviorism', or 'radical behaviorist'. I read as many of these articles as I could get with reasonable convenience, trying to see what the author appeared to mean by 'radical behaviorism'.

For 1950–84 I found twenty-eight articles whose topic description in the subject matter index contained the expression 'radical behaviorism'. Figure 1 shows the frequency of such articles as a function of five-year periods. It is clear from this figure that the frequency of topic descriptions containing the expression 'radical behaviorism' has been rising steadily in recent years.

In what follows I will identify and characterize the content of the earlier articles in Figure 1. Then I will classify the articles into groups, showing the variety of different uses the expression 'radical behaviorism' appeared to have in this sample of articles.

THE ARTICLES BY SCRIVEN AND BY JOHNSON

The single entry for the 1955–59 year-group was Scriven's paper on 'A Study of Radical Behaviorism' for Volume I of the *Minnesota Studies*, for which examples of Scriven's usage of 'radical behaviorism' were examined in some detail above. In essence, I took Scriven to mean by 'radical behaviorism' the kind of behaviorism advocated by Skinner, i.e., the inductive description of lawful relations between the environment and behavior, but where Skinner's objections to the use of psychological 'theory' were both inappropriate and unnecessary. The second article to be referenced in Figure 1, namely the single entry for 1960–64, is entitled 'Discussion: A Commentary on "Radical Behaviorism"' by Rochelle Johnson (1963). The abstract published in *Psychological Abstracts* reads as follows:

> Methodological arguments on Skinner's 'Radical Behaviorism' are upheld against the critique by Michael Scriven. The latter's insistence upon mental state and other state explanations stems from his confusing 'the analysis of terms for their ordinary meaning with the analysis of terms for their scientific explanatory value.' Issues relating to Skinner's antitheoretical views of science are discussed. (M. Turner [author of abstract] *Psychological Abstracts*, Vol. 38, 736–7)

Johnson's article begins in an interesting way, which may shed a slight amount of light on what was meant by 'radical behaviorism' in the early 1960s.

> B.F. Skinner is perhaps even more widely known for his views on science than for his experimental work. His comments on the role of theory in science have been labeled 'antitheoretical,' 'ultra-empirical,' 'non-theoretical,' 'radical,' and worse. His position appears to be both extreme and untenable. Scriven [1956] has given us a critique of Skinner that goes beyond

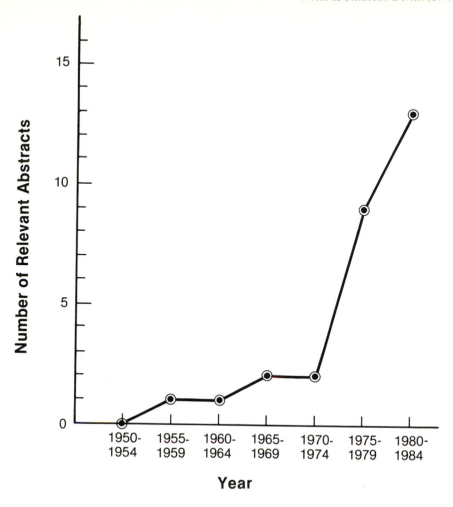

Figure 1. *Period of Subject-Matter Indexes Reviewed*

mere labeling; it is an examination of the assumptions and implications of such a position.

In some instances, however, Scriven's analysis is not entirely correct or is misleading. There are different interpretations of Skinner from those offered by Scriven and perhaps 'something more' in Skinner's point of view than has been caught by Scriven's analytic 'net.' (Johnson, 1963, p. 274).

TWO ARTICLES ON BEHAVIORISM AND PHENOMENOLOGY

I now ask the reader to consider the two articles that are referenced in Figure 1 for 1965–69. Here we have a truly remarkable thing! These two articles were each written on a different continent by people who had never heard of each other, each advancing the same, most extraordinary claim that Skinner's radical behaviorism is intrinsically compatible with phenomenology. Both authors argue this in spite of the general consensus among professional psychologists at that time

that behaviorism and phenomenology stood at opposite poles of intellectual perspectives in the field. The papers are: (first in order of publication) 'Skinner and Sartre', by Steinar Kvale and Carl Erik Grenness, which appeared in the *Review of Existential Psychology and Psychiatry*, Spring, 1967; and (second in order of publication) 'Radical Behaviorism in Reconciliation with Phenomenology', by me, which was published in the *Journal of the Experimental Analysis of Behavior*, 1969.

The composition of both these papers was stimulated by the same event, the Symposium on Behaviorism and Phenomenology held at Rice University in 1963 to celebrate the founding of Division 24 of the American Psychological Association, now called the Division of Theoretical and Philosophical Psychology. Both papers have been influential in the field: for some these papers have suggested new professional directions to take; but for others they have stuck offensively in the craw. However, our question here is: 'Yet how did these authors conceptualize radical behaviorism?' In answering this question let me move into the scheme of classification that I have used for ordering the body of articles that were identified by entering the subject-matter indexes of *Psychological Abstracts* in the manner described above.

Category I

It is not easy to describe the common property of the discriminative stimulation that governs the differential responding involved in my making the classifications which follow. However, in general it is clear that new classes become necessary as the intellectual climate in the profession changes with time. In Category I I place those papers in which 'radical behaviorism' is taken to refer to a particular type of *learning theory*. In this class there are only two papers: those by Scriven and Johnson. Radical behaviorism means in both these papers what we spoke of in the 1950s as 'Skinner's *system*', out of deference to Skinner's purported aversion to theory in psychology. One meant Skinner's systematic *position*, where this position was regarded as competing with other professional positions, or theories of learning, that were appropriately subject to intense intellectual scrutiny, as in the work of the Dartmouth Conference of 1950, out of which *Modern Learning Theory* emerged (Estes *et al.*, 1954).

By 1963 the work of the Rice Symposium showed the time was ripe for something else in the profession. At the Symposium, Sigmund Koch was supposed to have joined Skinner in standing up for the behaviorist perspective. But the opposite happened: Koch's paper was a diatribe *against* any and every form of behaviorism. Thus, in a sense Skinner was left alone to stand for behaviorism in the field. Consequently, to regard radical behaviorism as Skinner's systematic position, in the sense that it is to be contrasted with other systematic behaviorist positions, became inappropriate. The professional issue was the relationship between behaviorism, as now represented chiefly by Skinner, and phenomenology. This led Kvale and Grenness, and me also [from now on I will refer to my work as Day], to make a common move in addressing this issue, and it was a move which involved a very different conceptualization of radical behaviorism from that involved in the work of Scriven and then of Johnson.

Category II

The second category of conceptions of radical behaviorism is one I describe as conceptions of radical behaviorism that have been arrived at through an original, selective, and individualistic integration of Skinner's work on the part of the author of the paper. I regard the papers by Kvale and Grenness (1967) and Day (1969) as good examples in this category. They stand back a certain distance from the corpus of Skinner's work and then try to identify, and to explain, what they take to be those features of Skinner's thought that are most important in engaging the then-current professional scene. The following are representative of the important features of Skinner's radical behaviorism for Kvale and Grenness:

(a) Skinner ... strongly objects to what may be called 'the illusion of the double world,' inherent in most of contemporary psychology. It involves the assumption of an 'outer,' 'objective,' 'physical' world and its 'inner,' 'subjective,' 'psychological' copy .... Both radical behaviorism and phenomenology regard this doubling of the world as contradictory, and unnecessary for a scientific psychology. (Kvale and Grenness, 1967, pp. 129–30)

(b) A parallel to the illusion of the double world is what Skinner has termed 'the flight to the inner man.' ... Just as psychology had to create an inner world to account for perception, it had to construct an inner man to account for action. This inner man is a rudiment of the now unacceptable 'soul,' but in a disguised form .... Just as with the 'inner world,' the 'inner man' explanations lead to an infinite regress. The behavior of the inner man remains to be explained, this must be done by recourse to a new inner man, and so on indefinitely. (Kvale and Grenness, 1967, pp. 131–2)

(c) Knowledge Is Action[.] With an enlarged conception of behavior, our knowledge of the world comes to be our behavior with respect to the world .... Skinner puts the issue ... briefly and concretely [the following are quotations from Skinner].
 '... knowledge is action rather than sensing ... We "interpret" a stimulus as smoke insofar as we tend to respond with behavior appropriate to smoke ... our "perception" of the world — our "knowledge" of it — is our *behavior* with respect to the world.' (Kvale and Grenness, 1967, pp. 138–9)

(d) The Primacy of Description[.] The repudiation of inner entities and the focusing upon concrete observable behavior has led both Skinner and the phenomenologists to emphasize adequate description in psychology. Skinner finds psychological theorizing most often a refuge from the data, and he repeatedly stresses, 'But we must eventually get back to an observable datum.' (Kvale and Grenness, 1967, p. 140)

These quotations should give a reasonably good idea of the kind of notions Kvale and Grenness found in Skinner's work that they felt were centrally important and thus form the core of their conception of radical behaviorism. But this is not to say that Kvale and Grenness agree with everything they find in Skinner. They find his conception of 'the real world' or 'the world of physics' ambiguous. They also find that the problem of the inherent intentionality of behavior has not been dealt with satisfactorily.

There are a multitude of different behavioral relationships to the world and it is meaningless to choose one as the correct objective approach to the real world. But still, Skinner's belief in the primacy of the physical world seems unshaken. He himself becomes the victim of the prejudice of the physical world when he talks definitely about 'the world itself' and asserts that 'we operate in one world — the world of physics' [a quotation from Skinner]. Skinner must then assume that one reaction, namely the physicists', is a reaction to the 'real' world, and that every other perceptual reaction is an illusion, precisely the line of thinking he dismissed above. (Kvale and Grenness, 1967, p. 134)

When discussing the prejudice of the objective world, we saw that Skinner wavered between a physical and a 'perceptual' conception of the world. The same ambiguity is reflected in his concept of behavior. On the one hand Skinner conceives of behavior as mechanical

movements 'Watching a person behave in this way is like watching any physical or biological system' [quotation from Skinner]. He even applies his concept of behavior to microphysic particles when he compares the behavior of particles in a cyclothrone to human behavior in a culture .... On the other hand, in practical examples, Skinner often considers behavior a meaningful human action, e.g., 'the persistent behavior which we call teasing' [quotation from Skinner].

Skinner explicitly denies the intentionality of the behavioral and consciousness aspects of man's relation to the world. (Kvale and Grenness, 1967, pp. 137–8)

The point here is that Kvale and Grenness are not trying to come up with a definition of radical behaviorism *simpliciter*. It is *our* job to appreciate the conception of radical behaviorism that Kvale and Grenness had, and we can see this in themes in Skinner's work that they regard as genuinely important in the contemporary professional culture.

Day (1969) makes essentially the same move. His list of important features of radical behaviorism overlaps somewhat with those of Kvale and Grenness. For Day (1969) radical behaviorism is to be distinguished from conventional behaviorism in that associated with radical behaviorism is (1) a focal interest in functional relations between the environment and behavior — a primary interest in the control of behavior; (2) a focal awareness that all scientists are themselves behaving organisms — this amounts to a behavioral epistemology; (3) a focal interest in description; and (4) a focal awareness of the importance of environmental variables in giving an account of behavior. Day's conception of radical behaviorism is further elucidated in the paper by a list of four problems to be overcome in effecting a genuine reconciliation between radical behaviorism and phenomenology. These are: (1) a largely superficial knowledge of Skinner's work as a whole on the part of psychologists — examples would be mistaken views about Skinner's notion of operational definition and 'rampant' mentalism among practitioners of the experimental analysis of behavior; (2) a failure to differentiate between radical and conventional behaviorism; (3) the lack of training on the part of behaviorists in philosophy; and (4) practical problems in carrying out explicitly descriptive research, in view of the high professional value placed upon the experimental manipulation of independent variables.

Papers by McCorkle and Moore. I also classified three other papers in Category II, where a conception of radical behaviorism has been arrived at through an original, selective, and individualistic integration of Skinner's work. These are the two papers by Jay Moore (1975, 1981) and the dissertation of Marguerite McCorkle (1978). The work clearly belongs in this category because of the marked selectivity in regard to what it is that is really important about radical behaviorism that gives it its characteristic identity.

Category III

Time has passed since the concerns of the 1960s with phenomenology. Moore and McCorkle belong to another generation, and it is difficult for me to think of their work apart from a third category in my system of classification: papers involving a conception of radical behaviorism that is clearly derivative from, an advance beyond, or in some way at least closely related to the earlier work of Day on the

one hand, or Kvale and Grenness on the other. McCorkle's work is very closely tied to Day's thought, which is to be expected since she was his student; even so, it very clearly involves an advance. Yet there is a change, a hardening, in the way in which her conception of radical behaviorism engages the profession. The more gentle efforts of Day and Kvale and Grenness to explain to the profession what they take to be important about Skinner's work are very different from the strident insistence of these younger authors that the profession look at radical behaviorism in their particular light (and with their particular professional values). I, at least, find this same kind of dogged insistence upon a claim to the *correct* interpretation of Skinner, and a claim as to what radical behaviorism *should be*, to be present in the papers by Moore. Of course, the perspectives developed by McCorkle and by Moore are quite different from each other. From the perspective of someone like me, a person who is trying to look at how radical behaviorism has been conceptualized over the past thirty years, the big difference between the outlooks of Moore and McCorkle centers on the role of TEAB, the experimental analysis of behavior.

McCorkle's advance beyond Day is seen in the following material from her dissertation:

> Skinner's reconceptualization of 'knowledge' can be stated simply as that knowing is behaving, and it exists, as any other behavior, only as it occurs. The trained observer or behavior-analyst *knows* how to analyze a behavioral episode in terms of assessing controlling contingencies, where by 'knowing' reference is made to the observer's capacity to respond discriminatively under relevant conditions. (McCorkle, 1978, pp. 46, 48)
>
> Attention should be called in particular to the following methodological implications of the preceding theoretical rationale ....
>
> (1) The presentation of any verbal material whatsoever ... is made largely for the purpose of shaping desired discriminative behavior in the careful reader, and of influencing the reader's subsequent verbal behavior so that it functions effectively within relevant professional discourse.
>
> (2) The primary purpose of research is to put the researcher in a situation such that professionally interesting behavior can be directly observed by the researcher.
>
> (3) The adaptive function of the direct observation of behavior by the researcher is focused on the capacities of the observation to shape new, professionally relevant discriminations in the behavior of the researcher.
>
> (4) The primary professional obligation of the researcher who has acquired new discriminative repertoires as the result of direct observation of behavior is no more than simply to respond verbally under the control of what has been observed ....
>
> (5) The professional training of radical behaviorists leads them to bring to the behavior of direct observation a particular kind of conceptual equipment, which is the product of their professional training. Salient features of this conceptual equipment are: (a) a tendency to make sense of observed behavior in ways that avoid mentalism; and (b) a focal interest in spotting the functioning of environmental variables as they act to control behavior.
>
> (6) In informing others of the steps taken in the course of a program of research, the primary focus of attention is on the *behavior of the researcher* as the program happens to have been actually carried out .... Thus reports of research are largely descriptions of the researcher's behavior throughout the course of the research and of the environmental circumstances that have acted to control his/her behavior. (McCorkle, 1978, pp. 68–9)

The features of radical behaviorism that Moore highlights in his papers of 1975 and 1981 are quite different from those emphasized by McCorkle. I would not want to say that Moore's emphases are significantly derived from my own, although we met in 1974 and he was already familiar with my work at that time. His 1975 paper is ostensibly about 'the principle of operationism in a science of

behavior.' Moore wants to contrast the conventional interpretation of operationism with that of radical behaviorism. At the outset of his paper Moore links
Skinner's radical behaviorism with the interbehaviorism of J.R. Kantor to produce an integrated system which is spoken of henceforth as 'the behaviorist
position'.

> Although it may be difficult to claim that Kantor's interbehavioral psychology and Skin-
> ner's radical behaviorism are identical ..., they are nevertheless sufficiently alike as compared
> with traditional practices that they may be treated as representing a systematic behaviorist
> position. What then is the behaviorist [for our purposes, read 'radical behaviorist'] interpreta-
> tion of operationism, and how does it differ from the conventional interpretation? (Moore,
> 1975, p. 121)

The upshot is — and Moore's discussion is largely of what Skinner has to say
— that radical behaviorist operationism involves an account of the verbal behavior of the scientist that avoids mentalism, unlike the conventional conception
of operationism, which supports an inherent dualism in psychology. True to
Skinner's 1945 paper on operationism, in this paper Moore is careful to give a
detailed account of the nature and functioning of mental terms in the science of
behavior. Thus the spotlight, in bringing to the fore the salient features of radical
behaviorism, is put upon the account it gives of private events, or of terms
commonly taken to refer to mental processes involved in conscious experience.

However, in sharp contrast to McCorkle's approach, Moore seems never to
want operationism to move very far away from the behavior of the *scientist*, or
from TEAB, the experimental analysis of behavior. Explicit manipulation of
relevant variables, with the ultimate aim of prediction and control, seems always
to be in the background of Moore's analysis. On the other hand, the words can
easily be read as entirely consistent with McCorkle:

> The behaviorist interpretation of operationism may now be understood as a matter of
> assessing the conditions that lead the scientist to use the term in the way he does. In the sense
> that when a scientist performs an operation he interacts with certain elements of the environ-
> ment, then operationism consists of assessing the extent to which these elements, and their
> manipulations, influence the verbal behavior of the scientists. In psychological science, when
> talking about an operation, one is typically talking about the imposition of some set of stimulus
> conditions upon a person, and the observation of their effect. Operationism then consists of
> assessing the extent to which (1) these imposed stimulus conditions and (2) the response that
> the person makes to them, influence the psychologist's verbal description of the behavioral
> event. (Moore, 1975, p. 123)

> [B]ehavioral events are simply occurrences in the environment .... The fundamental problem,
> then, is to determine what elements in the environment participate in the event, and to sharpen
> the stimulus control of these elements over the verbal behavior of the scientist. (Moore, 1975,
> p. 135)

In the 1975 article Moore also considers the role of theory in radical behaviorism (although Scriven [1956] and Johnson [1963] are not cited):

> Consider ... the role of theory in science. Skinner's position is often referred to as atheoretic-
> al, and it is often alleged that his position inhibits scientific inquiry .... However, a closer
> examination of the facts reveals that Skinner has suggested that 'experimental psychology is
> properly and inevitably committed to the construction of a theory of behavior ....' (Moore,
> 1975, p. 130)

Thus one might say that the professional understanding of what is singular
about radical behaviorism is not its position in regard to theory in psychological

science, but its unique capacity, in contrast to other behavioristic approaches, to incorporate private events into the scientific account of behavior.

With respect to the later paper by Moore (1981), I can find in it no basic change in outlook from that presented in the 1975 paper. This paper seems to indicate an increasing frustration on Moore's part that the scourge of mentalism continues to frequent the halls of the experimental analysis of behavior. Moore concentrates on the intrinsic bond between radical behaviorism and anti-mentalism, rather than upon the radical behaviorist technique for operational definition of psychological terms. However, the paper does suggest what Moore understands 'radical behaviorism' to mean: 'Behaviorism, according to the Skinnerian point of view, or radical behaviorism, is not simply the scientific study of behavior, but rather an integrated and comprehensive philosophy of science, concerned with the subject matter, methods, and dimensions of psychology' (Moore, 1981, p. 75).

Before moving on to the next category, I want to include the papers of Eachus (1972) and Corriveau (1972) in Category III, as involving conceptions of radical behaviorism derived from Day (1969) or Kvale and Grenness (1967). (I trust that it is clear that the only articles I am considering are those that turned up in my survey of the subject-matter indexes of *Psychological Abstracts*.) Eachus at one time studied with me, so it is not surprising that he both speaks of himself as a radical behaviorist and takes it for granted that his manipulations and inter-pretations of behavior can be taken at face value as representative of radical behaviorism. His article is interesting, in that it involves an effort on his part to shape his own social behavior in a desired direction, in a social situation that was particularly sticky. The paper shows only a small slice of what radical behavior-ism means for him — in this case the interpretation of behavior as being largely under environmental control, and the appropriateness of shaping behavior in a desired direction by making reinforcement contingent upon desired behavior. Corriveau is a phenomenologist, and the aim of his paper is to show that radical behaviorism and phenomenology are not at all intellectually compatible. As far as his understanding of radical behaviorism is concerned, he is content simply to take Day's conceptualization (1969) at face value. His criticism is of Kvale and Grenness' conceptualization of phenomenology.

Category IV

I found that I wanted a special category of conceptualizations of radical behavior-ism calling focal attention to the analysis of private events, because I had six papers that would fit such a category. Moreover, I feel it is important to call special attention to the relevance of the analysis of private events because Skinner himself has often distinguished radical from methodological behaviorism on this basis. For instance, Chapter 1 of his popular book, *About Behaviorism* (1974), contrasts three 'strategies' used in psychology in a search for the causes of behavior. They are, in the order considered in the chapter, Structuralism, Methodological Behaviorism, and Radical Behaviorism. The section on Radical Behaviorism begins as follows:

> The statement that behaviorists deny the existence of feelings, sensations, ideas, and other features of mental life needs a good deal of clarification. Methodological behaviorism and some

versions of logical positivism ruled private events out of bounds because there could be no public agreement about their validity .... Radical behaviorism, however, takes a different line. It does not deny the possibility of self-observation or self-knowledge or its possible usefulness, but it questions the nature of what is felt or observed and hence known. It restores introspection but not what philosophers and introspective psychologists had believed they were 'specting,' and it raises the question of how much of one's body can one actually observe .... By dealing exclusively with external antecedent events it turned attention away from self-observation and self-knowledge .... Radical behaviorism restores some kind of balance [between mentalism and methodological behaviorism]. It does not insist upon truth by agreement and can therefore consider events taking place in the private world within the skin. It does not call these events unobservable, and it does not dismiss them as subjective. It simply questions the nature of the object observed and the reliability of the observations.

   The position can be stated as follows: what is felt or introspectively observed is not some nonphysical world of consciousness, mind, or mental life, but the observer's own body. (Skinner, 1974, pp. 16–17)

Because *About Behaviorism* appeared in 1974, and because it was widely read, it is undoubtedly not entirely coincidental that the curve in Figure 1 begins to accelerate sharply after 1975. The six papers I listed in Category IV were, in order from earliest to most recent date of publication, Moore (1975), Zuriff (1980), Moore (1981), Carbone (1981), Natsoulas (1983), and Day (1983). I have already had my say with respect to the two papers in this list by Moore. Let us dispense quickly with Day (1983). This paper, 'On the Difference between Radical and Methodological Behaviorism', is largely a review of the argument Skinner has used repeatedly in calling attention to the special feature of radical behaviorism that consists in its capacity to find a place for private events in a natural science. (This paper is also a pep-talk for increased effort to generate productive research in the analysis of verbal behavior, since Skinner's comfort with the place of private events in radical behaviorist analysis rests upon the capacity for a productive analysis of verbal behavior.) Let me, then, just give a short sentence or two from the papers by Zuriff (1980), Carbone (1981) and Natsoulas (1983) to illustrate their usage of 'radical behaviorism'.

   One can get a sense of Zuriff's approach from the following sentences, which are taken from his own abstract of the paper. 'In contrast with other varieties of behaviorism, radical behaviorism (RB) claims that it alone can deal with private events in science because it rejects the doctrine of "truth by agreement." However, several schools of behaviorism that are committed to an intersubjective agreement criterion of truth have nevertheless included private events in their theories ...' (Zuriff, 1980, p. 337).

   The article by Carbone (1981) appears to have been written with an audience of applied behavior analysts in mind. Its basic aim is to encourage the behavior modifier not to be trapped by an appeal to inner causes just because radical behaviorism finds a place for private events in a natural science. 'It is hoped that a sufficiently convincing argument has been presented so that the reader, when faced with a behavior control problem will not be distracted by inner causes but will move immediately to the external world for the explanation' (Carbone, 1981, p. 113). A further glimpse into the conception of radical behaviorism held by Carbone is given in a footnote at the end of this article: 'This paper has drawn heavily on the ideas and writings of B.F. Skinner. Without his development of the philosophical position called Radical Behaviorism, my repertoire would not have contained most of the responses found in this paper' (Carbone, 1981, p. 113).

   Natsoulas is well known in the profession for his painstaking analyses of

issues involved in the psychological study of conscious experience. In this article Natsoulas argues that Skinner is not correct about the problem of conscious content, even though the mistake does not necessarily invalidate the radical behaviorist position. The stance in trying to show that, in a certain way, the Skinnerian analysis is mistaken, even though this does not really affect the appeal of radical behaviorism, is reminiscent of the similar stance taken by Scriven (1956), as we have seen. The following quotations provide a sense of what is happening in the article and the usage of radical behaviorism that it contains:

> The claim of this final section of the present article shall be that Skinner has not got the problem of conscious content right. Moreover, it shall be claimed that Skinner was not in a position to get this problem right because of the impoverished conceptual apparatus which he had to put to work on the problem given the philosophy of psychology to which he stands committed. To be more accurate, Skinner's difficulties in this regard are not exactly due to the radical behaviorist philosophy. This seems to me to have greater potential than Skinner allows. His difficulties have more to do with how he chose to construe the philosophy which sustains his work and gives the work its particular quality and direction.
>
> It seems safe to say that Skinner has believed all along that the scientific philosophy of behaviorism which governs his scientific work leaves him no option than to treat of conscious content exclusively with concepts that pertain to stimuli and responses. This self-imposed condition for scientific endeavor is a costly one .... (Natsoulas, 1983, p. 19)

It seems to me that Natsoulas means by 'radical behaviorism' what there is in Skinner's overall conception of the nature of behavior that is intellectually coherent and internally consistent (even though the arguments specifically advanced by Skinner may from time to time be mistaken). The following paragraph contains instances of Natsoulas's usage of 'radical behaviorism.':

> Skinner (1974) was in effect suggesting that we can know more specifically what the problem of conscious content is for radical behaviorism by taking note of how the latter proposes to treat a larger problem, namely how it proposes to bring stimuli theoretically into the process by which operant behavior occurs. We have already seen, in the previous section, that this suggestion should not be taken to imply that radical behaviorism considers conscious content to be part of the actual process that works to bring behavior about. Although conscious content was admitted by Skinner (1953, 1974) to be part of such a process in the case of introspectively knowing of the occurrence of conscious content and in the case of using conscious content mentally to solve problems, the major part of behavior was held not to have conscious content among its causes. It follows that if the problem of conscious content for radical behaviorism amounts to the theoretical specification of how stimuli enter into the determination of operant behavior, this would be because working out the role of the stimulus will yield as a *by-product* a solution to the problem of conscious content, in the sense that conscious content will thereby find its proper location in the account.
>
> What is the role of the stimulus in an operant analysis? An answer to this question can be long and detailed, since this role has been one of the major preoccupations of the radical behaviorist scientific community .... (Natsoulas, 1983, p. 14)

Category V

Category V pertains to those papers which in one way or another want to link radical behaviorism with TEAB, or the experimental analysis of behavior. This is natural enough, since the experimental analysis of behavior had its origins in Skinner's work with rats and pigeons. Skinner put the matter forcefully in the Introduction to *About Behaviorism*:

... There must be some ... reason why behaviorism as the philosophy of a science of behavior is still so seriously misunderstood.

I believe the explanation is this: the science itself is misunderstood. There are many different kinds of behavioral science, and some of them ... formulate the field in ways which do not raise important behavioristic issues. The criticisms [of Skinner's behaviorism] listed above are most effectively answered by a special discipline, which has come to be called the experimental analysis of behavior. The behavior of individual organisms is studied in carefully controlled environments, and the relation between behavior and environment then formulated. Unfortunately, very little is known about this analysis outside the field. Its most active investigators, and there are hundreds of them, seldom make any effort to explain themselves to nonspecialists. As a result, few people are familiar with the scientific underpinnings of what, I believe, is the most cogent statement of the behavioristic position.

The behaviorism I present in this book [presumably radical behaviorism] is the philosophy of this special version of a science of behavior [the experimental analysis of behavior]. (Skinner, 1974, pp. 7–8)

Seven of the articles identified in my survey took for granted the firm connection between radical behaviorism and the experimental analysis of behavior. The following quotations illustrate the usage of 'radical behaviorism' by the seven members of this category:

... While such statements may be true of associationism, they certainly are *not* at present true of radical behaviorism. The radical behaviorist position continues to be that behavioral units are functionally defined. Units are not assumed in advance of observation (Catania, 1973; Skinner, 1935, 1938, 1953, 1957, 1966, 1974). The reliance on functional units has always been one of the distinguishing characteristics of radical behaviorism, and serves to differentiate it from associationistic or stimulus-response approaches to the study of behavior. (Branch, 1977, pp. 171–2)

While many psychologists view the current emphasis on cognitive behavior modification ... as a positive development, it may be that a complete conceptual divorce from the experimental analysis of behavior may occur as a consequence of the cognitive-behavioral movement. Such a divorce may be considered either positive or negative. The position taken here is that it is negative. To construe that the experimental analysis of behavior and its applied sibling, the applied analysis of behavior, is or has been incompatible with the analysis of internal behavior is an incorrect assumption (Skinner, 1974). However, due to the timeliness of cognitive-behavioral research, many workers who are not in touch with a radical behavioral view have been attracted to this area. (Jaremko, 1979, p. 547)

... This self-styled 'bypass' [of the thematic and methodological contributions of radical behaviorism and phenomenology in the paper by Kvale and Grenness] has the felicitous effect of extricating them from a far more difficult and less productive path for comparison, since the methods and themes in Skinner's experimental analysis of behavior have seldom resembled the work of the phenomenologist. [Giorgi] maintains that phenomenology has had a long history in its philosophy or approach, whereas it had comparatively less history as a psychological method, and that almost the opposite is true of behaviorism. This is certainly correct in the case of Skinner, who has recently become increasingly less involved with the experimental analysis of behavior and more involved with the exposition of behaviorism as a philosophy (cf. Skinner, 1974) .... Skinner's opposition to theory is an abiding part of his radical behaviorism ..., although one might argue that in some sense his programmable schedules of reinforcement are as much a theory as any mentalistic computer metaphor. (Anderson and Saeger, 1979, pp. 41, 48)

Skinnerianism, radical behaviorism, operant analysis, or the experimental analysis of behavior has been carried from its inception in large part by the work of one man, B.F. Skinner. The experimental analysis of behavior has changed from its positivistic origins to an almost entirely analytic orientation in its present form .... The experimental analysis of behavior has stood out from these background theories in psychology in general. Initially, it was more restrictively behavioristic, more operationally positivistic, and more experimentally based than any of the grand theories of learning. Currently, it is more analytic, hence more

fluid and less interested in constructing predictive models than the more specific modeling approaches to learning. (Kidd and Natalicio, 1982, pp. 41–2)

   Some radical behaviorists have expressed concern about the increasing use of cognitive constructs in the field of the experimental analysis of behavior. This cognitive movement involves language consonant with the computer metaphor and work in computer science is cited as a source of important ideas .... This dispute about the value of the computer metaphor for the experimental analysis of behavior can be seen as an example of the community in the throes of determining what it will let its members say ('warranted assertibility,' 'what it is good for us to believe'). (Lamal, 1983, p. 107)

   ... The Skinnerians, for their part, began moving in ways that Kantorians suggested. On this point, Fuller (1973) was most direct: 'Without the influence of Kantor, operant studies might have stayed exclusively in the animal laboratories for a long, long time.' ... Moreover, although radical behaviorists did not engage in extensive basic research with human subjects for a number of years, they did extend their concepts beyond the laboratory, as made evident by the publication of Keller and Schoenfeld's *Principles of Psychology* (1950) and of Skinner's *Science and Human Behavior* (1953) .... Today, the commitment of many radical behaviorists to the field of applied behavior analysis stands as clear evidence for their concern with broader human interests .... (Morris, 1982, p. 194)

I have already called attention to Moore's objection to what might be taken as mentalism in the conceptualization of certain research problems in the experimental analysis of behavior. For illustration of the way in which Moore holds the experimental analysis of behavior accountable to the precepts of radical behaviorism see Moore (1981), pp. 70–5.

Category VI

In a sixth category I have tried to single out those articles that appear to conceptualize radical behaviorism as essentially something practical, or socially useful. I placed four references in this category, the earliest of which was the abstract for the dissertation of J.J. Coulthurst from the University of Illinois at Urbana, 1973. The following quotation from the abstract (prepared by Coulthurst) makes clear the basis for its inclusion in this category:

   Given the increasing prominence of behavioral methods of analysis, prediction, and control of human behavior in many of our dominant institutions, the philosophy of radical behaviorism is examined as a means of understanding the assumptions and implications of this viewpoint for its continued application in our society. The work of B.F. Skinner is taken to be representative of the radical behaviorist's position. A thorough study of behavioral technology developed from his experimental work is examined, particularly as it is found in current industrial psychological and educational settings. (Coulthurst, 1974, p. 7638-A)

An article by J.M. Throne shows similarly that practical and utilitarian concerns can stand out as salient features of radical behaviorism:

   Learning disabilities inhere in the circumstances of the environment in which children function, not in children .... To the extent that the environment proves sufficient ... the learning [of a brain-injured or emotionally disturbed child] will improve. In either case it is the environment which makes the difference: causes the brain-injured or emotionally disturbed child to succeed or fail.
   This is the basic point of view of radical behaviorists ..., who take their lead from the basic research and writings of B.F. Skinner (1938, 1953, 1968). Radical, unlike traditional, behaviorists, regard learning disabilities to be caused by environmental, not organismic, variables. (Throne, 1976, p. 41)

Similarly focused on applied concerns is the following quotation from an article by Cullen, Hattersley and Tennant:

> The use of behaviour modification in the mental health field appears to be well established in this country [Great Britain] and it has been argued that behaviour modification is one aspect of a 'full functional analysis' .... Although terms such as 'functional analysis' and 'behavioural analysis' appear frequently in published reports, their meanings are far from clear. In our view behavioural intervention based upon radical behaviourism should have the following characteristics:
>
> 1. Identification and description of the behavioural episode and its part in the individual's total behavioural organization ....
> 2. Interpretation of the data in terms of a conceptual framework derived explicitly from an experimental analysis of behaviour (Skinner, 1953, 1972) ....
> 3. Intervention — based upon the interpretative stage, intervention involves the manipulation of the functional relationships to predicted ends, and thus is a process which is experimental in nature.
> 4. Assessment of the effects of intervention. (Cullen, Hattersley and Tennant, 1977, p. 65)

A last article is 'A Behaviouristic Base for an Ethic', by C.L. Roberts (1981). The following quoted material is interesting, not only because the author tries to give an explicit characterization of 'radical behaviorism', but also because he tries to press an interest in radical behaviorism to a consideration of how one deals with the practical concerns that arise in attempting to apply it towards productive changes in society.

> I will, in this brief paper, propose an ethic rooted in radical behaviourism. Therefore, I must characterize that term. In its most general sense radical behaviourism is a critique of traditional ways of explaining behaviour and an attempt to clarify the nature and purpose of a scientific analysis of behaviour. It is, then a philosophy of psychology. More specifically, it is the philosophy of that special discipline of psychology called experimental analysis of behaviour (Skinner, 1974, pp. 7–8). In the context of the present topic its significant facets are these: Radical behaviourism argues that the problems facing the world will be solved only if we improve our understanding of human behaviour; that such improvement requires the rejection of the concept of autonomous man and of mentalistic and other 'inner' causal accounts of behaviour, and the replacement of such accounts with one which explains behaviour in terms of phylogenic and ontogenic contingencies of selection. What this means, practically, is that for human behaviour to be changed the environment on which behaviour depends must be changed. Contingencies of selection must be brought to bear differentially on various classes of behaviour.
>
> Now, the commitment to contingencies of selection by radical behaviourism implicates survival as a value (cf. Skinner, 1974, p. 205) .... (Roberts, 1981, p. 80)
>
> I am doing nothing less here than proposing that we strive to create a culture based on the ethic outlined in this presentation, because people so acculturated have a better chance of surviving than those who accept too many things as 'O.K.' — those who say what people do does *not* matter. If such a proposal is deemed audacious, arrogant, presumptuous, then so be it. I am in very good company (see references, especially Michael, 1977).
>
> But there is a spectre here and I will close with a brief consideration of it. If we behaviourists believe *we* 'know' *what* is good, and why we should *be* good, and *how* to be good, will we be *allowed* to be good? There are many people 'out there' who also believe they know what is good and why it's good (and who may even agree with us on these points), but who leave 'how to *be* good' to 'will power,' 'moral force,' 'a sense of responsibility,' exhortation, and/or various forms of brutality. This is what makes the difference: the radical behaviourist advocates an *effective* 'technology of teaching': the differential reinforcement of desirable *behaviour*.
>
> But there are more mentalists and advocates of autonomous man than there are radical behaviourists, so behaviourists must hope that Napoleon was not necessarily right in saying that

God is on the side with the big battalions. In any event there are more battalions of mentalists than of radical behaviourists and those battalions are arrayed behind the walls of credulity. Behaviourists will not prevail in a frontal assault. Behaviourism must continue its seige and mine away at those walls. Behaviourists must continue to persuade, to argue, to debate, to reinforce appropriate behaviour, to stress principles, not just procedures, and, most of all, to provide data. In short, behaviourists must educate.

Whom must behaviourists educate? Statistically speaking behaviourists are not likely to have much impact on the well-established members of the four estates. The latter will not readily give up the gay apparel of mentalism for the almsman's garb of functional analysis. Nor will they easily foreswear the 'literature of freedom and dignity' for the unsettling, stark, and thrifty prose of B.F. Skinner, nor even for the ardent representations of Jack Michael, the relentlessly reasoned arguments of Israel Goldiamond, nor the graceful lucidity of Donald Baer. The technical literature, of course, is incomprehensible to them, and radical behaviourists do not seem to be in demand as scientific advisors to governments. But, the students of today become the legislators, the constitutional lawyers, and the nine old men of tomorrow — and the next day, and the next. (Roberts, 1981, p. 85)

Category VII

In a last category I placed those articles where basically what was meant by 'radical behaviorism' is Skinner's views, primarily 'philosophical' or systematic, taken collectively. Most of these articles also showed up in some other category. But, regardless of some other special emphasis, they seemed to indicate that the author(s) had developed a conception of radical behaviorism out of a consideration of the corpus of Skinner's writing. These articles are: Mischel (1976), Aronson (1976), Zuriff (1980), Anderson and Saeger (1979), Moore (1981), Carbone (1981), Kidd and Natalicio (1982), Lamal (1983), Natsoulas (1983), and Day (1983). We have already given examples of these authors' usage of 'radical behaviorism' in the categories reviewed above, apart from Mischel (1976) and Aronson (1976). Interestingly, both of these papers take a stance that is strongly anti-behaviorist.

Mischel's paper was a presentation for the Nebraska Symposium on Motivation, 1975, and it is carefully reasoned throughout. Mischel is thoroughly familiar with the corpus of Skinner's work. The following material, quoted from his paper, consists largely of topic sentences of the paragraphs as they occur, more or less successively, in his lengthy and careful development of Skinner's views. These excerpts should give a reasonably accurate picture of Mischel's conception of radical behaviorism. They are taken from a section of the paper that carries the major heading, 'Can Intentionalistic Explanations Be Eliminated from Psychology?', with a subheading, 'Methodological, Purposive, and Radical Behaviorism'. The material on radical behaviorism is preceded by Mischel's discussion of Tolman's 'purposive behaviorism', and these concluding sentences are also given here by way of establishing context:

> ... But what is at issue is not whether we can have excellent evidence for intentionalistic characterizations of behavior — indeed, we can — but whether such characterizations can be translated into extensional ones which make no reference to how things appear to be from the agent's point of view. The answer to that, most philosophers would now agree, is no, and that rules out the 'purposive behaviorism' Tolman envisaged.
>
> Skinner's radical behaviorism continues the attempt of earlier behaviorists to make psychology a science which eliminates the agent's point of view from descriptions and explanations of behavior, but radical behaviorists have a much clearer idea of what such a science would have to be like than did behaviorists like Watson .... Tolman's purposive behaviorism

sought to provide criteria for distinguishing the level at which, and the parameters in terms of which, psychological, as opposed to physiological, data could be identified and discriminated. But, as we have just seen, one cannot identify behavior intentionalistically, in terms of purposes and cognitions, and at the same time satisfy the conceptual and methodological restrictions behaviorists had imposed on themselves.

The problem is, however, overcome in Skinner's operant conditioning paradigm. Operants, far from being movements elicited in glands and muscles by physical stimuli, are simply 'emitted' by organisms; they are responses on the part of the organism and are defined as a class of behaviors in terms of the effect they produce — a bar press is any behavior that gets the lever down. Consequently, operant conditioning deals with molar behavior acts, while the basic stance of behaviorism is maintained since operants are defined from an external point of view, by the experimenter who does not raise any questions about what the situation may mean from the organism's point of view . . . .

This makes it possible for Skinner to claim that 'the distinction between voluntary and involuntary behavior is a matter of the kind of control. It corresponds to the distinction between eliciting and discriminative stimuli . . . voluntary behavior is operant and involuntary behavior is reflex' ([Skinner] 1953, p. 112) . . . . Consequently there is, according to Skinner, no basis for the charge that 'behaviorism has no place for intention or purpose' . . . far from it, 'operant behavior is the very field of purpose and intention . . . .'

Similarly, Skinner rejects the 'methodological behaviorism' of Watson and others which 'ignores consciousness, feelings, and states of mind' on the ground that they cannot be studied scientifically, because this merely avoids the mentalistic problem instead of dealing with it (1974, p. 4, 13ff.). In contrast, 'the heart of radical behaviorism,' according to Skinner, is its ability to deal with 'what is inside the skin,' and in so doing radical behaviorism 'provides an alternative account of mental life' . . . . A great deal of Skinner's writing is devoted to attempts 'to interpret a wide range of mentalistic expressions' . . . . 'I consider scores, if not hundreds of examples of mentalistic usage . . . . Many expressions I "translate into behavior" ' . . . .

Central to Skinner's 'translations' is the notion that mental states and processes can be construed as felt body states which are private, in the sense that only the person himself can, normally, feel or observe what is going on 'inside his skin' . . . . But 'no special kind of mind stuff is ·assumed. A physical world generates both physical action and the physical conditions within the body to which a person responds when a verbal community arranges the necessary contingencies' ([Skinner, 1974] p. 220).

This 'translation' of mentalistic concepts provides Skinner with a justification for bypassing the inner states to which they refer in the scientific analysis of the causes of behavior. For if desires, purposes, and other so-called 'mental states' are really physical states inside our own bodies, then they cannot initiate or direct behavior but must themselves be caused by other physical states and conditions . . . .

What emerges from Skinner's 'translations' and 'interpretations' of mentalistic concepts is a biologized version of the passive organism of association psychology, a picture according to which we never act, but always react to external contingencies . . . . it could not be otherwise, since the adoption of the explanatory framework of the physical sciences excludes the agent's point of view, and thus also the framework of concepts in which we can distinguish actions, which are initiated and directed by someone, from reactions that are caused to occur in him. As Skinner puts it, 'there is no place in the scientific position for a self as a true originator or initiator of action' . . . .

Skinner's theoretical achievement lies in showing how behavior *might* be due to the action of external contingencies even when it does not have any obvious environmental cause . . . .

Now if it is really true that complex human behaviors can be predicted and explained in terms of the operant paradigm, then Skinner's claim that mentalistic explanations are just inventions, . . . that to explain behavior one 'must look to the constructing environment, not to a constructing mind' . . . will have real force. The objection that what is important is not the physical stimulus or the topography of the behavior, but their meaning, will then be beside the point . . . .

While Skinner has, I think, succeeded in sketching coherent background assumptions for a possible program of psychological research, he talks of 'laws of the science of behavior' and 'recent advances in the experimental analysis of behavior' *as if* laws of the appropriate type had, in fact, been established for complex human behavior. But Skinner's claim that 'it is in the nature of an experimental analysis of human behavior that it should strip away the functions

previously assigned to autonomous man and transfer them one by one to the controlling environment' ... is certainly not supported by evidence showing that such an experimental analysis can, in fact, be carried through for complex human behavior. What Skinner has shown is that a surprising amount of animal behavior in the Skinner box, and a very limited range of human behavior, can be predicted and controlled in terms of the operant conditioning paradigm .... [A]t least with respect to human behavior, Skinner's talk about 'advances in the experimental analysis of behavior' is a promissory note, and what is at issue is the plausibility of thinking that it can be cashed. (Mischel, 1976, p. 158ff.)

Mischel has a balanced and, for a philosopher, an exceptionally well-informed conception of radical behaviorism as basically Skinner's views, primarily 'philosophical' or systematic, taken collectively. The above material has been severely abridged, but its balanced tone and manner of presentation are representative of the style maintained throughout Mischel's argument.

The paper by Aronson is of an entirely different nature. Indeed, I was not sure where I should place it in my classification. In some ways Aronson's conception of radical behaviorism is more similar to that of Scriven than to that of any of the other persons whose usage of 'radical behaviorism' we have considered. However, I placed the article here because it does not fit within the professional climate of the times when Scriven's paper was written, and it does involve a basically 'philosophical' assessment of the professional potential of Skinner's view:

In spite of the rejection of behaviourism in various circles in the philosophy of science, psychology and linguistics, many professional psychologists and social scientists still regard themselves as behaviourists. One reason why this is so is that they believe the alternative models of human behaviour have little or no effect on their scientific research. It is argued that even if there are mental states or cognitive structures which serve as intermediaries between stimulus and response, the existence of these 'entities' would not change the nature of the psychologist's scientific enterprise. That is, if the response is a function of the stimulus, whatever serves as a connection between stimulus and response plays a role equivalent to a middle term in a syllogism; whatever its nature, whether it be mental, physiological or otherwise, it need not be considered when it comes to psychologically explaining and predicting behaviour. Psychology, as a complete science, is thus *independent* of any speculation about what happens between stimulus and response .... This then is the fundamental assumption of radical behaviourism: the neurophysiological connection between stimulus and response is straightforward to the extent that inner states are rendered superfluous when it comes to the prediction, control, and explanation of behaviour. It is this assumption that allows the radical behaviourist to claim that individual behaviour is, in principle, completely predictable, accountable, and controllable by physical stimuli or environmental factors, and it is this assumption that will be questioned in this paper.

Radical behaviourism, then, assumes something about the nature of neuronal activity that allows the psychologist to make his investigations without having to worry about internal variables ....

But there are other possible working models of the brain, and these models may be contrary to the above fundamental assumption. It will be shown below that certain viable models of the brain are not coherent with radical behaviourism .... (Aronson, 1976, pp. 49–50)

I have been unable to obtain copies of three papers which were identified in my survey of the subject-matter indexes of *Psychological Abstracts*: Cullen (1975), Cullen (1981), and Stanley and Linke (1982). It is unfortunate that I am not able to report on these papers, in part because my best guess is that all three suggest that radical behaviorism in its applied aspects should try to avoid entanglement with epistemological features often attributed to TEAB, the experimental analysis of behavior. I am unable to resist reproducing material from the abstracts of these

articles. (The references following the quotations are to volume and page numbers of *Psychological Abstracts*.)

Cullen (1975):
> Questions the relevance of J.C. Quicke's (see PA, Vol. 54: 8247) criticism of radical behaviorism, specifically rebutting 2 points: that behaviorism is both mechanistic and reductionistic, and that it is not humanistic. (PA, Vol. 55, p. 352)

Stanley and Linke, (1982):
> Argues that the clinical practice of radical behaviorism has been dominated by the methodological imperative that Skinner initiated in 1938, while the epistemological imperative of 1945 has not received sufficient attention from clinicians. This latter approach offers an interpretive framework for examining cognitive behavior modification techniques, whose popularity results from the prevailing cognitive paradigm of experimental psychology. (PA, Vol. 70, p. 699)

Cullen (1981):
> Comments on W.D. Pierce and F.W. Epling's (1980) paper on the element of analysis in applied behavior analysis and points to a shift from the kind of 'science' that was once the hallmark of behavior modification. This shift is characterized by a trend toward data transformation and an increase in the use of mentalistic terms. The solution lies not in the flight to the laboratory, but in the application of radical behaviorism to problems of social importance.

In concluding, have I answered the question with which we started: what is radical behaviorism? My response is 'yes' in that I have provided information relevant to how people actually make use of the expression 'radical behaviorism'. We could go on to talk about the information I have displayed. I could point out that usage changes as a function of changes in the profession with the passage of time. I could point out that people are more likely to spend time thinking about certain problems in regard to radical behaviorism than about others. People think about the role of theory in radical behaviorism, about the role of private events in a natural science, and about mentalism, the use of 'mentalistic' terms, and what happens when such terms are given behavioral translation. People can become *really* worked up over how the experimental analysis of behavior engages what we want to make useful and to take advantage of in radical behaviorism.

But have I said what radical behaviorism really *is*? This is an ontological question which raises epistemological issues. Let us agree to leave those matters alone here. More relevant to this question when it is raised among people who refer to themselves as 'radical behaviorists' is this question: what *should* radical behaviorism be? In any case, whatever your question about radical behaviorism may be, if it can be answered by a relevant definition, I offer the following:

> When it comes to a statement of what radical behaviorism is, the most straightforward thing to say is that it is the attempt to account for behavior solely in terms of natural contingencies: either contingencies of survival, contingencies of reinforcement, or contingencies of social evolution. However, Skinner has [spoken] of radical behaviorism as the philosophy of a special discipline within psychological research spoken of as the experimental analysis of behavior. Yet it should be kept in mind that when Skinner attempts to characterize this philosophy, the account consistently involves a complex argument centering on practices of the verbal community in teaching us to talk about our behavior, both private and public.
>
> I myself prefer to take a somewhat different approach to conceptualizing radical behaviorism. For me, radical behaviorism is the effect that Skinner's thought happens to have on the behavior of people. To the extent that this effect involves establishing new repertoires of responding that seriously challenge the very old ideas we have in our culture about how behavior is to be explained, I believe that radical behaviorism is both interesting and important. (Day, 1983, p. 101)

NOTES

1   In an effort to keep the *Encyclopedia* reasonably current, a *Progress Volume* was published in 1983. The material concerning behaviorism appears under the entry 'Experimental Psychology: Recent Developments'. The upshot of the recent developments can be seen in the following excerpt.

> The review of materials points to two contrasting groups of words. On the one side were such nouns as associationism, elementalism, behaviorism, and operationalism. On the other side were such nouns as nonassociationism, holism, cognition and inferred constructs (or models). There can be little doubt that contemporary experimental psychology is best characterized by the latter, rather than the former, set of words .... For about a quarter of a century (roughly 1940–1965), B.F. Skinner's behaviorism was the most visible force in American psychology .... The basis of the Skinnerian appeal was (and still is) its strictly descriptive and positivistic approach to the study of behavior, a view increasingly regarded as deficient by substantial numbers of contemporary psychologists. Cognition and purpose were deliberately excluded: they were consequences, not determiners, of behavior .... An especially important [matter] seems to be that concern has shifted away from the sphere of 'action' to that of 'knowledge.' Witness the growth of research in the areas of perception, memory, attention, and psycholinguistics .... The foregoing developments led to substantial numbers of behavioral psychologists adopting a fresh outlook, one that included the examination of 'cognitive processes.' (Wolman, 1983, pp. 125–6)

There is no reference to 'radical behaviorism' in the *Progress Volume*. Instead, reference is to 'B.F. Skinner's behaviorism' and 'operant behaviorism'.

2   There is no reference to 'radical behaviorism' in Wolman's (1973) *Dictionary of Behavioral Science*.

REFERENCES

Anderson, S.J. and Saeger, W. (1979) 'Behavior, mind and existence: Toward a primary triangulation of human action', *Behaviorism*, 7(1), pp. 37–63.

Aronson, J.L. (1976) 'Some dubious neurological assumptions for radical behaviourism', *Journal of the Theory of Social Behaviour*, 6, pp. 49–60.

Boring, E.G. (1950) *A History of Experimental Psychology*, 2nd ed., New York, Appleton-Century-Crofts.

Branch, M.N. (1977) 'On the role of memory in the analysis of behavior', *Journal of the Experimental Analysis of Behavior*, 28, pp. 171–9.

Bridgman, P.W. (1927) *The Logic of Modern Physics*, New York, Macmillan.

Carbone, V.J. (1981) 'The inner world: A radical behavioral account', *Corrective and Social Psychiatry and Journal of Behavior Technology, Methods and Therapy*, 27, pp. 109–13.

Corriveau, M. (1972) 'Phenomenology, psychology, and radical behaviorism: Skinner and Merleau-Ponty on behavior', *Journal of Phenomenological Psychology*, 3 pp. 7–34.

Coulthurst, J.J. (1973) 'Behaviorism in education and society: The implications of Skinnerian ideology', unpublished doctoral dissertation, University of Illinois, Urbana-Champaign, Ill.

Cullen, C.N. (1975) '"Behaviorism and Education": A reply', *AEP (Association of Educational Psychologists) Journal*, 3(9), pp. 35–8.

Cullen, C.N. (1981) 'The flight to the laboratory', *Behavior Analyst*, 4, pp. 81–3.

Cullen, C., Hattersley, J. and Tennant, L. (1977) 'Behaviour modification: Some implications of a radical behaviourist view', *Bulletin of the British Psychological Society*, 30, pp. 65–9.

Day, W. (1969) 'Radical behaviorism in reconciliation with phenomenology', *Journal of the Experimental Analysis of Behavior*, 12, pp. 315–28.

Day, W. (1981) 'The historical antecedents of contemporary behaviorism', in Rieber, R. and Salzinger, K. (Eds), *Psychology: Historical and Theoretical Perspectives*, New York, Academic Press.

Day, W. (1983) 'On the difference between radical and methodological behaviorism', *Behaviorism*, 11, pp. 89–102.

Eachus, T. (1972) 'A radical behaviorist's view of humanistic psychology: Do you see what I see?' in Houts, P.S. and Serber, M. (Eds), *After the Turn on, What? Learning Perspectives on Humanistic Groups*, Champaign, Ill., Research Press.

Edwards, P. (Ed.) (1967) *The Encyclopedia of Philosophy*, 8 vols., New York, Macmillan.

Estes, W.K. *et al.* (1954) *Modern Learning Theory*, New York, Appleton-Century-Crofts.

Feigl, H. (1958) 'The "mental" and the "physical",' in Feigl, H., Scriven, M. and Maxwell, G. (Eds), *Minnesota Studies in the Philosophy of Science*, Vol. 2, Minneapolis, Minn., University of Minnesota Press.

Feigl, H. and Brodbeck (Eds) (1953) *Readings in the Philosophy of Science*, New York, Appleton-Century-Crofts.

Hempel, C. (1958) 'The theoretician's dilemma', in Feigl, H., Scriven, M. and Maxwell, G. (Eds), *Minnesota Studies in the Philosophy of Science*, Vol. 2, Minneapolis, Minn., University of Minnesota Press.

Jaremko, M.E. (1979) 'Cognitive behavior modification: Real science or more mentalism?' *Psychological Record*, 2, pp. 547–52.

Johnson, R.J. (1963) 'Discussion: A commentary on "radical behaviorism".' *Philosophy of Science*, 30, pp. 274–85.

Kaufman, A.S. (1967) 'Behaviorism', in Edwards, P. (Ed.), *The Encyclopedia of Philosophy*, Vol. 1, New York, Macmillan.

Kidd, R. and Natalicio, L. (1982) 'An interbehavioral approach to operant analysis', *Psychological Record*, 32, pp. 41–59.

Kvale, S. and Grenness, C. (1967) 'Skinner and Sartre', *Review of Existential Psychology and Psychiatry*, 7, pp. 128–49.

Lamal, P.A. (1983) 'A cogent critique of epistemology leaves radical behaviorism unscathed', *Behaviorism*, 11, pp. 103–9.

McCorkle, M. (1978) 'A radical behaviorist study of "women's experience of conflict",' unpublished doctoral dissertation, University of Nevada Reno, Reno, Nev.

Mischel, T. (1976) 'Psychological explanations and their vicissitudes', in Arnold, W.J. (Ed.), *Nebraska Symposium on Motivation*, 1975, Lincoln, Neb., University of Nebraska Press.

Moore, J. (1975) 'On the principle of operationism in a science of behavior', *Behaviorism*, 3, pp. 120–38.

Moore, J. (1980) 'On behaviorism and private events', *Psychological Record*, 30, pp. 459–75.

Moore, J. (1981) 'On mentalism, methodological behaviorism, and radical behaviorism', *Behaviorism*, 9, pp. 55–77.

Morris, E.K. (1982) 'Some relationships between interbehavioral psychology and radical behaviorism', *Behaviorism*, 10, pp. 187–216.

Natsoulas, T. (1983) 'Perhaps the most difficult problem faced by behaviorism', *Behaviorism*, 11, pp. 1–26.

Roberts, C.L. (1981) 'A behaviouristic basis for an ethic', *New Zealand Psychologist*, 10, pp. 80–5.

Scriven, M. (1956) 'A study of radical behaviorism', in Feigl H. and Scriven, M. (Eds), *Minnesota Studies in the Philosophy of Science*, Vol. 1, Minneapolis, Minn., University of Minnesota Press.

Skinner, B.F. (1938) *The Behavior of Organisms*, New York: Appleton-Century-Crofts.

Skinner, B.F. (1945) 'The operational analysis of psychological terms', *Psychological Review*, 52, pp. 270–7, 291–4.

Skinner, B.F. (1953) *Science and Human Behavior*, New York, Macmillan.

Skinner, B.F. (1964) 'Behaviorism at fifty (with discussion)', in Wann, T.W. (Ed.) *Behaviorism and Phenomenogy*, Chicago, Ill. University of Chicago Press.

Skinner, B.F. (1974) *About Behaviorism*, college ed., New York, Alfred A. Knopf.

Stanley, B. and Linke, S. (1982) 'Why we are not cognitive behaviour modifiers: The philosophical basis of applied behaviour analysis', *Behaviour Analysis*, 3, 3, pp. 14–25.

Throne, J.M. (1976) 'Learning disabilities: A radical behaviorist point of view', *School Psychology Digest*, 5, pp. 41–5.

Wann, T.W. (Ed.) (1964) *Behaviorism and Phenomenology*, Chicago, Ill. University of Chicago Press.

Wolman, B.B. (Ed.) (1973) *Dictionary of Behavioral Science*, New York, Van Nostrand Reinhold.

Wolman, B.B. (Ed.) (1977) *International Encyclopedia of Psychiatry, Psychology, Psychoanalysis, and Neurology,* 11 vols, New York, Van Nostrand Reinhold.

Wolman, B.B. (Ed.) (1983) *International Encyclopedia of Psychiatry, Psychology, Psychoanalysis, and Neurology: Progress Volume 1*, New York, Aesculapius Publishers.

Zuriff, G.E. (1980) 'Radical behaviorist epistemology', *Psychological Bulletin*, 87, pp. 337–50.

4. The Implications of Radical Behaviourism: A Critique of Skinner's Science of Behaviour and Its Application

GEOFFREY HALL

In his time J.B. Watson was referred to as '*the* behaviourist', a title which if used nowadays would undoubtedly have to be conferred on B.F. Skinner. But there is more than one behaviourism and Skinner cannot be held responsible for (or take the credit for) the achievements of many of them. If behaviourism is taken to be simply the insistence on objective methods of study in psychology, then the general acceptance of this doctrine is the legacy in large measure of Watson himself and would have occurred without Skinner. To say that this doctrine has been generally accepted prompts us to ask (along with Broadbent, 1964): by whom? Broadbent's answer is, 'by those people in the English-speaking countries who engage in pure academic research in psychology' (p. 35), and he quickly goes on to point out that this excludes many (in particular, a large number of psychiatrists) who are regarded by the public as authorities on human nature. Although Skinner has been in the forefront of those eager to carry a behaviourist message both to the public (as in *Beyond Freedom and Dignity*, 1972) and to the psychiatric community (see his 'Critique of Psychoanalytic Concepts and Theories', Skinner, 1954), these activities are not the unique outcome of his brand of behaviourism. The contributions of Eysenck, for instance, have been quite as prominent in this area (e.g., Eysenck, 1972).

But if some form of 'methodological behaviourism' is generally accepted by academic psychologists, not all have gone on to attempt to devise an all-embracing account of psychology from the systematic study of non-human animals in the laboratory. Again, however, although Skinner has been prominent among

41

those who have made the attempt (with his *Behavior of Organisms*, 1938), he has been one among many and the endeavour does not uniquely characterize his contribution. Equal importance must be granted to the work of Hull and Spence and of Tolman. The 'purposive behaviourism' of the last (Tolman, 1932) is clearly something rather different from any behaviourism that Skinner would want to espouse but so too is the 'neobehaviourism' of Hull and Spence (see Kendler and Spence, 1971; Spence, 1948). With its use of the S-R formula and of intervening variables, its insistence on the hypothetico-deductive method and its emphasis on mathematical theorizing, neobehaviourism incorporates many of the features that Skinner has been keen to exorcise from his own analysis of behaviour.

It is possible, therefore, to present a critique of Skinner's 'radical' behaviourism while retaining a commitment to the use of objective methods in psychology and acknowledging the achievements of the neobehaviourists and their successors. What we must consider, rather, are the features of Skinner's behaviourism that distinguish it from its rivals. These are many but have their source in one central doctrine: that what an organism does can and should be explained entirely in terms of what happens to it. Other behaviourisms are content to use behaviour as an index of something else (of the subject's state of mind, for instance, or of the strength of an S-R association), which is in turn invoked to explain observed behaviour. Radical behaviourism sweeps away these 'explanatory fictions': behaviour is to be studied in its own right and its causes sought in the environment.

Our task, then, is to provide a critical assessment of the 'central doctrine' of radical behaviourism and of its implications. We can best begin this task by examining the experimental work to which it gave rise. We will then consider the theoretical interpretation to which the empirical findings have been subjected, and finally the attempt to apply this theory more generally.

THE EXPERIMENTAL ANALYSIS OF BEHAVIOUR

For an avowed devotee of an experimental psychology who has bemoaned 'the flight from the laboratory' (Skinner, 1961), a surprising amount of Skinner's work, in particular, that on verbal behaviour (1957), has been based on more everyday and less systematic observations of the doings of his fellow men. But the analysis of human behaviour, it is asserted, has its foundation in those laboratory studies of the behaviour of non-human animals that constitute 'the experimental analysis of behaviour'.

Methods

The general methods of the behaviour analyst seem sensible enough and have been widely adopted by experimenters who reject the tenets of radical behaviourism. A convenient experimental subject (say a rat or a pigeon) is isolated in a special enclosure (let us call it a Skinner box) which allows environmental events (usually the presentation of tones, or lights, food, or electric shock) to be controlled totally by the experimenter who is thereby able to see how manipulation of these events determines what the animal does. The recording of behaviour

is simplified by concentrating upon measuring (usually) just one automatically scored activity — that of pressing a lever, say, or of pecking a 'key'.

Simplification, the stripping down of a complex phenomenon to its essentials, is the essence of a good scientific experimental procedure; but problems soon arise with Skinnerian methods not because of the restrictions imposed upon the subject, but because of further constraints that Skinner (e.g., 1966) wants to impose on the experimenter. According to strict Skinnerian practice, the experimenter must study the behaviour of individual animals and may not make use of the average performance of several subjected to the same procedure; he may not, therefore, compare (using statistical methods) the behaviour of two groups of animals subjected to different procedures but must investigate the behaviour of one individual given the different treatments at different times; and he should restrict his measure of behaviour to the rate at which the response occurs (see also Sidman, 1960).

The origin of some of these restrictions is perhaps discernible in the doctrine that behaviour should be studied in its own right. But whatever their origin, they provide a first hint of a narrowness of vision that seems to characterize radical behaviourism. They also seem to reveal a surprising lack of confidence. Cannot radical behaviourists trust themselves to make use of the methodology of their conceptual rivals when the need arises (as, for instance, in the study of a treatment, say the injection of a drug, that might have irreversible effects on behaviour) without fear of ceasing to be radical. If they cannot, their vision becomes narrowed so that they are then capable of working only on issues for which their methodology is appropriate. When we look at the outcome of studies using these techniques we will see that they have generated a system that finds no place for several important determiners of behaviour and that is inadequate to account even for animal behaviour in the laboratory, let alone the natural behaviour of all species including our own.

Findings

The Skinner box allows the experimenter to control his subject's environment and to see the change in behaviour that results. Many of the events available (the presentation of tones or of lights, say) do little more than elicit 'unconditioned' responses (a jump, or a turn of the head) and these do not seem to be the stuff of which everyday behaviour is made. But other events ('reinforcers') such as the presentation of food to a food-deprived animal can generate much more and more interesting behaviour and it is upon reinforcement that the behaviour analyst has concentrated.

Operant behaviour. A pigeon will not 'spontaneously' peck the key in a Skinner box. One way to train it to do so is to present food each time the bird makes a movement that approximates to that desired, requiring closer and closer approximations until the key-peck is 'shaped'. Behaviour thus changes as a result of stimulation, but, Skinner points out (e.g., 1938), it is not elicited by the stimulus and the S-R analysis of other behaviourists seems inappropriate. Rather, 'operant' behaviour, of which this is taken to be an example, is controlled by its consequences not its antecedents. Skinner was one of the first to make clear (see

also Miller and Konorski, 1928; Grindley, 1932) the distinction between this sort of conditioning and the 'respondent', classical, conditioning of Pavlov which for Skinner was a process 'concerned mainly with the internal physiology of the organism' (Skinner, 1953, p. 59) whereas operant behaviour concerned the interactions of the organism with its world. Operant behaviour was taken to encapsulate the essence of 'voluntary' behaviour — the proper subject matter of psychology.

Operant conditioning turns out, however, to provide at best an incomplete account of behaviour. Sometimes, for instance, properly applied reinforcement procedures simply fail to work. Thus Shettleworth (e.g., 1975) has found it nearly impossible to increase the rate of face-washing by food reinforcement in that otherwise tractable creature, the golden hamster. Faced with this sort of result the behaviour analyst can take refuge in definition by asserting simply that face-washing is not an operant since it is not susceptible to reinforcement. But in doing so he gives no real account of the phenomenon. Presumably the factors responsible for such failures can be discovered and specified, and any system that fails to find some place for them must be judged to be seriously deficient.

In some cases the operant reinforcement account can be shown to be not so much incomplete as wrong. We have described the shaping of the pigeon's key-peck in terms of the effect of reinforcement on the behaviour it follows. But evidence has now accumulated (Moore, 1973) to suggest that this training procedure is effective because it ensures that a particular sort of stimulation (reinforcement tends to be given when the pigeon's head is turned toward the lit key) precedes food. The procedure is that of classical conditioning in which one stimulus (food) is made contingent on another (the key-light) and the key-peck is best interpreted as a Pavlovian conditioned response. To accept this interpretation means also accepting that the most widely studied laboratory 'operant' (see, e.g., Ferster and Skinner, 1957) may in fact be controlled according to Pavlovian principles. And more, the discovery that classical conditioning can govern the behaviour of the whole animal and its movements about its environment means that its importance has been greatly underestimated by Skinner. If behaviour controlled by its past history of operant reinforcement can be validly labelled as 'voluntary', then it seems unfair to deny this label to the behaviour of approaching one event that has previously been associated with some other such as food. Given that much of our everyday behaviour can be construed as a series of movements governed by once-neutral events that have become signals for other events of motivational significance, it is unjustified to assert that the study of operant behaviour can be equated with that of voluntary behaviour.

Schedules of reinforcement. The restriction imposed by the operant methodology virtually forced upon Skinner his next step as an experimenter: that of investigating the behaviour governed by schedules of reinforcement (in which the reinforcer is presented only after a given time interval, or after a given number of responses have elapsed, and so on). The behaviour governed by such schedules is often impressively orderly and a large-scale industry has grown up in which behaviour analysts devise increasingly more complex and abstruse schedules. Schedules are perhaps the most prominent contribution of the behaviour analyst to the laboratory study of behaviour and it has been claimed (Reynolds, 1968, p. 60) that 'the study of schedules is central to the study of behavior' more generally.

We have no space to examine this claim in detail but it is important to establish that it is not generally accepted. Thus we may agree with Jenkins (1970) when he points out that schedules are not a 'given' that the psychologist must study, since 'neither men nor animals are found in nature responding repeatedly in an unchanging environment for occasional reinforcement' (p. 107). A possibility that Jenkins will allow is that schedules might constitute 'useful contrivances' that may be used in order to further our understanding of basic conditioning principles. But even in this respect they are far from ideal. In the next section we consider one attempt to analyze the behaviour produced by a 'fixed interval' schedule. This analysis reveals the justice of the assertion by Mackintosh (1974) that the fact that 'simple' schedules produce orderly behaviour carries no implication about 'the simplicity of the causal factors responsible .... However orderly the behaviour ... it is the product of a complex interaction between the subject's past and present behaviour and the particular pattern of reinforcement received ... schedules are far from being simple. They are frighteningly complex and not necessarily at all well suited to an elucidation of the important processes underlying instrumental behaviour' (Mackintosh, 1974, pp. 181–2).

THEORETICAL INTERPRETATION

Skinner created his experimental analysis of behaviour in defiance of the contemporary trend toward elaborate theorizing (Skinner, 1950). His own aim was to provide a purely descriptive system, a functional analysis in which the only terms allowed were independent variables (manipulable features of the environment) and the dependent variable (response probability, measured usually as response rate). His system was to consist only of verified facts about behaviour (as opposed to hypotheses susceptible to disconfirmation) and his contribution as 'theorist' confined to that of organizing these facts 'in such a way that a simple and convenient description can be given ...' (Skinner, 1938, p. 45). For this it was allowed that a 'system' was required.

Skinner's 'System'

The essence of Skinner's system is his 'three-term contingency'. Apart from the (largely neglected) 'respondents' that are directly elicited by stimuli, behaviour is taken to consist of operants, the likelihood of which is controlled by the presentation of reinforcers and also by the environmental stimuli in the presence of which reinforcements occur (although it is insisted that such 'discriminative stimuli' do not actually elicit behaviour). Operants become less likely when reinforcement is withheld (extinction) or the discriminative stimulus is changed. Reinforcers may be identified by the fact that they strengthen operants; operants are responses without eliciting stimuli that are susceptible to reinforcement; and a discriminative stimulus may be any event contiguous with operant reinforcement.

Armed with these and a few subsidiary notions, Skinner was prepared to attempt an analysis of the complex patterns of behaviour generated by reinforcement schedules (Ferster and Skinner, 1957). Thus, in order to explain the final pattern of responding (the rate is low immediately after reinforcement and

increases thereafter) generated by a 'fixed interval' schedule (in which the first response after a given time yields the reinforcer), the following processes, among others, are invoked. Responding will be occurring at a given rate when the reinforcer is delivered and this rate of response will therefore be differentially reinforced; the time since the previous reinforcer can come to act as a discriminative stimulus being present when reinforcement occurs; the stimuli associated with reinforcement can become discriminative stimuli constituting an occasion following which subsequent responses are never reinforced; and so on.

It is immediately apparent that what we are being given here is not simply a set of facts but the outline of a theory of sorts that attempts to explain them. The suggestions being made are open to empirical test and capable of being disconfirmed. Skinner was willing to allow (1950) that by this criterion no empirical statement is wholly non-theoretical, simply because evidence is never complete. But this is not the point at issue here. No one disputes the observation that, for instance, certain cues immediately follow reinforcement. What is at issue is the assertion that these cues play a critical part in producing the pattern of behaviour observed. Without going into the details of his experiments, it is enough to say that Jenkins (1970) has been able to demonstrate that performance on interval schedules cannot be reduced to operation of simple conditioning principles, to confirm the theoretical status of the system used by Ferster and Skinner.

We may even doubt that the basic three-term contingency has the atheoretical status claimed for it. A doubt is raised by the fact (already discussed) that a pattern of behaviour (the pigeon's peck to a lit key), confidently asserted to be a prime example of the operation of this contingency, can turn out to be nothing of the sort. As a further example, consider the suggestion that a discriminative stimulus is established simply by its temporal conjunction with reinforcement of the operant. Such a view leaves no place for the possibility that the animal might 'attend' to some aspects of an event and ignore others. But recent research (see Mackintosh, 1977) has convincingly shown that such 'stimulus selection' often occurs, and to this extent Skinner's account is disconfirmed.

The Role of Theory

There is no disgrace for a scientist in having his theory disproved. The examples just cited are intended merely to demonstrate that we should not take entirely seriously the image of Skinner as the great anti-theorist. Skinner himself (e.g., 1969) is willing to acknowledge his activities as a theoretician. He goes on, however, to point out that he has not involved himself with the sort of theory he has condemned elsewhere. He has no truck with 'any explanation of an observed fact which appeals to events taking place somewhere else, at some other level of observation, described in different terms, and measured, if at all, in different dimensions' (Skinner, 1950, p. 193). This definition adequately characterizes the theorizing of most experimental psychologists.

Why again this narrowness of approach? Given that well-established sciences operate for the most part by proposing and testing explanatory theories concerned with concepts or events other than those to be explained, why should the psychologist be banned from considering underlying mechanisms, whether these be expressed in physiological terms or merely as conceptual models? Crick and Watson were given a set of observations of the behaviour of a certain crystal

(diffraction patterns) produced by a particular sort of stimulation (X-ray irradiation). Their discovery of the structure of DNA and all that followed came about because they, quite literally, dared to build a model of the structure that might be responsible for the observations. Psychology might hope for an equivalent leap forward when its practitioners devise an equivalently powerful model (physical or conceptual) for behaviour. If the components of this theory can be linked to physiological processes, so much the better.

Does mistrust of such theorizing again betray a lack of confidence? Skinner writes that theories deal with intervening steps in the relationship between dependent and independent variables. 'But instead of prompting us to search for and explore relevant variables, they frequently have quite the opposite effect. When we attribute behavior to a neural or mental event, real or conceptual, we are likely to forget that we still have the task of accounting for the neural or mental event' (Skinner, 1950, p. 194). The argument is sound. Intervening events can, of course, be dispensed with; and if they are not, it is, of course, necessary to relate them to observables. But it seems implausible that serious students of behaviour are likely to forget this, and unduly restrictive to deny them a full range of theories in case they should do so.

APPLICATIONS

If Skinner had published nothing after *The Behavior of Organisms* (1938), his position as an important experimental psychologist would still be recognized among other experimental psychologists. His wider fame (or notoriety) derives from the activities of his later years in which with increasing urgency (from *Science and Human Behavior*, 1953, to *Beyond Freedom and Dignity*, 1972) he has urged the application of his 'science of behaviour' to human affairs. One aspect of this application is seen in the attempt to devise 'a technology of behaviour' in which the methods and empirical findings of the behaviour analyst are used directly to modify the behaviour of the inmates of schools, and factories, and psychiatric institutions. But equally noteworthy is the attempt to apply the concepts derived from the operant analysis to phenomena seemingly quite remote from the behaviour shown in the Skinner box: to all aspects of human social behaviour (Skinner, 1953), verbal behaviour (Skinner, 1957), and to thinking, perceiving, emotion and similar topics once thought to be the preserve of the mentalist (Skinner, 1974).

These attempts at application have provoked strong reaction in some quarters in spite of Skinner's insistence that an effective science of behaviour will not deprive man of his freedom and dignity. His defence of his philosophical position seems to me to be valid (see his 'Freedom and the Control of Men', Skinner, 1956). Much more dubious is the central assertion that Skinner's analysis of human issues genuinely reflects the proper application of a science of behaviour.

Application and Interpretation

When a schizophrenic who has remained isolated and mute for twenty years is taught to speak and interact with his fellows by a training technique in which approximations to the desired behaviour cause the patient to be given a stick of

chewing gum, it scarcely matters that the procedure is called 'shaping' and the gum a 'reinforcer'. We can applaud the outcome and acknowledge that the procedure might not have been tried but for the experimental work of behaviour analysts. But applied science implies more than the application of rules of thumb ('behavioural principles') derived from analogous laboratory situations. And when it is asserted that the behaviour of saying 'red' is a verbal operant, under the control of a discriminative stimulus (a red object) and reinforced by a listener (who says 'right!'), the terminology becomes all-important. For it is in the use of his three-term contingency to reinterpret behaviour usually described in other ways, that Skinner has made his most persistent attempts to apply his science.

We have already noted the 'functional' definitions of the terms of this contingency whereby a reinforcer, for instance, can be anything that reinforces (a smile, a word, a pellet of food, and so on). The flexibility of these definitions does not mean that a postulated operant can never be shown to be something else, but the relevant experimental technique (known as omission training) is rarely used outside the conditioning laboratory, and the elasticity of the three-term formula has allowed it to be applied almost universally. Its wide applicability can be taken to reflect the fact that, to use everyday language, people do the things they do because they find themselves in certain circumstances and because they expect their actions to have certain consequences.

If it is asserted that this application is *merely* a reinterpretation of established facts using an unfamiliar terminology, Skinner would in part agree. He has urged that understanding of behavioural processes is important not only for practical applications but because 'we can use it to *interpret* behaviour' (Cohen, 1977, p. 277). What he would dispute is the adverb 'merely'. A reinterpretation in unfamiliar terms can sometimes generate new insight and understanding — no one stigmatizes the theory of evolution as 'mere' redescription on the grounds that it constitutes only a way of organizing established facts according to an unfamiliar principle. Theories of this sort are not assessed in the ways of conventional science: it is difficult to think of empirical evidence that might make us want to dispense with them. Rather, they gain acceptance because they allow us to make new sense of a wide range of disparate facts. The widespread rejection of Skinner's theory (something Skinner himself has noted, Skinner, 1974) means that for most people it fails to enhance their understanding of human behaviour. Why should this be so?

Environmental Determinism

Skinner (e.g., 1972) is in no doubt about the answer. It is that an ingrained attachment to the notion of 'autonomous man', free to control his own destiny, prevents his critics from facing up to a truth that they might find unpalatable. But this can be, at best, only a partial explanation. A large number of practising psychologists are as wedded as Skinner to a determinist view of their subject matter. How could they hope to build any science of behaviour if they accepted that their dependent variable was not lawfully controlled by the influences acting upon the organism? What these scientists reject is not determinism but Skinner's narrow version of it. It is one thing to say that behaviour is 'determined'; quite

another to say that it is determined almost entirely according to the principles of operant conditioning.

Skinner's emphasis on the role of the environment leads him to neglect the other major determinant of an organism's behaviour — its genetic endowment. What something does depends not only on what happens to it but what it is to start with. The reinforcement contingencies sufficient to establish verbal behaviour in a human child do not work with any other species. Skinner (1969) is prepared to acknowledge that some patterns of behaviour can be said to be in some sense 'innate' but this scarcely comes to terms with the central issue which is that, of the two basic determinants of behaviour, one is simply omitted from Skinner's system.

An account of the role of genetic endowment need not be beyond the scope of the behaviourist's analysis. A genotype turns into a behaving organism only in interaction with an environment and we can trace the course of this interaction. This was just the message taken from the work of Watson by another of his followers, Kuo, a man with an interpretation of behaviourism every bit as radical as that of Skinner. His detailed analysis of the role of the environment in shaping the developing behaviour of the domestic chick (Kuo, 1967) should be heart-warming to the environmental determinist. But his work also makes clear that the environment can have its effect in ways quite different from those embodied in the principles of operant conditioning.

One possible reaction to these observations by the radical behaviourists is to try to bypass the whole issue — to take the developed organism as a 'given', to ignore the origins of behaviour and genetically produced differences between individuals, and to concentrate on the way in which the environment controls the changing behaviour of the mature individual. In this restricted area, at least, perhaps the theory of reinforcement might assume full command. It might, but it does not. Since the interpretation of human behaviour in operant terms is not readily open to empirical test, what we must do is return to the laboratory in which the theory was born and examine it in controlled conditions. What we find is that although operant principles are appropriately applied to some phenomena they are also clearly inadequate to account for a wide range of others (e.g., habituation, classical conditioning, observational learning, spatial learning, early learning, and so on) in which behaviour is modified by environmental events. There is no reason to suppose that principles so restricted in their applicability to laboratory behaviour can be universally applied to the behaviour of everyday life.

CONCLUSION

There are many things to admire in Skinner's work. Of these, two seem to deserve special mention. First, the account of behaviour he developed in his 1938 book introduced methods, findings, and concepts that constitute an important contribution to this branch of psychology. Second, in his later work he has taken on the challenge that other psychologists have been unwilling to accept — that of examining with courage and intellectual rigour the full implications of a determinist view of human behaviour. It is not clear, however, that his original findings constitute the comprehensive science of behaviour that he claims, nor, indeed, that his later writings constitute a genuine application of such a science. His

claims to the contrary have the unfortunate effect of generating opposition to his views not only from laymen but from experimental psychologists who might otherwise be expected to be sympathetic. Should this failure to control the behaviour of his critics be taken as one more piece of evidence against his analysis?

REFERENCES

Broadbent, D.E. (1964) *Behaviour*, London, University Paperbacks.

Cohen, D. (1977) *Psychologists on Psychology*, London, Routledge and Kegan Paul.

Eysenck, H.J. (1972) *Psychology Is about People*, Allen Lane, Penguin Press.

Ferster, C.B. and Skinner, B.F. (1957) *Schedules of Reinforcement*, New York, Appleton-Century Crofts.

Grindley, G.C. (1932) 'The formation of a simple habit in guinea pigs', *British Journal of Psychology*, 23, pp. 127–47.

Jenkins, H.M. (1970) 'Sequential organization in schedules of reinforcement', in Schoenfield, W.N. (Ed.), *The Theory of Reinforcement Schedules*, New York, Appleton-Century-Crofts.

Kendler, H.H. and Spence, J.T. (Eds), (1971) *Essays in Neobehaviorism*, New York, Appleton-Century-Crofts.

Kuo, Z-Y. (1967) *The Dynamics of Behavior Development*, New York, Random House.

Mackintosh, N.J. (1974) *The Psychology of Animal Learning*, London, Academic Press.

Mackintosh, N.J. (1977) 'Stimulus control: Attentional factors', in Honig, W.K. and Staddon, J.E.R. (Eds), *Handbook of Operant Behavior*, Englewood Cliffs, N.J., Prentice-Hall.

Miller, S. and Konorski, J. (1928) 'On a particular form of conditioned reflex', *Journal of the Experimental Analysis of Behavior* (1969), 12, pp. 187–9.

Moore, B.R. (1973) 'The role of directed Pavlovian reactions in simple instrumental learning in the pigeon', in Hinde, R.A. and Hinde, J.S. (Eds), *Constraints on Learning*, London, Academic Press.

Reynolds, G.S. (1968) *A Primer of Operant Conditioning*, Glenview, Scott Foresman.

Shettleworth, S.J. (1975) 'Reinforcement and the organization of behavior in golden hamsters: Hunger, environment, and food reinforcement', *Journal of Experimental Psychology: Animal Behavior Processes*, 1, pp. 56–87.

Sidman, M. (1960) *Tactics of Scientific Research*, New York, Basic Books.

Skinner, B.F. (1938) *The Behavior of Organisms*, New York, Appleton-Century.

Skinner, B.F. (1950), 'Are theories of learning necessary?', *Psychological Review*, 57, pp. 193–216.

Skinner, B.F. (1953) *Science and Human Behavior*, New York, Macmillan.

Skinner, B.F. (1954) 'A critique of psychoanalytic concepts and theories', *Cumulative Record*, rev. ed. (1961), New York, Appleton-Century-Crofts.

Skinner, B.F. (1956) 'Freedom and the control of men', reprinted in *Cumulative Record*, rev. ed. (1961), New York, Appleton-Century-Crofts.

Skinner, B.F. (1957) *Verbal Behavior*, New York, Appleton-Century-Crofts.

Skinner, B.F. (1961) 'The flight from the laboratory', reprinted in *Cumulative Record*, rev. ed. (1961), New York, Appleton-Century-Crofts.

Skinner, B.F. (1966) 'Operant Behavior', in Honig, W.K. (Ed.). *Operant Behavior: Areas of Research and Application*, New York, Appleton-Century-Crofts.

Skinner, B.F. (1969) 'The phylogeny and ontogeny of behavior', *Science*, 153, pp. 1205–13.

Skinner, B.F. (1972) *Beyond Freedom and Dignity*, London, Jonathan Cape.

Skinner, B.F. (1974) *About Behaviourism*, London, Jonathan Cape.

Spence, K.W. (1948) 'The postulates and methods of behaviorism', *Psychological Review*, 55, pp. 67–78.

Tolman, E.C. (1932) *Purposive Behavior in Animals and Men*, New York, Century.

Interchange

DAY REPLIES TO HALL

In my opinion it is the abstract of Geoffrey Hall's paper that is the key to what is forceful about the paper itself. As I read the paper, besides a number of relatively minor matters, Hall has basically two complaints to make in regard to Skinner's stance as leader and public defender of the scientific study of behavior. One: it is wrong of Skinner to give the impression that the major achievement of the experimental investigation of behavior is the analysis of operant behavior in terms of the well-known three-term contingency of discriminative stimulus, response, and reinforcing stimulus. Second: it is misleading of Skinner to create the impression that the practical achievements of 'applied behavior analysis' constitute the *bona fide* application to human affairs of behavior principles determined experimentally in the laboratory; instead, what Skinner is really doing is no more than giving a 'reinterpretation of known facts in the terminology of determinism and anti-mentalism.' In what follows I will comment on each of these complaints in turn.

The chief difficulty with Hall's first charge is that it involves contention with a straw man. For Hall, Skinner's behaviorism is to be distinguished from its rival behavioristic positions by its central doctrine that 'what an organism does can and should be explained entirely in terms of what happens to it.' Hall's man of straw consists of the conception that Skinner's science of behavior is restricted to analysis of operant behavior in terms of the three-term contingency, thus rendering it 'incomplete' and 'inadequate'. Yet Skinner's systematic views have always included room for organismic variables. *The Behavior of Organisms* (Skinner, 1938) contains a chapter devoted to 'Drive' and another chapter centered on the interaction of drive and conditioning. Similarly, in *About Behaviorism* (Skinner, 1974) there is a chapter devoted to 'Innate Behavior', and a subsection of this chapter carries the heading, 'Intermingling of Contingencies of Survival and Reinforcement'. Indeed, the plan of *About Behaviorism* is organized around Skinner's effort to respond to the most frequent criticisms of his work; in it twenty such criticisms are discussed. The second of these criticisms is similar to Hall's description of the 'central doctrine' of radical behaviorism: 'It neglects innate endowment and argues that all behavior is acquired during the lifetime of the individual.' Such a charge when made concerning his work is, says Skinner, 'simply wrong' (Skinner, 1974, p. 4).

Hall's paper gives the impression that the research and publications of Shettleworth (1975), Moore (1973), Jenkins (1970), and Mackintosh (1974) have generated results which in some sense overturn, or 'disconfirm', Skinner's system. Nothing could be farther from the truth. All this work takes its place very nicely in

the ongoing progress of what Skinner speaks of in *About Behaviorism* as 'a special discipline, which has come to be called the experimental analysis of behavior' (1974, p. 7). When it comes to stating the 'central doctrine' of radical behaviorism, it is important to keep one's eye on what must be for Skinner a very fundamental judgment: 'The behaviorism I present [in *About Behaviorism*] is the philosophy of this special version of a science of behavior [i.e., the experimental analysis of behavior]' (Skinner, 1974, p. 8). What types of research constitute the experimental analysis of behavior? The simplest way to answer this question is to survey the articles published in the *Journal of the Experimental Analysis of Behavior*, where any of the research cited by Hall would be comfortably at home. Another thing to do would be to look at the text *Learning* by A.C. Catania (1984), where the experiments referenced by Hall take their place quite naturally. The orientation developed in such texts as Catania's *is* the experimental analysis of behavior. It is true that some persons who speak of their own work as 'radical behaviorist' — and I include myself in this group — chaff at too close a connection between a conception of the heart of the radical behaviorist outlook and whatever philosophy may be taken to underlie the experimental analysis of behavior (e.g., Stanley and Linke, 1982, contrast the 'epistemologies of 1938 and 1945'). But contrasting an emphasis on the experimental analysis of behavior with an emphasis on interpretive practices in characterizing the heart of radical behaviorism does not involve a denigration of the long-range value of laboratory research.

Two more or less independent issues are connected with Hall's second objection to Skinner's radical behaviorism. The first is Hall's claim that a variety of other forms of learning exist besides simple operant conditioning, and these other types of learning are highly relevant to considering how principles of learning are best applied in solving concrete human problems. Hall identifies what he has in mind by the following list: '(e.g., habituation, classical conditioning, observational learning, spatial learning, early learning, and so on).' However, from a radical behaviorist perspective, Hall's mistake here is to look at operant conditioning as primarily a *type of learning*. The operant analysis of behavior is not a theory about the nature of the learning process: it is an analysis of *behavior*, an analysis of a certain type of relation that may exist between the environment and behavior. Radical behaviorist conceptual equipment is brought to bear in a variety of different ways upon the specific environment-behavior relations that may be operating in particular cases of 'learning'. The reader who is interested in seeing a representative example of how radical behaviorism is typically brought to bear on what are commonly taken to be different 'types' of learning should look at the pages referenced in the Index of Catania's book, *Learning*, under the heading 'learning' (Catania, 1984, p. 402). This would generate the following list of 'types of learning' for Catania that roughly approximate the kind of distinctions Hall wants to make: all-or-none learning, latent learning, observational learning, place *vs.* response-learning, sensory-motor learning, set learning, and verbal learning.

The other issue engaged by Hall's second objection to radical behaviorism is his claim that 'Skinner's analysis of human issues [fails genuinely to reflect] the proper application of a science of behavior' and that 'applied science implies more than the application of rules of thumb ... derived from laboratory situations.' Unfortunately Hall does not provide a clarification of what this 'more' is, or a

reference to where an elucidation can be found. I suspect that what is involved is certain supposedly formal relations that may be purported to obtain between a *theory* and the practical application of the theory. To be sure, there is a certain sense, as Skinner points out, in which the radical behaviorist conceptualization of behavior can be taken to be 'theoretical'. But this conceptualization is not theoretical in the sense that it is an hypothesis subject to experimental confirmation. It is, instead, a class of conceptual equipment that can be brought to bear on the analysis of behavior, it is a set of potential behaviors that constitute a particular way of interpreting or making sense of behavior.

Hall is correct when he says that Skinner 'has urged that understanding of behavioural processes is important not only for practical applications but because "we can use it to *interpret* behaviour." ... A reinterpretation in unfamiliar terms can sometimes generate new insight and understanding.' But Hall errs, in my opinion, when he claims that 'the widespread rejection of Skinner's theory ... means that for most people it fails to enhance their understanding of human behaviour.' It is an enormous advance in anyone's understanding of behavior to be able to make sense of it in a non-mentalistic way. It is an enormous advance to be able to place the understanding of behavior within the framework of an analysis of contingencies of reinforcement rather than to try to speculate about possibly relevant human motives. I argue that the force of Hall's paper is diminished, rather than advanced, by his speculations that radical behaviorists show a 'surprising lack of confidence' (*sic*) and 'a narrowness of vision' (*sic*) in wanting to restrict research to the study of behavior as a subject matter in its own right, and that they cannot 'trust themselves [*sic*] to make use of the methodology of their conceptual rivals ... without fear of ceasing to be radical.' In short, I argue that it is a virtue, not a defect, of radical behaviorism that in practical application it often consists 'in the reinterpretation of known facts in the terminology of determinism and anti-mentalism', to use Hall's words.

HALL REPLIES TO DAY

RADICAL BEHAVIOURISM: DEFINITION AND USAGE

When I began to write on radical behaviourism and its implications I was tempted to adopt the strategy of bypassing the issue of definition. I was tempted to declare simply that radical behaviourism is that version of behaviourism advocated by Skinner and to move on to a discussion of those features of Skinner's work that seemed most vulnerable to criticism. A good reason for succumbing to the temptation emerged when a cursory survey of Skinner's writings revealed (what Professor Day's much more systematic survey has confirmed) that Skinner himself uses the qualifier 'radical' only rarely and provides us with no very extended discussion of the distinction between radical and other forms of behaviourism. It became clear that in this case, as in many others, it is necessary to let the use of the word tell us its meaning — that a survey of the type provided by Day would be needed. Lacking the qualification to undertake such a survey I did not attempt it and I am most grateful that Day has been willing to perform the task.

Nonetheless, in the end I did essay a definition of a sort when I put forward the following as being the central doctrine of radical behaviourism: 'what an organism does can and should be explained entirely in terms of what happens to it'. What concerns me now is that, since I have supplied no formal justification for my definition, in criticizing this doctrine and its implications, I might be accused of attacking a straw man of my own fabrication. Here Professor Day comes to my aid. Far from wishing to reject his analysis, I think I can make use of it in justifying my own.

Day offers us seven categories of psychological usage for the term 'radical behaviourism'. As he points out, there is some overlap among them and accordingly I will not deal explicitly with each. Day would no doubt also allow that the categories he discusses are not all of the same general type. Sometimes the usage he identifies comes close to constituting a definition, e.g., when radical behaviourism is equated with a specific version of a theory of learning. Other examples are perhaps better seen as cases in which individual authors have selected those particular (incidental?) features of radical behaviourism that are of consequence for their immediate concerns — the philosopher showing a special interest in the analysis of the role of private events supplied by Skinner, the clinical psychologist in the fact that radical behaviourism might have practical application. These writers would not deny that radical behaviourism has other important features, nor would they assert that their interests lead to a fully adequate characterization. Thus, to attempt to *define* radical behaviourism as that version of behaviourism that generates socially useful consequences would be an insult to the work of those psychologists (H.J. Eysenck and N.E. Miller come to mind) who have attempted to derive useful applications from a version of behaviourism that is avowedly not of the radical variety.

It is, even so, a comfort to discover how readily most of the varied usages outlined by Day can be derived from my own attempt to summarize the essence of Skinner's thought. If we accept the assertion of the 'central doctrine' that what an organism does can be explained solely in terms of what happens to it, then the notion that we can control behaviour and change it in ways that will be socially beneficial follows directly. If we argue further that what an organism does *should* be explained in this way, then several things follow. First, as I tried to show in my contribution to this volume, this doctrine leads naturally to the use of a certain set of experimental techniques (those constituting 'the experimental analysis of behaviour'). Next, it generates a particular sort of learning theory: one that finds no place for entities, processes, or events other than descriptions of behaviour and of controlling environmental variables. Finally, it implies an outright rejection of mentalism and leads to a philosophy of psychological science that takes this rejection as its foundation stone.

What remains is the point emphasized by Day: that, because of its willingness to allow discussion of private (although not mental) events, radical behaviourism allows the possibility of creating its own productive phenomenology. Such a conclusion does not necessarily follow given my formulation of the central doctrine of radical behaviourism — a matter for concern since Skinner himself has given an important place to this notion in his few terse statements on the distinction between radical and other forms of behaviourism. In defence of my formulation I have space for just a few brief points.

First, it is not at all clear to me that we should want to deny the label 'radical

behaviourist' to a scientist who insisted on public verifiability while simultaneously accepting all the other tenets of radical behaviourism. To prove my point would require an analysis of usage as extensive as that supplied by Day. I can do no more than offer my suspicion that many practising (if philosophically unsophisticated) psychologists hold such views and do indeed regard themselves as radical behaviourists.

Next, Skinner is not alone in allowing that private, unobserved, and unobservable events can be determinants of behaviour. Among the neobehaviourists, for example, Hull made extensive use of postulated 'stimuli' (often response-produced) in his explanatory schemes. Such notions, therefore, do not uniquely characterize radical behaviourism. In his time Hull was roundly criticized for resorting to what was seen as a subterfuge. His response was perfectly reasonable (and akin to the argument proposed by Skinner). Private events are not mere inventions; their effects can be seen in behaviour and they are assumed to govern behaviour according to the same laws as those determined for the effects of publicly observable events. But, however reasonable the argument, since we no longer accept Hull's 'laws', so his account of the role of unobserved stimuli can now be discarded. Similarly, if my doubts about the validity of Skinner's theory of the control of behaviour by public events are justified, an equivalent fate may lie in store for his account of the place of private events in a natural science.

Part IV: *The Epistemology of Radical Behaviorism*

5. Knowledge As Action: The Epistemology of Radical Behaviorism

ROGER SCHNAITTER

When I was a boy I remember my grandmother saying, in the midst of some bother, 'When I think, I get confused'; and perhaps that thought should be taken more seriously than its notorious cousin, 'I think, therefore I am.' For if there is a common thread to modern epistemological orthodoxy it is that the problem of knowledge will be resolved in thinking about thought. But if there is one bit of advice in the work of B.F. Skinner, one insight that runs contrary to the mainstream, it is that something is badly muddled in this whole history of thought about thought. One can imagine Descartes, for instance, lying abed at dawn in a Stockholm winter pondering on the reality of his existence, and wondering if the world is genuine or if a demon has created a phantasm before his senses, and how he can come to know if any of that is true or not; but then the reverie is broken as Queen Christina summons him, and ruefully he departs from the warmth of his bedclothes for the frigid dressing room, where well he knows how to pull up his trousers and button his waistcoat, and how to frown imperiously at his manservant, and a few moments later how to show just the proper balance of authority and obsequiousness to maintain the Queen's favor. Descartes is not confused at all about the management of his practical life. But unfortunately he has failed to recognize that his practical life is full of certainty and it is only when he thinks that, like my Gram, he too becomes confused. Skinner, almost alone among those who have thought seriously about the problem of knowledge, finds the fundamentals of human knowledge to be founded on the realities of practical life. The certainties of life are sticks and stones; thought derives from them; life in the external world is primary; the world of the mind is a pale and imperfect shadow. We can learn immensely more about 'knowing' through observation of the prac-

tical life of ordinary people than through study of the ruminations of learned scholars. That is where Skinner's views that could be called epistemological begin.

It is not just Descartes. Philosophy, both in its rational and empirical traditions, holds that something about the life of the mind is primary. If Descartes thought that his thoughts were the only thing he could know for sure, then Hume thought it was his sensations; and while that might seem like a powerful difference, both were equally convinced that the problems of knowledge could be unravelled by solving problems intrinsic to the mind itself. Skinner, however, turns this traditional stance of mental primacy on its head. The world, and one's relation to it, are primary. The life of the mind is secondary and derivative.

The best case to be made for Skinner's position is demonstrative. If one is inclined to accept Samuel Johnson's refutation of idealism in which he kicked a chair across the room, then the comparable demonstrations of Skinner's case are easy enough to follow.

> It does not matter much what one *believes* about the appropriateness of stepping into the street; if one incautiously steps in front of an onrushing automobile one will be knocked flat.
> It does not really matter if one *thinks* one knows what horse will win the Derby when placing a bet; if the horse wins, one is likely to bet that horse again, or continue using the same system to make betting choices.
> It does not matter if one has the *idea* of brazenly challenging the boss's judgment; one will experience his or her displeasure on the basis of the overt act, not its internal causes.
> It does not really matter how strongly one *intends* to play 'Clair de Lune'; without a history of instruction at and practice on the piano the plan is doomed to failure. Meanwhile, the accomplished pianist can play 'Clair de Lune' while carrying on a conversation about the price of corn.

The world is a great equalizer of our mental conceits and pufferies. It will stroke us or pull us down, independently of our grandest thoughts and dreams. Perhaps that is why great thinkers have been loath to give it credit.

Knowledge As Action

Knowledge, as Skinner sees it, exists only to the extent that one has the capacity to act. Thought and self-reflection are forms of action that are private and internally executed in Skinner's view, but one is incapable of them without first having the capability of action in the world. Contemplative, reflective, introspective self-knowledge derives from action in the world.

> 'We do not act by putting knowledge to use; our knowledge *is* action, or at least rules for action. As such it is power, as Francis Bacon pointed out in rejecting scholasticism and its emphasis on knowing for the sake of knowing. Operant behavior is essentially the exercise of power: it has an effect on the environment . . . .
> There is room in a behavioristic analysis for a kind of knowing short of action and hence short of power. One need not be actively behaving in order to feel or to introspectively observe certain states normally associated with behavior. To say, 'I know a sea lion when I see one,' is to report that one can identify a sea lion but not that one is now doing so. A response

temporarily forgotten may still be claimed as knowledge, as when we say, 'I can't think of it at the moment but I know it as well as I know my own name.'

We also use 'know' to mean 'being under the control of,' a condition which is not the only determiner of our behavior. When we say, 'I went to the meeting knowing that X would be speaking' (where knowing could be replaced by believing, expecting, realizing, or understanding), we report that our behavior was affected by some prior indication that X would be at the meeting, but the behavior itself could not be called knowing that fact. (Skinner, 1974, pp. 139–40)

So Skinner's view is that knowledge is action, or the capacity to act. To know a thing in the world is to act or to have the capacity to act differentially with regard to it. To know a thing slightly is to have a limited capacity for differential action regarding the thing; to know a thing thoroughly is to have a comprehensive repertoire of behavior regarding it. To know *that* a thing is p or q is to have a second-order capacity, a capacity to respond differentially to a first-order capacity to respond differentially to a thing. So conceived, it does not seem that 'knowing that' necessarily requires linguistic capacities. In normal adult human behavior, however, this kind of knowledge that is usually expressed in terms of propositional content often involves the ability to say, or assert, or describe.

We come to know the world as we come to have the capacity to respond differentially to the world. We are born into the world with an innate set of capacities, and these are the basis on which our further capacities, those developed in our lifetimes, are acquired. These further capacities arise as we *interact* with the world. We act in regard to some aspect of the world, and that action is successful or unsuccessful as a function of its consequences in the world. So we learn, or acquire knowledge, as a function of these interactions. We learn less well about private, internal things than about public, external things, claims Skinner, because the functional consequences of differential action with regard to private and internal things are imprecise and unreliable (Skinner, 1972, pp. 370–84). So we know things in the external world better than things about our inner selves. One can see an aardvark for the first time and describe it more accurately and fluently than the most intimate qualities of one's own emotional life.

Actions Can Be Individuated by Reference to the External World

If there is one thing for which Skinner is justly famed, it is his elucidation of the effect of consequences on behavior. Behavior sensitive to its consequences is called operant behavior, and the consequences that result in such behavior changing in frequency are called reinforcers. Skinner has emphasized the subtlety of selection by consequences, as seen both in the processes of natural selection in the evolution of species and in the ontogeny of actions within an individual (Skinner, 1981). Science has only lately discovered it as a causal mode in nature. Furthermore, selection by consequences is distinctly different from the mechanical, push-pull pattern of causation amenable to description in quantitative laws that appears to operate in the phenomena of interest to the physical sciences. There have been three prongs to the radical behaviorist elucidation of the effect of consequences on behavior. The first is found in the experimental analysis of behavior, a scientific discipline that Skinner established with publication of his

book, *The Behavior of Organisms* (1938). The second is found in the applied analysis of behavior, a field in which Skinner's direct contributions have been more limited, but which is based on application of behavioral principles to human problems. The third is found primarily in Skinner's work again, in the interpretation of natural patterns of human activity from a behavioral point of view (e.g., Skinner, 1953, 1971, 1974).

Beyond any doubt, in the concept of reinforcement Skinner is on to something of immense importance. Even some of his most astute critics recognize it (e.g., Dennett, 1978). Less clear is the adequacy of the conceptual and methodological repertoire deployed in the description and analysis of reinforcing effects, and the resulting 'facts' of behavior as now recorded in the literature of the experimental analysis of behavior. Quite possibly, detailed analysis of the free operant via schedules of reinforcement (e.g., Ferster and Skinner, 1957; *Journal of the Experimental Analysis of Behavior*, 1958-present) has been of much less significance than its advocates believe. What need analysis are not arbitrarily synthesized categories of action, but natural kinds in which organisms engage to pursue their interests and live out their biological destinies. The experimental analysis of behavior has infrequently caught sight of that goal. After all, it has taken fifty years' study of food-reinforced lever-pressing and key-pecking by rats and pigeons for operant psychologists to recognize that their standard experimental model concerns foraging (e.g., Staddon, 1980)! Applied behavior analysis on the other hand (e.g., *Journal of Applied Behavior Analysis*, 1968-present), necessarily being accountable to human interests, has avoided the arbitrary extremes of the experimental analysis, and consequently has established a considerable degree of practical validity to its techniques and their applications. In interpreting examples of natural human behavior, Skinner has again kept his focus on relevant phenomena. My point is that the significant discovery of radical behaviorism has concerned the causal nature of behavioral consequences. Not all that radical behaviorists have done or said about such consequences is necessarily useful, however, or even correctly conceived.

Anyone committed to naturalism who considers the problem of knowledge must begin by recognizing that, both phylogenetically and ontogenetically, knowledge fundamentally concerns the manner in which organisms adapt to and function in their worlds. But if actions are understood primarily in terms of the relation between outer efforts and inner mental states such as intentions, then the naturalistic premise that actions are adaptive, functional categories through which organisms relate to the world has been obscured. Clearly, actions *can* be individuated by reference to their immediate (mental) antecedents, but as well they can be individuated by reference to the causal matrix whereby the actor stands related to the world in which he or she acts. The purpose of this section is to establish a perspective on individuating actions by reference to the external world rather than by reference to internal, mental machinery.

The operant, as a class of behavior individuated by a common reinforcing consequence, is the behavioristic action category (also see Zuriff, 1975; Lee, 1983). If it can be established that under some description actions are operants, and since operants are individuated by their consequences in the world, then it would follow that under some description actions can be individuated by reference to their consequences in the world. In general such a consequence must be caused by something the actor does, rather than being an accidental correlate of it

(the sun being a second of arc higher in the sky following some movement will not do). Furthermore, the consequence must exert a causal effect back on the actor, at least in the sense of leading to termination of the particular action-episode, and possibly by affecting the likelihood that the actor will do something similar when a comparable future situation arises. This second causal feature is the behaviorist's way of getting at the commonsensical notion that actions are performed to 'fulfill the intentions' of the actor. The operant, then, is at the core of the behavioristic analysis of purpose and intention. The following discussion, however, does not rely on any technical notion of the operant or of reinforcement.

Unsupported acts. This informal classification of action types begins with the least significant but most problematic case. Some acts do have the appearance of occurring without reference to any external conditions. Stretches and yawns are clear examples of unsupported acts, as are forms of emotional expression such as smiles, grimaces, frowns, and so forth. Stretches and yawns, however, are a kind of reflexive or self-referenced action. Their criterion of successful execution is some change in state of the executor of the action — relief from a cramp perhaps. Walking and other forms of locomotion may appear unsupported, but in fact are not identical with effector topographies. The topography must cause movement relative to an underlying surface to count as walking. To perform walking movements in water does not result in the act of walking but of treading water, and the 'space walks' of astronauts are walks only in a metaphorical sense. In regard to emotional expression, since Darwin these acts have normally been understood to serve a communicative function, rather than being instances of pure emotive self-expression. A smile, to effectively communicate pleasure or satisfaction, must work some effect on the observer or recipient of the smile. So it does appear that unsupported acts fall into types according to their effects, though perhaps in less than obvious ways.

Another category of unsupported act might be called private, this being acts performed covertly, or mentally (Schnaitter, 1984). Skinner's point here would be that such acts become possible only after the capacity to perform a range of worldly actions is established. One's game of 'inner golf' initially derives from outer golf, although eventually the relation may become reciprocal.

Directed acts. To pick an apple from a tree one must not only execute some kind of movement, the movement must produce a certain sort of effect on the environment. No matter what is in one's mind, one cannot pick an apple without an apple tree. The vast majority of ordinary human actions are of this sort. Consider a bit of daily routine: one gets out of bed, shaves, showers, dresses — that consisting of putting on various items of clothing, fastening snaps, buttons, and laces — eats toast, drinks coffee from a cup. These acts obtain their identity through relations existing between classes of movement and common functional effects on the world (which includes one's own body), not by particular mental antecedents. A man does not consult a mental state to ascertain if he has successfully buttoned his fly; he checks his fly.

Conventional acts. Certain acts — checkmating the king, inaugurating the President, christening an infant — have their identity not so much through functional

effects as by meeting external criteria characterized by rules, standards, protocols, or social (rather than natural) laws. These conventions are publicly shared by the social community for whom the conventional act is relevant. Checkmating is a convention among chessplayers, but not among children employing chess pieces as toy soldiers. Consequently, children playing soldiers with chess pieces do not perform checkmates. On the other hand a chess player playing a game performs a checkmate whenever the rules defining checkmate are met by his move, even if he has moved absent-mindedly or for other reasons has performed the checkmate unintentionally.

Speech acts. Does this approach also apply to those acts that are performed linguistically? It might be argued that one can *assert*, or *promise*, or *dissemble* purely on the basis of what is in one's mind, what one's linguistic intentions are, with no necessary reference to the world. Speech acts are perhaps unsupported acts — linguistic stretches and yawns, so to speak. While this issue is of great complexity, several grounds can be offered for thinking that the explication of speech acts will necessarily make reference to factors beyond the mind of the speaker.

First, linguistic tokens, to count as instances of various categories of act, must occur in the context of a hearer to whom they are directed. Just possibly one can *proclaim* in an empty room, but one surely cannot *promise* or *request* or *apologize in vacuo*. Furthermore, the tokens must be intelligible to and effective for the hearer. An aphasic speaker may intend to *warn* of danger, but if the intended utterance of 'Fire! Run for your lives!' is mumbled incoherently or comes out 'That's it! Do do do!', then a warning has not been given. Second, naked utterances underdetermine the kind of communicative act in which they play a role. A context shared by speaker and hearer can critically determine the interpretation of the utterance. Bach and Harnish (1977, p. 5) illustrate this point with the example of the expression, 'I love you like my brother.' The meaning of the utterance depends crucially on whether or not the speaker loves or hates his brother, for instance, or whether it is said by a young woman to a suitor, or by a man to a wartime buddy. Third, and this is by far the most important, the meanings of linguistic tokens are not to be found 'in the head', but in the relation between what speakers say and their worlds.

Meanings Are Not 'In the Head'

Skinner has developed a case for this claim in the book, *Verbal Behavior* (1957), and elsewhere, where he maintains that meaning, rather than being a property of an utterance itself, is to be found in the nature of the relationship between occurrence of the utterance and its context. It is important enough to put in his own words.

> ... meaning is not properly regarded as a property either of a response or a situation but rather of the contingencies responsible for both the topography of behavior and the control exerted by stimuli. To take a primitive example, if one rat presses a lever to obtain food when hungry while another does so to obtain water when thirsty, the topographies of their behaviors may be indistinguishable, but they may be said to differ in meaning: to one rat pressing the lever 'means' food; to the other it 'means' water. But these are aspects of the contingencies which

have brought behavior under the control of the current occasion. Similarly, if a rat is reinforced with food when it presses the lever in the presence of a flashing light but with water
when the light is steady, then it could be said that the flashing light means food and the steady
light means water, but again these are references not to some property of the light but to the
contingencies of which the lights have been parts.

The same point may be made, but with many more implications, in speaking of the
meaning of verbal behavior. The over-all function of the behavior is crucial. In an archetypal
pattern a speaker is in contact with a situation to which a listener is disposed to respond but
with which he is not in contact. A verbal response on the part of the speaker makes it possible
for the listener to respond appropriately. For example, let us suppose that a person has an
appointment, which he will keep by consulting a clock or a watch. If none is available, he may
ask someone to tell him the time, and the response permits him to respond effectively ...

The *meaning of a response for the speaker* includes the stimulus which controls it (in the
example above, the setting on the face of a clock or watch) and possibly aversive aspects of the
question, from which a response brings release. The *meaning for the listener* is close to the
meaning the clock face would have if it were visible to him, but it also includes the contingencies involving the appointment, which make a response to the clock face or the verbal response
probable at such a time ....

One of the unfortunate implications of communication theory is that the meanings for
speaker and listener are the same, that something is made common to both of them, that the
speaker conveys an idea or meaning, transmits information, or imparts knowledge, as if his
mental possessions then become the mental possessions of the listener. There are no meanings
which are the same in the speaker and listener. Meanings are not independent entities ...
(Skinner, 1974, pp. 90–2)

One does not have to take Skinner's word alone, however, for much current
philosophical work also leads to the conclusion that meanings are not in the head.
The issue extends beyond the problem of meaning construed as a linguistic
property to the problem of intentionality and the interpretation of mentality itself.
While the reasoning behind this claim is varied and complex, perhaps an analogy
with machine functions can be helpful here. A computer is a perfect example of a
system that performs meaningless syntactic operations. The electrical configuration of the addressable memory locations is just formal structures, without semantic significance to the computer either as numbers or as representations of numbers. All the computer does is change states automatically as electrical current
runs through its circuits. Despite the pure formality of its operations, however,
the computer (if designed and programmed correctly) will be truth-preserving
across computations: ask the thing to add 2 + 2 and it will give you a 4 every
time. But the numerical meanings we attach to the inputs and outputs do not
enter into and emanate from the computer itself. Rather, they remain outside the
system, in the interpretations that we as computer users assign to the inputs and
outputs of the machine's operations. Now, if one is inclined to a computational
view of mind, then by analogy much the same thing holds for the organic
computational systems we call our brains. Meanings are not in them, but exist in
the mode through which they in their functioning stand to the world.

Ironies begin to mount here. Brentano's claim that 'Intentionality' is the
mark of the mental is now widely accepted. Intentionality in its technical sense
has to do with the meaningfulness, the semantic content, of mental states. But the
argument is now made that cognitive operations and their objects are formal and
syntactic only, and do not themselves have semantic content (e.g., see Putnam,
1975; Fodor, 1980; and Stich, 1983, for a range of contributions to this viewpoint). Semantic issues do not concern internal mental mechanisms but concern
the mode of relation between individuals and their worlds. Such issues are not

really psychological at all, it is claimed, and are relegated to other fields of inquiry for whatever elucidation can be brought to them. For example, while belief is a canonical example of a mental, intentional state, Stich says, 'Believing that p is an amalgam of historical, contextual, ideological, and perhaps other considerations' (1983, p. 170). The net result of these recent moves in cognitive psychology and the philosophy of mind seems to be that the essence of mentality — its meaningfulness — is in the process of being disowned by modern mentalism! But Stich's ashbin of intentionality — historical and contextual considerations — is exactly what behaviorism seeks to address. Can it be that *behaviorism* will be the instrument called for final explication of Brentano's thesis of the mental? One's head spins to think it.

If, as Skinner argues, knowledge is action, and if actions can be individuated by reference to external circumstances, then it follows that knowledge can be understood by reference to the standing of organisms to their worlds. This does not mean that the radical behaviorist perspective in knowledge involves any sort of denial of the significance of inner states to knowledge, meaning, or other psychological problems, however.

Behaviorism Presupposes Inner States, and Is Inconceivable without Them

'The objection to inner states,' says Skinner, 'is not that they do not exist, but that they are not relevant in a functional analysis' (1953, p. 35). Well, perhaps. While we may grant that inner states are not relevant *in* the functional analysis Skinner has in mind, they are of paramount importance *to* a functional analysis, as we can see in the remainder of the well-known passage that begins with the remark above.

> We cannot account for the behavior of any system while staying wholly inside it; eventually we must turn to forces operating upon the organism from without. Unless there is a weak spot in our causal chain so that the second link is not lawfully determined by the first, or the third by the second, then the first and third links must be lawfully related. If we must always go back beyond the second link for prediction and control, we may avoid many tiresome and exhausting digressions by examining the third link as a function of the first. Valid information about the second link may throw light upon this relationship but can in no way alter it.

These remarks are usually taken to be an argument for the irrelevance of inner states, but that is an odd way to look at it.

All relations between environmental circumstances and behavior are mediated by inner states, for an organism's nervous system always intervenes between the environment and behavior. (Were it not so, then operants would have to have their own receptors when under stimulus control!) If a functional relation between an initial, environmental link and a terminal, behavioral link is to hold, then it must be mediated by an inner, second link which is lawfully coordinated with the initial external conditions on the one hand, and with the behavioral outcome on the other. Lawful relationships between the first and third links *depend* on the lawful relatedness of the second, inner link with the initial and terminal links. For a functional analysis of behavior to have any chance at all of working, inner states must exist which execute the orderly coordinations of external circumstances with behavior. This assumption is necessary to make a functional analysis of behavior even plausible. Thus, in an important sense be-

havioral analysis is founded on a presupposition of the existence and coherent functioning of inner states. It cannot work without them. Skinner uses the assumption of this lawfulness of inner states as the basis for dropping them out of his functional, behavioral laws. He makes a methodological point here, a point more related to the relative epistemic accessibility of inner states versus outer circumstances than to any ontological claim about what is or is not going on inside organisms.

If this is so, then how has Skinner come to be an antimentalist, opposed to any program of elucidation of the nature of these inner states? There are two basic reasons. One stems from his positivistic conviction that the goal of science is description rather than explanation. The goal Skinner has set for behaviorism is the description of behavior and its external circumstances at its own level, in its own right, in terms most appropriate to such a subject. Following Mach (1883) he is after the most economical account, and he believes that such economy cannot be achieved by introduction of considerations lacking immediate reference. Second, the important practical values of science, so far as Skinner is concerned, are prediction and control. The laws of science, he suggests, are not components of a scheme whose purpose is to provide a coherent explanation of a range of phenomena, but are rules for taking effective action in the real world (Skinner, 1974, pp. 123–4; Schnaitter, 1980). This essentially pragmatic view keeps Skinner's focus on the external world of objects and events, which can be manipulated effectively, rather than on the inner, mental world, which is inaccessible to direct manipulation and control.

Clearly, not everyone takes the goal of science to be pure description, but even if that might be science's goal it can be argued that significant sorts of description are necessarily abstract, requiring invention, hypothesis, and inference rather than the relatively direct Baconian consultation of the book of nature that Skinner seems to have in mind. Although in some sense the laws of science are rules for effective action, such effectiveness may be largely cognitive, limited to providing an explanatory scheme whereby otherwise puzzling phenomena are cast into an orderly pattern and coordinated with those phenomena of nature where understanding is more firmly established.

Thus, I have no particular reason to maintain that Skinner's philosophy of science is correct. Yet correct or not it is a position of much interest because it has certain important consequences so far as the problems that become of concern to those who hold it. These problems tend not to be caught sight of by persons holding other orientative attitudes or, once sighted, are quickly lost again. These problems concerning the coordination of behavior with its external, historical and current context are of manifold importance because they are deeply intertwined with such problems as knowledge and meaning, as I have suggested in earlier sections of this chapter. While psychologists and philosophers of other persuasions occasionally catch a glimpse of this truth, the standard mentalistic orientation most often results in such outward relationships being treated as the basis for inferring the nature of inner mechanisms, and then treating these outer phenomena as some kind of trivial product or consequence of such mechanisms — mere data, phenomena to be explained rather than phenomena of any explanatory value. As such, a thoroughgoing assessment of the comprehensive nature of the functioning of organisms *in their world* is neglected.

It is as if we can keep only two things clearly in mind, even when there are

three things before us. Such a malady afflicts behaviorists and mentalists equally. While Skinner acknowledges that any behaviorally effective external circumstances operate by changing the internal state of the organism, he doggedly resists specification of the details of what that change might be. Thus, the organism's behavior-mediating state is treated as one grand and glorious undifferentiated interaction (e.g., 'Behavior exists only when it is being executed. . . . The system was changed when the behavior was acquired, and it is the changed system which is "possessed."' Skinner, 1974, p. 137). On the other hand, mentalists are most inclined to address the relation between environmental circumstances and mental state as if that were the end of things. Such is particularly true among information-processing theories where the mind is conceived to accept and process informational input, but no more. That there may be a functionally significant loop from the processing of such information to the adaptive behavioral functioning of the organism in its environment is largely neglected.

The organism, its external circumstances, and what it does, form a three-term relationship that seems easiest to approach two at a time. Consequently, the behaviorist employs the model

$$(B \rightleftharpoons E)/O$$

where the organism provides the background or context over which behavior-environment interactions are played out. The mentalist, on the other hand, is inclined to employ the model

$$(E \rightarrow O)/B$$

where the organism's behavior serves only as an indicator of the significant information-processing functions performed in the organism on the environmental inputs. Occasionally, as when a psycholinguist takes an utterance to be the product of an internal sentence-generating mechanism that operates without reference to the external circumstances that give a speaker something to say, the mentalistic model becomes

$$(O \rightarrow B)/E.$$

Philip Hineline (unpublished) has spoken of such practices as not unlike a figure-ground perception, and that may indeed be a useful metaphor. What is ground for the behaviorist is part of the figure for the mentalist, and vice versa. In fact I hold no brief against any of these models. It is important to realize, however, that they are not the same models, and that they do not compete for analysis of quite the same phenomena.

It should now be apparent that the behavioral analysis of knowledge is as much a matter of conceptual necessity as it is a result of empirical considerations. In a system whose conceptual categories address properties of behavior and environment but not states of the organism, knowledge simply *must* turn out to be much what Skinner says it is. But as well, knowledge concerns states of the knowing organism: the inner states tacitly required to orchestrate the behavior-environment interactions and capacities identifiable through Skinner's outer perspective. What is true of knowledge in that regard must be true of psychological phenomena in general. Consequently, any position purported to be a complete psychology must include a psychology of inner states. In that sense Skinnerian behaviorism is but half a psychology, although its subject is an important and often neglected half. Eventually one hopes that a complementarity between the psychologies of inner states and outer life may emerge. (I make this case in two other ways in Schnaitter, 1986a and 1986b.)

Psychological Knowledge and Practical Life

The thing that fascinates about radical behaviorism is its thoroughgoing commitment to understanding organisms as they participate in a system of interactions with their world. This epistemology without hubris of the intellect, this orientation toward understanding organisms *living in the world*, is much more fundamental than the details of the conceptual apparatus current at any given time (e.g., discriminative stimulation, free operant responses, schedules of reinforcement), or what are purported to be the facts of behavior at any given time. The pragmatic positivism of Skinner — a view that is, in my estimation, his own unique synthesis — has kept the focus of radical behaviorists on this outside story from the 1930s to the present. During the first half of this period most leading neobehaviorists (e.g., Hull, Spence, Mowrer, and their followers) were developing a version of the psychology of inner life in terms of S-R mediational mechanisms. During the second half of this period the neobehaviorist position has been substantially deserted for the conceptually more rich cognitivist version of the inside story. Thus, even the majority of people who have thought themselves to be behaviorists have never been interested in a thoroughgoing (that is to say, *radical*) behaviorism. Truly, there *is* an inside story, and its telling is important to psychology. But there is an outside story as well, a story that seems to lack any sort of appeal to the majority of people calling themselves psychologists. It is thus quite remarkable that Skinner's position has kept the interests of a growing segment of the psychological community directed on this important but unprepossessing subject for five decades. The radical discontinuity between Skinner's epistemological views and those of the mainstream has no doubt been central in maintaining the identity of the radical behaviorist community.

REFERENCES

Bach, K. and Harnish, R. (1977) *Linguistic Communication and Speech Acts*, Cambridge, Mass., MIT Press.

Dennett, D. (1978) 'Why the law of effect won't go away', in Dennett, D. *Brainstorms*, Montgomery, Vt., Bradford.

Ferster, C. and Skinner, B.F. (1957) *Schedules of Reinforcement*, New York, Appleton-Century-Crofts.

Fodor, J. (1980) 'Methodological solipsism considered as a research strategy in cognitive psychology', *Behavioral and Brain Sciences*, 3, pp. 63–73.

Hineline, P. (unpublished) 'Organism/environment as reversible figure/ground relationship'.

Lee, V. (1983) 'Behavior as a constituent of conduct', *Behaviorism*, 11, pp. 199–224.

Mach, E. (1883) *The Science of Mechanics*, trans. 1960, LaSalle, Open Court.

Putnam, H. (1975) 'The meaning of "meaning",' in Gunderson, K. (Ed.), *Language, Mind, and Knowledge. Minnesota Studies in the Philosophy of Science*, Vol. 7, Minneapolis, Minn, University of Minnesota Press.

Schnaitter, R. (1980) 'Science and verbal behavior', *Behaviorism*, 8, pp. 153–60.

Schnaitter, R. (1984) 'Skinner on the "mental" and the "physical"', *Behaviorism*, 12, pp. 1–14.

Schnaitter, R. (1986a) 'A coordination of differences: Behaviorism, mentalism, and the conceptual foundations of psychology', in Knapp, T. and Robertson, L. (Eds), *Approaches to Cognition: Contrasts and Controversies*, Hillsdale, N.J., Erlbaum.

Schnaitter, R. (1986b) 'Behavior as a function of inner states and outer circumstances', in Thompson, T. and Zeiler, M. (Eds), *Analysis and Integration of Behavioral Units*, Hillsdale, N.J., Erlbaum.

Skinner, B.F. (1938) *The Behavior of Organisms*, New York, Appleton.

Skinner, B.F. (1953) *Science and Human Behavior*, New York, Macmillan.

Skinner, B.F. (1957) *Verbal Behavior*, New York, Appleton-Century-Crofts.

Skinner, B.F. (1969) *Contingencies of Reinforcement: A Theoretical Analysis*, New York, Appleton-Century-Crofts.

Skinner, B.F. (1971) *Beyond Freedom and Dignity*, New York, Knopf.

Skinner, B.F. (1972) *Cumulative Record*, 3rd ed., New York, Appleton-Century-Crofts.

Skinner, B.F. (1974) *About Behaviorism*, New York, Knopf.

Skinner, B.F. (1981) 'Selection by consequences', *Science*, 213, pp. 501–4.

Staddon, J.E.R. (Ed.) (1980) *Limits of Action*, New York, Academic Press.

Stich, S. (1983) *From Folk Psychology to Cognitive Science*, Cambridge, Mass., MIT Press.

Zuriff, G. (1975), 'Where is the agent is behavior?' *Behaviorism*, 3, pp. 1–21.

6. An Exercise in Triviality: The Epistemology of Radical Behaviorism*

J. JACQUES VONÈCHE

Classically three different sorts of criticism have been levelled against B.F. Skinner's position. The first assimilates Skinner's epistemology to a psychological version of Lamarckism. The foremost representative of this criticism is Jean Piaget. To him, Skinnerism is all genesis and no structures and, as such, the negative mirror-image of Gestalt which is all structure and no genesis. The second type of criticism is humanistic. It considers Skinnerism as an inauthentic substitute for love and will that puts humanity in the moral predicament of using tools such as the Skinner box on people it should have considered as total beings. The third sort of criticism has been expressed by Ivan Illich. It goes as follows: for today's leaders, diseases caused by the industrial society can only be cured by remedies manufactured industrially by technocrats. In other words, in education, medicine, management, warfare or psychology the only recipe to the industrial-technocratic poison is more of that poison under new labels such as programmed education, self-tutoring, behavior modification, and positive reinforcement.

These criticisms miss the point of Skinner's epistemology. Piaget's comparison of Skinner and Lamarck is inadequate on three grounds. First, Lamarck postulated a fixed scale of beings in his system (metaphysical argument) beside what he called circumstances (biological argument). Piaget overlooked completely the metaphysical fixed scale in favor of the inheritance of acquired characteristics (the role of circumstances). Second, theories of organic selection cannot be compared with cumulative records of contingencies of reinforcement, because they are at two different levels of analysis. Third, Skinner is clearly Darwinian (Skinner, 1981).

* For their critical commentary on an earlier draft, the author would like to express sincere appreciation to Howard E. Gruber, Fernando Vidal and Evelyn Aeschlimann.

The humanistic criticism of Skinnerism confuses Skinner's ability to train a pigeon to execute a complicated dance perfectly by means of behavior modification with the development of an interest in ballet. Skinner never claimed this last point. Illich's more substantial criticism is not specifically aimed at behaviorism but rather at its uses and abuses. The sort of criticism that I would like to formulate in the following pages is of a strictly epistemological nature. As Piaget showed (1942), any epistemology relies in the end upon either logic or sociology. My arguments will indeed be logical *and* sociological.

THE LOGICAL ARGUMENT

Methodologically, Skinner's system represents the most rigorous and consistent application of operationism to psychology with all the difficulties involved in such an undertaking. According to Skinner, operationism deals with: (1) observations; (2) computational and manipulative procedures entailed by observations; (3) the logical and mathematical steps taken from there on.

Such a form of operationism presents several difficulties. First it does not provide a criterion for the validation of knowledge, but a technique for the construction of concepts with a given empirical meaning. Therefore, it denies any validity to the logical analysis of scientific discourse in favor of a psychological one. A second difficulty is the requirement for the validity of any psychological theory that it predict and control behavior. Indeed Skinner defines his system as positivistic and limited to the description rather than to the explanation of behavior. A third difficulty is the replacement of causality by the relation between the modification of an independent variable (the 'cause') and the modification of a dependent variable (the 'effect').

Replacing causality with correlation is a matter of decision and not of description: causes and correlations are not given in the same way as facts. Moreover, a scientific law, even based on correlation, has to be unlimited or universal, and cannot be circumscribed to finite classes of individuals or to spatio-temporally defined events as is a Skinnerian scientific law. The fecundity of scientific knowledge relies not only on its empirical basis but also on its theoretical breadth, i.e., the establishment of principles of explanation and prediction in the form of general laws or theories. Theoretical terms are as essential to the growth of knowledge as observational ones. Any verification of a descriptive proposition is bound up with a context within which this proposition makes sense. This is true for every proposition including Skinner's. None of them makes sense independently of the other and their internal consistency is the best argument against Skinner's own epistemology.

After these methodological remarks, I would like to turn now to another form of the logical argument: the proof that a behavioristic explanation of external behavior is impossible.

In the framework of Skinner's system, animals could be considered as automata, more specifically as Turing machines where some physical objects verify some mathematical relations such as partially recursive functions. In fact, Skinner's system requires the exclusive use of external predicates for the description

of animal behavior, thus forming the S-R relation as a function independent of internal state.

Hence, for Skinner, animals represent finite transducers which are the least complex of all possible Turing machines. Finite transducers can be defined as a Turing machine moving only in one direction. Usually, a Turing machine consists of an infinite linear tape together with a mobile central body capable both of reading inputs (finite sequences of signs inscribed on the tape) and of producing outputs (new inscriptions on the tape, including cancellations of signs) and thus, new movements along the tape, either to the left or to the right. Finite transducers, beside being one-directional, have a finite number of states.

One could then interpret stimuli as inputs and responses as outputs. But if this is so, any given R corresponds to an internal behavioral readiness or to a dispositional property of the animal and not to an external stimulation only to which the animal reacts. Any language that lacks terms to denote internal dispositions is not sufficiently powerful to explain automatic behavior, since it can only explain the behavior of automata with an initial state. In other words, Skinner seems to answer only the question: 'To what does the animal respond?' and not, 'How does the animal respond?' But even the first question is not really answered by Skinner, since knowing to what the animal responds supposes the formulation of a formal system of rules for S-R correspondence. Still in other words, psychological explanations must be deductions of laws about S-R relations (external behavior) from higher theoretical laws about the internal structure of animals. The key point (overlooked by Skinner) is that S-R theory requires at least two internal states in the animal: an initial state after S and before R, and a final one after R. If these two states are not somehow differentiated, there is no behavior at all. This fact cannot be circumvented. Hence, the behavioristic explanation of external behavior leads to absurdity.

The third point about the epistemology of radical behaviorism is that it is *self-contradictory* in at least three ways. First, it attempts to explain behavior only by learning. To do this, it relies heavily on reflexes. Reflexes demonstrate no growth, however they are as brilliant in the end of a learning process as in its beginning. Second, learning is defined as a modification of behavior due to experience and not as the development of competences in dealing with new issues. There is no possible modification of behavior by mere exposure. Experience is something more than that. Third, there is a more basic contradiction in the system: reflexes, stimuli, responses are concepts. At two levels, at least, decisions about them are categorical in nature, not factual. One is the crucial decision of defining what, out of the vast world, will be an acceptable paradigm of a response, stimulus or reflex. The selection of 'responses', 'stimuli' or 'reflexes' as categories of behavior worthy of study is yet another categorical choice. Once again, Skinner tends to mistake the products of his predecessors' refined analysis for crude facts. Contrarily to Skinner's claim such categorical choices do not duplicate facts.

Another form of contradiction appears in the very language used by Skinner in his theorizing. It is self-contradictory to refuse interpretative discourse and to use words as interpretative as 'reinforcements' or 'contingencies'. Skinner's ideal language should be deprived of any metaphor, since his definition of a theory as appealing to 'events taking place somewhere else, at some other level of observa-

tion, described in different terms and measured, if at all, in different dimensions' applies exactly to metaphors. A language without metaphors being impossible, the predicament is total. Moreover, if theory duplicated reality, as Skinner claims, he would be right to throw out one of the two, with the sorry corollary for him that his own writings would be disposable from his viewpoint.

THE SOCIOLOGICAL ARGUMENT

What accounts for the successs of Skinner's views in spite of all their logical pitfalls? In my opinion, it is their adherence to a set of American values that are largely exported by the government of the USA along with other goods. This is no wonder in the field of psychology, which is largely dominated by American productions.

We will now review those aspects of American culture that are transparent in Skinner's writings, and then show how they lead to an American philosophical bestiary that has nothing to do with real animals but a lot with the way in which white middle-class America envisions the world. Then we will demonstrate the political role of behaviorism. The politics of behaviorism are interesting in two ways. First of all, as I witnessed it myself in Brazil, when the regime switched from the left to the right through a military *putsch* the Faculty of the National University of Brazilia was demoted and the United States of America sent in American experts with fifty-seven Skinner boxes for teaching 'real psychology'. There was some irony in this gift to a country where thousands of people were going to be sent to jails without any lever to depress but a lot to depress about. Second, there is another interesting paradox to Skinnerism as a solution for current social problems: it advocates the absence of negative reinforcers (punishment) as a remedy to contemporary social evils which are due to an excess of freedom in the education of children according to Skinnerists.

Besides these immediate aspects of the politics of Skinnerism, there are more profound ones interwoven into the fabric of American ideology. First, Skinner's discourse on theoretical constructs is largely disjunctive. It reveals the American cult of *versus*: nature versus nurture, theories versus atheoretical positions, facts versus speculations, and so on. This logic of exclusions typifies American choices in religion, politics, friendships and science.

Second, the logic of categorical oppositions is never made clear to the public in American society. When country clubs, universities and other American institutions reject applications from Afro-Americans, Jews, Catholics or Indians, they usually fail to justify their decision appropriately by the fear of contagion from these infectious populations. On the contrary, they usually praise them for their alleged typical qualities. In the same way, when Skinner rejects theories as duplicating empirical facts, he fails to make his own motivation clear. In fact, he shares the positivistic belief that the world is made of facts, not of values which he considers as superfluous superstitions. If this is not a value, what is?

Third, this attitude leads Skinner to believe that experimental manipulations carry the status of absolute proof; which is another form of the American cult of facts.

Fourth, the idea that learning is a mere change in the probability of response reflects the American consensus about the basic goodness of American society.

By making learning a series of local, evanescent, specific responses, Skinner censors the possibility of any revolution or long-term changes. It reflects the rapidity with which trends of all sorts follow each other in American society.

Fifth, Skinner's position is so consensual with American culture that it creates a bestiary that confirms American ideology: animals are up and doing in the box of the great shaper who shapes. 'In the Great Shaper we trust!' Compare these 'American' animals with those observed by Germans. The 'German' animals sit still and think, and at last evolve the solution out of their inner consciousness; admirable beasts who have learned to conform so perfectly to the national characteristics of their Masters that an 'objective' observation by scientists confirms all their stereotypes and prejudices. So much so that the question arises: are we faced with scientific knowledge or with a subvariety of prejudice?

The coincidence between Skinner's epistemology and American ideology raises two substantial questions: first, what about the fact that America produced James, Dewey and Baldwin as well as Skinner? Second, what about the replacement of behaviorism by cognitivism in American psychology? These two questions are objections indeed. They can be represented as a historical question about the succession of paradigms in American psychology and an epistemological one about the relation between epistemologies and theories.

As far as the historical question is concerned, the different personal psychologies of the nineteenth century in America were essentially mechanistic, natural-selectionist, and, as such, paved the road for Watson's behaviorism. But they were also European psychologies in exile and presented important similarities with European schools of psychology. Once the United States became established as a world power in 1917 (at the time of the Soviet revolution) American psychology became autonomous and, except for psychoanalysis (which is still the most important school of psychology in the States), radicalized a movement towards 'experimental' psychology started by W. James and G.S. Hall in direct opposition both to the structuralism of an Englishman, Titchener, and to the 'metaphysical' psychology of their times.

This answers the second question. Epistemologically, there is a rather strong continuity from early American psychology to current cognitivism including behaviorism in between.[1] But the interesting aspect of such a continuity is that it leads to rather different theories. In spite of a common reliance upon Darwinism, materialism and physiological mechanicism, the emphasis changed considerably over time. At first, the post-Darwinian epistemological complex served the function of reconciling the oppositions of biology and culture, the individual and society, thought and action, truth and value, by showing that they were rooted in the developing coordination of reason and reality. Then the very same epistemology discovered that this coordination generated the dichotomies between mind and body, subject and object, and reality and appearance, which were all rather bothersome. Hence, why not consider them as disposable and see what happens? Hence, Bridgman's operationism, Skinner's application of it to psychology, and Bridgman's strong reaction against this.[2] Piaget's operations appear to be a more fitting illustration of his theory in spite of Piaget's denial.

The coincidence of Piaget's arrival on the American scene with the technological breakthroughs in computer sciences led to a crucial reformulation of the same epistemology consisting of an incursion into the black boxes of automata but with the same atomistic and manipulative preoccupations as in behaviorism.

The history of the theoretical metamorphoses of the unchanged epistemological tenets of American ideology goes beyond the scope and limits of this
chapter. But it is an interesting issue, because it shows that apparent enemies in
the strife of systems are, in effect, brothers-in-arms. It demonstrates how the
construction of science is based upon deeply cultural metaphors. For instance, the
representation of the genetic code as an alphabet is very unlikely to occur where
people use ideograms. Finally, it demonstrates that the most interesting sort of
psychology is not the study of behavior but the analysis of the various representations of behavior.

CONCLUSION

The most pathetic error of behaviorism is that it wants to get rid of the most
fundamental principle of any science: the world is not well-known and our
relation to it is not primary.

NOTES

1   For a complete documentation of this continuity, see Hall, G.S. (1881) *Aspects of German Culture*,
    and Perry, R.B. (1935) *The Thought and Character of W. James*, Boston, Mass. Also think of
    James' theory of emotions; Dewey, J. (1910) *Influence of Darwin on Philosophy*; Broughton,
    J.M. and Freeman-Moir, D.J. (1982) *The Cognitive Developmental Psychology of James Mark
    Baldwin*; and, without being too pedantic, the James Papers, Houghton Library, Harvard
    University, Cambridge, where James listed all of these as hylozoic atomists who espoused a kind of
    atomistic identity of mind and matter.
2   See Perry Bridgman's autobiography; *The Way Things Are*.

REFERENCES

Piaget, J. (1942) *La Psychologie de l'Intelligence*, Paris, Armand Colin.
Skinner, B.F. (1981) 'Selection by consequences', in *Science*, 213, pp. 501–4.

Interchange

SCHNAITTER REPLIES TO VONÈCHE

What we have here is an argument to the effect that American practical values are inferior to Continental intellectualist values, and as Skinner's position is a product of these inferior values, it too is inferior. As Vonèche's chapter itself emanates from the Continental intellectualist tradition, it provides a working example of the kind of thought generated by this alternative value system. To a considerable extent the chapter speaks for itself and requires no critique beyond *caveat emptor*. But I cannot resist cataloging a selection of its more egregious errors. The shorter section, headed 'The Logical Argument', receives the main part of my attention.

1. Since Skinner is well-known for his rejection of Bridgemanian operationism, it is hard to tell just what Vonèche is asserting when he claims that Skinnerian behaviorism represents operationism's most rigorous application to psychology. If this claim is true, then it is true only in regard to Skinner's own special sense of operationism. This does not appear to be Vonèche's point.

2. Skinner's 'criterion for the evaluation of knowledge' has to do with one's effectiveness at getting along in that aspect of the world reflected in some putative domain of knowledge. One knows how to ride a bicycle if one *can* ride a bicycle, regardless of anything the 'logical analysis of scientific discourse' might have to say about it.

3. Contrary to Vonèche's claim, Skinner does not replace causality with correlation. What makes Skinner's views on causality somewhat distinct from much contemporary scientific thought is his rejection of mechanistic reductionism. But phenomena can be shown to stand in a causal relation even when not mechanically linked one to another.

4. The old chestnut that scientific laws must be 'unlimited and universal' is often rolled out in service of such arguments as that no social science can ever be real science, or that the theory of evolution is not a scientific theory. In fact it does not matter much if Skinner's or anybody else's laws are unlimited or universal. All a valid generalization must do is generalize over its own domain. If some philosophers of science want to restrict the appellation 'scientific law' to generalizations over universal domains, that is a matter of convention. It has nothing to do with the usefulness of law-like generalizations whose established domains fall somewhat short of the fringes of the universe.

5. Vonèche quite uncontroversially asserts that descriptive propositions (e.g., 'the apple is red') can be evaluated only in a context (I assume he means to include both a linguistic context — the English language in this case — and a material context). Vonèche then claims that this truism is inconsistent with Skin-

ner's epistemology! No reasons are given for drawing this conclusion; indeed, none can be given, as such a conclusion is entirely spurious.

6. On the whole Vonèche's discussion of automata theory is correct. However, in consequence of both misinterpreting Skinner's position and failing to note a subtlety of automata theory, his conclusions are incorrect. Automata theory has convincingly demonstrated that any adequate learning model must incorporate an 'internal' state concept analogous to the state table of a Turing machine. However, it must be noted that this notion of 'internal' state is a formalism, and does not rely on any particular mentalistic interpretation of such states. Contrary to Vonèche's claim, Skinner's 'exclusive use of external predicates' does not form 'a function independent of internal state', in the necessary formal sense of internal state. 'A *state* is simply an element of a *state-space*, which is characterizable purely mathematically in set theory', as Nelson puts it (1975, pp. 257–8). Particular interpretations placed on it are not relevant to the force of the formalism. It happens that Skinner's model interprets this formalism in terms of an environmental history rather than in terms of a current mental state. The nature of that interpretation is not at all critical to the claims of automata theory, however. Yet even with that said, Skinner *does* acknowledge that 'what an organism does will eventually be seen to be due to what it is, at the moment it behaves . . .' (Skinner, 1974, p. 249). If that does not count as an acknowledgment of internal states, I do not know what would. This and related issues are explored in greater depth in Schnaitter (1986). Also see Bealer (1978) and Nelson (1984).

7. Skinner does not attempt to explain all behavior through learning. He makes frequent reference to phylogenetic contributions to behavior.

8. Skinner does not rely heavily on reflexes in accounting for learning. (Even when he does they are dull American reflexes, never the 'brilliant' ones that apparently shine in Geneva.) One would think it beyond question that Skinner's major emphasis is on the modification of *emitted* (not elicited) behavior by its reinforcing consequences.

9. Radical behaviorism is not committed to the view that behavior cannot be modified through 'mere exposure' (e.g., observationally, or imitatively).

10. Skinner is not opposed to 'interpretive discourse', and quite explicitly and self-avowedly engages in it. The book *About Behaviorism* is almost exclusively interpretive.

11. Skinner does not claim that 'theory duplicates reality', whatever that might mean.

About 'The Sociological Argument', I have but two points to make. First, for those whose hearts swell to such refrains, the tune has been much better sung by others (e.g., Mishler, 1975; Schwartz and Lacey, 1982). Second, this kind of thing is going to give the *ad hominem* a bad name.

REFERENCES

Bealer, G. (1978) 'An inconsistency in functionalism', *Synthèse*, 38, pp. 332–74.
Mishler, E.G. (1975) 'Skinnerism: Materialism minus the dialectic', *Journal for the Theory of Social Behaviour*, 6, pp. 21–47.
Nelson, R.J. (1975) 'Behaviorism, finite automata and stimulus-response theory', *Theory and Decision*, 6, pp. 249–67.

Nelson, R.J. (1984) 'Skinner's philosophy of method', *Behavioral and Brain Sciences*, 7, pp. 529–30.

Schnaitter, R. (1986) 'Behavior as a function of inner states and outer circumstances', in Thompson, T. and Zeiler, M. (Eds), *Analysis and Integration of Behavioral Units*, Hillsdale, N.J., Erlbaum.

Schwartz, B. and Lacey, H. (1982) *Behaviorism, Science, and Human Nature*, New York, Norton.

Skinner, B.F. (1974) *About Behaviorism*, New York, Knopf.

VONÈCHE REPLIES TO SCHNAITTER

If I understood him correctly, Roger Schnaitter recognized in his chapter, 'Knowledge As Action: The Epistemology of Radical Behaviorism', that knowledge rests on acts; that radical behaviorism does not explain inner acts or thoughts; that Skinner's goal is the description, control and prediction of behavior instead of its explanation.

This position raises the following questions:

1 how do physical actions get truth-values attached to themselves once they become thoughts or arguments in a discussion?

2 can we still apply the term 'psychology' to a science that does not explain or describe inner life?

3 how does Skinner draw the line separating description, control and prediction from explanation, from a logical point of view?

By systematically refusing one of the two terms of such dialectical distinctions as objective and subjective meanings, facts and values or internal and external acts, Skinner, instead of founding a truly 'scientific' and 'objective' science, replicates the ideology of Puritanism. The central idea of Puritanism is the doctrine of predestination according to which salvation depends neither on true faith as in Lutheranism nor on good deeds and true faith as in Catholicism, but on God's unconditional election as in Calvinism. In such a view the only way to know that one has been chosen is by testing the signs of election by acting out (the famous Puritan work ethics) a sort of groping. If one's work leads to success, one has been elected; if not, one is doomed.

The knowledge of election or damnation rests on external acts; it is strictly objective knowledge. One's own faith, ideas or thoughts and inner acts are unnecessary. The mere description of one's own successes and failures (trials and errors or contingencies of reinforcement) is a better controller and predictor of God's election than any other type of explanation. What better illustration for his theology,[1] could my next-door neighbour on the rue Calvin, John Calvin, imagine than a Skinner box!

NOTE

1 I am fully aware that there are other aspects to Calvin's theological writings, but predestination is the main feature of the popularization of Calvinism. Another objection could be made that the strict experimental methodology to which Skinner adheres is also used by many others in the different scientific disciplines. To this objection I would answer that it is no accident that Sir

Francis Bacon organized the laws of scientific experimentation, that John Stuart Mill reorganized them, and that Charles Darwin rested his theory of evolution upon natural selection (a form of reasoning upon the consequences similar to Skinner's, as we have seen in my chapter). All three had, for different reasons, a strong training in Calvinism.

Part V: A Psychological Analysis: Political, Social and Moral Implications

7.   B.F. Skinner: The Pragmatic Humanist

JAMES WRIGHT

It has been said that one can only write one's autobiography; the veracity of this observation is evident in Skinner's writings. What is quite remarkable in Skinner's impressive 'autobiographical' output is the extent to which he has been able to maintain a clear and consistent theoretico-experimental perspective throughout his career. The main thrust of his operant perspective will be familiar to a wide audience but the technical and philosophical backgrounds will not. These will have to be mastered to an acceptable level, especially if the reader aspires to be a critic; but beware: '(I read this book — *The Technology of Teaching* — three times, making notes, because of the intellectual density, before I thought I knew all that was in it. This has happened to me with less than ten books in a lifetime of study.)' (Platt, 1973, p. 38). The importance the author attaches to adopting such a conscientious approach to mastering Skinner's perspective was established on the preceding page: 'In fact, considering its already visible effects on education and behavior, and its incipient effects on medicine, the law, and all our social structures, it may be the most important discovery of this century' (1973, p. 37). Although perhaps not as confident as Platt, others increasingly are according Skinner's work the intellectual seriousness merited by its achievements and importance. A recent issue of *Behavioral and Brain Sciences* and this volume are two examples supporting this claim.

The main task of my chapter for this volume is to relate the Skinnerian perspective to larger socio-ethical and moral issues. I have attempted to do this in the second and third sections below, 'Let Him Extrapolate Who Will' and 'Part of the Problem or Part of the Solution?' The two other sections, 'Brief Overview' and 'Future Directions', provide a larger contextual framework.

BRIEF OVERVIEW

Skinner has written clearly and succinctly on his methodology and his radical behaviouristic philosophy. I cite only four representative sources here and leave it to the reader to identify others as individual interest warrants: (Skinner, 1961, 1969, 1974, 1978). The cornerstone of methodological operant research is the principle of contingencies of reinforcement. Reinforcers are stimulus events that strengthen and maintain behaviour and as such are provided by the environment. Most of the voluntary behaviour that organisms (including humans) display is assumed to be under the control of particular reinforcing stimuli. Closely allied to the principle of reinforcement is the requirement that empirical functional operations be carried out. Thus, reinforcers are identified empirically on the functional criterion that they increase responding over baseline levels of responding. The basic laboratory paradigm for conducting empirical functional investigations is the so-called three-term contingency arrangement: $S^D \rightarrow R \rightarrow S^R$. This translates roughly to, if a response occurs in the presence of a certain stimulus (S^D = discriminative stimulus), that response will produce a reinforcer (S^R = reinforcing stimulus). What needs to be appreciated, minimally, at this time, is that a range of behaviours — simple and complex alike — can be reduced to this functional formulation and made the basis of any required experimental analysis that the scientist wishes. When this (the experimental analysis) is done carefully and systematically much of our everyday behaviour is revealed to be under the control of specifiable environmental contingencies. Functionally, the contingencies can be either positive (involve something we want) or aversive (involve something we do not want). The behavioural effects, however, turn out to be not so symmetrically tuned. Behaviour controlled and maintained by positive contingencies appears to be much more orderly and stable than behaviour under the control and maintenance of aversive ones. Skinner cites this fact along with a number of other undesirable side effects that occasion the use of aversive procedures as the basis of his commitment to a behavioural technology founded on positive reinforcement. In the applied operant domain many follow this lead totally.

The philosophical basis of operant theory is often referred to as radical behaviourism. Skinner's 1945 paper ('The Operational Analysis of Psychological Terms') as well as his 1974 book (*About Behaviorism*) are the best sources to consult. For our purposes we can accept the salient features summarized by Day (1980), and comment as appropriate: '(a) a focal interest in the study of behavior, *as a subject matter in its own right* [author's italics]; (b) antimentalism; (c) a commitment to biological evolutionism; and (d) a commitment to materialistic determinism' (p. 208). Many of Skinner's critics will have been unaware of his advocacy of (a) and (c) but I think, in the main, would not seriously wish to challenge him on those issues. The substantive items, then, from Day's list are (b) and (d). We take them in reverse order in the discussion that follows.

Even the most sympathetic of Skinner's critics have difficulty accepting Skinner's thoroughgoing deterministic stance (e.g. Platt, 1973; Sagal, 1981). The line usually taken is that for logical and ontological reasons determinism cannot obtain as a scientific principle. Grünbaum, however, in a careful pair of papers (1962, 1971) has been able to provide a valuable critique of the indeterminist's case. In particular he highlights a number of errors that the indeterminist is prone to

make. I comment on the three that are especially prominent in the criticisms of Skinner's stance.

One is mistakenly identifying determinism with universal predictability. There are at least two kinds of situations in which there may be no predictability even though determinism obtains. In the emergent situation, for instance, well-understood phenomena may interact in ways not predictable with reference to the current status of scientific laws. Obviously, the unpredictability here is only temporary and disappears as advances are made in uncovering the relevant scientific laws. The second kind of situation which may prevent predictability is the situation in which it proves physically impossible to obtain the information essential for the success of the prediction. The 'unpredictableness' of processes inside the so-called 'black holes' is an extreme example of this type. Thus, it is important not to equate determinism with universal predictability.

The second error highlighted by Grünbaum is the fallacious identification of determinism with fatalism. Briefly, the fatalist maintains that outcomes (consequences) are fixed and are always independent of our efforts. Outcomes, of course, are not immutable for the determinist, but indeed *are* dependent on our efforts under operant contingencies. In a respondent world things may be different.

The third error is that of confusing causal determination with compulsion. This error is evident, for example, in the claim that determinism becomes self-contradictory when applied to man. Proponents of this argument maintain that as determinism implies a causal determination of its own acceptance by its defender, the determinist cannot, by his own theory, help accepting determinism under the given conditions. Thus the determinist's acceptance of his own theory is viewed as having been forced upon him. The force or compulsion invoked here is of a literal nature, hence the error: identifying causal determination with literal compulsion. As a consequence of this kind of error, the possibility that the acceptance of determinism is due to the 'belief' that the available evidence supports determinism is not allowed. When this possibility is allowed, then the 'belief' can be considered 'forced' or 'compelled' only in the sense that the basis for the 'belief' is the available evidence. Of course, the 'belief' itself may be unwarranted; then, however, a different analysis would be required to ascertain that. On this interpretation, then, a demonstration of the deterministic basis for the deterministic advocacy cannot be used to undermine the deterministic doctrine. Rather, the obverse obtains: 'It follows that although the determinist's assent to his own doctrine is caused or determined, the truth of determinism is not jeopardized by this fact; if anything it is made credible' (Grünbaum, 1971, p. 310). Skinner's position, perhaps more reflective, is just as adamant: 'We cannot prove, of course, that human behavior as a whole is fully determined, but the proposition becomes more plausible as facts accumulate ...' (1974, p. 189).

The second feature we want to consider from Day's list is Skinner's antimentalism, his stance on which is as uncompromising as his stance on determinism: 'I am a radical behaviourist simply in the sense that I find no place in the formulation for anything which is mental' (Skinner, 1964, p. 106). Appeal to such mentalisms as purposes, goals, and intentions is regarded by Skinner 'as surrogates of histories of reinforcement' (1984, p. 578). His proscription of mentalism, however, does not extend to subjective, i.e. private, stimuli. This position, in-

terestingly, is in marked contrast to methodological behaviourism, since methodological behaviourism excludes private stimuli from its domain of study. (Was the 'empty organism' label misapplied?)

One final point of clarification is required in this section. The concept of the operant, properly considered, refers to a class of events — either of stimuli or of responses. Thus, the effect of reinforcement attaches to particular stimulus or response classes rather than exclusively to the light stimulus that acts as a discriminative stimulus or the terminal response on a schedule of reinforcement. This technical refinement allows us to talk about response strength in a generic sense and may prove helpful in the discussions to follow.

LET HIM EXTRAPOLATE WHO WILL

Some readers will recognize the above statement as coming from *The Behavior of Organisms*, a book dealing exclusively with the behaviour of rats in very simple laboratory situations. In time many came to accept the challenge implicit in that statement; none sooner or more ambitiously than Skinner himself. *Walden Two* (1948), *Science and Human Behavior* (1953), *Verbal Behavior* (1957), *The Technology of Teaching* (1968), and *Beyond Freedom and Dignity* (1971) are the best-known results of his 'extrapolations'. In these works the reader will soon discover a recognizable refrain: the human condition is amenable to a scientific, behavioural analysis; society should apply the behavioural technology based on this scientific analysis in the management of its affairs. Failure to do so may prove tragic — nay, *will* prove so: the demise of one's culture, in fact. So, we have Skinner, the dispassionate scientist, as well as Skinner, the pragmatic humanist. The humanistic label serves to underscore the beneficent consequences of his practical efforts as well as to remind us of the classical connotation of the saying: 'man is the measure of all things.' It is in this classical sense also that we can focus on some of the specific issues raised by others in their objections to Skinner's philosophical and technological behavioural science.

There can be little question that a behavioural technology based on operant principles works. Human operant work appears regularly in handbooks and in research and applied behavioural journals. A number of *Walden Two* communes has been established and although 'in general ... there is little concern with the scientific exactitudes of Frazier ...' (Ramsey, 1979, p. 155), Skinner, at least, views the approximate results rather optimistically: 'I think this is very encouraging and this is as close to *Walden Two* as I had any right to expect' (Young, 1978, cited in Ramsey, 1979, p. 154). Yet, in spite of an admittedly strong public accounting record, there is continuing resistance to a fuller adoption of this behavioural technology. The reasons are varied and diverse but in the main centre on the position that Skinner's view of man qua man is wrong. *Beyond Freedom and Dignity* (1971) is the work that has received the greatest critical attention; perhaps along with judicious readings from *Contingencies of Reinforcement: A Theoretical Analysis* (1969) and *Reflections on Behaviorism and Society* (1978), it is the best non-technical Skinnerian work to consult.

Man, according to Skinner, is controlled jointly, by his genetic and reinforcement histories. As adumbrated in his antimentalist stance, personal autonomy, ethical sentiment, intentions, and the like, are accorded no role as causative

agents in his formulation. This position is conveyed unambiguously: 'Science does not dehumanize man, it de-homunculizes him, and it must do so if it is to prevent the abolition of the human species. To man qua man we readily say good riddance' (1971, p. 196). Skinner offers to redefine questions of traditional ethics and values to questions about the way people behave. Value judgments ('This is good', 'That is bad') are simply statements that one has learned to make about particular environmental events in a manner analogous to the way in which one acquires responses such as 'red flower', 'cat', and 'I am tired'. All that is required in both instances is that the statements are descriptively 'accurate' in nature; the 'accuracy', however, is defined by the relevant verbal community. In practice it becomes clear that the things one describes as good turn out to correspond to things which function as positive reinforcers; things judged as bad turn out to correspond to negative reinforcers. One can easily shift from talking about the things to talking about the way one feels about them. In the latter case one is describing the effects of reinforcement. Thus under subtle 'shaping' by the verbal community one learns to distinguish between a thing and the reinforcing effect of a thing on the basis of positive and negative reinforcing contingencies. Values, then, are simply tacts (cf. *Verbal Behavior*, Ch. 5) and are not essentially different from the world of facts.

The question of ethical injunctions involves a similar overall process but is different in two important respects: (1) indirect reference to the relevant controlling contingencies in the speaker; and (2) indirect reference to the reinforcing contingencies affecting the listener. Although the reference to these two sets of controlling contingencies is indirect, factual information can be brought to bear on them and thereby establish the descriptive accuracy outlined for simple value statements above. Taking Skinner's example, 'You should (ought to) read *David Copperfield*' (1971, p. 111), translates roughly to, 'generally those who read *David Copperfield* are reinforced as a result of having done so.' Complexities soon occur, especially in terms of identifying the controlling contingencies with reference to the speaker and the listener. Nevertheless, the significance of such an analysis cannot be overstated as the beginnings of a social interaction (speaker-listener) have been given behavioural significance. Technically, most 'should' and 'ought' statements would be classified as mands (cf. *Verbal Behavior*, Ch.3) and have as a defining characteristic the aforementioned speaker-listener interaction.

The practical implications of this analysis are quite wide-ranging. Summarizing Day (1977), behaviourists should be prepared to offer evidence concerning three kinds of reinforcing contingencies that bear upon any particular recommendation they may want to make. The relevance of the three kinds of reinforcing contingencies can easily be seen once the recommendation has been translated roughly into the following behavioural form: '"If you are reinforced by such-and-such (x), you will be reinforced by doing such-and-such (y), and the reinforcement controlling this assertion on my part is such-and-such (z)"' (Day, 1977, p. 18). The first two sets of reinforcing contingencies are perhaps clear enough in the *David Copperfield* example given above.

The third set of reinforcing contingencies relates to factors determining the recommendation the behaviourist actually makes. In short, an examination of the contingencies governing the behaviour of the behaviourist is required. It is clear that all behaviourists have not been sensitive to this requirement (cf. 'Part of the

Problem or Part of the Solution?' below); it is equally clear, however, that any laxity that does occur is at variance with the formal behavioural model.

Ethics and moral codes are thus viewed as behaviour brought under the stimulus control of the verbal community. The a prioristic stance so characteristic of the traditional approach to these issues, as a consequence, is replaced by a thoroughgoing functional account. In this way the external conditions of which man's behaviour is a function are identified and brought within the purview of a scientific analysis, a radical behaviouristic analysis. Many objections have been raised against this account and some of these (objections) have been out of a sense of 'philosophical proprietorship'. But not all: (see especially Wheeler, 1973, and Krapfl and Vargas, 1977, for helpful critical papers). Even some of the 'proprietorship' type of criticisms are not without intellectual merit in that they at least force a legitimate examination from as wide a spectrum as possible of both the practice and philosophy of radical behaviourism. It is on the political front, however, that Skinner's ideas will encounter their most severe test and the issue of paramount concern will be that of potential abuse. As Wheeler notes in his introductory chapter, 'the political problem facing us is the same one that faces us when any powerful technology is developed: how to control it so that we can enjoy its benefits rather than suffer from its abuses' (1973, p. 20). Skinner, of course, is also aware of the necessity to be ever-vigilant against the technology being used discreditably: 'The misuse of a technology of behaviour is a serious matter, but we can guard against it best by looking not at putative controllers but at the contingencies under which they control' (1971, p. 179). Is this corrective mechanism sufficient?

PART OF THE PROBLEM OR PART OF THE SOLUTION?

Holland, noted for his independent and collaborative pioneering work with Skinner on programmed instruction (e.g., Holland, 1960, 1967; Holland and Skinner, 1961), has devoted considerable effort to documenting that in practice applied behavioural analysts, perhaps unwittingly, are often as prone to recommend unscientific behavioural programmes as non-applied behavioural analysts are (1977, 1978). A particularly revealing charge is the extent to which applied analysts readily adopt, in William Ryan's terms, a 'blaming the victim perspective'. This propensity is particularly apparent in programmes designed for alcoholics and criminals. The clear consequence of adopting such a perspective is that the 'problem' is analyzed and dealt with not in relationship to the maintaining environmental contingencies but rather in accordance with institutional requirements. The applied analyst is indicted further by Holland for insufficiently subjecting his own behaviour to an analysis in terms of its controlling contingencies. When this complete analysis is done, Holland concludes that 'the dire predictions of the civil libertarian and the social reformer are amply confirmed' (1978, p. 164). Not only is there a high proportion of behavioural programmes utilizing aversive contingencies, these contingencies are especially likely to be employed if the 'problem' behaviour is considered by society to be repugnant. Holland goes further and provides a fuller analysis within the context of sociopolitical reform. The core of this analysis is that the stratified social system that obtains in America contains the behavioural basis for many of the problems that

the applied analyst is asked to deal with; in his professional approach to these problems the applied analyst frequently aligns himself with the power elite of the society. In this sense applied analysts may be considered to be part of the problem. The solution recommended by Holland involves a more faithful adherence to radical behaviouristic principles along with a wider canvassing of alternative social systems.

Holland's ideas have not remained unchallenged. Culpability in 'blaming the victim' appears accepted (at least in part), but rather vigorous dissent has been registered with respect to other aspects of Holland's overall analysis. Harshbarger (1977) questions the narrowness of Holland's analysis and feels that it is ideological and non-data-based in some of its claims. Goldiamond is concerned that Holland has included non-behaviourists in his culpable net (the work with alcoholics cited by Holland was conducted by a psychiatrist) and in general implies that the 'part of the problem' element is overemphasized (cf. 1978, p. 182). In his fuller discussion Goldiamond summarizes themes he had developed on earlier occasions (1976, 1977) with respect to the concept of professionals as double agents. The applied analyst, for instance, has the patient or student as one client and the social system as the other. This tripartite functional unit operates in a trouble-free manner for the most part; difficulties may arise, however, when the patient-student requirements are not congruent with the requirements of the social system. Although for Goldiamond only a minority of the applied analytical work involves incongruence of this sort, it is imperative that the applied analyst makes explicit his role as a double agent in the programmes that he develops. Goldiamond's more extensive treatment of this notion of the professional as a double agent in his earlier sources should be consulted for more elaboration than can be provided here.

Thus Holland and critics alike seem agreed that there is a problem; the basic disagreement centres on the solution. While Holland would recommend fundamental institutional changes, Goldiamond, at least, recommends a much more thorough, 'fine-grain' analysis of the dynamics that obtain in the applied situations in which the analyst works. What is clear from both sides of the debate is that the behaviour of the agent (applied analyst) is no less immune to environmental contingencies than his patients-students (and in other circumstances rats and pigeons). It would seem, then, that by replacing Holland's 'or' with an 'and', we observe a vindication rather than a discrediting of Skinner's corrective principle. To be clear, Holland's analysis did not call into question the radical behaviouristic perspective, it simply failed to consider fully the scope for a solution within this framework.

FUTURE DIRECTIONS

Kendler in 1959 could write: 'In general, learning theorists understand each other better than did their ancestors of two decades ago. ... Skinnerians also find it easy to communicate among themselves' (p. 79). Such isolation no longer obtains, nor is it desirable that it should. Encouragingly, within the behavioural sciences barriers are receding as well, but not as rapidly as one would wish. As a result of an authoritative discussion of trends and directions in a recent issue of *Journal of the Experimental Analysis of Behavior* (Vol. 42, No. 3, 1984), I can offer observa-

tions of a more restricted range. I offer two below: (1) on *Verbal Behavior* and (2) an operant theory.

Skinner clearly regards *Verbal Behavior* as his most important work in psychology. After a slow start, interest in this work seems to be gaining momentum (even amongst linguists, psycholinguists, and philosophers). As data accumulate, required modifications will be made to the basic formulation, but already practical results are forthcoming from its application in clinical and applied work (Rozynko *et al.*, 1973; Michael, 1984). A particularly imaginative application of the model was utilized by Bem (1967) in his analysis of self-perception. Much more experimental data, of course, are required, but on present form Skinner's self-assessment may be realized.

I comment explicitly on operant theory because of the increased 'theoretical' behaviour of operant researchers over the last decade or so. There is no need to rehearse Skinner's careful advice on this issue, but rather to re-emphasize it while at the same time give a gentle nudge. In his *Notebooks* (1980) he regrets that he has failed in his writings to stress the importance of dimensional analysis in psychological work. This formal technique is used to great advantage in the physical sciences and has been assimilated successfully by biologists investigating problems of size and shape and metabolism (e.g., McMahon, 1973; Schepartz, 1980). In my (conservative) opinion this is the best avenue for translating our hard-won goals into greater advances on the theoretical front.

Finally, Skinner's closing comments in the 'Preface' to the seventh printing of *Behavior of Organisms* are appropriate here:

> So far as the facts are concerned, *The Behavior of Organisms* is out of date. It still seems to me a viable book, however, for it presents a useful formulation of behavior supported by a selection of illustrative experiments. It may also serve as a reminder that a conception of human behavior has been derived from an analysis which began with organisms in simple situations and moved on, but only as its growing power permitted, to the complexities of the world at large. (p. xiv)

REFERENCES

Bem, D.J. (1967) 'Self-perception: An alternative interpretation of cognitive dissonance phenomena', *Psychological Review*, 74, pp. 183–200.

Day, W. (1977) 'The philosophy and thought of B.F. Skinner', in Krapfl, J.E. and Vargas, E.A. (Eds), *Behaviorism and Ethics*, Kalamazoo, Mich, Behaviordelia, Inc.

Day, W. (1980) 'The historical antecedents of contemporary behaviorism', in Rieber, R.W. and Salzinger, K. (Eds), *Psychology, Theoretical Perspectives*, New York, Academic Press.

Goldiamond, I. (1977) 'Protection of human subjects and patients', in Krapfl J.E. and Vargas, E.A. (Eds), *Behaviorism and Ethics*, Kalamazoo, Mich., Behaviordelia Inc.

Goldiamond, I. (1978) 'The professional as a double-agent', *Journal of Applied Behavior Analysis*, 11, pp. 178–84.

Grünbaum, A. (1962) 'Science and man', *Perspectives in Biology and Medicine*, 5, pp. 483–502.

Grünbaum, A. (1971) 'Free will and laws of human behavior', *American Philosophical Quarterly*, 8, pp. 299–317.

Gunther, B. (1975) 'Dimensional analysis and theory of biological similarity', *Physiological Reviews*, 55, pp. 659–99.

Harshbarger, D. (1977) Commentary: 'Is institutional change necessary?' in Krapfl, J.E. and Vargas, E.A. (Eds) *Behaviorism and Ethics*, Kalamazoo, Mich., Behaviordelia, Inc.

Holland, J.G. (1960) 'Teaching machines: An application of principles from the laboratory', *Journal of the Experimental Analysis of Behavior*, 3, pp. 275–87.

Holland, J.G. (1967) 'A quantitative measure for programmed instruction', *American Educational Research Journal,* 4, pp. 87–101.

Holland, J.G. (1977) 'Is institutional change necessary?' in Krapfl, J.E. and Vargas, E.A. (Eds) *Behaviorism and Ethics,* Kalamazoo, Mich., Behaviordelia, Inc.

Holland, J.G. (1978) 'Behaviorism: Part of the problem or part of the solution?' *Journal of Applied Analysis of Behavior,* 11, pp. 163–74.

Holland, J.G. and Skinner, B.F. (1961) *The Analysis of Behavior,* New York, McGraw Hill.

Kendler, H. (1959) 'Learning', Annual Review of Psychology, *10,* pp. 43–88.

Krapfl, J.E. and Vargas, E.A. (Eds) (1977) *Behaviorism and Ethics,* Kalamazoo, Mich., Behaviordelia, Inc.

McMahon, T. (1973) 'Size and shape in biology', *Science,* 179, pp. 1201–4.

Michael, J. (1984) 'Verbal behavior', *Journal of the Experimental Analysis of Behavior,* 42, pp. 363–76.

Platt, J.R. (1973) 'The Skinnerian revolution', in Wheeler, H. (Ed.), *Beyond the Punitive Society,* London, Wildwood House.

Ramsay, D. (1979) 'Morning Star: The Values-Communication of Skinner's *Walden Two*', PhD thesis, Rensaelaer Polytechnic Institute, Troy, N.Y.

Rozynko, V. *et al.* (1973) 'Controlled environments for social change', in Wheeler, H. (Ed.), *Beyond the Punitive Society,* London, Wildwood House.

Ryan, W. (1971) *Blaming the Victim,* New York, Vintage Books.

Sagal, P.T. (1981) *Skinner's Philosophy,* Washington, D.C., University Press of America.

Schepartz, B. (1980) *Dimensional Analysis in the Biomedical Sciences,* Springfield, Ill., Charles C. Thomas.

Skinner, B.F. (1938) *The Behavior of Organisms,* New York, Appleton-Century-Crofts.

Skinner, B.F. (1945) 'The operational analysis of psychological terms', *Psychological Review,* 52, pp. 270–7, 281–94.

Skinner, B.F. (1948) *Walden Two,* New York, Macmillan.

Skinner, B.F. (1953) *Science and Human Behavior,* New York, Macmillan.

Skinner, B.F. (1957) *Verbal Behavior,* New York, Appleton-Century-Crofts.

Skinner, B.F. (1961) *Cumulative Record,* enlarged ed., New York, Appleton-Century-Crofts.

Skinner, B.F. (1964) 'Behaviorism at fifty (with discussion)', in Wann, T.W. (Ed.), *Behaviorism and Phenomenogy,* Chicago, Ill., University of Chicago Press.

Skinner, B.F. (1966) 'The phylogeny and ontogeny of behavior', *Science* 153, pp. 1205–13.

Skinner, B.F. (1968) *The Technology of Teaching,* New York, Appleton-Century-Crofts.

Skinner, B.F. (1969) *Contingencies of Reinforcement: A Theoretical Analysis,* New York, Appleton-Century-Crofts.

Skinner, B.F. (1971) *Beyond Freedom and Dignity,* New York, Alfred A. Knopf.

Skinner, B.F. (1974) *About Behaviorism,* New York, Alfred A. Knopf.

Skinner, B.F. (1978) *Reflections on Behaviorism and Society,* Englewood Cliffs, N.J., Prentice Hall.

Skinner, B.F. (1979) *The Shaping of a Behaviorist,* New York, Alfred A. Knopf.

Skinner, B.F. (1980) *Notebooks, B.F. Skinner,* Englewood Cliffs, N.J., Prentice-Hall.

Skinner, B.F. (1981) 'Selection by consequences', *Science,* 213, pp. 501–4.

Skinner, B.F. (1984) 'Coming to terms with private events', *Behavioral and Brain Sciences,* 7, pp. 572–81.

Wheeler, H. (Ed.) (1973) *Beyond the Punitive Society,* London, Wildwood House.

Young, V. (1978) *A World of Difference: B.F. Skinner and the Good Life,* Transcript of NOVA Videotape 603, narrated by Jean Richards, Boston, Mass., WGBH Educational Television.

8.   Scolding the Carpenter

DOUGLAS BETHLEHEM

It is with an acute sense of my own temerity that I take up my fountain pen to write an article highly critical of a major living behavioural scientist. It is the same fountain pen with which I passed my examinations in psychology years ago, for which I closely studied — with more than a decent respect, with a certain piety even (science and learning are not mere instruments to me) — the research and theories of the man whom I now disparage. I take my justification from Dr Johnson, who observed, to a self-deprecating friend, 'You *may* abuse a tragedy, though you cannot write one. You may scold a carpenter who has made you a bad table, though you cannot make a table' (Boswell, 1791/1949, p. 253). This volume is not, after all, a Festschrift.

Yet it is important to recall what roused my admiration as a student, and does to no less a degree today. Professor Skinner will be remembered, and deservedly so, in the histories of psychology that come to be written, for the penetrating thought, and the careful and assiduous research, which led to *The Behavior of Organisms* (1938), *Schedules of Reinforcement* (Ferster and Skinner, 1957), and perhaps for the orientation though not the detail of *Verbal Behavior* (1957). The first two have their monuments in the everyday usage of working psychologists: it is easy to forget, now that the terms are part of the psychologist's stock in trade, that '*operant* conditioning' and 'variable ratio' schedules were concepts that needed thinking out and defending.

But even as an undergraduate, I had misgivings. Hull's great work received a drubbing from Skinner (1944/1961); it was apparent that the teaching machines of the day were not all that wonderful, or specially Skinnerian; and there was a worrying lack of contact with ethical philosophy. These misgivings have been amplified by what I have read since. It is to these shortcomings of Professor Skinner, as a self-conscious scientist, as a political or moral philosopher, of his offerings on art and life, and of his tenets of belief regarding psychology, that I now turn.

CRITICISMS

Science

Skinner has a very limited view of science, and even of the science of psychology. The limitations come up again and again, and lead to other errors which in turn lead to other sets of limitations and errors. Indeed, the various sets of limitations and errors form a series of ·connecting staircases which appear always to be ascending, each one leading to the foot of the next, like those impossible figures associated with the artist Escher.

As a start, there is the curious, usually unstated, assumption underlying his work that, where psychology is concerned, 'natural science' is equivalent to 'radical behaviorism', dogmas and all. (I give the term 'behaviorism' its American spelling in this context as a proper noun, the copyright, as it were, of Skinnerians.) Thus, individual differences are given short shrift: they are ascribed to 'differences in the history of reinforcement' (1965, p. 196) or, offhandedly, to heredity and development — but so offhand is the reference to those factors that one might suppose behaviour genetics and developmental psychology did not exist in 1953 (when the passage was written)! But worse, he goes on to show the same appreciation of test theory and sampling as a fresher forced into doing psychology against his or her prejudices by an unsympathetic timetable. A score on an intelligence test, we are told, even when given as a standard score, is 'not a quantitative measure of a trait' since 'trouble will arise when we try to use such a measure in a different group' (1965, p. 198). Hence statistical sampling theory and its application in mental testing are ignored.

They are ignored in consequence of another of the staircases in the figure — the extraordinarily naive conception of 'cause'. Not that Skinner is alone in his naivety regarding *cause*. As far as almost all psychologists are concerned, Hume, and even Mill's careful analysis of how the term might be used (his famous five canons, 1843/1973), might never have existed. So Skinner is not alone: but it is an important factor in his writing and thinking, and sits uneasily for one who refers so frequently and familiarly to the great philosophers (e.g., 'Perhaps, like Jeremy Bentham and his theory of fictions, I ...' (1967, p. 408); 'Reading a short essay on morals by Montaigne ...' 'I thought I saw a bit of Bacon, a bit of Locke ...' (1980, p. 82); Hume, unsurprisingly, is seldom if ever mentioned). It follows from his incomprehension of the difficulties with the term that he cannot comprehend that traits, such as intelligence and introversion, do *explain* and predict behaviour, and that, while they do not *cause* behaviour, neither does an organism's reinforcement history, since the term *cause* is empty. To be sure, he does make a passing acknowledgment that 'the terms "cause" and "effect" are no longer widely used in science' (1965, p. 23), but shows no real comprehension of *why* they are not, nor does he pay more than this brief lip-service to their emptiness. Hence he is able to assert unblushingly that 'the experimental analysis of behavior goes *directly* to the antecedent *causes* in the environment' (1974, p. 30 — emphasis mine), as though the holy grail had at last been found: in the attic of the home of radical behaviorism, where else?

That takes us to another of the ever-ascending staircases in confusion of Skinner's philosophy: his epistemology. Of course, no one has evolved a complete-

ly satisfactory epistemology. Nonetheless, persons claiming to deal in science and its philosophy must come to grips with the problem. Skinner makes no real attempt to do so, and hence is able to provide no foundation for his radical behaviorism. Even the simple and obvious questions — of course, the answers are not to be described in those terms — of what the radical behaviorist is to take for his data, and how this decision is to be justified, while treated at length (see, e.g., Ch. 5 of *About Behaviorism*, 1974, a book supposedly dealing not with the science of behaviour but with 'the philosophy of that science', — p. 3), are dealt with very superficially. He comes to a conclusion consonant with the most simplistic form of realism. 'When operationism led to the study of the process of discrimination rather than of sensations, a person was regarded as looking at or listening to the real world. He was no longer reporting his perceptions or sensations; he was reporting stimuli. The world was back where it belonged' (1974, p. 86). This is a position which can be defended, or which can be adopted as a bluff matter of cutting Gordian knots. Skinner does neither. Moreover, he even qualifies this simple realism later (in fourteen lines on *Truth* — 1974, p.136 — he acknowledges that 'there is no way in which a verbal description of a setting can be absolutely true', but he does not seem to see the relevance of this statement to Skinner boxes or the vague analogies to these in human settings). He accepts that 'private' events — emotions, thoughts, etc. — can be part of the data of his psychology, since he rejects the more blatant demands for agreement among observers, at least as far as 'facts' or basic statements are concerned. He 'does not insist on truth by agreement and can therefore consider events taking place in the private world within the skin' (1974, p. 16). Yet he does not really accept the simple realism he espouses. How shall we know the world? — by an organism's responses to it. 'I could be said to know that this sheet of paper is really there because I pick up a pen and write on it, and that bright after-image which bothers me is not there because I do not try to brush it away' (1974, pp. 86–7). What he does not tell us is (1) what if a person *does* try to brush away the after-image? and, more important, (2) *how do we know the responses of the organism?* Hence a correspondence theory of truth is ruled out, since that requires the simple realism he goes on to doubt.

And he piles confusion upon confusion: '. . . knowledge is a repertoire of behavior' (1965, p. 409). It is behaviour 'which satisfies the contingencies [the world] maintains' (1969, p. 156) — i.e., adaptive behaviour — or it is 'the behavior controlled by contingency-specifying stimuli' (1969, p. 156). In other words, knowledge is simply responding adaptively or appropriately. Whence then the realism referred to above?

All these lead up in the ever-ascending staircases to the major landing: an incomprehension of the nature of science in its orthodox conception. It shows in his pragmatic conception of reinforcement as any stimulus which increases the probability of a response or the rate of responding. Perhaps it is a minor point to say that Skinner insists on a weak version of the law of effect — that is, one which is formally circular inasmuch as it defines (positive) reinforcement in terms of increase in probability or rate of response, and ascribes increase in probability or rate of response to (positive) reinforcement. It is saved from being a useless and foolish tautology by the commonsense recognition that certain things are reinforcing in many different circumstances: certain foods (provided the organism is ascribed the mentalistic quality of hunger), sugar, escape from pain, etc. How

do you know what will be reinforcing? *Put yourself in the place of the rat!* Of course, this form of extraspection is not recommended, and pages are devoted to attacking it. But I do not suppose Skinner tried at random all possible stimuli before finding what 'reinforces' behaviour. (The point that reinforcers are adaptive from an evolutionary point of view appears to be a *post hoc* empirical statement, not a statement of definition.)

But what these signs lead to is Skinner's incomprehension of science: the grand conception of science. He slammed Hull's *Principles of Behavior* (1944/1961); and never seems to have got rid of his contempt for Hull and his work; in his little autobiography (1967) he tells us that while he was at school he began a 'treatise' called *Nova Principia Orbis Terrarum*. Then he jeers in parentheses, 'That sounds pretentious, but at least I got it out of my system early. Clark Hull published his Principia at the age of fifty-nine' (p. 396). To be sure, much of what he has to say about Hull's work in the review of *Principles of Behavior* is quite justified: Hull's theory was, in a sense, a grand failure; and, to be fair, Skinner is not ungenerous in the review, referring in closing to the 'stimulating effect' of Hull's book, and the 'research which will certainly follow'. (It did, in a very big way.) The disturbing thing is that he shows no comprehension there, or elsewhere, of what Hull was trying to achieve: that is, a scientific theory, consisting of axioms and postulates, and an ascending system of hypotheses/laws/theories in which each lower level in the system is rigorously deducible from the higher levels, and the lowest levels are testable by comparison with observation. This lack of comprehension and the disparagement run through Skinner's works. In one of the most absurd passages, fashioning an hypothesis is compared to 'guessing who is calling when the phone rings' instead of lifting the receiver (1969, p. ix): as though the deity of science sat at the end of a telephone to say this or that conception is the true scientific solution: to say to Hull that operant conditioning is the answer to all questions relating to the science of behaviour, or to save an industrious and brilliant Fechner or Thurstone bother by putting them onto Fechner's Law or the modal discriminal process. Skinner refers quite frequently (e.g., 1974, p. 228; 'In the Psychiatrist's Chair', 1984) to *interpreting* behaviour outside the laboratory in terms of results in the laboratory. This form of words covers the inadequacy of his position by allowing him to evade recognition that the business of science is not to interpret — which any Marxist, Freudian, structuralist, etc., can and does do — but to *explain*, and that is done through theories. Elsewhere (1967, p. 409) he says, 'I am not interested in psychological theories, in rational equations, in factor analyses, in mathematical models, in hypothetico-deductive systems, or in other verbal systems which must be *proved* right [italics in original]'. Now, a passing acquaintance with Hume, or a cursory knowledge of the logic of science — through reading Popper, for instance — would lead him to recognize that theories cannot, in the nature of things, be proved. He might have been led to the realization that his tinkering with rat-boxes is only the first step — of course, essential — on the way to fulfilled science. Skinner does not recognize these things. Briefly discussing methodology, he recognizes that 'eventually . . . the experimenter must behave verbally' (1969, p. 113), and 'theories are fun' and '. . . the need for a formal representation of the data reduced to a minimal number of terms' (1949/1961, p. 69). But nowhere does he overtly recognize that in, e.g., discussing 'piecework pay' as a 'fixed-ratio schedule' (1953, p. 385) he is assuming some theory such as 'fixed ratio schedules

of reinforcement always have the effect on rate of response which is commonly exhibited by rats on fixed-ratio schedules in Skinner boxes.' Put like that it seems absurd: if he had bothered to theorize on those lines, we would probably have heard less of the confident assertion that schedules of reinforcement explain all behaviour in any circumstances whatever.

Political and Ethical Philosophy

If Skinner understands little of the philosophy of science, he understands less of political and ethical philosophy. *Walden Two* and *Beyond Freedom and Dignity* are about the dreariest in the long line of totalitarian advocacy and apology. They lack any kind of style and vigour; as philosophy, *Beyond Freedom and Dignity* is a non-starter, and as a novel *Walden Two* scarcely exists, being simply a tedious disquisition of the least believable utopia in the whole canon of utopian literature. Neither puts forward a new point of view, or offers new thoughts on the questions raised. Neither even attempts to answer the libertarian view, since their author seems hardly to be aware that the libertarian view exists. Skinner has not read Mill's *Logic*, and he certainly has not read that careful setting out of the importance of liberty in Mill's essay 'On Liberty' (1859/1910a), or Mill's justification of democracy (1861/1910b). Worse, he *has* read, presumably carefully, Thoreau's *Walden* (1886), and has failed to take its important messages. It is a paeon to quiet thought and non-conformity. 'Let every one mind his own business, and endeavour to be what he was made,' says Thoreau .... 'If a man does not keep pace with his companions, perhaps it is because he hears a different drummer. Let him step to the music which he hears, however measured or far away' (1886, p. 323). In Walden Two — the imaginary place — no one is allowed to hear a different drummer. Presumably, if they did, the sound would be reinforced right out of their heads, and they would be rendered back into good little conformists, making no waves.

Basically, Skinner takes the totalitarian position which justifies all illiberal regimes: 'I know what is good for you, and if you disagree or want to do things differently you are to be disregarded and coerced/controlled as either a fool or a knave.' Poor Professor Skinner, benign Jupiter as he would like to be, simply cannot see that there will always (thank goodness!) be some people who disagree, who prefer their own way, however unappealing that is to Skinner. The limitation of vision is nicely illustrated in the radio interview (In the Psychiatrist's Chair, 1984) referred to earlier. Dr Clare, the interviewer, asks Professor Skinner about rebels and anarchists in his scheme of things. Skinner replies: '... if IBM builds the *perfect* typewriter, and no part breaks down, that is a fault, because others have broken down? ... I would suppose that a well designed culture would not need rebels .... It would need experimental change and investigation — you never can stop with what you have .... But why you need rebels — the answer to that is that you haven't got a perfect system.' Exactly the same thing might be said by every blinkered nationalist and totalitarian apologist the world has ever seen. Every step away from liberal tolerance is a step towards totalitarianism. The only thing totalitarians differ on is the nature of the ideal. Doubtless we all favour despotism, provided '*I*' am the despot.

Democracy is discussed — and dismissed — in *Walden Two* (Ch. 30). The

tired old rationalizations come out. No single vote makes much difference, so people might as well not bother to vote: but look at regimes where regular and genuine elections do not take place. The people are stupid and ignorant: 'The people are in no position to evaluate experts', says the Skinner-surrogate Frazier (p. 251). In any case, voting is a sham: 'Voting is a device for blaming conditions on the people' (p. 250). He goes on in the chapter to deny fascism, but his metamorphosis of brute fascism to pseudo-democracy relies on two dogmatic fictions: one, that in Walden Two (the imaginary place) everyone's grievances are instantly looked into and remedied by the managers, is as credible as the land of the lotus eaters; the other, on which the first in a sense depends, is that the environment — in the particularly simplistic sense of the immediate physical surroundings (books and ideas seem not to count) — controls people's desires and behaviour ('. . . the observed fact that men are made good or bad and wise or foolish by the environment in which they grow', says Frazier, p. 257). It is implied that Skinner knows, or nearly knows, how to control that environment. Yet nowhere do we get a serious discussion of justice, in whose service the control would presumably be exercised.

The sad thing is that the vision is so paltry. What we are promised in *Walden Two* is not the spiritual fulfilment of Bunyan's Celestial City, nor even the more fleshly satisfactions of *Brave New World*, where the girls carried contraceptive belts and soma was always available, but a kind of dull, mid-western small town with a well-endowed arts centre. Beethoven's music, so freely available in Walden Two, would, alas, be well beyond the understanding of the inhabitants: they'd probably all go for the mechanical muzak on offer to the Deltas of *Brave New World*. Even the technology offered is irredeemably feeble. Skinner is a famous psychologist, so we are entitled to ask more of him than we do of, say, Aldous Huxley. And what are we offered? Constant references to his dogmas regarding the ineffectiveness of punishment and the all-controlling contingencies of reinforcement, and the inculcation of self-control in children by making them wait for their food. Oh dear!

Skinner is not by any stretch of the imagination a fascist. It is narrow and short-sighted, and, judging by his tone when he alludes to it, hurtful, to use that term of the man himself. The distinguishing feature of totalitarian/fascist ideology is that someone knows what is right, and all other views must be controlled as dangerous error. It is a pity that Skinner cannot see the implications of his ideas.

Views on Art and Life

Skinner presents himself as a man of wisdom beyond the mere laboratory, almost as a guru. Writings like *Beyond Freedom and Dignity* (1972), *Walden Two* (1976), *About Behaviorism* (1974), *Science and Human Behavior* (1965), and even *Contingencies of Reinforcement* (1969), many of his articles, and above all the *Notebooks* (1980), are writings on art and life, love and death, politics, philosophy, ethics, culture, and all. These form a considerable portion of his published work. And what he has to say on these great subjects is almost all appallingly banal. Nowhere is there a flash of insight, or an enlightening or amusing epigram. Most, particularly the *Notebooks*, are ponderous and dull. As just one small example, he quotes a stanza from Hardy (1980, p. 10), a poetic conceit on the immortality

of love; he then goes on to write a stanza, meant to be a satirical comment, which does not scan, or have a rhyme scheme comparable to the original, which is not amusing or pithy or pointed, and contains the word 'whooshingly', pointing out that missiles (they go 'whooshingly by') may kill everyone and put paid to the lovers and their love. As something said off the cuff in a pub it might have provoked a wry smile — provided the hour was late enough. But to allow it to be published in a book! Worse still, his comment ends, 'But [poetry] must not be taken seriously. Or permitted to interfere in serious matters' (1980, p. 11). What on earth does he consider 'serious matters' to be? You can see why he gave up creative writing!

But there is even worse to be found, without digging especially deep. He attributes the liking for dialogue in novels to an ease of identification with speakers 'because the recorded speech provides a direct source of strength for verbal responses and because these responses can be executed in any environment' (1965, pp. 216–17). The use of dialogue to allow us to infer things about the speaker or events in the narrative, the use of dialogue to convey irony (who could fail to relish the wretchedly hen-pecked Mr Bumble in *Oliver Twist* being told by Mr Brownlow that 'the law supposes that your wife acts under your direction'?), remain unremarked by Skinner. Indeed, irony seems to miss him altogether. Bertrand Russell's famous passage (1927, p. 33) about American experimental animals rushing frantically about 'with an incredible display of hustle (sic.) and pep' while German experimental animals 'sit still and think' is referred to (1974, p. 18) as though it were a solemn comment: the light irony of the passage passes him by. In the same book (1974, p. 49) he tells us that 'to "love" is to behave in ways having certain kinds of effects, possibly with accompanying conditions which may be felt.' Not only has he not read Thurstone and the literature on attitudes in psychology, he has not read — except perhaps to count the number of alliterations per line — *Antony and Cleopatra* or *Othello*. Of his novel he remarks, '*Walden Two* was not planned' (1967, p. 408). Comment is superfluous.

Skinner's Dogmas

Lastly, let us take a brief look at the dogmas which underlie and pervade Skinner's work. The most prominent is that contingencies of reinforcement can explain virtually all behaviour, and anything that is not behaviour or a reinforcement schedule is irrelevant. Even if it were true, the position would suffer all the problems associated with any reductionist position, especially the impossible complexity involved in discussing very complex phenomena in atomistic terms. But it is pure faith that it is true. His attempts to use the dogma to predict behaviour are only very marginally successful, apart from rats in boxes: hence his invoking of 'interpreting', rather than explaining and predicting, referred to above. A secondary dogma — for he is nothing if not benign — is that punishment is ineffective in reducing the probability of a piece of behaviour: that punishment works 'simply does not hold. It has been established beyond question', says Frazier in *Walden Two* (p. 244), and the view is echoed many times in Skinner's writing. Evidence for this extraordinary simplification is very short. Indeed his whole position is based on a dogma. Of Behaviorism — his own form, no doubt — he says: 'I have no doubt of the eventual triumph of the position —

not that it will eventually be proved right, but that it will provide the most direct route to a successful science of man' (1967, p. 410).

CONCLUSION

What are we to make of Skinner's work? I have detailed the debit side of the balance sheet. His lack of philosophy has allowed him to stray disastrously. Lack of early recognition, and his staunchness in working himself through that period, must have played a part in undermining his critical facility. Whatever accounts for his lack of discrimination, it has done him a dreadful disservice. No man is a hero to his valet; but what on earth could have possessed him to permit some function-ary of similar role and status to make public his notebooks, his least heroic foibles?

What is Skinner's legacy? A novel that is appalling qua literature and philosophy, and qua psychology serves only to assert empty dogma; teaching machines, which, like the pigeons he hoped would guide rockets, never got off the ground; behaviour therapy — but that owes much more to the despised Hull than to Skinner, as a glance at Wolpe (1958) will show. And a faith in the deity Radical Behaviorism, the chief effect of which is to put scientific psychology in disrepute with the uncritical world, because the publicity Skinner makes for a god who cannot deliver the goods obscures the real deities, the lesser ones like Thurstone's attitude theory and the greater and as yet unperceived ones, the grand theories that Hull groped searchingly towards.

His positive contributions are considerable, and of true and lasting value to science and technology: the work on operant conditioning and schedules of reinforcement, and the kernel of the musings on verbal behaviour. They should be — I hope are — a source of legitimate pride. These are the blocks which greater persons (or perhaps just later persons), will use to build and model grand and beautiful edifices which are the goal and true satisfiers of science. If Skinner had come to terms with the aims of science, had realized that *control* is something that grows out of explaining and predicting, not the growing stem of science — he would have recognized that you cannot simultaneously be inside a box and pick it up and move it around; that is, to elaborate the metaphor, it is foolish to say, 'All behaviour, *even this sentence*, is determined and explainable', since that makes nonsense of trying to explain or comprehend the sentence. The paradox must be accepted that as a scientist one accepts the working hypothesis that all behaviour is determined, but as a person one stands outside the determined system. Science must primarily be a plaything, and, treated as such, it can confidently be expected to have useful offshoots.

My quarrel, such as it is, is not with Professor Skinner the scientific research worker. His research is the kind of psychology that commands respect. If I have a quarrel, it is with Professor Skinner the guru, and with Professor Skinner the scientist in the largest sense of that word.

How the gods love to mock us! Skinner has worked hard from his boyhood. 'I try not to let any day "slip useless away"' (1967, p. 407), he tells us. '(Some of my first cumulative records are stamped December twenty-fifth and January first).' Who, counting up his *productivity*, could doubt it? The irony is, that if he had spent more time idly wondering, kicking stones about the yard with his hands

in his pockets, as it were, or fishing in Walden Pond, he might have lost some of the ponderous solemnity that so informs his work, and gained some perspective on literature and philosophy.

Alas, a remark made by a rueful John Broadus Watson (1936, p. 274) provides an apt summing up: 'God knows I took enough philosophy to know something about it. But it wouldn't take hold. I passed my exams but the spark was not there.'

REFERENCES

Boswell, J. (1949) *Life of Doctor Johnson*, Vol. 1, London, Dent, originally published in 1791.

Ferster, C.B., and Skinner, B.F. (1957) *Schedules of Reinforcement*, New York, Appleton-Century-Crofts.

'In the Psychiatrist's Chair', Radio Interview of B.F. Skinner by Dr Anthony Clare, BBC Radio 4, 8 September 1984.

Mill, J.S. (1910a) 'On Liberty', in *Utilitarianism, Liberty, Representative Government*, London, Dent; originally published 1859.

Mill, J.S. (1910b) 'Representative Government', in *Utilitarianism, Liberty, Representative Government*, London, Dent; originally published 1861.

Mill, J.S. (1973) *A System of Logic Ratiocinative and Inductive*, London, Routledge and Kegan Paul; originally published in 1843.

Russell, B. (1927) *An Outline of Philosophy*, London, Allen and Unwin.

Skinner, B.F. (1938) *The Behavior of Organisms*, New York, Appleton-Century-Crofts.

Skinner, B.F. (1957) *Verbal Behavior*, New York, Appleton-Century-Crofts.

Skinner, B.F. (1961) '*Hull's* Principles of Behavior', in Skinner, B.F. *Cumulative Record*, enlarged ed., London, Methuen, pp. 384–9; originally published 1944.

Skinner, B.F. (1965) *Science and Human Behavior*, London, Collier Macmillan.

Skinner, B.F. (1967) 'B.F. Skinner', in Boring, E.G. and Lindzey, G. (Eds), *A History of Psychology in Autobiography*, Vol. 5, New York, Appleton-Century-Crofts.

Skinner, B.F. (1969) *Contingencies of Reinforcement*, New York, Appleton-Century-Crofts.

Skinner, B.F. (1972) *Beyond Freedom and Dignity*, London, Jonathan Cape.

Skinner, B.F. (1974) *About Behaviorism*, London, Cape.

Skinner, B.F. (1976) *Walden Two*, London, Collier Macmillan.

Skinner, B.F. (1980) *Notebooks*, Englewood Cliffs, N.J., Prentice-Hall.

Thoreau, H.D. (1886) *Walden*, London, Walter Scott.

Watson, J.B. (1936) 'John Broadus Watson', in Murchison, C. (Ed.), *A History of Psychology in Autobiography*, Vol. 3, London, Humphrey Milford.

Wolpe, J. (1958) *Psychotherapy by Reciprocal Inhibition*, Johannesburg, Witwatersrand University Press.

Interchange

WRIGHT REPLIES TO BETHLEHEM

THE ILLUSION OF A CRITIQUE

In 1977 Skinner complained: 'When one has published nine books setting forth a scientific position it is disconcerting to find it misunderstood. To be misunderstood by a former student and present colleague is especially puzzling' (p. 1006). In a similar vein I find *my* colleague's comments puzzling and welcome this opportunity to '... try to set the record straight' (p. 1006).

Most critics of Skinner's works succumb to the easy temptation to score stylistic points while leaving the substance of his ideas insufficiently examined — if at all; those which are examined are subjected to such Procrustean tactics as to border on the scandalous. Bethlehem's chapter is no exception, and even contrives to introduce a novel criticism of Skinner: that of being right. How else are we to interpret the contorted discussion he offers regarding Skinner's review of Hull's *Principles of Behaviour*. Far from having 'slammed' Hull, the review is a model of restrained, critical, professional assessment of a fellow professional's efforts. Bethlehem apparently has not read Koch's (1954) review: '... probably the most mercilessly sustained analysis of a psychological theory on record' (Koch, 1974). This misrepresentation is compounded by gratuitously impugning Skinner's professional probity by interspersing such phrases as 'contempt for Hull' (p. 92) and 'the despised Hull' (p. 96). In truth, Skinner held Hull in very high regard, as can be seen from the 'Acknowledgments' in *The Behavior of Organisms* (1938) and the good-humoured comments in *The Shaping of a Behaviorist* (1979), the second volume of a large autobiography. There are numerous examples of a similar misrepresentational nature in Bethlehem's chapter. I will highlight two others but, because of space limitations, leave it to the reader to consult the cited texts directly for ultimate adjudication. Contrary to what Bethlehem (p. 95) implies, Skinner's (1974) use of Russell's statement is appropriate. The caricature Bethlehem (p. 92) offers of Skinner's (1969) example is more serious: it trivializes Skinner's eloquent and long-standing opposition to hypothetico-deductive methods in psychology. This example of misrepresentation also serves to underscore my charge of an 'illusion of a critique' for nowhere do I, as a student of operant theory (*caveat lector*), find Bethlehem has engaged Skinner's ideas in a credible manner. Even when he offers 'supportable', but highly biased, personal opinions, for example, on *Walden Two* and *Beyond Freedom and Dignity* (cf. p. 93), he misses the larger point: both were written as practical guides for establishing or dealing with societal problems from a science of behaviour point of

view. Fortunately, a few have not missed this larger point and the reader may wish to consult Ramsey (1979) for his in-depth study of *Walden Two* and Wheeler (1973) and Carpenter (1974) for helpful discussions of *Beyond Freedom and Dignity*.

When we look more closely at Bethlehem's chapter we find misrepresentational damage of a particularly disconcerting nature. The radical behaviourist label is allowed — and just as promptly ignored. Surely a critic would be expected to consider 'one of the most important theoretical articles Skinner ever wrote' (Meehl, 1984, p. 563). As a consequence of not consulting that 1945 paper ('The Operational Analysis of Psychological Terms') and cursorily dismissing *Verbal Behavior* ('It will, I believe, prove to be my most important work', Skinner, 1980b, p. 198), Bethlehem has drawn a number of inaccurate pictures regarding the basic tenets of radical behaviourism. First, the author of the respondent/operant distinction (1937), as well as papers on phylogenetic/ontogenetic contingencies (1966, 1981), would not be guilty of claiming 'that contingencies of reinforcement can explain virtually all behaviour' (p. 95). What he does claim is that much can be gained in developing a science of behaviour by investigating behaviour directly in the context of environmental contingencies (an operant analysis, in short). Second, the discussion of reinforcement (p. 91) reveals a failure to understand Skinner's emphasis on carrying out an empirical functional analysis. I suppose if Olds and Milner (1954) had, extraspectively, put themselves in the place of the rat (p. 92), the answer to the query, 'Would you find electrical stimulation of your brain reinforcing?', may well have been, 'NO!' Fortunately, Olds and Milner were empirical scientists. Third, the distinction between methodological behaviourism and radical behaviourism simply is not confronted critically. There are at least two distinctions crucial for our present consideration; taken together, they provide radical behaviourism a unique ontological status amongst the experimental sciences: that of being able to account for the behaviour of the scientist within the deterministic system that he (the scientist) espouses. We elaborate below.

The first distinction is that not only does radical behaviourism attach scientific significance to private as well as to public events; it further assumes that the two classes of events achieve their effects through similar psychological processes. Thus, the first-person-present tense ('I have a toothache')/third-person ('his hair is black') verification dichotomy set up by Malcolm (1964) does not apply to radical behaviourism but does apply to methodological behaviourism. Bethlehem is aware of the first half of this distinction but fails to take note of the second half. Thus he is unprepared for the second distinction, viz., a radical behaviouristic perspective embraces the behaviour of the behavioural scientist within its theoretical domain. *Verbal Behavior* deals imaginatively and lengthily with this psychological reality, Skinner (1980a), more succinctly: 'I used to represent the behaviourist's attitude toward himself by describing a lecturer who explains human behavior, including the behavior of other lecturers, and leaves the stage. Then he sticks his head out from the wings and says, "And I'm like that too!"' (p. 360). I have not attempted to organize my response to Bethlehem's chapter according to the four headings he employed — Skinner's sweep is much too dynamic for that sort of editorial approach. What I have attempted to do is raise the reader's intellectual curiosity enough above the operant-level so that he/she

will read Skinner's works more extensively and carefully then I claim Bethlehem
has. I conclude with the following sentiment for Bethlehem and me to contem-
plate.

> There is nothing I wou'd more willingly lay hold of, than an opportunity of confessing my
> errors; and shou'd esteem such a return to truth and reason to be more honourable than the
> most unerring judgment. A man, who is free from mistakes, can pretend to no praises, except
> from the justness of his understanding: But a man, who corrects his mistakes, shews at once the
> justness of his understanding, and the candour and ingenuity of his temper. (Hume, 1888/1978
> p. 623)

REFERENCES

Carpenter, F. (1974) *The Skinner Primer*, New York, The Free Press.

Hume, D. (1978) *A Treatise of Human Nature*, 2nd ed., with text revised and notes by P.H. Nidditch,
Oxford, Oxford University Press; originally published 1888.

Koch, S. (1954) 'Clark L. Hull', in Estes, W.K. *et al., Modern Learning Theory*, New York,
Appleton-Century-Crofts.

Koch, S. (1974) 'Psychology as science', in Brown, S.C. (Ed.), *Philosophy of Psychology*, London,
Macmillan.

Malcolm, N. (1964) 'Behaviorism as a philosophy of psychology', in Wann, T.W. (Ed.), *Behaviorism
and Phenomenology*, Chicago, Ill., University of Chicago Press.

Meehl, P.E. (1984) 'Radical behaviorism and mental events: Four methodological queries', *The
Behavioral and Brain Sciences*, 7, pp. 563–4.

Olds, J. and Milner, P. (1954) 'Positive reinforcement produced by electrical stimulation of septal area
and other regions of rat brain', *Journal of Comparative Physiology and Psychology*, 47, pp.
419–27.

Ramsey, D., (1979) 'Morning star: The values-communication of Skinner's *Walden Two*, PhD thesis,
Rensselaer Polytechnic Institute, Troy, N.Y.

Skinner, B.F. (1937) 'Two types of conditioned reflex: A reply to Konorski and Miller', *Journal of
General Psychology*, 16, pp. 272–9.

Skinner, B.F. (1938) *The Behavior of Organisms*, New York, Appleton-Century-Crofts.

Skinner, B.F. (1945) 'The operational analysis of psychological terms', *Psychological Review*, 52, pp.
270–7, 291–4.

Skinner, B.F. (1948) *Walden Two*, New York, Macmillan Company.

Skinner, B.F. (1957) *Verbal Behavior*, New York, Appleton-Century-Crofts.

Skinner, B.F. (1961) *Cumulative Record*, enlarged ed., New York, Appleton-Century-Crofts.

Skinner, B.F. (1966) 'The phylogeny and ontogeny of behavior', *Science*, 153, pp. 1205–13.

Skinner, B.F. (1969) *Contingencies of Reinforcement: A Theoretical Analysis*, New York, Appleton-
Century-Crofts.

Skinner, B.F. (1971) *Beyond Freedom and Dignity*, New York, Alfred A. Knopf.

Skinner, B.F. (1974) *About Behaviorism*, New York, Alfred A. Knopf.

Skinner, B.F. (1977) 'Herrnstein and the evolution of behaviorism', *American Psychologist*, 32, pp.
1006–12.

Skinner, B.F. (1979) *The Shaping of a Behaviorist*, New York, Alfred A. Knopf.

Skinner, B.F. (1980a) *Notebooks, B.F. Skinner*, Englewood Cliffs, N.J., Prentice-Hall.

Skinner, B.F. (1980b) 'The experimental analysis of operant behavior: A history', in Rieber, R.W.
and Salzinger, K. (Eds), *Psychology, Theoretical-Historical Perspectives*, London, Academic
Press.

Skinner, B.F. (1981) 'Selection by consequences', *Science*, 213, pp. 501–4.

Wheeler, H. (Ed.) (1973) *Beyond the Punitive Society*, London, Wildwood House.

BETHLEHEM REPLIES TO WRIGHT

My friend and colleague has produced the thoroughgoing defence of Skinner's operant work and underlying philosophizing that was to be expected. It indicates Skinner's position clearly, but its clarity also brings out the shortcomings in the philosophizing. To deal with just a few:

1 'Most of the voluntary behaviour that organisms (including humans) display is *assumed* [emphasis mine] to be under the control of particular reinforcing stimuli' (p. 80). Now an *assumption* like that is a necessary part of any scientific theory or system, and it is justified by the scientific results it yields, i.e., any increment in explanation and prediction. Skinner's virtue in this respect is the very great scientific value of his research into operant conditioning and schedules of reinforcement; where things go wrong is where the point is stretched to infiltrate areas quite beyond its powers to strengthen. Wright refers to some such empirical areas. Skinner has an aversion to punishment, followed 'totally' by 'many'; but then, again, many behaviour therapists follow a different path. Despite Wright's assertion, it is increasingly realized that operant principles are not at work in many situations. Token economies and the old teaching machines *have* come into question. I am afraid that Skinner's conception of human behaviour has indeed been extended to 'the complexities of the world at large' (p. 86) well beyond its 'growing power.'

2 The 'commitment to materialist determinism' (p. 80) to which Wright refers is essential to a thoroughgoing scientist *in the scientific role*. But you have to stand apart from that role or the role itself becomes meaningless. 'Outcomes . . . *are* dependent on our efforts under operant contingencies' says Wright (p. 81). What he does not go on to say is that an operant determinist must assert that the *effort itself* is under operant control. A determinist asserts the paradox that we can indeed do what we want to, but *what we want to do* is determined. 'The causal generation of a belief does not, of itself, detract in the least from its truth' (Grünbaum, p. 309). But the concept of truth only has meaning in contrast to non-truth. If all belief is determined, truth becomes irrelevant. If we *could not* believe anything but what we do believe, 'truth' is merely a synonym for 'belief'. The point about effort and the point about truth are analogous in that to appreciate them you need to be able to stand back and examine your assumptions and judgments. It is this standing back that Skinner has not given himself time or room for.

3 An allied point relates to ethics and values. Values are more than 'simply tacts' (p. 83). You cannot stick wholeheartedly to 'antimentalism' when dealing with truth and ethics, because the concepts themselves have no meaning outside a mentalistic framework. Plonk and a fine subtle claret are both reinforcing; a limerick and a great poem, and a child's drawing and a Velasquez are all reinforcing. The claret, the poem, and the Velasquez have revealing depths that stir us and have the potential to give us almost unique insights. To call these things 'reinforcers' may be true in a sense, but it entirely misses the point in a wider context — which is where Skinner tries to place his work. In similar vein one can accept that 'You should (ought to) read *David Copperfield*' means '*David Copperfield* is reinforcing'. But what about 'You should fight for your country/ ethnic group, etc. (even though you hate soldiering and even if you feel no

patriotic loyalty')? And 'You should not commit adultery (even though — one reads — the practice can be fun)'? In these examples, 'should/ought' takes on a meaning beyond the entailing of reinforcement.

The last two points take us outside the walled domain of science. I am sure that Skinner and Wright both know them in some sense and appreciate them. It is the reflective examination that is absent from Skinner's writings.

Putting judgments in perspective is very difficult. While I have written very critically of Skinner's work, I recognize him as a very important scientist whose work has passed into the language of our science. It is true that he has obscured some of the value of his scientific work with his lesser, untuned works. But he is acquainted at first-hand with the writings of the great minds of the past, and the problems they have wrestled with; he has written a commercially successful novel; reading his work is *de rigueur* for any psychologist worth his or her salt. All these accomplishments make him worth infinitely more than most of those psychologists who disparage, or worse, ignore him.

REFERENCE

Grünbaum, A. (1971) 'Free will and laws of human behavior', *American Philosophical Quarterly*, 8, pp. 299–317.

Part VI: Philosophy of Science and Psychology

9. Skinner on Science*

RICHARD E. CREEL

B.F. Skinner's interest in the nature of science is evidenced by the works he has read, the people with whom he has associated, and the writings he has published (1976, 1979, 1983). However, his ideas on the nature of science are scattered through more than forty years of publication. This is unfortunate because those ideas constitute a distinctive interpretation of science that is worthy of wide consideration. My objective here is to promote such consideration by presenting an exposition of the most salient features of Skinner's understanding of science.

SCIENCE AS BEHAVIOR: TOWARD A SCIENCE OF SCIENCE

It is common to distinguish between science as process and as product, but in neither case does science exist independently of scientists. Science as process exists only in the behavior of scientists at work. Science as product exists internally in the modified behavioral dispositions of the scientist and externally in aids and devices that have no significance apart from their potential for modification of behavior. Science both as process and product, then, exists in or in subservience to behavioral repertoires and activities.

Skinner contends that therefore an adequate understanding of science will not come through reflection on the concepts of science (1983, pp. 128, 240). To understand science we must look at what scientists do as scientists. Such doing is behaving that is under the control of different factors than is the behavior of the same individuals when they are engaged in other activities. Hence, we need to launch a duly empirical study of the behavior of scientists as scientists (1974, pp.

* I would like to thank Paul W. McBride and Stephen P. Schwartz, my colleagues, for extensive editorial help with this paper.

144–5; 1972, p. 213). The purpose of a science of science would be to identify the variables of which scientific behavior is a function so that scientific behavior might be shaped, maintained, and strengthened more effectively. A good way to begin the search for those variables is by seeking the roots of scientific behavior in unconditioned human responses to the world.

THE SHAPING OF A SCIENTIST

It is common to observe a baby become fascinated with some causal relationship that it discovers accidentally. Perhaps the baby strikes the handle on a jack-in-the-box, causing it to emit a brief musical sound. Ordinarily the baby will then begin (though perhaps not after the first accidental strike) to touch the handle with more frequency and for longer periods until the jack pops up. Many toys are designed to take advantage of our natural human fascination with causal relations (a fascination that has an obvious evolutionary explanation). Similarly, a well-designed science curriculum takes advantage of this natural fascination, confronting students with increasingly subtle and complex causal relations, equipping the students to discover and explore such relations, until finally some students are searching for such relations on their own.

In this process of scientific development the behavior of the scientist (whether beginner or pioneer) is brought about by the subject matter, and especially by certain features of it. Those features and the resulting behavior distinctive of the scientist are identified partially by the following terms: observation, accessibility, prediction, manipulation, control, lawfulness, cause/effect, functional relation, independent/dependent variable, regularity, order, discovery, confirmation, repeatability, knowledge.

Perhaps the most fundamental terms in this cluster are 'discovery' and 'lawfulness'. Science is behavior that is reinforced by the discovery of lawfulness, i.e., by the observation of new functional relations. It is not, however, the mere observation of lawfulness that is distinctive of scientific behavior; rather, it is fascination with the *discovery* of lawfulness (1972, p. 213; 1979, p. 282). Hence, a person is behaving as a scientist when ser behavior is under the control of past discoveries of lawful relations and is reinforced by steps that, according to past experience, hold some promise of confirming or disconfirming laws that others have claimed, or of discovering new laws.[1]

Skinner writes that as a psychologist he 'never faced a Problem which was more than the eternal problem of finding order' (1972, p. 112; 1967, p. 407). More generally, scientific behavior is behavior that is reinforced by new observations of order — not just any kind of order, of course, but that invariable or highly dependable kind that we denote by such phrases as 'cause and effect', 'independent and dependent variable', 'action and consequence', and 'natural law'.

Skinner accepts David Hume's analysis of causation (1953, p. 23; 1971, p. 218), but he is sensitive to the difference between incidental conjunction and causal conjunction. To the scientist the discovery of a causal conjunction is a positive reinforcer; the discovery that a conjunction is not causal, though it appeared to be, is a negative reinforcer, turning scientists away from that direction to others that are still viable. Perhaps the most aversive thing that can

happen to a scientist is to be discovered by others to have made a mistaken causal claim. Elaborate procedures have been developed by scientists to minimize the probability of mistaken causal claims. Direct access to the subject matter and manipulation of it are clearly important with regard to this objective. The more directly one has access to one's variables, and the more fully they can be manipulated, the less likely it is that one will make mistaken claims about dependent and independent variables.

Control of the subject matter is a reciprocal affair. As the behavior of the scientist comes under more subtle control of the subject matter, the subject matter will come under more discriminating control by the scientist. Scientific progress is generated by this practical dialectic between scientist and subject matter. The scientist as a repertoire of dispositions is changed by ser exposure to the subject matter. Consequently, ser behavior is under the control of steps that have led to the discovery of new causal relations or that are untried but because of past experiences are assayed to hold some promise of disclosing new causal relations.

The goal of scientific investigation is new scientific knowledge. Scientific knowledge resides in the acquired dispositions of a person who has been modified by contingencies such that se is henceforth able to discern and take advantage of causal relations of which se was hitherto unaware.

The proper modality of scientific claims is probability, not certainty. The natural scientist has couched ser discoveries in probabilistic statements since the advent of modern physics, and the social scientist need claim no more (1957, pp. 22, 28, 52–3). This means that the scientist, natural or social, is reinforced not only by 100 per cent accuracy but also by *increases* in accuracy of prediction and control.

Scientists are reinforced by the repeatability of results because therein lies confirmation of their belief that they have identified a causal relation. Without the repetition of results there can be serious doubt whether the *relata* of a functional relation were identified correctly. Manipulation of the independent variables together with repetition of the results increases the likelihood that a *bona fide* causal relation has been identified. If other scientists can repeat the result, it is even more likely that a new causal relation has indeed been discovered.

SCIENCE AND THE LARGER COMMUNITY

The individual scientist operates ordinarily within a community of scientists, which operates within a yet large community. We must examine the relation between these two communities if we are to understand science more adequately.

Humans have become the dominate species on earth because, among other things, of the extent to which they are sensitive to causal relations, reinforced by their discovery, able to take advantage of them, reinforced by doing so, and able to communicate their discoveries to one another. Because of the practical importance of many causal relations, the community at large is not indifferent to individuals who make causal discoveries. Indeed, it seems plausible to think that even in the most ancient communities individuals who discovered valuable causal relations were rewarded. There were certainly people who *claimed* to know of and have control over causal relations of enormous importance to the community.

Generally those people were religious functionaries who were honored and rewarded because they were thought to know better than others how to anticipate, assuage, and please the gods and goddesses, thereby averting disaster or bringing prosperity to the community. We may dismiss such beliefs as superstition, but we should not fail to appreciate how strongly convinced the community was that some of its members could control, at least to some extent, the factors that determined the welfare of the community, and how deeply the community was involved in identifying and rewarding individuals who were thought to have such abilities. The larger community has been involved in that enterprise to this day — and presumably will be as long as humans are reinforced by survival and propagation.

The larger community is involved also in trying to ensure the integrity and reliability of the scientific community. Ordinarily when an experiment does not produce results valuable for the discovery of new causal relations, the behavior involved extinguishes. Sometimes, however, scientists lie about their findings or claim results that cannot be reproduced because of procedures that were poorly recorded, thought out, or executed. Upon public exposure such scientists are usually rebuked sharply — presumably because scientific research uses a significant part of a community's resources, and because action on the basis of a mistaken scientific claim can cause great damage (1957, pp. 429–30).

The primary police force surrounding the individual scientist is, of course, the network of ser colleagues. Scientists scrutinize one another in part because of their dependence on the larger community for accreditation and resources. One irresponsible scientist inadequately critiqued by ser colleagues could raise questions within the larger community as to the reliability of the entire group, resulting in loss of time and funds for research. Consequently, scientists are conditioned by teachers and peers, as well as the larger community, to take reasonable steps to ensure that a claim is not mistaken and that the procedures followed to establish it are described so that others can repeat the result.

RESEARCH, TECHNOLOGY, AND THE LABORATORY

The purpose of scientific research is to discover new causal relations. Sometimes such relations are discovered by accident. Skinner emphasizes that there is no special virtue in a causal relation discovered by accident or in waiting for causal relations to be disclosed by accident. Accident does not generate scientifically revealing events frequently; when it does generate them we may not be there to observe; if we are, the conditions of observation may not be conducive to learning. Scientific research endeavors to overcome these problems by speeding up the rate at which events of a novel type occur and by optimizing the conditions of observation.

The products of technology contribute to this process by bringing the observational behavior of the scientist under the control of factors that are more and more remote from unaided observation because of their speed of occurrence (too fast or slow), minuteness, complexity, distance, danger, etc. Technology also extends the scientist's powers of manipulation. These increases of ability to observe and control nature enable the scientist to discover functional relations where our ancestors saw only miracles. Hence, science and technology are related

dialectically: by means of new instruments of technology scientists discover new natural laws, and by means of new natural laws technologists create more sophisticated instruments of observation and control.

The laboratory is an environment under the control of past successes at the discovery of natural laws. It is designed as a consequence of those successes so as to maximize the probability of discovering new laws and exposing mere coincidence. The importance of technology in constructing such an environment is obvious. Sometimes a laboratory is set up to accelerate under conditions of optimal observation the revealing accidents that occur so rarely and haphazardly in nature. In such a case the scientist is 'running out the permutations', that is, working quickly through all of the relevant variations of, for example, temperature, solution concentration, stress, etc., that give promise of revealing something significant. By contrast, sometimes one solution to a problem stands out among others as having a significantly higher probability of being correct, and so a 'crucial experiment' is conducted.

Clearly, then, Joseph Wood Krutch had things quite backwards when he warned that in a scientifically designed culture it would be 'impossible for the unplanned to erupt again' (1983, p. 106). A scientifically engineered culture will *accelerate* the rate at which scientifically relevant accidents occur, and it will accelerate their occurrence under conditions conducive to learning from them. To be sure, scientists occasionally learn important things from sheer accident, but that is serendipity, not science.

We should distinguish, however, two types of accident. A *passive accident* is *not* precipitated by the behavior of the person to whom it occurs, as, for example, when a pedestrian is struck by a falling part from an airplane. An *active accident is* precipitated by the behavior of the agent, but whereas the agent intends to do what triggers the accident, there is an unexpected result that se does not intend. Consider someone who pushes a switch in an unfamiliar house and causes a garage door to crash down on the owner's car. Se may plead that it was an accident. Yes, se meant to push the switch; no, se did not mean to damage the car. That was an accident; se thought the switch was for an overhead light. Similarly, when physicists first reduced the temperature of a metal to a level approximating absolute zero, they intended the reduction of the temperature of the metal, but they did not intend the subsequent behavior of the metal because they did not know what it would be.

Science is the art of *generating* active accidents under conditions optimal for learning new causal relations from them. Scientists want to *minimize* the occurrence of passive accidents because they are more often wasteful than not and can be disastrous as well as fortuitous. However, no one can prevent them from occurring altogether, and so, willy nilly, scientists shall continue to learn from them.

Science is associated in the popular mind with the laboratory. That is entirely appropriate because the laboratory is the area in which scientists ordinarily engage in the most intense, direct contact with their subject matter. Skinner emphasizes that the best teacher of the scientist is the subject matter itself. We should not mistake the study of verbal behavior about the subject matter (for example, reading journal articles and books about DNA) for scientific study of the subject matter (for example, studying DNA). Verbal behavior about a subject matter should not be studied unless there is good reason to think that it will result

in fruitful engagement with the subject matter itself. This stricture holds even when the subject matter is verbal behavior (1983, pp. 406–7; 1979, p. 306; 1967, pp. 409–10; 1957, p. 420).

This, then, should be the first principle of science education: put the student into contact with the subject matter as early as is fruitful and as directly as is safe in such a way that the student is brought quickly and increasingly under the control of its causal complexities. Further, the scientist — budding or mature — should be conditioned and supported so that se acts according to this fundamental of scientific research: 'When you run onto something interesting, drop everything else and study it' (1972, p. 104; 1983, p. 400). After all, the purposes of scientific research are to discover novelty and disclose pretense. When anything gives promise of leading to either, 'business as usual' should come to a screeching halt.

EXPLANATION, THEORY, AND INTERPRETATION

To explain the occurrence of an event is to relate it to its causes; it is to cite a functional relation between a dependent variable and an independent variable. For an explanation to be scientific it must provide a causal account in terms of physical factors that have been observed directly or that can be postulated plausibly on the basis of something that has been observed directly. Two reinforcers of scientific explanation are simplicity and unity. Regarding *simplicity*, the fewer concepts that an explanation employs, all other things being equal, the more reinforcing it is. This preference has an obvious evolutionary explanation: the more efficient an explanation is, the less energy is expended on it and the more energy there is for other things. A scientific explanation is *unified* when no part of it involves an appeal beyond that which is physical and lawfully determined. Such unity is reinforcing because it gives the scientist something to work with. Explanations that involve a subjectively free agent cannot yield scientific knowledge because of the unpredictability of free actions. Explanations that appeal to non-physical factors — such as God, gods, the mind, soul, or spirit — cannot yield scientific knowledge because the causal status of a non-physical factor cannot be confirmed or falsified by observation or manipulation. Nor can its status be clarified by appealing to established physical principles. A purported variable must make or suggest some lawful practical difference in order to be scientifically useful. Consequently, scientists are reinforced by explanations that are unified on the physical level of explanation.

Because non-physical factors are not accessible to observation or manipulation, the name of a non-physical factor that is included as a cause in an explanation can function only as an empty reference to what it is — natural or supernatural, personal or impersonal — which accounts for the effect that is being explained. Thus Skinner says, '... mentalistic explanations explain nothing' (1974, p. 224; 1971, p. 195; 1953, p. 33).[2]

Mentalistic explanations have piggybacked on the natural human tendency to invent an explanation when none is obvious. The survival of this tendency is understandable. If we have no explanation, and therefore no response to a situation, we are entirely its victim. If we have an explanation, then we have at least one chance of responding effectively. This seems to have been such a crucial lesson of evolution that many humans find not having an explanation aversive.

A non-physical explanation is not better than nothing, however; it is worse because it explains nothing and discourages the development of a physical explanation. Hence, scientific progress in a culture involves critical rejection of all explanations that employ non-physical factors. It also involves development of operational means for testing the appropriateness, value, and economy of explanations that employ *theoretical* physical factors (1972, pp. 69–100; 1938, p. 44).

Ideally scientists would not need theories, that is, explanations that employ speculative entities; ideally scientists could observe, that is, discern directly, functional relations among the components of a subject matter. For various reasons that is not always possible, so theoretical explanations emerge at the frontiers of science. However, whereas observation is under the control of the subject matter, speculation is not. It is a creative attempt to fill in where observation fails.

Because theory is speculative, not descriptive, more than one theory can explain the same data. Hence, as long as we are speculating, we do not know that there are such entities as our theory postulates. Further, we are justified in postulating theoretical entities only insofar as they increase the effectiveness of our ability to predict or control events, that is, only insofar as they bring the theorizer under more discriminating control of the subject matter, or suggest lines of research that promise such an increase of effectiveness. Obviously we cannot know in advance which speculations will be scientifically fruitful, but by empirical investigations we can identify those types of speculation that are likely to be fruitful and those that are not. Non-physical explanations have not been fruitful.

Theory should come into play only after the failure of attempts to understand the subject matter in terms of accessible physical factors. Moreover, even when theory does prove useful, the goal of science is to go beyond it, so as to have an explanation in terms of the subject matter itself, as known directly, rather than by speculation that might be mistaken in some ways despite being useful in others. Hence, the scientist is ambivalent about speculation. It is reinforcing because it might extend our knowledge; it is aversive because it might contain a mistake. The scientist can rest only in knowledge, that is, in dispositions shaped by observation of the subject matter itself and confirmed by the ability to predict and, where possible, control the subject matter.

There is, however, no ambivalence about speculation in its proper place. Speculation is the grappling hook that scientists throw into otherwise inaccessible places. There is ample evidence that they can pull themselves forward in this way. Moreover, because scientists are reinforced by the discovery of lawful connections, it is inevitable that they will continue to engage in scientific speculation because they will want to know for each newly discovered independent variable of what factors it is a dependent variable. Insofar as a newly established independent variable is just inside the limits of current observational and manipulative powers, scientists must, in order to understand it as a dependent variable, speculate beyond it and wait for technological advances to enable them to ratchet forward from theory to knowledge. Hence, there is no reason to think that scientists will ever abandon speculation.

Finally a few words about *interpretation*. In all sciences there are events that scientists would like to explain but cannot for lack of adequate evidence. In such cases they may resort to interpretation, that is, to understanding the subject

matter in terms of relevant physical principles, but without being able to demonstrate that those principles provide a correct explanation. Obviously interpretation is not as satisfactory as explanation, but it is not arbitrary. As Skinner points out, 'our interpretation will have the support of the prediction and control which have been possible under other conditions' (1974, pp. 176, 209). Later, in *About Behaviorism*, Skinner uses human behavior to illustrate the nature and value of interpretation.

> Obviously we cannot predict or control human behavior in daily life with the precision obtained in the laboratory, but we can nevertheless use results from the laboratory to interpret behavior elsewhere. Such an interpretation of human behavior in daily life has been criticized as meta-science, but all the sciences resort to something much like it. As we have just seen [earlier in *About Behaviorism*], the principles of genetics are used to interpret the facts of evolution, as the behavior of substances under high pressures and temperatures are used to interpret geological events in the history of the earth. What is happening in interstellar space, where control is out of the question, is largely a matter of interpretation in this sense. (1974, pp. 228–9)

Interpretation is acceptable, then, where explanation is not possible, and it can serve to suggest research by means of which explanation might supersede interpretation. Further, it is a way of integrating into a cohesive, comprehensive world-view the findings of the different sciences.

THE SUCCESS AND SURVIVAL OF SCIENCE

Skinner suggests in *About Behaviorism* that the evolution of philosophies as well as species can be understood best in terms of random mutations and environmental selection. Noting the diversity of explanatory models in psychology Skinner states, 'Perhaps this diversity is healthful: different approaches could be regarded as mutations, from which a truly effective behavioral science will eventually be selected' (1974, p. 249). Along the same lines, he says in *A Matter of Consequences*, '. . . a scientist is only science's way of making more science. Variations in genes and in the environments of person and group are the sources of novelty or, to use Darwin's word, the *origin* of things' (p. 408).

   Skinner's point about competing models for psychology applies also to competing models for the acquisition of knowledge. From the welter of such models (religious, astrological, intuitive, scientific, etc.) the selection will not be made on the basis of eloquence, emotional appeal, logical proof, coherence, comprehensiveness, or intersubjective agreement. The determining factor will be which model eventuates in more effective and efficient prediction and control of the world and ourselves (1967, pp. 409–10). Obviously, by this criterion science is the odds-on favorite.

   There are, of course, different models of science, as well as of knowledge and psychology. Skinner believes that science understood in the operationist mode is the most promising model for the pursuit of knowledge. Operationism insists that the concepts, claims, and procedures of science be interpretable in terms of physical properties and operations. It seeks 'an effective experimental approach' to each subject matter. This approach is encouraging because its primary concern is demonstrable prediction and control, not communication or disputation. It places little value on argument or logical dialectic. Its aim is not to win the

agreement of others; it is to increase our control over nature (1972, p. 383).

Control is not equally reinforcing to every person or society, but those to whom it is less reinforcing will be at a disadvantage relative to those to whom it is more reinforcing. The latter — all other things being equal — will be aware of a larger number of causal relations and thus be more likely to cope successfully with problems posed by nature and society. Hence, individuals and societies spend their time and resources on non-scientific explanations to their disadvantage. From an evolutionary point of view it is understandable that communities place a high value on persons and practices that they believe able to promote the survival of their members, their progeny, and their way of life. For its well-being the community needs to identify and motivate those youngsters who are most strongly reinforced by the discovery of causal relations, who are most sensitive at discerning them, and who are most effective at discovering new ones on their own.

In conclusion, it should not be surprising that the scientific approach to explanation has strengthened so dramatically over the last several centuries while alternative forms of explanation have weakened. The alternatives have not provided us with effective, growing control over our situation; science has. Further, science will continue to prosper because those societies that are reinforced by it will have a survival advantage over those that are not, and those that do it more effectively will have an advantage over those that do it less effectively. In brief, because science is increasing our control over the world, its control over us is increasing.

NOTES

1 It seems to me that the best way to deal with the fact that the English language does not have non-sexed personal pronouns is to invent some. I shall use 'se' for 'she or he', 'ser' for 'his or her', and 'mer' for 'him or her'. This also provides non-sexed personal pronouns for God, angels, and appropriate creatures that genetic engineering will almost certainly bring forth.
2 For a fuller discussion of Skinner's position on non-physical explanations see my (1980) 'Radical Epiphenomenalism: B.F. Skinner's Account of Private Events' in *Behaviorism*, 8, 1 (Spring), pp. 31–53.

REFERENCES

Skinner, B.F. (1938) *The Behavior of Organisms*, New York, Appleton-Century-Crofts.
Skinner, B.F. (1953) *Science and Human Behavior*, New York, Macmillan.
Skinner, B.F. (1957) *Verbal Behavior*, New York, Appleton-Century-Crofts.
Skinner, B.F. (1967) 'B.F. Skinner', in Boring, E.G. and Lindzey, G. (Eds), *A History of Psychology in Autobiography*, Vol. 5, New York, Appleton-Century-Crofts.
Skinner, B.F. (1969) *Contingencies of Reinforcement*, New York, Appleton-Century-Crofts.
Skinner, B.F. (1971) *Beyond Freedom and Dignity*, New York, Knopf.
Skinner, B.F. (1972) *Cumulative Record*, 3rd ed., New York, Appleton-Century-Crofts.
Skinner, B.F. (1974) *About Behaviorism*, New York, Knopf.
Skinner, B.F. (1976) *Particulars of My Life*, New York, Alfred A. Knopf.
Skinner, B.F. (1978) *Reflections on Behaviorism and Society*, Englewood Cliffs, N.J., Prentice-Hall, esp. Chs 6–9 and 13–14. Ch. 14, 'The Force of Coincidence', is very brief but extremely valuable.
Skinner, B.F. (1979) *The Shaping of a Behaviorist*, New York, Alfred A. Knopf.
Skinner, B.F. (1983) *A Matter of Consequences*, New York, Alfred A. Knopf.

10. The Limits of Skinner's Philosophy of Science and Psychology

MICHAEL WESSELLS

In his autobiography B.F. Skinner describes an encounter in graduate school with Alfred North Whitehead. 'He told me that a young psychologist should keep an eye on philosophy, and, remembering Bertrand Russell, I told *him* that it was quite the other way around — we needed a psychological epistemology ...' (1979, p. 29). Skinner clearly psychologizes philosophy, and he is not a philosopher of science in the traditional sense. He does not address traditional problems such as the nature of scientific laws and the problem of induction. He has never attempted to construct a formal philosophy of science, and he does not employ traditional philosophical methodology. Yet Skinner is concerned deeply over philosophy, stating that 'behaviorism is not the science of human behavior; it is the philosophy of that science ...' (1974, p. 3). An assessment of his philosophy of science and psychology is therefore of central importance in evaluating his radical behaviorism.

Unfortunately, psychologists have not analyzed Skinner's philosophy of science and psychology extensively. Among radical behaviorists a detailed evaluation might seem unproductive because of our limited understanding of the antecedents of philosophical verbal behavior and because of epistemological skepticism about the possibility of analyzing adult verbal behavior completely. Nevertheless, Skinner's behavior analysis rests on numerous assumptions which must be evaluated if radical behaviorism is to be assessed fairly and modified appropriately. The aims of this chapter are to outline Skinner's philosophy of science and to criticize it in the hope of stimulating additional dialogue.

SKINNER'S PHILOSOPHY

Skinner's philosophy of science is both prescriptive and analytical. It consists first of an orientation toward behavioral science and a set of conceptual imperatives regarding the proper way to analyze behavior. It also consists of an empirical attitude toward philosophy (Day, 1983) founded upon a theoretical analysis of the contingencies governing verbal behavior. In this section I shall sketch the prescriptive and the analytical facets of Skinner's philosophy.

Before describing Skinner's approach, a caveat is in order. Skinner's philosophy of science has changed markedly over his distinguished career. For example, he introduced hypothetical constructs such as the reflex reserve in his early analyses (1938, pp. 26, 83–96), but subsequently rejected them (1969, p. 82). Similarly, Skinner flirted with operationism in 1938, but by 1945 he had abandoned it (Flanagan, 1980). Because of space limitations, I shall focus not on the evolution of his position but on central features that he has maintained over the years.

Prescriptions for Behavioral Science

Since the mid-1930s Skinner has published many empirical and conceptual papers, which function as shared exemplars in the community of behavior analysts, model problem-solving efforts which point the way toward an effective science of behavior (Kuhn, 1972). Analyzing his own investigative behavior, Skinner has formulated numerous prescriptions about how to do psychology and about how to maintain effective scientific behavior. Although these prescriptions are rules that exert instructional control over practices in the community of behavior analysts, they may also be viewed as descriptions of conventions regarding research in the radical behaviorist community. Because they direct one's questions, methods and theories along behaviorist channels, they constitute a radical and important part of Skinner's philosophy of science and psychology, and they reflect Skinner's unique history as a scientist.

Skinner's main prescriptions may be condensed into approximately ten interrelated injunctions, which are listed below, though not necessarily in order of importance.

1   Regard behavior as the proper subject matter (1938, *passim*). For example, he states that 'behavior is not simply the result of more fundamental activities, to which our research must therefore be addressed, but an end in itself ...' (1972, p. 326).
2   Subject behavior to a functional analysis (1938, p. 8), identifying controlling external variables, 'the causes of behavior' (1953, p. 35). In this approach, the aims are to predict and to control behavior.
3   Search for general laws of learning by analyzing relatively simple responses under well-controlled conditions, avoiding the botanization of reflexes (1938, pp. 10–12, 46–7; 1969, pp. 101–24).
4   Proceed inductively and avoid hypothesis-testing (1938, pp. 44, 437; 1969, pp. xi–xii; 1972, p. 112).
5   Analyze the behavior of individual subjects, avoiding the averaging of data and the use of statistics (1938, pp. 442–4; 1953, p. 19; 1969, pp. vii–xii, 93; 1972, pp. 112–15, 119–20, 319–21).

6 Focus on accessible, manipulable variables (1969, p. 199; 1972, p. 70; 1974, pp. 12, 44, 165, 208, 210, 213).

7 Stay close to observables and avoid loosely defined theoretical constructs and metaphors (1938, pp. 23, 368, 377, 441; 1969, pp. 269–97; 1974, pp. 102–10).

8 Reject inner causes and explanations, particularly mentalistic ones; look to the environment for the causes of behavior (1938, pp. 418–44; 1953, pp. 23–35; 1957, pp. 3–10; 1969, pp. 236–40, 269–96; 1972, pp. 239–48; 1974, *passim*; 1977, *passim*). For Skinner, 'The contingencies explain the behavior …' (1974, p. 94).

9 Translate and, when necessary, revise mentalistic statements and every-day explanations into behavioral statements (1953, pp. 257–82; 1972, pp. 370–84; 1974, *passim*). Speaking of non-behaviorist statements, Skinner states that 'some can be "translated into behavior," others discarded as unnecessary or meaningless' (1974, p. 17).

10 Regard private events as physical and lawful, and treat subjective states and events as collateral by-products (1953, pp. 257–82; 1969, p. 258; 1972, pp. 370–84; 1974, pp. 17–32, 207–18).

These prescriptions blend methodological, theoretical and meta-theoretical considerations. Items such as 4 and 5 above are methodological, whereas items such as 7 and 8 are meta-theoretical (cf. Schnaitter, 1983), stipulating appropriate types of theories and explanations. In Skinner's view, these imperatives stand upon the success of his theoretical analysis, to which we turn next.

Theoretical Analysis

Skinner's (1969, 1974) theory asserts that behavior is determined jointly by contingencies of natural selection and by contingencies of reinforcement. Of course, Skinner applies this theory not only to the behavior of rats and pigeons but also to the behavior of scientists and philosophers, including his own. Skinner uses this theory radically to reformulate questions about science and philosophy.

First consider his analysis of science (Skinner, 1953, 1957, 1969, 1972; Schnaitter, 1983). Science consists primarily of scientists' investigative responses, many of which are non-verbal, and scientists' verbal responses, including vocal and textual responses, graphs, equations, and so on. It also includes the contingencies that govern scientists' behavior, some of which are provided by nature (in contingency-shaped behavior), and some of which are arranged by the scientific community (in rule-governed behavior). Ultimately, however, the theoretical verbal behavior of scientists is shaped by natural contingencies. In particular, verbal statements of functional relationships (e.g., laws) and abstractions (e.g., concepts) are reinforced if they extend the scientists' range of effective action. Otherwise, they suffer extinction and are neglected or revised by the scientific community.

Skinner seldom comments upon literature in the philosophy of science, but his views on verbal behavior may be extended in a straightforward manner. In particular, the philosophy of science consists of the verbal behavior of philosophers under the control of contingencies arranged by the community of philosophers of science. Ideally, these contingencies establish verbal behavior that

accurately describes the practices of the scientific community and that evaluates the logic of scientists' verbal behavior. But Skinner's analysis also recognizes that the contingencies governing philosophical verbal behavior may differ from those governing scientific behavior. Consequently, a gap may emerge between the philosopher's statements about science and what scientists say and do. For example, philosophers often analyze the logic of explanation, whereas scientists typically judge their explanations more by empirical criteria than by logical ones. For this reason and others, Skinner avoids formalistic treatments of the scientific process (1972, p. 102).

By any standard this is a radical reconceptualization of the philosophy of science. By analyzing philosophy as verbal behavior, Skinner psychologizes philosophy, putting it on a behavior analytic footing. Questions in philosophy become questions about the contingencies that control the verbal behavior of philosophers. For example, questions about the nature of explanation become questions about the verbal behavior said to be explanatory and the contingencies that govern it. This approach is radical not only because it revises philosophical questions but also because it stands upon a behavior theory that is subject to empirical evaluation. For this reason radical behaviorism is a philosophy that must be held with an empirical attitude. While this may seem more like functional analysis than philosophy (Day, 1983), Skinner himself speaks repeatedly of the philosophy of radical behaviorism.

SKINNER EXAMINED

Skinner's provocative analysis has numerous strengths. For example, it directs the philosophy of science away from abstract, logical analyses, which too often bear little relation to what scientists actually do, and focuses instead on the behavior of scientists and the antecedents thereof. Further, it invites examination of the contingencies governing behavior in a scientific community. This program might elucidate the origin and the maintenance of scientific paradigms, particularly their disciplinary matrices (Kuhn, 1972).

On the other hand, nearly all of Skinner's prescriptions are problematic in one respect or another, and his view of philosophy encounters serious objections, some of which have been reviewed elsewhere (Flanagan, 1984; Scriven, 1956; Wessells, 1981, 1982). In this section I shall forego an exhaustive critique and concentrate instead on several central problems which have not received the attention they deserve. I attempt neither to disparage Professor Skinner nor to condemn radical behaviorism but to raise issues which must be resolved if behaviorism is to advance.

Empirical Status

Skinner's philosophy of science is imperialistic in that it psychologizes philosophical questions and theories, treating them as verbal behavior to be explained through analyses of contingencies of reinforcement. This imperialistic approach stands or falls on the strength of his functional analysis of verbal behavior. Despite Chomsky's (1959) polemics, Skinner's functional analysis does have

substantial interpretive power (MacCorquodale, 1970). Unfortunately, radical behaviorists have done very little research on complex human verbal behavior. Consequently, his philosophy lacks a solid empirical base.

One might object that his philosophy is a straightforward application of principles that have been well-established in the laboratory. But the generality of the laws of conditioning cannot be assumed so lightly. The existence of biological constraints on conditioning is well-established (Shettleworth, 1972), and no one knows just how far or under what conditions the principles of conditioning will generalize. Moreover, it is a mistake to generalize from extant studies of verbal operant conditioning, many of which involve relatively simply responses (e.g., Greenspoon, 1955) and are open to cognitive interpretations (Brewer, 1974). Whether complex responses in natural settings obey the same laws that govern simpler responses in laboratory settings is an unresolved empirical question. At present the great conceptual weight assigned to the functional analysis of scientific and philosophical verbal behavior is incommensurate with the few ounces of available data. Consequently, Skinner's analysis of verbal behavior remains a plausible hypothesis, not a compelling base for a philosophy of science.

Another possible objection is that there are epistemological limits on our ability to specify the antecedents of adult verbal behavior. Perhaps it is as impossible for the behaviorist to identify and to control the multitude of variables that influence verbal behavior as it is for the physicist to predict the path of a falling leaf. On this view, it is unreasonable to expect behavior analysts to provide exhaustive empirical analyses of verbal behavior of the complexity one observes in science and philosophy.

This argument, however, encounters fatal objections. First, cognitive theories are moving ahead in predicting and explaining complex adult behavior (Anderson, 1983; Kosslyn, 1980). If behavior theory is limited epistemologically, so much the worse for radical behaviorism. Second, the empirical evaluation of Skinner's theory of verbal behavior does not require the detailed analysis and explanation of the verbal behavior of particular adults. What are required are successful experimental analyses of the contingencies governing relatively complex verbal responses. Even if performed under controlled laboratory conditions, these analyses would extend the generality of Skinner's account. Equally important, it is simply too early to assume the existence of epistemological limits. When the existence of these limits is assumed prematurely, empirical inquiry is discouraged. In turn, this limits the extension of behavior analysis and relegates Skinner's analysis to the status of a large promissory note. In science epistemological postulation is no substitute for sustained empirical analysis.

Overall, Skinner's functional analysis is best regarded as a plausible working hypothesis about verbal behavior. Though plausibility invites further inquiry, it provides unstable footing for an encompassing philosophy.

Psychologism

Like all scientific approaches, Skinner's approach stands on philosophical assumptions, which cannot be justified from within his system. For example, he assumes that 'an explanation is the demonstration of a functional relationship between behavior and manipulable or controllable variables' (1964, p. 102). Since these

manipulable variables are in the environment, not inside the organism, explanations must appeal to environmental variables (cf. Wessells, 1982). As Skinner says, 'in an acceptable explanatory scheme the ultimate causes of behavior must be found *outside* the organism' (1972, p. 325).

The idea that acceptable explanations must appeal to environmental variables may appear to be a theoretical tenet established by careful experimentation showing that external events do in fact control behavior. But this idea is equally a conceptual, philosophical commitment regarding what *counts* as an explanation. Consider a hypothetical example concerning a young child learning to say 'dog'. Assume that in the presence of a collie, the parent said 'dog', that the child then said 'dog' for the first time, and that the parent replied, 'That's right.' Assume also that following this episode, the child frequently said 'dog' in the presence of the family's collie. Presumably, the verbal response 'dog' was imitative initially, but once it occurred, it was reinforced and brought under the control of the visual properties of the dog.

Even if this account withstood careful experimental scrutiny, it would *not* constitute an acceptable explanation from the cognitive perspective. A cognitive psychologist would demand an account of the inner processes that occurred in the episode — the internal representation of the object dog and the verbal stimulus 'dog', the retrieval of lexical information concerning the word 'dog', and so on. From this perspective, the behaviorist account is not wrong but incomplete and non-explanatory since it identifies no inner processes. In other words Skinner and cognitivists disagree at the meta-theoretical level over what counts as an explanation. As a result, behaviorist accounts will never satisfy cognitivists (and vice versa), and each type of account will appear superfluous by the standards of the other. In this sense, Skinner's frequent assertion that cognitive theories are unnecessary is not strictly theoretical but also philosophical.

It now seems clear that Skinner's attempt to base his philosophy of science strictly upon his behavior theory is unjustified. Since his behavior theory itself stands on philosophical assumptions, it will not do to analyze all philosophical assumptions as phenomena to be explained by behavior theory. By virtue of his psychologistic attitude, Skinner has diverted attention away from his assumptions and neglected his philosophical duties as a scientist. Philosophy cannot be dispelled so easily by a wave of the behaviorist wand.

Prediction, Control and Explanation

Skinner's assumptions regarding what counts as an explanation are both unusual and questionable. By stating that the goal of functional analysis is to predict and control behavior (1953, p. 35) and that functional analyses of contingencies explain behavior (e.g., 1974, pp. 38, 94, 235), he assumes that explanation is closely related to prediction and control. The linkage which Skinner sees between prediction, control and explanation is spurious, and it runs counter to the explanatory practices in other sciences. For example, the concept of fitness in evolutionary theory has explanatory power despite the limits on its usefulness in prediction and control (Scriven, 1959). Similarly, geological theories can explain volcanic eruptions in terms of underground flow of magma, pressure increases, and so on. Yet the strength of these theories does not derive from their success in

predicting and controlling volcanic eruptions. In general, the explanatory power of a scientific theory cannot be equated with its utility in prediction and control.

Conversely, a functional relationship that provides significant power in prediction and control does not therefore provide an adequate explanation. For example, a functional relation exists between the ingestion of aspirin and the alleviation of everyday headaches. Knowing this, one can predict the effects of taking aspirin on headaches and actively decrease headaches by administering aspirin to the patient. But it does not follow that the functional relationship is therefore explanatory. After all, why does aspirin alleviate the headache? Perhaps the discovery of other functional relationships would resolve this issue. The point remains, however, that functional relations do not necessarily explain.

Throughout Skinner's works and his discussions of explanations, there is an overriding emphasis upon the control of behavior through the direct manipulation of environmental variables (Scriven, 1956; Wessells, 1981). This emphasis gives Skinner's behaviorism a methodological (though not in the Watsonian sense) and pragmatic character. His pragmatism is apparent in his statement that 'when we have achieved a practical control over the organism, theories of behavior lose their point ...' (1972, p. 120). Similarly, in discussing the nature-nurture issue, he states, 'The question is not whether human procreative behavior is primarily instinctive or learned, or whether the behavior of other species is relevant, but whether the behavior can be controlled through accessible variables ...' (1969, p. 199). His pragmatic emphasis pervades works such as *Walden Two* and *The Technology of Teaching*.

Skinner's pragmatism has substantial benefits, not the least of which is the development of an effective technology. But because it colors his views on non-technological matters such as explanation and theory construction, his pragmatism is overextended. In advanced disciplines such as physics and biology, theory is not dictated by which variables are accessible. Indeed, genes and atoms were useful theoretical constructs well before they became relatively accessible (Carlson, 1966; Dunn, 1966). Judging from activities in the other sciences, then, explanatory success does not follow from pragmatism and the emphasis on accessible variables. It is difficult to see why matters should be any different in psychology. Further, in biology it was theorizing about inaccessible events which resulted in the current genetic engineering technology. The exclusive focus upon accessible variables does not necessarily enhance one's practical control in the long run. Rather, explanatory successes pave the way for pragmatic undertakings, providing the theoretical basis for effective technology. In sum, Skinner has inappropriately allowed pragmatic concerns to take precedence over explanatory ones.

Theory

Skinner assumes that acceptable psychological theory must consist of an analysis of the contingencies that govern behavior. In his ongoing critique of theories referring to events occurring in a non-behavioral dimension, he has been particularly condemnatory of theories involving inferred inner events, saying 'the most objectionable practice is to follow the causal sequence back only as far as a hypothetical second link ...' (1953, p. 34). This view, which militates against

both cognitive and neurophysiological theories, is excessively restrictive.

Consider first Skinner's critique of cognitive theory. Throughout his works, he argues that cognitive theories are incomplete, logically circular, misleading, vague, fictional and unnecessary, and they obscure important details, focus attention on events that are difficult to observe and manipulate, provide a spurious sense of order, allay the experimenter's curiosity prematurely and impede the development of effective behavioral technology. This critique fails, however, as I have argued in detail elsewhere (Wessells, 1981, 1982). Some mentalistic theories that originated outside experimental psychology may be flawed in the ways that Skinner contends. But in contemporary cognitive psychology, some well-tested, respectable scientific theories have been developed, and they appeal to inferred processes. Although Skinner objects that they are incomplete, unnecessary, fictional, and so on, many of these criticisms presuppose the legitimacy of his views regarding explanation, which were found lacking above.

In general, the measure of an acceptable scientific theory is not whether it appeals to observable, accessible events but whether it explains the phenomena it is intended to explain, fits with the available evidence, makes significant predictions, avoids logical circularity and inconsistency, and achieves parsimony. In evaluating psychological theory, then, it is inappropriate to reject mentalistic concepts in principle, as Skinner does. Further, Skinner's rejection of inferred inner processes disregards practices in other branches of science. Contemporary theories in physics refer to many inferred subatomic particles, some of which are inherently unobservable. As stated previously, genetic theory was useful well before genes had been identified physically. Why should psychology rule out inferred processes when these have contributed to successful scientific theory in other disciplines?

In addition, there are good reasons for wanting to construct theories that appeal to inferred inner processes, as is illustrated by the following analogy. Imagine a fifth-generation computer that includes a robot capable of learning through reinforcement and punishment and of modifying its responses through extensive internal processing. Perhaps one could, following Skinner's approach, analyze the robot's behavior in terms of its conditioning history. But this analysis leaves many important questions unanswered. What internal events intervene between environment and behavior and allow contingencies to exert their effects? What events bridge the temporal gaps between a conditioning episode and subsequent behavior? What are the capacities of the system, not only for conditioning but also for remembering and for processing internally? Following the approach of cognitive psychologists, these questions may be analyzed by making inferences about the functional architecture and the internal processing of the system (Anderson, 1983; Kosslyn, 1980). For example, accurate inferences regarding the program guiding the behavior of the system would clarify the nature of the inner events. A theory of inner events might explain the constraints on conditioning, and it might also explain behavior that, like much human behavior, involves extensive inner processing and is not the product of a discernible three-link causal sequence.

As this example illustrates, the capacities and the inner workings of a system may be analyzed on a conceptual level as well as on a physical one. Moreover, analysis on a conceptual level does not entail the acceptance of dualism, as Skinner mistakenly suggests (e.g., 1974, p. 211) Contemporary cognitivists are

physicalists, but they analyze the system on a conceptual level, just as computer scientists analyze physical systems at the program level. Skinner (1969, 1974, 1977) criticizes this approach for being metaphorical. But metaphorical theories have been used successfully in other sciences, and they have a legitimate place so long as they satisfy the usual criteria of explanatory power, predictive success, and so on.

With regard to neuroscience, Skinner endorses physiological analysis since it will fill in the temporal gaps in functional analyses (1974, p. 215). Yet he relegates physiology to a secondary status, pointing out that laws of physiology will not supersede laws of behavior. What Skinner overlooks here is that physiological analyses can corroborate and clarify the basis of functional relations between environment and behavior. For example, if an operant response could be brought under stimulus control of some hues more readily than others, analysis of the visual system might indicate why this is. In this case and many others, physiological analysis identifies the physical bases of the organism's capacities. It is at least conceivable (and quite likely in the eyes of many) that a physiological theory will achieve greater explanatory and predictive power than behavior theory. In a field as young as psychology Skinner's restrictions on inferred processes and on neurophysiological analyses are premature and excessively confining.

It is no small irony that while Skinner has helped to put psychology on a scientific footing, he has simultaneously opposed the kinds of practices that have been productive in other sciences. One wonders whether behaviorism will achieve its potential while bounded by the excessive constraints that Skinner imposes.

REFERENCES

Anderson, J.R. (1983) *The Architecture of Cognition*, Cambridge, Mass., Harvard University Press.

Brewer, W.R. (1974) 'There is no convincing evidence for operant or classical conditioning in adult humans', in Weimer, W.B. and Palermo, D.S. (Eds), *Cognition and the Symbolic Processes*, Hillsdale, N.J., Erlbaum, pp. 1–42.

Carlson, E.A. (1966) *The Gene: A Critical History*, Philadelphia, Pa., W.B. Saunders.

Chomsky, N. (1959) 'A review of B.F. Skinner's *Verbal Behavior*', *Language*, 35, pp. 26–58.

Day, W. (1983) 'On the difference between radical and methodological behaviorism', *Behaviorism*, 11, pp. 89–102.

Dunn, L.C. (1966) *A Short History of Genetics*, New York, McGraw-Hill.

Flanagan, O.J. (1980) 'Skinnerian metaphysics and the problem of operationism', *Behaviorism*, 8, pp. 1–13.

Flanagan, O.J. (1984) *The Science of the Mind*, Cambridge, Mass., MIT Press.

Greenspoon, J. (1955) 'The effect of two spoken sounds on the frequency of two responses', *American Journal of Psychology*, 68, pp. 409–16.

Kosslyn, S.M. (1980) *Image and Mind*, Cambridge, Mass., Harvard University Press.

Kuhn, T.S. (1972) *The Structure of Scientific Revolutions*, 2nd ed., Chicago, Ill., University of Chicago Press.

MacCorquodale, K. (1970) 'On Chomsky's review of Skinner's *Verbal Behavior*', *Journal of the Experimental Analysis of Behavior*, 13, pp. 83–99.

Schnaitter, R. (1983) 'Science and verbal behavior', *Behaviorism*, 11, pp. 153–60.

Scriven, M. (1959) 'Explanation and prediction in evolutionary theory', *Science*, 130, pp. 477–82.

Scriven, M. (1956) 'A study of radical behaviorism', in Feigl, H. and Scriven, M. (Eds), *Minnesota Studies in the Philosophy of Science*, Vol. 1, Minneapolis, Minn., University of Minnesota Press, pp. 88–130.

Scriven, M. (1959) 'Explanation and prediction in evolutionary theory', *Science*, 130, pp. 477–82.

Shettleworth, S. (1972) 'Constraints on learning', in Lehrman, D.S. *et al.* (Eds), *Advances in the Study*

of Behavior, New York, Academic Press.
Skinner, B.F. (1938) *The Behavior of Organisms*, New York, Appleton-Century-Crofts.
Skinner, B.F. (1948) *Walden Two*, New York, Macmillan.
Skinner, B.F. (1953) *Science and Human Behavior*, New York, Macmillan.
Skinner, B.F. (1957) *Verbal Behavior*, New York, Appleton-Century-Crofts.
Skinner, B.F. (1964) 'Behaviorism at fifty', in Wann, T.W. (Ed.), *Behaviorism and Phenomenology*, Chicago, Ill. University of Chicago Press, pp. 79–108.
Skinner, B.F. (1968) *The Technology of Teaching*, New York, Appleton-Century-Crofts.
Skinner, B.F. (1969) *Contingencies of Reinforcement*, New York, Appleton-Century-Crofts.
Skinner, B.F. (1972) *Cumulative Record*, 3rd ed., New York, Appleton-Century-Crofts.
Skinner, B.F. (1974) *About Behaviorism*, New York, Knopf.
Skinner, B.F. (1977) 'Why I am not a cognitive psychologists', *Behaviorism*, 5, pp. 1–10.
Skinner, B.F. (1979) *The Shaping of a Behaviorist*, New York, Knopf.
Wessells, M.G. (1981) 'A critique of Skinner's views on the explanatory inadequacy of cognitive theories', *Behaviorism*, 9, pp. 153–70.
Wessells, M.G. (1982) 'A critique of Skinner's views on the obstructive character of cognitive theories', *Behaviorism*, 10, pp. 65–84.

Interchange

CREEL REPLIES TO WESSELLS

PHYSIOLOGY, EXPLANATION, AND CONTROL

Wessells' article is admirably researched and penetrating. It has me thinking new thoughts. Still, I believe that Wessells' assessment of Skinner's philosophy of science is inadequate in some ways and mistaken in others.

Wessells claims that 'the capacities and the inner workings of a system may be analyzed on a conceptual level as well as on a physical one.' The conceptual analysis of which he speaks takes the form of speculative explanation in non-physical terms; hence, it is not an analysis of the inner workings of a physical system. We might do a conceptual analysis of an unfamiliar computer program and discover that whenever we input a number, it outputs another number that is the cube of the input number. But to do a conceptual analysis of what the machine went through to produce its output, i.e., of its inner workings, would be futile because there is an infinite number of ways in which it could have produced that output. Hence, it is not true that 'accurate inferences regarding the program guiding the behavior of the system would clarify the nature of the inner events.' Accurate inferences regarding the program would tell us about relations between input and output, but they would tell us nothing about how that output was produced.

Physiology must tell us that part of the story. Skinner insists that there will not be a complete science of behavior until physiology explains how input into an organism is processed into output. Does this mean that he 'relegates physiology to a secondary status'? Certainly not in any pejorative sense. Skinner's point is that in the division of labor for the study of behavior it is the psychologist who isolates the terms between which the physiologist seeks the connections. It is somewhat like the detective who determines the crime (output) and the suspect (input) but turns certain evidence over to a forensic technician for analysis. Yes, the lab work has a secondary status; it serves the larger process of determining guilt and innocence, but it is no less important for that. Neither is the work of the physiologist.

Wessells adds in criticism that according to Skinner, 'laws of physiology will not supersede laws of behavior.' Two replies are in order. First, the discoveries made by the physiologist will help us understand how the input of a functional relation discovered by the psychologist is processed into and through the organism into output — accounting eventually for susceptibility and insusceptibility to reinforcement, satiation curves, etc. Hence, the discoveries of the physiologist will not supersede those of the psychologist. Rather, they will be subsumed within

the broader framework of the latter — as forensic analysis is subsumed within detective work. Second, Skinner states clearly that physiologists may develop sophisticated techniques that bypass traditional modes of stimulation to the organism, but, again, that would not mean that the laws of physiology had superseded the laws of behavior. Those new laws and tools would simply enrich the resources available to the behaviorist (*Contingencies of Reinforcement* [1969], p. 283).

Wessells argues also that the behaviorist account of a learning episode, such as a child learning to say 'dog', is 'incomplete and non-explanatory'. Skinner would agree that the behaviorist account is incomplete — because it does not include a physiological account of the causal connections that mediate input and output. But what could anyone add of scientific value to the joint work that the behaviorist and the physiologist would do in providing an account of the individual's behavior?

Regarding the purportedly non-explanatory character of behaviorist accounts, Wessells allows that a functional analysis might disclose, for example, that aspirin alleviates headaches. But such an account, he adds, would not tell us *why* aspirin alleviates headaches. Apparently Wessells believes that in science we can get at something more than functional relations that are ultimately opaque. I do not believe we can. No matter how sophisticated our understanding of the effectiveness of aspirin becomes, it will never consist of more than a sequence of functional relations, each of which is a fact that we must just accept.

Finally, Wessells states that Skinner confuses explanation with prediction and control. It is true that Skinner has long been concerned with the practical value of psychology, but his emphasis on prediction and control in experimentation is strictly for the sake of understanding, not application. Only through successful prediction and control of a subject matter can we be confident that we have achieved a correct understanding of it, that is, that we have identified correctly the variables of which its properties and behaviors are functions and that we have identified correctly the causal relations among those variables, properties, and behaviors. This kind of understanding *is* scientific understanding — as distinguished from poetic, religious, and metaphysical understanding. From such understanding our most fruitful and durable scientific explanations arise, and to it they return.

WESSELLS REPLIES TO CREEL

Creel's description of Skinner's views on science agree remarkably well with my own, though we emphasize different facets of Skinner's analysis. We disagree extensively, however, on the validity of Skinner's views, particularly those regarding theory and explanation. Lacking the space for an exhaustive analysis, I shall examine several prominent areas of disagreement.

Creel portrays mentalistic explanations as dualistic accounts that, like those which invoke God, soul or spirit, appeal to non-physical factors. Like Skinner, he rejects non-physical accounts because they are difficult to confirm or to falsify by observation and manipulation and because they discourage the development of physicalist accounts. This criticism applies effectively to many unscientific, menta-

listic theories, some of which continue to be accepted both inside and outside psychology. The trouble, however, is that it simply does not apply to cognitive psychology, the central arena within which mentalistic theories are being developed today.

Many cognitive theories attempt to explain behavior by appealing to inferred inner processes whose physical bases are unknown. Yet cognitive theorists as diverse as Chomsky, Pylyshyn and Anderson assume that mental processes are physical in nature, so they are clearly not dualists. They assume that the activities of a physical system such as a computer system may be analyzed physically in terms of magnetic, electrical and mechanical events. But this level of analysis is too cumbersome to be useful in analyzing very complex events, just as analysis at the level of quantum mechanics is too cumbersome to be useful in analyzing global weather patterns. Consequently, they choose to analyze physical systems conceptually in terms of capacities and processes, much as a computer scientist might analyze a computer system in terms of capacities and programs. Thus mentalism does not entail dualism, yet it may be pursued fruitfully on a non-physical level.

The issue here is not whether the system is physical but how best to construct scientific theories about it. Although some may prefer theories that emphasize directly manipulable variables, scientific theories should be judged according to the usual criteria of empirical confirmation, generality, testability, internal consistency, parsimony, and so on. Some cognitive theories fare well by these criteria, and they explain many phenomena that are beyond the range of Skinner's theory. By Skinner's standards, cognitive theories may appear non-explanatory since they do not appeal to external, directly manipulable variables. But neither did the initial genetic and atomic theories, yet who would want to claim that these were scientifically ill-conceived or unproductive?

Creel's chapter and mine are informed by very different conceptions of the role of theory and of the relation between observation and theory. He states that ideally scientists would not need theories involving 'speculative entities' and that 'theory should come into play only after the failure of attempts to understand the subject matter in terms of accessible physical factors . . .' Unfortunately, as in the case of early genetic theory, the postulation of unobserved entities or events may help to guide research in highly productive directions. Further, analyses of accessible physical factors may enhance significantly one's ability to predict and to control phenomena, but this approach overlooks the most important function of theory — explanation. As I pointed out, it cannot be assumed that functional relations between environment and behavior are explanatory.

In addition, in stating that '. . . observation is under the control of the subject matter, speculation is not', Creel implies that observations are the more objective and are free of theory. The problem is that observation, theory and meta-theory are tightly interwoven. Which observations one makes or takes as important depend largely upon one's theoretical conceptions and preconceptions. In the context of particular cognitive theories, functional relations between stimulus exposure time and the number of correct verbal responses might be highly important, whereas these observations are relatively unimportant in the context of Skinner's theory. Moreover, Skinner's preconception that the goals of psychology are to predict and control behavior leads naturally to the search for environmental antecedents, as does the preconception that functional relations count as explana-

tions. As my chapter indicates, however, these preconceptions are both unusual in the house of science and unnecessary for the construction of scientific psychological theory. Skinner's position remains very much in need of additional philosophical analysis and support.

Part VII: Variation and Selection: The Evolutionary Analogy in Skinner's Theory

11. Variation and Selection: The Evolutionary Analogy in Skinner's Theory

MARC RICHELLE

SKINNER AND BIOLOGY

Many aspects of Skinner's thinking have been persistently misinterpreted by his opponents. His views on the role of the environment or on verbal behaviour are cases in point. Skinner has been classified among S-R psychologists, in spite of his numerous explicit statements to the contrary (Skinner, 1953, 1969). Few contemporary psycholinguists, still confident in Chomsky's influential attacks (Chomsky, 1959), would recognize that their current research is exactly fulfilling Skinner's suggestion that the 'global episode' of verbal exchanges between speaker and listener should be considered. However, no misrepresentation of Skinner's views seems more difficult to eradicate than that concerning the relation of a science of behaviour to biology.

Skinner's position toward biology and biological thinking is usually represented in terms that can be summarized as follows:

1 Skinner has neglected, and, worse, has even denied the interest of what goes on in the brain; he has advocated a 'black-box' psychology, that has become more and more outdated as neurosciences have progressed;

2 Skinner's environmentalism has been blind to the role of heredity, and, given the place of genetics in modern biology, his theory is at odds with biology;

3   by claiming that laws of conditioning are universal, and that they work for any species and for any response — *operants* are, for that matter, totally arbitrary — he has cut behaviour analysis, as practised by himself and his followers, from ethological thinking, and has completely overlooked the important problems raised by species-specific behaviour and by the evolution of behaviour, including the evolution of capacities for learning.

These misrepresentations are most surprising — though not without explanation if one looks at the history of the field — since Skinner has repeatedly made it clear that the study of behaviour is a part of biology. He even defined behaviourism not as the science of behaviour, but a philosophy of science concerned with the subject matter and methods of psychology that make psychology 'part of biology, a natural science for which tested and highly successful methods are available' (Skinner, 1963a). Was he, at that time, biologically naive to such point as to think of himself as a sort of biologist, while ignoring fundamental tenets of the biological approach?

IN DEFENCE OF THE BLACK BOX

I shall not comment on Skinner's defence of a behavioural science proper within the framework of the natural sciences. His arguments, as presented in two famous methodological papers (Skinner, 1947, 1961), were clear enough, and they contained no denial of the importance of physiological and psychophysiological research. He simply insisted that there is a place — and an important place — for a study of behaviour; that progress in brain physiology is tied to some extent to progress in the study of behaviour; and that, from the point of view of psychology and physiology as well, one should regret the flight from the psychological to the neurophysiological laboratory of many first-rate experimenters who were tempted to join a field already rich with expert researchers. These arguments should, of course, be seen in their historical context, when experimental psychology was much less developed than it is now, and when integrated neuropsychological approaches were, for technical and theoretical reasons, far less familiar and less efficient than they are today. However, in spite of the rapid changes that have taken place in the neurosciences, Skinner's warnings that 'both (physiological and psychological) sets of facts are *equally* important' are still relevant. Contemporary neurosciences, while favouring real brain-behaviour approaches — often based, as far as *behaviour* is concerned, on sophisticated techniques developed by 'black-box' behaviour analysis in the past thirty years or so — also foster a trend towards 'neurological reductionism', which implies that looking into the brain will tell us everything about behaviour (Changeux, 1983). Such a 'self-contained' brain research philosophy logically leads to denying any interest in an analysis at the level of behaviour. It finds some support from a certain brand of cognitivism, for which behaviour is, at best, an indication of inferred mental processes that are taken as the very subject matter of psychology.

It is worth noting that objections to neurological reductionism come not only from the psychologists who still think of their science as the science of behaviour (with all the qualifications of sophisticated behaviourism), but also from psy-

chologists and psychophysiologists of very different style as well. Most significant in this respect are the solicited comments by D. Hebb on Bunge's essay on the *Mind-Body Problem* (Bunge, 1980). With the courteousness that fits an invited post-script to Bunge's book, the great psychophysiologist, who is not suspect of obedience to radical behaviourism, undertakes to rehabilitate behaviourism, and, echoing 1980 Skinner's *Flight from the Laboratory* (1961), expresses some reservations about neurological triumphs:

> As for the idea that psychological theory would be in better shape if it became more neurological and more mathematical, I am myself somewhat skeptical. Ultimately, nonneurological 'black-box' formulations must be capable of translation into neurological terms, if consciousness and thought are, as I believe, a state or activity of the brain; but in the present state of knowledge, black-box theory can in some situations be the most effective way of making progress (Hebb, 1983, p. 222 in Bunge, 1980; see also Hebb, 1980).

ENVIRONMENTALISM

As to the second point, Skinner's environmentalism, this is essentially an affirmation that behaviour is, by definition, an interactive process. This has nothing to do wtih a denial of genetic endowment. The point has been discussed on several occasions by Skinner himself (see, among a number of other sources, 1953 and 1966). What is important is the crucial role of the environment both in selecting particular genic structures and in shaping particular combinations of behaviour units (Skinner, 1975). Skinner's environmentalism, therefore, cannot be dissociated from his view on the learning mechanism, as summarized in the 'evolutionary analogy' (discussed below).

It is also related to the solution given to the problem of the evolution of learning capacities. If higher capacities for individual learning are recognized in some species (*Homo sapiens* possibly being one such species), the environment to which the individual is exposed might be relatively more important for these species than the environment in which the species evolved. To say that what the species can learn is programmed is not a sufficient account (see the next section).

SPECIES-SPECIFIC CONSTRAINTS AND THE EVOLUTION OF LEARNING

The neglect of species-specific differences in behaviour appears to throw more serious doubt on Skinner's biological claims. In retrospect, the emphasis on the 'arbitrariness' of the operant response reflects an astonishing ignorance of, or indifference to cross-species comparisons. However, this should again be put in historical perspective. Besides the fact that 'arbitrary' is best defined in Skinner's writing with reference to Pavlovian conditioned reflexes (rather than to what is now called 'biological constraints'), there is no reason why we should expect Skinner, in the thirties or forties, to have been more aware of the ethological dimension than any of the great learning theorists (Hull, Tolman, Guthrie, etc.), whose concern was to derive general psychological laws from animal subjects selected for experimental convenience, just as physiologists did, not without success.

The central question here — but it addresses Skinner no more than the

majority of other American psychologists, not exclusively in the behaviourist tradition — is why it took so long for ethological thinking to become known and integrated into psychology. Important as the question is for a history of psychology, it is beyond the scope of this chapter. However, Skinner cannot be taken as peculiarly responsible for that state of affairs. He was, on the contrary, more receptive than others to early concern with species-specific behaviour, as shown by Breland and Breland (1961). The controversy in the late seventies suggests that his students and followers gave more importance than he did to the idea that species-specific characters could be ignored when dealing with operant conditioning (Herrnstein, 1977a, 1977b; Skinner, 1977; see also Skinner, 1983); consequently, ethology came to them as a revelation, while it had been included in any psychologist's training in most European universities.

Skinner was interested initially in the nature of learning mechanisms, not in the evolution of learning capacities. However, after interaction between the behaviourist tradition and ethology was established, mainly from 1960, first in a rather conflictual fashion that softened with time, he devoted much thought and many pages to the issue of the relation between phylogenetic and ontogenetic mechanisms accounting for behavioural repertoires. We shall return to some of the problems raised in that debate, especially the existence of one (or a small number of) basic learning mechanism(s) as against a plurality of species-specific mechanisms. But we should turn first to a more crucial point if we want to evaluate the place of biological thinking in Skinner's theory: the reference to biological evolution.

SKINNER AND DARWINISM

The recent crossfertilization of learning theory and ethology was by no means the first occasion on which Skinner appealed to the theory of evolution. Darwin's mode of explanation is explicitly referred to in his work much earlier, for instance, in *Science and Human Behaviour* (1953). From then on it is invoked repeatedly with two different, but equally important, purposes. The first is related with antimentalism, one of the major tenets of Skinner's radical behaviourism. Darwinism provided biology with an alternate to finalism. Adaptive functions in living organisms were no longer seen as goal-seeking mechanisms, but as by-products of a past history of selective pressures. Similarly, behaviour was to be explained, not by resorting to mental entities (mental 'fictions') such as purpose, desire, will, familiar to commensense psychology and to many psychological theories as well, but by tracing it to the environmental history that shaped it. Commenting on Thorndike's contribution, Skinner points to his making it 'possible to include the effects of action without using concepts like purpose, intention, expectancy, or utility'; he goes on: 'Thorndike's solution was probably suggested by Darwin's treatment of phylogenic purpose. Before Darwin, the purpose of a well-developed eye might have been said to be to permit the organism to see better. The principle of natural selection moved "seeing better" from the future into the past' (Skinner, 1963b). Evolution theory is, in this case, an inspiring precedent, that helps in solving an old problem in a radically different manner. It might be nothing but an analogy, though a very valuable one — as analogies in scientific thinking can both suggest fresh solutions to the scientist and assist him or

her in persuading reluctant colleagues of the plausibility of a solution.

The evolutionary analogy was brought in concurrently in another, though closely related, context. Skinner suggested that his analysis of operant responses, as a basic mechanism in the shaping and maintenance of behaviour, parallels, at the level of the individual, the process of natural selection at work in biological evolution, a process that has been accepted as a satisfactory account of the emergence of new living forms. As is well-known, a large part of Skinner's efforts at both theoretical and empirical levels, has been devoted to the notion of the *selective* action of the environment. The idea was already germinating in Thorndike's *law of effect*, but Skinner has made it the key concept in understanding learning mechanisms not reducible to Pavlovian (Type S) conditioning. Operant responses are not elicited as reflexes are, or as some motor actions of variable complexity can be, in so-called *Fixed Action Patterns*. They are emitted, and eventually followed by reinforcement. They must, as Skinner emphasized, occur for some other reason if the selective action of the environment is ever to take place. 'In both operant conditioning and the evolutionary selection of behavioural characteristics, consequences alter future probability. Reflexes and other innate patterns of behaviour evolve because they increase the chances of survival of the species. Operants grow strong because they are followed by important consequences in the life of the individual' (Skinner, 1953, p. 90).

THE EVOLUTIONARY ANALOGY: SUPERFICIAL OR SUBSTANTIAL?

Since that early (first?) statement, the evolutionary analogy as applied to operant behaviour has been widely developed by Skinner in his theoretical writings; it has been put to use to explain the emergence of novelty and creative behaviour, such as artistic production (Skinner, 1970, 1971); and it has merged with his reflections on the place of learning in evolution. Recent papers (1981, 1984) are devoted exclusively to the issue; they make it clear that what might have been initially no more than a metaphor is now viewed by Skinner as a much deeper common point in mechanisms proper. In 'Selection by Consequences' (1981) Skinner argues that the same kind of process, involving variation and selection, is at work at three different levels: biological evolution (or level of species), operant behaviour (level of the individual organism), and social practices (level of culture). There are, of course, fundamental differences between the three levels: genes, behavioural units and cultural traits are not one and the same thing, and the process involved must be qualified accordingly. There is no question about that. But all three levels exhibit a typical 'causal mode' found only in living systems, levels 2 and 3 taking over the principle at work at level 1 — *variation and selection* — while extending and amplifying its potentialities by applying it to other material, at another time and with specific qualifications.

It can be objected that these qualifications are so important that whatever might seem similar among the three levels is, at best, mere analogy. However, the case for a substantial continuity in basic mechanisms, in spite of all agreed differences, has been made by a number of scientists, possibly of a less purist inclination. Piaget has argued strongly in favour of the continuity hypothesis and of a basically common mechanism transposed from one level to another, with new structural features reorganizing the system without eliminating the common

mechanisms (see Piaget, 1967). This applies, in his constructivist theory, to cognitive developmental stages as well as to the passage from primitive forms of life to the highest products of human intelligence. Comparison of Piaget's and Skinner's writings reveals interesting convergences (Richelle, 1976).

Schools of thought in cultural anthropology also resort to the variation-selection evolutionary model, as in the classical work of Leslie White, in a way that has nothing in common with nineteenth century social Darwinism. When the French biologist, Monod, in his preface to the French translation of Popper's *Logic of Scientific Discovery*, compares the progress of scientific knowledge to biological evolution, it is not clear that he means it only as an analogy (Monod, 1973).

In the face of such an issue, scientists have the choice between investigating a given level in order to qualify it with more and more accuracy or exploring the analogical path, which is obviously more adventurous but by no means less promising, as the history of science has shown repeatedly. The second alternative may remain for ever at a stage where generality equals vagueness, but it may also unveil unsuspected connections between fields of research traditionally kept apart.

VARIATION: THE NEGLECTED HALF OF THE LEARNING PROCESS

Let us concede that at present the evolutionary analogy is nothing but a crude analogy, and that it is of no help in building an integrative theory of living systems from cell to culture. This would not preclude the fruitfulness of the analogy in the particular domain of a science of behaviour. If the analogy is instrumental in reformulating the problem of individual learning and adaptation, and leads to new hypotheses and experiments, it will have proven its heuristic value. On these grounds I would contend that the evolutionary analogy, if taken seriously, is one of the most stimulating conceptual contributions of Skinner, and one that should inspire future behavioural research.

However, it has not yet yielded empirical work to prove its fecundity. If the analogy is to be taken seriously, research should focus equally on its two complementary aspects, *variation* and *selection*. Little attention has been given to variation, the emphasis in experimental analysis of behaviour being put, during the last fifty or so years, on the selective action of the environment. The nature and sources of variation have been given only occasional attention. The reasons are to be found in three different directions. First, dealing with variation in its own right is a risk that few scientists are eager to take, as long as they can move on without it. Variation is the sort of thing one wishes to get rid of, unless confronted with it as a basic property of nature which cannot be avoided. Psychologists, who have been and still are in search of scientific respectability, have been particularly reluctant to venture into the uncertainties of intra-individual behavioural variation. The field of inter-individual variation — differential psychology — has been reserved essentially to applied psychology, with little impact on experimental and theoretical psychology.

Second, if one has recognized as important a process of variation-selection, one is still confronted with the intrinsic difficulties of dealing with variation, and it

is more appropriate to concentrate on *selection* first, leaving *variation* for later inquiry. Biologists have long explored selective pressure in much greater detail than the sources of variation, the study of which had to wait for population genetics and molecular biology. It is no wonder that psychologists have followed the same course of action. They were encouraged in the experimental analysis of behaviour (as Skinnerian psychologists like to label their area of research) by the experimental technology developed by Skinner himself. This is the third category of reasons, and deserves further comment.

If we look at the history of the field, it is obvious that impressive efforts have been devoted to describing all sorts of selective action of the environment under the general labels of 'contingencies' and 'schedules of reinforcement'. It seemed important to experimenters in the fifties and later to demonstrate the lawfulness of operant control, so variation within an individual's behaviour was usually overlooked. (There are, however, some early exceptions: Schoenfeld *et al.*, 1966; Keller and Schoenfeld, 1950; and of course the descriptive work of Ferster and Skinner, 1957). This trend was facilitated by the automatization of experimental devices and the consequent neglect of what goes on in the subject's behaviour besides the operant recorded responses. The emphasis on *rate* at the expense of *topography* or *structure* of behaviour was another favourable condition. The experimenter was likely to ignore variation if he relied exclusively on rate recording, at least when automatic equipment was still limited in capacity. With computer technology entering the operant laboratory, it has become possible to record events at a much more refined level and, eventually, to approach variation systematically. Recording of 'spontaneous' variation in duration, or force, or position, within the specified class of responses as a function of operant schedules is a case in point (Antonitis, 1951; Boren *et al.* 1978; Eckerman and Lanson, 1969; Herrnstein, 1961; McCray and Harper, 1962).

Concurrently, and partly under the growing influence of ethology, researchers became more interested in response topography on the one hand and in what goes on between operant responses on the other. The seminal paper by Staddon and Simmelhag (1971) undoubtedly marked a decisive turn by drawing attention to the *variation* aspect of the operant model. The authors clearly stated the factors responsible for behaviour upon which reinforcement exerts its selective action. They proposed the label 'principles of behavioural variation for all such factors that originate behaviour'. Giving Skinner credit for the original idea (they refer to Skinner, 1966, 1969; they might have included Skinner, 1953), they worked out the evolutionary analogy to a point beyond that reached by Skinner at that time. Other theoretical contributions appeared along the same lines (see among others Segal, 1972).

Experimental work was carried out, but the focus was not so much on variation proper as on the sources of the units of behaviour from which operants are eventually built. So-called adjunctive, collateral or schedule-induced behaviours were analyzed mainly within the general concept of species-specific behaviour and the related constraints on learning. Variation proper was given only occasional attention by a handful of experimenters (Vogel and Anau, 1973; Eckerman and Lanson, 1969; Boulanger, 1983; El Ahmadi, 1983; Périkel, 1982; Schwartz, 1980, 1981, 1982a, 1982b). We still have a long way to go, however, before we fully understand the nature and sources of behavioural variation.

VARIATION AND THE EVOLUTION OF LEARNING

What has to be accounted for is the fact that individual learning gave some advantages for survival so that built-in variability mechanisms eventually developed. For reasons that can be traced, in principle, to phylogenetic history, members of various species might be endowed, to various degrees correlated with the species potentialities for learning, with what could be called, metaphorically, a 'generator of variability'. It would have a more important role in species with an 'open programme' for learning, as compared with species with a 'closed programme' in Lorenz's terms. Conspicuous instances of behavioural variability can be found in exploratory activities and play in animals and humans. Lorenz (1978), among others, has pointed to a plausible relation between exploratory behaviour and learning. Bovet (1979), in another context, has developed the hypothesis of the survival value of foraging strategies based on maximized variability (i.e., tending toward randomness). Of course, the 'generator of variability' need not be a purely random machine. This would be an extreme case. Usually constraints defining the system at a given point leave only a limited range of variation; as Staddon and Simmelhag put it, it is 'organized production of novelty'.

Viewed in this perspective, operant behaviour has little to do with the repetition of stereotyped responses which has become the popular representation of it. It is a highly dynamic process grounded in behavioural variation. Novel and creative behaviour, and problem-solving do not raise particular difficulties in this view, which is close in some respects to Piaget's theory. (The concept of *desequilibration*, which has an essential part in the constructivist account of development, raises a similar issue, i.e., the sources of variation in behaviour.) But how does it fit with current conceptions of the evolution of learning?

No decisive theory is available at present. Three main categories of solutions are still competing: (1) there is one or a few fundamental mechanisms of learning, appearing early in biological evolution and remaining throughout, whatever the level of complexity of behaviour being learned; (2) behaviour exhibits increasing complexity as biological forms become more complex (at least among vertebrates); and one should distinguish as many learning mechanisms as there are levels of behavioural complexity; (3) learning capacities have evolved in a species-specific context, and cannot be reduced to one or a few basic mechanism(s), nor can they be ordered according to some hierarchy.

The first solution has been adopted by most classic learning theorists, including Pavlov and Skinner. The latter has emphasized the distinction of two basic processes, respondent and operant, and has maintained the distinction in his most recent writings (Skinner, 1981). There are, within this category of solutions, several variants which are still a matter of debate, as to the number of processes involved (just one, two, or three?) and as to their nature (Type I, Type II or something else?). In spite of important divergences on these and other points, there is a common denominator: the process or processes retained are seen as the adequate model(s), whatever the structural level of the behaviour being considered — which means that the model is cross-specific and cross-levels. This does not imply that qualifications are not needed for each level or for each species, but these qualifications are seen as secondary to the basic common mechanism(s).

The second type of solution has been worked out by Razran (1971), among others, who draws a hierarchy of levels from habituation and sensitization (preas-

sociative learning) to higher symbolizing, through associative mechanisms corresponding to Type I and Type II conditioning broken down into more than two classes. This view dispenses with the important problem faced by the first solution above, i.e., how does a simple, basic process apply to structures of increasing complexity? Here learning gradually merges into the psychology of intelligence, cognition and language, with a sense of continuity, but with the clear consequence that processes recognized at lower levels can be forgotten as higher structures are reached.

The third solution derives from interest in the last two decades in the biological or species-specific constraints on learning. The generality of the laws of learning were first shaken by the observation that responses, stimuli and contingencies are not equivalent in all species, but are related to the species-specific repertoire, so that a correct description and explanation of learning potentialities in a given species requires a good knowledge of its natural repertoire. This insertion of learning in the ethological description and explanation is now widely accepted, even by advocates of a single learning mechanism, as pointed out above. But this third solution implies much more than a species-specific qualification of some general process(es). In its most extreme version it goes as far as to suggest that there is no such thing as general processes; that learning is, in essence, no less species-specific than the peculiar morphology of, say, claws or eyes. There are as many learning processes as there are species which learn (see Plotkin and Odling-Smee, 1982). There is no place for learning theory distinct from a theory of species-specific behaviour. Whatever might look common to various species with respect to learning would be mere superficial convergence or analogy (in the biological, not epistemological, sense of the word).

None of these three types of account is supported by unquestionable evidence, be it empirical or logical. Explanations of the first category still prevail among traditional learning psychologists, who show great flexibility in adjusting their theories to new facts or concepts, as testified by the wide acceptance of biological constraints as modulators of learning processes. The second class of explanation appeals to many psychologists who define themselves as cognitivists, and are mainly interested in higher processes in humans. While recognizing the importance of habituation, Pavlovian and operant conditioning in animals and, at the level of elementary responses, in humans, they feel they can do without them when dealing with verbal memory, abstract problem-solving and the like. The third solution appeals to those who emphasize the neglect of species diversity by traditional learning theories and who resort to arguments from comparative ethology.

The vogue of the last two types of solution might reflect a swing of the pendulum rather than some real advance in our understanding of learning. Learning theories of a more classical brand, i.e., the first class, have been in disgrace because of a contemporary concern for non-reductionist accounts in which preserving levels of complexity and species diversity often means, indirectly, preserving man's self-esteem.

There is nothing implausible in the idea that one basic process is at work throughout numerous levels of complexity or in a wide variety of living species. The same fundamental mechanism is called upon in evolutionary biology to account for the simplest and for the most complex living forms. The same is true of the basic principles governing the genetic code. One basic principle is accept-

able if it provides for structural diversification. This is exactly what the variation-selection process does in biological evolution. But the observed diversity must not hide the basic process that produces it. The same might be true of behaviour.

Skinner's use of the evolutionary analogy still offers interesting heuristic prospects both to account for the evolution of learning capacities and to elucidate the ways in which individual behaviour grows richer.

REFERENCES

Antonitis, J.J. (1951) 'Response variability in the white rat during conditioning, extinction and reconditioning', *Journal of Experimental Psychology*, 42, pp. 273–81.

Boren, J.J., Moersbacher, J.M. and Wayte, A.A. (1978) 'Variability of response location on fixed ratio and fixed interval schedules of reinforcement', *Journal of the Experimental Analysis of Behavior* 30, pp. 63, 67.

Boulanger, B. (1983) 'Contribution à l'etude de la variabilité comportementale chez l'adulte', unpublished MA thesis, Lab. Exp. Psychol., Liège.

Bovet, P., (1979) 'La valeur adaptative des comportements aléatoires', *L'Année Psychologique*, 79, pp. 505–25.

Breland, K. and Breland, M. (1961) 'The misbehavior of organisms', *American Psychologist*, 61, pp. 681–4.

Bunge, M. (1980) *The Mind-Body Problem*, Oxford, Pergamon.

Changeux, J.P. (1983) *L'Homme Neuronal*, Paris, Fayard.

Chomsky, N. (1959) 'Review of Skinner, B.F. *Verbal Behavior*', *Language*, 25, pp. 26–58.

Eckerman, D.A. and Lanson, R.N. (1969) 'Variability of response location for pigeons responding under continuous reinforcement, intermittent-reinforcement, and extinction', *Journal of the Experimental Analysis of Behavior*, 12, pp. 73–80.

El Ahmadi, A. (1983) 'Contribution, à l'étude de la variabilité comportementale chez l'enfant', unpublished MA thesis, University of Liège.

Ferster, C.B. and Skinner, B.F. (1957) *Schedules of Reinforcement,* New York, Appleton-Century-Crofts.

Hebb, D.O. (1980) 'Epilogue: A behavioral approach', in Bunge, M., *The Mind-Body Problem*, Oxford, Pergamon, pp. 220–3.

Hebb, D.O. (1983) *Essay on Mind*, Hillsdale, N.J., Lawrence Erlbaum.

Herrnstein, R.J. (1961) 'Stereotypy and intermittent reinforcement', *Science*, 133, pp. 2067–69.

Herrnstein, R.J. (1977a) 'The evolution of behaviorism', *American Psychologist*, 32, pp. 593–603.

Herrnstein, R.J. (1977b) 'Doing what comes naturally. A reply to Professor Skinner', *American Psychologist*, 32, pp. 1013–16.

Keller, F.S. and Schoenfeld, W.N. (1950) *Principles of Psychology*, New York, Appleton-Century-Crofts.

Lorenz, K. (1978) *Grundlagen der Ethologie*, Wien, Springer.

McCray, C.L. and Harper, R.S. (1962), 'Some relationships of schedules of reinforcement to variability of response', *Journal of Comparative and Physiological Psychology*, 55, pp. 19–21.

Monod, J. (1973) Preface to K.R. Popper, *La Logique de la Découverte Scientifique*, Paris, Payot.

Perikel, J.J. (1982) 'Le microprocesseur dans l'expérimentation psychologique. Application à l'étude de la variabilité comportementale', unpublished MA thesis, University of Liège.

Piaget, J. (1967) *Biologie et Connaissance*, Paris, Gallimard.

Plotkin, H. C. and Odling-Smee, F.J. (1982) 'Learning in the context of a hierarchy of knowledge gaining processes', in Plotkin, H.C. (Ed.), *Learning, Development and Culture*, Sussex, Wiley, pp. 443–71.

Razran, G. (1971) *Mind in Evolution*, Boston, Mass., Houghton Mifflin.

Richelle, M. (1976) 'Constructivisme et behaviorisme', *Revue Européenne des Sciences Sociales*, 14, pp. 291–303 (volume d'hommage à J. Piaget à l'occasion de son 80e anniversaire).

Schoenfeld, W.N., Harris, A.M. and Farmer, J. (1966) 'Conditioning response variability', *Psychological Reports*, 19, pp. 551–7.

Schwartz, B. (1980) 'Development of complex, stereotyped behavior in pigeons', *Journal of the Experimental Analysis of Behavior*, 33, pp. 153–6.

Schwartz, B. (1981) 'Control of complex, sequential operants by systematic visual information in pigeons', *Journal of Experimental Psychology: An. Processes*, 7, pp. 31–44.

Schwartz, B. (1982a) 'Failure to produce response variability with reinforcement', *Journal of the Experimental Analysis of Behavior*, 37, pp. 171–81.

Schwartz, B. (1982b) 'Interval and ratio reinforcement of a complex sequential operant in pigeons', *Journal of the Experimental Analysis of Behavior*, 37, pp. 349–57.

Segal, E.F. (1972) 'Induction and the provenance of the operants', in Gilbert, R.M. and Millenson, J.R. (Eds), *Reinforcement Behavioral Analysis*, New York, Academic Press, pp.1–34.

Skinner, B.F. (1947) 'Current trends in experimental psychology', in *Current Trends in Psychology*, Pittsburgh, Penn., University of Pittsburgh Press.

Skinner, B.F. (1953) *Science and Human Behavior*, New York, Macmillan.

Skinner, B.F. (1961) 'The flight from the laboratory', in *Current Trends in Psychological Theory*, Pittsburgh, Penn., University of Pittsburgh Press.

Skinner, B.F. (1963a) 'Behaviorism at fifty', *Science*, 140, pp. 951–8.

Skinner, B.F. (1963b) 'Operant behavior', *American Psychologist*, 18, pp. 503–15, (in Honig, W.K. (Ed.) *Operant Behavior: Areas of Research and Application*, New York, Appleton-Century-Crofts, 1966, and reprinted in Skinner, B.F., *Contingencies of Reinforcement*, New York, Appleton-Century-Crofts, 1969).

Skinner, B.F. (1966) 'The phylogeny and ontogeny of behavior', *Science*, 153, pp. 1205–13.

Skinner, B.F. (1969) *Contingencies of Reinforcement* New York, Appleton-Century-Crofts.

Skinner, B.F. (1970) 'Creating the creative artist', in *On the Future of Art*, New York, Solomon R. Guggenheim Museum.

Skinner, B.F. (1971) 'A lecture on having a poem', lecture given at the Poetry Center, New York, 1971.

Skinner, B.F. (1975) 'The steep and thorny way to a science of behavior', *American Psychologist*, 30, pp. 42–9.

Skinner, B.F. (1977) 'Herrnstein and the evolution of behaviorism', *American Psychologist*, 32, pp. 1006–12.

Skinner, B.F. (1981) 'Selection by consequences', *Science*, 213, pp. 501–14.

Skinner, B.F. (1983) *A Matter of Consequences*, New York, Alfred A. Knopf.

Skinner, B.F. (1984) 'The evolution of behavior', *Journal of the Experimental Analysis of Behavior*, 41, pp. 217–21.

Staddon, J.R. and Simmelhag, V.L. (1971) 'The "superstition" experiment: A reexamination of its implications for the principles of adaptive behavior', *Psychological Review*, 78, pp. 3–43.

Vogel, R. and Anau, Z. (1973) 'An operant discrimination task allowing variability of reinforced response patterning', *Journal of the Experimental Analysis of Behavior*, 20, pp. 1–6.

12. The Evolutionary Analogy in Skinner's Writings*

HENRY PLOTKIN

The use of the evolutionary analogy as a means of illuminating problems of individual learning, thinking and problem-solving, as well as in the analysis of socio-cultural processes, goes back over a century. It is still being used today. Skinner began to allude to the analogy in the 1950s, and it became a relatively consistent feature of his writings from the mid-1960s. Thus it may be seen as an important part of Skinner's thinking in the later years of an exceptionally long and prolific career. I will deal with the analogy and Skinner's use of it in two parts. First, I will outline very briefly the history of the evolutionary analogy and where it has led us. This is important because reading Skinner alone will lead one to believe that the analogy begins and ends with him, whereas it has been used and developed by some of the most distinguished of biologists and psychologists to help resolve some of the most fundamental problems in the field. I will argue that though the analogy is an analytical device it also reflects an identity of process. Second, I will evaluate Skinner's use of the analogy against that background. I will conclude that by and large Skinner referred to the analogy merely to point to surface similarities and consequently that he never employed it to any real conceptual advantage.

THE EVOLUTIONARY ANALOGY

The heart of the evolutionary analogy is as follows: whatever process or set of processes accounts for biological evolution (i.e., adaptation and speciation), there is a similar process or set of processes that accounts for other knowledge-gaining

* My thanks to Donald Campbell, Celia Heyes, Justin Joffe and John Odling-Smee for commenting on an early draft of this chapter.

or generating phenomena such as learning, thinking and culture. I will later 'harden' this analogy into an identity of process, but for the moment we can take it that the evolutionary analogy has been used like any other analogy. That is, an understanding of one process is used as a model, as an illumination, of another process. Nagel (1961) provides a classic account of the role of analogy in scientific thinking.

It must follow that the account of learning, thinking and culture that results depends upon the theory of evolution that is espoused as the model upon which the analogy is to be based. (Of course, it assumes that our understanding of evolution is more advanced than our understanding of learning and thinking. This may not be true. But if my argument for identity of process is correct, it does not matter which way we run the analogy — our understanding of how evolution works can and should be illuminated by our understanding of cognitive processes in the individual or cultural interactions between individuals.) Thus Spencer's pre-Darwinian psychology was essentially Lamarckian and held that a progressive, directed, evolution had resulted inevitably in the perfection of the mind of nineteenth century man. However, the great impetus for a biological psychology, including the use of the evolutionary analogy, came from the success of Darwinian theory and so it is with these post-Darwinian developments that we are concerned.

After 1859 some of the earliest uses of the evolutionary analogy are to be found in the parallels that were drawn between the Darwinian notion of the struggle for existence amongst the myriad forms of a species and a struggle for existence between the parts of developing organisms. Oppenheim (1982) cites a review by T.H. Huxley in 1869 of one of Haekel's books as an early example; and in 1881 a book by Roux bore the title *The Struggle of the Parts of the Organism*. The first use of the evolutionary analogy in the context of learning, thinking and culture that I know of is by William James: 'A remarkable parallel, which to my knowledge has never been noticed, obtains between the facts of social evolution and the mental growth of the race, on the one hand, and of zoological evolution, as expounded by Mr. Darwin, on the other' (James, 1880, p. 441). Following an extended argument for the undirected nature of evolution (i.e., the variant forms are unrelated to selection pressures), he concluded that:

> . . . new conceptions, emotions and active tendencies which evolve are originally produced in the shape of random images, fancies, accidental outbirths of spontaneous variation in the functional activity of the excessively unstable human brain, which the outer environment . . . *selects* . . . just as it selects morphological and social variations due to molecular accidents of an analogous sort. (p. 456)

It is of interest that, unlike later writers, James explicitly denied the application of the evolutionary analogy to the 'lower strata' of the mind, which includes the 'entire field of habit and association by contiguity' (p. 455) which, in his view, appeared to be 'passively plastic'. Thus for James the analogy held for ideation but not for learning. It was Baldwin who extended the analogy to learning: 'The individual's learning processes are by a method of functional "trial and error" which illustrates "natural" in the form of "functional selection"' (Baldwin, 1910, p. 32). He also introduced the notion of organic selection by envisaging a confluence of genetic predisposition and some developmental disequilibrium that reinforces the expression of that disposition in the phenotype.

Baldwin influenced (or at least forms a historical bridge with) the thinking of Piaget, who argued over several decades for an identity of process between human cognition and evolution, rather than mere analogy. For example, in his principal work on biology he wrote that 'our main hypothesis is the supposition that cognitive mechanisms are an extension of the organic regulations from which they are derived' (Piaget, 1971, p. 346). It is well-known that Piaget was critical of the central tenet of Darwinian theory, namely its undirected nature. That, however, is beside the point here. For Piaget the processes responsible for adaptive organization are the same at all levels — genetic, epigenetic, individual learning and thinking.

Other writers from a variety of fields have used the evolutionary analogy, notably Popper and Ashby. The interested reader can find a complete review in Campbell (1974). For our purposes, the work of two individuals merits special mention — that of Lorenz and of Campbell himself.

One of the most persistent and central problems of psychology has been the relationship between nature and nurture and how each in some way determines behaviour. The behaviourist tradition never denied the existence of innate or instinctive behaviour, the very acknowledgment of which powerfully perpetuated the notion of a dichotomy between nature and nurture. Skinner recognized that animals may be predisposed to learn certain things and quite frequently referred to such predispositions, for example, 'An innate capacity to be reinforced by damage to others traceable to phylogenic contingencies' (Skinner, 1969, p. 211) when writing about aggression; and 'a susceptibility to reinforcement by proximity to the mother' (Skinner, 1966a, p. 5) when discussing imprinting. Yet the significance and implications of such learning predispositions were never discussed or analyzed by him.

Lorenz (1965) recognized that resolution of the nature-nurture problem lay in eliminating the dichotomy. This he achieved by arguing that learning (nurture) is itself innately, phylogenetically determined. That is, nature and nurture are not separate — learning is innately caused and hence so too is what is learned. Whatever the relationship is between nature and nurture, the idea (or the metaphors implying) a separateness of influence or cause will not describe it. Rather, nature and nurture appear to be different components of some larger, more inclusive process, and that process is described in terms of the evolutionary analogy — some kind of trial-and-error or trial-and-success algorithm.

Learning was thus seen by Lorenz as just one of several components of what he termed 'adaptive modifications', and all show the properties of adaptation which 'is a process which molds the organism so that it fits its environment in a way achieving survival' and 'any molding of the organism to its environment is a process so closely akin to that of forming, within organic structure, an image of the environment that it is completely correct to speak of information concerning the environment being acquired by the organism' (Lorenz, 1965, p. 7). So all adaptations are partly the end-products of knowledge-gaining processes, and learning has the curious property of being simultaneously both one of those processes and a product of knowledge-gain at some other level.

Donald T. Campbell's contribution was made in an important series of papers in which he argued for a nested hierarchy of knowledge processes, all of which operate identically by generating variants, selecting certain of these variants and then propagating the selected variants. Like Lorenz, Campbell's use of the evolu-

tionary analogy assumed an identity of process at whatever level knowledge is being gained, be it at a fundamental genetic level, or at a more elevated level such as non-mnemonic problem-solving, the formation of habits, learning by imitation, or even the operation of science. A very important feature of Campbell's position is that the nested hierarchy allows 'shortcuts' between levels. Knowledge gained at a more fundamental level of the hierarchy by possibly lengthy and laborious repetition of the *a posteriori* selective-retention algorithm may then appear at a less fundamental level where it may seem to be *a priori* knowledge. In this way Campbell's scheme can explain all notions of evolutionary Kantianism and in particular Lorenz's innate bases of learning that guide learning to its adaptive outcomes. Campbell's best-known work, as well as some subsequent developments in the use of the analogy, can be found in Plotkin (1982).

Whether one uses the analogy as an analytical device or adopts the stronger view that there is an identity of process, the analogy clearly sets certain empirical questions and directions, even if few of them have yet been substantially investigated. If we consider only learning, these include understanding the precise nature of the relationship between learning and other knowledge-gaining processes, notably development and socio-culture; the way in which different learning forms arise out of the mix of component subprocesses of the analogy and how these relate to the dimension of stereotypy and innovation; and the relationship of the component subprocesses to the processes postulated by traditional learning theory. Only Staddon (1983) has pursued an empirical programme of any depth. Obviously, if the analogy is allowed to run its full course, for example embracing cultural evolution as well, then many other empirical issues are raised.

I have tried in this half of the chapter to show how even a brief survey of the use of the evolutionary analogy reveals a conceptually rich area with a potentially powerful role to play in synthesizing theory across diverse parts of biology; and that the analogy is not empirically empty. With this as our background, we are now in a position to evaluate the way in which Skinner used the analogy.

SKINNER AND THE EVOLUTIONARY ANALOGY

If science is a way of thinking about the world, and if that thinking is partly and importantly guided and disciplined by attempts to match that thinking to what is actually out there, then there is point to the argument that the evolutionary analogy is not yet a part of science — its empirical day has yet to come. This is no less the case for Skinner than for anyone else who has used the analogy, but it is much the stranger since Skinner has been the most important and consistent exponent of the positivist-empiricist tradition in the behavioural sciences. Why did Skinner of all people not cash in the analogy for some real empirical payoff? In what follows I will argue that there were two reasons for this. One is that it was only in the last ten years (which in the Skinnerian timescale is recent) that the force of the analogy as reflecting an underlying identity of process was realized by him. Before that the analogy was referred to in a loose and casual manner. The second is that when it might have been of real use to him the analogy was simply incompatible with a behaviourist approach to learning.

Because of the length of time over which Skinner has been writing, and because of his very large output, it is helpful to get some kind of chronological

perspective on his references to the evolutionary analogy. I have not read every-thing that he wrote and so cannot claim absolute accuracy for the next few sentences, but I have read enough to know that it is essentially correct. *The Behavior of Organisms* (1938) contains no reference to the analogy. Neither can I find any mention of it in the first edition of *Cumulative Record* (1959), about half of which contains papers first published prior to 1950. However, *Science and Human Behavior* (1953) attributes the apparent purposefulness of behaviour to the fact that 'in both operant conditioning and the evolutionary selection of behavioral characteristics, consequences alter future probability' (p. 90). This was an important issue for Skinner, and I shall refer to it later as the teleology problem. In the same book he argues that a selection-of-variants notion applies not only to biological evolution and operant learning (p. 340), but that 'the evolution of cultures appears to follow the pattern of the evolution of species' (p. 434). *Contingencies of Reinforcement* (1969) contains numerous references to the analogy between operant learning and evolution as it appeared in essays published over the ten or fifteen years preceding that date; *The Technology of Teaching* (1968) contains passages extending the analogy to cultural evolution; and the third edition of *Cumulative Record* (1972) extended the analogy to discussions of creativity. In Skinner's *Notebooks* (1980) I found eight references to the analogy, these being dated 1966, 1969, 1969, 1972, 1975, 1976, 1976, and 1977. In a personal note to me Skinner wrote that he thought the 1966 and 1981 *Science* papers the 'main things' that he had written about the analogy. I will treat these and the 1975 paper on 'The Shaping of Phylogenic Behavior' separately because of their importance.

The above is not an exhaustive listing. The analogy, for example, also appears in *Beyond Freedom and Dignity* (1971) and in *Reflections on Behaviorism and Society* (1978). Doubtless it is present in other publications too. The point of all these dates is that there does seem to be a pattern: no references to the analogy before 1950, and then only sparing references before the 1960s; from the mid-1960s it becomes a common feature of his writings; in 1981 the analogy is written of in terms of an identity of process operating at all (in his scheme, three) levels of living systems. I would claim that there is a discernible drift towards the 'identity view' over the preceding twenty years. But I will argue that what identity he establishes is at some cost and does not constitute a coherent system of thinking.

The Respondent-Operant Distinction

The distinction between elicited respondent behaviour and emitted operant behaviour (Skinner, 1935, 1938) is the cornerstone of Skinner's writings. His emphasis on the pre-eminence of operant behaviour is what marks Skinner off from other major learning theorists, and the way he formulated the problem of understanding operant behaviour is, it seems to me, what inevitably led him to the evolutionary analogy. I am not concerned here with whether the distinction between respondents and operants can or cannot be maintained. What is impor-tant is that Skinner's description of these two kinds of behaviour and their associated forms of learning, corresponding roughly to Pavlov's conditioning and Thorndike's trial-and-error learning, implies the existence of two fundamentally

different processes. When respondent behaviour enters into a learning relationship it is explained by a process of 'instruction'. That is, some stimulus or stimulus configuration becomes associated with a reinforcing stimulus and comes to elicit (in some way cause) a response similar to that previously elicited by the reinforcing stimulus. What is learned is an absolutely determined association between stimuli and reflexive responses — the learning does not, cannot, go beyond these explicit events and the temporal parameters that relate them. This is what I mean by 'instruction'. It is important to note that Skinner seems never to have doubted the existence of respondent learning.

Operant learning is quite different according to Skinner. Responses are emitted spontaneously. 'I do not mean that there are no originating forces in spontaneous behaviour but simply that they are not located in the environment. We are not in a position to see them, and we have no need to' (Skinner, 1938, p. 20). If an operant is followed by a reinforcing event then the strength of that operant is increased and it is more likely to occur in the future. Because operants seem to be spontaneously generated (' . . . there is always an element of mystery in the emission of any operant response' (Skinner, 1968, p. 137)) what learning an operant enters into depends upon the temporal relationship that that operant bears to a reinforcer — the reinforcer 'picks out' the operant by virtue of that relationship, and hence the operant need not be causally related, at least non-trivially, to the reinforcer. 'The consequences of action change the organism regardless of how or why they follow' (Skinner, 1966b, p. 14). However, usually the relationship *is* one of non-trivial causation. Furthermore, 'the greater part of the conditioned behaviour of the adult organism' (1938, p. 19) is of this sort.

So most learning depends, at least initially, on the spontaneous generation of operants, the selection of these operants by reinforcers, and as a result their probability of future occurrence is increased. Spontaneous generation seems to have a chance element about it, as does the selection process itself. For these reasons operants are not determined with the precision of respondents. The learning may be described as 'selective' and works on an algorithm of generating random variants, their selection by reinforcement, and their selective retention for some future reoccurrence due to a weighting that alters their probability of occurrence. This, of course, is a statement of the principal processes of Darwinian evolution. That is the form of the evolutionary analogy that Skinner came increasingly to refer to when discussing operant learning — even if he employed slightly different phrases.

Did Skinner Really Use the Analogy?

I have written of Skinner's 'references' to the analogy. But did he ever *use* it in the sense described earlier? That is, did what is known of the evolutionary process stand for Skinner as a model to illuminate operant learning and help in understanding some of the problems that it presents? Did the analogy inspire an empirical programme? The answer to all these questions is 'no', and the reason is not difficult to find.

Consider first the problem of teleology. Skinner rejects an explanation of the seeming end-directed nature of behaviour in terms of a knowing learner that has purposes and intentions and hence acts as if having knowledge of the future.

But his explanation for the seeming end-directedness of learned behaviour in terms of the Law of Effect is itself teleological. How can the consequences of an act alter that act? In his own words, 'Some effects seem to throw light on the behavior which produces them, but their explanatory role has been clouded by the spectre of teleology' (Skinner, 1966b, p. 12). That statement referred to purposes or goals, but are not reinforcers the same kinds of 'effects' as purposes or goals? Skinner clearly sees the difficulty because he offers two ways around it. One is to suggest that operants and their reinforcers are 'approximately simultaneous' (Skinner, 1966b, p. 12), a formulation that is offered in a number of places with slight variation of the phrasing. But this is simply incorrect. The whole spirit of Skinner's enterprise is that animals act upon their environment, change it, and are changed in turn by the consequences of their actions (see the opening sentences to *Verbal Behavior*, 1957). Operant behaviour *causes* certain effects, and some of these are reinforcers. There can be no simultaneity — the arrow of time moves in just one direction for biology. So a strict behaviourist account seems to be dangerously close to teleology. It would not be so if it took the evolutionary analogy seriously, since the teleological trap is avoided by postulated or known entities that are conserved across the troublesome time interval between the appearance of a phenotypic attribute and its selection. For evolutionary biology genetic structures and their expression as enduring phenotypic structures provide a continuity in time upon which selection can act without any contra-causal implications. The relationship between operants and reinforcers could be treated analogously. But to do so requires the postulation, in a causal capacity, of enduring internal (cognitive and/or physical) states. Since this is contrary to the behaviourist credo, Skinner cannot do this and so the evolutionary analogy has no role to play in this way.

Another way out of the teleological trap for Skinner is to argue, as he does, that 'it is not correct to say that operant reinforcement "strengthens the response which precedes it". The response has already occurred and cannot be changed. What is changed is the future probability of responses of the same *class*. It is the operant as a class of behavior, rather than the response as a particular instance, which is conditioned' (Skinner, 1953, p. 87; see also Skinner, 1966b). This is sound argument and it directly relates to the point made in the previous paragraph because a response 'class' smacks of something that has the property of being enduring. But it is also a postulated, unobserved, covert entity. Skinner is saving his position on teleology by having recourse to a hypothetical construct and so straying from the straight and narrow path of radical behaviourism (see Verplanck, 1954, for demonstrations of other deviations of this kind). And very importantly, Skinner fails to tell us how to set the limits on response classes. How are we to know that a succeeding response belongs to the same class as one that preceded it?

There is a second, serious, difficulty for Skinner to which the evolutionary analogy, properly used, could have provided a solution. This is the question of the origin of the operants. Where do they come from? It is worth repeating Skinner's curious phrase that 'there is always an element of mystery in the emission of any operant response.' The mystery lies partly in no operant ever being wholly under stimulus control, and partly because within Skinner's scheme it is the spontaneity of the operants that provides behaviour with its rich diversity and with the potential for 'newness', originality, creativity.

Skinner attempts to account for the provenance of operants by extraordinarily vague references to evolutionary theory, sometimes with regard to the origin of the species and other times to the origins of novel phenotypic attributes. 'The key term in Darwin's title is Origin' (Skinner, 1972, p. 353). Indeed so. Also:

> It once seemed necessary to attribute the extraordinary diversity of living things to a creative mind — until genetic and evolutionary theories of the origin of species provided an alternative. It is not surprising that anthropocentric explanations should be abandoned last of all in accounting for novel forms of human behaviour, but alternative explanations are available. New responses are generated by accidental arrangements of variables as unforseeable as the accidental arrangements of molecules'or genes. Scientific discovery and literary artistic inventions can often be traced to a kind of fortuitous programming of necessary contingencies. (Skinner, 1968, p. 180)

Especially revealing is his essay 'Creating the Creative Artist' (1972, pp. 333–44), which is replete with references to devices for generating 'mutations' and how 'selection' operating on these then results in a 'creation', a work of art. The entire piece is built upon the evolutionary analogy. But it is fatally flawed conceptually because Skinner's adherence to radical behaviourism places him in a position identical with that of the pre-Mendelian evolutionist. He knows that something is generating the novel forms (the cognitive equivalents of genetic processes) but, unlike the pre-Mendelian who was merely ignorant, Skinner is wilfully disregarding. Surely Skinner must know that the modern synthesis arose through the marrying of the concept of natural selection with genetics. Proper use of the evolutionary analogy requires a similar synthesis between an autoselection kind of process, i.e., an internally mediated selection of environmental contingencies analogous to natural selection (Plotkin and Odling-Smee, 1981), and the generation of variants (operants if one prefers). The latter can only emerge from processes occurring inside the heads of learners, just as the genetic processes partly responsible for variant phenotypes occur inside cells.

One can press the criticism further. Skinner is not just like the pre-Mendelian evolutionist. He is also like the post-Mendelian geneticist who refuses to believe that the phenotypic attributes that are manipulated by selective breeding experiments, and their statistical properties, can ever be explained in terms of what is happening inside the nuclei of cells. That is, he sees the effects, systematically controls them and then declares that they are adequately explained by his manipulations rather than by some as yet unobserved processes. Refusing to recognize the essential contribution of these internal processes not only deprives Skinner of a proper account of a phenomenon like creativity, but it also leaves him without an empirical programme. The 'mutations' that Skinner rightly sees as essential to creativity are not available for study. All that he can suggest are ways by which artists can increase their 'mutation rates'. But he tells us nothing of how the mutations may be investigated in terms of their provenance, their frequencies relative to different kinds of activities (operants), or how they are expressed behaviourally. We are not even told how to measure the diversity caused by these mutations. Contrast this with the evolutionary biologist for whom 'diversity is the basis of ecosystems and the cause of competition and symbiosis; it also makes natural selection possible', and 'what is particularly significant is that one can ask very similar questions concerning diversity at each hierarchical level, such as the extent or variance of the diversity, its mean value, its origin, its functional role, and its selective significance' (Mayr, 1982, p. 133). All of this is denied Skinner

whose conceptual position is impossible — he is an evolutionist who refuses to accept the relevance of genetics and epigenetics to evolution. That is why Skinner can only acknowledge the evolutionary analogy. He can never use it.

Three Important Essays

'The Phylogeny and Ontogeny of Behavior' (1966b) fails because Skinner never states a view as to what the relationship is between phylogeny and ontogeny. Again, the reason for this is the same as that given in the previous section — the failure is inherent in radical behaviourism. Whatever its reason, it leaves us with an implicit dichotomy between nature and nurture. This is so retrograde a step that the parallels between evolution and ontogeny that are drawn, and which are no better in this piece than they are elsewhere, lose all their force. In my view this essay is amongst the worst of Skinner's writings on the evolutionary analogy and adds nothing to his previous work (see Plotkin, 1984, for a lengthier criticism of this paper).

'The Shaping of Phylogenic Behavior' (1975) is a very different matter. Here Skinner provides us with the only attempt that I know of (apart from his own earlier note in Skinner, 1969, p. 217) to run the analogy in the reverse direction. That is, he uses what is known about how behaviour with complex topography can be shaped by appropriate contingencies of reinforcement to help understand the way in which continental drift has shaped, through the action of natural selection, the seemingly bizarre migratory behaviour of turtles, eels and salmon. That continental drift can account for certain aspects of migratory behaviour is not a new idea. What *is* novel in Skinner's hands is that the explanation of 'phylogenic' behaviour is successfully achieved by his use of the evolutionary analogy. This paper is Skinner's only real achievement with — his only real *use* of — the evolutionary analogy.

'Selection by Consequences' (1981) is potentially important because it is in this essay that Skinner clearly establishes an identity of process among biological evolution, operant learning and cultural evolution. The identity revolves around all three 'levels' operating on the basis of an identical 'causal mode', i.e., selection by consequences. Apart from the unresolved teleology problem at the second level, the potential of the paper is lost partly because Skinner seems not to understand the dynamic, reciprocal nature of selection processes (see Plotkin and Odling-Smee, 1984, for a more detailed comment on this point), and partly because of what Dennett (1983) refers to as Skinner's curious form of 'bland assertion'. Skinner, in this paper, seems to have given up any kind of analysis, formal or otherwise. We are simply told, and the telling is unconvincing and inadequate.

There is a further curious feature of the *Science* papers. Both, especially the 1981 piece, give a sense of attempting a synthesis in an important sense; both seem to be statements by Skinner that are meant to have real generality. Yet that synthesis has no room for respondent conditioning which, in Skinner's scheme, lies outside the selection-by-consequences framework. This means either that the synthesis that Skinner attempts is inherently incomplete, or that the level of analysis is so poor that the omission is not noticed. I suspect that it may be both.

So while Skinner may feel that the *Science* papers are his principal contribu-

tions to the evolutionary analogy, I would beg to disagree with him. If I were to direct readers to just two of his papers which illustrate Skinner's involvement with the analogy, I would suggest 'The Shaping of Phylogenic Behavior' for its success, and 'Creating the Creative Artist' for the way that essay highlights the difficulties that a radical behaviourist will always have when attempting to use the analogy.

CONCLUSIONS

I have tried to show that, though the evolutionary analogy became an increasingly prominent part of Skinner's writing, his radical behaviourism was always an obstacle to its adequate implementation. Skinner never achieved what Lorenz, Piaget or Campbell achieved with the analogy because the latter had no conceptual scruples about thinking about unobservables. Few scientists do. But radical behaviourism is not rational in this respect; it is idealogical and that is no way to do science. The very fact that Skinner never refers to the use of the analogy by others shows the extent to which his own work was forced to an isolationism born of an idealogical stance.

On the other hand, in writing this piece I have had to read more Skinner than I ever done before, and I confess to emerging with a much greater respect for his work. If Skinner had been able to wed his exposition of the operant to a more tolerant, dare I repeat, rational, view of internal processes, then his application of the evolutionary analogy might have yielded quite profound success.

REFERENCES

Baldwin, J.M. (1910) *Darwin and the Humanities*, London, Allen and Unwin.

Campbell, D.T. (1974) 'Evolutionary epistemology', in Schilpp, P.A. (Ed.), *The Philosophy of Karl Popper*, Book 1, La Salle, Open Court, pp. 413–63.

Dennett, D.C. (1983) 'Intentional systems in cognitive ethology', *The Behavioural and Brain Sciences*, 6, pp. 343–90.

James, W. (1880) 'Great men, great thoughts and the environment', *Atlantic Monthly*, 46, pp. 441–59.

Lorenz, K. (1965) *Evolution and the Modification of Behaviour*, Chicago, Ill., University of Chicago Press.

Mayr, E. (1982) *The Growth of Biological Thought*, Cambridge, Mass., Harvard University Press.

Nagel, E. (1961) *The Structure of Science*, London, Routledge and Kegan Paul.

Oppenheim, R.W. (1982) 'Preformation and epigenesis in the origins of the nervous system and behaviour', in Bateson, P.P.G. and Klopfer, P.H. (Eds), *Perspectives in Ethology*, Vol. 5, London, Plenum, pp. 1–100.

Piaget, J. (1971) *Biology and Knowledge*, Edinburgh, Edinburgh University Press.

Plotkin, H.C. (1982) *Learning, Development and Culture: Essays in Evolutionary Epistemology*, Chichester, Wiley.

Plotkin, H.C. (1984) 'Nature and nurture revisited', *The Behavioral and Brain Sciences*, 7, pp. 695–6.

Plotkin, H.C. and Odling-Smee, F.J. (1981) 'A multiple-level model of evolution and its implications for sociobiology', *The Behavioral and Brain Sciences*, 4, pp. 225–68.

Plotkin, H.C. and Odling-Smee, F.J. (1984) 'Linear and circular causal sequences', *The Behavioral and Brain Sciences*, 7, pp. 493–4.

Skinner, B.F. (1935) 'Two types of conditioned reflex and a pseudotype', *Journal of General Psychology*, 12, pp. 66–77.

Skinner, B.F. (1938) *The Behavior of Organisms*, New York, Appleton-Century-Crofts.

Skinner, B.F. (1953) *Science and Human Behavior*, New York, The Free Press.

Skinner, B.F. (1957) *Verbal Behavior*, New York, Appleton-Century-Crofts.

Skinner, B.F. (1959) *Cumulative Record*, 1st ed., New York, Appleton-Century-Crofts.

Skinner, B.F. (1966a) 'The phylogeny and ontogeny of behavior', *Science*, 153, pp. 1205–13.

Skinner, B.F. (1966b) 'Operant behavior' in Honig, W.K. (Ed.), *Operant Behavior*, New York, Appleton-Century-Crofts, pp. 12–32.

Skinner, B.F. (1968) *The Technology of Teaching*, New York, Appleton-Century-Crofts.

Skinner, B.F. (1969) *Contingencies of Reinforcement*, New York, Appleton-Century-Crofts.

Skinner, B.F. (1971) *Beyond Freedom and Dignity*, London, Jonathan Cape.

Skinner, B.F. (1972) *Cumulative Record*, 2nd ed., New York, Appleton-Century-Crofts.

Skinner, B.F. (1975) 'The shaping of phylogenic behavior', *Acta Neurobiologia Experimentalis*, 35, pp. 409–15.

Skinner, B.F. (1978) *Reflections on Behaviorism and Society*, Englewood Cliffs, N.J., Prentice-Hall.

Skinner, B.F. (1980) *Notebooks*, ed. Epstein, R., Englewood Cliffs, N.J., Prentice-Hall.

Skinner, B.F. (1981) 'Selection by consequences', *Science*, 213, pp. 501–4.

Staddon, J.E.R. (1983) *Adaptive Behaviour and Learning*, Cambridge, Cambridge University Press.

Verplanck, W.S. (1954) 'Burrhus F. Skinner', in Estes, W.K. *et al.* (Eds), *Modern Learning Theory*, New York, Appleton-Century-Crofts, pp. 267–316.

Interchange

RICHELLE REPLIES TO PLOTKIN

Plotkin has summarized, in a concise and illuminating manner, the history of the evolutionary analogy as applied to learning processes. That part of his chapter could, appropriately, serve as an introduction to my own contribution. His account of that particular aspect of Skinner's theory reflects a careful, sympathetic and critical reading of Skinner's work, as elegantly mentioned in the last paragraph of his conclusion. Plotkin uses essentially the same references as I do in Skinner's writing chronology. Divergences on minor points will not be discussed here because of lack of space (for instance, I do not agree that it was only in the last ten years that Skinner realized *the identity of process*; he has done since 1953, if we want to retain written evidence only).

We differ on one fundamental point, to which I shall devote the present commentary. Plotkin points, as I do, to the fact that Skinner has not really used the evolutionary analogy in empirical research that would have demonstrated its heuristic value within his theory. I have argued that the reasons for this were historical[1] and methodological. Plotkin contends that the main reason is to be found in the behaviourist approach itself, which is of an ideological rather than rational nature. He admits that Skinner came close to the truth, but that he remained blind to it because he was biased by his adhesion to the behaviourist credo — something similar to the Jews not being able to acknowledge the Messiah.

Unfortunately, Plotkin does not tell us clearly how he defines the behaviourist ideological stand. We have to guess from indirect or implicit qualifications which, I feel, do not apply fairly to Skinner. There is nothing in Skinner's view that excludes *enduring states* of the organism, that would provide the link between operants and reinforcers. Skinner has insisted that when an operant is shaped, the subject is changed; and that it is this changed organism that behaves afterwards, and so on. He has dealt with the important problem of the time gap — which can be months or years — between effective selection of an operant by reinforcer and its emission on a later occasion showing evidence of its increased strength. That these changes could be described as physical states — potentially in the language of physiology — was also obvious for Skinner. All this Plotkin denies to Skinner because he (Plotkin) assimilates the enduring internal states to *cognitive* states. The conflict seems to be between some sort of cognitivism and some sort of behaviourism and it would take more than 800 words to clarify it. The term 'cognitive states' would require precise qualifications no less than the term 'behaviourist approach'. Though the problem of intentionality remains one of the

most difficult issues in psychology, Skinner's formulation of behaviour is typically teleonomic, in Pittendrigh's sense, and definitely non-teleological. Plotkin rightly mentions the concept of *response class* in relation to this issue. It is, as is well-known, an early and crucial concept in Skinner's thinking; it is crucial with respect to the evolutionary analogy in that it provides the 'range of freedom' in which behavioural variation will occur.

Skinner, as I have argued in my chapter, cannot be blamed for not having elucidated the provenance of the operant. True, he might have drawn more specifically from some fields of psychology and ethology to be less vague about the 'element of mystery', as some others have done (see my references to Segal, 1972, and to Staddon and Simmelhag, 1971, and also, of course, Plotkin's reference to Staddon, 1983). I still do not think that what we know of those 'processes occurring inside the heads of learners' is comparable to what is known of genetic processes today. We might be closer to pre-Mendelian ignorance than Plotkin has us believe. My divergence from Plotkin might be reducible to difference in our respective ways of looking at and judging Skinner's contribution to science. Plotkin takes it as a closed system, based on some *a priori* ideology (radical behaviourism) that has doomed to sterility the most promising intuitions throughout a whole intellectual career, and has 'forced' Skinner to isolationism. 'The fact that Skinner never refers to the use of the analogy by others' is given as an unambiguous sign of the weight of the ideological stance. What is precisely the demarcation between ideology, as Plotkin uses the word here, and paradigm?

Evaluated by such criteria, many great scientists could be suspected of the same sin. I have pointed to the *reciprocal* ignorance of Piaget and Skinner (see my reference to Richelle, 1976; and also Richelle, 1977). Another case is Popper, also mentioned by Plotkin, who wrote a whole essay aimed at accounting for knowledge in an evolutionary framework (Popper and Eccles, 1981) and did not even mention Piaget, whose *Biology and Knowledge* (1971) is available to any English graduate student. Great theorists seem to exhibit a tendency to ignore some of their fellows. Let us face it: maybe this behaviour has some evolutionary advantage.

Unlike Plotkin, I think of Skinner's work, as of the work of any influential scientist, as an open and dynamic system. Parts of it that might look imperfectly worked out in some respects might prove most stimulating for future research and most fruitful in generating a theory to integrate previously isolated pieces of the puzzle of behaviour.

NOTE

1 In addition to historical reasons already mentioned in my chapter, one should recall that, by the time he first realized the importance of the evolutionary analogy, Skinner was busy with the final stage of his career as an experimenter, fully devoted to the analysis of reinforcement schedules (the *selection* half of the analogy). From 1960 he did very little experimental work himself, and did not supervize much either. This was a matter of personal choice, and he cannot be blamed because his students did not immediately and spontaneously start experimenting on *variation*. Piaget, who had a much more directive style, continued until his death to give his co-workers instructions for experiments.

REFERENCES

Piaget, J. (1971) *Biology and Knowledge*, Chicago, Ill., University of Chicago Press.
Popper, K. and Eccles, J. (1981) *The Self and Its Brain*, Berlin, Springer.
Richelle, M. (1977) *B.F. Skinner ou le Péril behaviouriste*, Brussels, Mardaga.

PLOTKIN REPLIES TO RICHELLE

Richelle asks whether Skinner was biologically naive, and if so, how naive. Doubtless Skinner himself will have the last word on this. My judgment, which is based on his writings from about 1950 to 1980, which is when his references to the evolutionary analogy were developing and changing in character, is that he *was* biologically naive, and quite considerably so. I see no references in his own writings to suggest that he was widely read in biology. At times he showed at best elementary, at worst deficient, understanding of specific and central issues in evolutionary biology, for example, the notion of homology (Skinner, 1969, p. 101) and the interpretation of Waddington's work on genetic assimilation (Skinner, 1969, p. 204). I know of no single instance of his referring to the use of the evolutionary analogy in the writings of others. So not only would I judge him to have been naive with respect to biology, but I think that he was unscholarly and isolated as well. Richelle is right to emphasize the potential empirical and theoretical payoff of studies on variation during learning. In doing so he shows a keener appreciation of the uses to which the evolutionary analogy can be put than did Skinner, whose references to the analogy tended to focus on selection. But overall I reject Richelle's assessment of Skinner's use of the evolutionary analogy as being praiseworthy. In my view it is precisely because of Skinner's biological naivety that his exposition on the analogy is one of the more trivial in the literature. It does not begin to compare with the conceptual depth that Lorenz, Piaget and Campbell brought to their use of the analogy.

I also cannot agree with Richelle on a more specific point. He cites some of my own work (Plotkin and Odling-Smee, 1982) as an instance of the view that 'there are as many learning processes as there are species which learn.' I have never written in this vein because I have never held that position. Two points must suffice here. The first is that, contrary to Richelle's assertion, I certainly *do* believe that a general theory of learning is possible. What I do not believe is that the associationist framework into which most of general process theory is cast is adequate. Something like the evolutionary analogy operating via different mechanisms at different levels in a hierarchy of knowledge-gaining processes is what I consider to be the appropriate conceptual scheme for a general theory of learning. Skinner's 1981 *Science* paper is clearly a movement in that direction, but it is a piece entirely without analytic content. Second, the biological boundaries approach has failed to make an impact because its findings were not placed in the context of some more general theory of adaptation. That is why Revusky's jibe about evolutionarily oriented learning theorists aggrandizing minor science at the expense of major science was so potent. But a hierarchy of knowledge-gaining

processes, one of the levels of which corresponds to individual learning, is a general theory of adaptations that explains the findings on the constraints on learning. And it is major science by Revusky's own definition as that which seeks for generality of explanation. I fully concede that Skinner may have had that kind of vision. However, he seemed not to have been able to implement it in any kind of coherent analysis or theory.

REFERENCES

Plotkin, H.C. and Odling-Smee, F.J. (1982) 'Learning in the context of a hierarchy of knowledge gaining processes', in Plotkin, H.C. (Ed.) *Learning Development and Culture*, Sussex, Wiley, pp. 443–71.

Skinner, B.F. (1969) *Contingencies of Reinforcement*, New York, Appleton-Century-Crofts.

Skinner, B.F. (1981) 'Selection by consequences', *Science*, 213, pp. 501–4.

Part VIII: *The Explanatory Power of Skinnerian Principles*

13. The Explanatory Power of Skinner's Radical Behaviorism*

HOWARD RACHLIN

To assess the absolute explanatory power of Skinner's radical behaviorism would require clearer conceptions than we now have of radical behaviorism, on the one hand, and what it means for a theory to have explanatory power, on the other. An easier task is to compare the explanatory power of radical behaviorism to that of other psychological viewpoints. Therefore, radical behaviorism will be discussed here along with three other viewpoints — mentalism, physiologism and cognitivism.

THE DOMAIN OF PSYCHOLOGY

Like radical behaviorism, mentalism, physiologism and cognitivism are rather points of view, within the scope of which particular theories may be constructed, than theories themselves. As points of view, they differ with regard to the domain over which they extend. Mentalism, for instance, sees the domain of psychology as the inner mental life of human beings. A mentalist deals with behavior only as an indication or 'ambassador' of the inner mental world and denies the behaviorist's claim that the proper sphere of psychology is the overt behavior of human beings and other animals.

* This paper was prepared with the help of a grant from the National Science Foundation.

155

Whatever 'explanatory power' means, it might be expected that each psychological viewpoint would have, within its own domain, maximum explanatory power, diminishing when extended into the domains of other viewpoints. Yet (I claim) radical behaviorism not only has high explanatory power as applied to the overt behavior of human beings and other animals, a point which has usually been conceded by mentalists, but also explains the mental life of human beings — the very field claimed by mentalists as their own — better than mentalism does. To put it another way, mental terms are more meaningful when translated or interpreted by behavioral theories, particularly Skinner's radical behaviorism, than when they are left uninterpreted and used in their everyday, mentalistic, sense.

Unlike mentalism, physiologism and cognitivism may well be superior to behaviorism within their own domains (the physical properties of the nervous system and the simulation of mental processes by computers) but neither theory has the explanatory power of behaviorism as applied to overt behavior of intact animals (behaviorism's own domain) or as applied to the mental life of human beings.

Since other points may be conceded by mentalists, physiologists and cognitivists, this essay will concentrate on the relative explanatory power of the four viewpoints in only one domain — people's mental life. Following is a brief definition of each viewpoint as it incorporates mental terms:

Mentalism: the belief that mental terms refer to internal, instrinsically private events that mediate between environment and behavior and may be revealed by introspection. This is by far the most common of the four viewpoints. It is the viewpoint of common sense as carried by the English language, at least, and possibly by most extant languages. The other three views have made little headway against it.

Physiologism: the belief that mental terms refer to internal events that occur in an organism's nervous system; moreover, that it is proper to use mental terms *only* to refer to internal physiological events. These events are revealed, not by introspection, but by physiological investigation.

Cognitivism: the belief that mental terms refer to internal events, reliably revealed neither by introspection nor by physiological investigation but by overt behavior including verbal behavior. From a careful analysis of overt behavior it is possible to infer the existence of internal events as one might infer the program of a computer from its inputs and outputs. Just as a given computer program may be instantiated in hardware in any number of ways (a computer memory with a given function in the program may consist of bubbles, transistors, vacuum tubes, relays or other devices) cognitivists are not committed to any particular physiology.

Behaviorism: the belief that mental terms refer to overt behavior of intact organisms. Behaviorism differs from the other three viewpoints in that mental events are not supposed to occur inside the organism at all. Overt behavior does not just *reveal* the mind — it *is* the mind. Each mental term stands for a pattern of overt behavior. This may include such mental terms as 'sensation', 'pain', 'love', 'hunger', and 'fear' (terms considered by the mentalist to be 'raw feels') as well as more complex mental states such as 'belief' and 'intelligence' that are sometimes

said to be 'complex mental states' and sometimes 'intentional acts'. Behaviorists differ among themselves as to whether 'raw feels' are overt or covert behavior (Skinner sees them as covert behavior), but the essence of radical behaviorism is the belief that intentional acts are nothing but patterns of overt behavior.

EXPLANATORY POWER

The explanatory power of a theory can be judged along several dimensions. First, the theory itself must be sound relative to others. It should be conceptually elegant, simple, symmetrical, amenable to mathematical or logical expression; it should be easier to remember than the multitude of facts that it is supposed to explain. In other words, it should be aesthetically pleasing by the standards of the society in which it is promulgated. Simplicity and symmetry, presumably, were the features that made Copernican theory win out over Ptolemaic theory which equally well explained the then known astronomical facts.

Second, a theory ought to have a laboratory base of some kind, a sphere, however artificial, where it can be tested. Otherwise, like Freudian theory, it will have to await the fortuitous occurrence of natural events which, due to their complexity, can never be decisive.

Third, a theory ought to have some plausibility as it is extended outside the laboratory. The theory should be able to *interpret* natural events even while it may never wholly explain or predict them. The path of an individual leaf, as it floats down from a tree, for instance, is awkwardly but plausibly interpretable by classical physics in terms of gravity and aerodynamics even though it cannot be predicted as the path of a leaf in a vacuum can be. Plausibility, however, is not the ultimate criterion of a scientific theory. It is plausible that the earth is flat, that the sun moves around the earth and that the deity has a direct influence in individual human affairs ('God punished you', will be our eternal cry whenever a person does something bad and then has an accident). Many of us agree, nevertheless, on other grounds, to reject these ideas in favor of less plausible ones.

Fourth, a theory should have meaningful application in the real world; it ought to prove useful in everyday life. This is the bottom line for a scientific theory. Although it is here presented last, it logically stands first. Other criteria (conceptual elegance, testability, and plausibility) are, pragmatically, subcategories of this one. A theory with good explanatory power must alter human activity in some way for the better. Otherwise it will lose out, eventually, to other scientific theories that do have this effect or, failing their appearance, to custom or common sense.

Let us now turn to Skinner's radical behaviorism and see how it stands, relative to mentalism, physiologism and cognitivism, on these criteria.

RADICAL BEHAVIORISM

Skinner's radical behaviorism, taken by itself, is not a particularly elegant theory. As presented in Skinner's (1938) *Behavior of Organisms* radical behaviorism is little more than an expression of faith that all behavior of humans and animals is composed of respondents, correlated with immediately antecedent events (stimu-

li) and operants, correlated with immediately consequent events (reinforcers). All learning, according to Skinner, consists of respondent conditioning (Pavlovian or 'classical' conditioning) and operant conditioning. The latter can best be understood, Skinner has claimed, by observation of cumulative records wherein patterns of responding are revealed; each type of contingency (schedule of reinforcement) produces a characteristic pattern. Operant conditioning consists of alternation of pattern as reinforcement contingencies are changed. Learning, in this view, is nothing but a shaping or molding of behavior by the environment. The inelegance of this version of the theory (however effective it might be in other respects) is nowhere more clearly exhibited than in Ferster and Skinner's (1957) *Schedules of Reinforcement*, a vast compendium of cumulative records of pigeon subjects with hardly a connecting thread, preditive rule or mathematical description.

This lack of elegance has disappointed Skinner's followers who share (1) his faith that behavior consists of nothing but respondents and operants and (2) his rejection of previous theories of behavior including those of the behaviorists, Hull (1943) and Tolman (1932), on the grounds that they were concerned too much with unobservable inner entities and too little with behavior as such. (Skinner has gone so far in this direction as to reject his own 'reflex reserve' theory as too remote from behavior.) Attempts by Skinner's followers to explain the action of the environment on behavior in a more lawlike (i.e., quantitative) manner include the conception of reinforcement of interresponse times (Shimp, 1982, following Skinner's own suggestion), the conception that animals match aspects of their behavior to the reinforcing patterns of the environment (Herrnstein, 1970), the conception that behavior is governed by economic laws (Rachlin, 1978), the conception that the laws of behavior correspond to the laws of evolution (Staddon, 1979) and the conception that the laws of operant conditioning are subcategories of the laws of respondent conditioning which, in turn, are subject to quantitative expression (Gibbon and Balsam, 1981). It is possible to view all of these conceptions as attempts to organize and predict the effects of schedules of reinforcement on behavior. In this view they are all elaborations of Skinner's original behaviorist program. Among themselves these theories range considerably in simplicity, symmetry, quantitative expression and predictive power. The best of them (which they are will vary with the observer) are easily comparable with any current physiological or cognitive theory in sophistication, mathematical complexity and internal consistency. On these grounds alone there seems to be no reason to adopt behaviorism — rather than physiologism or cognitivism. With regard to mentalism, however, a quantitative, a logical or even an imprecisely formulated theory does not currently exist. To adopt a mentalistic view of psychology, then, is to abandon psychology as a science, to believe what our introspections tell us individually about the working of our minds and to trust to tradition and custom in the guidance of our behavior. Since introspections differ widely among individuals and customs, among societies, mentalism is the psychological equivalent of the tower of Babel.

We turn now to laboratory application of theory. Here Skinnerian radical behaviorism is far superior to all of the other viewpoints principally because Skinner established a standard set of laboratory conditions in which behavior takes certain standard forms. There have been arguments that these conditions are so restrictive that they bear no meaningful relation to conditions in the real

world. We will discuss such arguments later. But there is no question that within the laboratory the principles enunciated by Skinner and the rules, laws and equations discovered by Skinner's followers are generally true. In the past objections have been raised (e.g., Seligman, 1970) that even under the very laboratory conditions specified by Skinner, Skinnerian principles have only limited applicability. But, much as friction and air resistance (originally thought to be limiting factors) have been incorporated into classical physics so as to illuminate rather than contradict its principles, such apparently anomalous phenomena as autoshaping, species-specific defense reactions, instinctive drift, taste-aversion learning and imprinting have been incorporated into radical behaviorist theories (see, for instance, Staddon and Simmelhag, 1971). By comparison, physiological psychology and cognitive psychology have no *standard* laboratory testing ground. Physiological psychology borrows its tests from physiology and biology. To the extent that specifically psychological questions are dealt with by physiological theory, the best laboratory testing procedures have been borrowed from operant conditioning. Cognitive psychology not only has no agreed upon laboratory testing ground, it seems to have as many theories as it has experimental tests of theories, none with any relation to another. This state of affairs may be just a reflection of a current turmoil within cognitive psychology but until agreement is reached on a common laboratory test, the plethora of current cognitive theories, ranging from cognitive decision theory (Kahneman and Tversky, 1984) to imagery theory (Shepard, 1984) to memory theory (Johnson, 1984) to attention theory (Sperling, 1984) cannot be compared with each other, let alone tested against each other.

Mentalistic theory, based on introspection, has, in psychology's distant past, been tested in standard laboratory situations (Titchner, 1896). The problem was that, however rigidly environmental conditions were held constant, introspections would vary unpredictably among individual subjects. Since the object of study (the mind) was supposed to be located inside the subject, this variability became intolerable and the effort to provide a standard laboratory test for introspection collapsed.

With regard to plausibility, behaviorism looks worse than any of the other theories. It seems implausible that a mental event such as a 'hope' could originate outside us and that our behavior, rather than being only a sign or indication of what we hope, is itself the hope. We understand very little about mental events such as hopes. Mentalism, with its vague and shaky reliance on introspection, accurately mirrors our current vague and shaky understanding of mental events. This is what lends mentalism its plausibility. The problem is that mentalism imperializes its own vague and shaky understanding; it provides no path to a more coherent model of the mind.

Physiological psychology is not much more plausible than behaviorism. It uncomfortably marries the molecularity of physiology to our molar mentalistic vocabulary. It does not seem right to say that a hope or a dream is nothing but a chemical reaction in our brains. The mind seems to be something more than that.

Behaviorists have raised the objection to physiological psychology that a mental event such as a belief or an expectation depends on the integration of all the parts of a person as that person interacts with the environment. To expect to find a belief or a hope inside a person is like expecting to find a little automobile inside an automobile. The interior components of a person might be expected to

have their own principles of operation and their own functional characterization, different from those of the person as a whole, just as the carburattor has principles of operation and functional characterization different from those of the car as a whole. Yet the recent discovery of certain interior neural mechanisms in animals (neural structures of *Aplysia* that may be classically conditioned: Hawkins and Kandell, 1984) and the success (albeit poorly understood) of drugs such as lithium in treatment of psychological disorders have lent physiological psychology a degree of plausibility.

Cognitive psychology borrows plausibility in recent times from the success of computers. To the extent that computers have succeeded in simulating human mental functioning, cognitive psychology has become more plausible. In this regard, cognitive psychology is more plausible than it deserves to be. While computers have achieved enormous success in simulating certain elements of human behavior, they are still very far from simulating the complexity of its *functional* (goal-directed) characteristics. Yet it is precisely the functional characteristics of human behavior that make us see it as *mental*; the more distant the goal, the more mental the behavior seems to be. As computers grow more powerful they do *not* grow more human as might have been suspected. A person, even a computer programmer, is much more likely to ascribe malignant intention to a radio or coke machine or an automobile that is out of order at a critical time than to a computer that prints out the message, 'I hate you.' A wagon with a squeaky wheel that 'needs' oil is much more likely to be perceived as in 'pain' than a computer that prints out the message, 'I am in pain'. Because most of us believe that a squirrel cannot think (or cannot think much), we assume that it buries nuts because of 'instinct' — i.e., that the forces that cause it to behave as it does are immediate and innate. But let a squirrel be found that can learn to save 'tokens' of some kind by behaving in some non-natural way, with no other reward than the obtaining of food in two months' time, and the squirrel will suddenly emerge as a thinking animal.

Much of the initial interest in computers by psychologists was based on the supposition that language is the essential ingredient of thought. But now that computers can in all essential respects speak, we see that they *still* cannot think. If this is granted, then the critical component of thought cannot be language. The critical component of thought, behaviorism suggests, is the action of *distant* rewards on current behavior — what we call 'self-control' (and it is the non-humanity of the digital computer that makes this clear). Language (including logic and mathematics) is a highly useful tool for thought. It is undoubtedly an essential tool for abstract forms of human thought, but it is not what we *mean* by thought. As computers become more familiar, their limitations may become more apparent (as has occurred with telephone switching systems and other abandoned mechanical models of thought), and cognitive psychology may become less plausible. Be that as it may, plausibility is the least reliable criterion of explanatory power. Let us turn now to the most reliable criterion: application in the world.

It may seem perverse to argue that mentalism has no meaningful application in the real world since it claims the real world (as opposed to the laboratory) as its area. Yet if we require for meaningful application of a theory (1) that it suggest actions different from those that would have been performed had the theory not been available and (2) that it be distinguishable in its suggested applications from other theories, mentalism fails on both counts. Its problem is that it is much too

flexible. It rationalizes *any* action ('I did it because I wanted to do it', is a prototypical mentalistic rationalization) and it suggests none. Mentalistic language is useful in human communication, not because it expresses an inner state but because it helps us predict each other's behavior. A child who says, 'I want a bicycle', usually will do something to obtain the bicycle or will act happy or show gratitude (sooner or later) after its receipt. If none of these actions occurs, the statement, 'I want a bicycle', serves no function. As it retreats from overt behavior to its home *inside* people, mentalism loses its function in the world. Why, then, do so many of us accept it? Because it provides a convenient cover for our ignorance. When we are ignorant of the cause of one of our own actions it is more convenient to say, 'I did it because I wanted to', than to say, 'I don't know why I did it.' This circumlocution does have an immediate function: it closes off questioning by others when we may want to get on with what we are doing. But its long-term effect is negative — it also closes off our *own* inquiry into our own behavior. More importantly, it closes off inquiry into behavior in general. Just as belief in the deity's direct manipulation of physical objects conveniently hid our previous ignorance of physical laws and closed off physical science for hundreds of years, so the belief in the mental origin of behavior conveniently hides our present ignorance of behavioral laws and closes off behavioral science. This has always been the core of the non-mentalist's argument against mentalism, an argument which no one has made more forcefully or consistently than Skinner.

With regard to meaningful application, both physiological psychology and cognitive psychology are easily disposed of — there has been no meaningful application of either viewpoint. Even if drug therapy for psychological disorders, electroconvulsive shock therapy or psychosurgery are considered to be successful (and all have been severely criticized), none arises in any meaningful way from empirical work or theoretical constructs of physiological psychology. They are rather outgrowths of medical techniques that were found to affect behavior.

Cognitive psychology can claim no more applications in the real world. Perhaps surprisingly, educational practice has been almost untouched by it. Although Piaget's theory of cognitive stages has found wide acceptance among educators, lack of agreement on what constitutes a stage and whether anything can be done to advance a child from one stage to another has hampered meaningful application. So far, cognitive theory seems to have provided only a vocabulary to describe various previously instituted practices. In other words it fails to suggest actions different from customary ones and it is not distinguishable in its suggested applications from other theories, particularly mentalism.

There does exist something called 'cognitive behavior therapy' (Mahoney, 1974). 'Cognitive' is a currently fashionable appellation in American psychology. But cognitive therapy owes absolutely nothing to either the theory or the practice of cognitive psychology. It is rather a superimposition onto behavior therapy of a mentalistic vocabulary and a mentalistic justification of poorly understood practices. For instance, as applied to treatment of chronic pain, cognitive behavior therapy instructs patients to think pleasant thoughts or imagine oneself to be Superman, etc. There is no evidence that any of these 'cognitive' techniques are effective (Turk, Meichenbaum and Genest, 1983).

What, then, of Skinnerian behaviorism in terms of meaningful application? With regard to the two previously mentioned criteria — does it suggest practices different from custom? and do its suggestions differ from those of other theories?

— Skinnerian behaviorism does apply meaningfully to everyday life. In its most general form behaviorism suggests that when behavior does not obviously depend on its antecedents in the world, it depends on its consequences in the world. This emphasis on consequences in theory, in the laboratory and in the real world is behaviorism's central difference from the other three theories. When no *immediate external antecedent* stimulus is discovered for a given act, all three other theories assume that an *immediate internal antecedent* stimulus exists (a mental event, a cognitive event, a brain state) that must have caused the act. The job of all three other theories is to invent such stimuli when none is apparent. Skinnerian behaviorism declines to invent internal causes and instead infers past *external consequences* ('reinforcement history') as the fundamental cause of the action. (For Skinner the inferred consequences must have immediately followed the act. For some of Skinner's followers, although immediate consequences are held to be strongest, consequences distant from an act, but correlated with it, may also alter its frequency.)

How does this difference in theory result in a difference in application? Consider, for instance, a person in chronic pain. Suppose, as is often the case, no apparent stimulus (no sharp or burning object, no cancer, no nervous inflammation) is found antecedent to the pain (or the pain persists chronically after such a stimulus is removed). Then the pain must, according to Skinnerian behaviorism, be an operant. Therefore, the pain must be maintained by its actual overt *consequences* in the environment. These consequences may be immediate — the administration of drugs, for instance — or distant in time from the pain behavior — avoidance of social duties, reduction of work, avoidance of temptation, restructuring of family interactions, etc. Whatever in the real environment is correlated with the behavior in question (the pain, in this instance) may be maintaining that behavior. Skinner's radical behaviorism suggests courses of 'treatment' for such maladaptive behavior, different from custom and those suggested by other theories: first, because a mental event is an overt behavioral event, and a person is no better (and often worse) at observing his or her own behavior than an outside observer, behavioral treatment of maladaptive behavior has often consisted of the provision of feedback (verbal description of contingencies, record keeping, calculation, etc.). Feedback increases the salience of what may have been an initially obscure relationship between behavior and its negative consequences. Many actions (overeating, drug-taking, smoking, etc.) have salient, immediate positive consequences but non-salient, delayed, negative consequences. Feedback helps increase the salience of the more distant consequences, thereby enhancing their control over behavior. Second, when a positive consequence has been maintaining a maladaptive act (as when attention and affection from one family member have been contingent on sickness or pain or aggression of another) behavior therapy has been concerned to remove the dependency of the reward on the maladaptive act while maintaining the reward by making it dependent on a non-maladaptive act. Such behavioral techniques have worked in reduction of chronic pain (Fordyce, 1976) and form the basis for many procedures in family therapy (Jacobson and Bussod, 1983). More recent developments in the operant laboratory have suggested other techniques. For instance, Herrnstein's (1970) matching law suggests ways to manipulate behavior indirectly by rewarding alternative behavior (McDowell, 1984). There is no space here for an extended recounting of the successes of the application of behavioral theory. The point is

that there have been such successes and that these are truly meaningful extensions of Skinner's radical behaviorism to the non-laboratory world.

THE CONSEQUENCES OF APPLYING A THEORY

A theory that is taken out of the laboratory and applied to the real world will, of necessity, apply most easily to those real-world situations that most resemble the laboratory. Thus, classical physics applies better to stones dropped from the leaning tower of Pisa than to feathers dropped from the leaning tower of Pisa. Similarly, Skinner's radical behaviorism, dealing as it does with prediction and control of behavior, applies in a more straightforward way to situations in the real world where the forces of control are most direct — prisons, factories, armies and the like. Radical behaviorism applies less obviously in situations such as family relationships where control is less obvious. But, as indicated above, it does apply meaningfully in those situations too. Other theories do not even apply in areas where control of behavior is obvious. This *should* be a cause for suspicion of those other theories, not for condemnation of behaviorism. If we condemn a theory because it explains a phenomenon that may be an evil phenomenon, we would have to condemn classical physics because it explains the action of cannons better than religion does, and modern physics because it explains the hydrogen bomb better than classical physics does. If mentalism, cognitivism and physiologism, worse as they are admitted to be at explaining factory and prison behavior, were somehow better than radical behaviorism at explaining family behavior or at helping people deal with chronic pain, then there might be a reason to adopt those alternative theories. But the degree of success of mentalism, cognitivism and physiologism in explaining family behavior or at helping deal with chronic pain (or at development of educational methods or at controlling bad habits or at curing mental illness or at achieving world peace) is commensurate with the degree of success of religion in explaining the operation of cannons. If Skinner's radical behaviorism has no explanatory power in the real world, then nothing has. Fortunately, however, there is good reason, in the further development of radical behaviorism, for optimism.

REFERENCES

Ferster, C.B. and Skinner, B.F. (1957) *Schedules of Reinforcement*, New York, Appleton-Century-Crofts.

Fordyce, W.E. (1976) *Behavioral Methods for Chronic Pain and Illness*, St. Louis, Mo., C.V. Mosby.

Gibbon, J. and Balsam, P. (1981) 'Spreading association in time', in Locurto, C.M., Terrace, H.S. and Gibbon, J. (Eds), *Autoshaping and Conditioning Theory*, New York, Academic Press, pp. 219–54.

Hawkins, R.D. and Kandel, E.R. (1984) 'Is there a cell-biological alphabet for simple forms of learning?' *Psychological Review*, 91, pp. 375–91.

Herrnstein, R.J. (1970) 'On the law of effect', *Journal of the Experimental Analysis of Behavior*, 13, pp. 243–66.

Hull, C.L. (1943) *Principles of Behavior*, New York, Appleton-Century.

Jacobson, N.S. and Bussod, N. (1983) 'Marital and family therapy', in Hersen, M., Kazdkin, A.E. and Bellack, A.S. (Eds), *The Clinical Psychology Handbook*, New York, Pergamon Press.

Johnson, M.K. (1984) 'A multiple entry, modular memory system', in Bower, G.H. (Ed.)., *The Psychology of Learning and Motivation: Advances in Research and Theory*, Vol. 17, New York, Academic Press.

Kahneman, D. and Tversky, A. (1984) 'Choices, values and frames', *American Psychologist*, 39, pp. 341–50.

McDowell, J.J. (1984) 'The importance of Herrnstein's mathematical statement of the law of effect for behavior therapy', *American Psychologist*, in press.

Mahoney, M. (1974) *Cognition and Behavior Modification*, Cambridge, Mass., Ballinger.

Rachlin, H. (1978) 'A molar theory of reinforcement schedules', *Journal of the Experimental Analysis of Behavior*, 30, pp. 345–60.

Seligman, M.E.P. (1970) 'On the generality of the laws of learning', *Psychological Review*, 77, pp. 406–18.

Shepard, R.N. (1984) 'Kinematics of perceiving, imagining, thinking and dreaming', *Psychological Review* 91, pp. 417–47.

Shimp, C.P. (1982) 'Reinforcement and the local organization of behavior', in Commons, M.L., Herrnstein, R.J. and Rachlin, H. (Eds), *Quantitative Analyses of Behavior II: Matching and Maximizing Accounts*, Cambridge, Mass., Ballinger.

Skinner, B.F. (1938) *The Behavior of Organisms*, New York, Appleton-Century.

Sperling, G. (1984) 'A unified theory of attention and signal detection', in Parasuraman, R. and Davies, D.R. (Eds), *Varieties of Attention*, New York, Academic Press.

Staddon, J.E.R. (1979) 'Operant behavior as adaption to constraint', *Journal of Experimental Psychology: General*, 108, pp. 48–67.

Staddon, J.E.R. and Simmelhag, V.L. (1971) 'The "superstition" experiment: A reexamination of its implications for the principles of adaptive behavior', *Psychological Review*, 78, pp. 16–43.

Titchner, E.B. (1896) *An Outline of Psychology*, New York, Macmillan.

Tolman, E.C. (1932) *Purposive Behavior in Animals and Men*, New York, Appleton-Century.

Turk, D.C., Meichenbaum, D. and Genest, M. (1983) *Pain and Behavioral Medicine: A Cognitive-Behavioral Perspective*, New York, The Guilford Press.

14. The Explanatory Power of Radical Behaviorism*

HUGH LACEY AND BARRY SCHWARTZ

B.F. Skinner's radical behaviorist program has always been bold, distinctive, significant, and far-reaching. It has also been controversial, for it has involved commitments to the following views.

1   All human behavior is lawful. It is explicable in terms of principles (laws, regularities, generalizations) that can be discovered and confirmed in experimental studies in the laboratory.
2   For the bulk of human behavior, including verbal and purposive behavior, these generalizations involve only current relations between behaviors and environmental factors, together with a person's past history of such relations. Other variables, whether from physiology or from cognitive psychology, are not needed to express these generalizations (see Skinner, 1945, for qualifications of this view).
3   In the light of these generalizations significant controls may be exerted over human behavior, controls that, as they are progressively implemented, promise to resolve major social problems.
4   The achievement of widespread control, both experimental and technological, is a crucial factor, alongside prediction, in evaluating the explanatory claims of a research program.

Skinner recognized that these commitments presuppose a particular view of the human person. He summed it up in these words: 'A person is not an originating agent; he is a locus, a point at which many genetic and environmental variables come together in a joint effort' (Skinner, 1974, p. 168). Acknowledging this view led him to propose a fundamental revision of our discourse about human

* This paper was prepared with the help of National Science Foundation grants SES-838604 (to HL) and BNS82-06670 (to BS).

persons and societal relations, a revision that challenges the assumptions that maintain liberal social and political institutions, and indeed the way we think about moral and political issues in general. This chapter is motivated by the question: is there sufficient support, either theoretical or empirical, for Skinner's commitments for one to take his views as a serious guide to action? We will be concerned principally with evaluating the *comprehensiveness* of the explanatory power of radical behaviorist principles.

EVALUATING COMPREHENSIVENESS

How, then, can the comprehensiveness of behavior principles be assessed? Many refuse to address this question, regarding it as nothing more than distracting speculation, incapable of serious answer until the radical behaviorist research program is much further along. Indeed some become impatient even with Skinner himself when he draws out far-reaching, and thus far unsupported, implications of radical behaviorism. They perceive that such speculation provides an easy target for criticism, while doing little to further the science of behavior. Therefore, before we present our main argument about how comprehensive radical behaviorist principles are, a little needs to be said about why an assessment of comprehensiveness is important, even, or perhaps especially, at this stage of scientific development. There are at least three important reasons for assessing comprehensiveness. They apply to any research program, in any science.

1   A research program (Lakatos, 1978; see Lacey, 1980, for application to behaviorism) provides positive guidelines for research, in large part by constraining what constitutes proper research — what are proper methods, research strategies, and hypotheses. It can be said to be defined by an object of inquiry (e.g., behavior), and by a broadly sketched class of parameters whose effects it systematically and progressively investigates to include more, more complex, and more significant features of the object of inquiry within its explanatory compass. It provisionally assumes that the class of parameters it investigates is broad enough to encompass the object of inquiry. Without a preliminary charting of the general, fundamental features of the object of inquiry, and a plausibility argument that the parameters in question could fully explain it, there is no ground for restricting inquiry in the manner required by the research program. General methodological arguments, dissociated from the specific object of inquiry, cannot provide such a ground (see Lacey, 1974). Thus, for example, the study of behavioral and environmental parameters, and not of cognitive ones, requires a substantive and not just a methodological defense.

2   As Skinner (1971) makes clear, there is a contradiction between the conception of human behavior that informs the behaviorist research program and that which informs dominant social practices. If the latter conception is correct, the behaviorist program cannot produce a comprehensive explanatory account of behavior. Alternatively, if the behaviorist conception is correct, and if it were to become widely accepted, social practices justified by the other conception would be undermined and

displaced. There is no room for compromise here: either the behaviorist program is importantly incomplete, or important social practices are ill-conceived. If the research program is incomplete, sound research must extend beyond it to those features of behavior that cannot be encompassed by the program. In order to uphold any claim to the *priority* of the behaviorist program then, a strong plausibility argument supporting its comprehensiveness is essential.

3   Behaviorists tend to pursue vigorously the application of their discoveries, and for many application constitutes the principal rationale of experimental inquiry. An application is licit only if two conditions are met: first, that it succeeds in bringing about the desired effect; and second, that it does not produce any undesired side-effects. Experiment can settle the first condition. To settle the second, one needs to explore the range of variables on which the applied procedure could have an impact. Suppose, for example, that it is true that behavior is almost exclusively controlled by prevailing contingencies of reinforcement coupled with the organism's past history of reinforcement. If so, one need not look beyond the scope of behaviorism to check for side-effects, and we could reasonably expect that a procedure that merely recasts the prevailing contingencies would not produce adverse effects on human beings. But our expectancy would be different if important behaviors were not explicable in terms of behavioral principles, but instead required, let us say, an appeal to principles of cognitive psychology. Then, achieving control through an applied procedure could well involve the modification of cognitive factors that behavioral principles do not encompass though they may be of central human significance. An example of this sort of side-effect is Schwartz's (1982) demonstration that a history of reinforcement for successful individual responses impaired people's ability to discover generalizations efficiently. Since applied behavior analysts rarely evaluate the licitness of applications in the light of the posits of rival research programs, or the presuppositions that underlie dominant social practices, it follows that their presumption of the licitness of routine application of behavioral principles rests upon a positive assessment of the comprehensiveness of the behaviorist program (see Lacey, 1979).

IS BEHAVIORISM COMPREHENSIVE?

Now that it is clear that an assessment of behaviorism's comprehensiveness is important, it is time to make the assessment. Skinner has maintained that his commitment to comprehensiveness is required if one adopts a scientific stance towards human beings. Certainly, its apparent plausibility is supported by the success of radical behaviorism's scientific research program. It has now been demonstrated in countless experiments that there are principles of the type cited by Skinner, and the range of their manifest exemplification continues to expand (see Schwartz, 1984, for a review). Equally important has been the success of applied behavior analysis, the application of experimentally derived principles to generate control in certain institutions and social contexts.

However, these successes do not tell us how comprehensive radical behavior-

ist principles are. That is because experimental and applied settings, those in which the explanatory power of behavioral principles is clear, have significant characteristics that are lacking in a large and important class of ordinary social settings. They tend to be relatively simple, with few salient variables operating. They are constructed by some human beings to satisfy certain explicit ends, ends that involve the successful control of other human beings (or experimental animals). How comprehensive behavior principles are cannot be settled only by investigation of experimental and applied settings, just as the comprehensiveness of the physics of motion is not settled by the study of objects in a vacuum, or by the construction of cannons. We believe that there are clear limits to the comprehensiveness of behavior principles, and we now turn to the kind of argument that can support this negative assessment. The issue is difficult and complex; it is the kind of issue where a missing of the minds frequently occurs. The reason for this is that we are not asking whether behavior principles currently *are* comprehensive. On this there is virtually no disagreement; everyone acknowledges that there is still much work to be done. Rather, what we are asking, and answering negatively, is whether behavior principles are *in principle* comprehensive. To show that behavior principles cannot produce a comprehensive account of behavior, we must show that there are behaviors that principles consistent with the constraints of the research program cannot explain. How can this be done?

There is both constancy and change as a research program unfolds. Its conception of the object of inquiry and of the parameters worthy of investigation remains more or less constant. The behaviorist commitment to behavior as the object of inquiry, and to certain current and past environmental factors as parameters, is an example of this constancy. While this formulation of the constraints of the research program is quite general, it does conflict with other conceptions, for example, that verbal and purposive behavior are expressions of mental events. While what should be studied is not logically entailed by the behaviorist conception, it does set limits. Reinforcement, punishment, discriminative control, etc. can be studied; mental states cannot. The research program imposes constraints; it rules out some things.

On the other hand, the appropriate, specific set of parameters can change. It can expand, as when Skinner added the domain of operant to that of respondent conditioning. Or it can be transformed in a more fundamental way, as in recent attempts to incorporate behavioral principles into the broad framework provided by micro-economic theory (e.g., Rachlin *et al.* 1976). Such attempts should be viewed as progressive developments of the behaviorist research program, rather than as the introduction of a rival, because (1) the parameters employed in the economic model all fit the radical behaviorist constraints; (2) the economic model retains previously established behavioral principles as special cases, not as *ad hoc* additions; (3) it has expanded the range of phenomena of which behavioral principles offer explicit and detailed explanations; and (4) it opens up new, potentially fruitful areas of research. Given the possibility of this kind of transforming change *within* the behaviorist program, it is even more important to emphasize that any argument for the limits of behaviorist explanation must be applicable to the general conceptions that define the program, and not merely to the specific set of principles currently known.

We expect a serious argument for the inherently restricted explanatory power of the radical behaviorist research program to spring not from a formal proof that

behaviorist principles must be inconsistent with certain data, but from the positive achievements of an alternative scheme. The relevant positive achievements would be the following.

1 The alternative offers explicit and detailed explanations of a certain class of phenomena.
2 These explanations employ parameters that violate the constraints of the behaviorist program.
3 These explanations have some empirical support.
4 Behavioral principles currently offer no explanation of this class of phenomena.
5 The class of phenomena that the alternative scheme explains consists of behavior that is reasonably regarded as characteristically human.
6 The alternative scheme is fruitful, either with respect to defining and solving research problems, or with respect to providing an aid to practical concerns.
7 The alternative scheme produces the current behavioral principles as special cases, obtained when either one or more specified variables are held constant, or under special, explicitly stated, environmental conditions.
8 The presuppositions or theoretical principles of the alternative scheme imply that there exist regularities relating behavior to environmental factors, past and present, *only* in settings in which specified variables are held constant or in which specified environmental conditions obtain.
9 Repeated efforts to extend the behaviorist research program, as a generator of fruitful research, to settings in which the specified variables are not held constant, or specified environmental conditions do not obtain, have failed.

We regard the demonstration of this list of achievements by an alternative scheme to behaviorism as necessary and sufficient to show that behaviorism is inherently incomplete. Moreover, such achievements would also serve to define positively the limits of behaviorist explanation, by specifying which variables had to be held constant, or which environmental conditions had to exist, for behavioral principles to provide a satisfactory explanation of behavior. The production of such an alternative scheme would not logically compel the rejection of behaviorism. However, it is not easy to see what grounds could be used to defend continued allegiance to behaviorism. One could not appeal to comprehensiveness since, in the stipulated circumstances, behaviorism has been shown not to be as comprehensive as the alternative. One could not appeal to fruitfulness since, again by stipulation, there is at least one significant domain in which the alternative scheme is more fruitful. And one could not appeal to the power to control behavior that behavior principles yield since, once more by stipulation, that power is restricted to a specified set of situations.

AN ALTERNATIVE TO BEHAVIORISM

A suitable alternative to behaviorism could, in principle, come from either of two sources. It could come from a rival scientific research program, such as cognitive

psychology. Or it could come from an explanatory scheme whose origins lie in practical life rather than experimental research, such as that of teleological explanation (Taylor, 1964). Whether or not they actually meet our stringent requirements, it is fair to construe the critical arguments against behaviorism by Chomsky (1959) and Fodor (1975) as attempts to provide an alternative scheme from psycholinguistics and cognitive psychology. This is certainly a proper source of an alternative to behaviorism if one shares with behaviorism the commonplace scientific presupposition that behavior is lawful. We will not here evaluate arguments that spring from rival scientific research programs.

Instead, we will point to the limits of behaviorist explanation from the perspective of the explanatory framework universally used in the deliberations of practical life — that of teleological explanation. Let us begin by acknowledging that behaviorist principles are manifestly exemplified in settings (both experimental and applied) in which control is established. These settings exhibit the following characteristics: only a few reinforcers are available, and usually one has special salience; the experimenter (behavior modifier) has control over conditions of deprivation and access to the reinforcers; there is only one, or at most a few, available means to the reinforcers; the performance of clearly defined, specific tasks is reinforced; different tasks are effectively interchangeable for the one that is reinforced; the schedule of reinforcement is externally imposed and varied by agents not themselves being subjected to the contingencies; there are no effective alternatives to being in the setting.

We will call settings that exhibit these characteristics *closed settings*. Clearly, settings can be more or less closed. The argument that follows suggests that the exemplification of behavior principles should become increasingly discernible as the setting becomes increasingly closed. Demonstrating that behaviorism has explanatory success in closed settings does not suffice to show that its explanatory principles are comprehensive, if not all settings are closed. And many ordinary social settings are not. We now sketch an argument, the details of which can be found elsewhere (Schwartz and Lacey, 1982, Ch. 9; Schwartz, Schuldenfrei and Lacey, 1978) that the explanatory power of behaviorism is limited to closed settings. The argument is empirical in character, though primarily based on sociological and historical rather than experimental considerations.

Experimental and applied settings are closed, and they were constructed by behavioral psychologists in order that control be obtained in them. As a step toward exploring the possible exemplification of behavioral principles in *open* (that is, non-closed) settings, we asked if they are manifestly exemplified in any setting of our society that was not constructed in the course of applying known behavioral principles. There is one such setting, parts of the modern, factory workplace. If this setting were paradigmatic of social settings in general, we would be well on the way to defending the comprehensiveness of behaviorism. But it is not, for two reasons. First, while this setting is ubiquitous in the modern world (decreasingly so in the first world, increasingly so in the third), there are important courses of action (for example, creating and running the factory, or engaging in science) that are not encompassed by it. That is, behaviorists may be able to account for the person's behavior within the closed setting, but they cannot account for their own behavior in establishing it. Second, this setting, as a significant social phenomenon, is a recent historical development, and is wide-

spread only in industrial societies. We reached this second conclusion on the basis of the following observations (Schwartz, Schuldenfrei and Lacey, 1978).

1 Medieval work, the precursor to modern work, cannot be analyzed as exemplifying behavioral principles, because it was variegated, flexible, and socially integrated.
2 Important features of the modern factory workplace emerged slowly during the nineteenth century. As they emerged, certain customary and traditional work practices were suppressed and gradually replaced by wages as the worker's predominant concern in the workplace.
3 Only with the suppression of these traditional practices did behavior in the workplace become describable and explicable in informative detail in terms of behavioral principles.
4 The structuring of the modern workplace was completed under the heavy influence of the scientific management movement at the turn of this century, in the light of principles virtually identical to those of behaviorism.

We conclude from these observations that those settings in which behavioral principles are manifestly exemplified are not generally characteristic of human societies, but have been constructed in the course of recent history. Moreover, although they are not the product of applied behavior analysis as we know it today, they are also closed settings, in which money is the salient reinforcer. The factory workplace, then, does not constitute evidence that behavioral principles are exemplified outside closed settings. That this is so is bolstered by the fact that as one moves to more open settings, in which external control is minimized, desired outcomes are the product of lengthy, variegated, and often novel activities, and plans and actions are shaped in the course of study and discussion, behaviorist descriptive categories become less and less useful for providing illuminating descriptions. Instead they become more metaphorical, more parasitic on other conceptual schemes, and more dependent upon appeals to the complex or unknown. A striking example of this is how 'reinforcement' tends to take on a vague, metaphorical usage, marred by an oft-repeated conceptual confusion.

Radical behaviorists often assert that their fundamental principle is: 'behavior is under the control of its consequences', which they usually take to be equivalent to: 'behavior is under the control of contingencies of reinforcement.' Thus, any consequence that controls behavior necessarily becomes a reinforcer, from which it is often inferred that any goal of a human action is a reinforcer. Since behavior in most open settings is goal-directed, that is, is performed in order to bring about certain consequences, the inference would imply that this open-setting, goal-directed behavior is controlled by reinforcement. In order to see that this inference is invalid, note that within behavior theory, 'behavior is under the control of contingencies of reinforcement' has the very precise meaning: 'behavior occurs because of the contingencies of reinforcement in which earlier instances of the behavior have been involved.' But behavior may occur in order to bring about a certain consequence without previous instances of the same kind of behavior ever having been reinforced, or even having occurred. The invention of the 'Skinner box', for the convenient study of free-operant behavior, and of concurrent reinforcement schedules, for the convenient study of choice,

and of 'mands' and 'tacts' for the analysis of verbal behavior are just a few examples. Also, within behavior theory something is a reinforcer only if it increases the probability of the behaviors on which it is contingent. But there are many goals for which a person may act that do not have this property, goals that, once achieved, render irrelevant or unnecessary the further repetition of the behaviors that eventuated in the achievement of the goals. For example, once Skinner and his collaborators reached the goal of having discovered generalizations about schedules of reinforcement, they moved to other experimental inquiries. Such goals are not reinforcers.

We have concluded that there is no evidence that behavioral principles are exemplified outside closed settings, and that in open settings, radical behaviorism offers neither explanations nor illuminating descriptions. For completeness, our argument would require demonstrating the inadequacy of Skinner's 'interpretations' of verbal behavior (Skinner, 1957), but we lack the space to do so here (see Lacey, 1974). In contrast, teleological categories (goal, expectancy, plan, reason, intention, etc.) are routinely successful in capturing order in human action, and in expressing the detail, sequence, novelty, and significant variation that human behavior displays. They are used in historical inquiry and social commentary, and universally in charting the human environment as an apt guide to action. The framework of teleology satisfies all the criteria we identified earlier that a serious alternative to behaviorism would have to meet.

1   It offers explicit and detailed explanations of a certain class of phenomena — goal-directed behaviors in open settings.
2   These explanations employ parameters (intention, purpose, deliberation, etc.) that violate the constraints of the behaviorist program.
3   These explanations have empirical support; we use them effectively to make sense of most aspects of daily life.
4   Behavioral principles currently offer no explanation of this class of phenomena, as we have argued above.
5   The phenomena that the teleological framework explains are characteristically human.
6   The teleological framework is fruitful; it provides the categories that enable effective interaction and deliberation in practical life.
7   It treats current behavioral principles as special cases, generalizations that obtain when, and only when, the conditions defining closed settings obtain. In these settings behavior is still purposive; that it exhibits law-like regularities is a consequence of the limited options and means to bring them about that characterize closed settings. Behavior in these settings is a special, albeit in our historical epoch, common case. Put another way, goals become reinforcers only under the conditions of closed settings, and behavioral principles are exemplified only when key conditions that prevail in open settings are suppressed.
8   More generally, the presuppositions of teleological explanation (see below) imply that there exist regularities relating behavior to environmental factors, past and present, only when environmental conditions are held sufficiently constant that intelligent variation of goals is not likely to occur.

9 Repeated efforts to extend the behaviorist research program to open settings have failed.

We want to emphasize that while behavioral phenomena in open settings are more complex than those in closed settings, complexity is not the key to our argument. Closed settings are not the simplest cases on which to build additively in order eventually to encompass complex, open cases, which is what most behaviorist researchers assume. Rather, they are special, degenerate cases that are properly intelligible only in the light of the teleological categories that also illuminate open settings.

The logic of teleological explanations is quite distinct from the logic of explanations obtained by subsuming a phenomenon under general laws, a goal to which all behaviorist explanations aspire (see Taylor, 1964). When we say, '*A* had the goal *X*, and *A* did *Y* because *A* believed that doing *Y* would (contribute to) bring about *X*', we do not imply that there are internal states, *A*'s having goals and beliefs, that are instances of variables in a law that subsumes *A*'s doing *X*. Thus, for example, the explanatory import of 'in the 1950s, Skinner engaged in a sustained, collaborative program of experimentation systematically investigating schedules of reinforcement, because his goal was to formulate a comprehensive set of behavioral principles, and he believed that reinforcement schedules were significant variables in that set, and that his available experimental techniques could uncover the principles of reinforcement schedules' does not depend upon finding laws (regularities, generalizations) linking those goals and beliefs to the sequence of actions that constituted the carrying out of the research program. The having of goals and beliefs is not a hypothesized internal state that has a causal role that is explicated by laws. Rather, the connection between the having of goals and beliefs and action is closer to a logical relation, expressed in what some philosophers have called a 'practical syllogism'. The idea (considerably simplified) is this: if I say that I have the goal *X* and that I believe that doing *Y* will bring about *X*, but yet I don't do *Y*, then I am involved in a 'practical contradiction', unless I can show that there were countervailing considerations (for example, another goal that overrode *X*, another means to *X*, that I was prevented forcibly from doing *Y*). Put another way, *certeris paribus* not doing *Y* is public evidence that either I did not have the goal or I did not have the belief. This is an instance of how there are public 'criteria' for the having of goals and beliefs (Wittgenstein, 1958). The existence of these public criteria makes possible the empirical confirmation of attributions of goals and beliefs to a person. In addition, the order that is discernible among actions in the course of teleological explanation does not derive from classifying actions (behaviors) and displaying the members of the class as regularly following members of a class of antecedent events, as would be the case in law-like generalizations. The order derives instead from relating actions to goals, and it varies in richness depending on its capacity to display a wide variety, pattern, and sequence of actions as leading to the same goal. Since there is a kind of logical ('criterial') connection between the having of goals and beliefs and action, connections do not have to be defined in terms of regular successions of classes of events; teleological explanation can rest with unique descriptions of particular actions and still reflect order.

To challenge our argument about the limits of behaviorist explanation, it is

necessary to show that there are settings, beyond the boundary conditions we specified in our discussion of closed settings, in which behaviorist principles are clearly exemplified. One must show how the teleological framework, in which relations between explanatory factors and actions are 'logical' rather than causal, can be replaced by causal laws of the behaviorist research program.

WHAT HUMAN BEINGS ARE

We have used the categories of teleological explanation, those that we use routinely to illuminate most of practical life, in order to define positively the boundaries of the explanatory power of behaviorist principles, and our mode of argument has involved sociological and historical analysis. Although our analysis is not 'scientific', in the sense in which science is conceived as involving the representation of phenomena as lawful, it serves the indispensible scientific function of defining the limits or boundary conditions of known generalizations. Our procedure is not *ad hoc*; it is entirely appropriate in the light of the kind of beings that humans are. To conclude, we will briefly outline our conception of human beings, contrasting it with the general conception of radical behaviorism.

Like behaviorists, we regard the analysis of the relation between persons and the environment as essential for understanding human behavior. Unlike them, we deny that this relation can be captured in a set of regularities involving behavior and environmental variables, except in closed settings. Characteristically, the relation between a person and the environment is mediated by the person's interpretation (perceptions, beliefs) of the environment, and intentions with respect to modifying it. Interpretations and intentions may be thought to be the province of cognitive psychologists. But they, like behaviorists, are normally in search of laws, and we do not believe that interpretations are any more lawful than actions are in open settings (see Fodor, 1983, for a supporting argument). Consequently, except in closed settings, human behavior is marked by variability and a certain novelty.

Affirming the explanatory significance and indispensibility of interpretations and intentions does not diminish the importance of the environment. The environment is both a constraint on behavior and the object of behavior. It limits what it is possibile to do, and what can be done is always a modification of the environment (never the product of 'pure volition'). Modification of the environment is the explicit object of intentions; virtually all acts presuppose a multiplicity of environmental conditions, and all acts are expressed in a material medium. Beyond this we also maintain that the very obtaining of behavioral regularities depends upon the presence of certain environmental conditions (broad socio-economic structures that convert many settings into closed ones). On this view different regularities may obtain within different socio-economic structures, so that the obtaining of regularities has an essential and ineliminable historicity, and requires a social-historical analysis for its explanation. When regularities are detached from socio-economic structures, human nature comes to be viewed as identical with its manifestation in the particular socio-historical locale in which it is being examined. Psychological inquiry dissociated from history always runs the risk of this misidentification.

In other ways, too, we emphasize the social and historical character of human action. Human beings are social beings. What they do reflects their social positions and social roles, and much of what they do is directed toward generating and maintaining various kinds of social relations. Much deliberation about what to do concerns what is possible and appropriate given one's social position and role, and the positions and roles to which one can reasonably aspire. The explanation of a person's goals involves locating that person in the social nexus. The social nexus in turn requires that the person participate in certain practices, *or* be subjected to certain controls. Compare, for example, the role of professor in a psychology department, which requires participation in the practice of scientific research, with that of a worker earning piece rates in a factory, which requires performing tasks set by management in accordance with schedules controlled by management.

Within a practice such as scientific research, goals are understood in terms of their appropriateness given the current state of development of a particular research program — whether, for example, the research in question contributes to solving an outstanding problem, to refuting a rival hypothesis, to exploring a significant new phenomenon, to confirming a prediction that was generated by a theory, and so on. What it makes sense to do at one time is often quite different from what it makes sense to do at another. To understand why a researcher performs a particular experiment, one needs to locate its relevance to the historical unfolding of the research program. Actions that derive from practices become fully articulated only in teleological and historical terms.

Within a practice, goal-setting is not merely an individual matter, for judgments of appropriateness ultimately involve the collective wisdom of the body of practitioners, and novices are apprenticed into the practice in the context of this collective authority. So proposed goals may be varied, challenged, and changed. Goals may be changed for various reasons, for example, conditions for realizing the goal (funding, outlets for publication) may be removed. Paradigmatically, however, within a practice goals are changed because of criticism, argument, the presentation of evidence — in general, through participation in dialogue. How the practice develops is crucially the outcome of this dialogue among the practitioners, and so a practice develops appropriate social relations among its members to facilitate and enhance such dialogue. In contrast, dialogue among the members of the work-force is essentially irrelevant to the setting of goals in a closed setting like the factory, and social relations that facilitate control rather than dialogue are thus developed.

There has always been a moral impulse behind Skinner's driven and unrelenting commitment to behaviorism, a belief that the implementation of systematic behavioral controls will contribute quickly to solving the big social problems of the modern world (Skinner, 1971). And much of his philosophical writing has been devoted to arguing that persons are the kind of beings defined by relations of control. We too have a moral motive. It is that relations of dialogue in all aspects of life are better for everyone than relations of control. So it is important for us to take as the appropriate objects of psychological inquiry persons who are capable of rich, dialogical relations, and to give an empirical basis to the claim that settings in which relations of control dominate are products of historically contingent socio-economic structures. We have tried to do so here, and to suggest that

human beings are what the explanatory scheme with the greatest comprehensiveness — the teleological scheme — says they are, and that where they appear to be otherwise, important features of humanity have been suppressed.

REFERENCES

Chomsky, N. (1959) 'Review of B.F. Skinner's *Verbal Behavior*', *Language*, 35, pp. 26–58.
Fodor, J.A. (1975) *The Language of Thought*, New York, Crowell.
Fodor, J.A. (1983) *The Modularity of Mind*, Cambridge, Mass., MIT Press.
Lacey, H.M. (1974) 'The scientific study of linguistic behavior: A perspective on the Skinner-Chomsky controversy', *Journal for the Theory of Social Behavior*, 4, pp. 17–51.
Lacey, H.M. (1979) 'Skinner on the prediction and control of behavior'. *Theory and Decision*, 10, pp. 353–85.
Lacey, H.M. (1980) 'Psychological conflict and human nature: The case of behaviorism and cognition', *Journal for the Theory of Social Behavior*, 10. pp. 131–55.
Lakatos, I. (1978) *The Methodology of Scientific Research Programmes*, Cambridge, Cambridge University Press.
Rachlin, H., Green, L. Kagel, J.H. and Battalio, R.C. (1976) 'Economic demand theory and psychological studies of choice', in Bower, G.H. (Ed.), *The Psychology of Learning and Motivation*, Vol. 10, New York, Academic Press, pp. 129–54.
Schwartz, B. (1982) 'Reinforcement induced behavioral stereotypy: How not to teach people to discover rules', *Journal of Experimental Psychology: General*, 111, pp. 23–59.
Schwartz, B. (1984) *The Psychology of Learning and Behavior*, 2nd ed., New York, W.W. Norton.
Schwartz, B. and Lacey, H. (1982) *Behaviorism, Science, and Human Nature*, New York, W.W. Norton.
Schwartz, B., Schuldenfrei, R. and Lacey, H. (1978) 'Operant psychology as factory psychology', *Behaviorism*, 6, pp. 229–54.
Skinner, B.F. (1945) 'The operational analysis of psychological terms', *Psychological Review*, 52, pp. 270–7.
Skinner, B.F. (1957) *Verbal Behavior*, Englewood Cliffs, N.J., Prentice-Hall.
Skinner, B.F. (1971) *Beyond Freedom and Dignity*, New York, Knopf.
Skinner, B.F. (1974) *About Behaviorism*, New York, Knopf.
Taylor, C. (1964) *The Explanation of Behaviour*, London, Routledge and Kegan Paul.
Wittgenstein, L. (1958) *Philosophical Investigations*, Oxford, Blackwell.

Interchange

RACHLIN REPLIES TO LACEY AND SCHWARTZ

For Lacey and Schwartz, as mentalists, an observer of another person sees only that person's behavior and must *infer* the person's hidden internal mental state which 'mediates' between the behavior and the environment. For me, as a behaviorist, an observer of another person may actually see that person's mental state — the mental state is an observable pattern of behavior-environment interaction — and must *infer* the historical pattern of contingencies of reinforcement behind it. Thus, perhaps paradoxically, for the mentalist behavior is the only objectively and directly observable datum, while for the behaviorist a mental state is directly and objectively observable.

Mentalistic reasoning attempts to get behind the surface of behavior to the underlying mental state, while behaviorist reasoning attempts to get behind the surface of mental state to the underlying contingencies of reinforcement. The mentalist infers current internal mental events (perceptions, beliefs, expectancies) as the causal focus of current behavior, and the behaviorist infers past external behavior-environment interactions (stimuli, responses, reinforcers, punishers) as the causal focus of current behavior (including current perceptions, beliefs and expectancies). It is not true, as Lacey and Schwartz seem to think, that mentalistic vocabulary is forbidden to the behaviorist. Mentalistic vocabulary is no more forbidden to the behaviorist than the terms 'stimulus,' 'response' or 'reinforcement' are forbidden to the mentalist. The behaviorist who talks about mental states is no more 'parasitic' on mentalism than the mentalist who talks about behavior is parasitic on behaviorism.

The critical difference between the mentalist and the behaviorist lies in the point where explanations may stop. For a mentalist, explanations of behavior may stop when they have been traced to a current internal cause ('I ate the spinach because I believed it would be good for me'). For a behaviorist, explanations of behavior (or mental states) may stop only when they have been traced to a previous external cause ('I ate the spinach, and believe it is good for me, because when I used to eat spinach as a child it pleased my mother and when my mother was pleased she was kind').

Lacey and Schwartz claim that, although it may capture behavior-environment *regularities*, the behaviorist vocabulary is insufficient to capture behavior-environment *irregularities* (i.e., novelty and variability). Since human behavior, especially human dialog, is characterized by novelty and variability, behaviorism is insufficient (Lacey and Schwartz say) to capture the 'richness' of human nature. This argument assumes that there exist human behaviors (aside from simple reflexes) that cannot, 'in principle', be traced to underlying conting-

encies of reinforcement. Scientific discovery is Lacey and Schwartz's paradigmatic case of such behavior. As an example of a scientific discovery they cite Skinner's own invention of the Skinner box. This was perhaps an unfortunate choice since, in the second volume of his autobiography (*The Shaping of a Behaviorist*), Skinner makes a point of showing how this particular invention arose by degrees from earlier reinforced behavior. It is no more difficult, *in principle*, to make such interpretations than it is to explain the fall of a leaf in terms of gravity and aerodynamics. Whether a particular effort at interpretation is worthwhile is another question.

It would seem, from the success of current applications of behaviorism to everyday life, especially to situations involving self-control, that interpretation in open settings is worthwhile and that human life, in all its richness, may be more regular than Lacey and Schwartz suspect.

Let us now turn briefly to the supposed superiority of the mentalistic vocabulary as applied to open settings. Lacey and Schwartz claim that the richness of the teleological (i.e., mental) explanation 'depends on its capacity to display a wide variety, pattern and sequence of actions as leading to the same goal.' If this is a statement about psychology (as opposed to physics or biology), it needs to be accompanied by a method to ascertain why a person believes certain actions to be appropriate to a given goal. Otherwise, what stops a person from believing *any* action is appropriate to *any* goal? No such method is provided by Lacey and Schwartz or, indeed, by any mentalist. Lacey and Schwartz believe that people may act in accordance with what they are told or contrary to what they are told, in accordance with a set of logical principles or contrary to a set of logical principles, in accordance with their nature or contrary to their nature, in accordance with what is good for them or contrary to what is good for them, etc. At what point does an explanation become too rich? Lacey and Schwartz reject the notion that belief is governed by any set of potential rules, no matter how complex. For them it is impossible to understand how people acquire their beliefs, it is impossible to know for sure what their beliefs are, hence it is impossible for Lacey and Schwartz to understand why people behave as they do.

LACEY AND SCHWARTZ REPLY TO RACHLIN

ON THE APPLICABILITY OF APPLICABILITY

Rachlin identifies practical application, the achievement of control, as the pre-eminent criterion for assessing the explanatory power of a theory. In this he is consistent with arguments made many times over the years by Skinner. In our response we will focus on this one point. But let us first be clear on where we do not take issue with Rachlin. First, we agree with Rachlin that radical behaviorist theories have generated significant practical applications, arguably more so than the alternatives he discusses. Second, an acceptable theory must generate practical applications. However, the necessity here is neither logical nor methodological, but social. Practical applications are a requirement for the social support that makes rapid theory development possible. Third, 'mentalism', as characterized by

Rachlin, is indeed trivial. It is not a serious alternative to radical behaviorism.

With these areas of agreement clear, let us turn to the significance of practical application for validating theories. The view that the power generated by a theory, manifested by the extent to which it allows us to control things, is a reflection of the explanatory power of a theory is deeply rooted in contemporary scientific culture. The argument for it is apparently simple and compelling. Power results from having discovered the laws of nature, or of a relevant domain of nature, such as behavior. When we exercise control, we are merely bringing about the boundary conditions within which those laws are known to be operative in the given domain. Conversely, if there are some putative explanatory principles that do not allow us to achieve control, it must be because these principles do not actually represent laws of the domain. So application, through control, allows us to separate the wheat from the chaff; to distinguish the actual laws of nature from the pretenders.

We will evaluate this argument only with respect to the domain of behavior, though our remarks could be extended to other domains. Clearly, there is something right about the argument. Its weakness lies in the difficulty and ambiguity of specifying the 'relevant domain' over which the explanatory scheme is meant to operate. The possibility of implementing behavioral controls is a consequence of having discovered the regularities (laws) of some domain. The question is: which domain? We have argued that the controls (successful applications) engendered by radical behaviorism have occurred only in what we called 'closed settings'. On this argument the regularities expressed in radical behaviorist theories are just the laws of behavior in closed settings. We have further argued that, from the perspective of teleological explanation (which is not 'mentalist' as Rachlin defines the term), behavioral regularities of the sort described by behaviorists *only* occur in closed settings. So the laws are laws that operate in the domain of closed settings, and the applications are applications that work in the domain of closed settings. That the domain of operation of laws and the domain of successful application line up is hardly a defect of the theory — in itself.

However, what our argument makes clear is that the mere fact of successful control itself tells us nothing about the extent of the explanatory power of the principles that underlie this power to control. That the principles enable control of behavior in closed settings implies nothing about whether or not they are salient principles for explaining behavior in general. Whether they do the job in open settings is an empirical question. If they do not, their explanatory scope will depend upon the relative frequency of closed and of open settings in the environments in which people typically find themselves — another empirical issue.

We are not making a skeptical point here, or attempting to forestall on ordinary, inductive move from simple to complex cases. We have argued from the perspective of teleology, a scheme that not only offers concrete explanations where behaviorism offers only gestures, but also serves to define the limits of applicability of behaviorist principles, portraying behavior that is under the control of those principles as a degenerate case of purposive behavior. It is true that a teleological scheme has the conceptual resources to explain every action, but that is not the vice that Rachlin suggests, since it does not offer the sort of trivial 'explanations' that Rachlin's mentalistic straw person does. Moreover, it makes a difference — a practical, everyday difference. Accepting teleology in broad outline implies interacting with other human beings differently from the way implied

by the behaviorist outline; emphasizing relations of dialogue rather than control.

Rachlin seems to offer two responses to this argument. First, he suggests that there are clear instances of the application of operant principles in open settings, for example, procedures of 'self-control' and the treatment of pain. Elsewhere (Schwartz, 1984, Ch. 7; Schwartz and Lacey, 1982, Ch. 8), we argued that a number of applied behavioral procedures like those of 'self-control' could not properly be regarded as exemplifications of operant principles; that they make sense only in terms of teleological categories. Lacey (1985) made a similar argument concerning Rachlin's (1985) behavioral analysis of pain and its treatment. We note, however, that arguments of this type are of the required kind, if they are successful, to undermine our conclusion.

The second response is to suggest that mentalistic terms, presumably including teleological ones, can be translated into behaviorist terms, though the translations may be rather complex and cumbersome. Our argument suggests that such 'translations' are impossible, at least if they are to have any explanatory role, since we have used the teleological scheme in part to identify the limits of behaviorist explanation. Over and above this general, and admittedly arguable, point we can only deal with such translations as are explicitly and specifically offered. Rachlin offers none.

REFERENCES

Lacey, H. (forthcoming) 'Pain behavior: How to define the operant', *The Behavioral and Brain Sciences*.

Rachlin, H. (forthcoming) 'Pain and behavior', *The Behavioral and Brain Sciences*.

Schwartz, B. (1984) *Psychology of Learning and Behavior*, New York, W.W. Norton.

Schwartz, B. and Lacey, H. (1982) *Behaviorism, Science, and Human Nature*, New York, W.W. Norton.

Part IX: Skinner and the Unit of Behavior

15. Skinner and the Unit of Behavior*

JOHN HINSON

B.F. Skinner has become the most famous psychologist of his time through his exposition of radical behavorism, and his creation of operant conditioning. To some extent Skinner's notoriety has obscured his more substantial contributions to psychology. In trying to reach the broadest possible audience through popular writings, it was, perhaps, inevitable that Skinner's position would become over-simplified. Also his promotion of unusual or controversial social doctrines has made Skinner the object of unfounded criticism. Polemic attacks are usually based on Skinner's popular sources, rather than his more thoughtful works.

It is harder to account for the misunderstandings and misrepresentations of Skinner's views by psychologists. It may be that his accomplishments are so familiar that they seem ordinary. However, the problem seems to run deeper. For many operant theory is the commonsense application of a few principles of reward, punishment, and association to the study of behavior. Praise is generously apportioned for the technical innovations of operant theory, such as improved methods for the control of behavior and schedules of reinforcement. But concern with the *conceptual* framework of operant theory usually extends only as far as to relegate Skinner's radical behaviorism as a historical curiosity. Unfortunately the rationale for the enterprise seems to have been lost in the maze of technical achievements.

In truth Skinner's operant theory provided a tremendous conceptual advance which allowed him to avoid a number of serious problems encountered by his predecessors and contemporaries. Skinner's achievement is most evident in his

* This research was supported by funds from Washington State University. I thank F.K. McSweeney for helpful comments on earlier versions of the manuscript.

treatment of the problem of determining behavioral units of analysis. His resolution of this problem appeared in the early works which laid the groundwork for modern operant theory. While it is difficult to do justice to the subtlety of his reasoning in a small space, it is possible to provide a historical outline of Skinner's position. It is my contention that Skinner reached his answer to the problem of units of analysis because of his commitment to radical behaviorism. I begin my discussion by noting briefly the behaviorist position which provides the impetus for Skinner's theory. I then summarize Skinner's resolution of the units of analysis problem, followed by a brief summary of the different approach taken by Clark Hull. Finally, I consider some problems created by Hull's theory, but avoided by Skinner's theory. This comparison indicates why Skinner ultimately achieved ascendancy, and why his operant approach is worth following.

THE HISTORICAL IMPORTANCE OF BEHAVIORISM

Operant theory is commonly believed to be synonymous with behaviorism. However gratifying this may be for Skinner, it is certainly a mistaken identity which he has been compelled repeatedly to correct. Behaviorism is a philosophy of psychology and should not be confused with any particular theory (e.g., Skinner, 1964). Since its introduction, behaviorism has suffered a kind of guilt by association with the combative and acetic John B. Watson. However, the tenets of behaviorism laid down by Watson (1913) in his initial manifesto seem quite tame by modern standards.

Watson wanted to establish psychology as a branch of natural science, a goal shared by Wundt, Titchener, and the American functionalists, Angell, Dewey, and James. However, Watson was convinced that the main obstacle to progress toward this goal was the quandary produced by the introspective method of analysis of consciousness, a method common to structuralists and functionalists. He argued that most questions addressed by this method were not simply unimportant, but *senseless*, in that there was no basis for agreement or disagreement. In this regard psychology would be better off excluding all *reference* to consciousness, a much misunderstood suggestion. In place of the analysis of consciousness, Watson suggested that psychology concern itself with the activity of humans and animals in their adjustments to the environment, or what Watson called a consistent functionalism. This course alone offered hope of experimental treatment. As progressively better methods were developed, more complex forms of behavior such as imagination, reasoning, and judgment could also be studied in a fashion consistent with objective science (Watson, 1913, p. 174).

While Watson offered an unequivocal alternative to introspectionism, he was unable to develop a consistent behavioral theory during his unexpectedly brief academic career. Through his association with Yerkes, Watson (1916) introduced Pavlov's conditioned reflex method to a receptive audience. But despite the revolutionary change of perspective from the analysis of consciousness to the study of behavior, and the use of Pavlov's terms and techniques, experimental psychology lacked a coherent program.

Like many of his contemporaries, Skinner desired a system in which behavior would serve as a scientific datum. But unlike others, Skinner wanted to insure that behavior would be treated as *significant* in its own right, and not simply as a

manifestation of underlying nervous system structures, or inner mental entities; this position is radical behaviorism (Skinner, 1945). One error to be avoided was the mere translation of older mentalistic terms, since a science based on such translations would perpetuate the conceptual problems of earlier times (Skinner, 1938, p. 7). Skinner's alternative was to eliminate older metaphorical concepts, and to retain or create terms purely descriptive of behavior. His concern with the use of terms in the analysis and description of behavior led to his first theoretical contribution, an operational analysis of the concept of the reflex.

EXTENSION OF THE REFLEX CONCEPT

An operational analysis of the reflex concept seemed a good place to begin, since this concept was central to physiological studies most clearly concerned with objective, scientific method. Although he did not present an exhaustive history of the reflex concept, Skinner's (1931) analysis did focus on two important historical developments. The first of these was the introduction, by Descartes, of the concept of the stimulus. Recognition of the role of the stimulus obviated, in theory, the requirement of an internal causal entity responsible for behavior. The second important step was the distinction between reflex and voluntary activity. Common experience seemed to dictate the distinction between voluntary and involuntary, with the reflex concept confined to the involuntary mode of causation.

However, when Skinner examined the actual circumstances in which the reflex concept was employed in the description of behavior, he found that the usual characterizations of reflex activity as involuntary or unconscious were gratuitous. Moreover, the concept did not refer specifically to physiological events. The defining characteristic of the reflex concept was the observed correlation between a stimulus and a response. The reflex, so defined, was applicable to all of the behavior of the living organism. Therefore, Skinner argued that the reflex was the general *form* of description of the functional relation between the events acting on the organism, and the response of the organism to external events. Scientific investigation of behavior involves the identification of reflex units, i.e., observed correlations between stimuli and responses (Skinner, 1931, p. 445). In addition, the investigation of behavior also identifies changes in these correlations due to the operation of what Skinner termed their variables, i.e., any antecedent conditions which affect the observed correlation.

SKINNER'S SYSTEM OF EXPERIMENTAL ANALYSIS

Having established the reflex as the general form of description of behavior, Skinner next proposed a systematic experimental approach to the study of behavior. Like Watson, Skinner (1938, p. 6) suggested a broad definition of behavior along three lines: (1) that which an organism is observed to do; (2) that aspect of an organism engaged in acting upon, or having commerce with, the environment; (3) the effects of the organism in its environment, as opposed to the action itself.

One of Skinner's tasks was to identify specific types of analytic units of

behavior. Simple enumeration of all functional relationships which occur between behavior and environment was clearly pointless, i.e., the so-called 'botanizing' of reflexes. As an alternative, Skinner suggested that types of reflex units could be identified on the basis of the static and dynamic laws applicable to each. The static laws are those governing single occurrences of the reflex, while the dynamic laws are those governing repeated reflex occurrences. In addition to the classic dynamic laws of reflex activity, Skinner included the laws of conditioning and extinction of Type S, which were meant to account for the type of reflex unit studied by Pavlov. Skinner called this type of unit a *respondent*, and the dynamic laws governing such units the laws of *respondent conditioning* (1938, p. 18).

The dynamic laws of respondent conditioning provided an account for a large body of behavior. Nonetheless, the specification of an additional type of analytic unit seemed necessary. Respondents clearly depend on the prior occurrence of a stimulus, or in other words they are elicited by an antecedent stimulus. Another type of behavior seems to have no readily identifiable eliciting stimulus. Instead, this type of behavior is freely emitted at a certain spontaneous rate. Other theorists had attempted to force emitted behavior into the respondent mold. But Skinner argued that this attempt was not only undesirable, but unnecessary. Freely emitted behavior could be shown to be consistent with the reflex account in another way.

As noted earlier, the defining characteristic of the reflex is a correlation between aspects of behavior and environment. Respondents are reflex units in that they are defined by the specific relationships (i.e., dynamic laws) between a response and an eliciting, antecedent stimulus. Spontaneous behavior is, by definition, not elicited. But it can be analyzed into reflex units if consistent relationships (i.e., dynamic laws) can be established between the behavior and *consequent* events. The dynamic laws appropriate to spontaneous behavior Skinner called the laws of conditioning and extinction of Type R (1938, p. 21). The law of conditioning of Type R was Skinner's version of the law of effect. The consequent event which defines the unit is called a reinforcer, and the unit itself is called an *operant*. Thus the laws of *operant conditioning* govern the establishment of operant units of behavior, operants being defined by the law of effect.

SKINNER'S METHOD FOR IDENTIFYING ANALYTIC UNITS

Establishing the existence of operants and respondents is only part of Skinner's system of analysis. Another important aspect of analysis is to discover the defining properties of the stimulus and response which yield a reproducible analytic unit. The key to identification of defining properties is recognition of the fact that the terms 'stimulus' and 'response' refer to *classes* of events (Skinner, 1935). Hence, the units of analysis must describe a correlation between these classes. Moreover, the appropriate level of analysis at which the defining properties of these classes appear must be determined through observation of the obtained functional relations. The defining properties of these classes cannot be deduced in advance.

For example, after establishing a functional relationship between aspects of behavior and environment, one can progressively restrict the defining properties of both. Some of these restrictions lead to a more orderly form of dynamic

function relating behavior and environment, while others do not. At some point before all the properties of the stimulus and response classes have been specified, there will be no further increase in the consistency of the relationship between the classes. This point of specificity, where the dynamic changes between stimulus and response approach an *optimal* degree of orderliness, ultimately determines the appropriate level of analysis (1935, p. 55). In Skinner's words, operants and respondents are analytic units that are '... defined at levels of specification marked by the orderliness of dynamic changes' (1938, p. 40).

Skinner's system of operant analysis is a purely descriptive enterprise. In the beginning the task is to identify a consistent set of concepts which are descriptive of behavior. Next, by observing the dynamic functions which relate stimulus and response classes, the investigator identifies specific analytic units, such as operants and respondents. Any time an operant is identified, reinforcing conditions are also identified. Further observation and experimentation lead to the development of higher-order concepts which integrate separate observations, while still remaining descriptive of behavior. The mission of operant theory is to seek out appropriate units of analysis by discovering the relevant aspects of the environment controlling behavior. Only by investigation of the activity of interest can we discover the relevant properties of the response and stimulus classes involved. The inductive method is important because the *effective* properties of these classes are not typically identical to their physical properties. For instance, response *topography* is generally less important than response *function*. Also, the effective stimulus may not correspond to a simple physical value, and may be exceedingly abstract (see also Verplanck, 1954).

This summarizes the conceptual basis of Skinner's system. Skinner was keenly aware of the strictures of stimulus-response approaches to psychology, and was determined to offer a reasonable behaviorist alternative (e.g., Skinner, 1938, pp. 433–8). The stimulus-response approach in twentieth century psychology was the culmination of the philosophies of empiricism and associationism of the nineteenth century. The apotheosis of this approach appeared in the theory of Clark Hull. The difference between the theories of Skinner and Hull is most striking in their respective treatments of the units of analysis problem.

HULL'S ALTERNATIVE SYSTEM OF BEHAVIOR

Like other behaviorists, Hull (1937) wanted to substitute the experimental method of settling disputes for the pointless argumentation which seemed to characterize psychological debates. Unlike Skinner, Hull was a methodological behaviorist. For the methodological behaviorist the world is divided into public and private realms. The scientific requirement of inter-subjective reliability dictates publicly observable behavior as the subject matter of psychology. But behavior is interpreted as an indication or a manifestation of significant events, and is not treated as significant in its own right. For instance, according to this viewpoint, we can infer the existence of memory from an appropriate response after a delay, but memory itself is not directly observable. This position is able to preserve events of the private realm, such as memory, as explanations, while dealing only with events of the public realm, such as the movements of muscles and secretion of glands (Hull, 1943b, p. 30).

In contrast to Skinner's descriptive system, Hull proposed a highly formal, or formalistic, system. Like formalists before him, Hull believed that with the right formal notation system otherwise difficult problems would settle themselves, and any remaining uncertainties could be resolved by simple, experimental test (cf. Koch, 1954). Hull began his theory by explicitly assuming that with which everyone would agree. These commonly accepted assumptions served as postulates in a formal deductive theory. His own reading of the history of science convinced Hull that the formal deductive method was the only proper way of adhering to Bacon's adage that 'truth comes sooner from error than confusion'. By rigorously deducing the implications of the postulates, and by submitting these deductions to experimental test, the theory would be both progressive and self-correcting (Hull, 1943b, pp. 1–15).

Hull conceived of living organisms as adaptive machines produced by natural selection. To remove all doubt about his position, Hull at one time suggested as a 'prophylaxis against anthropomorphic subjectivism' that we consider the behaving organism as a completely self-maintaining robot (1943b, p. 27). It was clear to Hull that activity has evolved to support needs of the organism. Because of the variety and unpredictability of situations to which a living organism must adapt, Hull believed that truly adaptive organisms could not be equipped solely by natural selection. Learning was viewed as the adaptive means by which novel reactions could be established in the service of biological emergencies (1943b, p. 17). The adaptive basis of action left no room for 'the doctrine of despair' of emergentism. Any seemingly emergent properties of behavior, such as purpose or foresight, must eventually be reducible to fundamental adaptive processes, or 'mere movement and secretion' (1943b, p. 26).

HULL'S UNIT OF ANALYSIS

Hull suggested that significant correlations between behavior and environment occur at the most primitive levels of the nervous system. All forms of behavior were conceived to be associative connections between a physical stimulus trace and a physically defined response by the organism (1943b, p. 66). Some of these associative connections are unlearned, while others are acquired through experience. The objective of Hull's theory was to show how complex activity could be ultimately reduced to combinations or elaborations of these simple receptor-effector units, or, in the theory's terms, stimulus-response habits.

The implications of this reductionistic analysis are clear in an early attempt to provide a mechanistic account of the acquisition of knowledge (Hull, 1930, 1931). Hull represented the environment as a sequence of discrete stimulus events. Corresponding to each effective stimulus was a response by the receptive organism. In turn each response produced a characteristic internal stimulus. For Hull the correspondence of events in the organism to the sequence of events in the world was the organism's 'knowledge' of the world (1930, p. 514). Events inside and outside the organism were connected through redintegration. Redintegration is an archaic term which refers to a version of the principle of association by contiguity, or the ability of part of a stimulus complex to evoke the whole. Each event in a sequence of responses would be more or less contiguous in time with the next event in the sequence. Repeated exposure would lead to the ability of

prior events in the series to evoke following events in the series. However, redintegration alone could account only for the increasing fixation of a chain of responses in the presence of characteristic stimulation.

Finally, Hull added a stimulus component which was common to all responses in the sequence. This stimulus component was his representation of purposiveness, or the 'persisting core of sameness in stimulus complexes' (1930, p. 519). While all responses in a sequence leading to a goal would occur in close temporal proximity with the persisting stimulus core, some responses would benefit by association more than others. By intra-serial competition, later responses in the chain could occur earlier in the series. This 'short-circuiting' of the chain would solve for Hull the puzzling problem of 'foresight', or how an organism can respond to an 'impending' event (1930, p. 514).

From adaptive considerations, the formula was quickly revised to specify more clearly the role and nature of the 'persisting core of sameness'. The persisting state of the organism that makes an event a goal was termed a drive stimulus, while the effect of the organism's congress with the goal object was the reduction of the drive stimulus (1931, p. 489). Drive reduction became the basis of Hull's version of the law of effect. Another hypothesized effect of primary reinforcement was the fractional antedating goal response which served as a mediational mechanism for anticipation (1931, p. 495).

Hull (1935) was confident that his principle of primary reinforcement provided a unitary explanation of Pavlov's conditioned reflexes as well as the so-called 'associative reactions' studied by Thorndike. The mechanical reinforcement process was held to be fundamental, and even able to account for the 'striving' which seemed to precede it. Hull argued that in nature responses which precede particular states of affairs are likely to be causes of them. Therefore, causal stimulus-response sequences are almost always strengthened by primary reinforcement. The result is 'that the organism through the mere process of conditioning will come to strive for states of affairs which are positively reinforcing' (1935, p. 822).

DIFFERENCES BETWEEN SKINNER AND HULL

Practical implications of the theoretical differences between Skinner and Hull can be illustrated by the following brief examples: (1) the role of the law of effect; (2) the importance of schedules of reinforcement; (3) accounts of complex behavior.

The Role of the Law of Effect

Hull's postulate of primary reinforcement, which he considered the central postulate of his theory (cf. Koch, 1954), was a redefinition of Thorndike's law of effect. In Hull's theory the concept of reinforcement was the ultimate explanation of all changes in behavior, determining which stimulus-response linkages were strengthened and which weakened. Reflecting his adaptive viewpoint, Hull used the drive stimulus and drive reduction as the common factors in all cases of reinforcement. Hull's view of behavioral units required a persisting drive stimulus complex to explain the properties of lengthy response chains. Also drive reduc-

tion was required both to eliminate the persisting stimulus complex and to insure that correct response chains would be increasingly probable on future occasions. Hull's general drive reinforcement mechanism was eventually discredited by many findings, such as latent learning. The function of reinforcement in the theory was radically altered in later versions (Hull, 1950), reducing what was formerly the foundation of the theory to a secondary role.

Skinner remained aloof from these controversies because his concept of reinforcement was purely definitional. Operants are *defined* by their relationships with consequent events. Reinforcers are simply the consequent events which can be shown to change subsequent behavior. From this standpoint there is no reason to expect that all reinforcers will have a common property such as drive reduction, no matter how biologically attractive that may seem. What is common to reinforcing conditions is a set of operations which produces the effects, and the consistency of the changes in response classes as a result of the manipulation of reinforcing consequences (Skinner, 1950, p. 200).

Much of the criticism of Skinner's empirical law of effect, e.g., its presumed circularity, seems wide of the mark. Also the *significance* of the empirical law of effect often seems to be missed. For example, it is generally believed that Meehl's (1950) major contribution in his defense of the empirical law of effect is the concept of trans-situationality of reinforcers. While it is true that the law would be of less interest if no reinforcers were trans-situational, this is a minor point. Meehl rightly notes that the empirical law of effect, as a definition, cannot be proved or disproved. Detractors of the inductive approach seem to want laws of behavior stated before their discovery. The law of effect is a useful definition which aids the discovery of important classes of events. It proves its worth to the extent that it is helpful in organizing our observations. The empirical law of effect is not the final word, but the beginning, a way of *framing* the problems to be addressed (see also Malone, 1975).

Equally important is Meehl's recognition that reinforcement as defined by Skinner cannot be a *discrete* event. Rather, all instances of reinforcement involve what Meehl (1950) calls *schedule-reinforcer combinations*. Any time a putative reinforcer is made available, it occurs against a background of prior opportunities extending through time. The schedule of opportunities is as important as the biological significance of a reinforcer. It is the event *and* its schedule which determine when a reinforcer will be efficacious. The drive concept is unnecessary as well as misleading, in that it leads to the notion of a unitary state underlying reinforcement. Instead, the *context* in which an event occurs seems to be most important. Thus, the empirical law of effect emphasizes the temporal structure of events, and the diversity of context variables which determine reinforcement.

The Importance of Schedules of Reinforcement

One finding problematic for Hull's theory was the 'partial reinforcement effect'. The greater resistance to extinction found with less reinforcement presented something of a paradox. According to the theory, each response in a chain has an effective strength which is the result of its past proximity to primary reinforcement, or stimuli associated with primary reinforcement (Hull, 1943b, p. 97). But intermittent reinforcement produced fewer reinforced and more unreinforced

responses. Because of the theory's commitment to independent and isolated units of analysis, the gulf between the occurrence of the response and a reinforcer had to be bridged with hypothetical, and implausible, secondary reinforcers. Hull's (1931) fractional anticipatory goal response mechanism served as the general model for explanations of how behavior could be maintained in the face of asynchrony between responses and primary reinforcers.

The paradox for Hull's theory was the basis for one of the achievements of Skinner's theory, development of schedules of reinforcement. Continuous reinforcement represents only one type of reinforcement schedule. Since schedules are the fundamental contingent relations between behavior and environment, the characteristic behavior produced by the schedule tells us something important about the organism. If the environment is orderly at all, then by definition reinforcers are available on a schedule. With changes in the quantitative or qualitative aspects of the operative schedule, we expect to see a change in the behavior under the control of that schedule. Thus, the *pattern* of behavior produced by a schedule can be considered an appropriate behavioral unit, e.g., the 'scalloped' rate profile for a fixed-interval schedule, and does not need to be reduced to any more fundamental units. This pattern need not be explained by any underlying mechanisms. It is explained fully by the *pattern* of reinforcement produced by that behavior, i.e., the contingent relationship between behavior and environment (Skinner, 1950).

The advance in behavioral analysis and control produced by schedules of reinforcement was dependent on Skinner's conception of units of analysis. In Hull's theory predictions were based on measurements in terms of reinforced or non-reinforced trials. The concept of a trial is appropriate only if units of analysis refer to discrete events in time. However, in Skinner's theory opportunities for available reinforcement vary continuously through time, even in those cases in which the experimenter tries to establish discrete trials. The appropriate dependent measure from this point of view is rate of behavior, not merely because it was easier to employ than probability, but because time is implicit in the measure (Skinner, 1950, p. 198) Appropriate units of analysis describe relationships between variations in rate of behavior and variations in rate of reinforcement.

Accounts of Complex Behavior

Hull believed that all complex behavior could be reduced to simple stimulus-response associations. Since the fundamental units of analysis are simple, the complexity of overt behavior is translated into complexity of underlying, mediating events. Despite variation in the kinds of mechanisms employed, this translation is typical of all forms of methodological behaviorism. Viewed in this fashion, many cognitive theories are actually forms of methodological behaviorism. This point was not missed by Hull (1943a), when he explicitly compared the use of intervening variables in his theory with their similar function in the theories of Tolman and Brunswik.

On the other hand, Skinner did not believe that all behavior can be reduced to one level of analysis. Because he was committed to a treatment of behavior as significant in its own right, Skinner's units of analysis were defined at different levels, depending solely on the orderliness of observed relations. This being the

case, intervening variables such as the reflex reserve and drive were deemed unnecessary, and were eventually eliminated from the system. Although originally considered convenient summary terms, intervening variables divert attention from the search for functional relationships, and often themselves become the explanation for behavior (e.g., Skinner, 1950, p. 194).

Since stimulus and response classes as defined by Skinner can be arbitrarily abstract, operant analysis can be applied directly, rather than by analogy, to complex activity (cf. Verplanck, 1955). As one example, Skinner's operant approach does not try to reduce human verbal behavior to simple stimulus-response chains. But it also recognizes that saying people internalize rules of language structure does not really accomplish anything. Understanding how to use an internal rule would, presumably, require another rule, and it in turn another. Rules are *established* through the activities of a verbal community, by means of the characteristic consequences governing the occurrence of verbal responses (Skinner, 1957). The proper study of verbal behavior is the functional analysis of the contingencies employed in the acquisition and maintenance of verbal responses. Like any other response class, the verbal response class is defined by the dynamic laws which govern its occurrence in the verbal community. Physical aspects of the response class, such as its phonetic structure, cannot be assumed to be defining characteristics (Skinner, 1945, p. 273).

The functional approach to verbal behavior is general enough to deal with subjective expressions which refer to private events, a topic considered crucial by Skinner (1945, p. 274). As with any other expression, the use of expressions descriptive of private events must be established by the verbal community on the basis of three-term contingency. The problem of gaining verbal control over private events cannot be solved by 'inferring' the private stimulus in question, nor by the use of more precise physiological measurement. If a subjective expression such as 'I have a pain' can be used consistently in ordinary life, then the means must be available for the verbal community to provide contingent reinforcement for such expressions. Because of the limited possibilities for differential reinforcement, and because of the inadequate means of protection against deception, Skinner notes that our own knowledge of these private events must be severely limited (Skinner 1945, p. 278, 1964, p. 84).

CONCLUSION

Skinner's position is often confused with that of methodological behaviorism. However, Skinner has consistently argued that this form of behaviorism maintains an illegitimate distinction between public and private worlds (e.g., Skinner, 1945). Radical behaviorism, on the contrary, concerns only one world, the world in which living creatures interact with their environment. Skinner's operant theory is based on the tenets of radical behaviorism, and concerns itself solely with the important functional relationships which occur between behavior and environment.

To a certain extent the use of a common set of terms such as stimulus, response, and reinforcer has made Skinner's theory seem more similar to other behavioral theories than it really is (see also Verplanck, 1954). In fact, the stimulus-response theory of Hull is widely considered to be the prototype of

behavioral theory. Nonetheless, operant theory is different in fundamental ways, primarily because of its foundation of radical behaviorism. Skinner's commitment to radical behaviorism resulted in his unique solution to the units of analysis problem. Rejecting reductionistic associationism, operant theory defines the appropriate level of analysis for behavioral units at the point of optimal orderliness between environment and behavior. Thus, the observer discovers through investigation the appropriate level of analysis, rather than trying to force the behavior he observes into the slots of a preconceived stencil.

Skinner's admonitions against the inappropriate use of theory also follow from his radical behaviorism. One of the prime functions of theory is to bridge temporal gaps between events (Skinner, 1956). If analytic units are arbitrarily defined in terms of discrete, physical properties, and only contiguous events can affect one another, then intervening events, such as memory, must be postulated to explain behavior. However, if analytic units are properly defined, the significance of the temporal dimension of behavior is also included. In this way the functional approach of operant analysis addresses the 'natural lines of fracture' between behavior and environment, not the arbitrary lines drawn for the sake of theory.

By accepting the potential complexity of behavior, and by resisting the temptation to reduce behavior to associations between simple physical events, Skinner avoided a number of problems encountered by Hull. Strangely enough, many of the criticisms of the operant approach seem to be addressed to limitations of the approach typified by Hull (see MacCorquodale, 1970). It is also ironic that many cognitive theories, which are supposed to go beyond the limitations of behaviorism, posit underlying mechanisms, different in degree but similar in function, to those employed in Hull's theory. While Skinner's inductive approach has often has criticized for its lack of theoretical structure, honest poverty is always preferable to suspicious wealth.

REFERENCES

Hull, C.L. (1930) 'Knowledge and purpose as habit mechanisms', *Psychological Review*, 37, pp. 511–25.

Hull, C.L. (1931) 'Goal attraction and directing ideas conceived as habit phenomena', *Psychological Review*, 38, pp. 487–506.

Hull, C.L. (1935) 'Special review: Thorndike's *Fundamentals of Learning'*, *Psychological Bulletin*, 32, pp. 807–23.

Hull, C.L. (1937) 'Mind, mechanism, and adaptive behavior', *Psychological Review*, 44, pp. 1–32.

Hull, C.L. (1943a) 'The problem of intervening variables in molar behavior theory', *Psychological Review*, 50, pp. 273–91.

Hull, C.L. (1943b) *Principles of Behavior*, New York, Appleton-Century-Crofts.

Hull, C.L. (1950) 'Behavior postulates and corollaries — 1949', *Psychological Review*, 57, pp. 173–80.

Koch, S. (1954) 'Clark L. Hull', in Estes, W.K. *et al.*, *Modern Learning Theory*, New York, Appleton-Century-Crofts, pp. 267–317.

MacCorquodale, K. (1970) 'On Chomsky's review of Skinner's *Verbal Behavior*', *Journal of the Experimental Analysis of Behavior*, 13, pp. 83–9.

Malone, J.C. Jr (1975) 'William James and B.F. Skinner: Behaviorism, reinforcement, and interest', *Behaviorism*, 3, pp. 140–51.

Meehl, P. (1950) 'On the circularity of the law of effect', *Psychological Bulletin*, 47, pp. 52–75.

Skinner, B.F. (1931) 'The concept of the reflex in the description of behavior', *Journal of General Psychology*, 5, pp. 427–58.

Skinner, B.F. (1935) 'The generic nature of the concepts of stimulus and response', *Journal of General Psychology*, 12, pp. 40–65.

Skinner, B.F. (1938) *The Behavior of Organisms*, New York, Appleton-Century-Crofts.

Skinner, B.F. (1945) 'The operational analysis of psychological terms', *Psychological Review*, 52, pp. 270–77, 291–4.

Skinner, B.F. (1950) 'Are theories of learning necessary?' *Psychological Review*, 57, pp. 193–216.

Skinner, B.F. (1956) 'What is psychotic behavior?' *Cumulative Record*, New York, Appleton-Century-Crofts.

Skinner, B.F. (1957) *Verbal Behavior*, New York, Appleton-Century-Crofts.

Skinner, B.F. (1964) 'Behaviorism at fifty', in Wann, T.W. (Ed.), *Behaviorism and Phenomenology*, Chicago, Ill., University of Chicago Press.

Verplanck, W.S. (1954) 'Burrhus F. Skinner', in Estes W.K. *et al.*, *Modern Learning Theory*, New York, Appleton-Century-Crofts, pp. 267–317.

Verplanck, W.S. (1955) 'The operant, from rat to man: An introduction to some recent experiments on human behavior', *Transactions of the N.Y. Academy of Sciences*, 17, 8, pp. 594–601.

Watson, J.B. (1913) 'Psychology as the behaviorist views it', *Psychological Review*, 20, pp. 158–77.

Watson, J.B. (1916) 'The place of the conditioned reflex in psychology', *Psychological Review*, 23, pp. 89–116.

16. Skinner, the Behavioral Unit, and Current Psychology

JOHN C. MALONE JR

Skinner is clearly aware of the current sad state of psychology, as he showed in a recent and lively paper (Skinner, 1983). A 'new' cognitive orientation is indeed with us; unfortunately, it takes the form of new wrinkles on an old associationism and the positing of simple faculties, such as memory. One would think that Skinner's (1963) 'Behaviorism at Fifty' had never been written. Along with cognition, the discovery that pigeons do not require careful training to learn to peck a key has led to the small science of autoshaping, a development that may puzzle posterity; and, if one judges from Mackintosh (1983), 'blocking' may emerge as the phenomenon of the decade. These and other 'advances' suggest that history and systems may better be taught in reverse chronological order if progress is to be shown.

Skinner may be partly responsible for the 'shambles' that he calls current psychology. He has consistently failed to appreciate what seem to be obvious implications of his early analysis of the behavioral unit, and he has failed to emphasize adequately the difference between his analysis and simple S-R associationist psychology. This ensured that when the latter very vulnerable position came under strong attack, the experimental analysis of behavior would be considered part of the target. The problem was compounded by Skinner's frequent and paradoxical emphasis on molecular behavior and momentary contingencies (contiguous causality), which is utterly incompatible with his analysis of the behavioral unit.

As his efforts became more devoted to plausibility arguments for the analysis of complex behavior and less to daily collection and analysis of data, he abandoned a number of 'theoretical' terms, such as the reflex reserve. The few allowable terms that remained seemed sparse indeed when offered as sufficient for the analysis of behavior in general. This left us in the embarrassing position of

being unable to answer in a plausible way the simple questions posed by colleagues; we can avoid 'explanatory fictions' without being restricted to speaking only of 'emitted operants reinforced in the presence of ...'.

Skinner has been misinterpreted by sympathetic colleagues of long standing (e.g., Herrnstein, 1977), and I expect that I will misinterpret him as well. Perhaps greater clarity and consistency on his part would avoid such misinterpretation and avoid much misdirected criticism. The urgency of the matter is illustrated when one considers some recent critics.

CRITICS OF THE ANALYSIS OF BEHAVIOR: CAUSE FOR CONCERN?

Skinner's critics fall into four rough groups, ranked in order of increasing sophistication; the first two may be ignored, but the second two warrant attention. Thus, one need not be concerned with the first group, including Chomsky, Koch, and the like. Such critics, like Skinner's (1983) psychiatrist friend, either have no idea what they are talking about or they are concerned with matters other than objective psychology and will be receptive to no argument that treats them as 'organisms'.

The second, 'biological boundaries' group of critics seems more knowledgeable about its target, seems to know Pavlov's and Skinner's works, and includes former advocates of Skinner's program. However, it is now clear that their target has been the leftovers of Hull's S-R theory, that became everyone's naive 'behaviorism' by the 1960s (see Malone, 1982). Many of these critics were themselves former advocates of the simple associationist view they attack, who evidently never distinguished it from behavior analysis.

The third group lies in behavior therapy, which is strange, since that is where the power of the EAB has been obviously shown and where there seems no reason for theoretical debates. But what an odd view of behavior analysis is held by many behavior therapists! According to Mahoney (1977), they all pass through clinical training programs constituting 'behavioral boot camp', where they are taught that *behavior* is movement in space. If one teaches patients to monitor their own behavior (as Skinner does his), set goals, imagine various things, or set their own contingencies, s/he is not a good behaviorist. Hence, we have 'cognitive behavior therapy', which is thought by its practitioners to be fundamentally different from radical behaviorism. How could such gross misunderstanding possibly have occurred? Perhaps if Skinner had not waited until he retired in 1963 to publish 'Behaviorism at Fifty', the message of radical behaviorism might have been received earlier and more effectively.

Of course, *some* cognitive behavior therapy *is* non-behavioral. That occurs when it is based on a mixture of simple S-R theory and very naive cognitive psychology. Bandura's (1977) 'central processor of efficacy information' is a prime example of this, and some of the same errors are shared by Staats' (1981) lesser-known 'social behaviorism'. Staats proposed nine levels of analysis, ranging from animal learning to humanism, each with its own principles, thus missing more than one point. Conditioning and associationism are for the animals, while the question of freedom applies to the humanism end. It is exasperating when students see such 'social learning theories' as a perfect blend of behavioral and cognitive views.

If the misunderstandings of behavior therapists and social learning theorists are of concern, those of the fourth group are cause for real concern. These critics include former associate editors and editorial board members of the *Journal of the Experimental Analysis of Behavior* (*JEAB*). Some contributed to Hulse, Fowler and Honig's (1978) *Cognitive Processes in Animal Behavior*, a volume reviewed favorably in *JEAB*, though not without dissent (Malone, 1982). Most contributing authors criticized 'behaviorism', conceived as the crassest possible S-R associationism. One wrote that behaviorists believe that only movements or glandular secretions can be learned and the tone of individual chapters suggested that others agreed. Is that behaviorism? And is the only alternative the 'translating, organizing, storing, and reprocessing' of stimulation, as Honig suggested in his preface?

H.M. Jenkins is a distinguished former associate editor of *JEAB* who contributed an authoritative chapter on the history of theory and research in animal conditioning and learning to a volume sponsored by the Psychonomic Society (Jenkins, 1979). In it he described the main characteristics of behavior analysis fairly, but with little fervor. Its accomplishments were noted in a very few sentences, praise was vanishingly faint, and attention was turned to more popular current trends. He was probably accurate in identifying these trends and they were clearly outside and largely irrelevant to the analysis of behavior.

Jenkins made it clear that simple association theory has been and is the dominant 'theoretical schema'; even Pavlov is now cast as an S-R theorist. (It still seems a wonder that anyone could read Pavlov and reach the conclusion that bare principles of association were an important part of his thinking [Pavlov, 1932].) Current researchers seem anxious to trade the simple associationism of the 'outside story' for a similar associationism of the 'inside story', which is somehow more 'rich and complex' and involves 'conceptual associations encoding knowledge'. Jenkins clearly did not endorse this trend, though his repeated contrasting of 'knowledge-centred' and 'response-centered' approaches seemed to favor the former. While the inner/outer associationists battle it out, the analysis of behavior can continue to attempt to 'control' people and animals and do whatever it does with schedules of reinforcement.

Schwartz is a capable researcher and former member of the *JEAB* editorial board who has recently been castigated by Skinner (1983) and by others. As co-author of a recent text (Schwartz and Lacey, 1982), he presented behaviorism, including Skinner's, as so crude an S-R associationism that even Hull would have found it repellent. It came as no surprise that he and Lacey had little difficulty in progressively demolishing this 'behaviorism' through the book. Amazingly, they pointed to conspicuous successes in behavior therapy as failures, since the version of behaviorism they presented could not account for them.

It gives one pause to realize that critics in this, the most sophisticated, group seem to see little difference between Skinner and Hull! Is behavior analysis that easily confusable with S-R associationism? Can the analysis of behavior not handle the 'rich and complex'? What happened since 1935 that left Skinner and Hull sharing paragraphs in many recent texts? What happened to the concept of the operant?

ARE THERE ONLY TWO CHOICES?

Do *I* misunderstand? *Is* the analysis of behavior essentially equivalent to the leftover Hullian psychology that is recent S-R assocationism? Or does the present state of affairs mean that the awful choice that James (1890) described is still the *only* choice for most of us? James contrasted the 'rationalist/soul' theory with the associationism of his day and found both wanting. But those were the choices of 1890. Do many today feel that our choice is thus constrained? Is it a question of simple associationism versus 'powerful central determinants'? Is the analysis of behavior equated with the former choice?

Consider Bandura (1977), who contrasted 'connectionist/peripheral' and 'cognitive/central' viewpoints. Citing the matching law and the demonstrated importance of contingency over contiguity, he rejected the former viewpoint (in which he included behavior analysis) in favor of the latter, which he developed as his 'central processor of efficacy information'. James' two poor alternatives were the only choices he could envision. Many others, in addition to those mentioned above, seem to share the same view.

Assuming that all these critics are genuine, we can only conclude that Skinner's message has not been received. It is extremely important to recognize that behaviorism in general has been interpreted as S-R connectionism by the general public, by virtually every college student, by its critics, *and* by many behaviorists, including former supporters of the analysis of behavior noted above. As the deficiencies of that view have become apparent, alternatives have been sought, as is proper. But the alternatives tend to be of the 'rationalist/soul' kind or of forms otherwise incompatible with radical behaviorism.

Some sophisticated critics are concerned with the organization of behavior, which they feel the analysis of behavior unequipped to deal with and which makes 'central determinants' seem attractive. It may be that the view of reflex organization described by Sherrington (1906), and adopted in large part by Pavlov (1927), could have provided some of the organization they find lacking. But Skinner's (1938) harsh treatment and Hull's (1943) 'translation and trivialization' of Pavlov ensured that these views would not be influential. In any event, if Skinner's program is not S-R connectionism, as it is not, we must make it clear just what it *is*. Did Skinner fail to grasp his own message well enough to communicate it clearly and consistently?

THE CONCEPT OF THE OPERANT

Skinner (1931, 1935) published an analysis of the reflex, concluding that it was really a conceptual expression referring to a kind of correlation between stimulation and responding. There are rules for the discovery of reflexes that tell us when we have isolated one and the demonstration of a reflex constitutes an explanation for the behavior involved. We isolate 'physiological' reflexes by showing that an observed correlation of stimulation and responding obeys the static and dynamic laws that define reflexes in general.

Pavlovian CRs may also be defined by appeal to static and dynamic laws, with the latter including the laws of conditioning and extinction of Type S. The discovery of conditioned reflexes thus accounts for that much more of an organ-

ism's behavior. Skinner used the same strategy to show 'reflex order' in what seemed spontaneous behavior, for which there are no obvious eliciting stimuli. To make a long story short, we find that such behavior is often influenced by its consequences and that by manipulating them we may show orderly changes in the occurrence of such behaviors. Thus, the laws of conditioning and extinction of Type R may be used as dynamic laws to define a unit of 'operant' behavior. If orderly changes occur as we manipulate schedules of reinforcement, 'motivation', and so on, we may be certain that we have identified an operant and thus extended the lawfulness of the reflex to the level of freely-occurring behavior.

Our unit, therefore, is not determined in advance, as was Hull's S-R habit. We seek eliciting stimuli or consequences that influence a behavior and then refine our definition of stimulation and behavior until we discover the classes that covary in an orderly way. In practice the discovery of response classes may reveal some behaviors as members that we could not have foreseen. For example, training a child to keep a room neat may influence an operant class including punctuality, personal cleanliness, and so on (cf. Rachlin, 1976). The organism, not the experimenter, defines the response class.

What does this mean? It seems clear that the intensive study of 'representative' units, such as the rat's bar press, is aimed at the discovery of regularities that we may use as guides when we examine more complex behavior. In the search for order in behavior, whether animal or human, we may find the operant appearing at a molecular level, as in the demonstration of operant muscle contractions (Hefferline and Keenan, 1963). In other cases the operant may be describable only in more molar terms, as temporally-extended behavior, showing the inadequacy of a thoroughgoing emphasis on molecular units and contiguous causes.

Recent research shows clearly that order often appears only when one looks at the relation between contingencies and behavior over time. For example, it is noteworthy that Mackintosh (1983), who squeezed the last drops from simple associationism, finally seemed to agree that Herrnstein and Hineline's (1966) demonstration that responding may be established and maintained by a molar consequence (reduction of overall shock frequency) cannot be explained in molecular terms. Morse and Kelleher (1977) reviewed very important data showing the maintenance of clear patterns of behavior over periods of weeks with only powerful response-produced electric shock as the reinforcer. Barrett and Stanley (1980) showed that electric shock may maintain one behavior that produces it, while concurrently maintaining a second behavior that avoids shock. And, depending upon the contingencies, hungry subjects may respond to avoid food, just as others respond to avoid shock (Clark and Smith, 1977). To the non perceptive these are sideshow tricks. In fact, they demonstrate the important influence of behavioral history and current contingencies on behavior extended in time. Neither simple S-R theory nor cognitive theories are useful in accounting for such data.

Research of this kind, and much of that done on higher-order reinforcement schedules, seems to follow directly from Skinner's 1931 and 1935 papers; the behavioral unit may be molecular or molar, but it is always defined by the organism. It is surely inappropriate to define the response class by reference to *both* experimenter-set contingencies and the organism's behavior, as suggested by Catania (1973). Whatever the experimenter's requirements, the response class must be defined by the organism, or the sense of the behavioral unit is lost (cf.

Staddon, 1967). We need not repeat Hull's (1943) error and specify our units in advance. (If this interpretation of Skinner's analysis seems incorrect or unclear, interested readers may consult Staddon, 1967, pp. 377–87 for an excellent treatment of the concept of the operant.)

SKINNER AFTER 1935

Skinner (1938) inadvertently illustrated his (1953) thesis that we are 'many selves' or 'repertoires of behavior'; his first two chapters appear to have been written by different authors. After summarizing his 1931 and 1935 papers describing the strategy for the discovery of functional behavioral units in the first chapter, he considered *chaining* in the second. He noted that once a simple chain is established, such as a rat's approaching a lever, pressing it, seizing a food pellet, and eating it, it 'appears' that its members form a functional unit. Any reader who understood the preceding chapter would agree. If we vary the rat's food deprivation, or its sleep cycle, or if we give it drugs, we might expect to find orderly changes in the performance of the sequence. Surely it becomes a functional unit, and is not best viewed as a series of discrete units!

Incredibly, Skinner insisted that however unitary a chain may seem, it is not a unit, as may be seen by interrupting it at different points. What an odd conclusion. What is a critic, such as Chomsky, to assume concerning Skinner's interpretation of verbal sequences? Many years later Skinner's views changed, though glacially slowly. Skinner (1953) non commitally wrote that we often think of a chain as a single response and in the 1960s he noted that a series of turns or a run of musical notes function as one response, though learned bit by bit (Skinner, 1980).

Trying to show that Skinner is more consistent than he appears, sympathetic authors, such as Zeiler (1977), point out that Skinner long ago (1938) suggested that *patterns* of responding typically occurring under specific reinforcement schedules may be treated as units. This would exemplify the point of his early analysis of the behavioral unit, which suggests that the functional unit is defined at that level, molecular or molar, where order appears. But one may search Skinner's writings over the years, vainly seeking such statements, and the 1938 reference is disappointing. On page 300 he did suggest that the response pattern typical of fixed-ratio schedules may be treated as a unit, but on the two succeeding pages he dismissed this possibility and decided that each response was better viewed as an independent unit, with the series held together by conditioned reinforcement!

In later works he showed a continued and puzzling preference for molecular interpretations. How could the author of the 1931 and 1935 papers, who in 1938 emphasized the importance of response *rate* as a datum and who popularized the use of the cumulative recorder, prefer molecular units of behavior and contiguous causation? Skinner (1983) reiterated such a preference, referring approvingly to the emphasis Ferster and Skinner (1957) placed on the importance of conditions prevailing at the precise moment of reinforcement.

Jenkins (1970) attempted to account for behavior generated by simple reinforcement schedules, using the terms of molecular S-R associationism, such as conditioned reinforcement, chaining, delay of reinforcement, and the like. He concluded that even simple schedule behavior was not interpretable in those

terms. Corroborating evidence shows that he was certainly correct, and one hopes that Skinner will eventually reach the same conclusion.

Herrnstein (1977) illustrated another inconsistency in Skinner's views. He interpreted Skinner's concept of the 'stimulus class' as equivalent to the empirical generalization gradient. He *was* mistaken, though anyone who read Skinner's papers of the early thirties would make the same inference. For Skinner (1938) the relation of the stimulus to the 'pseudoreflex', or discriminated operant, could have been clearer, but his 'law of induction' clearly specified that a generalization gradient reflected a spreading (inducing) of the effects of reinforcement to *related reflexes*. This means that a response to 500 Hz and an 'induced' response to 510 Hz are different behavioral units (though the treatment of discrimination and the reserve on page 229 leaves the matter obscure).

Skinner's molecular emphasis has surely not aided our understanding of stimulus control. The remarkable history of research on behavioral contrast and the attempt to account for it in molecular terms were competently covered in a section of a review by Williams (1983) and show that the analysis of behavior is still inept in the study of stimulus control. Skinner may have emphasized the 'three-term contingency' for decades, but his relative lack of concern for stimulus control was manifested in the work of Guttman and his colleagues, who used Skinner's methods but Hull's hypotheses (Guttman, 1963).

All of this suggests that Skinner's argument for the functional unit of behavior was not even very influential on *his* thinking. He is known for his arguments against 'mental way stations', as unnecessary fillers of temporal gaps (e.g., 1963), and that would seem to indicate that he clearly opposes exclusive reliance on molecular interpretations and contiguous causes. But there is enough of both in his writings to convince the non dedicated reader that Skinner is little different from Hull. The language of behavior analysis adds to this impression.

A COMMON QUESTION AND A MAJOR INFERENCE

An intelligent colleague on his way to class recently asked me 'a quick question'. This was, 'Does Skinner believe that learning always depends on reinforcement?' What does one answer in the thirty seconds available? 'Yes, ultimately, but ... a reinforcer may be anything, from food to tactual contact or any other consequence ... skilled repertoires of behavior established in childhood may survive intact over half a lifetime, though unused ... the class of behaviors involved may include unforeseen members, as in verbal behavior ... behaviors extended in time, such as verbal passages and motor sequences, may act as units.' One gropes for words, concluding with, 'the best way to look at it is in terms of contingencies effective over the species' and individual's histories.'

The colleague was probably wondering about latent learning or whether a conspicuous reinforcer was necessary for thinking or problem-solving. But when all one can say is, 'yes, but there is more to it ...', it is natural to wonder whether we have not progressed past the simple terms that Skinner (1938) found to characterize 'the most convenient formulation at the present time'.

In considering the common behavior of an adult human with an unknown history of exposure to 'contingencies' we must make the same inference that Skinner (1966a) pointed to as a disadvantage in interpreting behavior controlled

by phylogenic factors. Just as we must infer selection of such 'instinctive' behavior in the distant past, we must also infer similar selection during the individual's lifetime. Are the terms we use to describe such selection, for example, discriminative stimuli, operants, and reinforcers, the best terms to describe the product? Why not follow Holt (1915), who emphasized the reflex *basis* of behavior, as a prophylactic against supernatural causes, but who proposed different descriptors for the behavior of the whole organism?

Much seeing *is* operant, but 'operant seeing' will never be acceptable to many. 'Functional seeing' might well be acceptable. Verbal behavior is largely functional, but the 'emitted verbal operant' will always conjure up the bar-pressing rat. One can almost hear Skinner asking, 'What's wrong with that?', but he knows the answer. This was evident in his (1966b) proposal that *rule-governed behavior* be distinguished from *contingency-shaped behavior*. A space scientist guiding in a satellite exemplifies the former, while a baseball player fielding a fly ball represents the latter. The single term, 'rule', represents the wisdom imparted to us by society that makes it unnecessary for us to directly experience the contingencies to which they refer. Such rules do not exist in verbal form for much contingency-shaped behavior. But Skinner still called rules 'discriminative stimuli' and so the step in the right direction was a small one.

THE FUTURE

Why not call a rule a rule and leave the discriminative stimulus to refer to discrete and simple stimuli? J.R. Kantor was even more careful than Skinner to avoid any possibility of mentalism or other fictional causes, yet even he criticized the experimental analysis of behavior for assuming that the use of common language terms would mean their instant reification (Kantor, 1970). What is wrong with speaking, reading, seeing, thinking, remembering, hoping, and the like? We can retain the point of radical behaviorism without the constant baggage of operants and reinforcers. Why not assume that histories of reinforcement are *ultimately* the causes of behavior without appearing to insist that they are still effective moment by moment, thus requiring us to resort to arguments that seem thin and fishy, as we point to hypothetical reinforcers? We would be wise to dispense with 'conditioned reinforcement', which has already done enough spurious service.

There are good reasons for following the advice of Holt and Kantor. First, those who are concerned with Lloyd-Morgan's 'inside story' or with associations, cognitive maps, processors, marginal utility, or encoding will go (or have gone) their way in any event. Second, if we follow the logic of the concept of the reflex, units are of whatever form or temporal extension that show orderly relations with contingencies. Research already cited by Herrnstein and Hineline, Morse and Kelleher, and others represents what may be the best illustration of the Skinnerian viewpoint. That is, they show that in many cases order may exist only at a molar level, not at the molecular level of S-R associationism. Even the matching law illustrates this principle, insofar as it emphasizes the influence of temporally-extended variables. The law of effect becomes a relative law, and order appears most clearly when relative behavior over time is related to relative consequences over time. A lot of fudging is necessary to make this law generally true and a

more molecular analysis is always possible. But in all these cases description in terms of operants and reinforcers is difficult.

Third, the analysis of behavior must make contact with kindred views in other areas of psychology, where terminology is now a barrier. Bem (1967) probably did not think of himself as a behavior analyst, but he correctly interpreted radical behaviorism and ingeniously proposed his theory of 'self-perception', which played a large part in eradicating cognitive dissonance theory. No references to operants or reinforcers were necessary. Neisser (1976) abandoned his earlier information processing orientation and suggested that cognitive activity is more usefully conceived as a set of acquired skills, while perception is 'something we do', requiring no internal mechanisms. Gibson (e.g., 1966) specified the conditions necessary for ordinary perception, without recourse to internal processing (cf. Costall, 1984). Many other examples of congenial viewpoints exist, but our terminology makes the analysis of behavior seem fundamentally different.

Our analyses cannot continue indefinitely to be cast in basic conditioning terms; they do not do justice to the phenomena and they are all too easily construed as a variant of S-R associationism. This will be the case, however energetic the counterargument, as long as 'discriminative stimulus' and 'operant' can be construed as 'S' and 'R'. To the public and to our colleagues this will remain the language of the animal trainer, and they will turn to accounts that seem better fitted to deal with 'the complexity and richness' of behavior and experience.

One is reminded of Watson, who was far more reasonable than Skinner and others have concluded. He had no problem with the use of ordinary language descriptors, as long as they were behavioral, rather than cast in the language of the introspectionists. Skinner (1938) accused him of avoiding the mental by turning to the neural, but this suggests only that Skinner never seriously read Watson (1919). Watson began to argue against using neural explanations in the preface, where he explained the lack of neurological illustrations, pointing out that they promote a static rather than a dynamic conception. Later, on page 349, he criticized those who drag in the nervous system 'by its hair'. He was by no means a molecular S-R associationist and he anticipated, albeit crudely, Skinner's later argument for the behavioral unit by using 'stimulus' and 'response' to refer to either molecular or molar things, depending upon the phenomenon under consideration. What *is* wrong with 'botanizing reflexes', if that is done as Watson proposed, using common language *behavioral* descriptors and seeking order in phenomena of interest to us?

REFERENCES

Bandura, A. (1977) 'Self-efficacy: Toward a unifying theory of behavioral change', *Psychological Review*, 84, pp.191–215.

Barrett, J.E. and Stanley, J.A. (1980) 'Maintenance of responding by squirrel monkeys under a concurrent shock-postponement, fixed-interval shock-presentation schedule', *Journal of the Experimental Analysis of Behavior*, 34, pp. 117–29.

Bem, D.J. (1967) 'Self-perception: An alternative interpretation of cognitive dissonance phenomena', *Psychological Review*, 74, pp. 183–98.

Catania, A.C. (1973) 'The concept of the operant in the analysis of behavior', *Behaviorism*, 1, pp. 103–16.

Clark, F.C. and Smith, J.B. (1977) 'Schedules of food postponement: II. Maintenance of behavior by food postponement and effects of the schedule parameter', *Journal of the Experimental Analysis of Behavior*, 28, pp. 253–69.

Costall, A.P. (1984) 'Are theories of perception necessary? A review of Gibson's *The Ecological Approach to Visual Perception*', *Journal of the Experimental Analysis of Behavior*, 41, pp. 109–15.

Ferster, C.B. and Skinner, B. F. (1957) *Schedules of Reinforcement*, New York, Appleton-Century-Crofts.

Gibson, J.J. (1966) *The Senses Considered As Perceptual Systems*, Boston, Mass., Houghton Mifflin.

Guttman, N. (1963) 'Laws of behavior and facts of perception', in Koch, S. (Ed.), *Psychology: A Study of a Science*, Vol. 5, New York, McGraw-Hill, pp. 114–78.

Hefferline, R.F. and Keenan, B. (1963) 'Amplitude-induction gradient of a small-scale (covert) operant', *Journal of the Experimental Analysis of Behavior*, 6, pp. 307–15.

Herrstein, R.J. (1977) 'The evolution of behaviorism', *American Psychologist*, 32, pp. 593–603.

Herrnstein, R.J. and Hineline, P.N. (1966) 'Negative reinforcement as shock-frequency reduction', *Journal of the Experimental Analysis of Behavior*, 9, pp. 421–30.

Holt, E.B. (1915) *The Freudian Wish and Its Place in Ethics*, New York, Holt.

Hull, C.L. (1943) *Principles of Behavior*, New York, Appleton-Century.

Hulse, S.H., Fowler, H., and Honig, W.K. (Eds) (1978) *Cognitive Processes in Animal Behavior*, Hillsdale, N.J., Erlbaum.

James, W. (1890) *The Principles of Psychology*, New York, Henry Holt.

Jenkins, H.M. (1970) 'Sequential organization in schedules of reinforcement', in Schoenfeld, W.N. (Ed.), *The Theory of Reinforcement Schedules*, New York, Appleton-Century-Crofts.

Jenkins, H.M. (1979) 'Animal learning and behavior theory', in Hearst, E. (Ed.), *The First Century of Experimental Psychology*, Hillsdale, N.J., Erlbaum.

Kantor, J.R. (1970) 'An analysis of the experimental analysis of behavior (TEAB)', *Journal of the Experimental Analysis of Behavior*, 13, pp. 101–8.

Mackintosh, N.J. (1983) *Conditioning and Associative Learning*, New York, Oxford University Press.

Mahoney, M.J. (1977) 'Cognitive therapy and research: A question of questions', *Cognitive Therapy and Research*, 1, pp. 5–16.

Malone, J.C. Jr (1982) 'The second offspring of general process learning theory: Overt behavior as the ambassador of the mind', *Journal of the Experimental Analysis of Behavior*, 38, pp. 205–9.

Morse, W.H. and Kelleher, R.T. (1977) 'Determinants of reinforcement and punishment', in Honig, W.K. and Staddon, J.E.R. (Eds), *Handbook of Operant Behavior*, Englewood Cliffs, N.J., Erlbaum.

Neisser, U. (1976) *Cognition and Reality*, San Francisco, Calif., W.H. Freeman.

Pavlov, I.P. (1927) *Conditioned Reflexes*, trans. G. V. Anrep, London, Oxford University Press.

Pavlov, I.P. (1932) 'The reply of a physiologist to psychologists', *Psychological Review*, 39, pp. 91–127.

Rachlin, H. (1976) *Introduction to Modern Behaviorism*, San Francisco, Calif., W.H. Freeman.

Schwartz, B. and Lacey, H. (1982) *Behaviorism, Science, and Human Nature*, New York, Norton.

Sherrington, C.S. (1906) *The Integrative Action of the Nervous System*, New Haven, Conn., Yale University Press.

Skinner, B.F. (1931) 'The concept of the reflex in the description of behavior', *Journal of General Psychology*, 5, pp. 427–58.

Skinner, B.F. (1935) 'The generic nature of the concepts of stimulus and response', *Journal of General Psychology*,, 12, pp. 40–65.

Skinner, B.F. (1938) *The Behavior of Organisms*, New York, Appleton-Century.

Skinner, B.F. (1953) *Science and Human Behavior*, New York, Macmillan.

Skinner, B.F. (1963) 'Behaviorism at fifty', *Science*, 140, pp. 951–8.

Skinner, B.F. (1966a) 'An operant analysis of problem solving', in Kleinmuntz, B. (Ed.), *Problem Solving*, New York, Wiley.

Skinner, B.F. (1966b) 'The phylogeny and ontogeny of behavior', *Science*, 153, pp. 1205–13.

Skinner, B.F. (1980) *Notebooks*, Englewood Cliffs, N.J., Prentice-Hall.

Skinner, B.F. (1983) 'Can the EAB rescue psychology?' *The Behavior Analyst*, 6, pp. 9–17.

Staats, A.W. (1981) 'Paradigmatic behaviorism, unified theory, unified theory construction methods, and the Zeitgeist of separatism', *American Psychologist,* 36, pp. 239–56.

Staddon, J.E.R. (1967) 'Asymptotic behavior: The concept of the operant', *Psychological Review,* 74, pp. 377–91.

Watson, J.B. (1919) *Psychology from the Standpoint of a Behaviorist,* Philadelphia, Pa., Lippincott.

Williams, B.A. (1983) 'Another look at contrast in multiple schedules', *Journal of the Experimental Analysis of Behavior,* 39, pp. 345–84.

Zeiler, M. (1977) 'Schedules of reinforcement', in Honig, W.K. and Staddon, J.E.R. (Eds), *Handbook of Operant Behavior,* Hillsdale, N.J., Erlbaum.

Interchange

HINSON REPLIES TO MALONE

The commentary by Malone is clear and forceful, and in general I believe that his arguments strengthen my own. I should first like to summarize the most important points, while noting my agreements and disagreements with the issues raised by Malone.

Skinner's commitment to radical behaviorism is clearly the key to any interpretation of his work. Unfortunately many psychologists and philosophers have a difficult time understanding radical behaviorism. Part of the confusion may occur because of the normal distinction drawn between methodological and radical behaviorism, as though they were two varieties of the same general line of thought. In fact, methodological behaviorism is a dualistic philosophy, and it is this very dualism that radical behaviorism is trying to combat. Dualism serves as the framework for discourse about the unknowable, and inevitably leads to philosophical skepticism, as surely now as it did in Descartes' time. But from the dualistic perspective radical behaviorism seems to be a form of monism, since it excludes the mental and seemingly concerns itself only with events defined along physical dimensions.

Modern cognitive psychologists, who are uniformly critical of Skinner, also contribute to the misunderstanding of radical behaviorism. While seeing their discipline as a reaction to narrow behaviorist orthodoxy, they are, in fact, mostly methodological behaviorists, being either unabashedly or implicitly Cartesian. If any group is in direct lineage to S-R associationism, it is surely the cognitive psychologists. While the specific types of association mechanisms employed by cognitive psychologists are more complex and subtle, the form of explanation is the same as that of classic associationism. For instance, perception is the result of internal information processing mechanisms which act on the impoverished physical stimulus. Behavior is the result, and an imperfect indicator, of the action of these internal mechanisms. Thus, what is important for cognitive psychologists are events taking place between stimulus and response which cannot in themselves be known, but what is measured and manipulated is behavior.

While I believe Malone would agree with my foregoing statements, he would also add that Skinner has contributed to the confusion, primarily by reliance on the explanatory principle of temporal contiguity. Temporal contiguity is essential to associationist explanation, and is the impetus for the creation of internal mechanisms that, for instance, bridge temporal gaps (memory), or provide cohesiveness in the perception of an event on different occasions (stimulus equivalence). It is difficult to disagree that the principle of temporal contiguity seems out of place in the context of Skinner's analysis of behavioral units. Yet, as far as

Skinner is concerned, there is no more heralded result than the 'superstition' experiment. For many years adventitious reinforcement was held to be the paradigm of operant behavior.

Furthermore, Malone would make the argument that a restricted set of explanatory or integrative concepts, such as discriminative stimulus, reinforcer, conditioned reinforcer, has hindered rather than aided the analysis of behavior. Instead of a real analysis, often what has been given is a redefinition of terms. It also difficult to disagree with this point. In my reading, Skinner often uses the term 'contingencies of reinforcement' as a literary device, and many alleged analyses take the form of plausibility arguments for a potential analysis. I have no argument with the use of common terms in the analysis of behavior, so long as they are descriptive of behavior. Indeed, such an approach could easily deflect many superficial criticisms of behavior analysis.

I have argued that Skinner's operant analysis follows from his commitment to radical behaviorism. But a commitment to radical behaviorism does not require a joint commitment to operant analysis. For instance, Skinner's concept of reinforcement, as defined by the empirical law of effect, is obviously his central and most logically primitive explanatory concept. But as Malone rightly points out, other radical behaviorists, such as Kantor, have not found the reinforcement concept to be of overwhelming importance.

Despite my broad agreement with Malone's criticisms, I maintain that Skinner's approach to the analysis of behavioral units is cogent. I would draw the distinction between Skinner's theoretical contribution, that is, his treatment of the conceptual problems of psychology, and his specific contributions within that conceptual framework. Many of his specific inquiries are of questionable value, such as his summary dismissal of the existence of behavioral contrast, his odd reliance on temporal contiguity, and his promiscuous employment of conditioned reinforcers. On the other hand, his conceptual approach to the problems of psychology still provides the best available alternative for the analysis of behavior.

MALONE REPLIES TO HINSON

Hinson clearly understands radical behaviorism, which immediately identifies him as a member of a tiny and rapidly shrinking group of people. This also means that he appreciates Watson's virtues, even though it has become almost mandatorily fashionable to criticize Watson and not to read him. Similarly, Hinson agrees that secondary reinforcement (or conditioned reinforcement) is a concept of questionable virtue. Most important (and most surprising to me), Hinson agrees that many 'cognitive' viewpoints are actually exemplars of methodological behaviorism! He is correct so often that criticism seems hard to conjure up.

Actually, Hinson illustrates the problem that I stressed; it is apparent in the first pages of his chapter. He discusses Skinner's early thoughts on the behavioral unit (and he assumes that Skinner remembered them for more than a few months). He seems absolutely accurate to me, though sometimes the argument (Skinner's, not Hinson's) seems too abstract; one cannot be too optimistic that the average reader will put up with such stuff for long.

But then all that changes and the sun comes shining through as Hinson, clearly having an easier time of it, discusses Hull. By comparison Hull is clear, direct, and, as the AMA would assure us, Hull was essentially correct! How awful is truth. Skinner's best ideas are difficult to understand (even for him) and Hull is easy to understand. Hull represented simple concrete mainstream thought in his day and it appears that that simple view is still with us. Three chilling recent developments illustrate this; there are undoubtedly many other equally chilling developments of which I am unaware, but these are bad enough.

The biggest problem in psychology is the failure to progress beyond naive cognitive psychology and naive behaviorism, which share offensive characteristics. One alternative to both is radical behaviorism, which has nothing to do with S-R associationism and which deals with cognition far better than do most cognitive theories, as Bem and others have shown.

Given that, it is depressing to receive the 'future directions' issue of the *Journal of the Experimental Analysis of Behavior* (November, 1984) and find stimulus control treated even more primitively than I suggested it was, i.e., purely in terms of S-R associationism. Another treat was provided by a second author, who spoke for naive cognitive psychology, inexplicably arguing that the analysis of behavior has to deal with molecular units of behavior and that we therefore need a faculty of memory to account for organization in behavior! Future directions? This is the journal that is supposed to represent the analysis of behavior; are there no limits to tolerance, especially in an issue that points out future directions? What is a naive reader to think?

The second interesting development is the publication of an edited collection of Clark Hull's theoretical papers; I will not give the reference, but the interested reader should have no trouble finding it. This book was published in late 1984 — need I point out that someone thought it would receive a warm reception in the eighties?

Though some may disagree, a second volume could serve as a companion to the Hull collection. This is a 1982 collection of papers on the subject of animal cognition; again, I cannot bear to give the reference but it may be easily found. Within its covers one learns three things. First, that radical behaviorism will never be understood by most people and will always be identified with S-R associationism (as the author of the fourth paper illustrates). Second, it is apparently possible to understand radical behaviorism and still prefer naive congitive psychology, as does the author of the first chapter. Third, the field of conditioning and learning seems to have de facto become the field of 'cognitive' psychology, as many of the other contributors illustrate.

Hinson must know of these depressing recent developments, and he must see that Skinner's lack of consistency has fostered the confusion that has led to them. Hinson describes a wise and consistent Skinner, who seems to have spent half a century vainly arguing for radical behaviorism. He provides citations to support his rendition of Skinner's career and he knows that those citations are hard to come by. It is far easier to find citations that stress molecularism, devices such as conditioned reinforcers and chains, and things that we 'find reinforcing'.

Skinner has received credit enough so that I do not worry when I say that Hinson is too kind to him. Skinner gave us a version of radical behaviorism more sophisticated than the one Watson provided in 1919, and for that we should be grateful. But he also gave us a particular conditioning theory and a vocabulary which should long since have been abandoned.

Part X: Skinner's Position against Theory and against Mentalism

17. Mentalism, Private Events, and Scientific Explanation: A Defense of B.F. Skinner's View*

STEVEN C. HAYES AND AARON J. BROWNSTEIN

In describing the experimental analysis of behavior, Skinner has said:

> The experimental analysis of behavior is also generally characterized by an unhurried attitude toward the as-yet-unexplained. Criticism often takes the line that the analysis is oversimplified, that it ignores important facts, that a few obvious exceptions demonstrate that its formulation cannot possibly be adequate, and so on. An understandable reaction might be to stretch the available facts and principles in order to cover more ground, but the general plan of the research suggests another strategy. Unlike hypotheses, theories, and models, together with the statistical manipulations of data which support them, a smooth curve showing a change in probability of a response as a function of a controlled variable is a fact in the bag, and there is no need to worry about it as one goes in search of others. The shortcomings and exceptions will be accounted for in time. (Skinner, 1969, p. 84)

In the twenty years since Skinner described this unhurried attitude, criticism of behavior analysis has not diminished. In fact, we now find among the critics individuals who have formerly been sympathetic. A greater urgency is evident in attitudes toward the as-yet-unexplained. The 'understandable reaction' referred to above appears imminent. This would not be of concern if the alternatives being proposed advanced the goals of science as seen by behavior analysts. Sadly, that does not appear to be the case.

The purpose of this chapter is to examine critical issues in psychological analysis in view of recent criticism of the behavioral approach which seem to suggest a more rapid path to the 'as-yet-unexplained'. We will examine the purpose of science, the nature of explanation, the role of private events, and the

---

* In memory of Aaron J. Brownstein, 1932–86.

objection to mentalism. Our main point will be that behavior analysis is a powerful and viable approach to psychology when evaluated against its own goals.

THE PURPOSES OF SCIENCE: PREDICTION AND CONTROL

> The terms 'cause' and 'effect' are no longer widely used in science . . . . The terms which replace them, however, refer to the same factual core. A 'cause' becomes a 'change in an independent variable' and an 'effect' a 'change in a dependent variable.' The old 'cause-and-effect connection' becomes a 'functional relation.' . . . Any condition or event which can be shown to have an effect upon behavior must be taken into account. By discovering and analyzing these causes we can predict behavior; to the extent that we can manipulate them, we can control behavior. (Skinner, 1953, p. 23).
>
> We undertake to predict and control the behavior of the individual organism. This is our 'dependent variable' — the effect for which we are to find the cause. (Skinner, 1953, p. 35).

Skinner has consistently claimed that prediction and control are the end products of science. According to this view, scientific practices and beliefs are worthwhile to the extent that they contribute to our ability to predict and control. Other purposes might be well served by different scientific practices and beliefs.

Many arguments seem to dissolve when differences in goals are made evident. If the goal is the development of a hypothetico-deductive system, for example, behavior analysis will fall short. We can, of course, argue about what the nature of scientific explanation 'should be'. Such an argument goes beyond the purposes of this chapter, and in any case is likely to be fruitless. It seems only fair to evaluate radical behaviorism against the goals it sets for itself. Thus, what is at issue is whether radical behaviorism is overly restrictive regarding practices that contribute to the prediction and control of behavior.

In talking of prediction and control Skinner has indicated a much stronger correspondence between the two goals than might generally be emphasized. He seeks an analysis of behavior in terms of events that are of a kind that at least potentially allow *both* prediction and control simultaneously. Much of the failure to appreciate the thrust of the behavioral approach may be the result of failing to emphasize the word 'and' in the phrase 'prediction and control'. Some kinds of events *in principle* can only directly allow prediction and not control. Other kinds of events can allow both in principle, though for practical reasons control may presently be impossible. Skinner prefers the latter set of variables due to his pragmatism, and his view of the proper division of labor among the sciences.[1]

Skinner's calls this second set of variables 'environmental variables', or 'external variables'. For example: 'The external variables of which behavior is a function provide for what may be called a causal or functional analysis. . . . Our 'independent variables' — the causes of behavior — are the external variables of which behavior is a function' (Skinner, 1953, p. 35). Skinner is concerned that our science move toward more and more thorough accounts of behavior. Discovering variables that in principle cannot perform the full functions required of a scientific analysis is not objectionable because the information is useless (often it is not) but because it necessarily fails to provide a complete account. 'We cannot account for the behavior of any system while staying wholly inside it; eventually we must turn to forces operating upon the organism from without' (Skinner, 1953, p. 35).

Thus, for Skinner the elements of a predictive formulation and a controlled

formulation ultimately should be the same. Both ultimately must involve relationships between external events and behavior. To the extent that we can manipulate the external variables we can control behavior. In this pragmatic sense of explanation events are fully explained when prediction and control based on external events are possible.

Much of the argument would have vanished had Skinner simply emphasized control as the defining property of science. Others would have disagreed, but to the extent that it was pursued, control would force us to emphasize external variables that are functionally related to the behavior. This is so because it is impossible to manipulate events other than real, physical events external to the behavioral system. But often we cannot manipulate events because of technical limitations on our ability to do so. The fact that we cannot manipulate these events should not lead us to view predictive relationships as incomplete when prediction is based upon external variables ('external' in the sense that the variables are in the domain in which control is at least *theoretically* possible), because in principle they can provide a complete account.

It is Skinner's pragmatic insistence that all the functions of science be served that prohibits the organism itself, or behavior itself, from being an initiating cause. We are, and can only ever be, in other people's environment. Since scientific laws are meant to guide our behavior, they must start where we are — in the environment: 'In practice, all these ways of changing a man's mind reduce to manipulating his environment, verbal or otherwise' (Skinner, 1969, p. 239). Thus, explanations such as ' . . . anxiety and worry are useful clues only if they can be explained in turn' (Skinner, 1974, p. 63).

Many popular scientific practices are clearly inadequate when seen from this point of view. For example, it is useless to 'explain behavior by appealing to independent variables which have been inferred from the behavior thus explained' (Skinner, 1969, p. 264). Such variables are not externally available. In principle they cannot directly allow prediction *and* control. This is, in large part, Skinner's objection to theories which emphasize hypothetical constructs and intervening variables.

Keat (1972) offers interesting argument in support of the explanatory value of this kind of inferred mental item. Analyzing it will help draw a clearer distinction between Skinner's and others' view.

> For although it may be true that our only evidence for (other people's) mental items is behavioral, there is no good reason to believe that, in explaining any particular piece of behavior, it is *that* behavior which provides our only evidence for the explanatory mental item. For example, I may attempt to explain someone's dropping a cup in terms of her feeling of anxiety, and use the way she was moving her hands prior to that event as evidence for the mental item; the evidence is behavioral, but not the *same* behavior as that which is being explained. (p. 61)

He recognizes that mental causes must be based on behavior, but he claims that mental events can be based on *other* behavioral events than the one explained and thus mental cause may be viewed as independent from the behavior it explains. If we review this strategy, it is clear first of all that the inferred anxiety does not enable us to predict the dropping of the cup any better than does 'the way she was moving her hands prior to the event'. We have dressed up a predictive behavior-behavior relationship in a way which makes it appear to be a relationship between non-behavioral events and some behavior.

Obviously, the behavior-behavior relationship is useful. One would be ill-advised to use one's best china under such circumstances, for example. But psychologists would presumably wish to explore those events that control the way she was moving her hands and modify them if possible. Anxiety per se cannot be manipulated. At best we can manipulate events to manipulate anxiety. Thus, using anxiety as an explanation leaves unspecified factors that provide control (the 'and' in prediction and control has not been properly emphasized). Explanations which do not go outside the behavioral system are necessarily incomplete in this sense. The ultimate cause must be other than behavior (and other than simply inferences from behavior) if the entire sequence is to be of greater value than behavior-behavior relationships.

A simple test can be formulated as to whether an analysis has proceeded to a point of completeness that is acceptable. When we have identified some event which enables us to predict and control (if we could manipulate it) some target behavior of an individual, ask whether the responsible event is within the domain of events that we, as psychologists, aspire to predict and control regarding that individual. If it is, then our account is not complete because our account is still within the domain we originally sought to explain. If it is not, then our account is complete. Obviously, there is nothing ultimate about such an account, but that was never the desired end, nor is such a request made of alternative accounts.

The problem with some recent formulations of reciprocal determinism (Bandura, 1978, 1981) highlights this issue. It is to the credit of this view that it emphasizes the dynamic relationship between behavior and the environment (a view championed by behavior analysis). In this ongoing process it is impossible to determine an initiating event in some ultimate sense. This impossibility, however, would be an improper argument for choosing *any* event at all. Lawful relationships should not contain behavioral events (of the same individual) as their antecedents for two reasons. First, as we have been emphasizing, these events cannot themselves directly produce the desired end products of science: prediction *and* control. Skinner's view of causality is largely pragmatic: 'The second link is useless in the control of behavior unless we can manipulate it' (Skinner, 1953, p. 34). It is true, of course, that behavior influences the environment so as to influence behavior further. But reciprocal determinism misses the point. If I tell you an environmental cause, I have given you a rule you can in principle use directly; given the technical ability to manipulate it, effective action can be based on it. If I tell you a behavioral 'cause', this might help you find the environmental cause, but it is also likely, if you are not careful, to stop the search for causes that could permit a complete account. In Skinner's words:

> It has been objected that we must stop somewhere in following a causal chain into the past and we may as well stop at a psychic level . . . . It is true that we could trace human behavior not only to the physical conditions which [cause it] but also to the causes of those conditions and the causes of those causes, almost ad infinitum, but there is no point in going back beyond the point at which effective action can be taken. That point is not to be found in the psyche. (Skinner, 1974, p. 210)

Thus, 'the *initiating* action is taken by the environment' (Skinner, 1974, p. 73, emphasis added; see also Skinner, 1984).

The second problem with behavioral causes is that these are themselves the events which we seek to predict and control in this same individual. Skinner is quite sensitive here to the proper division of labor among the sciences. If we

explain behavioral events in terms of events that are in the domain of other sciences, we move toward the comprehensive knowledge that we desire. But if we designate some events as not behavioral, and these events are themselves actually the legitimate topic of the behavioral sciences, then a significant gap is left.

One defense against the charge of incompleteness of an account is to deny that the antecedent event is in need of prediction and control (that is, to deny that it is itself in the domain of the events to be explained). This, for example, is often exactly the stance taken with regard to private events by non-behaviorists, a topic to which we now turn.

THE NATURE OF PRIVATE EVENTS

One convenient way to understand Skinner's position on private events is to concentrate on what kind of events can be 'behavioral' events in his and other systems. 'Behavior' is commonly taken to refer to a certain subset of human action. For example, it is quite typical to see theorists speak of 'thoughts, feelings, and behavior', as if behavior can be easily distinguished from events called 'thoughts' or 'feelings'.

Confusion over this issue can in part be attributed to Watson. Watson's position (as it was understood by others) actually had two parts: one was methodological behaviorism. Essentially it said scientists must be behaviorists because science can only deal with the publicly observable. Since only behavior is publicly observable, we can only deal with behavior, even though other kinds of human action may exist. This position might be thought of as implicitly dualistic because it recognizes that behavior is only a subset of human action, but contends that science can only deal with that subset, rather than the entire set, due to rules of proper scientific methodology. Skinner is not fond of this perspective:

> One solution, often regarded as behavioristic, is to grant the distinction between public and private events and rule the latter out of scientific consideration. This is a congenial solution for those to whom scientific truth is a matter of convention or agreement among observers. It is essentially the line taken by logical positivism and physical operationism. (Skinner, 1969, p. 226)

Watson also made a second, somewhat contradictory point. He was understood to be saying that even if we could solve the problem privacy presents to a scientific analysis, behavior is still all that could be studied because only behavior exists. Serious students of Watson believe that he meant only to say that non-spaciotemporal events do not exist, but he was commonly taken to mean that thoughts, feelings, and other private events are not real. The position that thoughts and feelings do not exist, while behavior does, can be termed 'Watsonian metaphysical behaviorism'.

It is important to note that the definition of the word 'behavior' keeps changing. In methodological behaviorism, behavior is defined as a subset of human action that is publicly observable and is therefore subject to a scientific analysis. In Watsonian metaphysical behaviorism, behavior is defined as the totality of human action, but there is once again the implication that only events which are publicly observable (at least potentially) should be thought of as real.

Radical behaviorism can be distinguished from these other types of behavior-

ism in part by the view it takes on the definition of 'behavior' (Skinner, 1945, 1963). Like Watsonian metaphysical behaviorism, behavior is taken to be the set of all human action. Unlike this earlier position, however, there is no commitment to public observability per se as the defining characteristic of scientific observations (Skinner, 1945) and because of this, private events are given scientific legitimacy: '[Radical behaviorism] does not insist upon truth by agreement and can therefore consider events taking place in the private world within the skin. It does not call these events unobservable, and it does not dismiss them as subjective' (Skinner, 1974, p. 16). Rather, scientific observations are termed 'scientific' because of the contingencies surrounding the observation. The purpose of scientific methodology is to insure that scientific observations are tacts, controlled by events in the subject matter of the science, and not by states of deprivation, audience factors, or other such sources of control over verbal events (Moore, 1981). Since public agreement provides no assurance of this, and since private observations can be tacts given the proper prior history, private events are no more or less scientific than public events based on their privacy per se. In radical behaviorism, behavior can thus be defined as all observable human action, not all publicly observable human action (cf. Heidbreder, 1933, and her discussion of the flaws of classical behaviorism).

In this view, then, no objection can be made to talk of events such as thoughts or feelings. This talk is not trivialized by insisting it is only the talk itself that is scientifically legitimate (Skinner, 1945). Thoughts and feelings are themselves viewed as scientifically accessible events: covert behavior. The term 'covert behavior' may be a less than desirable label. It presents itself as a paradox. As we have just seen, most definitions of behavior contain some reference to public observability, hence the paradox. The term 'behavior' as used by Skinner refers to what organisms do that is appropriate to the domain of psychology even if not sharing the obvious physical properties of behavior as it is usually defined.

While many non-behavioral accounts would concur with the assignment of the referential events to the domain of psychology, they question whether they are best regarded as behavior. Why insist that these events be so regarded when the physical properties appear so different? The justification is that by referring to these events as behavior we emphasize that it is the task of psychology to predict and control them. Their explanation is our assignment, and no matter how dynamically they may be intertwined with other clearly behavioral or less behavioral events, they (the covert behavior) do not represent an adequate explanatory account. It is not simply that regarding these events as behavior is parsimonious, but rather it is an insistence upon our need to explain these events that prompts our labeling them as behavior. The criticism that some cognitive accounts direct our attention away from the study of behavior (Branch, 1982) is probably better understood as a concern for needed explanation rather than an insistence upon being concerned only with overt behavior.

However justifiable, the use of the term 'covert behavior' will probably continue to appear paradoxical. Some other term that would also emphasize the responsibility of psychology in accounting for these events would do equally well, but no less troublesome term suggests itself. Thus, when a radical behaviorist is less than enthusiastic about an account of behavior that predicts that someone will respond in a given way after thinking in a given way, it is an absence of enthusiasm resulting from the incompleteness of the account rather than the

reference to thinking. The immediate question then becomes what are the determinants of thinking.

It is often missed, but this type of objection is not just to covert behaviors playing such a role. The view that a thought causes an overt behavior distills down to the view that one behavior can cause another. But this would be just as objectionable if the intertwined behaviors were all overt. Skinner's (1953) excellent discussion of self-control, for example, concludes by re-emphasizing the external variables which control the overt controlling behavior. Since our job as behavioral scientists is to explain behavior, explanations of behavior with more behavior must necessarily be incomplete. 'We may object, first, to the predilection for unfinished causal sequences' (Skinner, 1969, p. 240).

It would be inappropriate to assume that all research generated by non-behavioral psychologists results in incomplete analyses (see, for example, Ornstein and Naus' (1978) discussion of work on rehearsal strategies in young children; recall was increased after the manipulation of environmental events controlling overt rehearsal). Conversely, behavioral analyses that implicate covert behavior are incomplete if they fail to extend the analysis to environmental variables. We must guard against responding to the quality of language rather than to the quality of the analysis. If our description of radical behaviorism is correct, that is what is stressed by the approach rather than an attempt to urge that some simple physical correspondence exists between private and public behaviors.

MENTALISM

The dominant alternative to a behavioral analysis of private events is mentalism. A mentalistic account from our perspective is clearly incomplete. A more detailed analysis may reveal other ways in which it may be deficient with regard to the goals of the behavioral approach and scientific accounts in general. Objections to mentalism can be placed in two basic categories: metaphysical and meta-theoretical. The metaphysical objections are directed at the concept of literal dualism.

The Scientific Unacceptability of Literal Dualism

Originally psychology was the study of the soul. The *Oxford English Dictionary* defines 'soul' as 'the spiritual part of man', and 'spirit' as an 'incorporeal or immaterial being' and as a 'being or intelligence distinct from anything physical'. The word 'physical' comes from a word for nature (thus the science of physics) and is defined as 'of or pertaining to the phenomenal world of the sense; matter'. Thus, if you take the words literally, 'soul' and 'spirit' are inherently dualistic terms, because they oppose matter and non-matter. We might label this 'literal dualism'. Literal dualism is the belief that there are two kinds of stuff in the world: one type exists in space and time, while the other is non-spatiotemporal.

As psychology shifted to an emphasis on the study of the mind, this type of literal dualism was simply transferred to a new way of talking about psychological topics. The *OED* defines 'mind' as 'the mental or psychical being or faculty'. An

elaborating definition explains that 'mind' is 'the seat of a person's consciousness, thoughts, volitions, and feelings; also, the incorporeal subject of the psychical faculties, the spiritual side of a human being; the soul as distinguished from the body. ... Mental being; opposed to matter.' The spiritual meaning of 'mind' is also shown by the fact that God has long been referred to as 'mind', for example, 'That eternal infinite mind, who made and governs all things' (Locke, 1690). Thus, it is widely understood that the stuff of the mind is fundamentally different from the stuff of the physical universe; that is, it is explicitly based on literal dualism.

Such an account appears to place the prediction and control of mental events outside the domain of psychology and more generally outside the domain of science. The knowledge gap referred to above is clearly evident. Who is to predict and control the occurrence of these mental events and relate them to behavioral events if they are not in the purview of science?

Thus, one objection to literal dualism is simply that such a view is not scientifically tenable. Furthermore, it raises the impossibly difficult issue of how non-spatiotemporal events can cause physical events to occur. To the extent that terms like 'mental' or 'mind' are literally dualistic, Skinner objects to them vigorously on such grounds: 'But where are these feelings and states of mind? Of what stuff are they made? The traditional answer is that they are located in a world of nonphysical dimensions called the mind and that they are mental. But ... how can a mental event cause or be caused by a physical one?' (Skinner, 1974, 10). It is important to realize that Skinner is not here rejecting covert behavior: 'Not only does a behavior analysis not reject ... "higher mental processes"; it has taken the lead in investigating the contingencies under which they occur. What it rejects is the assumption that comparable activities take place in the mysterious world of the mind' (Skinner, 1974, p. 223). It is hard to see how a scientific view could take any other perspective on literal dualism.

Other objections to dualism are more specific to radical behaviorism. Dualism is rejected because all behavior is to be interpreted through contingency analysis: 'A behavioristic analysis rests on the following assumptions: A person is first of all an organism ... possessing a genetic endowment which [is] the product of contingencies of survival to which the species has been exposed .... The organism [then] acquires behavior under ... contingencies of reinforcement' (Skinner, 1974, p. 207). Note that these are specifically said to be assumptions: they are not answers, they are frameworks for answers. Within a contingency analysis the relationship between behavior and the events that proceed and follow it in the lifetime of the species, culture, or individual is examined in order to understand the behavioral events. This same analysis is also applied to our own verbal behavior, and thus dualistic talk will be understood by examining the contingencies controlling that kind of talk.

Such a thoroughgoing form of contextual analysis is inherently monistic. *All* behavior is said to be subject to contingency analysis. Contingencies are the relationships among behavior and the distinguishable events that precede and follow behavior. Any event that can be discerned is being observed in the world of space and time and must in that sense be thought of as 'physical'. This is not an argument about terms. If someone wanted to call all events 'mental' there could be no objection, though it would distort our normal understanding of the term.

The concern is more directed at literal dualism: 'What is lacking is the bold and exciting behavioristic hypothesis that what one observes and talks about is always the "real" and "physical" world (or at least the "one" world)' (Skinner, 1945, p. 276). Thus, radical behaviorism's contingency analysis is necessarily physicalistic in the sense given above, and it is monistic in that it applies the same method of analysis to all behavioral events, without recognizing any fundamental distinctions in the stuff of those events.

Mental Physiology

In recognition of the problems of literal dualism a variety of tactics have been used to try to bring scientific legitimacy to dualistic perspectives. One method is to create a pseudophysiological analysis to stand in for mentalism. In this way the scientist can appear to be interested in physical events while at the same time using these terms mentalistically.

It is very popular to use the word 'mind' to mean 'brain'. Television shows or magazine articles on the action of the human brain, for example, are almost always said to be about 'the human mind'. A recent authoritative text on cognitive psychology asserted that in cognitive psychology 'the contemporary view [is] that mental processes are synonymous with brain processes' (Ellis and Hunt, 1983, p. 11). Study of the brain and the nervous system is, of course, worthwhile and relevant to a behavioral analysis. But it is no less mentalistic simply to substitute the word 'brain' for 'mind' and then to engage in precisely the same kinds of analyses as before. Cognitivists use talk of the brain primarily to claim that 'mental functioning is not a mysterious, nonphysical event' (Ellis and Hunt, 1983, p. 7). It is clear that they do not intend to study the brain:

> Of course, brain activity can be studied psychologically, but cognitive psychologists use a different approach. Since the brain activity of interest cannot be directly observed (for example, we have no idea what happens in the brain when a person remembers a grandmother), we must infer the existence of these processes and then describe the processes in abstract language. (Ellis and Hunt, 1983, p. 7)

Speaking of the brain, however, does not make the view non-mentalistic, if the way the term is being used is the same as in mentalistic accounts. Skinner puts it this way:

> Usually [the mind is said to be] the thinking agent. It is the mind which is said to examine sensory data and make inferences about the outside world, to store and retrieve records, to filter incoming information, to put bits of information in pigeonholes, to make decisions, and to will to act.... it has been possible to avoid the problems of dualism by substituting 'brain' and 'mind.' The brain is ... the agent which processes incoming data and stores them in the form of data structures. Both the mind and the brain are not far from the ancient notion of a homunculus — an inner person who behaves in precisely the ways necessary to explain the behavior of the outer person in which he dwells. (Skinner, 1974, p. 117)

Thus, while it seems to avoid problems of literal dualism, it is used in the same way literally dualistic analyses are used.

Skinner insists that his objection to mentalism is not an objection to true physiological or structural analyses, but to literal dualism, pseudostructural analyses, and to the false causality both engender:

> What is felt or introspectively observed is not some nonphysical world of consciousness, mind, or mental life, but the observer's own body. This does not mean ... that introspection is a kind of physiological research, nor does it mean (and this is the heart of the argument) that what are felt or introspectively observed are the causes of behavior. An organism behaves as it does because of its current structure, but most of this is out of reach of introspection. (Skinner, 1974, p. 17)

Thus, if private events allowed direct access to the current structure of an organism, there could be no objection. Skinner makes it clear that a thorough-going knowledge of current structure is preferable to the more indirect 'historical analysis' for which he is best-known. But for several reasons (discussion of which is beyond the scope of this chapter), he rejects the view that observations of private events are direct observations of current structure.

Because of his view of causality and scientific explanation, he rejects the causal role of private events, at least as initiating causes. Much of his concern with mentalism boils down to a concern over what in his system are pseudocauses. As we have already shown, Skinner believes (we think correctly) that an improperly placed concern over private causes, behavioral causes, or any 'cause' that is in principle non-manipulable, will slow our progress because it diverts our efforts toward necessarily incomplete analyses. Mentalism virtually always has this effect in Skinner's view:

> One of the most tragic consequences of mentalism is dramatically illustrated by those who are earnestly concerned about the plight of the world today and who see no help except in a return of morality, ethics, or a sense of decency, as personal possessions .... But what is needed is a restoration of social environments in which people behave in ways called moral. (Skinner, 1974, p. 196)

Even the most literally dualistic terms can be examined from within a behavior analytic system. For example, we can translate terms such as 'spirit' (Hayes, 1984) or 'unconscious' into scientifically sensible terms. But even then nothing is caused by 'agents' such as spirit or the unconscious. As discussed above, the primary benefit to be gained from such a translation is that it emphasizes that the analysis is incomplete. 'What behaviorism rejects is the unconsciousness as an agent, and of course it rejects the conscious mind as an agent, too' (Skinner, 1974, p. 154). That Skinner does not mean to impune the reality of private events by this is shown by his insistence that organisms cannot initiate public events either, even though no one would deny their reality: 'A scientific analysis of behavior must, I believe, assume that a person's behavior is controlled by his genetic and environmental histories rather than by the person himself as an initiating, creative agent. [We assume that] human behavior as a whole is fully determined' (Skinner, 1974, p. 189).

Skinner is quite clear that his concern over mentalism is primarily the limited type of science it allows:

> How are we to decide between [behavior analysis and mentalism]? We cannot say that one is simpler that the other ... [but] accessibility [for use in control] is another matter. No one has ever directly modified any of the mental activities or traits ... for most practical purposes they are changed only through the environment .... A decision [between the two positions] is perhaps more difficult if we simply want to predict behavior .... [Traits] are ... useless in control but they permit us to predict one kind of behavior from another kind. (Skinner, 1974, pp. 208–9)

> In its search for internal explanations, supported by the false sense of cause associated with feelings and introspective observations, mentalism has obscured the environmental antecedents which would have led to a much more effective analysis. (Skinner, 1974, p. 165)

We believe that much of the criticism of the behavioral approach arises from a failure to recognize its goals. Other goals make alternative practices and beliefs justifiable, and with these we can have no quarrel, provided only that the researcher honestly states what these goals are. For example, if a particular field of psychology wishes to eschew control as the end product of science, it has the obligation to make that clear to all, whether the person is a psychologist or a taxpayer helping fund federal research. If an approach embraces prediction *and* control as legitimate goals of science, it should show how its practices advance the achievement of these goals. We see no relative disadvantage for a behavioral approach, when these goals are being pursued. As Skinner has argued, and we have tried to show, its practices seem more directly related to these goals than other perspectives.

Another, and perhaps more legitimate, criticism of the behavioral approach has been its apparent lack of experimental involvement with behaviors of special significance for understanding human interaction. The reasons for this are many and go beyond the scope of this chapter. We raise the issue because much of the frustration with a behavioral position has arisen from this apparent lack, and it has often been falsely attributed to the fundamentals of Skinner's view on scientific explanation and private events. To the contrary, we believe that as radical behaviorists become more involved with complex human behaviors (as they should), they must not inappropriately relinquish the framework of a behavioral approach and its advantages. It is precisely in these areas that it is most needed and is most likely to lead to innovations in our understanding of human behavior.

NOTE

1 Skinner's emphasis on control may also be understood as a natural result of his apparent philosophical embrace of contextualism (cf. Pepper, 1942). In a comprehensive contextualistic account any event is to be understood and even defined through a contextual analysis. The three-term contingency of radical behaviorism is a dynamic contextual unit — none of the terms can be defined independently of any of the others. Skinner has added to the non-mechanistic nature of this view by insisting that even the behavior of scientists as they conduct such analyses is to be understood through such analyses (Skinner, 1945). Any such thoroughgoing contextualistic analysis can easily be paralyzed by the need to analyze context, and then to analyze the context of the analysis of context, and so on *ad infinitum*. Skinner avoids being caught in such a whirlpool by insisting on control as a goal of science, thus providing an end to the analysis that goes outside the realm of pure verbal analysis. If prediction were by itself a reasonable goal, a thoroughgoing form of contextualism would not know when to stop reflecting on its own analyses.

REFERENCES

Bandura, A. (1978) 'The self system in reciprocal determinism', *American Psychologist*, 33, pp. 344–58.

Bandura, A. (1981) 'In search of pure unidirectional determinants', *Behavior Therapy*, 12, pp. 30–40.

Branch, M.N. (1982) 'Misrepresenting behaviorism', *Behavioral and Brain Sciences*, 5, pp. 372–3.

Ellis, H.C. and Hunt, R.R. (1983) *Fundamentals of Human Memory and Cognition*, Dubuque, Iowa, Brown.

Hayes, S.C. (1984) 'Making sense of spirituality', *Behaviorism*, 12, pp. 99–110.

Heidbreder, E. (1933) *Seven Psychologies*, New York, Appleton-Century-Crofts.

Keat, R. (1972) 'A critical examination of B.F. Skinner's objections to mentalism', *Behaviorism*, 1, pp. 53–70.

Locke, J. (1690) *An Essay Concerning Human Understanding*.

Moore, J. (1981) 'On mentalism, methodological behaviorism, and radical behaviorism', *Behaviorism*,

9, pp. 55–77.

Ornstein, P.A. and Naus, M.J. (1978) 'Rehearsal processes in children's memory', in Ornstein, P.A. (Ed.), *Memory Development in Children*, Hillsdale, N.J., Erlbaum.

Pepper, S.C. (1942) *World Hypotheses*, Berkeley, Calif., University of California Press.

Skinner, B.F. (1945) 'The operational analysis of psychological terms', *Psychological Review*, 52, pp. 270–6.

Skinner, B.F. (1953) *Science and Human Behavior*, New York, Free Press.

Skinner, B.F. (1963) 'Behaviorism at fifty', *Science,* 134, pp. 566–602.

Skinner, B.F. (1969) *Contingencies of Reinforcement: A Theoretical Analysis*, New York, Appleton-Century-Crofts.

Skinner, B.F. (1974) *About Behaviorism*, New York, Knopf.

Skinner, B.F. (1984) 'Reply to Catania', *The Behavioral and Brain Sciences*, 7, pp. 718–19.

18. Emergent Behaviorism*

PETER R. KILLEEN

Skinner vacillated in his views on the nature and causal efficacy of events that occur inside an organism. In his reply to Blanshard he stated that 'ideas, motives and feelings have no part in determining conduct and therefore no part in explaining it' (Blanshard and Skinner, 1967, p. 325), and several years later 'the mental laws of physiological psychologists like Wundt, the stream of consciousness of William James, the mental apparatus of Sigmund Freud have no useful place in the understanding of human behavior' (Skinner, 1972, p. 19). Why then do thoughts and feelings seem to cause behavior? 'They usually occur in just the place that would be occupied by a cause .... For example, we often feel a state of deprivation or emotion before we act in an appropriate way. If we say something to ourselves before saying it aloud, what we say aloud seems the expression of an inner thought' (1972, p. 19). For some reason Skinner never considered that through classical conditioning such precursors to action might come to elicit it.

Not everywhere does Skinner deny the efficacy of private events: 'It is particularly helpful to describe behavior which fails to satisfy contingencies, as in 'I let go too soon' or 'I struck too hard'. Even fragmentary descriptions of contingencies speed the acquisition of effective terminal behavior, help to maintain the behavior over a period of time, and reinstate it when forgotten' (1969, p. 143). 'There are good reasons, then, why a speaker ... should turn his verbal behavior upon himself. The result is close to thinking ...' (1957, p. 445). How can he admit that 'verbal behavior has practical effects upon the speaker as listener'? (1957, p. 440), yet deny the causal efficacy of ideas, thoughts, and feelings? Part of the reason is that, like Bertrand Russell whom he admired, Skinner preferred not to use the term 'cause' (all mentions of it in the index of *Science and Human Behavior* refer to pejorative discussions), and he found it

* I thank R.J. Herrnstein, P. Prins, K. Benyamini and G. Graham for comments on this chapter. A number of the issues raised here have also been discussed by Sober (1983).

219

especially problematic in referring to intermediate links of causal chains. 'Effects' seem to have given him less trouble. Another part of the reason must be that he recognized that a science of behavior is prior to a science of logic, and he respected the laws of conditioning more than the 'laws' of valid inference. He wished to bring his verbal behavior under the control of his data, even if that required some inconsistencies, given our current state of knowledge. For what we witness is not a slow shift in position as Skinner's perspective changed. There is no monotonic relation between the degree of causal efficacy given covert events and the year in which that opinion was published.

Many of Skinner's objections to 'Mental Way Stations' are to ad hoc and untestable 'explanations' loosely inferred from casual introspection, not to the possibility of 'practical effects' deriving from covert behavior. These and other objections are clearly stated in his article 'Behaviorism at Fifty' (1963), where he notes that Mental Way Stations (MWS) are often accepted as terminal data, and thereby abort the search for environmental causes of the MWS, or, going in the other direction, the existence of its putative consequences. Even when the MWS is anchored to both prior stimuli and consequent responses, 'various things happen at the way station which alter the relation between terminal events. ... Mental states alter one another. ... Dissonant cognitions ... will not be reflected in behavior if the subject can "persuade himself" that one condition was actually different. ...' (It is left ambiguous as to whether he believes that such interactions occur, or whether they are precipitated out as one of the unclean and unnecessary byproducts of a cognitive vocabulary.) 'The effects still provide a formidable stronghold for mentalistic theories designed to bridge the gap between dependent and independent variables' (p. 240).

With what engines does he assault that stronghold? The methodological objections are: (1) to the predilection for unfinished causal sequences; (2) that MWS 'burdens a science of behavior with all the problems raised by the limitations and inaccuracies of self-descriptive repertoires' (p. 241); and (3) 'Perhaps the most serious objection. ... Responses which seem to be describing intervening states alone may embrace behavioral effects'. That is, inferences about MWS may be based in part on the observation of our subsequent overt behavior. As we shall see, these are weak objections.

What rule will Skinner establish once the stronghold is breached? He notes: 'These disturbances in simple causal linkages between environment and behavior can be formulated and studied experimentally as interactions among variables; but the possibility has not been fully exploited' (p. 240). He deals briefly with multiple causation in *Science and Human Behavior* (1953), and much more extensively throughout his monumental *Verbal Behavior* (1957). The product was a series of astute observations, but they have not been adopted by many students as an effective approach to these issues. In part this is because of the enormous difficulty of the subject; in part because in *Verbal Behavior* Skinner 'put the reader through a set of exercises for the express purpose of strengthening a particular verbal repertoire. ... I have been trying to get the reader to behave verbally as I behave' (p. 455). He succeeded in that attempt for many of us; what he did not provide was an *experimental* analysis of complex cases such as verbal behavior. It was all talk, often brilliant talk, and he left us talking, often somewhat less brilliantly. His citations are primarily to intellectuals and men of

letters, and this is the model he provides us, not that of an experimenting scientist.

OBJECTIONS TO MENTALISM

Random House defines behavior as 'the aggregate of observable responses of an organism to internal and external stimuli'. This was the domain of Skinner's early work, as reported in *The Behavior of Organisms* (1938). But Skinner was always eager to address the most sophisticated aspects of human behavior. To do that, he could either devise new analytical tools, or he could adopt those of others, or he could assert that no new tools were needed. In attempting to extrapolate the laws of conditioning to humans, Skinner clearly took the last course. It was an optimistic gambit; the combination of a few simple principles can easily generate complex outcomes in any field of investigation. His principles were based on 'movements of an organism or of its parts in a frame of reference provided by the organism itself or by various external objects or fields of force' (1938, p. 6). His independent variables were reinforcement contingencies defined in terms of schedule parameters, motivational operations defined in terms of deprivation operations, and stimuli defined in terms of both physical parameters and the nature of the behavior that they controlled.[1] Skinner's 'generic', or functional, definition of stimuli and responses provided a trapdoor to escape from the problems that would otherwise be posed by attention, elaboration, and other mental processes. Unfortunately it was a route that he seldom took, preferring to study behavior where physical definitions of stimuli and responses were usually good enough.

This early history of reinforcement shaped Skinner's approach to the analysis of human behavior. Skinner recognized that 'mental states alter one another', and repudiated them for that reason.[2] But the omission of such states left him with an inadequate vocabulary, which he then expanded by moving some stimuli inside the organism ('private stimuli'), and by treating all other aspects of mental states as responses. Seeing became behavior, and imagination became 'seeing without the thing seen'.[3] But these are assertions, not demonstrated facts. They may serve as the axioms of a parsimonious behaviorial system, and that is largely how Skinner used them. But they cannot also be used as arguments against other systems, or against behavioral systems with augmented axioms, such as the assumption that covert events are sufficiently different from overt ones to deserve separate treatment as a separate category of events. The competition between such systems is in terms of explanatory power, not in terms of whose axioms are least objectionable to those who do not hold them.

Let us, nonetheless, review Skinner's objections to the inclusion of mental events in his (and anyone else's) system. Keat (1972) summarizes them; for Skinner mentalism is to be rejected because:

1 it lacks 'explanatory power';
2 it involves the employment of 'theories';
3 it tends to invoke 'homunculi', or 'inner agents', regarding man as an 'autonomous agent';
4 it distracts our attention from the study of behavior;
5 it involves a dualistic ontology of the 'mental' and the 'physical' (p. 55).

To these we may add those mentioned above and not included here: the limitations of a self-descriptive repertoire, and the contamination of descriptions of internal states by discriminations based on overt behavior. What of these?

Explanatory Power

Skinner notes that after we have explained a response in terms of mental states or activities or feelings, we still need to explain the mental state. But there is nothing wrong with that. Experimental analysis of one of the links in a causal chain should not necessarily be faulted because it does not include the previous ones; analysis must inevitably stop at some point short of the ultimate cause. We might infer from a person's pale face, hand over stomach, and low moan that he is in pain, and thus seek aid for him. We do not attempt to move the hand, nor silence the moans, nor rouge the face: the inference of an internal state of distress is more likely to be useful to him. Nor do we yet need to infer that it was something he ate, or that it was the 'flu that is going around, or that he was punched. Such determinations will certainly help, but we can take immediate and effective action based on our inference alone. Are we more likely to be helpful if we know that he ate strange food, but deny that he is in distress? Similarly, there are many things that might make us angry, and knowledge of that internal state will be much more effective in explaining subsequent behavior than knowledge of the (often seemingly innocuous) stimuli that preceded it. We might get by without telling others of our needs, our goals, our ideas and ideals, and merely be viewed as a 'private' person; were we to convey in their place our reinforcement histories and immediate stimulus context, unflavored by our subjective evaluations of them, we would be condemned either as tedious obscurants, or, if taken seriously, as unreflecting pawns of our history.

Theories

Skinner has stated that 'whether experimental psychologists like it or not, experimental psychology is properly and inevitably committed to the construction of a theory of behavior. A theory is essential to the scientific understanding of behavior as a subject matter' (1969, pp. vii–viii). What he objects to are particular types of theories: 'any explanation of an observed fact which appeals to events taking place somewhere else, at some other level of observation, described in different terms, and measured, if at all, in different dimensions' (p. vii). But what is wrong with such theories? Although we should not try to model our scientific discipline too closely on others, for our problems are different, we can evaluate this general statement by asking whether the condemned types of explanation are used in other fields. Any reasonable interpretation of Skinner's words shows that they are not only used, but that they consititute some of the most powerful and elegant theories that we know! Newton's theory of universal gravitation explained the tides on earth by events 'taking place somewhere else'; about as elsewhere as one can get. Skinner should be the last to want to posit some hypothetical stuff that bridges the spatial gap in order to avoid action at a distance.

  It is not clear how to interpret 'at some other level of observation', other

than as observations that employ instruments to aid our senses. But then we must include the germ theory of disease, a theory greatly abetted by the microscope. Should we give that up for fear of a behaviorist's censure, and hope that holistic medicine will be ready for us when we need it?

'Described in different terms' is often a strength of theories. Theories are a map, or metaphor, and serve us by providing a coherent frame of reference within which to view the phenomena, along with the rules to develop specific models. If events are not recondite, we seldom think of them in terms of theories. I do not seek theoretical explanation for why my dog barks at cats. But I do generate hypotheses about why he howls at railroad whistles. And those involve theories that use 'different terms' — speculation about evolutionary constraints and wolves howling to gather for a hunt. In general a failed description elicits another attempt in other terms ('Let me put it this way'). We all know that many successful theories involve descriptions in other terms: chemists explain molar physical properties of substances in terms of internal states, such as the valence of atoms, polarization of molecules, and so on.

'Measured, if at all, in different dimensions'. Differences in the dimensions used to describe a phenomenon may indicate a basic and insurmountable incommensurability. Or they may indicate an arbitrary historical decision or a matter of style or convenience. We may record motion and shape in Cartesian or polar coordinates; we may quantify sound waves in terms of their energy over time, or in terms of their power spectrum. In this latter case it is the insight provided by Fourier's Law that reveals the equivalence between the two representations. It is this realization of the unity of phenomena behind the apparently different dimensional frames that provides some of the most potent rewards for scientists and inspiration for their audience. What more beautiful evidence of this could one want than that symbol of twentieth century physics, Einstein's equation relating energy to mass and the speed of light?

'Perhaps', you say, 'Skinner was merely trying to assert that things like emotions don't have dimensions that would support conversion to the dimensions of things like running speed.' They do not currently, although some people 'get so mad they could spit', thus providing latency and ballistic measurements. In a similar manner atoms sometimes emit particles, whose latency and trajectory can tell us how 'excited' they were. Of course, one need not assume that excitation is nothing more than the propensity to emit an electron, nor that the level of excitation should be characterized only in terms of one type of cloud-chamber tracing. A similar analysis holds for emotions and other types of inner causes. It may be true that good measures of emotional states and their strengths are not yet available. However, we should not elevate this current deficiency into a permanent dogma, or we shall never have them. Let us instead look to theory to suggest new types of dimensions and new ways of relating them.

Homunculi

Skinner objects to mentalism because it leads us to invoke homunculi. But it needn't do that, nor is the doing of that necessarily bad. Part of Skinner's objection here is the unfinished-causal-sequence argument, for he does not want us to view humans as 'autonomous agents' (Skinner, 1974). As suggested above,

one can defer the analysis of prior links in the causal chain without denying their existence. In fact, one can be a determinist and still believe that it is useful to treat humans as autonomous, or 'self-governing' (Audi, 1976). The governors (e.g., traits and values) may have been aligned by nature and nurture, but the individual's interactions with his or her current environment may be treated more effectively by a theory of internal rules and set-points than by untested reference to histories of reinforcement. Not that such behavior is uncaused, but that more might be derived from focusing on the internal, self-reflective dialog as cause than by focusing on bells, whistles, and cumulative records. Histories of reinforcement are often reconstructed through verbal report of individuals who are less than disinterested observers, and they thus suffer some of the same liabilities as introspective reports, 'History of reinforcement' is a critical construct in Skinner's theory, but has received little critical analysis. In the study of human behavior it often serves as generic explanation, of the same order as 'inner man'.

Skinner's problem with homunculi is that he never took them seriously enough. What he seems to mean by them are small creatures with all the capacities of larger ones, who live inside and make the decisions — *homo ex machina*. Clearly, there would be a problem packing them in — all the more so since they would need their own homunculi, and they theirs. The implication is that an infinite number would be needed, thus forstalling any specification of the machinery that might actually get the job done, and thereby reducing this type of explanation to absurdity. Skinner is objecting to the hypostatization of a solution, in the manner of Molière's doctor who explained the soporific properties of opium as being due to their *virtus dormitiva*: 'The function of the inner man is to provide an explanation which will not be explained in turn' (Skinner, 1971, p. 14). If this is its only function, then it is certainly counterproductive. But not all infinite series are regresses, nor do all of them carry us infinitely far from the starting point. If enough tasks are accomplished by each homunculus before it passes its output to the next higher demon, then the job will be done with a finite number of levels; the series will converge, and it may converge quickly.

But why bother with such a hierarchy? Simon (1973) provides the most eloquent answer, and Dawkins (1976) discuss hierarchies in greater detail. Just as computer programs based on subroutines are easier to write, to troubleshoot, and to modify, behavioral programs are more effective when arranged hierarchically (Dennett, 1978). Cognitive psychologists analyze the role of 'scripts', 'schemas', and 'prototypical actions' in the control of behavior (Abelson, 1981); behaviorists speak of higher-order stimulus control, but seldom attempt to explain that in turn.

The computer subroutine metaphor is useful, not only because such programming shares features will behavioral programming, but because of the way in which people characterize the actions at each level. As Dennett (1978) has observed, a single line of code is discussed mechanistically. So might be a single subroutine. But for sufficiently large systems, whether they control petroleum refineries or play chess, programmers revert to functional ('in order to') and intentional ('it is attempting to') discourse. (Of course, this could be folly, responsible in part for the high costs of gasoline and our inability to write a grand master chess program!) Similarly, for reflexive or automatized behavior it is natural to speak mechanistically, in terms of short chains of cause and effect. But why believe, against the everyday evidence afforded by the ordinary verbal

behavior of even the most sophisticated radical behaviorists, that the emergent language of function and intention is not a superior mode of discourse concerning complex human behavior?

Distraction from the Study of Behavior

This is patently a behaviorist's complaint. But since behavior is 'what an organism is observed by another organism to be doing' (Skinner, 1938, p. 6), an organism may be doing many interesting things that do not qualify as behavior, yet may be fit for scientific study. If we broaden the definition by annexing private events, it has to be demonstrated why 'response-produced private stimulus' is a better label for the object of your mind's eye than 'image'. If the answer is that we do not have a 'copy' in our head, then we must ask clarification of the nature of 'private stimuli'; either they carry the meaning of copy/image, or an important phenomenon — our images, and our ability to inspect them — will be left unaccounted for.

Behaviorism has helped us to focus on the environmental context of actions, and that has been all to the good. It is all too easy to invent unverifiable 'mental' causes even when the precipitating environmental events are obvious to any who would look. Radical behaviorism provides excellent discipline. But, like discipline, it is not something one should major in. The world is bountiful with substantive issues, to which behaviorism can contribute important perspectives and methodologies. It is by focusing on these issues that the perspectives and methodologies will be improved. We should study behavior, but we should also study what goes on inside organisms. To call that 'behavior' is a theoretical commitment; it certainly is not what gets measured in most Skinner boxes; labeling it 'behavior' is at least a metaphorical extension, if not a magical mand. Perhaps other terms would be better. 'The decision as to whether to limit psychological theory to stimulus-response relationships . . . or to admit non-behavioral theoretical terms would seem to depend only on the heuristic values of the two approaches' (Zuriff, 1976, p. 51).

Dualism

This is not a simple issue, but it is not solved by claiming that 'my toothache is as physical as my typewriter' (Skinner, 1972, p. 384). How can that be? Is not a toothache in that limbo of 'some other level of observation, described in different terms, and measured . . . in different dimensions', along with theories and other embarrassments? Skinner's verbal behavior here appears to be more under the control of formal properties (alliteration) than physical properties. We may wish to avoid the long, usually dense, sometimes tedious, philosophical analyses of the mind/body issue by such a fiat. But the difference between toothaches and typewriters remains. Now we must invent some new dimension along which to differentiate them. Whatever we label that dimension, it will have two ends (or at least directions), and thus support a new charge of dualism.

'Mental' need not be equated with angels, uncaused causes, and other superstitions. It is a convenient rubric for many of the phenomena that led most of us into the field of psychology, and which remain fit subjects for study, despite our

insights as hypotheses, and therefore in need of testing. Thinking of a speculation as a hypothesis helps us to disengage from it if it turns out to be wrong. If we think of it as an assumption or take it to be axiomatic, its invalidation will threaten the whole system, and we are more likely to cling tenaciously to it, and to become doctrinaire — or worse, bellicose. Witness the recent review of Gibson's work by Costall (1984), who questions the existence of cognitive structures, and seeks 'an alternative scheme that does not merely question the solutions put forward by cognitive psychologists but converts their very problems from implicit to conspicuous nonsense' (p. 112). Cognitive psychologists are not innocent of confusion and error, both of the types that Skinner has identified, and of others as well (Sampson, 1981). But denigration such as Costall's is more likely to hurt the behaviorist movement than the cognitivist, for it places us in the roles of confounder, critic and saboteur, less seemly and less productive postures than that of originator. Science must be self-correcting, but since so much is provisional and since all systems contain flaws, the demonstration of a superior approach is much more effective in bringing about correction than is fault-finding. Let us agree with Wessells (1981) that 'it is premature to depict cognitive accounts as inherently flawed and unworthy of the serious, dispassionate attention of radical behaviorists' (p. 167).

THE POSSIBILITY OF EMPIRICAL MENTALISM

Behaviorism's success was not due to the fact that it was atheoretical (it was not — it was merely inchoately theoretical), nor that it was anti-mentalistic (spitting into that wind has kept us from studying some of the most intriguing phenomena). Its success was due to its empiricism — its respect for data, and its insistence that discourse be not too far removed from it. The Queen told Alice that she could believe as many as six impossible things before breakfast; when analysis is stacked onto more than one or two tenuous assumptions, behaviorists lose their taste for the meal. This is not to say that theory is thereby denied them. Anyone current with the discussions of maximizing versus matching in the analysis of choice, of economic behaviorism, of optimal foraging, of behavioral momentum, will recognize that the name of the primary journal may soon have to be changed to the *Journal of the Experimental and Theoretical Analysis of Behavior*. I think this is excellent progress.

The study of mind has proceeded from the opposite direction — speculative and unempirical. That is its problem, not that it involves a four-letter word. With some practice, it is possible to say 'mind' without a shudder of revulsion, and even to consider that it might be preferable to 'covert behavior', the first term of which has the synonyms 'clandestine', 'surreptitious', and 'furtive', suggesting the overthrow of elected governments and the mining of harbors. The second term seduces us into believing that the same experimental techniques that have served in the study of overt behavior will be adequate for events at some other level of observation, described in different terms, and measured in different dimensions. They may, but why limit ourselves?

'The objection to inner states is not that they do not exist, but that they are not relevant in a functional analysis' (Skinner, 1953, p. 35); 'the major behaviorist objection to cognitive or mental explanations is not that they are not objective, or

that they are based on introspection, . . . but rather that they . . . decrease the probability of investigation of manipulable variables' (Branch, 1982, p. 373); 'Mentalistic ideas are so seductive that one is in danger of being led by them down the garden path of introspection and mysticism . . . perhaps only a tough minded behaviorist can afford to entertain the seductress' (Pavio, quoted in Catania, 1982, p. 375). Is that all that Skinner and other radical behaviorists have been objecting to, a dalliance with unproductive ideas? (Do not dismiss that warning by noting that ideas, as collateral byproducts, cannot cause behavior. It is the texts in which you read them, and what you say about them to yourself and to others, that has the behaviorists worried, not the ideas themselves!) But what if this concern is misplaced? What if invocation of inner states and mental explanations turns out to be useful? What if Skinner was right when he said that 'part of human progress has been the improvement of our description of these things [internal states]' (1964, p. 106)?

We know the importance of chains of conditioned reinforcers; 'Unless the gap between behavior and the ultimate reinforcer is bridged with a sequence of conditioned reinforcers, other behavior will occur and receive the full force of reinforcement' (Skinner, 1958, p. 95). What about the gap between stimulus and response? How do humans mediate long gaps there, if not by talking to themselves, visualizing objects in familiar locations, and performing other mental gymnastics? Behaviorists accept such feats, preferring only that we call them behavior: seeing behavior, choice behavior, imagining behavior. But that qualification must take some of the fun out of it, for few behaviorists study those covert chains that mediate so much of human behavior.

Other researchers, less certain about the irrelevance of internal states, have attained insights about them that even behaviorists must applaud, if only briefly, before they attempt to 'translate' them, or with Costall, 'reduce them to explicit nonsense'. Posner (1982) has outlined the rich interaction of models and data in the development of attentional theory. E.R. John, a critic of the behavioristic minimization of research on mental phenomena, has traced stimuli into the brain by measuring the evoked responses to rhythmic stimuli, tagged by their own rhythmicity. Among his findings are: localization of the areas responding to the stimuli, and their spread during conditioning; upon introduction to the experimental chamber the rhythmic brain activity commences, 'as if the animal were rehearsing the experience of the meaningful stimulus'; activation of that evoked response when the event is expected but absent; in differential conditioning, errors preceded by the rhythm appropriate to the incorrect (and not displayed) stimulus (John, 1976).

The elegant work of Shepard and his students on mental transformations should by now be well-known to all psychologists. In an accessible introduction to his work Shepard (1978) notes the important role that imagery has played in the physical and life sciences. Shepard and Podgorny (1978) document and demonstrate many of the pervasive parallels between cognitive and perceptual processes. In his paper, 'Psychophysical Complementarity' (Shepard, 1981), he argues that evolutionary constraints have shaped the nature of our perceptual and cognitive processes, and that these achieve a rapid 'mesh' with the environment via certain predispositions that guide our inferences in uncertain situations. These are unexceptional arguments, perhaps, but he makes exceptional use of them. This view is parallel with that of Land (1978), a most practical scientist, who argues that

animals evolved in a 'polar partnership' with the world around them, with an inner order related to an outer order, related, Shepard would say, as a key to a lock. Many of Shepard's critical papers are collected and discussed in Shepard and Cooper (1982), where one finds scores of demonstrations such as: the time taken to decide whether two figures are the same depends not only on how many degrees one must mentally rotate them to align them, it depends also on whether one rotates them the short way or the long way; when the subject is given a head-start on rotating an image before a second figure is presented, if it is presented when the subject should have reached that orientation with their image, reaction time is uniformly short and independent of that orientation; subjects can rotate an image of a concrete object, but not of a frame of reference; rotation is either continuous or, if not, the size of the discrete steps must be less than thirty degrees. Other transformations, such as dilation, contraction, translation, and translation of attention to different parts of the image, are also reported (see also the work of Kosslyn, e.g., 1980). The wealth of creative experiments and systematic analyses thwarts simple summary. More than Skinner ever did, Shepard and his associates are treating seeing as behavior. They seem not at all hampered by their resolution that the 'thing' to which 'seeing without the thing seen' refers is an image, and that subjects need not do without it — to the contrary.

But behaviorists have never been very much interested in perception (Kantor, 1970); perhaps we should leave imagery to those who have a head-start on us, both experimentally and conceptually (for the latter, see Block, 1981). Our interests have been pragmatic, concerning 'manipulable variables of which behavior is a function' — behavior modification. Even there imagery will sometimes intrude. Covert sensitization and desensitization involve imagery, but except for the inconvenience those procedures could be effected overtly. Presumably covert behavior 'behaves' in the same fashion as overt behavior — but perhaps not always: Meichenbaum (1974) reviews studies where the covert processes do not respond to contingencies in the same fashion as overt behavior. Given the untoward overt responses of some animals to contingencies of reinforcement, and their recalcitrance to ordinary conditioning procedures (Breland and Breland, 1966), we should not be surprised to find that there are special constraints on cognitive conditioning. But with few exceptions (e.g., Catania, Matthews and Shimoff, 1982; McGuigan, 1978; Neuringer, 1981) behaviorists have not been looking. 'If those espousing a so-called radical behavioristic approach to cognition are to convert those whom they label cognitivists, then they will have to do so with experimentation and data' (Wasserman, 1983). 'If and when we assay that shift from rhetoric to research, we may be in for some surprises' (Longstreth, 1971).[4]

But, finally, does not the study of mental phenomena, in cognitive terms, force us into a dualistic metaphysics? No, it does not. As Bunge (1980) notes, 'rejecting psychophysical dualism does not force us to adopt eliminative or vulgar materialism . . . i.e. the thesis that mind and brain are identical, that there is no mind. . . . Psychobiology suggests . . . emergentism, i.e., the thesis that mentality is an emergent property possessed only by animals endowed with an extremely complex and plastic nervous system . . . this is not saying that minds constitute a level of their own, and this simply because there are no disembodied (or even embodied) minds, but only . . . minding animals . . . one can hold that the mental is emergent relative to the merely physical without reifying the former' (pp.

216–17). Emergent materialism; what is the difference between this and mentalism? 'The difference boils down to this: whereas mentalism has (simple) explanations for everything mental in mental terms alone, materialism gropes for (usually complex) explanations of the mental in terms of brain processes and possibly social circumstances as well' (Bunge, 1980, p. 214). It appears that what I have been calling empirical mentalism Bunge would call emergent materialism. Call it by either name, it is time for 'tough-minded behaviorists' to entertain the notion. It is time for them to become 'emergent behaviorists'.

PRINCIPLES OF EMERGENT BEHAVIORISM

What would emergent behaviorism be like? It would not be a 'methodological behaviorism' that draws a boundary for its subject co-extensive with the skin. Nor would it be a cognitive psychology that, at its worst, draws the same boundary but stays inside it. Nor would it be a radical behaviorism that has been short-sheeted by its own parsimony, contorting its basic theoretical terms to cover areas that are out of their reach.

It would be behavioral. Our roots are in the study of animal behavior, and in the rejection of introspective mental models for its explanation. An impressionistic theory of human motivation provides a poor foundation for a theory of animal behavior. Conversely, a theory of the behavior of non-verbal animals provides a problematic basis for the study of human behavior, including that covert behavior called mental activity. Our behaviorism would be emergent because it recognizes the causal relevance of mental states, and thus utility of having theoretical terms within the system to refer to those states.

It would be inductive. But its induction would be Peirce's (Rescher, 1978), not Skinner's (Verplanck, 1954). It would involve the generation of hypotheses based on observed regularities ('abduction'), and the modification of those hypotheses based on empirical tests ('retroduction'). Insofar as these hypotheses may concern events 'at another level', this constitutes a rejection of Skinner's positivism.

Like Skinner's behaviorism, it would be pragmatic (Platt, 1973). It would recognize that 'the rationality and progressiveness of a theory are most closely linked — not with its confirmation or its falsification — but rather with its problem solving effectiveness' (Laudan, 1977, p. 5). The same is true of research traditions; those that are successful are those that lead to the solution of an increasing range of empirical and conceptual problems. Emergent behaviorism would result from a cumulation of successful theories and the problem domains that they have addressed — not by fiat, nor by aping the traditions of other sciences, nor by proscribing certain techniques on doctrinal grounds. This may seem unexceptional, but I believe that the commitment of operant behaviorists to description rather than problem-solving has thwarted such development.[5]

It would be prudent with its resources, but not parsimonious. Parsimony is a better criterion for choosing competing theories than for generating new ones. The conceptual stinginess that it entails impoverishes exploration and thus stifles progress. It puts all the emphasis on cost, rather than cost-effectiveness. New constructs should be viewed as new parameters in a regression equation; they involve a real cost, for they decrease the degrees of freedom in the data-theory

system. But if the data are sufficiently strong and numerous, such constructs may greatly improve our ability to comprehend them. Gratuituous and ad hoc explanations are to be rejected, whether they are mentalistic or behavioral, simply because they do not pay their way (Rescher, 1978). They dilute the explanatory power of the theory by introducing a 'parameter' that can account for only a small domain of the data under purview.

In sum, emergent behaviorism would focus on behavior, not on parascientific theories about it such as those derogated by Skinner in the first lines of this paper. Its goals are to develop successful theories of behavior, and it recognizes that those theories may involve mental terms. Its methods would include hypothesis generation and testing. It would be pragmatic, not parsimonious, asking first what we can do, and only second what it will cost. Finally, because it opens the door to new freedom in theory construction, requiring only that the products pay their way, it should restore the excitement that some in our field have been searching for at the back door of cognitivism.

NOTES

1   Some of these constructs are operationally defined (contingencies and motivational operations) and some are functionally defined (stimuli and responses). Thus, a Fixed Ratio 1000 schedule that is ineffective in maintaining behavior remains a Fixed Ratio 1000 schedule, but a 'stimulus' that is ineffective in controlling behavior is not a stimulus. This is a curious mix of types. Certainly motivational constructs can be defined functionally (see, e.g., Bolles, 1967). So can reinforcement contingencies, although that is more difficult and requires a feedback/control language (Staddon, 1980, 1983). Stimuli and responses can be defined operationally — as Skinner and subsequent experimental analysts of behavior routinely reported experiments using lights of some color, counting lever-presses of some force and so on. Unless we designed explicit experiments (e.g., as did Reynolds, 1961), we could not know that responses of a slightly different topography were under the control of different aspects of the same stimulus. No matter how much admired, such analyses are usually undertaken only when the experimenter runs into trouble (see, e.g., Sidman, 1958). Thus while the operant is in theory an act (i.e., it is defined functionally), in reality it is usually defined operationally as the closure of three switches in sequence — those of the cue, the operandum, and the feeder.
2   Without such interaction there would be little need for the constructs. In cases where behavior becomes habitual or automatized, and therefore more resistant to modification, the more complex control provided by internal events such as self-instruction has given way to simpler chains of behavior; guidance by mental events vanishes, and with it the need for corresponding theoretical terms. But there are many occasions, the most characteristically human, where such control is present: the ability to guide, speculate, calculate and evaluate. Skinner discusses these different sources of control in his important article on rule-governed versus contingency-shaped behavior (1969). Unfortunately, few behaviorists followed him on this venture into *terra cognita*.
3   This arresting assertion is like a Zen koan, involving the nice contradiction that transitive verbs need not have predicates. Why Skinner should deny that 'private stimuli' can be 'seen' is unclear. He denies the name 'image' to an ensemble of them for fear of our seduction by the belief that there is a physical copy present in the brain. However, experiments cited below suggest that functionally the best way to treat such private events may be as images, because of the many properties they share with the referents of that term in its natural language use.
4   The conditions that optimize learning in animals also satisfy Hume's conditions for inferring causality — contiguity in space, precedence in time, and constancy of conjunction (Killeen, 1981). But these are transcended and modified by mental activity, just as Korte's laws for perceived motion of flashing lights are modified by placing an arced 'path' above the lights (Shepard, 1982).
5   One of the few such elaborations I have seen recently is Michael's introduction of the construct 'establishing stimulus' (1980; see also Sidman, 1979). I believe that it was Skinner's contempt for (other people's) theory that left his students unprepared to develop his own.

REFERENCES

Abelson, R.P. (1981) 'Psychological status of the script concept', *American Psychologist*, 36, pp. 715–29.

Audi, R. (1976) 'B.F. Skinner on freedom, dignity, and the explanation of behavior', *Behaviorism*, 4. pp. 163–86.

Bem, D.J. (1972) 'Self-perception theory', *Advances in Experimental Social Psychology*, 6, pp. 1–62.

Blanshard, B. and Skinner, B.F. (1967) 'The problem of consciousness — a debate', *Philosophy and Phenomenological Research*, 27, pp. 317–37.

Block, N. (1981) *Imagery*, Cambridge, Mass., MIT Press.

Bolles, R.C. (1967) *Theory of Motivation*, New York, Harper and Row.

Branch, M.N. (1982) 'Misrepresenting behaviorism', *The Behavioral and Brain Sciences*, 5, pp. 372–3.

Breland, K. and Breland, M. (1966) *Animal Behavior*, New York, Macmillan.

Bunge, M. (1980) *The Mind-Body Problem: A Psychobiological Approach*, New York, Pergamon.

Catania, A.C. (1982) 'Antimisrepresentationalism', *The Behavioral and Brain Sciences*, 5, pp. 374–5.

Catania, A.C., Matthews, B.A. and Shimoff, E. (1982) 'Instructed versus shaped human verbal behavior: Interactions with nonverbal responding', *Journal of the Experimental Analysis of Behavior*, 38, pp. 233–48.

Cialdini, R.B., Petty, R.E. and Cacioppo, J.T. (1981) 'Attitude and attitude change', *Annual Review of Psychology*, 32, pp. 357–404.

Costall, A.P. (1984) 'Are theories of perception necessary? A review of Gibson's *The Ecological Approach to Visual Perception*', *Journal of the Experimental Analysis of Behavior*, 41, pp. 109–15.

Creel, R. (1980) 'Radical epiphenomenalism: B.F. Skinner's account of private events', *Behaviorism*, 8, pp. 31–53.

Dawkins, R. (1976) 'Hierarchial organization: A candidate principle for ethology', in Bateson, P.P.G. and Hinde, R.A. (Eds), *Growing Points in Ethology*, New York, Cambridge University Press, pp. 7–54.

Dennett, D.C. (1978) *Brainstorms*, New York, Bradford Books.

Goffman, E. (1971) *Relations in Public: Microstudies of the Public Order*, New York, Basic Books.

John, E.R. (1976) 'A model of consciousness', in Schwartz, G.E. and Shapiro, D. (Eds), *Consciousness and Self-Regulation*, New York, Plenum. pp. 1–50.

Kantor, J.R. (1970) 'An analysis of the experimental analysis of behavior (TEAB)', *Journal of the Experimental Analysis of Behavior*, 13, pp. 101–8.

Keat, R. (1972) 'A critical examination of B.F. Skinner's objections to mentalism', *Behaviorism*, 1, pp. 53–70.

Killeen, P.R. (1981) Learning as causal inference', in Commons, M.L. and Nevin, J.A. (Eds), *Quantitative Analysis of Behavior, Vol. 1: Discriminative Properties of Reinforcement Schedules*, Cambridge, Mass., Ballinger, pp. 89–112.

Kosslyn, S.M. (1980) *Image and Mind*, Cambridge, Mass., Harvard University Press.

Land, E.H. (1978) 'Our "polar partnership" with the world around us', *Harvard Magazine*, January/February, pp. 23–6.

Laudan, L. (1977) *Progress and Its Problems: Toward a Theory of Scientific Growth*, Berkeley, Calif., University of California Press.

Lazarus, R.S. (1982) 'Thoughts on the relations between emotions and cognition', *American Psychologist*, 37, pp. 1019–24.

Lazarus, R.S. (1984) 'On the primacy of cognition', *American Psychologist*, 39, pp. 124–9.

Longstreth, L.E. (1971) 'A cognitive interpretation of secondary reinforcement', in Cole, J.K. (Ed.), *Nebraska Symposium on Motivation*, Lincoln, Neb., University of Nebraska Press, pp. 33–80.

Lowe, C.F. (1983) 'Radical behaviorism and human psychology', in Davey, G.C.L. (Ed.), *Animal Models of Human Behavior*, New York, John Wiley and Sons. pp. 71–93.

McGuigan, F.J. (1978) *Cognitive Psychophysiology: Principles of Covert Behavior*, Englewood Cliffs, N.J., Prentice-Hall.

Meichenbaum, D. (1974) *Cognitive Behavior Modification*, Morristown, N.J., General Learning Press.

Michael, J. (1980) 'Untitled presentation', *Behaviorism*, 8, pp. 161–3.

Natsoulas, T. (1983) 'Perhaps the most difficult problem faced by behaviorism', *Behaviorism*, 11, pp. 1–26.

Neuringer, A.J. (1981) 'Self-experimentation: A call for change', *Behaviorism*, 9, pp. 79–94.

Nisbett, R.E. and Wilson, T.D. (1977) 'Telling more than we know: Verbal reports on mental processes', *Psychological Review*, 84, pp. 231–59.

Platt, J.R. (1973) 'The Skinnerian revolution', in Wheeler, H. (Ed.), *Beyond the Punitive Society*, San Francisco, Calif., Freeman, pp. 22–56.

Posner, M.I. (1982) 'Cumulative development of attentional theory', *American Psychologist*, 37, pp. 168–79.

Rescher, N. (1978) *Peirce's Philosophy of Science*, Notre Dame, Ind., Indiana University Press.

Reynolds, G.S. (1961) 'Attention in the pigeon', *Journal of the Experimental Analysis of Behavior*, 4, pp. 203–8.

Sabini, J. and Silver, M. (1981) 'Introspection and causal accounts', *Journal of Personality and Social Psychology*, 40, pp. 171–9.

Sampson, E.E. (1981) 'Cognitive psychology as ideology', *American Psychologist*, 36, pp. 730–43.

Shepard, R.N. (1978) 'The mental image', *American Psychologist*, 33, pp. 125–37.

Shepard, R.N. (1981) 'Psychophysical complementarity', in Kubovy, M. and Pomerantz, J.R. (Eds), *Perceptual Organization*, Hillsdale, N. J., Lawrence Erlbaum Associates, pp. 279–341.

Shepard, R.N. and Zare, S. (1983) 'Path-guided apparent motion', *Science*, 220, pp. 632–4.

Shepard, R.N. and Cooper, L.A. (1982) *Mental Images and Their Transformations*, Cambridge, Mass., MIT Press.

Shepard, R.N. and Podgorny, P. (1978) 'Cognitive processes that resemble perceptual processes', in Estes, W.K. (Ed.), *Handbook of Learning and Cognitive Processes*, Vol. 5, Hillsdale, N.J., Lawrence Erlbaum, pp. 189–237.

Sidman, M. (1958) 'By-products of aversive control', *Journal of the Experimental Analysis of Behavior*, 1, pp. 265–80.

Sidman, M. (1979) 'Remarks', *Behaviorism*, 7, pp. 123–6.

Simon, H.A. (1973) 'The organization of complex systems', in Pattee, H. H. (Ed.), *Hierarchy Theory*, New York, Braziller, pp. 1–27.

Skinner, B.F. (1938) *The Behavior of Organisms*, New York, Appleton-Century.

Skinner, B.F. (1953) *Science and Human Behavior*, New York, Free Press.

Skinner, B.F. (1957) *Verbal Behavior*, New York, Appleton-Century-Crofts.

Skinner, B.F. (1958) 'Reinforcement today', *American Psychologist*, 13, pp. 94–9.

Skinner, B.F. (1963) 'Behaviorism at fifty', *Science*, 140, pp. 951–8.

Skinner, B.F. (1964) 'Comments at Symposium', in Wann, T.W. (Ed.), *Behaviorism and Phenomenology: Contrasting Bases for Modern Psychology*, Chicago, Ill., Chicago University Press, pp. 97–108.

Skinner, B.F. (1969) *Contingencies of Reinforcement: A Theoretical Analysis*. New York, Appleton-Century-Crofts.

Skinner, B.F. (1971) *Beyond Freedom and Dignity*, New York, Knopf.

Skinner, B.F. (1972) 'Humanism and behaviorism', *The Humanist*, July/August, pp. 18–20.

Skinner, B.F. (1974) *About Behaviorism*, New York, Knopf.

Skinner, B.F. (1975) 'The steep and thorny way to a science of behavior', *American Psychologist*, 30, pp. 42–9.

Sober, E. (1983) 'Mentalism and behaviorism in comparative psychology', in Rajecki, D.W. (Ed.), *Comparing Behavior: Studying Man Studying Animals*, Hillsdale, N.J., Lawrence Erlbaum Associates, pp. 113–42.

Staddon, J.E.R. (1980) *Limits to Action: The Allocation of Individual Behavior*, New York, Academic Press.

Staddon, J.E.R. (1983) *Adaptive Behavior and Learning*, New York, Cambridge University Press.

Verplanck, W.S. (1954) 'Burrhus F. Skinner', in Koch, S. *et al.*, *Modern Learning Theory*, New York, Appleton-Century-Crofts, pp. 267–316.

Wasserman, E.A. (1983) 'Is cognitive psychology behavioral?' *Psychological Record*, 33, pp. 6–11.

Wessells, M.G. (1981) 'A critique of Skinner's views on the explanatory inadequacy of cognitive theories', *Behaviorism*, 9, pp. 153–70.

Zajonc, R.B. (1980) 'Feeling and thinking: Preferences need no inferences', *American Psychologist*, 35, pp. 151–75.

Zajonc, R.B. (1984) 'On the primacy of affect', *American Psychologist*, 39, pp. 117–23.

Zuriff, G.E. (1976) 'Stimulus equivalence, grammar, and internal structure', *Behaviorism*, 4, pp. 43–52.

Zuriff, G.E. (1979) 'Ten inner causes', *Behaviorism*, 7, pp. 1–8.

Interchange

HAYES AND BROWNSTEIN REPLY TO KILLEEN

IS THIS THE KIND OF FLEXIBILITY WE NEED?

In discussing radical behaviorism in contrast to emergent behaviorism we find ourselves comparing a proposal for a science of behavior and some products of this proposal with only a proposal. What is made clear by Killeen's comments is that accounts offered by radical behaviorists can suffer from the same shortcomings as mentalistic accounts. Accounts within the behavioral camp have at times been incomplete and ad hoc. It is to the credit of the behavioral approach that such accounts are easily detected by virtue of the clearly expressed criteria for an adequate account — prediction and control.

What about the products of emergent behaviorism? We can only guess how they will measure up. Killeen's aspirations for emergent behaviorism are consistent in large part with those of radical behaviorism. The proposed approach appears to be more permissive than radical behaviorism, but Killeen intends for this flexibility to be tempered by evaluating scientific activities relative to their intended functions. If this actually worked, who could disagree with such a proposal? Surely not radical behaviorists since for them the issue is not the form of science but its function. A radical behavioral view may *appear* needlessly restrictive by comparison, but Killeen's portrayal of the approach makes it appear as though a similar set of evaluative processes was not involved in the development of the tenets of radical behaviorism. This is not the case. The radical behavioral view is meant to be flexible precisely to the degree required to meet the legitimate goals of science.

Killeen is offering a return to a more theoretical venture with inclusion of mental events. He would superimpose the criterion of pragmatic value on these activities, so we will not return to the juncture from which radical behaviorism originally emerged. But theory construction and attendant activities are at best way-stations on the path to more pragmatic activities. It has to be shown that they actually contribute to prediction and control. Skinner's objection to certain types of theories is largely that these types seem to become ends in themselves. When this happens, they are no longer pragmatically useful. His objections to mentalism are, as we tried to show in our chapter, based on the same concerns, and we believe with good reason. That these objections are not due to a rejection of flexibility per se is shown unequivocally by his permissive post-1945 attitude toward the definition of scientifically legitimate events. Perhaps Killeen is right that an emergent behaviorism could have its mentalistic cake and pragmatically eat it too, but we doubt that this would be so. As we tried to show, allowing

behavioral causes (made seemingly less incomplete by calling them 'mental') ultimately tends to stop causal analysis before effective action is possible. We see nothing in Killeen's proposal that would deal with this problem.

This is not to say that Killeen is incorrect to insist that we must get on with the important tasks at hand. We fear that his proposal is the wrong solution made for the right reasons. Killeen is fairly clear why he wants to have mental events included: he wants us to proceed with an analysis of significant human events. He lists many: talking to oneself, imagining, an analysis of verbal behavior and so on. With this we heartily agree. It is true that at times radical behaviorists have translated such important issues into behavioral language only so as to dismiss them, and at other times they may have acted as if difficult phenomena are explained merely by translation even though that may not be so. This is perhaps understandable because of the cautious attitude toward the as-yet-unexplained inherent in this inductive approach, as we noted in our chapter. Yet an embrace of mentalism is not a sure road to an appreciation of the richness of these phenomena, and trivialization is not the necessary result of behavioral translation. One can reject mentalistic terms precisely in order to study the phenomena associated with them in a more thorough and scientifically satisfying way. It is out of our concern that Killeen's topics be addressed adequately that we suggest radical behaviorism as a solution.

Current research in the *Journal of the Experimental Analysis of Behavior* and elsewhere shows that behaviorists are venturing out from a study of animal behavior and its straightforward extension into the direct experimental analysis of human behavior. The discipline supplied by the assumptions inherent in radical behaviorism is needed most in exactly such difficult endeavors, not in order to pursue discipline for its own sake, but in order to develop original insights of lasting value. Mentalism may provide a quick thrill, but it is one that seems doomed to fade. Like a husband or wife who finds that a spouse of many years, when approached in the proper way, continues to be a solid source of wonder and inspiration, we suggest that psychologists interested in significant human behavior will find more long-term value in a fresh look at radical behaviorism than in seeking 'excitement ... at the back door of cognitivism' (Killeen, this volume, p. 232).

KILLEEN REPLIES TO HAYES AND BROWNSTEIN

RADICAL BEHAVIORISM UNDER THE MICROSCOPE: CLARITY GAINED, DEPTH OF FIELD LOST

Hayes and Brownstein offer a clear and coherent statement of a behavioral system. However, it is only one of the many that we may infer from Skinner's writings. The virtue of specificity has cost them the blessing of universality to which Skinner aspired, and which he attained by inconsistency in the way he talked. Skinner's genius lies in his acute observations of environmental events that may be treated as causes of behavior, in lieu of the more convenient, more fallible, and less manipulable 'inner causes'. It is out of admiration for that approach that

I became and remain a behaviorist. It is the same theme of environmental determinism that excites Hayes and Brownstein, and which they choose as the cornerstone of their analysis. But what is invaluable as an attitude may prove uncertain and restrictive as a basis for a system.

The authors argue that prediction and control are the goal of radical behaviorism, and that we should argue not over the appropriateness of that goal, but only about how well it is realized. Because hypothetical constructs are not directly manipulable, they should play no role in the discipline. Only events that are not part of the subject matter of the discipline should be treated as causes (behavior, therefore, whether covert or overt, should not be taken as a cause of other behavior). They object to mentalism because it introduces a different kind of 'stuff' than the physical, and because all behavior is to be interpreted through contingency analysis.

This is an excellent basis for a technology of behavior, but inadequate for a science of behavior. Science is about understanding, and employs prediction and control as tests of adequate understanding. Understanding is intrinsically metaphorical — as Einstein said, it involves reducing a phenomenon to models that we already have intuitions about. There is nothing wrong with being an engineer, but it is difficult to attain the goals of science, as generally understood, if one is an engineer who has denied the propriety of those goals.

Hypothetical constructs may be manipulated as directly as behavior, however directly that may be. I might manipulate Hayes' and Brownstein's anxiety by pointing out a logical fallacy in their arguments, and could do so with approximately the same degree of control with which I might reinforce the raising of a fist or elicit blushing. The evidential basis for knowing that I have manipulated their anxiety is one step removed, so the construct must have compensating strengths — it must tie together a number of variables, and reduce the information load of the theory. (To know that five operations will produce a state, and the state will produce five behaviors, requires ten inferences rather than the twenty-five required without the construction of a state.) Such inventions may be viewed either as convenient fictions (intervening variables) or as occurrent events (hypothetical constructs). Both are ubiquitous in the physical sciences; to deny their reality because they are based on inference would be as useful as denying magnetism because 'it is inferred from the phenomenon it is said to cause.'

Skinner does not share the authors' reluctance to view behavior as a cause of behavior: 'In self control and creative thinking, ... the individual is largely engaged in manipulating his own behavior ...' (1953, p. 229). Although he looks to an ultimate explanation in enviromental terms, he realizes the utility of the provisional use of convenient fictions: 'Meanwhile, the term "self" will be used in a less rigorous way' (1953, p. 230). Although homunculi are out, we are given 'the self which is concerned with self-knowing functions concurrently with the behavioral system which it describes ... Other kinds of relations between personalities are evident in the process of making a decision, solving a problem, or creating a work of art' (1953, p. 287). These are the very phrases Skinner would derogate, coming from any other psychologist. But I regard these chapters as Skinner at his best, and this is what Hayes and Brownstein would discard.

Although one may object to 'mind' because some people associate it with non-physical 'stuff', one need not so reify the construct, just as behaviorism does not require a non-physical storehouse for lever presses when they are not being

made. It is process that psychologists study — minding and behaving. Whereas it is parsimonious to say that these are the same thing, it may be as useful as saying that fire and water are the same thing. Monism reduces the number of things you have to remember, but it gives you less to say about it.

The opposite of a small truth, they say, is a lie, but the opposite of a great truth is another truth. Radical behaviorism gives us many great truths. Consider: 'We cannot account for the behavior of any system while staying wholly inside it', and then replace 'inside' with 'outside'. Physicists can stay outside objects and predict their trajectories after a collision only if the bodies are inelastic; if they deform like rubber balls or silly putty, their internal properties must also be studied. We too must go inside our system, and to not forget where we are or what we study, we might call phenomena there by a different name. If 'mental states' has too chequered a history, let us coin new terms, such as 'mentate'. However we call them, let us not solve the spectrum of challenges we face by placing them under a single wavelength and then asserting that all is green.

REFERENCES

Skinner, B.F. (1953) *Science and Human Behavior*, New York, Free Press.

Part XI: Skinner and the 'Virtus Dormitiva' Argument

19. Skinner Re-Skinned

ULLIN PLACE

DENNETT, SKINNER AND THE CASE AGAINST MENTALISM

This chapter differs from most in this book in that criticism is not directed at the work of B.F. Skinner himself. It is directed instead at a recent criticism of Skinner's position by Professor Daniel C. Dennett which appears under the title 'Skinner Skinned' as Chapter 4 of his recent book, *Brainstorms* (Dennett, 1978).

Dennett begins his critique with the observation that for most psychologists Skinner's behaviourism is no longer a fashionable standpoint. He acknowledges, nevertheless, that at one time Skinner's position commanded a considerable following, and presents his critique as a diagnosis of what went wrong. For Dennett, Skinner's psychology stands or falls on the case for repudiating the use of mentalistic idioms in developing a scientific explanation of the behaviour of living organisms. Skinner, he acknowledges, 'has a strong gut intuition that the *traditional* way of talking about human behaviour — in "mentalistic" terms of a person's beliefs, desires, ideas, hopes, fears, feelings, emotions — is somehow utterly disqualified' (Dennett, 1978, p. 54). In speaking of this prejudice as 'an intuition', Dennett implies that Skinner is right to repudiate the use of mentalistic idioms in a scientific psychology; though by describing it as 'a gut intuition' he also implies that the reasons which Skinner gives for that repudiation leave much to be desired.

Having drawn attention to Skinner's habit of indiscriminately piling up arguments against mentalism with little regard for their cogency or their consistency with one another or with positions he himself adopts elsewhere, Dennett (pp. 55–6) lists four arguments against mentalism put forward by Skinner, the details of which need not concern us, which he dismisses on one or other of these grounds. He then goes on to discuss in greater detail two other arguments which Skinner does not formulate in so many words, but which, in Dennett's view, are implicit in what he does say. These we may call the *virtus dormitiva* and inten-

tionality arguments respectively. The *virtus dormitiva* (Skinner, 1938, p. 427; Dennett, 1978, pp. 56–9) is a reference to Molière's play, *Le Malade Imaginaire*, in which the learned doctor offers its possession of a *virtus dormitiva* as an explanation of why opium puts people who take it to sleep. This explanation of why opium puts people to sleep is plainly vacuous. Dennett must therefore be right to claim, as he does (p. 57), that Skinner's repudiation of mentalism would succeed if he could show that mentalistic explanations of behaviour are similarly vacuous. However, mentalistic explanations of behaviour, according to Dennett, are not vacuous. He does not tell us what it is about them that saves them from vacuity; any more than he tells us what it is that makes the *virtus dormitiva* vacuous in the first place. He simply relies on our linguistic intuitions to tell us that to explain Tom's taking the uptown bus in terms of his desire to go to Macy's and his belief that Macy's is uptown is not similarly vacuous (p. 59).

The only argument which Dennett (pp. 60–1) recognizes as providing a good reason for repudiating the use of mentalistic explanations in a scientific psychology is the contention that they involve what he calls, following Chisholm (1957), 'intentional idioms'. These he evidently equates with Quine's (1953) 'referentially opaque contexts', while endorsing Quine's (1960) view that such idioms are incompatible with the language of 'physical' science.

In opposing Dennett I shall not try to defend Skinner against Dennett's criticism of the reasons he gives for repudiating mentalism for the purposes of a scientific psychology. My quarrel is not with the claim that something is wrong with Skinner's defence of his position; it is rather with Dennett's diagnosis of what is wrong and with the resulting prognosis for the patient's future. I shall argue that Dennett fails to appreciate or, if he has appreciated, fails to point out:

1   that what Skinner thinks is objectionable about mentalistic idioms is that they involve the ascription of dispositional properties to the behaving organism;
2   that the *virtus dormitiva* and
3   intentionality arguments are both arguments against the use of dispositional property ascriptions in scientific explanation;
4   that, since dispositional property ascriptions are essential to any causal explanation, Dennett has failed to provide a good reason for endorsing Skinner's repudiation of mentalism; and
5   that what is objectionable about mentalistic explanations of behaviour is that their use presupposes that the behaviour to be explained is 'rule-governed' in Skinner's (1969) sense; this implies control of behaviour by a verbal specification of the relevant contingency which is contrary to fact in cases where the behaviour to be explained is 'contingency-shaped'.

STRATAGEMS USED BY SKINNER TO AVOID ASCRIBING DISPOSITIONS TO THE BEHAVING ORGANISM

Defining Dispositions in Terms of Their Causes

Skinner nowhere states that it is their dispositional character which for him renders mentalistic idioms unacceptable as a scientific explanation of behaviour.

Nevertheless, the remarkable collection of stratagems he adopts in order to avoid ascribing dispositional properties to the behaving organism in his own theoretical formulations makes it tolerably certain that this is his belief. The first of these stratagems is that in which a dispositional property is defined in terms of its causes rather than its effects. This stratagem is illustrated by the replacement of the concept of 'drive' which made a brief appearance in Skinner's first major book, *The Behavior of Organisms* (1938), but which was later replaced by the concept of 'a state of deprivation' which emphasizes what Michael (1982) calls the 'establishing condition', which has the effect of directing the organism's behaviour towards making good that deficiency.

Response Probability

The concept of 'drive' was, briefly, the sole survivor within Skinner's radical behaviorism' of a whole galaxy of dispositional concepts which formed part of the 'principles of behavior' proposed by Skinner's immediate predecessor in the behaviourist tradition, Clark L. Hull (1943), against whose elaborate attempt at mathematical theory construction Skinner was consciously reacting. Hull referred to these dispositional concepts as 'intervening variables' and they included, besides the concept of 'drive', such notions as 'habit strength', 'excitatory potential', 'inhibitory potential' and 'reaction potential'. But just as the concept of 'drive' survives in Skinner's later work in the form of the concept of 'a state of deprivation', so Hull's notions of 'habit strength' and 'reaction potential' have their counterpart in Skinner's concept of 'response probability'. This is the device which Skinner uses to express the strength of the organism's disposition or propensity to behave in a particular way. But in order to avoid ascribing such a disposition to the organism, he talks instead of the strength of the probability that a particular response will be emitted by the organism. In other words, in order to avoid attributing the disposition to the organism, he talks instead in terms of the strength of the observer's expectation that the response in question will appear.

Response Class

If the notion of 'response probability' is Skinner's way of characterizing the strength of a disposition to behave in a certain way, the notion of 'response class' is his way of characterizing the range and variety of different ways of behaving which, if they were emitted by the organism, would constitute what Ryle (1949) calls 'exercises' of the disposition in question. By talking about this range of possible behaviour in terms of the notion of response class, Skinner contrives to suggest that what he is talking about is the class of actual responses emitted by the organism in the past rather than a range of possible responses which it may or may not emit in the future.

The Law of Effect

Skinner's account of what determines both the probability that a given response will be emitted and the nature and breadth of the class of responses whose

emission probability is thereby increased or diminished is a version of the Law of Effect in which both aspects of the behaviour are determined by the consequences which similar behaviour has had in the past. What is actually strengthened or weakened by those consequences is the organism's disposition to emit similar behaviour on an indefinite number of possible occasions in the future. However, by talking as if the behaviour whose probability of emission is increased or strengthened by reinforcement is the same behaviour as that which produces the reinforcing consequences, Skinner contrives to suggest that all he is talking about is behaviour that has actually occurred in the past.

Dispositional Properties Ascribed to Stimuli

The absurdity of Skinner's attempt to avoid ascribing dispositional properties to the behaving organism is most apparent when he ascribes dispositional properties, such as those of being 'discriminative', 'aversive' or 'reinforcing', to environmental stimuli. The evident purpose of this is to avoid having to ascribe to the behaving organism dispositional properties such as the ability to discriminate, an aversion for or an addiction to the stimuli in question. He can do this because, although our normal linguistic practice constrains us to ascribe the dispositional property to only one of the entities involved, dispositional properties invariably involve an interaction between two distinct entities, a causal agent which acts and a causal patient which is acted upon. In some cases, like the magnetic properties we attribute to an iron bar or the ability to put people to sleep which we attribute to opium, the property is attributed to the causal agent. In other cases, like Ryle's favourite example of the brittleness of glass, they are attributed to the causal patient. But it is always possible to do things the other way round and talk of the propensity of the iron filings to be attracted to the magnet, of the propensity of human beings and other organisms to be put to sleep by opium or of the propensity of missiles to break glass. On this analogy there can be no serious objection to Skinner's practice of ascribing discriminative, aversive and reinforcing properties to the causal agent, the stimulus, instead of ascribing them, as we ordinarily do, to the causal patient, the organism. But while this way of construing the matter cannot be ruled out of order, it has arguably little to recommend it apart from indulging Skinner's prejudice against the ascription of dispositional properties to the behaving organism.

THE VIRTUS DORMITIVA AND THE CASE AGAINST DISPOSITIONAL PROPERTY ASCRIPTIONS

Although Dennett does not mention the fact, he can hardly be unaware that the *virtus dormitiva* has to be construed as an argument against the use for explanatory purposes of a certain kind of dispositional property ascription. Not only is the *virtus dormitiva* an obvious example of a dispositional concept, but Peter Geach (1957), the first philosopher to make use of this example in contemporary philosophical debate, used it as part of a criticism of Ryle's account of dispositional statements (statements ascribing a dispositional property to an entity) as concealed hypothetical statements about what is liable to happen, if certain con-

tingencies are fulfilled.

No one would want to deny that dormative power is a dispositional property or the vacuity of attributing opium's tendency to put those who take it to sleep to its dormitive power. There is disagreement, however, about what it is about that attribution that makes it vacuous. For Skinner, to judge by his discussion in *The Behavior of Organisms* (Skinner, 1938, p. 427) where he refers to 'Molière's "coup de grâce" to verbalism', what the *virtus dormitiva* example shows is the vacuity of *any* purported explanation which relies on the ascription of a dispositional property to the entity in question. According to Geach, on the other hand, such dispositional property ascriptions are vacuous as explanations only insofar as they cannot be backed up by an account of what it is about the microstructure of the entity in question which makes it true that if certain conditions are fulfilled it will behave in the manner described. Thus in the case of the *virtus dormitiva* the explanation would have been saved from vacuity had it been backed up by an account of what it is about the chemical composition of the drug which interacts with the biochemistry of the human brain to produce the effect in question.

Dennett does not tell us what he thinks makes the attribution of a *virtus dormitiva* vacuous; but it is difficult not to believe that he endorses Geach's interpretation, since its methodological implications for psychology are very much in line with his own methodological prescriptions, as outlined in the remainder of the book. For it would seem that on this interpretation of the argument the only way to avoid the vacuity of *virtus dormitiva* explanations in psychology is to rely on explanations involving a detailed specification of what it is about the microstructure of the brain and the central nervous system which makes the organism behave as it does.

Now it has to be conceded that the only non-vacuous account of what it is about opium that puts people who take it to sleep is an account in terms of its chemical composition and the effect of that chemical composition on the biochemistry of the brain. Likewise, as, according to Dennett (1978, p. 56), even Skinner concedes, the only non-vacuous account of what it is about a living organism that gives it its behavioural capacities and propensities is an account in terms of the microstructure of the brain. It is also true that the learned doctor in Molière's play is using the impressive-sounding Latin phrase, *virtus dormitiva*, as a cover for his ignorance of what it really is about opium that puts people to sleep. Nevertheless, it is not this ignorance which makes the explanation vacuous. What makes it vacuous to attribute opium's propensity to put people who take it to sleep to its *virtus dormitiva* is that the would-be explanation is a pure tautology. To say that opium has a *virtus dormitiva* or, in modern pharmacological parlance that it has hypnotic properties, is to say no more and no less than has already been said by saying that it tends to put people who take it to sleep.

This being the case, we cannot claim either, as Skinner evidently wants to do, that every explanation that relies on the ascription of a dispositional property to the entity in question is bound to be vacuous or, with Geach, that dispositional property ascriptions are only saved from vacuity insofar as they are backed up by a theoretical understanding of the state of the microstructure of the entity in question on which the dispositional property depends. If it is its tautological character which accounts for the vacuity of a *virtus dormitiva* explanation, the fact that such explanations are also dispositional in character is entirely beside the point. The fact that a dispositional property cannot be used to explain itself under

another description cannot be used as evidence that dispositional property ascriptions are invariably vacuous. If what is to be explained is a particular event or state of affairs, for example, someone's falling asleep on a particular occasion after taking opium, there is nothing vacuous about explaining *that* in terms of the dormitive virtue or hypnotic properties of the drug. By the same token there is nothing vacuous about explaining the particular event constituted by Tom's taking the uptown bus (Dennett, 1978, p. 59) in terms of the dispositions constituted by his desire to go to Macy's, and his belief that Macy's is uptown.

INTENTIONALITY AS THE MARK OF THE DISPOSITIONAL

According to Dennett (1978, pp. 60–1), Skinner is right to repudiate mentalistic explanations for scientific purposes, because such explanations rely on what he calls, following Chisholm (1957), 'intentional' or what Quine (1953) calls 'referentially opaque' idioms. Moreover, his reason for endorsing Skinner's belief that the use of such idioms is unacceptable in a genuinely scientific explanation is that, according to Quine (1960), such idioms 'refuse to "reduce" to the sentences of the physical sciences' (Dennett, 1978, p. 61).

Contrary to the view which I expressed in an earlier paper (Place, 1981), I would no longer wish to dispute Dennett's claim that Skinner is mistaken in believing that it is possible to provide non-intentional (i.e., referentially transparent) translations of intentional or referentially opaque idioms. What I do dispute is Quine's view that there is some radical and unbridgeable discontinuity between intentionality and referential opacity, on the one hand, and the language of physical science, on the other. Quine's view, it seems to me, is based on a confusion between the language of physical science and the first-order predicate calculus. The first-order predicate calculus is an extensional logic in which Leibniz's Law is taken as an axiomatic principle. Such a logic cannot admit 'intensional' or 'referentially opaque' predicates whose defining characteristic is that they flout that principle. But, as far as I can see, there are no particular reasons, other than the prejudices of a lifetime, for thinking that the language of physics either is or can be adequately represented in terms of the first-order predicate calculus or any other purely extensional logic. On the other hand, there are very good reasons for thinking that intentionality and referential opacity are an essential feature of any genuine explanation in any empirical science including physics.

The first step in the argument which shows that intentionality is an essential ingredient in all explanation in the empirical sciences is to show that so far from being, as Brentano (1874) thought, the mark of the mental, the intentional is the mark of the dispositional. Intentionality, as (thanks to Dr John Burnheim[1]) we now understand it, is the 'teleological' feature of dispositions whereby they involve an orientation of the entity to which the disposition belongs towards the occurrence of a kind of event, an 'exercise' of the disposition, as Ryle calls such things, if at any time certain broadly specifiable conditions are fulfilled. Thus the brittleness of a pane of glass is intentional-with-a-t insofar as it involves an orientation of the glass towards the occurrence of an event, its breaking, which has not yet occurred, may never occur (at the end of the day it may just melt in some final conflagration), but which may occur at any time, if it is subjected to the required degree of stress.

But not only are dispositional properties intentional-with-a-t; dispositional predicates are intensional-with-an-s or referentially opaque. For suppose that this particular pane of glass actually breaks on 24 August 1986, we cannot say, nor is it true, that its brittleness consists in the propensity for the event to occur which will actually occur or has actually occurred on that date. For brittleness consists in the propensity for that event to occur *at any time* given that the required conditions are fulfilled and not just at the time when those conditions are in fact fulfilled.

THE ROLE OF DISPOSITIONAL PREDICATES IN CAUSAL EXPLANATION

Given that intentionality is the mark of the dispositional rather than the mark of the mental, the second step in the argument is to show that a causal explanation is necessarily incomplete if it fails to mention the relevant dispositional properties of the entities involved. The argument here relates to the counterfactual nature of causal necessity. To say that a state or event *A* is a cause of the existence or occurrence of another distinct state or event *B* is to say that *B* would not have existed or occurred, as and when it did, if *A* had not existed or occurred. But since we can never hope to observe how things would have been, if things had been different, it follows that we can never hope to establish the truth of any causal judgment on the basis of observation alone. The only way to establish the truth of the kind of counterfactual claim that is involved in every causal judgment is by deducing it from some kind of universal law statement. These so-called 'covering laws' which are required to sustain the counterfactuals involved in causal judgments do not need to be wide-ranging principles like the law statements of science which apply to all individuals of a particular kind at all times and at all places. As Nelson Goodman (1955) first pointed out, all that is required in order to yield a counterfactual is to be in the position to assert that, *if at any time* within a period of time, which may be as restricted as you like provided it covers the period to which the counterfactual relates, an event or state of affairs of the cause type occurs or exists, an event or state of the effect type is liable to occur or exist. In other words, all that is required is that over that limited period a particular dispositional statement be true of one or both of the individuals involved in the causal relationship. Moreover, the fact that mentalistic explanations of behaviour frequently rely on the ascription of individual mental dispositions of extremely short duration, such as the belief that it is going to rain or the need to defecate, does not, in my view and contrary to what would appear to be Donald Davidson's (1970) opinion, disqualify the ascription of individual short-term dispositions from providing the sort of support for the counterfactual claim that is needed in a genuinely scientific causal explanation.

Given that intentionality is the mark of the dispositional and that dispositional property ascriptions are an essential ingredient in all causal explanations, all that is required in order to deduce the principle that intentionality (and hence the referentially opaque idioms required to express it) is an essential feature of the language of any empirical science, including physics, is the principle, which seems to me self-evidently true, that all explanations in the empirical sciences are causal explanations. That being the case, nothing is left of the claim, endorsed implicitly by Skinner and explicitly by Quine and, following him, by Dennett, that it is their intentionality or referential opacity which disqualifies the use of mentalistic explanations in the context of a scientific psychology.

MENTALISM AND THE PRESUPPOSITION OF RATIONALITY

On the other hand, what is also undermined, given that intentionality is the mark of the dispositional rather than the mental, is Dennett's claim (1978, p. 61) that the use of intentional idioms 'presupposes rationality'. But, since in this passage Dennett is evidently equating 'intentional idioms' with mentalistic notions like 'knowing', 'believing', 'wanting', 'intenting', etc., the claim that these mentalistic notions presuppose rationality is unimpaired. In Dennett's view, moreover, because rationality is 'the very thing psychology is supposed to explain ... if there is progress in psychology, it will inevitably be, as Skinner suggests, in the direction of eliminating ultimate appeals to beliefs, desires, and other intentional items from our explanations' (Dennett, 1978, p. 61). I find this an extremely puzzling suggestion. It is as if we were told that, because digestion is one of the things that physiology is required to explain, progress in the physiology of digestion will inevitably be in the direction of eliminating the use of terms like 'digestion' and other terms which presuppose it, presumably such terms as 'stomach', 'gastric juices', 'indigestion', etc. from our explanations of the process.

But while he is obviously mistaken in thinking that progress towards explaining a phenomenon entails eliminating the terminology used to describe it from our scientific vocabulary, Dennett is equally certainly right to think that it is the presupposition of rationality that disqualifies the use of mentalistic explanations, not indeed in all but at least in a great many branches of psychological science. For, as I see it, mentalistic explanations presuppose the rationality of the behaving organism in two senses. In one sense they presuppose that behaviour in question has been initiated as a result of a process of what Aristotle called 'practical reasoning', in which the agent formulates the consequences of the various courses of action open to him or her in the form of a series of sentences, and decides on a course of action which is again specified verbally in the form of a sentence. In the other sense mentalistic explanations presuppose rationality in that they assume that the behavioural strategies of the agent are worked out in terms of an organized system of verbally formulated beliefs. The rationality of this system of beliefs, and hence the assurance that most of its constituent beliefs are true, derives, in accordance with the fundamental logical principle of non-contradiction, from the internal consistency of or lack of dissonance (Festinger, 1957) within the system. Rationality in this sense requires consistency not only between the different beliefs constituting the individual's *Eigenwelt* (von Uexküll, 1926), but also between those beliefs and the shared beliefs of the verbal community (Skinner, 1957, Appendix). These shared beliefs of the verbal community constitute what Binswanger (1947) calls the *Mitwelt*; and it is on this system of shared beliefs, as Strawson (1959) points out, that we depend for our ability to refer to and hence convey information about objects, states and events remote from the context of utterance.

If I am right in thinking that mentalistic idioms presuppose the rationality of the agent in either or both these two senses, it follows that mentalistic explanations of behaviour can only be used with their full literal meaning in those cases where the behaviour to be explained is what Skinner (1969) calls 'rule-governed' as opposed to 'contingency-shaped'. 'Rule-governed behaviour' in Skinner's sense is behaviour controlled by a verbal specification of the contingency of which that behaviour forms part, where a contingency comprises the relation between a set

of antecedent conditions, the behaviour called for under those conditions and the consequences of so behaving. Such verbal specifications of the contingency may be formulated by the agent himself or herself on the basis of past experience, or may be received ready-made as information derived from another speaker. In either case the agent need not have had any previous encounter with the contingency in question. In this respect rule-governed behaviour contrasts with contingency-shaped behaviour which develops as a result of repeated exposure and consequent moulding or shaping of behaviour to the contingency itself. Empirical evidence demonstrating the reality of this distinction and the dependence of rule-governed behaviour in the growing child on the acquisition of linguistic competence has been summarized recently by Lowe (1979, 1983).

If it is true that mentalistic explanations of behaviour presuppose that the behaviour to be explained is rule-governed or verbally controlled rather than contingency-shaped, two things appear to follow. On the one hand, no serious objection can be raised to the use of mentalistic explanation in cases where this presupposition holds good, where the behaviour in question is in fact rule-governed or verbally controlled. On the other hand, where the behaviour is contingency-shaped, either, as in the case of animal or infant behaviour, because the agent lacks the relevant linguistic skills or, as in the case of verbal behaviour and the exercise of a motor skill like driving a car or playing tennis, because verbal control has little or no application in such case, the use of mentalistic explanations is ruled out for serious scientific purposes on the grounds that such explanations presuppose what is demonstrably not the case, that the behaviour is verbally controlled.

I conclude from this that there is a place within psychology for mentalism in providing a molar explanation of rule-governed behaviour. There is clearly a place for the kind of investigation of the functions of the brain and its constituent parts to which most of the remainder of Dennett's book is devoted, in providing a molecular explanation of the general dispositional properties of both rule-governed and contingency-shaped behaviour. But there is also a place within psychology for a non-mentalistic molar theory such as Skinner's in order to be able (1) to state, though not explain, the general dispositional properties of contingency-shaped behaviour; (2) to explain particular behavioural events insofar as the behaviour in question is contingency-shaped; and (3) since verbal behaviour itself is for the most part contingency-shaped, to explain the verbal control of non-verbal and other verbal behaviour and hence the very foundations of mentalism which cannot themselves be explained in mentalistic terms on pain of circularity.

NOTE

1   Of the Department of General Philosophy, University of Sydney, in an unpublished paper (Burnheim, *c* 1969) presented to the then united Department of Philosophy at Sydney (personal communication from Professor David Armstrong). I was personally converted to this view through discussions with Professor C.B. Martin of the University of Calgary (Martin and Pfeifer, 1986).

REFERENCES

Binswanger, L. (1947) *Ausgewälhlte Vorträge und Aufsätze*, Bern, Francke.

Brentano, F. (1874) *Psychologie vom empirischen Standpunkt*, Leipzig, Duncker and Humblot.

Burnheim, J. (*c* 1969) 'Intentionality and materialism'. Unpublished paper presented to the Department of Philosophy, University of Sydney.

Chisholm, R.M. (1957) *Perceiving: A Philosophical Study*, Ithaca, N.Y., Cornell University Press.

Davidson, D. (1970) 'Mental events', in Foster, L. and Swanson, J.W. (Eds), *Experience and Theory*, Amherst, Mass., University of Massachusetts Press, pp. 79–101.

Dennett, D.C. (1978) *Brainstorms: Philosophical Essays on Mind and Psychology*, Montgomery, Vt., Bradford Books.

Festinger, L. (1957) *A Theory of Cognitive Dissonance*, Stanford, Calif., Stanford University Press.

Geach, P.T. (1957) *Mental Acts*, London, Routledge and Kegan Paul.

Goodman, N. (1955) *Fact, Fiction and Forecast*, London, University of London Press.

Hull, C.L. (1943) *Principles of Behavior*, New York, Appleton-Century.

Lowe, C.F. (1979) 'Determinants of human operant behaviour', in Zeiler, M.D. and Harzem, P. (Eds), *Advances in the Analysis of Behaviour, Vol. 1: Reinforcement and the Organisation of Behaviour*, Chichester, Wiley, pp. 159–92.

Lowe, C.F. (1983) 'Radical behaviourism and human psychology', in Davey, G.C.L. (Ed.), *Animal Models and Human Behaviour*, Chichester, Wiley, pp. 71–93.

Martin, C.B. and Pfeifer, K. (1986) 'Intentionality and the non-psychological', *Philosophy and Phenomenological Research*, XLVI, pp. 531–54.

Michael, J. (1982) 'Distinguishing between discriminative and motivational functions of stimuli', *Journal of the Experimental Analysis of Behavior*, 37, 1, pp. 149–55.

Place, U.T. (1981) 'Skinner's Verbal Behavior I — why we need it', *Behaviorism*, 9, 1, pp. 1–24.

Quine, W.V.O. (1953) *From a Logical Point of View*, Cambridge, Mass., Harvard University Press.

Quine, W.V.O. (1960) *Word and Object*, Cambridge, Mass., MIT Press.

Ryle, G. (1949) *The Concept of Mind*, London, Hutchinson.

Skinner, B.F. (1938) *The Behavior of Organisms*, New York, Appleton-Century.

Skinner, B.F. (1957) *Verbal Behavior*, New York, Appleton-Century-Crofts.

Skinner, B.F. (1969) *Contingencies of Reinforcement*, New York, Appleton-Century-Crofts.

Strawson, P. (1959) *Individuals*, London, Methuen.

von Uexküll, J. (1926) *Theoretical Biology*, London, Kegan Paul, Trench, Trubner.

20. Skinner Placed: A Commentary on Place's 'Skinner Re-Skinned'

DANIEL C. DENNETT

Before turning to the substantive and interesting question of what Skinner is right or wrong about, I must first address the record-keeping question of who said what about what Skinner is right or wrong about. Place's paper attempts to correct some of my criticisms of Skinner and some of my defenses of Skinner, but he does not get my views quite right, so his criticisms fall wide of the mark. Place sometimes ends up proclaiming against me just the view I also expressed. It is probably my fault, for writing too allusively the first time around (Dennett, 1978[1]), so to make amends I will first attempt to set out, more straightforwardly, what I take the issues to be as they arise in Place's chapter. This will permit me to summarize, for Skinner's reaction, the joint and several objections Place and I have raised to his work.

Place has five points to make, and I will comment on each in turn.

(1) 'What Skinner thinks is objectionable about mentalistic idioms is that they involve the ascription of dispositional properties to the behaving organism.' It is certainly true that this is one of the central themes in Skinner's attack. I drew attention to it in a footnote, where I noted that, for example, in *About Behaviorism*, 'a particularly virulent attack of operationalism tempts him to challenge the credentials of such innocuous "scientific" concepts as the *tensile strength* of rope and the *viscosity* of fluids' (1978, p. 328, fn. 12). Place illuminates Skinner's antipathy for dispositional terms by reminding us that Skinner should be viewed as reacting to Hull's profligate postulation of intervening variables (a point I alluded to on p. 57). So I agree that one of Skinner's objections to mentalism is its postulation of dispositional properties. But that is not all there is to it, for Skinner or for Place. For to say of a stimulus that it is aversive or reinforcing is to attribute a dispositional property to it (as Place notes), and Skinner obviously has no quarrel with that dispositional property. It is rather the postulation of covert,

'internal' dispositional properties *of or in the organism* that Skinner objects to (as I said, p. 56).

When Skinner tries to lodge all the dispositional properties in the external stimuli, he gets into more trouble than Place acknowledges. Unlike iron filings and magnets, or projectiles and brittle vases, stimuli and organisms are related in complicated ways that defy this peripheralist treatment. How can Skinner explain the routine fact that the very same stimulus can be aversive to one organism and not to another (of the same species, etc.)? He may not want to admit that this is to be explained by a difference 'inside the organisms', and he can direct our attention instead to the different *histories* of reinforcement the organisms have had (as if the histories did not have their current effect via some internal trace), but he cannot just say blandly that the stimulus has the dispositional property of being *aversive-to-x-and-not-to-y* — not if he wants to do credible science. (It is also true that a vase can lose its brittleness — by being heated, for instance — so that even in the case of the simplest dispositions the trade-off between agent and patient suggested by Place is costly.)

(2) '. . . the *virtus dormitiva* has to be construed as an argument against the use for explanatory purposes of a certain kind of dispositional property ascription.' Of course not just any kind of dispositional property ascription, but a vacuous — that is, tautological — ascription. Is the only escape from vacuity the identification of the responsible physical microstructure as Geach suggests? No. What is functionalism, if not the insistence that one can non-vacuously analyze complex dispositional states (e.g., competences) into interacting complexes of other dispositional states (e.g., beliefs, desires,) without ever descending to the level of physical microstructure? Thus, to repeat the moral of the example Place alludes to, it is not vacuous to cite Tom's belief that Macy's is uptown and his desire to go to Macy's when explaining Tom's taking the uptown bus; on the other hand, it would be vacuous, as I noted, to explain his taking the bus by citing some special 'uptown-bus-affinity' in him (p. 57). So I agree, and have agreed all along, with Place's second point.

(3) 'Intentionality arguments are . . . arguments against the use of dispositional property ascriptions in scientific explanation.' Place obtains this conclusion, so far as I can see, by the simple expedient of redefining intentionality so it turns out to be a ubiquitous property of dispositions. First, Place says that I say that 'Skinner is right to repudiate mentalistic explanations for scientific purposes', which would be a fairly amazing thing for me to say, given my many defenses of mentalistic (intentional) explanations in psychology. Place draws this conclusion from my alluding to Skinner's 'gut intuition' on this score: 'in speaking of this prejudice as "an intuition", Dennett implies that Skinner is right.' If I had ever thought anyone would reason this way, I would have used another phrase, since I meant to 'imply' no such thing. I was attempting to show that Skinner was *wrong* about this. What I said Skinner was right about (almost) was that the use of intentional idioms presupposes rationality, which raises a particular danger of vacuity *for some but not all enterprises within psychology*.

Place will find he is in good company declaring that Quine's alignment of the language of science with the first-order predicate calculus is tendentious at best. Many have said so, and I have never denied it. So we agree on this larger point, even though Place's discussion of this matter is confusing to me in many ways. For instance, since so far as I know this incident has never before been reported in

print, I have no idea what revelation was vouchsafed to Dr John Burnheim that convinced him (and others, apparently) to use the word 'intentionality' in the way Place describes. Here in the free world I won't quarrel with their right to use the term as they choose, but I must point out that they court major confusion among those of us who use the term more restrictively to allude to what one might call the 'aboutness' of some phenomena (but not, e.g., the brittleness of glass, which surely is not about anything).

I also cannot follow Place's remarks about intensionality (with an 's'), so I am left uncertain as to their bearing on his third point.

(4) '... since dispositional property ascriptions are essential to any causal explanation, Dennett has failed to provide a good reason for endorsing Skinner's repudiation of mentalism.' Indeed I do not think there is a good reason for endorsing Skinner's repudiation of mentalism, and I agree with Place that dispositional property ascriptions are here to stay. I even agree with him that Quine is wrong to think that referential opacity disqualifies the mentalistic idioms from use in science (as I argue in 1978, Ch. 1, see esp. p. 19).

(5) (There are several different expressions of Place's final main point.) Roughly, he claims, I am right in claiming that the use of mentalistic (intentional) idioms presupposes rationality, but since rationality 'implies control of behaviour by a verbal specification', and since such a specification is only sometimes present, explanations relying on such ascriptions are only sometimes warranted.

There is, I think, a fairly clearcut distinction between behaviours controlled 'by a verbal specification' and behaviours not so controlled, but no one but Place, to my knowledge, has tried to limit all 'rational' behaviours to the former class. (When Fodor suggests the clearly related view that practical reasoning is a matter of the explicit framing and considering of hypotheses about actions, he is speaking of framing such hypotheses 'in the language of thought' — not natural human language.) In fact, as Lewis Carroll noted long ago, any such attempt is doomed to failure (see for instance my discussion in 1978, Ch. 1, p. 11). The idea that rationality is dependent on 'verbally formulated beliefs' instead of vice versa is hardly the uncontroversial claim Place takes it to be. Even the most extreme positions — e.g., Fodor's — have insisted that the capacity for rational thought and action is a precondition for language acquisition, not the other way around. So Place may proclaim that 'mentalistic explanations of behaviour can only be used with their full literal meaning in those cases where the behaviour to be explained is what Skinner (1969) calls "rule-governed" as opposed to "contingency-shaped"', but he proclaims this without apparent support and in the face of a chorus of unacknowledged contrary opinion. So in this instance I must shrink from Place's agreement with my position, since what he means by rationality is so different from what I mean when I assert that all intentional explanation presupposes rationality.

With all that sorting out of positions behind us, I can attempt a summary. Place and I agree that Skinner has not given us a good reason to shun dispositional properties, not even dispositional properties of the organism. Science thrives on such properties (operationalism notwithstanding), and so long as one avoids the outright tautological postulation of such properties, they can be put to good use.

Place and I would agree, I gather, that even the *virtus dormitiva* of opium

could be cited non-vacuously to help explain *something* — if not its capacity to put people to sleep, then perhaps its capacity to anaesthetize, or to diminish arithmetical competence, or impair performance on memory tests. There are other ways of achieving anaesthesia aside from putting to sleep; opium, unlike novocain, might be said to anaesthetize thanks to its *virtus dormitiva*. That is not very informative, but it is a start.

Place and I also agree that mentalistic explanations, even if they cannot be reduced to formulations in the first-order predicate calculus, can have their place in science. That is not so much a disagreement with Skinner as with Quine. We also agree, but only superficially, that mentalistic explanations presuppose rationality, and that this is what creates the problems about their status in psychology. I attributed this insight to Skinner as well, but not in the version Place accepts. I would certainly be interested to know which version, if any, Skinner now maintains. The question for Skinner, in my opinion, is this: of all the criticisms he has leveled against 'mentalism', which strikes him as most important, most telling? Since there are ready rebuttals to many, if not all, his charges in this vein, it would be a useful focusing of attention if we knew which of his arrows strikes closest to the bull's-eye, in his opinion. Is it that mentalistic explanations

1 are dualistic (imply non-physical processes),
2 imply a non-existent privacy,
3 invoke inferred as opposed to observable entities ('intervening variables'),
4 invoke internal as opposed to external dispositional properties,
5 are vacuous in the fashion of the *virtus dormitiva*,
6 presuppose rationality and hence are circular in psychology,
7 simply are dispositional (Place's reading)?

These are obviously somewhat related ways of getting at whatever one might find suspect in mentalistic or intentional explanations. Skinner has not chosen to distinguish his view sharply within this space of possibilities up to now. Does he wish to do so how? Does he think the issue is important? Place and I think so.

NOTE

1 All references are to Place's paper in this volume, and to Daniel C. Dennett (1978) *Brainstorms*, Cambridge, Mass., MIT Press and Brighton, Harvester Press, Chs. 1 ('Intentional Systems') and 4 ('Skinner Skinned').

Interchange

PLACE REPLIES TO DENNETT

SKINNER RE-PLACED

While it is clear from Dennett's reply that we are in substantial agreement about what is wrong with Skinner's reasons, both explicit and implicit, for repudiating mentalism, we are still far apart on the nature of mentalism and on the question of whether there are any circumstances under which the use of mentalistic explanations needs to be repudiated for the purposes of science and, if so, what those circumstances are. This is an important issue because, if I am right, Skinner's analysis of behaviour survives more or less intact, it is only the reasons he gives for adopting that analysis which are threatened; whereas, if Dennett is right, there is no room for the analysis either.

Since Dennett has responded to my paper by discussing each section in the original order, I shall respond to his detailed criticisms in the same order.

(1) I accept that I was wrong to suggest that it is a matter of indifference whether we ascribe a dispositional property to the causal agent or the causal patient. Although I am not sure that I know what it is, I am confident that there is some general principle which determines which of the two a dispositional property is assigned to in ordinary language. I am sure that Dennett is right to suggest that our ordinary practice in assigning appetites and aversions to the behaving organism, rather than to the stimuli towards or away from which the behaviour in question is directed, has a basis in the fact that 'one man's meat' can be and often is 'another man's poison'. I am persuaded nevertheless that Skinner's alternative way of construing the matter is not only perfectly legitimate (after all, it is no different from describing a stimulus event as pleasant or unpleasant), it can also be a valuable corrective to an excessive reliance on imputing intractable behavioural dispositions to the individual in excusing one's failure to deal adequately with a problem of disruptive or maladaptive behaviour.

(2) Although he accepts my contention that it is its tautological character that accounts for the vacuity of arguments of the *virtus dormitiva* type, Dennett does not accept my account of what saves the explanation from vacuity in the case where we explain Tom's taking the uptown bus in terms of his desire to go to Macy's and his belief that Macy's is uptown. On my account this explanation is saved from vacuity by the fact that a particular event, Tom's taking the uptown bus, is explained by reference to one or more dispositional properties *which are ascribed to the individual in question*. According to Dennett what saves the explanation from vacuity is its functionalist character. Functionalism, he maintains, consists in 'the insistence that one can non-vacuously analyze complex

dispositional states (e.g., competences) into interacting complexes of other dispositions (e.g., beliefs and desires) without ever descending to the level of the physical microstructure.' The explanation is saved from vacuity on this view by the fact that it involves two interacting dispositions, a belief and a desire. It would have been vacuous had it consisted in ascribing a single disposition such as an 'uptown bus affinity'.

This view seems to be mistaken on two counts. In the first place there is nothing vacuous, as I see it, in attributing Tom's taking an uptown bus to his uptown bus affinity. Human nature being what it is, uptown-bus-travelling buffs are no doubt rare. But that does not alter the fact that to attribute Tom's behaviour to such an addiction is a perfectly good non-vacuous single disposition alternative to an explanation in terms of a combination of a belief and a desire. Second, Dennett's account of functionalism seems to me plainly defective. Functionalism I take to be the position which has been advocated for many years by Hilary Putnam (1975), which seeks to account for the behavioural dispositions (e.g., competences) of the organism or system as a whole (not, as in this case, a particular behavioural act) in terms of the dispositional properties of and relations between a set of subsystems within the on-line computer that controls the system as a whole (the brain in the case of living organisms), where the dispositional properties of the subsystems are specified in such a way as not to prejudice the particular type of hardware (electronic circuits, electromagnetic relays, hydraulic valves or neurons) used to instantiate the controlling computer in the particular case. The fact that in Dennett's own peculiar version of functionalism the dispositional properties of the subsystems are specified in terms of the metaphor of a team of homunculi, each with its own set of desires and beliefs (1978, p. 80), is entirely beside the point.

(3) In connection with the thesis which I attribute to Dr John Burnheim (*c.* 1969), it is unfortunate that Dennett has not, as I have, had the opportunity of reading Burnheim's paper as well as an advance copy of an important paper on this topic by C.B. Martin and K. Pfeifer (1986). What both these papers show, to my satisfaction at least, is that physical causal dispositions and the idioms which ascribe such properties to objects qualify as intentional by every criterion of intentionality and intensionality that has ever been suggested in the literature on this difficult and controversial issue. In the light of this evidence we are faced with a choice. One alternative is to retain the view that intentionality is whatever it is that distinguishes the mental from the non-mental. Assuming, of course, that there actually *is* some one thing which distinguishes the mental from the physical, the effect of adopting this alternative is to make intentionality into something very different from what it has traditionally been taken to be. Thus Martin and Pfeifer, who take this alternative, propose that intentionality be redefined in terms of sensory experience. The alternative which I favour is that we abandon altogether the notion that intentionality is the mark of the mental, in favour of the view that intentionality is the mark of the dispositional. This has the great advantage of allowing us to retain all the traditional criteria of intentionality and intensionality, including the principle whereby alternative descriptions of the same object or event cannot be substituted within an opaque or intensional context without endangering the truth of the sentence of which it forms part. The purpose of the example which Dennett fails to understand was simply to illustrate the application of that principle to the case of the physical disposition of brittle-

ness. As Martin and Pfeifer point out, a physical disposition like the brittleness of a pane of glass is 'about' the event (the breaking of the pane) towards which the disposition is directed and whose occurrence constitutes its satisfaction in exactly the same way that the mental disposition of, say, wanting an apple is 'about' the event of getting an apple in that is the event towards which the disposition is directed and whose occurrence constitutes its satisfaction.

(4) No contest.

(5) I certainly do not think, as Dennett suggests I do, that 'the idea that rationality is dependent on "verbally formulated beliefs" instead of vice versa is ... uncontroversial'. If I gave that impression, it is only because limitations of space did not and do not now permit an adequate defence of what is currently a profoundly unfashionable view. It was not always so. Before the model of the computer came to dominate philosophical and psychological thinking in this area, it was possible for a philosopher like Ayer (1947, p. 7) to declare that 'the process of thought can[not] be validly distinguished from the expression of it'.[1] If that principle is taken seriously, we have to conclude not only that there can be no genuine thought in the case of beings who do not communicate with one another by means of a public language but also that there is no place within science for an explanation which involves attributing thoughts to an agent, unless there are good reasons for thinking that the behaviour to be explained is in fact under verbal control.

If I am not deterred from holding this view by the big battalions arrayed against me, it is partly because, to mix metaphors, this is not the first time that I have been a lone voice crying in the wilderness (Place, 1956). But a more compelling reason for this confidence is that I can see no other sustainable justification for Skinner's project in constructing a non-mentalistic language for the description and explanation of the behaviour of organisms at the molar level. Since for him Skinner's project has no intrinsic merit to recommend it, it stands or falls for Dennett on the cogency of the reasons given for adopting it. That is a view which I cannot share. It seems to me that the value of Skinner's project has already been amply demonstrated by the results achieved from its application. As is predicted by the theory that mentalistic explanations presuppose verbal control of the behaviour to be explained, these results are most impressive in areas such as animal behaviour and the behaviour of the mentally handicapped, where the behaviour is either entirely or predominantly 'contingency-shaped' and thus un-complicated by the superimposition of verbal control. I also believe, although here I cannot yet point to any concrete results, that once the defects of Skinner's (1957) initial attempt have been put right (Place, 1982, 1983), behaviour analysis will provide us for the first time with a fully integrated theory of language which incorporates phenomena at the pragmatic as well as the semantic and syntactic levels of analysis, linguistic performance as well as linguistic competence. That, of course, is a confidence that I cannot yet expect others to share. But since my evaluation of Skinner's project does not depend on the reasons he gives for adopting it, I have no wish to join Dennett in urging Skinner to settle for one of the various alternative reasons for repudiating mentalism which he lists in his final paragraph.

NOTE

1 I am indebted to Mr Jonathan Cohen of Queen's College, Oxford for drawing my attention to this quotation.

REFERENCES

Ayer, A.J. (1947) *Thinking and Meaning: Inaugural Lecture*, London, H.K. Lewis.
Burnheim, J. (*c.* 1969) 'Intentionality and materialism'. Unpublished paper presented to the Department of Philosophy, University of Sydney.
Dennett, D.C. (1978) *Brainstorms: Philosophical Essays on Mind and Psychology*, Montgomery, Vt., Bradford Books.
Martin, C.B. and Pfeifer, K. (1986) 'Intentionality and the non-psychological', *Philosophy and Phenomenological Research*, XLVI, pp. 531–54.
Place, U.T. (1956) 'Is consciousness a brain process?' *British Journal of Psychology*, 47, pp. 44–50.
Place, U.T. (1982) 'Skinner's *Verbal Behavior* III — how to improve Parts I and II', *Behaviorism*, 10, pp. 116–36.
Place, U.T. (1983) 'Skinner's *Verbal Behavior* IV — how to improve Part IV, Skinner's account of syntax', *Behaviorism*, 11, pp. 163–86.
Putnam, H. (1975) *Mind, Language and Reality, Philosophical Papers*, Vol. 2, Cambridge, Cambridge University Press.
Skinner, B.F. (1957) *Verbal Behavior*, New York, Appleton-Century-Crofts.

DENNETT REPLIES TO PLACE

Dennett's *main* contribution is in the form of a reply to Place's chapter.

Part XII: Rule-Governed Behavior: A Formulation in Terms of Complex Human Behavior

21. Rule-Governed Behavior and Higher Mental Processes*

MARGARET VAUGHAN

The behavior now called rule-governed was first discussed by Skinner when he gave the distinguished William James Lectures at Harvard University in 1947. His topic was verbal behavior, emphasizing the behavior of the speaker. The behavior of the listener was also discussed but only in terms of explaining the behavior of the speaker. As Skinner (1957) noted: '... the behavior of the listener is not necessarily verbal in any special sense. It cannot, in fact, be distinguished from behavior in general, and an adequate account of verbal behavior need cover only as much of the behavior of the listener as is needed to explain the behavior of the speaker' (p. 2). Thus, only a small section in his lectures and later a section in *Verbal Behavior* (1957), were devoted to, as he called it then, conditioning the behavior of the listener.

It was not until 1965 that Skinner first referred to this behavior as rule-governed (1966). In doing so, he emphasized a different aspect of the listener's behavior. He no longer talked about conditioning the listener's behavior; rather, he talked about the practical effects of this conditioning process. This change in

* I am indebted to Jerry Zuriff and Jack Michael for their critical reading of an earlier version; however, they cannot be held responsible for the chapter's present form.

emphasis brought new meaning to the concept and hence importance — the behavior of the listener was being considered in its own right.

Now, twenty years later, rule-governed behavior is emerging as a critical class of behavior in analyzing complex human behavior. The descriptive power of the concept is especially revealing (and appealing) when one is analyzing some of the activity referred to by cognitive psychologists as higher mental processes (e.g., Lachman, Lachman and Butterfield, 1979). For under these conditions such behavior is brought within the realm of a science of behavior, subject to measurement in quantifiable terms.

This chapter is an attempt to elucidate how rules work in facilitating behavior. Since verbal behavior is the foundation of rule-governed behavior, the first section will briefly outline its role. The next section will delineate, for practical purposes, two types of operant verbal behavior, contingency-shaped and rule-governed, while acknowledging the important fact that the latter is based upon the former. In so doing, a distinction is drawn between behavior under the control of a rule and behavior under the control of other forms of verbal stimuli. Finally, rule-governed behavior will be analyzed in terms of an individual engaging in some of the activities often referred to as showing higher mental processes. It is hoped that this analysis will illustrate the increased efficacy and parsimony of such a concept over the currently fashionable ways of talking about rational behavior.

THE ROLE OF VERBAL BEHAVIOR

Skinner's 1938 book, *The Behavior of Organisms*, formally launched the science of the experimental analysis of behavior and the philosophy of radical behaviorism. It was a systematization of the lawfulness found in the behavior of organisms, the foundation of a science of behavior. The title of the book was not a misnomer, nor was it meant to be pretentious (Skinner, 1979, p. 231). Skinner was confident that the orderly relations reported in the book would prove to be representative samples of behaving organisms with one possible exception — human verbal behavior. In *The Behavior of Organisms* Skinner states:

> Whether or not extrapolation is justified cannot at the present time be decided. It is possible that there are properties of human behavior which will require a different kind of treatment. We can neither assert nor deny discontinuity between the human and subhuman fields so long as we know so little about either. If, nevertheless, the author of a book of this sort is expected to hazard a guess publicly, I may say that the only differences I expect to see revealed between the behavior of rat and man (aside from enormous differences of complexity) lie in the field of verbal behavior. (p. 442)

Perhaps this statement was written in a somewhat modest vein, for Skinner had begun to write *Verbal Behavior* four years prior to the publication of *The Behavior of Organisms* (Skinner, 1957, p. 457). It is quite clear from various parts of *Verbal Behavior*, especially the last paragraph of the book (p. 452), that Skinner saw language as a part of a larger field. *Verbal Behavior* was written as an extension of the basic principles of behavior outlined in *The Behavior of Organisms*. It was an exercise in analyzing complex human behavior and showing that the basic principles of non-verbal behavior were sufficient in explaining it.

In distinguishing this subfield of behavior Skinner (1957) states that non-verbal behavior 'alters the environment through [direct] mechanical action, and its properties or dimensions are often related in a simple way to the effects produced' (p. 1). Verbal behavior, on the other hand, refers to behavior that 'acts only indirectly upon the environment from which the ultimate consequences of behavior emerge' (p. 1). Its first effect is upon other people. Specifically, it is defined as 'behavior reinforced through the mediation of other persons' (p. 2).

Both verbal and non-verbal behavior are products of contingencies. Non-verbal behavior is shaped and maintained by the immediate mechanical world; verbal behavior is shaped and maintained by contingencies established by the verbal community. But with verbal behavior a new class of behavior can emerge. Via instruction (rules), one can behave appropriately to a new set of conditions without having been exposed to them first. The long process of contingency shaping can then be by-passed. 'The evolution of verbal behavior has made possible the formulation of rules and hence the emergence of man as a rational animal' (Skinner, 1983, p. 284).

DISTINGUISHING BETWEEN CONTINGENCY-SHAPED AND RULE-GOVERNED BEHAVIOR

Behavior that is contingency-shaped is behavior that has been directly shaped by its consequences. Today few psychologists (Skinnerian or otherwise) deny the importance of consequences in shaping and maintaining non-verbal behavior (with the general exception of respondent behavior). The emergence of cognitive behaviorism as a field is a case in point (e.g., Bandura, 1974).

We do what we do because of what follows when we have done it. As children, we gradually learn how to reach and grab objects appropriately because of the consequences of earlier attempts. Watching a small toddler learn to pick up a cooked pea can be frustrating but instructive. Each new attempt shows slight refinements over the last. Eventually, the child is able to capture the pea intact, but only after several, perhaps messy, attempts.

To a Skinnerian psychologist — and here is where we often part company with other brands of psychology — verbal behavior is learned in a similar fashion. The same toddler learns to say 'mama' because of the reinforcing consequences which follow. It appears that simple forms of verbal behavior can be explained in terms of direct contingency shaping. But because of the unique feature of verbal behavior not requiring environmental support (e.g., you can talk about your exercise bicycle in its absence), more elaborate, complex verbal behavior is possible.

In addition, Skinner (1957) asserts: 'As a function of verbal behavior you can extend both the sensory powers of the listener, who can now respond to the behavior of others rather than directly to things and events, and the power of action of the speaker, who can now speak rather than do' (p. 432). Skinner is pointing to the natural benefits of verbal stimuli acquiring control over the listener's verbal or non-verbal behavior. But a verbal stimulus, or more specifically, a special kind of verbal stimulus, can do more. In addition to the control verbal stimuli exert over behavior as traditional discriminative stimuli, some may

also function, because of an extensive conditioning history, as repertoire-altering stimuli — altering the future probability of other behavior, evoked by different contingencies.[1]

A few examples of this distinction may be useful. Suppose, as you are walking across Brattle Street, you see an old friend. You stop. The friend serves as a non-verbal discriminative stimulus for stopping, with the consequence being a long overdue friendly chat. Likewise, if as you are walking across Brattle Street a weary traveller says, 'Excuse me, could you help us find a restaurant?' you stop. Here the discriminative stimulus, however, is verbal and perhaps more complicated, but, like the other example, it functions as an evocative stimulus; you are responding to the stimulus change resulting from the traveller's verbal behavior. These two examples can be contrasted with the final case. As you are walking across Brattle Street a police officer says, 'When you get to Church Street, would you please stop until the funeral procession passes by,' you don't stop; you nod. But when you get to Church Street you stop. The verbal stimulus in this example altered your behavior with respect to Church Street. By pairing a verbal stimulus ('Church Street') with a stimulus ('Stop') already showing some control over a response, we have altered the listener's future behavior with respect to the first stimulus. That is, the behavior appropriate to 'Stop' is now brought under the control of Church Street. It occurs via stimulus-stimulus pairings (Skinner, 1957, pp. 357–62).

Given the necessary history, one responds appropriately not only to requests or commands which serve as verbal discriminative stimuli (e.g., 'Please put your dirty dishes in the kitchen sink.') but also to advice and instructions which are verbal repertoire-altering stimuli (e.g., 'If you wish to avoid the grid-lock near Sumner Tunnel on your way to Logan Airport, take McGrath Highway'). It is the latter case that defines rule-governed behavior.[2]

When a speaker describes a state of affairs (a verbal stimulus), the listener can now behave differently (and ideally, more appropriately) to the state of affairs without having had direct contact with it. That is, the speaker can alter the behavior of the listener via a verbal stimulus and thus avoid the long process of contingency shaping. Of course, such a process is possible only because of a long, complicated conditioning history. Nonetheless, such stimuli prepare an organism for a future unlike its past. Unfortunately, the future cannot be too different from the past, for the process is limited by the extent of the change demanded (see Skinner, 1957, pp. 365–7).

In his article, 'An Operant Analysis of Problem Solving' (1966), Skinner states that a rule is 'a contingency-specifying stimulus . . . an object in the environment.' That is, it is a verbal stimulus that describes some contingency and, in so doing, can effectively alter behavior with respect to that described contingency.

Comparing rule-governed to contingency-shaped behavior, Skinner (1976, pp. 138–9) notes three advantages of the former:

1   rules can be learned more quickly than the behavior shaped by the contingencies that the rules describe (e.g., learning to drive a car with a stick shift);

2   rules make it easier to profit from similarities between contingencies (e.g., it drives like a BMW);

3 rules are particularly valuable when contingencies are complex or unclear (e.g., using the rules of a different language).

Although only a beginning, the analysis of rule-governed behavior seems to be useful in clarifying some instances of complex human behavior. Unfortunately, this analysis has been overlooked by most cognitive psychologists. As a result, they have found Skinnerian pyschology unable to account for examples of behavior implying higher mental activity (Bandura, 1974; Chomsky, 1959; de Villiers and de Villiers, 1977).

The analysis of rule-governed behavior here has only covered the behavior of separate speakers and listeners. Although such interactions are important in developing and maintaining complex human activity, they address only a few of the issues involved in some cognitive processes. To look at other forms of higher mental activity we need to consider the speaker and listener within the same skin. By doing so, the stage is set for an interchange that brings us even closer to a more parsimonious understanding of rational behavior.

RULE-GOVERNED BEHAVIOR AND HIGHER MENTAL PROCESSES

When the separate repertoires of speaker and listener merge within one organism, the opportunity exists for that organism to engage in forms of complex behavior often called problem-solving or, more generally, rational behavior. This does not mean that one organism acting as both speaker and listener can engage in behavior that is otherwise not possible for separate speakers and listeners. It just means that, to the degree that our covert behavior is verbal, we speak to ourselves as we speak to others and respond to the product of our verbal behavior just as we do to the product of others' verbal behavior.

Throughout the day we talk to ourselves about various things. We talk about what we are doing, what we have done, and what we will do. Much of this is probably no more than a running account — collateral behavior — of our activity, having no effect in evoking or altering our behavior.

Some self-generated verbal stimuli may, however, evoke behavior — behavior which is either uncommitted or a part of a weak contingency. A verbal stimulus — a response-product of saying something to oneself — may be a more powerful discriminative stimulus for some non-verbal behavior than the non-verbal stimulus which evokes the verbal behavior. For example, saying to oneself, 'You must start dinner now,' may serve as the needed stimulus which evokes the behavior of cooking.

Why one ever begins to talk to oneself about the prevailing contingencies and, as a result, alters the strength of some behavior, does not seem so difficult to understand. Behavior that involves minimal energy and clarifies or accentuates the behavior necessary to satisfy a contingency seems reasonable. The response is briefer, more defined and thus, as a response-product, can provide a more sharply defined discriminative stimulus.

The relevant question here is: can an individual also emit verbal behavior with the response-product serving as a verbal stimulus which *alters* his/her own repertoire with respect to other contingencies? That is, can an individual generate his/her own rule-governed behavior?

It has been suggested by some writers (e.g., Zettle and Hayes, 1982; Catania, 1983) that this question is impossible to answer, at least for the present, because it is virtually impossible to determine whether the self-generated rule was actually contingency-shaped. That is, the self-generated rule may be nothing more than a verbal link in a well established chain of behavior, not responsible for the behavior in question. Nevertheless, given the present analysis as to how rules work, the answer to the question seems to be 'yes'. By describing some contingency, perhaps an unclear contingency, and thereby clarifying it, an organism may be changed in terms of engaging in more effective behavior with respect to it. Whether one's tendency to describe the contingency has been contingency-shaped or instructed does not seem to be the relevant issue. It all eventually comes down to behavior shaped by contingencies of reinforcement, including rule-following and rule-stating. What is important is that some verbal stimulus, the response-product of talking to oneself, may alter one's future behavior with respect to some other contingency. The distinction between evocative and repertoire-altering stimuli becomes less clear when the speaker and listener are the same, but the practical advantages in making the distinction still seem useful.

Examples of this type of behavior can be found in everyday life. Saying to yourself, 'If I am not going to be home until 4:00 tomorrow, I had better take the roast out of the freezer the first thing in the morning so it will be ready to cook when I get home', alters your repertoire with respect to tomorrow morning and roasts. Likewise, planning your day so that you will accomplish all of your errands takes on rule characteristics. 'If I leave my office at 3:45, I can stop at the post office and the market and still make the 4:45 commuter train to get home.' Your repertoire has now been altered with respect to the time, 3:45, the post office and the market. That is, some of the behavior relevant to post offices and markets is now brought under the control of 3:45.

In both of these cases the activities ultimately engaged in could have occurred prior to emitting the rule, but the probability of such behavior was undoubtedly low. Now, however, as a function of emitting the rule, a repertoire has been altered with respect to stimuli that otherwise would have had little or no tendency to evoke the necessary behavior.

Decision-making involves a similar process. If a student keeps falling asleep during lectures, deciding on the appropriate action requires an analysis of one's options and the various consequences of each. What particular option settled upon may have been contingency-shaped (it had been successfully used before) or rule-governed (someone recommended that when such a problem occurs, ask the student a question) but the resulting change in one's repertoire, with respect to the next time this particular unappreciative student falls asleep, is rule-governed.

Attempting to predict some future event, or hypothesizing about what you will do given a possible set of circumstances, also exemplifies self-generated, rule-governed behavior. For example, knowing that the US dollar is strong and that the country is witnessing a bull market, you take money out of your Individual Retirement Account to buy stocks in America so as to boost your net worth. Describing these various contingencies (even though perhaps faulty) alters your repertoire with respect to stocks and bonds.

A more complicated example of problem-solving involves knowing what one knows. If for any reason a stimulus is unable to evoke appropriate behavior, any behavior which clarifies the stimulus conditions (and hence the contingencies) will

be useful and thus reinforcing. One may move closer to the object or manipulate it in some way. But by talking to oneself about the object, additional supplementary stimuli can be produced which alter one's repertoire with respect to the object. For example, 'Is the print a Modigliani or a Cezanne?' may be answered, if one has been instructed on both artists, by describing the defining features of each. This exercise does not alter what one knows, but alters the extent to which one knows it. As a result, all behavior appropriate to Cezanne is brought under the control of the new print and the puzzlement is resolved.

The child development literature, although not analyzed in these terms, is replete with research that appears to support the claim that talking to oneself can alter one's repertoire with respect to some contingencies (e.g., Kendler and Kendler, 1962; Kuenne, 1946; Luria, 1961; White, 1965). And, although it is a relatively new area of investigation within the field of the experimental analysis of behavior, there is now some behavioral literature on the topic (Catania, Matthews and Shimoff, 1982; Lowenkrown, 1984; Vaughan, 1985; see also Zettle and Hayes, 1982, for an analysis in terms of cognitive behavior therapy).

SUMMARY

The above discussion interprets in behavioral terms some aspects of cognition — or everyday intellectual behavior. There has been relatively little mention of non-verbal behavior, which, of course, is also a part of intellectual activity (e.g., perceiving). Rather, verbal behavior with special attention to rule-governed behavior has been emphasized. This was done for two related reasons. First, it appears that most cognitive research and theory has completely neglected the role of verbal behavior in facilitating intellectual activity (cf. Fischer, 1980), or has treated it as only one component of a range of cognitive activity, rather than as a vehicle for much cognitive activity (Lachman, Lachman and Butterfield, 1979). Ironically, however, and this is the second reason, much of the research in cognitive psychology is research on verbal behavior and the verbal contingencies which shape and maintain it. More specifically, much of the research involves instruction — rule-giving and rule-following (for example, see Estes, 1972; Kosslyn, 1980; Tversky and Kahneman, 1981).

Skinnerian psychologists have begun to study cognitive activity. In so doing, they have discovered the importance of instruction and self-instruction in clarifying weak stimuli, strengthening weak behavior, and generating new configurations of behavior. Cognitive psychologists have been studying cognitive activity for some time. Unfortunately, they have not acknowledged the role of verbal behavior and the contingencies of which it is a function. As a consequence, they have cast their analysis in terms of unmeasurable processes out of reach in a science of behavior.

NOTES

1 For a thorough discussion of the distinction between evocative and repertoire-altering affects of stimuli see Michael (1982).

2 It is perhaps important to acknowledge that some examples commonly used to illustrate rule-governed behavior do not easily fit this distinction.

REFERENCES

Bandura, A. (1974) 'Behavior theory and the models of man', *American Psychologist*, pp. 859–69.

Catania, A.C. (1983) 'Behavior analysis and behavior synthesis in the extrapolation from animal to human behavior', *Animal Models of Human Behavior*, New York, John Wiley and Sons, pp. 51–69.

Catania, A.C., Matthews, B.A. and Shimoff, E. (1982) 'Instructed versus shaped human verbal behavior: Interactions with nonverbal responding', *Journal of the Experimental Analysis of Behavior*, 38, pp. 233–48.

Chomsky, N. (1959) 'Review of *Verbal Behavior* by B.F. Skinner', *Language*, 35, pp. 26–58.

de Villiers, J. and de Villiers, P. (1977) *Language Acquisition*, Cambridge, Mass., Harvard University Press.

Estes, W.K. (1972) 'Reinforcement in human behavior', *American Scientist*, 60, pp. 723–9.

Fischer, K.W. (1980) 'A theory of cognitive development: The control and construction of hierarchies of skills', *Psychological Review*, 87, pp. 477–531.

Kendler, T.S. and Kendler, H.H. (1962) 'Inferential behavior in children as a function of age and subgoal constancy', *Journal of Experimental Psychology*, 64, pp. 460–6.

Kosslyn, S.M. (1980) *Image and Mind*, Cambridge, Mass., Harvard University Press.

Kuenne, M.R. (1946) 'Experimental investigation of the relation of language to transpositional behavior in young children', *Journal of Experimental Psychology*, 36, pp. 471–90.

Lachman, R., Lachman, J.L. and Butterfield, E.C. (1979) *Cognitive Psychology and Information Processing: An Introduction*, Hillsdale, N.J., Lawrence Erlbaum Associates.

Lowenkrown, B. (1984) 'Coding responses and the generalization of matching to sample in children', *Journal of the Experimental Analysis of Behavior*, 42, pp. 1–18.

Luria, A.R. (1961) *The Role of Speech in the Regulation of Normal and Abnormal Behavior*, London, Pergamon Press.

Michael, J. (1982) 'Distinguishing between discriminative and motivational functions of stimuli', *Journal of the Experimental Analysis of Behavior*, 37, pp. 149–55.

Michael, J. (1983) 'Evocative and repertoire-altering effects of an environmental event', *VB NEWS*, 2, pp. 21–3.

Skinner, B.F. (1938) *The Behavior of Organisms*, New York, Appleton-Century-Crofts.

Skinner, B.F. (1957) *Verbal Behavior*, New York, Appleton-Century-Crofts.

Skinner, B.F. (1966) 'An operant analysis of problem solving', in Kleinmuntz, B. (Ed.), *Problem Solving: Research, Method, and Theory*, New York, John Wiley and Sons.

Skinner, B.F. (1976) *About Behaviorism*, New York, Vintage Books.

Skinner, B.F. (1979) *The Shaping of a Behaviorist*, New York, Alfred A. Knopf.

Skinner, B.F. (1983) *A Matter of Consequences*, New York, Alfred A. Knopf.

Tversky, A. and Kahneman, D. (1981) 'The framing of decisions and the psychology of choice', *Science*, 211, pp. 453–8.

Vaughan, M. (1985) 'Repeated acquisition in the analysis of rule-governed behavior', *Journal of the Experimental Analysis of Behavior*, 44, pp. 175–84.

White, S.H. (1965) 'Evidence for a hierarchical arrangement of learning processes', in Lipsitt, L.P. and Spiker, C.C. (Eds.), *Advances in Child Development and Behavior*, Vol. 2, New York, Academic Press, pp. 187–219.

Zettle, R. and Hayes, S. (1982) 'Rule-governed behavior: A potential theoretical framework for cognitive behavior therapy', in Kendall, P.C. (Ed.), *Advances in Cognitive-Behavioral Research and Therapy*, Vol. 1., New York, Academic Press, pp. 73–118.

22. Rule-Governed Behavior: An Implicit Analysis of Reference

LINDA J. PARROTT

The rule-governed/contingency-shaped dichotomy was constructed as a means of accounting for innumerable instances of behavior that did not appear to have been acquired by way of direct exposure to contingencies of reinforcement. In all of these instances the conditions setting the occasions for behaviors were constituted of verbal stimuli. Despite the enormous utility of the concept of rule governance, the dichotomy remains a source of difficulty because there is no basis in behavior analytic theory on which to propose a genuine distinction between rule-governed and contingency-shaped behavior. From a strict behavior analytic standpoint the dichotomy is spurious.

When a system admits of a systemically spurious distinction on utilitarian grounds, something is amiss. That something, I believe, is not the rule-governed/contingency-shaped dichotomy, but rather the analysis of verbal behavior which renders this dichotomy spurious. My purpose is to show how Skinner's analysis of verbal behavior is in conflict with his analysis of rule governance, and to show how the former may be brought into line with the latter.

As mentioned above, certain observations of behavior appear to demand a rule-governed interpretation. We may begin by examining the circumstances under which a rule-governed interpretation has seemed necessary and has proven useful.

RULE-GOVERNED BEHAVIOR

Generally speaking, behavior is interpreted as rule-governed when it appears to be maintained despite 'defective' contingencies of reinforcement. Defects may be found among the antecedent or consequent conditions, although more often

among the latter. Specifically, consequences may be unlikely, negligible, or long-deferred (Skinner, 1969, pp. 166–71; 1974, pp. 125–8). With respect to unlikely consequences, Skinner (1969, p. 168) cites perseverant behavior which is, by definition, a continuation of behavior in the absence of reinforcement. With regard to consequences of a negligible sort, he mentions the fact that people wear seat belts even though the likelihood of any one person making contact with the consequences of failing to do so is very low. By far the most often cited defect in contingencies, however, is the lack of *immediate* consequences for behavior. For example, people quit smoking cigarettes even though the negative consequences of continuing to smoke are long-deferred. Likewise, people behave virtuously even though the ultimate consequences of virtuous conduct are remote, at best. In addition to maintenance despite defective contingencies of reinforcement, rule-governed behaviors all occur in the presence of a particular type of antecedent condition. Specifically, all occur in the presence of a description of a contingency of reinforcement, that is, a description of behavior to be executed, the conditions under which it is to be executed, and its likely consequences. (An incomplete rule is also a possibility.)

Behavior occurring in the presence of verbal stimulation of this form and for which immediate consequences appeared to be lacking did not seem to fit the pattern of contingency-shaped behavior, giving rise to the new category of rule-governed behavior. As is the nature of the behavior analytic system, a new category of behavior implied a new explanation for its occurrence. The explanation for the occurrence of rule-governed behavior amounted to a shift to antecedent conditions the control ordinarily exerted by consequent conditions. Rule-governed behavior is, as the name suggests, behavior under the control of the antecedent stimulation supplied by a contingency-specifying rule.

Once formulated, the new category of rule-governed behavior proved very useful. In our enormously complex culture, our survival depends in large part on our ability to acquire knowledge indirectly through the experiences of others. Rules permit us to do so. To paraphrase Skinner (1974, p. 124), rules carry us beyond personal experience and beyond the defective sampling of nature inevitable in a single lifetime. They also bring us under the control of conditions which could play no part in shaping and maintaining our behavior. Rules, however, are simply stimulus objects. How it is that behavior comes under their control remains to be analyzed.

How Rules Govern Behavior

The temporal relations of rules to the behaviors they control suggest that rules may be operating as discriminative stimuli. However, the discriminative functions of stimuli are established when behaviors are reinforced in the presence of those stimuli; hence, if rules are to be conceptualized as discriminative stimuli, the reinforcers for rule-governed behavior must be identified.

Two problems become apparent at this point. First, we are confronted with the dilemma of having to conceptualize rule-governed behavior as contingency-shaped behavior in order to account for the control exerted by rules. This being the case, we must question the necessity for the new category, rule-governed behavior. If, on the other hand, we ignore the issue of systemic necessity and

accept the rule-governed/contingency-shaped dichotomy on utilitarian grounds, we are faced with the problem of identifying the consequences for rule-governed behavior despite the fact that it was the apparent absence of immediate consequences for such behavior that led to the concept of rule governance in the first place.

Let us deal with the second problem first: what are the consequences of rule-governed behavior? In addressing this problem it becomes obvious that the consequences specified in a rule are not typically the consequences responsible for the control exerted by that rule. That is, while a contingency may be specified in a rule, the behavior under the control of that rule is subject to another contingency. For example, the eventuality of lung cancer — a specified consequence of continuing to smoke cigarettes — does not account for the cessation of smoking. Nor do more immediate social consequences of smoking cessation account for it, since the effect of these consequences may only be seen in subsequent occurrences of this behavior, and rule-governed behavior is distinguished by its not having been subject to such consequences. Instead, the consequences responsible for the occurrence of rule-following behavior are those that have attended rule-following behavior in the past (Skinner, 1969, p. 148). We follow rules because we have been reinforced for following rules in the past. In short, Skinner's solution to the problem of how rules govern behavior is achieved by considering rule governance to be an operant, of which individual instances of rule-governed behavior may be considered members.

This is, of course, a parsimonious solution. However, are there really no differences between rule-governed and contingency-shaped behavior? Is not rule governance at least a special subdivision of the contingency shaped category, and may we not expect further difficulties if we fail to overlook the differences between behaviors of this subdivision and those of the superordinate category? Skinner himself appears to believe that differences between these two categories exist and ought to be acknowledged. Unfortunately the differences identified by him are relatively trivial. Furthermore, the logic of his comparisons of rule-governed and contingency-shaped behaviors, by which these differences are revealed, is not at all clear. We may find support for these contentions by reviewing Skinner's views as to the differences between rule-governed and contingency-shaped behaviors.

Differences between Rule-Governed and Contingency-Shaped Behaviors

Skinner (1969, 1974) contends that while a given instance of rule-governed behavior may appear topographically similar to its contingency-shaped counterpart, the two episodes of behavior differ in several important respects. Specifically, they occur under the control of different antecedent conditions (1969, p. 166), may be maintained by different reinforcers (1969, p. 169), and may be subject to different motivational operations (1969, p. 169). In other words, they are instances of different operants. Moreover, despite the apparent similarity between the two response forms, closer examination reveals that a rule-governed response may be less precise, less complete, and less variable than corresponding contingency-shaped behavior (Skinner, 1969, pp. 167–70). In summary, Skinner's argument amounts to an assertion that an instance of one operant differs from an

instance of another. That is, an operant involving a rule differs from one which does not involve a rule; and, not surprisingly, it differs along those dimensions that define an operant, namely, the antecedent, reinforcing, and motivational conditions attending the response in question.

Apart from the bias implicit in comparative statements about the adequacy of the response topography in each case (i.e., response topographies are not incomplete, imprecise, or otherwise defective — they are what they are), there is nothing particularly objectionable about Skinner's position as to the differences between contingency-shaped and rule-governed behaviors. There is nothing particularly substantive about it either: he might as well have argued that an operant involving a red light is different from one involving a green light, with the main difference being the color of the light.

The lack of substance here is a function of the items selected for comparison and the logic of their selection. Skinner compares contingency-shaped response *classes* with individual *instances* of rule-governed behavior rather than with the operant, rule governance. As a result the nature and operation of rule-governed behaviors become ambiguous, and useful distinctions cannot be made. Skinner (1974, pp. 123–8) claims that rule-governed behavior occurs under conditions that would not allow for contingency shaping, implying that such behavior is not a product of contingency shaping. This is a statement made with respect to an *instance* of rule governance, and even here it is not entirely accurate. It means, essentially, that the consequences specified in rules are not immediate or probable enough to maintain the behaviors specified in rules. However, the consequences specified in rules are not the consequences responsible for the maintenance of rule-governed behavior. The consequences responsible for rule-governed behavior must be identified at the level of the operant, rule governance, not with respect to individual instances, as previously argued. At this level rule-governed behavior is conceptualized as contingency-shaped behavior, maintained by the generalized consequences of following rules, as it is only by way of such a conceptualization that the discriminative control exerted by rules may be accounted for. This ambiguity as to the nature of rule-governed behavior is eliminated when contingency-shaped operants are compared with the operant, rule governance. When comparisons of these two *classes* are undertaken what emerges as the only consistent difference between rule governance and contingency-shaped operants is the fact that in the former case the antecedent stimuli are always verbal in nature.

To illustrate further Skinner's comparison of instances with classes in this context, and to understand his reasons for doing so, we may examine the criteria by which episodes of behavior are selected by him for comparison. Do these criteria concern antecedent stimuli, response topographies, consequent stimuli, or some other commonality among episodes of behavior? We may eliminate the criterion of antecedent conditions. Skinner is careful to select contingency-shaped behaviors having non-verbal antecedents for the purpose of comparison so as to avoid unnecessary confusion. Likewise, similarities among consequent stimuli may be eliminated as a criterion for the selection of comparable episodes: to whatever extent the consequences of rule-governed behavior resemble those of contingency-shaped behavior, and become relevant to the maintenance of rule-governed behavior, that behavior ceases to be rule-governed. Topographical similarity of responses does not appear to serve as a criterion either, at least not

in isolation. It is none of these. Instead, it is only when a contingency involving one response is described by a rule governing another that the two episodes are compared for the purpose of illustrating the differences between rule-governed and contingency-shaped behaviors. It appears, then, that Skinner's comparison of rule-governed and contingency-shaped behaviors is based on an assumption that a special relation exists between patterns of verbal stimulation (i.e., rules) and occurrences to responses under particular circumstances producing particular consequences (i.e., contingencies); and further, that this relation is one of 'description', 'specification', or 'reference'. That is, rules *describe* contingencies and, because they do, a rule-governed counterpart of a contingency-shaped behavior may be identified for the purpose of their comparison. Herein lies a paradox: the rule-governed counterpart of a contingency-shaped behavior is identified by way of a referential interpretation of the relation between verbal and non-verbal events, yet a rule is a product of verbal behavior, which, according to Skinner (for example, see 1957, p. 82), does not 'refer' to anything.

Skinner makes no attempt to eliminate this inconsistency in his position — possibly because he does not recognize it as such or, alternatively, because to recognize it would call for significant changes in his analysis of verbal behavior, which he is not prepared to make. To understand his commitment to a non-referential analysis of verbal behavior and the problems this analysis produces with respect to rule following, in particular, we may now turn to Skinner's analysis of verbal behavior.

VERBAL BEHAVIOR

Relations of Reference

In the context of verbal behavior relations of 'description', 'specification' or 'reference' between verbal and non-verbal events are explicitly denied, as the following discussion of the tact indicates:

> It may be tempting to say that in a tact the response 'refers to', 'mentions', 'announces', 'talks about', 'names', 'denotes', or 'describes' its stimulus. But the essential relation between response and controlling stimulus is precisely the same as in the echoic, textual, and intraverbal behavior. We are not likely to say that the intraverbal stimulus is 'referred to' by all the responses it evokes, or that an echoic or textual response 'mentions' or 'describes' its controlling variable. The only useful functional relation is expressed in the statement that the presence of a given stimulus raises the probability of occurrence of a given form of response. This is also the essence of the tact. (Skinner, 1957, p. 82.)

Skinner's insistence upon a non-referential interpretation of the tact is somewhat difficult to understand. On the one hand, he is opposed to traditional views of reference because they implicate the involvement of mental events. The traditional view holds that words symbolize mental events called 'ideas' and are used as a means of referring to those ideas. Accordingly, the meaning of a word is the idea to which it refers. On the other hand, it is not only the implication of mental events that concerns him because, were this the only problem, he might have been inclined to suggest that words do refer to events, but not events of a mental sort. Rather, words refer to things and events of the natural word. By this analysis

the meaning of a word would have become the actual thing or event to which it referred. However, Skinner rejects this interpretation as well, primarily because of its limited applicability. Only the tact may be conceptualized as exemplifying a referential relation of this sort. The remaining verbal operants exemplify relations not between words and things, but between words and other words (excluding the mand). In these cases the only useful relation, Skinner argues, is expressed in the statement: '. . . the presence of a given stimulus raises the probability of occurrence of a given form or response' (1957, p. 82). Because the tact may be described in precisely the same manner, the concept of reference is rendered superfluous.

The above logic applies to the behavior of a speaker. The speaker simply emits verbal behavior under the control of some set of antecedent conditions (including conditions of the speaker's psychological history), just as he/she would emit non-verbal behavior under the control of some other set of antecedent conditions. The control exerted in each case is the same, and if a concept of reference is not required for an undertstanding of the relation sustained between antecedent conditions and non-verbal behavior, neither is one required for an understanding of such relations involving verbal behavior.

Rule-governed behavior is not verbal behavior though, at least not principally; it is behavior under the control of verbal stimuli. It is the behavior of the listener, not the speaker, that is of primary concern in this context. Hence, if we are to understand the implications of Skinner's rejection of the concept of reference for the analysis of rule governance, we must also examine his logic as it applies to the behavior of the listener.

Reference and the Behavior of the Listener

Traditional views of reference from the standpoint of the listener's behavior hold that one's behavior with respect to a word-symbol is, up to a point, that which the object symbolized would have occasioned (Russell, 1960, p. 82). Skinner disagrees with this analysis. He explains his position with a fox hunting example, arguing that one 'turns and looks' under the control of the word 'fox', whereas one 'rides after' an actual fox (Skinner, 1957, pp. 87–8).

This difference clearly prevails, however such differences are entirely a matter of the behaviors isolated for analysis under the two sets of circumstances. Were one to look at the behavior of seeing, for example, the response to the word and to the animal would be quite similar, except that in the former case the response involves imagining (i.e., seeing in the absence of the thing seen) as opposed to a perceptual reaction system. Skinner mentions behaviors of this sort, and further acknowledges that the word and the animal may elicit similar responses of the respondent type. In other words, according to Skinner, the word 'fox' may be regarded as a substitute for an actual fox only so long as the *respondent* behaviors of the fox hunter are concerned. Turning and looking under the control of the word 'fox' is not an example of respondent behavior. It is a discriminated *operant*, and this difference is important to Skinner. His argument is as follows:

> The verbal stimulus 'fox' is not a substitute for a fox but an occasion upon which certain responses have been, and probably will be reinforced by seeing a fox. The behavior which is

controlled by the fox itself — looking toward and riding after — cannot be evoked by the verbal stimulus, and there is therefore no possibility of a substitution of stimuli as an analog of sign or symbol. (Skinner, 1957, p. 88)

There is no question that the hunter's operant or practical behavior with respect to these two circumstances is different. However, the logic of focusing on operant behaviors, apart from the opportunity it affords for argument, is unclear. In the first place, if it is Skinner's intention to focus only on the 'practical' activities of the listener, it is unclear why the behavior of 'seeing' (i.e., imagining) a fox upon hearing the word 'fox' is not considered relevant. 'Seeing' a fox upon hearing the word 'fox' orients the listener with respect to an actual fox in the sense of bringing the listener's repertoire with respect to foxes into play (Parrott, 1984), and may be regarded as practical behavior for this reason. Second, traditional theories of reference are applied to listener activities quite unlike those to which Skinner's analysis is applied. Traditional theories of reference are concerned with the listener behaviors of listening and understanding, not with the operant or practical activities occurring subsequent to listening and understanding. While there is likely to be little disagreement with Skinner's arguments concerning the listener's operant behavior under the control of verbal stimuli, there is also likely to be little feeling among traditional theorists that it is relevant to the issue of reference.

Whether or not a concept of reference would prove useful in the analysis of listening and understanding is not addressed by Skinner, because he attempts no analysis of listening and understanding. As far as Skinner is concerned, the listener's role in a verbal episode is to act in such a way as to mediate reinforcement for a speaker's behavior. It is this action and this action alone that is subjected to analysis, and because a concept of reference does not appear to be required for an analysis of reinforcement mediation, the concept is abandoned.

In practice, however, a concept of reference is so important to an understanding of behavior under the control of verbal stimulation that it is not easily abandoned. In fact, it is not abandoned at all; it simply appears in disguised form, as is exemplified by the statement: 'rules describe contingencies'. In short, despite Skinner's denial that relations among verbal and non-verbal stimuli are referential in nature, his interpretation of rule governance is implicitly referential.

This inconsistency has two sources. First, because the traditional interpretation of reference implicates the involvement of mental entities, Skinner takes the position that a scientific understanding of verbal behavior as well as behavior under the control of verbal stimuli may be achieved without the use of this concept. The mistake here is to confuse an objectionable interpretation of a concept with the concept itself. A thoroughly naturalistic interpretation of this concept is possible. Skinner has no interest in making such an interpretation, however, because he does not recognize fully the circumstances under which it might prove useful. The concept is of use in the analysis of listening and understanding activities, to which he does not address himself. This is the second source of difficulty. The result is to make one analysis of verbal behavior and behavior under the control of verbal stimuli, and another analysis of rule governance. This difference is intolerable, however, because rule governance is nothing more than verbal behavior (i.e., rule-statement) and behavior under the control of verbal stimuli (i.e., rule-following).

To eliminate this inconsistency, two things must be done: the circumstances

under which a concept of reference is useful must be elucidated; and a naturalistic interpretation of this concept to be used under these circumstances must be formulated. It is to these issues that we may now turn.

Behavior under the Control of Verbal Stimuli

A listener's reaction to verbal stimuli is constituted of several segments of activity occurring in succession, the last of which Skinner describes as mediating reinforcement for a speaker's action. Prior to the occurrence of reinforcement mediation, the listener must become oriented with respect to the source of stimulation and must make perceptual contact with the stimulation arising from this source. That is, the listener must hear or see the stimulus in question. Let us assume that the stimulus in question is the auditory product of a vocal response having the form 'please pass the salt'. It is at this point in the sequence that Skinner suggests an overt reaction occurs: the listener reaches for the salt and passes it to the speaker, thereby reinforcing the speaker's request. What is not explained by Skinner is how the audient activity of the listener coordinated with the sound of the request gives rise to the reaching and passing reactions coordinated with the salt-shaker. We know, for example, that were the request to be made in a language foreign to the listener, he/she would have had no difficulty *hearing* this stimulus but would, nonetheless, be quite unlikely to pass the salt. We would say that the listener did not understand what was requested of him, raising the issue of what understanding means in this context. In other words, we must ask: how does a verbal stimulus give rise not only to an audient reaction on the part of the listener, but also to a non-verbal action coordinated with a completely different stimulus object? (This question might have been phrased: how does a rule give rise not only to the behavior of hearing the rule, but also to the behavior of following the rule occurring with respect to the stimulus conditions specified in the rule?) To answer this question we must examine in more detail the nature of verbal responding and its products. Specifically, we must address the operation of verbal action and the reasons for its facility in acquiring the functions of other stimuli, beginning with the latter issue.

Acquisition of Other Stimulus Functions by Verbal Stimuli

Verbal stimuli are able to acquire the functions of other stimuli more readily than non-verbal stimuli for two reasons. First, because verbal responding is ineffectual with respect to the non-social environment, it does not interfere with the execution of non-verbal behavior coordinated with the same stimuli as much as does other non-verbal behavior. For example, we may say 'salt' while passing a salt-shaker more easily than we may fill a salt-shaker while passing a salt-shaker. As a result, verbal action occurs in conjunction with other response events more often than do non-verbal actions coordinated with the same stimuli. Furthermore, because perceptual activities (seeing, hearing, etc.) are inevitable components of all non-verbal responses, verbal responses occur in conjunction with perceptual activities more often than with any other type of non-verbal responding (for a more detailed description see Parrott, 1984).

Frequent conjunctive occurrence of verbal and perceptual responding has important implications. Specifically, whenever different types of responding occur in conjunction or close temporal proximity with sufficient frequency, the subsequent occurrence of one type of activity may give rise to reactions of the other type. That is, upon saying 'salt' (or hearing it said) one may have a tendency to see a salt-shaker even when there is no-salt shaker to be seen in the immediate situation. Likewise, upon seeing a salt-shaker one may have a tendency to say 'salt' despite the absence of an appropriate social context for this response. While this process is not peculiar to conjunctions of verbal and perceptual action, the effect is more prevalent in the verbal field because of the ineffectual character of verbal behavior and its resulting lack of interference with the occurrence of other behavior. Moreover, because of a second feature of verbal responding, our actions with respect to things in their absence may be especially precise and differentiated in form. We may now turn to this second feature.

Verbal responding displays an arbitrariness of form not shared by its non-verbal counterparts. This is the case because verbal responding is ineffectual with respect to the non-social environment, and its form is thereby not conditioned by the physical properties of non-social stimuli in the same way as is non-verbal responding (Parrott, 1984). As a result, verbal response forms exist in great variety. This variation in form allows for a specificity of correspondance with aspects of the physical environment, such that each physical object or event, as well as each of its properties, may become coordinated with a verbal response having a form peculiar to that object and that object alone. Consequently, verbal responding not only allows for the occurrence of actions historically occurring in conjunction with it, but because of the specificity of correspondances between verbal response forms and features of the physical environment, these conjoint actions may be quite precise and differentiated. That is, upon saying or hearing said the word 'salt-shaker', one may see a salt-shaker in its absence with unusual clarity. On the other hand, were one to attempt to produce salt-shaker-seeing responses on the part of another person by fanciful shaking responses, seeing a salt-shaker would be no more probable than seeing a pepper-shaker. In summary, we are able to engage in actions with respect to things in their absence, notably perceptual reactions, and to do so in a highly specific way by means of verbal stimulation. Stimulation of other sorts, employed for this purpose, cannot produce such highly differentiated action, and is less effective for this reason.

Understanding Reactions and the Concept of Reference

Having addressed the acquisition of other stimulus functions by verbal stimuli, we may now return to the issue of understanding. What does it mean to say, 'the listener understands the speaker's request for salt'? Quite simply, it means that upon hearing the word 'salt', the listener engages in actions which have frequently occurred in conjunction with hearing this sound, among which are the perceptual activities of 'seeing' a salt-shaker, 'tasting' salt, as well as vestigial motor reactions of various sorts. It is the occurrence of the reactions to the sound 'salt' which orients the listener to the object, salt-shaker, as opposed to other objects in the immediate environment (see Parrott, 1984, for further discussion). These reactions have no independent causal status with respect to subsequent reinforcement

mediational activities of the listener; the listener may understand what is requested of him/her but not comply with the request. Rather, they constitute a phase in a sequence of events, in the absence of which the final component of passing the salt could not occur. Moreover, a tendency to 'see' a salt-shaker prior to making visual contact with a salt-shaker, influences the speed with which the listener comes into contact with this object as it restricts his/her search to objects of a particular size and shape as well as to locations in which salt-shakers have been seen in the past.

It is this orientation of the listener with respect to the things spoken of that is implied by the concept of reference. A referential response of the verbal type is one which produces reactions on the part of a listener with respect to stimuli other than the stimulus products of verbal responding — it produces reactions to the things spoken of. This is essentially what is involved in rule-following behavior, as discussed in the next section.

Rule-Following Behavior

In order to account for the behavior of following a rule, we must review exactly what it is we are trying to explain. For behavior to be rule-governed, it must not have occurred previously as contingency-shaped behavior. Instead, it must be behavior occurring for the first time under the control of verbal stimuli have the form of a contingency specification. That is, a rule must be part of the circumstance under which rule-following takes place. Rule-following is more than just listening to a rule, however. It is the *behavior specified in the rule*, occurring with respect to the *stimuli specified in the rule*. What requires explanation, then, is how one configuration of stimuli — the rule — brings about not only the response of hearing this stimulus, but also a totally different response under the control of a totally different stimulus complex.

Skinner's suggestion in this regard, namely, that rule-following is simply doing what a rule tells one to do, is not very helpful. It amounts to an assertion that a rule orients a listener with respect to the stimuli specified in the rule which, in turn, set the occasion for the behavior specified in the rule. In other words, it amounts to an acknowledgment, in commonsense terms, of the referential function of verbal stimuli. It does not explain *how* the rule-follower becomes oriented with respect to these other stimuli, nor what it means to suggest that stimuli or behaviors are *specified* in rules. An explanation for rule-following by way of the concept of reference is available, however.

A person following a rule is essentially a listener, that is, one who acts in such a way as to mediate reinforcement for a speaker's action. The speaker, in this case, is the person formulating the rule. (Whether or not this speaker is a part of the immediate situation is of no consequence to this analysis; the activities of a listener are *acquired* under social circumstances but do not depend on such circumstances for their continued occurrence. Moreover, a listener is also a speaker, and he/she may occupy both roles in a given verbal episode.) The listener's activities, as previously discussed, must be conceptualized as occurring in three distinct phases, the first being a perceptual interaction with the rule as an auditory (or visual) stimulus. An understanding reaction constitutes the second phase. It is during this phase that the listener's repertoire with respect to stimuli

other than those making up the rule is brought into play. For example, if the rule is an auditory stimulus having the form, 'If it rains, take an umbrella to stay dry', the listener's repertoire with respect to such things as rain and umbrellas would become available in the moment of contact with this stimulus. The listener would 'see' umbrellas, 'smell' rain, 'feel' wet or dry, and so on. It is the occurrence of actions of this sort that is implied when we suggest that contingencies are *specified* in rules: rules specify contingencies in that they give rise to behaviors normally occurring with respect to the stimuli making up those contingencies. They do so because the non-verbal stimuli making up those contingencies have occurred in conjunction with those making up the rule in the history of a particular listener, whereby the functions of those non-verbal stimuli were acquired by the stimuli making up the rule. If one does not hear the rule or otherwise make perceptual contact with a rule as a stimulus, no opportunity exists for an understanding reaction of this sort. In this sense, this second phase of rule-following depends on the occurrence of the first phase.

The third phase of rule-following, which may be considered rule-following proper, is analogous to the reinforcement mediational activity of the listener as discussed in the context of verbal behavior. It is the act, in this case, of taking the umbrella under conditions of rainfall. Whether on not this action occurs is a function of the listener's history of reinforcement for rule-following in general. Still, however, if one does not understand a rule, no opportunity exists for following a rule. A given instance of rule-following, therefore, depends on the occurrence of a previous understanding reaction, regardless of the strength of the rule-following operant.

CONCLUSION

Skinner's analysis of verbal behavior is primarily an analysis of the behavior of a speaker and, as such, the listener's response in a verbal episode is reduced to only those activities directly influencing the speaker, namely, reinforcement mediation. Because the listener's actions are conceived in this manner, however, the conditions under which a referential interpretation of verbal behavior and its products might prove most useful are not confronted. Consequently, a concept of reference is abandoned as lacking in utility as well as for systemic reasons. Little problem arises as a result, and *Verbal Behavior* (Skinner, 1957) remains an important contribution to our understanding of the speaker's action.

The problem of reference resurfaces under another name and in disguised form, however. Much complex behavior cannot be accounted for by appeal to a history of contingency shaping. Hence contingency-shaped behavior comes to be differentiated from a new class — rule governance. Rule governance, in essence, is behavior occurring under the control of verbal stimuli. In short, it is the behavior of the listener. The analysis made of listener behavior in the book, *Verbal Behavior*, is not sufficient to account for behavior under the control of rules, however. One solution to this problem would have been to provide a more complete analysis of the behaviors of the listener, including the acts of listening and understanding, but no such attempt was made. Instead, rules are assumed to have the special characteristic of reference: they are said to *describe* contingencies. Accordingly, behavior occurring under the control of a rule is analyzed as

doing what the rule tells one to do. It is here that a problem arises. Rules are not only rules, they are verbal stimuli; and if verbal stimuli are not regarded as having a referential character in the context of verbal behavior, how is it that they can have this character in the context of rule governance? Skinner does not resolve this controversy.

The conflict can be resolved, however. It is simply a matter of recognizing the conditions under which a concept of reference might prove useful, that is, in analyzing the behavior of the listener; and formulating an interpretation of this concept in terms acceptable to the systemic underpinnings of radical behaviorism.

REFERENCES

Parrott, L.J. (1984) 'Listening and understanding', *The Behavior Analyst*, 7, pp. 29–39.
Russell, B. (1960) *An Outline of Philosophy*, New York, Meridian Book Company.
Skinner, B.F. (1957) *Verbal Behavior*, New York, Appleton-Century-Crofts.
Skinner, B.F. (1969) *Contingencies of Reinforcement: A Theoretical Analysis*, New York, Appleton-Century-Crofts.
Skinner, B.F. (1974) *About Behaviorism*, New York, Alfred A. Knopf.

Interchange

VAUGHAN REPLIES TO PARROTT

Skinner (1966) distinguished between behavior which is directly shaped by contingencies of reinforcement and behavior which occurs as a function of a description of such contingencies, the latter case being rule-governed. Rules, or descriptions of contingencies, establish some stimulus change as reinforcement. A person's history of reinforcement for following rules and, in particular, the history of reinforcement for following rules verbalized by the present rule-giver, provide the necessary motivation. The rule-following repertoire is a result of a long and complicated learning history, but its operational building blocks are nothing more than contingencies of reinforcement. Nonetheless, the distinction has had enormous utility within the experimental analysis of behavior as researchers begin to dissect complex human behavior.

Parrott finds this distinction (and perhaps any distinction within a science based upon practical convenience) 'spurious' and 'trivial'. She argues for a 'genuine' distinction (a distinction based upon two different kinds of stuff?) between contingency-shaped and rule-governed behavior. She asserts that the relation between verbal and non-verbal events is special and requires some additional principle beyond those that the experimental analysis of behavior has uncovered in studying non-verbal activity. She argues that by incorporating the concept of reference as a basic principle, we can specify what the relation is between verbal and non-verbal events and, in so doing, clearly distinguish rule-governed from contingency-shaped behavior.

Parrott's solution to the situation she finds wanting, however, is doomed from the start: she must slip something inside the organism to explain behavior on the outside, but once in she can never get back out; she is forced to answer an endless regress of questions related to private events.

Specifically, Parrott is concerned with answering the following question (a question she believes Skinner has yet to address): how does a rule evoke not only the behavior of hearing the rule, but also the behavior of following the rule with respect to the stimulus conditions specified? In response to this she formulates a three-phase process — listening, understanding, and mediating. Phase One, listening, involves orienting to the source of stimulation and making perceptual contact with it. That is, one must see a written rule or hear it before any action takes place. Phase Two, understanding, involves the momentary strengthening of the repertoire called forth in the rule. The specific repertoire would include all behavior that has in the past been associated with the stimulus object now specified in the rule (e.g. seeing salt, seeing salt-shakers, tasting salt, etc.). 'It is the occurrence of the reactions to the sound "salt" which orients the listener to

the object, salt-shaker, as opposed to other objects in the immediate environment. These reactions ... constitute a phase in a sequence of events, in the absence of which the final component of passing the salt could not occur' (pp. 273–4). The final phase, reinforcement mediation, is simply Skinner's analysis of the listener in explaining the behavior of the speaker.

The heart, and downfall, of Parrott's position is summarized in these two sentences: 'It is this orientation of the listener with respect to the things spoken of that is implied by the concept of reference. A referential response of the verbal type is one which produces reactions on the part of a listener with respect to stimuli other than the stimulus products of verbal responding — it produces reactions to the things spoken of' (p. 274). But these 'reactions' do not explain anything; they are representations inside the head, historical summaries of contingencies of reinforcement. They only evoke further questions. For example, what is the origin of such reactions? Parrott suggests that they are a function of a history of reinforcement and respondent conditioning. But then why cannot the rule that evokes the representations (perceptual reactions) directly evoke the behavior described in the rule? Or more revealing: how does the organism know which response to engage in, given the perceptual reactions? Do the perceptual reactions include 'seeing' the behavior described in the rule? How does the organism know that it knows, and so on.

But the most important question is: what is gained by such an analysis? We are forced to rely on introspection to confirm such a theory and, even if we could agree on this, how does it help control and predict behavior? How does it make us more effective in dealing with our subject matter? In proposing her theory, Parrott takes on the role of a neurophysiologist. In so doing, perhaps our goals diverge. But if we are in the business of a science of behavior, we must be content with observable, manipulable events and leave what is going on inside, and what might be intervening, to those interested in anatomy and physiology.

In conclusion, I am not sympathetic with Parrott's description of the necessary organismic history from which she asserts rule-following emerges. I do not believe an appeal to private events brings us any closer to predicting or controlling the behavior in question. But I believe it is equally true that behavior analysts have not articulated in similar detail an alternative description. It is all too obvious how important such an exercise would be in further developing the verbal and non-verbal behavior of those interested in the relation between complex stimulus control and complex human behavior.

REFERENCE

Skinner, B.F. (1966) 'An operant analysis of problem solving', in Kleinmuntz, B. (Ed.), *Problem Solving: Research, Method and Theory,* New York, John Wiley and Sons.

PARROTT REPLIES TO VAUGHAN

Vaughan identifies two functions of rules as stimuli: a discriminative function, wherein a rule sets the occasion for responding in the immediate circumstance; and a repertoire-altering function, wherein a rule alters the 'future probability of other behavior, evoked by different contingencies' (p. 260). Her intent is to distinguish between these two functions, and to illustrate the utility of the concept of rule governance in the analysis of so-called higher mental processes. These conceptualizations of rule governance imply processes of stimulus function transfer, from verbal stimuli to non-verbal stimuli and from one verbal stimulus to another, however, and Vaughan makes no serious attempt to account for these processes. She looks instead, at instances of each function observed at a moment in time, describing their differences by appeal to the immediately obvious stimulus objects participating in each, and then extends this understanding to specific instances of persons operating with respect to self-generated rules. I do not believe that an adequate understanding of rule governance may be achieved by these means. If we are to understand rule governance, we must be prepared to account for the role of current stimulating conditions in the occurrence of rule-governed behavior, and to do so we must appeal to the historical circumstances responsible for their stimulational properties in the moment.

With that introduction, we may examine Vaughan's analysis in more detail, beginning with her description of the discriminative function of rules. In this context Vaughan, like Skinner, discusses the control exerted by verbal stimuli over responding in much the same way as that exerted by non-verbal stimuli. That is, a verbal stimulus sets the occasion for responding in some particular way due to a history of reinforcement for responding in that way in the presence of that particular stimulus. Verbal stimuli, however, are said to exert a unique form of control in that they are capable of evoking behavior not previously reinforced in their presence (p. 259). This unique feature, we are told, has something to do with the fact that verbal behavior requires no environmental support (p. 259). What, exactly, it has to do with this we are not told. The best explanation we find for the emergence of these more complex relations involving verbal stimuli is a reference to 'an extensive conditioning history', the details of which are not discussed.

The discriminative control exerted by verbal stimuli is a complex issue. It often involves responding with respect to stimuli other than those which appear to give rise to the response, as, for example, when one passes the salt-shaker upon being asked to do so. In these cases it is incumbent upon the analyst to account for the control exerted by the salt-shaker. How is it that one is able to act with respect to the salt-shaker upon being confronted not with the salt-shaker but with verbal stimulation having the form 'please pass the salt'? Moreover, the other stimulus involved may be one with which a person has never had previous contact. In Vaughan's words: 'When a speaker describes a state of affairs (a verbal stimulus), the listener can now behave differently (and ideally, more appropriately) to the state of affairs without having had direct contact with it.' How is one able to react to a state of affairs without having had contact with that state of affairs, and further, how is one able to do so by way of stimulation of an entirely different sort? These are important questions, and to answer them by casual reference to 'an extensive conditioning history' is of little service. We know

that an extensive conditioning history is involved; what we do not know is of what it consists.

Turning to Vaughan's analysis of the repertoire-altering function of rules, we are told that a rule can alter the future probability of other behavior, evoked by other contingencies. The events from which this description is drawn are simply that at time *A* one is confronted with stimulus condition *X* and presumably responds in some manner, and then, at time *B*, in the presence of stimulus condition *Y*, one responds in some other manner. How do we get from these events to the suggestion that stimulus condition *X* alters the likelihood of other behavior in the presence of condition *Y*? Underlying Vaughan's argument in this context is an assumption concerning the causal efficacy of stimuli beyond the circumstances of their actual occurrence, to which I shall return. The argument itself is that repertoire-altering occurs by way of stimulus-stimulus pairings. That is, by pairing stimulus *Y* with stimulus *X*, the behavior that would normally occur with respect to the former may be evoked by the latter.

Vaughan's example does not conform to this pattern, however. In her example, one is confronted at time *A* with a verbal stimulus ('when you get to Church Street, stop') to which one nods; and at time *B*, in the presence of a non-verbal stimulus (Church Street), one stops. At no time, however, was the non-verbal stimulus of Church Street paired with the verbal stimulus, 'when you get to Church Street, stop'. Moreover, it is unclear what behavior normally occurs with respect to either of these stimuli. If we look more closely at Vaughan's example, we find that the paired stimuli are not the verbal instruction and the non-verbal events referred to in the instruction, but rather two aspects of the instruction itself ('Church Street' and 'Stop'). Vaughan explains: 'By pairing a verbal stimulus ('Church Street') with a stimulus ('stop') already showing control over a response, we have altered the listener's behavior with respect to the first stimulus' (p. 260). The first stimulus, however, is a verbal stimulus. It is not the non-verbal event of Church Street, and it is the act of stopping upon confronting this non-verbal event that Vaughan is attempting to explain. The problem here is the same problem we encountered in attempting to understand the discriminative control of verbal stimuli. That is, how are we able to act with respect to non-verbal stimuli as a function of confrontation with verbal stimuli? Vaughan does not address herself to this issue in either context. Instead she refers the reader to a section of Skinner's *Verbal Behavior* wherein related issues are discussed at some length. Unfortunately, Skinner does not attempt, in this section, to explain how non-verbal stimuli acquire control over non-verbal behaviors as a function of prior verbal stimulation. In short, Vaughan's analysis is incomplete and pages 357–62 of Skinner's *Verbal Behavior* do not make it complete.

We may return now to the assumption underlying Vaughan's analysis of the repertoire-altering function of rules concerning the causal efficacy of stimuli beyond the circumstances of their occurrence. Vaughan asserts that stimulus events at time *A* have an impact on the probability of response events at time *B*, despite their absence from the situation at time *B*. How can this be? The usual explanations for statements of this sort, from a Skinnerian standpoint, make reference to a change in the organism brought about at time *A* which then moves with the organism to time *B* and thereby has a place in the effective present. This is not what Vaughan is implying, however. Rather, given that the future probability of behavior (i.e., the occurrence of behavior at time *B*) is a function of future

stimulus conditions (i.e., the stimulus conditions present at time *B*), Vaughan is suggesting that the stimulus events at time *A* affect changes in the stimulus events present at time *B*. How such changes are effected is explained by way of stimulus-stimulus pairings. However, again, this explanation falls short of its objective. More specifically, stimulus-stimulus pairings cannot begin to account for these changes unless the stimuli at times *A* and *B* are in fact paired, and they are not.

In summary, Vaughan attempts to account for rule-following by isolating two functions of rules as stimuli. Neither function is adequately identified, however, because the central question of how non-verbal stimuli acquire control over non-verbal behaviors, given immediate confrontation with only verbal stimuli, is never explicitly addressed. As a result, more complex circumstances, involving actions with respect to stimulus objects — verbal or otherwise — that are absent from the immediate situation, cannot be explained satisfactorily.

Despite these difficulties, Vaughan proceeds to an analysis of certain activities traditionally of interest to cognitive psychologists, among them the activities involved in self-instruction and problem-solving. Her discussion here focuses on the issue of whether or not one can act in such a way as to provide discriminative or repertoire-altering stimuli for one's own behavior; and while she does provide examples that illustrate these possibilities, I am not convinced by her arguments as to how such acts are engendered. For example, with regard to discriminative control over behavior, accomplished by way of self-instruction, Vaughan argues that such occurs because the activities involved in self-instruction are briefer, require less energy, and provide a more sharply defined discriminative stimulus (p. 261). It is a comparative statement. Unfortunately it is not clear to what self-instruction is being compared in these terms.

With regard to the issue of acting in such a way as to alter one's own repertoire, Vaughan argues, by way of example, that such can occur. However, she does not attempt to *account* for the occurrence of such behavior except to say that 'any behavior which clarifies the stimulus conditions (and, hence the contingencies) will be useful and thus reinforcing'. While this is no doubt true, it does not account for the occurrence of such behavior in the immediate situation since no explanation for the role of current stimulating conditions is provided. What circumstances set the occasion for acts of clarifying other stimuli, and how has this control been established in the history of the individual? Vaughan does not address these issues.

In summary, Vaughan does not appear to have properly identified her analytical responsibilities with respect to self-instruction and problem-solving. These are acts not of rule-*following* but of rule-*stating* and, as such, she must attempt to account for the role of stimulating conditions in the occurrence of rule-stating. Little is offered toward this end. Instead, she focuses her analysis on acts of following self-generated rules, which is, in my view, irrelevant to the issue at hand.

In conclusion, rule governance involves processes of stimulus function transfer whereby the control exerted by verbal stimuli comes to be exerted by other verbal and non-verbal events. Vaughan makes no serious attempt to analyze these processes, accounting for the occurrence of rule governance by appeal to an amorphous 'complex conditioning history'. Little understanding of rule governance is accomplished by this means and, as a result, little contribution is made to the understanding of higher mental processes. In short, Vaughan's analysis, like

Skinner's, is only nominally functional. A genuinely functional analysis is more than a description of temporal relations among stimuli and responses observed in a given episode of their occurrence. It is an analysis of stimulation with respect to responding — an analysis of functions — and functions can only be understood by way of an explicit and specific account of their historical development.

Part XIII: Skinner's Analysis of Perception/Cognition

23. Perception and Action

TERRY J. KNAPP

A textbook on learning, or psychotherapy, or educational psychology, or animal behavior, or industrial psychology is likely to be deemed deficient to the degree that it makes little or no mention of B.F. Skinner's views. Yet no contemporary textbook on the subject of perception contains a chapter, segment, or paragraph on the views or contributions of B.F. Skinner, or for that matter on the contributions of those who research and publish under the banner of the experimental analysis of behavior. The circumstances are much the same for those books which bear titles such as *Cognition* or *Cognitive Psychology*. It is as if the person regarded by historians as responsible for the second most significant development in psychology since World War II (Gilgen, 1982) had nothing to say on the matters taken up by such textbooks. Does radical behaviorism have nothing to contribute to an understanding of perceptual processes? Are perceptual processes (or the physics and physiology which underlie such behavior) largely irrelevant to the goals of radical behaviorism? Have psychologists, for whatever reasons, simply ignored what Skinner and workers in the experimental analysis of behavior have had to contribute to the field of perception? Is there little value in a behavioral analysis of the problems of perception?

To seek the answers to even some of these questions in the works of Skinner is not easy. His writings on perception — comments might be a better term — are widely scattered. The index to any one of his books will provide little guidance in locating the relevant sections (*Notebooks* is an exception in this regard), and only *About Behaviorism* (1974) offers a chapter directly on the topic. To be sure, he has written some individual papers on related themes, but most of these remain obscure even to many of those associated with his analysis. The earliest of this genre is a brief note (Skinner, 1932) on the visual effects of a black and white figure which yields under low white-light conditions the appearance of color. He suggests an explanation (a functional-element theory of color vision) and an experimental procedure to test it. Several years later he turned his attention to

auditory perception (Skinner, 1936) and studied verbal responses produced by
subjects as they listened to recordings of mixed meaningless patterns of vowels
against a background of noise or when such patterns were played at a low volume.
At the time Skinner wrote that the device used to produce the stimuli (which he
called a verbal summator) 'ought to become a standard apparatus for any clinical
psychiatrist [a kind of auditory Rorschach], for it would cut the time required to
locate complexes to a mere fraction' (1979, p. 176). The operant chamber and not
the verbal summator was to become a standard apparatus in psychology. Some
clinical testing was stimulated by the procedure (Shakow and Rosenzweig, 1940),[1]
and it is the only work by Skinner that I have ever seen cited in a textbook on
perception. Sekuler and Blake (1985) include it in a section on 'resolving auditory
blur'.

In both of the preceding papers Skinner was concerned with 'perceptual
processes' in the human. But he had earlier studied discriminative responding in
lower organisms (Skinner, 1938) and it is such work that is offered as a third
instance of his research on perception. While a number of papers could be
mentioned, the chapter on 'Stimulus Generalization in an Operant: A Historical
Note' (Skinner, 1965) is the most relevant. This is a report on a portion of the
data from *Pigeons in a Pelican* (Skinner, 1960), the World War II project to teach
pigeons to guide missiles. The studies reported concern about the properties of
the visual patterns on which the birds were first trained. 'Which of these properties are important in controlling the pecking response? How much induction
[generalization] will be shown to a pattern that differs with respect to any one
property?' (1965, p. 194). In the current cognitive era this work is likely to be
regarded as a study of selective attention.

A final contribution by Skinner to the analysis of perceptual phenomena
is contained in a paper (Skinner, 1941) on 'The Psychology of Design'. The Phi
Phenomenon, apparent movement, is suggested as an explanation for our reaction
to certain paintings. Those 'with lines at different angles should appear lively, and
those with parallel lines quiet . . . As one looked from one figure to another in
Daumier's Don Quixote with Sancho Panza Wringing His Hands, . . . Panza seems
to pull back . . . and Don Quixote to throw himself forward on his horse in part
because of "Phi"' (Skinner, 1979, p. 238).

Each of these examples suggests the range of perceptual issues on which
Skinner has published, though they fail to convey explicitly his analysis of perception, which is the central concern of this chapter. I shall turn to it shortly. First,
several preliminary considerations are in order.

CONCEPTUAL, BIBLIOGRAPHIC, AND HISTORICAL CONTEXT

Originally I had intended that this chapter be entitled 'Perception and Cognition'
because the predominant contemporary paradigm in the field — information
processing psychology — holds that these processes are continuous. It 'stresses
that sensation, perception, and higher mental processes — such as memory —
must be treated within a single system' (Matlin, 1983, p. 8). There are several
good reasons, however, for limiting the discussion to the topic of perception. It is
not at all evident that perception and cognition are best regarded as continuous
with each other (Robinson, 1985), but more to the point, Professor Skinner has

written sufficiently on both topics to warrant restricting our limited space to the narrower, though nonetheless difficult, issue of perception.

More significantly, however, perception and action as a title suggests what is at issue in an understanding of radical behaviorism (the behaviorism of B.F. Skinner), whereas perception and cognition as a title suggests the kind of explanations to which radical behaviorists object. Too many psychologists make perception the cause of actions (e.g., we act on the basis of what we perceive and know), as though the world of stimuli and behavior is explained by activities taking place in the world of phenomenal experience, or the world 'as perceived', or the world as 'represented'. The analysis of perception as a causal antecedent to behavior is an old one and has been usefully criticized by Ryle (1949, especially in Ch. 7, 'Sensation and Observation'). It will be argued later that perception does name a controlling relationship, and in that sense is a 'cause' of behavior, but it is behavior or action which is primitive, not perception.

It would profit the interested reader to consult earlier attempts which relate the concept of perception to the experimental analysis of behavior. The issues are not new, and it would be difficult to improve upon the discussion offered by Guttman (1963) in his 'Laws of Behavior and Facts of Perception' or in two other early papers sympathetic to Skinner's analysis, 'Behavior and Perception' by Schoenfeld and Cumming (1963) and 'Perception' by Goldiamond (1962). Three chapters (Rilling, 1977; Mackintosh, 1977; Blough and Blough, 1977) in Honig and Staddon's *Handbook of Operant Behavior* are relevant in that they serve to update the earlier chapters (Terrace, 1966; Blough, 1966) in the first Honig volume and provide a review of recent work on 'perception' from the perspective of the experimental analysis of behavior. An excellent summary of the extensive operant literature on stimulus control is available in Rodewald (1979).

E.G. Boring (1950) in his *History of Experimental Psychology* helps to place in context, though not addressing Skinner in particular, the general tenor of American psychology from its inception as a transformed German heritage to a mid-twentieth century science.[2] 'America', he says (Boring, 1950), 'has taken over from Germany, and attention within psychology has shifted from sensation and perception to action and conduct' (p. 385). When Skinner formally began to take up the topic of psychology,[3] interest in sensation, perception, psychophysics, and related issues could readily be found, but the 'reaction' tradition was also well established by the experimental work of Thorndike and Pavlov, by the theoretical analysis of Watson (and more to the point for Skinner, of Bertrand Russell), and by the soon to emerge or emerging works of Tolman, Hull, Guthrie, and other minor figures who took as the fundamental problem of psychology the explanation of response acquisition, and with Skinner's work, the maintenance of varied response rates under varied stimulus conditions.

When Hilgard (1948) summarized the field of learning at the close of the 1940s, he included a contrast between those theorists with a preference 'for a reaction psychology (laying emphasis upon movements) as over against a cognitive psychology (emphasizing perception-like and idea-like processes)' (pp. 12–13). The former, he said, without identifying any one theorist, 'prefer to speak of discriminatory reactions rather than of perceptions' (p. 13). This was partly to avoid 'the subjective or introspective connotations of the word perception', but also because of what 'appear to be the facts of the case so far as learning is concerned' (p. 13). Hilgard's remarks reflect the renewed interest in perception as

a consequence of the influx of the Gestalt psychologists and his remarks forecast the 'new look' in perception which was said to have occurred in the 1950s. His distinction may also reflect a temperamental dichotomy in one's approach to psychology, something on the order of William James' contrast between the 'tender minded' and the 'tough minded'.

PERCEPTUAL PSYCHOLOGY, PSYCHOLOGY OF PERCEPTION, AND STIMULUS CONTROL

When psychologists say they are interested in perception, one of three issues (or all three) may be intended. They may be reflecting a commitment to constructing a *perceptual psychology* in the sense that the concept of perception (a constructed view of the world which determines and hence explains our actions) is primitive. The problems of perception, for example, illusions, depth, form, etc., are not given any special attention or status because *all* of psychology is *the* problem of perception, that is, is the problem of explaining how our actions are determined by our perceptions. The now dated work by Snygg and Combs (1949) is a good exemplar of this approach, as is much of the work of Piaget. The view is an old one and is one way of being a cognitive psychologist. The issues are broad (Skinner, 1977), and other chapters in the present volume are highly relevant.

A second way in which a psychologist might be interested in perception is in the 'problems of perception'. These usually form the basis of textbooks on the topic, and there is nothing about the problems per se that is incompatible with a behavior analysis. Sometimes the problems of perception are treated in a manner which suggest they are problems in physics and physiology (Cornsweet, 1970). On other occasions they are treated as phenomenologically grounded (Rock, 1975) in the sense that one can argue for different explanations of a perception problem by exposing the audience to varied perceptual experiences produced by distinctively different physical stimuli (or the same set of stimuli which produce alternating descriptions as in ambiguous figures). On still other occasions the problems of perception are embedded in a larger context, how we come to know the world, and such a strategy usually results in a cognitive psychology which studies 'all the processes by which the sensory input is transformed, reduced, elaborated, stored, recovered, and used' (Neisser, 1967, p. 4).

Today what may be regarded as traditional textbooks on perception (Matlin, 1983; Sekuler and Blake, 1985) contain a hodge-podge of material ranging from sensory neurophysiology, to psychophysic methods, to signal detection methods, to information methods, to perceptual problems (constancy, form), to non-visual categories of perception (space, time, motion), to cognitive, developmental, and motivational influences on perception, to topics deserving a textbook in their own right, e.g., attention. In treatments such as these, perception at times seems to be a category of explanation, and at other times a category requiring explanation.

A radical behaviorist would be interested in perception in a fourth way, as we shall see: in how stimuli present at the occasion on which a response is reinforced come to control the response with some degree of probability. This kind of interest in perception is never treated systematically in textbooks on the topic.[4]

Before we proceed to examine the last analysis as the positive contribution which Skinner has made to perception, an overview of his critical thoughts is

offered. These are usually introduced in his works as the 'copy theory' (Skinner, 1953, pp. 275–80; 1969, pp. 230–6, 247–51; 1974, pp. 80–1).

THE COPY THEORY

When we seek to understand the relationship between an organism and its 'environment', we may treat the latter term as naming the objects, properties, and events around us which influence the organism directly (e.g., when the red light is on, the rat stops bar-pressing). Alternately, we may treat the term 'environment' as naming these same categories, but assign to it a less direct role, that of the environment as mediated by the organism's own construction, i.e., the stimulus as perceived as opposed to the stimulus per se. Sometimes this mediated component is quite innocent, as when it is a short-hand reminder that each organism brings to its relationship with the environment a unique history that is necessarily reflected in the resultant interaction (e.g., naive rats do not stop or start bar-pressing when a red light is turned on). But it is rarely this abbreviated way of speaking about the 'mediated stimulus', as an indirect reference to its history of interaction with the organism's behavior, that commentators use. Rather, they wish to make room for some form of representationalism, the view that the behavior of the organism is only explained by reference to the influence of the representation of the environment constructed by the organism.[5] The organism copies the environment and in doing so modifies it. Often this alleged copying process is loosely referred to as perception, or more commonly, when the influence of more remote or complex variables is involved, as cognition. Sometimes conceptual arguments are given to advance representationalism, but in psychology empirical studies of great diversity are more often cited (Mahoney, 1974). At other times the evidence for the view is taken as so well-founded as to make a challenge appear incredible.

So far as I am aware Skinner's (1953) earliest description of the copy theory occurs in *Science and Human Behavior*.

> It is usually held that one does not see the physical world at all, but only a nonphysical copy of it called 'experience.' When the physical organism is in a contact with reality, the experienced copy is called a 'sensation,' 'sense datum,' or 'percept'; when there is no contact, it is called an 'image,' 'thought,' or 'idea.' Sensations, images, and their congeries are characteristically regarded as psychic or mental events, occurring in a special world of 'consciousness' where, although they occupy no space, they can nevertheless often be seen. (p. 276.)

In 'Behaviorism at Fifty' (Skinner, 1963) the origin of the theory is attributed to the Greeks. They 'could not explain how a man could have knowledge of something with which he was not in immediate contact. . . . Copies of the real world projected into the body could compose the experience which a man directly knows' (p. 231).

Skinner's objections to the copy theory take a variety of forms.

1   The metaphor is seductive when considering visual stimuli, but much less so in the case of auditory, olfactory, or tactile stimuli (1974, p. 83).
2   The 'perception' of the inner copy remains to be explained, a process as difficult as explaining the original case of perception (1974, p. 83).

3 Attempts at operationalizing sensation, percept, etc. will result in intervening variables, a state of affairs not acceptable to a science of behavior (1953, p. 278).

4 The causal status assigned to the copies will thwart the search for the actual controlling variables of behavior (1953, p. 278).

5 Finally, and perhaps most importantly, as the current chapter title suggests, perception comes to replace action. 'At some point the organism must do more than create duplicates. It must see, hear, smell, and so on, as forms of *action* rather than *reproduction*. *It must do some of the things it is differentially reinforced for doing when it learns to respond discriminatively*' (1969, p. 232).

It would be easy to dismiss what Skinner has written about the copy theory as a diatribe against a straw person, for it is the case that 'copy theories' might be a better expression given the variety of ways in which one can hold such a view, and the equal variety of ways in which one finds psychologists speaking about perception.[6] I find comfort in acknowledging these qualifications until I encounter statements such as the following from the introductory section of a contemporary textbook on perception. We are told that 'perception is really a puzzle that has mystified philosophers and psychologists for centuries. Basically, it is difficult to explain how the qualities of objects out there in the world can be recreated inside our own heads' (Matlin, 1983, p. 2). Am I to understand this as loose talk, or perhaps as an adequate formulation for undergraduates, *or* as a formulation of the fundamental problem of perception: how do we copy the world? If the last is the case, I am inclined to agree with Skinner and Ryle as to why the puzzle has remained for so long. It is not a mystery, but a mystification that is the source of the puzzle.

THE CASE FOR PHYSICS AND PHYSIOLOGY

It is fair to recognize, evident in any standard textbook of perception or sensation and perception, that a great deal of what is at issue is better suited as an object of study for the physicist or the physiologist. 'The sequence of physical and physiological events which are involved when an organism perceives an object is, of course, a legitimate subject for study. The first stage, between the object and the surface of the perceiver, is part of physics. The second, the optics of the eye, is the physics of an anatomical structure. The third is physiological' (Skinner, 1969, p. 249). Much of what can be regarded as progress in the field, making sensation and perception textbooks of 1980 different from those of the 1930s, is best regarded as neurophysiology.

A science of behavior receives the organism with certain capacities, for movement or locomotion, for example. The explanation of these capacities may be left to other disciplines. A part of what we mean by perception is just such a capacity. Few psychology textbooks devote any space to the musculoskeletal system, but many describe in detail the anatomy and physiology of the visual system and then proceed to describe the stimulus as it is 'processed' by this system. No book contains a description of behavior as a 'response' flowing out of the musculoskeletal system. That capacity is left to other sciences.

LOCATING PERCEPTION AMONG THE THREE-TERM CONTINGENCY

The three-term contingency of reinforcement, comprised of a discriminative stimulus which sets the occasion for a response, the response identified by its consequence as a member of a class of responses, and the stimulus reinforcer which determines the probability of the response class, is fundamental in sketching Skinner's analysis of behavior. Any complexity evident in an action is a matter of complexity in the contingencies of reinforcement (and punishment). Multiple sources of discriminative control, multiple and independent schedules of reinforcement, concurrent response classes under independent discriminative control, reinforcing stimuli which may be terminated rather than applied are ways of getting to the complexity of behavior from the seeming simplicity of the three-term contingency (Skinner, 1953).

The delivering of consequences through the behavior of another organism, whose response has been shaped for precisely that purpose, introduces the complexity of verbal behavior (Skinner, 1957). When the discriminative stimuli are in the form of rules which specify a contingent relationship themselves, a further level of complexity arises. Any analysis of perception which Skinner might offer must be related in a fundamental way to his analysis of contingencies of reinforcement.

Where is 'perception' in the analysis of behavior through a three-term contingency of reinforcement? A part of what leads us to talk about an organism perceiving is when its responding is systematically related to changes in a stimulus. We speak of the monkey seeing the light, hearing the tone, feeling the sandpaper, when some aspect of its behavior can be made discriminative to some value of the named stimuli through differential reinforcement. Stimulus control is the name for the fact that the organism's behavior has been brought to bear a systematic relationship to values of the stimulus. For a radical behaviorist the study of perception *is* the study of stimulus control or discriminative operants.

But how does the organism come to respond differentially — pecking a blue key when a slide contains a human figure, and a red key when it does not? Through differential reinforcement arranged by the experimenter, or in other examples by the natural environment. But how is it able to 'see the difference'? Physics and physiology provide one set of answers, as we have seen; the history of differential reinforcement, *given* the organism's capacity for the development of differential responding (blind pigeons are handicapped in just this regard with visual stimuli), provides the other part of the answer. Is there more to the story? Yes, but only in terms of the complexity that can be developed in regard to discriminative responding. No, if what is sought is a copy (or representation) of the stimulus to which the pigeon is *really* responding. No, if what is sought is a description of the hypothetical processes which mediated the effects of differential reinforcement at a level other than the physiological or behavioral. No, if independent and dependent variables are confused, as in such expressions as 'perception causes behavior', 'explains it', 'or produces it in some manner'. Perception is the relationship between a certain class of responses and a certain class of controlling variables.

But it is not merely simple discriminative responding which leads psychologists to speak of perception. Often the organism's response is complex, and we may be inclined to say that it perceives relationships — largely on the basis of

rejecting the possibility of discriminative responding to relative differences.

Perhaps it can be agreed that the organism 'sees' lights in the sense of coming under discriminative control, but such an account, it is said, is not applicable to 'seeing connections', 'relations' or 'contingencies' in the environment. The argument leads to making perception primitive and causal, in an operant analysis responding is primitive, and the 'causes' are located in the individual's genetic endowment, history of contact with environmental antecedents and consequences, and current environmental antecedents and consequences.

But what about examples where the organism is not responding?

> People interested in perception often criticize a behavioristic analysis on the grounds that it doesn't cover simple looking without doing. Contemplation, the enjoyment of 'perception' — how can these be treated as behavior? But the shortcoming is on the other side. What *is* looking? What does one *do* in contemplating something. The answer is to be found in the discriminative contingencies. What is differentially reinforced as one learns to see? The development of 'eye-hand' coordination and of spatial relations is one example. One sees *where* a thing is by acquiring all the behavior under its control as a stimulus. These survive in contemplation. (Skinner, 1980, p. 309)

We have seen the manner in which perceptual problems are incorporated into the three-term contingency. The conceptual analysis is backed by a methodological recommendation. 'I see no reason why any problem in perception cannot be converted into an exploration of the range of stimuli which give equivalent responses. But it is always a response that is being studied, not what you see' (Skinner, in Evans, 1968, pp. 15–16). Once the traditional formulation is dismissed, 'so far as behavior is concerned both sensation and perception may be analyzed as forms of stimulus control' (1969, p. 235).

THE ANALYSIS OF 'SEEING AS BEHAVIOR'

The controlling relationship described in the previous section does not cover all the instances in which psychologists speak of perception. Many would hold that it does not cover the most critical and difficult cases which evoke perceptual talk, that is, cases of seeing, hearing, tasting, smelling, when one is concerned with the private or conscious experience allegedly entailed by such terms. Skinner's analysis in such usages is captured in his phrase: 'The behavior of seeing'.

The intended contrast is between treating seeing as a perceptual-representational process versus treating it as a kind of response. At issue is 'what *is* seeing?' For Skinner, 'seeing does not imply something seen' (1969, p. 224). Representationalism is not assumed. Skinner writes, 'It took a long time to understand that when one dreamed of a wolf, no wolf was actually there. It has taken much longer to understand that not even a representation of a wolf is there' (1969, p. 955). The heart of what some psychologists mean by perception is the representation of the world on which the organism or its 'perceptual processes' operate. Skinner is not a representationalist; in this respect his work bears some similarity to the views of J.J. Gibson (1966).

CONDITIONED AND OPERANT SEEING

Skinner's analysis of 'conditioned' and 'operant' seeing has found little acceptance, perhaps because it is such a radical shift from our ordinary language way
of talking about perceptual phenomena, i.e., with perceptual language rather than
a language seen as appropriate only for behavior. The most systematic discussion
of these concepts by Skinner is contained in *Science and Human Behavior* (1953,
pp. 266–75). If seeing is treated as a response, then such responses may be
susceptible to respondent and operant conditioning. 'A man may see or hear
stimuli which are not present on the pattern of the conditioned reflex: he may see
X, not only when X is present, but when any stimulus which has frequently
accompanied X is present' (1953, p. 266). Skinner has suggested that such an
analysis explains a variety of perceptual phenomena, including the 'laws of
perception' derived from the Gestalt psychologies. Seeing incompleted rings as
completed may be merely consistent with 'the world according to one's previous
history'. If his analysis is correct, Skinner says 'seeing a completed ring would
presumably not be inevitable in an individual whose daily life was concerned with
handling incompleted rings, as might be the case in manufacturing certain types of
piston rings' (1953, pp. 267–8). Operant seeing differs from conditioned seeing in
the manner that respondent conditioning differs from operant. In the latter
instances reinforcement and deprivation are the relevant controlling variables.
Thus, the analysis is used to handle such cases as seeing 'dogs while looking at ink
blots' (p. 271), or under strong sexual deprivation seeing 'sexual objects or
activities in the absence of relevant stimuli' (p. 272).

THE VALUE OF STUDYING PERCEPTION

Skinner has not placed a high priority on the problems of perception that have
occupied many psychologists, both historically and contemporarily. His commitment to the analysis of action, and perception as action, is evident in an unpublished manuscript, *A Sketch for an Epistemology*, written during the early 1930s.
Portions have appeared in *The Shaping of a Behaviorist* (Skinner, 1979), and the
following excerpt seems to foretell Skinner's subsequent treatment of perception:

> In approaching the study of, say, human behavior, one of the *last* things we would do is study
> those fine discriminations which comprise the subjects of 'Vision' and 'Audition'. ... It is easy
> to understand the lack of sympathy of end-organ specialists with behaviorism. ... But end-
> organ study is going over to physiology anyway. ... To the practicing behaviorist whose
> interests are determined by the logical development of his science the typical questions of
> experimental psychology are of no pressing importance. (1979, p. 118)

The experimental analysis of behavior generates its own set of issues and
problems even though its methods have been widely applied in general psychology. In one sense this is most evident in *Walden Two*. The variables which control
repeatable behaviors (some problematic, others desirable) are analyzed to produce a better culture. The kind of 'psychology' which seeks to understand illusions, or depth perception, or the structural principles of closure, grouping, etc.,
is not much in evidence because the 'problems' are not deemed relevant to such
an end.

For Skinner the tradition in psychology which has taken the study of perception as its object is the result of a philosophical heritage of both ancient and modern origin. Among his most concise statements on this matter are those found in an interview with R.I. Evans published as *B.F. Skinner: The Man and His Ideas*. They warrant quotation at length:

> ... what British Empiricists felt was going to lead to an analysis of knowledge turned out to be a matter for physiology, that is, how the end organs work. But there remain all those curious activities which are assigned to perception rather than sensation, where the end organs themselves don't seem to account for the transformation between the physical environment and something inside. The study of perception suffers from the notion that somehow or other one is indeed relating experience to reality. People look into a distorted room, for example, and see it one way from one angle and another way from another, and they feel they have seen it both as it appears to be and as it really is. But that's nonsense. Both are the way it seems to be, if you want to put it that way. I don't at the moment particularly care about that kind of experiment, because I don't feel that one should answer the most difficult questions in a science first. People study perception because they're intrigued by perceptual phenomena. The Gestalt psychologists have been studying intriguing visual illusions for more than fifty years. New illusions are added, and more people become fascinated by them, but little real progress is made. There are subtleties in perceptual phenomena which will have to wait to be explained when our analytical machinery has become more powerful. I could guess how one would deal objectively with size constancy, for example, but I don't. I don't recommend anyone doing it now. I feel that scientific progress comes about by a progression from the more easily answered questions to the more difficult. (pp. 13–14)

CONCLUSION

B.F. Skinner's analysis of perceptual processes and the problems of perception has been, unlike his many other contributions, largely ignored by the psychology community. Skinner has published relevant papers and research on both visual and auditory 'perception', has articulated a critical analysis of a widely accepted theory of perception, and has offered an analysis of perception as stimulus control through differential reinforcement of discriminative responding. Moreover, he has suggested an analysis of 'seeing' as behavior and traced the implications of respondent and operant conditioning when applied to seeing as a response.

It is perhaps fitting to close this account of his contributions with a description of an encounter at the American Psychological Association meeting in 1940 between Skinner, Kurt Lewin, and Wolfgang Kohler. They were having lunch, when 'a hell of a violent argument' ensued in an attempt to 'convert' Skinner to Gestalt psychology. Kohler was arguing for the givens of visual perceptual experience, when Skinner 'suggested that [they] talk about a blind organism to simplify things.' Kohler shouted, 'Ah, ha! He admits he cannot handle perception!' (p. 246). Many today seem to have adopted Kohler's judgment, despite Skinner's extensive discussion of perceptual issues, and despite related studies of perceptual phenomena by operant psychologists.

NOTES

1   The verbal summator procedure was used in several unpublished studies and a visual analogue of the device was made by W.K. Estes; see Skinner (1979, p. 362).

2 Other relevant historical material may be found in Bevan (1958), Hochberg (1979), and Pastore (1971).
3 Skinner's instruction on perception came from E.G. Boring, and he received an 'A' by composing 'twenty mnemonic sentences, representing the twenty topics covered in the course with the names of the psychologists who had worked on them' (Skinner, 1979, pp. 47–8).
4 Introductory psychology textbooks written from the perspective of the experimental analysis of behavior have included material on traditional topics of perception (e.g., depth perception and perceptual constancies). See Malott and Whaley (1976), Salzinger (1969), and Keller and Schoenfeld (1950) for examples. A good discussion of the relationship of sensation, perception, and stimulus control may be found in Nevin (1973).
5 Though the concept of representation has long been central to many varieties of cognitive psychology, it is only relatively recent that any attempt at conceptual articulation and clarification of the concept has occurred (Palmer, 1978).
6 Representationalism and perception are not synonymous categories inasmuch as one may hold views on perception which are non-representational (e.g., Gibson), and inasmuch as representationalism may include phenomena regarded as non-perceptual (e.g., cognition, long-term memory, imagery). For a discussion of representationalism from a radical behaviorist perspective see Catania (1982) and Epstein (1982). Additional criticism may be found in Gergen (1985).

REFERENCES

Bevan, W. (1958) 'Perception: Evolution of a concept', *Psychological Review*, 65, pp. 34–55.
Blough, D.S. (1966) 'The study of animal sensory processes by operant methods', in Honig, W.K. (Ed.), *Operant Behavior: Areas of Research and Application*, New York, Appleton-Century-Crofts, pp. 345–79.
Blough, D.S. and Blough, P. (1977) 'Animal psychophysics' in Honig, W.K. and Staddon, J.E.R. (Eds), *Handbook of Operant Behavior*, Englewood Cliffs, N.J.; Prentice-Hall, pp. 514–39.
Boring, E.G. (1950) *A History of Experimental Psychology*, New York, Appleton-Century-Crofts.
Catania, A.C. (1982) 'Antimisrepresentationalism', *Behavior and Brain Sciences*, 3, pp. 374–5.
Cornsweet, T.N. (1970) *Visual Perception*, New York, Academic Press.
Epstein, R. (1982) 'Representation: A concept that fills no gaps', *Behavioral and Brain Sciences*, 3, pp. 377–8.
Evans, R.I. (1968) *B.F. Skinner: The Man and His Ideas*, New York, E.P. Dutton.
Gergen, K.J. (1985) 'The social constructionists movement in modern psychology', *American Psychologist*, 40, pp. 266–75.
Gibson, J.J. (1966) *Senses Considered As a Perceptual System*, Boston, Mass., Houghton-Mifflin.
Gilgen, A.R. (1982) *American Psychology since World War II: A Profile of the Discipline*, Westport, Conn., Greenwood.
Goldiamond, I. (1962) 'Perception', in Bachrach, A.J. (Ed.), *Experimental Foundations of Clinical Psychology*, New York, Basic Books, pp. 280–340.
Guttman, N. (1963) 'Laws of behavior and facts of perception', in Koch, S. (Ed.), *Psychology: A Study of a Science*, New York, McGraw-Hill, pp. 114–78
Hilgard, E.R. (1948) *Theories of Learning*, New York, Appleton-Century-Crofts.
Hochberg, J. (1979) 'Sensation and perception', in Hearst, E. (Ed.), *The First Century of Experimental Psychology*, Hillsdale, N.J., LEA.
Keller, F.S. and Schoenfeld, W.N. (1950) *Principles of Psychology*, New York, Appleton-Century-Crofts.
Mackintosh, N.J. (1977) 'Stimulus control: Attentional factors', in Honig, W.K. and Staddon, J.E.R. (Eds), *Handbook of Operant Behavior*, Englewood Cliffs, N.J., Prentice-Hall, pp. 481–513.
Mahoney, M.J. (1974) *Cognition and Behavior Modification*, Cambridge, Mass., Ballinger.
Malott, R.W. and Whaley, D.L. (1976) *Psychology*, New York, Harper and Row.
Matlin, M.W. (1983) *Perception*, Boston, Mass., Allyn and Bacon.
Neisser, U. (1967) *Cognitive Psychology*, New York, Appleton-Century-Crofts.
Nevin, J.A. (1973) 'Stimulus control', in Nevin, J.A. (Ed.), *The Study of Behavior*, Glenview, Ill., Scott, Foresman.

Palmer, S.E. (1978) 'Fundamental aspects of cognitive representation', in Rosch, E. and Lloyd, B. (Eds), *Cognition and Categorization*, Hillsdale, N.J., LEA.

Pastore, N. (1971) *Selective History of Theories of Visual Perception: 1650–1950*, New York, Oxford University Press.

Rilling, M. (1977) 'Stimulus control and inhibitory processes', in Honig, W.K. and Staddon, J.E.R. (Eds), *Handbook of Operant Behavior*, Englewood Cliffs, N.J., Prentice-Hall, pp. 432–48.

Robinson, D.N. (1986) 'Cognitive psychology and philosophy of mind', in Knapp, T.J. and Robertson, L.C. (Eds), *Approaches to Cognition: Contrasts and Controversies*, Hillsdale, N.J., LEA.

Rock, I. (1975) *An Introduction to Perception*, New York, Macmillan.

Rodewald, H.K. (1979) *Stimulus Control of Behavior*, Baltimore, Md., University Park Press.

Ryle, G. (1949) *The Concept of Mind*, New York, Barnes and Noble.

Salzinger, K. (1969) *Psychology: The Science of Behavior*, New York, Springer.

Schoenfeld, W.N. and Cumming, W.W. (1963) 'Behavior and perception', in Koch, S. (Ed.), *Psychology: A Study of a Science*, New York, McGraw-Hill.

Sekuler, R. and Blake, R. (1985) *Perception*, New York, Knopf.

Shakow, P. and Rosenzweig, S. (1940) 'The use of the tautophone ("verbal summator") as an auditory apperceptive test for the study of personality', *Character and Personality*, 8, pp. 216–26.

Skinner, B.F. (1932) 'A paradoxical color effect', *Journal of General Psychology*, 1, pp. 481–2.

Skinner, B.F. (1936) 'The verbal summator and a method for the study of latent speech', *Journal of General Psychology*, 2, pp. 71–107.

Skinner, B.F. (1938) *Behavior of Organisms: An Experimental Analysis of Behavior*, New York, Appleton-Century-Crofts.

Skinner, B.F. (1941) 'The psychology of design', in *Art Education Today*, New York, Bureau Publications, Teachers College, Columbia University, pp. 1–6.

Skinner, B.F. (1953) *Science and Human Behavior*, New York, Macmillan.

Skinner, B.F. (1957) *Verbal Behavior*, New York, Appleton-Century-Crofts.

Skinner, B.F. (1960) 'Pigeons in a pelican', *American Psychologist*, 15, pp. 28–37.

Skinner, B.F. (1965) 'Stimulus generalization in an operant: A historical note', in Mostofsky, D.I. (Ed.), *Stimulus Generalization*, Stanford, Calif., Stanford University Press, pp. 193–209

Skinner, B.F. (1969) *Contingencies of Reinforcement: A Theoretical Analysis*, New York, Appleton-Century-Crofts.

Skinner, B.F. (1974) *About Behaviorism*, New York, Knopf.

Skinner, B.F. (1977) 'Why I am not a cognitive psychologist', *Behaviorism*, 5, pp. 1–10.

Skinner, B.F. (1979) *Shaping of a Behaviorist*, New York, Knopf.

Skinner, B.F. (1980) *Notebooks*, Ed. by R. Epstein, Englewood Cliffs, N.J., Prentice-Hall.

Snygg, D. and Combs, A.W. (1949) *Individual Behavior: A New Frame of Reference for Psychology*, New York, Harper.

Terrace, H.S. (1966) 'Stimulus control', in Honig, W.K. (Ed.), *Operant Behavior: Areas of Research and Application*, New York, Appleton-Century-Crofts, pp. 271–344.

24. A Cognitive Approach to Behavior*

LYNN C. ROBERTSON

One of the problems with a dialogue such as the present one is that the schism between radical behaviorists and cognitive psychologists occurred several decades ago. In the ensuing years a great deal of work has been done within each area, but seldom has the same issue been studied with a similar paradigm nor are the same goals involved except in some broad sense of understanding behavior. Typically radical behaviorists plot learning curves representing how animals may learn to discriminate or categorize certain stimulus objects, but they would not bother to initiate questions about 'natural categories' and prototypes as Rosch (1973) so elegantly did. On the other hand, cognitive psychologists might plot the perceived similarity between items (Krumhansl, 1980; Shepard, 1957; Tversky, 1977) but neglect to ask how or even if environmental contingencies have anything to do with the observed relationship between items. Thus, there are few examples in which radical behaviorists and cognitive psychologists have worked on similar issues in similar ways. Perhaps this is because they are simply asking different questions. The radical behaviorist asks how behavior can be accounted for by the apparent history of the organism, and the cognitive psychologist asks how it can be accounted for by the structure and transformation of knowledge which the individual appears to possess.

Exceptions to this divergence have recently begun from the behaviorist's end and are best exemplified by the work of Robert Epstein. In collaboration with Skinner and others (Epstein, Lanza and Skinner, 1980a; Epstein, Lanza and Skinner, 1980b; Epstein and Skinner, 1981; Epstein, Kirshnit, Lanza and Rubin, 1984), Epstein has directly investigated such cognitive concepts as insight, self-

* Preparation of this chapter was partially supported by US Public Health Service grant award #AA 06637 to the author. I wish to thank Marvin Lamb for his invaluable comments on previous versions of this chapter.

awareness, and communication by manipulating animals' histories. The results are intriguing because they demonstrate that something like insightful behavior can be performed by such animals as pigeons, and that the probability of such behaviors can be changed by the environmental history of the animal. On the basis of such data Epstein (1986) argues that there is no need for a cognitive construct such as 'insight', because a complete account of insightful behavior can be made by reference to the history of the organism. In the present chapter I will discuss Epstein *et al.*'s work on insight to make my points because some radical behaviorists seem to believe it questions the fundamental bases of cognitive psychology and because it is one of the few instances where the differences and similarities between a cognitive and radical behaviorist approach can be examined with reference to fairly common procedures.

Since Epstein's findings will be a major focus of attention, I will first describe the results and place them within an historical perspective. This will be followed by a discussion of the important role that perception must play in interpreting the findings. I will end with an outline of why psychologists now feel comfortable with words such as 'mind'.

INSIGHT IN PIGEONS

A recent program begun by Skinner and Epstein is based upon demonstrating that after careful contingency control pigeons can produce behavior that many of us would call cognitive. For instance, if a pigeon is taught to push a box toward a green dot to receive food in some training sessions and taught to climb on the box to peck a caricature of a banana in another set of sessions, it will, when given the box and the banana separated in the chamber, push the box under the banana, climb onto the box and peck the banana. It will not push the box randomly about the chamber but will push it in the direction of the banana and will stop pushing when the box is under the banana. When pigeons are not trained to climb on the box, they do not 'solve the problem' in the experimental session, nor do they do so when they are not taught to push the box directionally.

The interpretation of these results is in terms of the history of the animal. That is, both Skinner and Epstein suggest that all that is needed to explain insightful behavior in the pigeon is a reference to its behavioral repertoire as a result of its environmental history. This explanation, however, avoids the larger issue of how two behaviors are combined to form a new behavior and how the 'correct' behaviors are selected from the entire behavioral experience. It is here that perception comes into play. The perception versus environmental history debate actually has its roots in an earlier period, and before I make the case for perception, a brief overview of the arguments may be enlightening.

In 1926 Higginson published an article entitled 'Visual Perception in the White Rat'. Helson followed in 1927 with 'Insight in the White Rat' and Maier reported a series of studies in 1929 on 'reasoning in the white rat'. This was also the era of Tolman who with Honzik wrote a paper entitled 'Insight in Rats' (1930). All of these studies demonstrated insightful behavior in species other than primates.

Papers such as these were met with harsh rebuttal by behaviorists, and what followed was a lively debate concerning how to characterize such high abilities in

animals with such small brains and, indeed, how to define 'insight' at all. Although the debate cut across several categories of cognition, the arguments surrounding 'insight' often employed references to perception. This occurred for various reasons, not the least of which was that Gestalt psychologists (including, of course, Kohler who performed the original studies on insight in apes) had always argued against the notion that different categories of behavior were governed by different principles. Insightful behavior referred to an animal *perceiving* the world in a new way and followed the same rules as those of perception in general. Although perception was not a function of learning, the Gestalt psychologists did not deny that experience was necessary; nor do contemporary cognitive psychologists. They only denied (and deny) that learning was (is) sufficient to understand the phenomena in full (see Robertson, 1986, for a discussion of the relationship between the Gestalt views of perception and contemporary views).

This scenario is again playing prime time in 1986. Epstein, Kirshnit, Lanza and Rubin's published paper is entitled 'Insight in the Pigeon'. Photographs of pigeons being 'insightful' have graced the pages of *The New York Times* (Science Watch, 17 April 1984) and can be seen on film at various professional meetings and in introductory classes across the country. The debates concerning the significance of this work have appeared both in the literature (Gallup, 1983; Riley, Brown and Yoerg, 1986) and face-to-face (Robertson, 1983, 1984; Epstein, 1983, 1984).

'Insight in Pigeons' is part of a series of studies, the goal of which is to demonstrate that cognitive phenomena can be explained through the history of the animal. Reminiscent of the Gestalt psychologist's position, I will argue that without a concept like perception, the interesting questions cannot be fully addressed. I will leave for others the discussion of possible methodological flaws or distinctions between Epstein's and Kohler's work (e.g., Ettinger, 1984). Instead, I will assume that pigeons do produce 'insightful' behavior similar in nature to Kohler's apes. I will grant Epstein and Skinner their claims and then address the issues of relevance concerning those claims.

PERCEPTION AND CONTINGENCIES

In this section I develop the idea that contingencies are only effective as perceived, and I examine how the perception of contingencies in one situation affects the perception of contingencies in a subsequent situation. The argument has relevance for both behavioral and cognitive approaches. On the one hand, I will freely admit that the probability of perceiving certain controlling variables *can* be a function of the environmental history of the organism, but in a way which has not readily been considered by radical behaviorists. On the other hand, my reference to perception is a reference to the organizing ability of the perceptual system, and I will argue that this is best understood within the framework of a cognitive psychology.

Before I address these issues I will summarize my understanding of the radical behaviorist position so there will be no confusion about where my arguments apply: any living organism behaves as it does due to the contingencies of reinforcement (that is, due to the antecedents and consequences of its behavior). Other behaviors in humans are derived from the verbal community which controls

rule-governed behavior — it can tell us what the rules are. Both reinforcement histories and the verbal community change the brain. The controls are assumed to be physical and, therefore, directly measurable. In the physical brain we measure physiology and neuroanatomy. The radical behaviorist's position is that the scientist cannot know the representation of something like a ball except as a pattern of neural firing. Although the change in brain firing, or more abstractly the change in the state of the organism, only correlates with changes in contingencies, the behaviorist's bias is to view the process as unidirectional. Contingencies are first and, therefore, change the brain. The brain does not change contingencies through, for instance, the perception or reconception of such contingencies.

Behaviorists often refer to mental processes as fiction, because they feel the word 'mental' clouds the issue of representation — namely brain processes. There are no cognitive mechanisms, there are only neurophysiological mechanisms, and these are changed by the antecedents to and consequences of behavior. Memory can be redefined as a change in the organism that increases the probability of a response, (for example, behaviorists feel their position is supported if memory is associated with the hippocampus), but the control of interest originates in the environment outside the organism.

Superficially, work such as Epstein *et al.* has suggested that at least one cognitive construct — namely insight — can be explained by the reinforcement history of their subjects. It is fascinating that pigeons can produce insightful behavior, but I do not see how demonstrating insight in pigeons after careful shaping of behavior clarifies the question of how behavior we call 'insightful' is derived. I do know that Behavior X (pushing a box) and Behavior Y (climbing on a box) must be available (that is, they must be in the behavioral repertoire). I also know that these behaviors can be available by introducing Contingency X and Contingency Y into the animal's environment. But the real question is: where does Behavior Z come from? All we have in this known world is Contingency X, Contingency Y, Behavior X, Behavior Y and an integration that is represented by Behavior Z. Whether the integration is derived from Contingencies X and Y or Behaviors X and Y or some combination thereof, the result is the formation of a relationship where no prior relationship existed. There can be no Behavior Z except by a relationship between Contingencies X and Y and/or Behaviors X and Y. It is this *relationship* that puts the problem of insight back into the organism. Contingencies X and Y are not and never have been related in the external environment, nor have Behaviors X and Y. The relating must come from somewhere else. When a pigeon is placed in a novel environment where Contingency X and Contingency Y are no longer operative, and Behavior X and Behavior Y alone do not do the job, what happens? Behavior Z emerges. In order for this to occur, the animal must somehow register the possibility of a new contingency, and it must produce a new string of behaviors. The emergent property of Z is particularly important. An emergent behavior is not a simple chaining because aspects of Behavior Z are not represented in Behaviors X and Y (e.g., the ordering of X and Y, the spatial relationship between pushing and climbing, etc.). Something more is needed — something that integrates or relates X and Y. I shall call this something 'perception' because it appears that the organism must perceive (not to be confused with awareness) the environment and the behavioral relationship to that environment in a new way. It is the perception of relationships that counts. It is this change in perception that can result in a

reorganization of behavior that can be called insightful. I would never say that this is independent of brain changes, but I think I get to the essence of the issue by using the word 'perception' rather than describing the neurophysiological changes that occur while perceptual reorganization takes place. (More will be said of this in the section on 'Levels of Analysis'.)

It may appear that I am using the word 'perception' rather loosely. I am using the term 'perception' when referring to contingencies because I do not see how the activity is much different from discovering that a subset of energy in a given location is a unit such as a chair, which may co-vary with some subset of energy in another location such as a table. In both contingency perception and form perception a naive system must discover the potential afforded by the environment. This is, of course, limited by the environmental energy and the structure of the brain.

The conceptual change that I have made from talking about contingencies as they exist and contingencies as they are perceived brings me to a second issue which centers on the notion that contingencies and their relationship to behavior are stimulus events that can be perceptually organized and represented just like any other event. The concept of 'contingencies of reinforcement' is highly abstract despite the comfortable feeling that antecedents and consequences appear more objective than internal events and, therefore, so much easier to measure. But contingencies are simply *potential* changes that must be uncovered by a behaving system. A naive system must discover how the energy outside itself will react to its movements. The consequences of behavior manifest themselves through the act of behaving, but contingencies only exist for the organism once relationships are perceived, not merely experienced. Different organisms/species may experience the same contingencies but perceive them differently.

My use of the word 'perception' to refer to discovering contingencies is not new. There is experimental evidence that supports the use of the concept in this regard. The line of research has typically been categorized as the investigation of 'learned helplessness' and, as such, has been more in line with clinical interests. The term was popularized by Martin Seligman (1975), based on data collected by Steven Maier and himself (1967). They showed that when an animal is placed in an environment where a relationship is difficult to form between an outcome and a behavior, the animal will be less likely to respond to contingencies in another environment where a relationship potentially exists. This 'learned helplessness' effect occurs whether the original conditions include aversive or appetitive stimuli (Engberg, Hanson, Welker and Thomas, 1973; Gamzu and Williams, 1971; Welker, 1976), whether the required behavior is action or inhibition of action (Maier, 1970) and whether the subjects are rats or humans (Hiroto, 1974; Roth and Kubel, 1975). On the basis of findings such as these Seligman suggested that there was a cognitive component to the phenomenon, and John Watson at the University of California, Berkeley has suggested that 'learned helplessness', at least in some cases, is produced by interference in *perceiving* contingencies.

Watson placed mobiles over the cribs of 8-week-old babies for several weeks. One group of infants could control the mobile with a head movement (reinforcement-dependent), while for another group the mobile moved only a proportion of the time that an infant moved its head (reinforcement-independent), and the rest of the time the mobile moved when the infant was doing something else. Infants in the reinforcement-dependent condition later

showed better learning performance in a different task compared to those in the reinforcement-independent condition.

Watson claimed that infants in the reinforcement-dependent condition perceived the relationship between their environments and their behavior while those in the reinforcement-independent condition did not. His notion, then, is that the probability of perceiving a relationship between behavior and contingencies can be a function of a prior reinforcement schedule. What seems to have occurred during this schedule, however, is the instantiation of an abstract notion — namely that contingencies can be perceived in different ways if one only looks.

An unfortunate side effect of lack of perceiving relationships can be depression. This is probably why the findings have become so interesting to clinical researchers, and, in turn, have needlessly become less interesting to cognitive psychologists. But when we ask, 'how are contingencies perceived?', the problem becomes a cognitive one. The learned helplessness literature has shown that perceiving no relationship in one situation interferes with the perception of relationships in a second situation. Despite the fact that the stimulus, response and outcome may have occurred in the external environment with equal frequency, a relationship is formed only when a reinforcement-dependent schedule has been experienced. Thus, a reinforcement-dependent schedule appears to set the stage for a subsequent cognitive process — relation formation.

There can be little doubt that discovering contingencies in one's environment is beneficial for the general well-being if not survival of the organism. A pigeon who does not see a way of obtaining hanging food will not survive long if the only source of food is high above its head. Furthermore, although the exact experiment has not been done, it appears that a pigeon would be less likely to manifest 'insightful' behavior if it had previously been frustrated in forming a relationship between some other behavior and some other outcome on a previous occasion despite having appropriate behaviors in its behavioral repertoire and despite the fact that the other behavior and other outcome had occurred many times before. It is not behavior that is disrupted *directly*, but the ability to form a relationship that is deficient. Thus, the reinforcement history has its effect on some process which forms relationships. Similarly, it is not the reinforcement history that determines overt behavior *directly*. It is the reinforcement history that determines the probability of forming a relationship. The motivation to use a cognitive process is couched in the history of the organism, but relating two objectively unrelated elements or events rests on the act of integration.

In sum, insightful behavior relies on the perception of contingencies in a novel situation which, in turn, relies on the perception of contingencies in a previous situation. If what we mean by perception is the formation of relationships from differences or changes in energy, then the word 'perception' seems to be an accurate reference. Relationships do not functionally exist in the energy outside the organism. One event does not follow the other in some external space. 'Following' is a word organisms use to impose structure on a change in energy, not the other way around.

These processes depend in part on perceptual organization which places them under the cognitive banner. The fact that insightful behavior can, at least in part, be predicted by a particular reinforcement history does not remove it from the cognitive category. While the data from Epstein *et al.*'s pigeons are intriguing and important, they have little to say about the viability of cognitive explanations. To

believe that data such as theirs somehow shake the foundation of cognitive psychology is to misunderstand the fundamental nature of such a psychology.

In the next section I will therefore outline the general framework which has been used to justify cognitive psychology, including the role of the computer metaphor. I want to emphasize that one need never have touched a computer to operate within this metaphor. The conceptualization could have been developed without the advent of the computer, although the computer made the concepts salient and credible.

LEVELS OF ANALYSIS AND BEHAVIOR

Although there have been other systems in the past which could have generated enthusiasm over the concept of levels of analysis in psychology (see Knapp, 1986), the machine which actually did so was the computer. The computer has a hardware and a software level of operation. One need know virtually nothing about hardware in order to understand software and vice versa. There is a level of analysis which defines the hard-wired parts of a computer, and there is a level of analysis which defines the programs. Different types of programs can be compatible with several different sorts of hardware. It is clear, of course, that for a program to run, a physical system is necessary. This is the essence of the computer metaphor and its 'solution' to the so-called mind-body problem. There are different levels of analysis for the act of thinking. The brain is the hard-wired apparatus on which 'programs' run. Thus, we can describe an act of the brain as a neurophysiological event embedded in the language of anatomy and physiology, or we can describe it as a series of logical operations. 'Mind' in this sense is not a fiction unless the very words we use to describe all events are fictions (in which case there are no distinctions between those words describing an electrical or chemical event in physical terms and those describing it in psychological terms). There is no mind-body dualism. There are only different levels at which events are analyzed. However, analyzing or describing events at different levels ultimately leads to different discoveries, partly because the dimensions at one level can be represented differently from the dimensions at another. For instance, events can be parsed cognitively that appear continuous neurophysiologically (e.g., the 'beginning' of a sentence). I want to emphasize that the computer metaphor does not mean we are computers. We clearly are not. Rather we are information processing systems as are computers. Within the information processing view of cognition it is only at this level of description that computers and people are at all alike. (See Palmer and Kimchi, 1986, for a thorough discussion of the assumptions that underlie the information process approach to cognition.)

The levels notion was not invented by cognitive psychologists. Skinner in fact argues from a similar footing when he notes that the study of behavior is independent from the study of physiology. In fact, behavior by definition, whether overt or covert, is always at a different level of analysis from physiology. It appears that Skinner (e.g., 1984) may understand this, but his students have often lost touch with his insight, and have argued distinctly contradictory points when talking about cognition. Skinner claims that thinking is 'simply more behavior which needs to be explained' (1974, p. 104), while other radical behaviorists often argue that 'mental processes' are only explainable as neurophysiology (e.g., Epstein,

1981). If cognition is behavior, the relationship between overt behavior and physiology must be the same as between 'cognitive behavior' and physiology. These are descriptions at a different level of analysis from the ones used by the neurophysiologist or the physicist. Cognition including perception need not be reduced to physiology any more than overt behavior need be reduced to physiology. The issue is not whether thinking is or is not a fiction or whether it is best described as neurophysiology or cognitive psychology. The issue is how behavior emerges.

EMERGENT BEHAVIOR

In the past few years Skinner's strongest objection to cognitive psychology has centered on its causal role in behavior. His argument is something like this: cognition *is* behavior, so how can it *cause* behavior? One answer is that the mechanisms of cognition (its subcomponents) can 'cause' behavior in the sense that they are necessary for emergent behavior to occur. There is nothing magical or unrealistic about the use of the word 'cause' in this regard. If the question is: can behavior cause emergent (or new) behavior?, the answer is 'yes'. Interactions between smaller units of behavior are necessary conditions for the emergence of a more extensive new behavior which is not present in the individual parts themselves. Would one really want to argue, for instance, that using the hand as a paddle to push oneself through the water does not, in part, cause swimming. Of course it causes swimming when in a particular spatio-temporal relation to other parts. It is a subbehavior which is part of a unit of activity that we more generally call swimming. In the insight experiments I discussed earlier, Epstein *et al.*'s pigeons produced a new behavior from distinct behaviors in their behavioral repertoire configured in a certain spatio-temporal relation, and the history of the animals indeed caused, at least in part, the novel behavior, but again only in the sense that the behaviors were necessary for the new behavior to emerge. This does not mean, however, that the original behaviors were an exhaustive list of the necessary components for new behavior to emerge.

As I argued in an earlier section, the intriguing question is how new behavior emerges from the combination of previous behaviors. This has been a prevailing issue for cognitive psychologists in an analogous form for some time. Part of what a cognitive psychologist may want to know is how subparts (modules or stages) of a system can create conditions from which a new result emerges. How do the individual components of a system interact to produce a distinct whole, and what parts are relevant in what ways for such an occurrence?

This issue cuts across several disciplines and across several categories of interest. I am most familiar with it as it relates to perception, and this is where I will focus my comments. However, I want to emphasize that the general problems found in understanding emergent properties in perception are relevant for any domain in which parts appear combined into wholes. When two behaviors are integrated to produce novel behavior, two parts are combined from which new behavior emerges just as two elements can be perceived in isolation but can lose their individuality in a new form when combined.

This was the theme of the Gestalt psychologists early this century when they noted that 'the whole is different from the sum of its parts'. Some contemporary

cognitive psychologists have translated the Gestalt statement into 'the whole is prior to the parts' with 'prior to' meaning 'processed before'. In fact, several studies have found that reaction times are longer when subjects are asked to respond to parts than when they are asked to respond to wholes (Navon, 1977; Robertson and Palmer, 1983; but see Pomerantz, 1981, for a discussion of qualifications in the conditions under which this will occur). The fact that this is ever the case suggests that all the details or parts need not be articulated (although they must of course be present) for the whole to emerge. Hue and saturation must be present for color to emerge, yet what we see is color. Color is an emergent property (Garner, 1974). A forest is created from a collection of trees, yet we perceive a forest. It is visible, and we need not perceive its constituent parts even when individual trees are clearly in view. There are also some brain damaged patients who do not see the parts of a stimulus which can be seen by normals, yet can perceive the emergent properties (Delis, Robertson and Efron, 1986; Robertson and Delis, in press). In all cases the parts must necessarily exist in the stimulus energy, but whether they will be seen as individual parts is a matter of attention, effort, perspective and the limitations of the system. There is no reason why individual behaviors which emerge into a new behavior do not require equivalent concepts.

There are also conditions in which wholes do not emerge from parts (e.g., Kimchi and Palmer, 1982; Goldmeier, 1972/1936; Pomerantz, 1981). When subjects are asked to respond whether a single parenthesis '('faces leftward or rightward, it is easier to do so in '(('vs'))' than in '(('vs'()' (Pomerantz and Garner, 1973). The element maintains its individuality in the first shape but must be separated from the whole in the second. Again, there are some brain damaged populations that do not synthesize elements to form an emergent whole (Delis, Robertson and Efron, 1986; Robertson and Delis, in press). The mere existence of the elements is not sufficient to explain their combination, just as the mere existence of two behaviors is not sufficient to explain their combination.

Although the answers to how these phenomena occur are not altogether clear, the issues they point to are relevant any time we ask the question: how do things change when two elements come together? We could ask this when considering atoms, chemicals, features or behaviors. It may be that in some conditions something like 'insight' behavior in pigeons is the simple addition of two behaviors. In other conditions the component behaviors must be integrated to produce an emergent behavior that does not exist in the two components independently. The type of situation in which Epstein's pigeons or Kohler's apes found themselves can only be evaluated through careful experimentation.

SUMMARY

Operant and cognitive psychologists have been operating in their individual arenas far too long. Cognitive psychology could benefit from operant psychology by addressing the question of how cognitive mechanisms may change as a function of a subject's history. Does the very use of a particular cognitive process depend on environmental contingencies in the past? The evidence from the studies of contingency perception suggests it might. I have examined one such process — relation formation — and have argued that operant psychologists should consider

such a mechanism in discussing how something like 'insight in pigeons' takes place. We need not describe this process at a neurophysiological level in order to understand how it works any more than we need to describe overt behavior at a neurophysiological level to understand how it works. The level at which one operates depends critically on the question one wishes to address and the type of phenomenon that one is studying.

REFERENCES

Delis, D.C., Robertson, L.C. and Efron, R. (1986) 'Hemispheric specialization of memory for visual hierarchical stimuli', *Neuropsychologia*, 24, pp. 205–14.

Engberg, L.A., Hanson, G., Welker, R.L., Thomas, D.R. (1973) 'Acquisition of key-pecking via autoshaping as a function of prior experience: "Learned laziness"?' *Science*, 179, pp. 1002–4.

Epstein, R. (1981) 'On pigeons and people: A preliminary look at the Columban simulation project', *The Behavior Analyst*, 4, pp. 43–55.

Epstein, R. (1983) 'An experimental analysis of cognition', paper presented at Western Psychological Association, San Francisco.

Epstein, R. (1984) 'Bringing complex phenomenon into the behavioral laboratory', paper presented at Rocky Mountain Psychological Association, Las Vegas.

Epstein, R. (1986) 'Bringing cognition and creativity into the behavioral laboratory', in Knapp, T.J. and Robertson, L.C. (Eds), *Approaches to Cognition: Contrasts and Controversies*, Hillsdale, N.J., Lawrence Erlbaum.

Epstein, R. and Skinner, B.F. (1981) 'The spontaneous use of memoranda in pigeons' *Behavior Analysis Letters*, 1, pp. 241–6.

Epstein, R., Kirshnit, C.E., Lanza, R.P. and Rubin, L.C. (1984) '"Insight" in the pigeon: Antecedents and determinants of an intelligent performance', *Nature*, pp. 61–2.

Epstein, R., Lanza, R. and Skinner, B.F. (1980a) 'Symbolic communication between two pigeons', *Science*, 207, pp. 543–5.

Epstein, R., Lanza, R.P. and Skinner, B.F. (1980b) '"Self-awareness" in pigeons', *Science*, 212, pp. 695–6.

Ettinger, G. (1984) 'Humans, apes and monkeys: The changing neuropsychological viewpoint', *Neuropsychologia*, 22, pp. 685–96.

Gallup, G.G. (1983) 'Toward a comparative psychology of mind', in Mellgren, R.L. (Ed.), *Animal Cognition and Behavior*, New York, North-Holland.

Gamzu and Williams (1971) 'Classical conditioning of a complex skeletal response', *Science*, 171, pp. 923–5.

Garner, W.R. (1974) *The Processing of Information and Structure*, Hillsdale, N.J., Lawrence Erlbaum.

Goldmeier, E. (1972/1936) 'Similarity in visually perceived forms', *Psychological Issues*, No. 29; originally published in *Psychologishe Forschung*, 1936, 21, pp. 146–208.

Helson, H. (1927) 'Insight in the white rat', *Journal of Experimental Psychology*, 10, pp. 378–96.

Higginson, G.D. (1926) 'Visual perception in the white rat', *Journal of Experimental Psychology*, 9, pp. 337–47.

Hiroto, D.S. (1974) 'Locus of control and learned helplessness', *Journal of Experimental Psychology*, 102, pp. 187–93.

Kimchi, R. and Palmer, S.E. (1982) 'Form and texture in hierarchically constructed patterns', *Journal of Experimental Psychology: Human Perception and Performance*, 8, pp. 521–35.

Knapp, T.J. (1986) 'The emergence of cognitive psychology in the latter half of the twentieth century', in Knapp, T.J. and Robertson, L.C. (Eds), *Approaches to Cognition: Contrasts and Controversies*, Hillsdale, N.J., Lawrence Erlbaum.

Krumhansl, C.L. (1978) 'Concerning the applicability of geometric models to similarity data: The interrelationship between similarity and spatial density', *Psychological Review*, 85, pp. 445–63.

Maier, N.R.F. (1929) 'Reasoning in white rats', *Comparative Psychology Monographs*, 6, No. 3.

Maier, S.F. (1970) 'Failure to escape traumatic shock: Incompatible skeletal motor responses or learned helplessness?' *Learning and Motivation*, 1, pp. 157–70.

Navon, D. (1977) 'Forest before trees: The precedence of global features in visual perception', *Cognitive Psychology*, 9, pp. 441–74.

Palmer, S.E. and Kimchi, R. (1986) 'The information processing approach to cognition', in Knapp, T.J. and Robertson, L.C. (Eds), *Approaches to Cognition: Contrasts and Controversies*, Hillsdale, N.J., Lawrence Erlbaum.

Pomerantz, J.R. (1981) 'Perceptual organization in information processing', in Kubovy, M. and Pomerantz, J.R. (Eds), *Perceptual Organization*, Hillsdale, N.J., Lawrence Erlbaum.

Pomerantz, J.R. and Garner, W.H. (1973) 'Stimulus configuration in selective attention tasks', *Perception and Psychophysics*, 14, pp. 565–9.

Riley, D.A., Brown, M.F. and Yoerg, S.I. (1986) 'Understanding animal cognition', in Knapp, T.J. and Robertson, L.C. (Eds), *Approaches to Cognition: Contrasts and Controversies*, Hillsdale, N.J., Lawrence Erlbaum.

Robertson, L.C. (1983) 'Do reinforcement histories have implications for cognitive psychology?' Paper presented at the Western Psychological Association, San Francisco.

Robertson, L.C. (1984) 'The perceptual organization of contingencies', Paper presented at the Rocky Mountain Psychological Association, Las Vegas.

Robertson, L.C. (1986) 'From gestalt to neo-gestalt', in Knapp, T.J. and Robertson, L.C. (Eds), *Approaches to Cognition: Contrasts and Controversies*, Hillsdale, N.J., Lawrence Erlbaum.

Robertson, L.C. and Delis, D.C. (in press) '"Part-whole" processing in unilateral brain damaged patients: Dysfunction of hierarchical organization', *Neuropsychologia*.

Robertson, L.C. and Palmer, S.E. (1983) 'Holistic processes in the perception and transformation of disoriented figures', *Journal of Experimental Psychology: Human Perception and Performance*, 9, pp. 203–14.

Rosch, E.H. (1973) 'On the internal structure of perceptual and semantic categories', in Moore, T.E. (Ed.), *Cognitive Development and the Acquisition of Language*, New York, Academic Press.

Roth, S. and Kubel, L. (1975) 'Effects of noncontingent reinforcement on tasks of differing importance: Facilitation and learned helplessness', *Journal of Personality and Social Psychology*, 32, pp. 680–91.

Seligman, M.E.P. (1975) *Helplessness*, San Francisco, Calif., W.H. Freeman.

Seligman, M.E.P. and Maier, S.F. (1967) 'Failure to escape traumatic shock', *Journal of Experimental Psychology*, 74, pp. 1–9.

Shepard, R.N. (1957) 'Stimulus and response generalization: A stochastic model relating generalization to distance in psychological space', *Psychometrika*, 22, pp. 325–45.

Skinner, B.F. (1974) *About Behaviorism*, New York, Alfred Knopf.

Skinner, B.F. (1977) 'Why I am not a cognitive psychologist', *Behaviorism*, 5, pp. 1–10.

Skinner, B.F. (1984) 'Behaviorism at fifty', *Behavior and Brain Sciences*, 7, pp. 615–67.

Tolman, E.C. and Honzik, C.H. (1930) '"Insight" in rats', *University of California Publications in Psychology*, 4, pp. 215–32.

Tversky, A. (1977) 'Features of similarity', *Psychological Review*, 84, pp. 327–52.

Welker, R.L. (1976) 'Acquisition of a free-operant-appetitive response in pigeons as a function of prior experience with response-independent food', *Learning and Motivation*, 7, pp. 394–405.

Interchange

KNAPP REPLIES TO ROBERTSON

I believe it is accurate to say that the kinds of general concerns which guide the activities of contemporary cognitive psychologists as well as the general experimental psychologists who preceded them are fundamentally different from what has guided Skinner's research and writing. It may also be true that some drift has occurred among those who are associated with the experimental analysis of behavior such that it is difficult at times to see how their activities and concerns differ all that much from the larger community of experimental, particularly animal, psychologists. This trend has not always pleased the radical behaviorist community, and a number of commentators have lamented it, while others have attempted more direct corrective action.

The role which Robertson wishes to make for perception is a broad one and is in no fashion limited to the 'problems of perception' but rather results in a 'perceptual psychology'. In this regard her case is better understood, I believe, as a set of arguments for a particular form of representationalism, one that I find hard to distinguish from the earlier cases made in psychology for intervening variables or hypothetical constructs. The issues are thus old ones, and I wonder where the work of Skinner or the experimental analysis of behavior would be had the time been taken to engage them fully. Whatever the ultimate fate of radical behaviorism, I believe it probably has benefited by its isolation from mainstream psychology.

Robertson wants to know how two or more repertoires of behavior are integrated. Epstein, Skinner, and co-workers have given one kind of a reasonable answer by discovering the necessary and sufficient conditions to produce the 'integration', that is, the novel behavior. Another kind of answer may someday be provided by neurophysiologists. How does a behind-the-scenes story add to either of these kinds of answers?

Wondering how an organism 'perceives' a contingency is not far from wondering how a species 'perceives' evolution. The environment selects. To be sure an organism can come under the discriminative control of a visual stimulus, and presumably can be made to come under the discriminative control of a 'relation', or 'contingency'. Do organisms form relationships, or are the relationships formed as arrangements in the environment? It is the old matter of locating the associations where they occur, rather than having the organism 'make' the associations.

Skinner has discussed in sections which were not reviewed in my chapter the problem of knowledge, and the difficulties arising from knowledge conceived as a possession. When cognitive psychologists take up such matters it usually leads to a

kind of structuralism. The problems with this view are also discussed by Skinner. If any possibility of common agreement exists in this regard between radical behaviorists and cognitivists, it may be the manner in which some cognitive psychologists have now come to perform what behavior analysis terms 'task analysis'. This is usually done for purposes of constructing the representation employed by the subject, but the analysis itself can be useful and in some respects necessarily leads the cognitivist back to the environment and to the responses of the organism.

ROBERTSON REPLIES TO KNAPP

Knapp's analysis of perception versus response psychologies is important and revealing. At this level of discussion I believe we are in agreement. There is no question that reinforcement histories influence behavior. There is also no question that the way one perceives the world influences behavior. It is not sufficient, however, to attribute perception to stimulus control. After all, perception functions not only on the antecedent side of contingencies but also on the consequence side. Something must detect an antecedent as a potential for reinforcement and register the change in environmental energy as a result of behaving. It must also detect the co-variation of energy before and after behaving. Whether or not one calls this detection 'perception', it is reasonable to assume that there is some internal mechanism which mediates antecedents and consequences. As I discussed in my chapter, some data have supported a perceptual role in the effectiveness of contingency control.

In response to the issue of internal representation (which I did not address in my chapter), Skinner's infinite regress argument may have been relevant for earlier views of representationalism but is inadequate against recent theories (e.g., Marr, 1982; Johnson-Laird, 1983). A cognitive representation is nothing more than a set of computations that are related to each other in some way that mimics the relationships between structures in the world. We are not looking at copies of what we see. We are looking at the world but make sense of it through a computational system. This is analogous to a digital computer which computes the world in base 2 because any other base would simply be impossible for that system. A digital computer does not make copies of copies, each of which it must examine. Rather, as a result of the computations (limited by the input, the base and the routines it uses), a certain type of representation emerges. If a digital computer could respond to contingencies, it too would be represented in base 2 and limited in the same way. This, of course, does not mean that people represent the world in base 2. It simply demonstrates that whatever means we use, it does not require copies of copies.

Finally, when Skinner is pushed to address issues of cognition such as perception he often resorts to arguments concerning value or importance. He may ask: even if cognitive psychologists are discovering something interesting, is it useful? Once the role of something like perception is even considered in contingency effectiveness, its possible importance must be included in all Skinner's examples of value. For instance, who can say whether it is the environment or the percep-

tion of the environment that has created conditions such that the human race can extinguish itself at any moment? Who is to say whether changes in the environmental history, changes in the perception and representation of those environmental histories or either will reduce this prospect? To argue that one is more important than another in solving the ills of society (whether because one is more difficult to study or because it just seems less important) is (1) like playing only one number on the roulette table and (2) to ignore the fact that the political arena is impervious to arguments by scientists unless they meet existing goals. I am not opposed to a sense of value in addressing scientific issues, but arguments based on bias or utopian ideals that one type of research has more value than another should be left to novels. These are not appropriate bases from which to argue for scientific omission or revision.

REFERENCES

Johnson-Laird, P.N. (1983) *Mental Models*, Cambridge, Mass., Harvard University Press.
Marr, D. (1982) *Vision*, San Francisco, Calif., W.H. Freeman.

Part XIV: Naturalistic Ethics

25. Naturalist Ethics

GERALD ZURIFF

What is the reason for the oft-noted difference between human progress in science and the abysmal lack thereof in solving social and political problems? Perhaps a fundamental distinction between scientific and ethical knowledge bears responsibility. Science involves matters of empirical fact to which all must accede while ethics deals with values over which there is not only general disagreement, but also no means for achieving consensus. Therefore, thinkers have long sought ways to derive an ethical system from factual matters of science, to deduce what one *ought* to do from what *is* the case, to distill evaluations from descriptions. In this tradition of naturalist ethics, Skinner (1953, Ch. 28; 1971, Ch. 6) contributes a version based on his behaviorist vision of society. His proposed science of ethics, supported by his science of behavior, promises to resolve ethical questions by the objective, empirical, and naturalistic methods of science. My purposes are threefold. First, I shall explicate what I take to be Skinner's Naturalist Deduction, that is, his methods for deriving ethical judgments from statements of scientific fact. Second, I shall examine what this Naturalist Deduction does and does not accomplish. Third, I shall elaborate on his behaviorist ethics.

THE NATURALIST DEDUCTION

Skinner's analysis begins with the observation that generally the things people tend to call 'good' are positive reinforcers, defined as stimuli which strengthen the behavior they follow. Among these positive reinforcers Skinner distinguishes two types: those which are reinforcing for an individual and those which are reinforcing for members of society in general. For example, lying in a particular instance may be reinforcing for an individual who therefore calls it 'good', but the other members of society not reinforced by this individual's lying will instead call honesty 'good'.[1] In addition, Skinner notes, some things, not necessarily reinforcing to the individual or to others, are also called 'good', namely, things which contribute to the long-term survival of the culture.

Let us define the property R as the property of being (1) reinforcing to the individual *or* (2) reinforcing to others *or* (3) contributory to the long-term survival of a culture. Skinner's analysis appears to show that goodness can be identified with R. Since R is a natural, empirically observable property, the good can be scientifically determined. Questions of value can be settled empirically by science, in particular by the science of behavior which specializes in studying reinforcement and cultural survival.

Because Skinner's ethical system allows the derivation of 'X is good' from 'X has R', it is a naturalist ethics in one important sense. There is, in addition, a second sense in which it is a naturalist ethics. The derivation of 'X is good' from 'X has R' is mediated by a suppressed premise:

For all X, X is good if and only if X has R.

Let us call this premise, the essence of Skinner's ethics, the 'Naturalist Principle'. This Naturalist Principle is a value judgment; it tells us what is good. What is the justification for the Naturalist Principle? If the Naturalist Principle is itself derived from scientific matters of fact as Skinner implies, then his ethical system is naturalistic in what I shall term the 'strong sense' (see Frankena, 1939, for a discussion of the different senses of naturalism). This derivation of the Naturalist Principle from matters of fact is what I call the 'Naturalist Deduction' which can be reconstructed roughly along these lines:

1   People say 'X is good' if and only if X has R.
2   Therefore, X is good if and only if X has R.
3   One ought to do the good.
4   Therefore, one ought to do X if and only if X has R.

In this derivation, the conclusion (4), an ought-statement, is derived from the first premise (1), an is-statement in the form of an empirical description, although currently only a plausible hypothesis. The derivation is mediated by (3), a tautology. The second premise (2) is, of course, the Naturalist Principle, and it is derived from (1) by a suppressed premise to the effect that if people correctly use the word 'W' to refer to Y, then the meaning of 'W' is Y. One could, along with G.E. Moore (1903/1966, p. 12), question this derivation of (2) from (1) and ask whether the fact that people *say* something is good necessarily implies that it *is* good, but this is not my present concern, and I will grant the derivation (for a fuller discussion see Hocutt, 1977).

What I do wish to examine is a striking paradox in Skinner's *Beyond Freedom and Dignity* and the implications of this paradox. As shown above, Skinner's Naturalist Deduction begins with an observation about verbal behavior, about how people emit the word 'good'. However, the book is not merely, or even chiefly, a dispassionate analysis of behavior. Instead, it is a remarkable appeal for *changes* in human behavior. Skinner urges his readers to adopt forms of action to promote the survival of the human species. Most of the book is an elaboration of what these actions are and how certain traditional ideas have impeded their adoption. The paradox is this: on the one hand, Skinner takes our normal use of the word 'good' as definitive and as the basis for his notion of good, but on the other hand, he uses his notion of good to argue for a change in our use of 'good'. If Skinner accepts verbal behavior as it is, then all he can do is describe it and not

evaluate it. If, on the other hand, he uses his science to evaluate and promote a change in verbal behavior, then the justification for his value judgment must come from a source other than verbal behavior as it is.

CONFICTS AMONG VALUE COMMUNITIES

One possible resolution to this paradox is to suggest that Skinner is not making a value judgment, but is rather clarifying matters of fact. Perhaps he is merely explaining the consequences of various courses of action so that speakers have more accurate information about the R properties of the options available to them. Given this information, people will adopt the social practices Skinner advocates.

This suggestion, however, does not resolve the paradox. It is clear from the widespread reaction of the readers whose behavior Skinner is trying to change that the conflict between him and his critics is not over consequences or other matters of fact. The most poignant illustration of this is seen in the response to Skinner's (1953) suggestion: 'A scientific analysis may lead us to resist the more immediate blandishments of freedom, justice, knowledge, or happiness in considering the long-run consequence of survival' (p. 436). Skinner's critics respond that they would prefer not to survive if survival means giving up the values, such as freedom and justice, they most highly cherish. Survival for its own sake possesses little value for them. Their disagreement with Skinner is not over matters of fact.

Disagreements of this sort do not, in themselves, undermine the Skinnerian analysis of behavior. They are explained in terms of histories of social reinforcement. Skinner's critics come from communities in which behavior, including verbal behavior, contributing to freedom and happiness is highly socially reinforced, while Skinner and his supporters belong to communities in which behavior promoting cultural survival is highly socially reinforced. Hence the groups differ in what they find reinforcing and therefore good. Each group constitutes a 'value community', each with its own contingencies of social reinforcement.

Indeed, a good number of the important moral and ethical dilemmas facing us today (e.g., abortion, pacifism, homosexual rights, affirmative action) are not primarily disagreements about consequences and other matters of fact but represent clashes among conflicting value communities. In such cases it appears that all a science of behavior can do is confirm that each side of a moral conflict acts in ways that are reinforcing to it, but the science cannot tell us which side is correct; it cannot tell us what we ought to do (cf. Hinman, 1979). The science cannot appeal to survival as a criterion to decide among differing points of view because the survivability criterion is precisely what is at issue. People do not, in fact, currently use survivability as the ultimate criterion to decide ethical questions, as Skinner admits. Therefore, a naturalist ethics based on empirical observations of behavior cannot justify survivability as a criterion to resolve ethical questions (Waller, 1982; but cf. Rottschaefer, 1980).

INTRA-INDIVIDUAL CONFLICTS

What is true for conflicts between members of different value communities is also true of conflicts within an individual. In making an ethical decision an individual will normally have available many courses of action, all of which have *R*. There will be many options that are personally reinforcing, many that are reinforcing to others, and some which contribute to cultural survival. Although (4), the conclusion of the Naturalist Deduction, purports to give necessary and sufficient conditions for what one ought to do, clearly it fails to give sufficient conditions since conflicting actions have *R*. But unless there is some means for choosing among the options, Skinner's naturalist ethics cannot fulfil its promise of empirically determining what one ought to do.

Several methods for resolving such conflicts immediately suggest themselves. Perhaps, for example, one ought to choose the action that maximizes one's reinforcement. But this solution raises a host of empirical and theoretical questions. First, there is the issue as to whether organisms necessarily do whatever maximizes reinforcement (see Commons, Herrnstein and Rachlin, 1982). According to the Skinnerian experimental analysis of behavior, an organism's response is always the result of a history of reinforcement. So in one sense the organism is always doing whatever behavior has the greatest response strength, i.e., has had the greatest past reinforcement. Consequently, Skinnerian ethics has no role, since individuals already and necessarily do the good, ie., that which maximizes reinforcement.

On the other hand, if it is possible for organisms to act in ways that do not maximize their reinforcement, Skinnerian ethics may play a role in guiding behavior. Then the question is how to quantify reinforcement and which dimensions to maximize. Although this is an unanswered question of great complexity, let us grant for the moment that it can be answered. To be ethical, then, one ought to act in ways that maximize reinforcement. The critical question for my purposes is: what is the source of this rule? It is not derived from observation of behavior, because by hypothesis we have assumed that people do not necessarily maximize reinforcement (Waller, 1982). Even if it could be so derived, it still does not uniquely specify what one ought to do. Besides the course of action which maximizes the individual's reinforcement, there is also the action which maximizes reinforcement for other members of the community, as well as the action which maximizes the culture's chances of survival. How ought one to choose among these?

I do not deny that rules, in fact, reasonable rules, can be formulated to decide these questions (see the debate between Graham, 1977, 1983, and Garrett, 1979, on this issue). My point is that whatever these rules, and however sensible their rationale, their source must be other than the observation of how people currently use the words 'good' and 'ought'. Therefore, these rules do not constitute a naturalist ethics in the strong sense.

For Skinner one source of ethical rules is a prediction about behavior. He argues that those societies which adopt practices which promote cultural survival will be the ones that will survive in a kind of cultural form of natural selection among societies. Therefore, he claims, in the future cultural survival will be the ultimate criterion for choosing among actions which have *R*. However, if and when Skinner's prediction is fulfilled, the Naturalist Deduction will have no role.

People in this future society will already and necessarily act in ways to promote
the survival of their culture. To be sure, a science of behavior can clarify for them
which practices are likely to be effective in this regard, but it cannot justify the
survivability criterion before such a criterion is adopted.

Therefore, it appears that the Naturalist Deduction cannot achieve what
many had hoped it would be: a guide to action. If it takes as initial premise (1) the
verbal behavior of some future society as predicted by Skinner, then it will advise
that society to do what it is already and necessarily doing. If it takes as its initial
premise (1) *current* verbal behavior, then it cannot include strict rules for choosing among goods. Without these rules it can give necessary but not sufficient
conditions for the good, and it, therefore, fails to tell us what we ought to do. If,
on the other hand, the ethical system includes these rules, then it is not based on
the Naturalist Deduction. It may be a very appealing and reasonable system,
perhaps even a morally good system, but its justification is not based on empirical
fact. It is a behaviorist ethics but not a naturalist ethics in the strong sense.

INDIVIDUAL DIFFERENCES

Another way to see that the Naturalist Deduction provides only necessary but not
sufficient conditions for what one ought to do is to consider differences among
individuals. Something might, for example, be a reinforcer for the behavior of an
Eskimo, or a masochist, or a cat, but most people will not call it good. Yet this
fact contradicts the initial empirical premise (1) of the Naturalist Deduction. To
save (1) it is necessary to relativize it to individual histories of reinforcement.
Thus, (1) should be revised to:

   5   For any speaker S, S says 'X is good' if and only if X has R for S.

This revision requires a modification of (2), the Naturalist Principle:

   6   X is good relative to S if and only if X has R for S,
       and a revision of (4):
   7   S ought to do X if and only if X has R for S.

The phrase 'relative to S' in (6) is ambiguous. It might mean that it is good
for S to do X, i.e. S's doing X is good. Under this interpretation, consider a
particular person P, and assume an act Q which has R for P. According to (6), P's
doing Q is good. However, if we substitute 'P's doing Q' for X in (5) we get:

   8   For any speaker S, S says 'P's doing Q is good' if and only if P's doing Q
       has R for S.

But from (8) in conjunction with (6) all that follows is:

   9   P's doing Q is good relative to S if and only if P's doing Q has R for S.

Thus, the fact that a particular act Q has R for a particular person P does not
imply that P's doing Q is good. Whether or not P's doing Q is good depends on
the speaker making the ethical judgment. If P's doing Q has R for the speaker S,
then S will judge it to be good, otherwise not. Thus, it is incorrect to interpret
'relative to S' in (6) as meaning that it is good in some absolute sense for S to do
X.

Another interpretation of 'relative to S' in (6) is that X is good *according* to S, i.e., in S's view. Under this interpretation, however, problems arise in deriving (7) which does not follow from (5), (6), and (3). To deduce (7), (3) must be revised to:

10   One ought to do what is good in one's own view.

But (10) is certainly open to debate and is not, at the very least, a tautology. Without (3), (7) is not derivable, and the Naturalist Deduction collapses.

LIMITS OF THE NATURALIST DEDUCTION

Several points emerge from these considerations. First, if the Naturalist Deduction refers to current verbal behavior, then its conclusion gives us necessary but not sufficient conditions for what we ought to do. Second, the Skinnerian ethical system with its emphasis on the survivability criterion is either a prediction about the future or it is a recommendation by Skinner, not a naturalist deduction from a behavioral science. Skinner (Rogers and Skinner, 1956) readily admits this: 'Do not ask me why I want mankind to survive. I can tell you why only in the sense in which the physiologist can tell you why I want to breathe' (p. 1065). In dealing with the question: 'why should I care whether my government survives long after my death?' Skinner (1971) answers: 'The only honest answer to that kind of question seems to be this: There is no good reason why you should be concerned, but if your culture has not convinced you that there is, so much the worse for your culture' (p. 137). If contributing to cultural survival is what Skinner recommends, that is, what he finds to be good, then from (8) we can conclude that for him actions which contribute to survival are reinforcing. This is because of his own reinforcement history and because of the contingencies of social reinforcement in the value community formed by him and his supporters.

Returning now to the paradox described at the beginning of this chapter, we see that *Beyond Freedom and Dignity* is not merely an empirical analysis but is indeed a book of ethics. It is an attempt to change our behavior by telling us what we ought to do. To understand how this is possible, I wish to suggest a behavioral analysis of the verbal behavior of making ethical judgments.

BEHAVIORAL ANALYSIS OF ETHICAL JUDGMENTS

One of the most important discriminative stimuli for human behavior is the verbal behavior of others. When a speaker tacts (Skinner, 1957, Ch. 5) stimuli in the environment, this verbal response may function as a discriminative stimulus for the non-verbal behavior of the listener. For example, the verbal tact, 'It is raining', on the part of a speaker may set the occasion for the response of getting an umbrella on the part of the listener. People learn to emit verbal behavior which brings about behavior on the part of the listener which is reinforcing to the speaker. In forms of intellectual self-management and self-control, the speaker and listener may be the same person.

Tacts are not always effective in bringing about listener behavior which is

reinforcing to the speaker. For example, the tact, 'It is raining', will not bring about any behavior on the part of the listener unless the listener has a conditioning history in which that tact, or similar ones, played a role in a contingency of reinforcement. Therefore, speakers can make their verbal behavior more effective in controlling the behavior of the listener by emitting a verbal response which functionally establishes a contingency of reinforcement. This can be accomplished by tacting a contingency. For example, the speaker may say, 'If you take an umbrella, you won't get wet.' This verbal response, which I shall label a 'contingency establishing verbal response', is more effective than 'It is raining' in bringing about the desired behavior on the part of the listener because it specifies both the desired behavior and the reinforcing consequence for the listener. In Skinner's (1969, Ch. 6) analysis such verbal responses are 'rules', 'warnings', or 'advice'.

Although a tact of reinforcement contingencies is an improvement, it still has certain weaknesses. For one thing it will succeed in bringing about the desired behavior only if the consequence specified is indeed a reinforcer for the listener. If, for example, staying dry is not a reinforcer for the listener, the warning will have no effect. Similarly, the effectiveness of the warning depends on the listener's states of satiation and deprivation with respect to the specific reinforcement.

A more powerful controlling stimulus would be a verbal response which establishes a contingency virtually independent of the listener's idiosyncratic history of reinforcement and drive states. An analogy with Skinner's concept of the generalized conditioned reinforcer is helpful here. Skinner (1957, pp. 52–4) introduces this concept to describe a conditioned reinforcement, such as social approval, which has been associated with so many different unconditioned reinforcers so many times, that it is effective regardless of the subject's motivational states and reinforcement history. It is a kind of universal reinforcement. Analogously we might speak of a '*generalized* contingency establishing verbal response' which has been associated with so many contingencies of reinforcement so many times that it is effective in establishing such a contingency regardless of the listener's motivational states and reinforcement history.

The most common form of generalized contingency establishing verbal response is the ethical or moral imperative. 'You ought to do X' does not specify a particular contingency of reinforcement, but it functions to establish a generalized one. Doing what one ought to do has been associated with many reinforcers, including social approval, escape from punishment, and other rewards. Therefore, it is extremely effective in establishing a contingency of reinforcement. Its effectiveness is enhanced by the fact that because of its association with many powerful reinforcing and aversive stimuli, it probably functions also as a Pavlovian conditioned stimulus to elicit autonomic emotional responses in the listener.

The more generalized the contingency, the more the verbal response enters into the realm of the ethical and moral. 'You ought to eat at Gino's if you like Italian food', is a contingency establishing verbal response, but the behavior and reinforcement mentioned are specific, and consequently the advice can hardly be called ethical. In contrast, 'You ought to be kind' establishes a contingency with a generalized reinforcement and response, and it is ethical in nature. There is thus a continuum between the purely prudent and the purely ethical depending, in part, on how generalized is the contingency established.

IMPLICATIONS

This behavioral analysis of value judgments clarifies several points about behaviorist ethics. First, note that in an ethical imperative, 'You ought to do X', there are *two* reinforcements involved. One is the reinforcement, specific or generalized, entering into the contingency for the listener. The other is the listener's behavior, specified in the contingency, which is reinforcing to the *speaker*. Indeed, the verbal behavior of telling others what they ought to do is maintained by the resulting listener behavior which is reinforcing to the speaker.

Second, if it is true that ought-statements are maintained in this way, then we have a behavioral analogy to the traditional distinction between 'ought' and 'is'. It has often been claimed that an ought-statement cannot be deduced from an is-statement. The latter kind of statement is analogous to the tact which, in a sense, describes stimuli. As argued above, a pure tact is not effective in modifying the behavior of the listener without a contingency of reinforcement. An ought-statement establishes such a contingency of reinforcement, and it therefore controls behavior. However, it does not merely describe, or tact, this contingency because a pure tact is maintained solely by generalized reinforcement (Skinner, 1957, pp. 81–90), while an ought-statement is maintained, in addition, by the listener's behavior which is reinforcing to the speaker. Therefore, the ought-statement has characteristics of a mand. Thus, the distinction between 'is' and 'ought' is reflected in the difference between a pure tact and a contingency establishing mixed tact-mand (Skinner, 1957, pp. 151–2; and see Day, 1977, and Begelman, 1977).

Because the ought-statement retains some of the characteristics of the tact, it is also descriptive. It describes a contingency of reinforcement, generalized or specific, and it can do so accurately or inaccurately. Therefore, an ought-statement can be true or false in the Skinnerian sense of truth: it can lead to either effective or ineffective behavior on the part of the listener (see Zuriff, 1980, for a discussion of Skinner's view of truth).

Third, if it is true that ought-statements are maintained by listener behavior that is reinforcing to the speaker, then it follows that people will not consider something ethical unless they are reinforced by it. Compare this conclusion with (5) which states that people call something good if it has R, and R refers not only to the property of being reinforcing to the individual, but also to that which is reinforcing to others or contributory to the survival of the culture. It appears from the present analysis that when people call something that is either reinforcing to others or contributory to cultural survival 'good', they do so only if it is also personally reinforcing to them, perhaps because the good of society and its survival are personally reinforcing to them. Thus, R can be reduced to the one quality of being personally reinforcing (cf. Graham, 1977).

CONCLUSIONS

We can now pull together the strands of the current discussion and evaluate the accomplishments of Skinnerian ethics. First, Skinner provides a behavioral interpretation (Zuriff, 1985, Ch. 10) of the behavior of making ethical judgments. This interpretation consists of a number of plausible empirical hypotheses based on an

extrapolation from behavioral laws discovered through the Skinnerian experimental analysis of behavior. Second, Skinner offers a prediction, also extrapolated from his experimental analysis of behavior, as to what will come to be the values of society in the future. Third, Skinner, in addition, makes recommendations about what ought to be our culture's current values. These recommendations, as opposed to his predictions, are not derived from the science of behavior and are, therefore, not a naturalist ethics in the strong sense. Only if his recommendations were to be adopted would we have an ethics in which ethical questions can be answered by the objective and empirical methods of science. Currently, his ethics are a 'redefinitional naturalism' (Harmon, 1977, p. 20) in which a precise naturalist system is suggested as a replacement for our present vague one.

Although Skinner's ethical recommendations are not a logical deduction from the behavioral science, they perhaps are related to that science in another way. In a behavioral interpretation science is seen as the behavior, verbal and non-verbal, of scientists. These scientists form a community, both a verbal community (Skinner, 1957, Ch. 18) and a value community. It is possible that exposure to the contingencies of reinforcement prevailing in this community leads one to espouse the values Skinner proposes. This shaping of value judgments might come about partly as a result of the contingencies of social reinforcement practiced by scientists. However, these social contingencies are only secondary, and are, of course, themselves in need of explanation. Perhaps the more basic contingencies arise in the very study of behavior itself. Scientists may come to value the survival of their culture and their species when they discover the beauty, the adaptiveness, and the potential of human behavior.

NOTE

1 Strictly speaking a reinforcement is a stimulus not a response, and it reinforces behavior not persons. However, for the sake of convenience I shall speak of a behavior as reinforcing for persons. By this I shall mean that (1) a person's behavior is followed by a reinforcement, or (2) a person's behavior is a reinforcing stimulus for another person's behavior, or (3) the stimulus consequences of a behavior are either conditioned or unconditioned reinforcers, and the behavior is 'self-reinforcing' (see Vaughan and Michael, 1982).

REFERENCES

Begelman, D.A. (1977) 'Commentary', in Krapfl, J.E. and Vargas, E.A. (Eds), *Behaviorism and Ethics*, Kalamazoo, Mich., Behaviordelia, pp. 24–8.

Commons, M.L., Herrnstein, R.J. and Rachlin, H. (1982) *Quantitative Analyses of Behavior, Vol. 2: Matching and Maximizing Accounts*, Cambridge, Mass., Ballinger.

Day, W. (1977) 'Ethical philosophy and the thought of B.F. Skinner', in Krapfl, J.E. and Vargas, E.A. (Eds), *Behaviorism and Ethics*, Kalamazoo, Mich., Behaviordelia, pp. 7–23.

Frankena, W.K. (1939) 'The naturalistic fallacy', *Mind*, 48, pp. 464–77.

Garrett, R. (1979) 'Value conflict in a Skinnerian analysis', *Behaviorism*, 7, pp. 9–16.

Graham, G. (1977) 'On what is good: A study of B.F. Skinner's operant behaviorist view', *Behaviorism*, 5, pp. 97–112.

Graham, G. (1983) 'More on the goodness of Skinner', *Behaviorism*, 11, pp. 45–51.

Harmon, G. (1977) *The Nature of Morality: An Introduction to Ethics*, New York, Oxford University Press.

Hinman, L.M. (1979) 'How not to naturalize ethics: The untenability of a Skinnerian naturalistic ethics', *Ethics*, 89, pp. 292–7.

Hocutt, M. (1977) 'Skinner on the word "good": A naturalistic semantics for ethics', *Ethics*, 87, pp. 319–38.

Moore, G.E. (1903/1966) *Principia Ethica*, Cambridge, Cambridge University Press.

Rogers, C.R. and Skinner, B.F. (1956) 'Some issues concerning the control of human behavior: A symposium', *Science*, 124, pp. 1057–66.

Rottschaefer, W.R. (1980) 'Skinner's science of values', *Behaviorism*, 8, pp. 99–112.

Skinner, B.F. (1953) *Science and Human Behavior*, New York, Macmillan.

Skinner, B.F. (1957) *Verbal Behavior*, New York, Appleton-Century-Crofts.

Skinner, B.F. (1969) *Contingencies of Reinforcement*, New York, Appleton-Century-Crofts.

Skinner, B.F. (1971) *Beyond Freedom and Dignity*, New York, Alfred A. Knopf.

Vaughan, M.E. and Michael, J.L. (1982) 'Automatic reinforcement: An important but ignored concept', *Behaviorism*, 10, pp. 217–27.

Waller, B. (1982) 'Skinner's two stage value theory', *Behaviorism*, 10, pp. 25–44.

Zuriff, G.E. (1980) 'Radical behaviorist epistemology', *Psychological Bulletin*, 87, pp. 337–50.

Zuriff, G.E. (1985) *Behaviorism: A Conceptual Reconstruction*, New York, Columbia University Press.

26. Practical Reason and a Science of Morals

RICHARD GARRETT

G.E. Moore argued that any inference by anyone (scientist or metaphysician) from an *is* to a moral *ought* is illicit and so guilty of what he described as 'the naturalistic fallacy'.[1] In an essay entitled 'Science and Religion' Albert Einstein expressed a similar view, saying that '... knowledge of what is does not open the door directly to what should be.'[2] Einstein went on to explain that science can only give us knowledge of the means we ought to employ in seeking this or that end, but that it cannot give us a knowledge of the ultimate or final ends we ought to seek in the first place. Today few philosophers and few scientists would disagree with Moore or Einstein on this matter. B.F. Skinner stands out as the most notable and most important exception to this rule.

Skinner agrees that other sciences do not have answers to questions about moral oughts, but argues that a science of human behavior is uniquely qualified to bridge the is/ought gap. In particular, he maintains that his own principles of human behavior hold the very key that can open the door separating the *is* from the *ought*. I am inclined to think there is something to this claim of Skinner's, and in this chapter I shall say why I think this way. However, although I am inclined to believe that his principles do hold the key that can open the door separating the is from the ought, I do not think the door has yet been opened. That is, I do not think Skinner has yet shown us how to get a moral-ought from his psychological-is. It will be essential to my showing how I think this can be done to make it clear why I think Skinner has not yet done this. Accordingly the chapter falls into two parts: in the first I will show why I believe Skinner has not yet shown us how to get from his psychological-is to our sought-for moral-ought; in the second I will outline an approach that I think is a viable means of going from Skinner's psychological-is to a genuine moral-ought.

I. The problem underlying Skinner's approach to bridging the is/ought gap can be seen in his comments on a passage in which Karl Popper defends the claim that you cannot get an 'is' from an 'ought'. Popper argues as follows:

In face of the sociological fact that most people adopt the norm 'Thou shalt not steal', it is possible to decide to adopt either this norm, or its opposite; and it is possible to encourage those who have adopted the norm to hold fast to it, or to discourage them, and to persuade them to adopt another norm. It is impossible to derive a sentence stating a norm or a decision from a sentence stating a fact; this is only another way of saying that it is impossible to derive norms or decisions from facts.[3]

In response to this passage Skinner makes the following comment:

The conclusion is valid only if indeed it is 'possible to adopt a norm or its opposite.' Here is autonomous man playing his most awe-inspiring role, but whether or not a person obeys the norm 'Thou shalt not steal' depends upon supporting contingencies, which must not be overlooked.[4]

This counter-argument of Skinner's may be rested as follows. (1) We are not autonomous (i.e., all of our voluntary behavior, including following a norm, is a function of the contingencies of reinforcement). (2) But if we are not autonomous, then it is impossible for us to adopt a norm or its opposite. (3) Finally, the validity of Popper's argument rests upon the assumption that we can adopt a norm or its opposite. Conclusion: therefore, Popper's argument is invalid.

This is a formally valid argument, as anyone with an elementary knowledge of logic could quickly determine. So if you accept premises (1)–(3), you must accept the conclusion. Now premise (3) is obviously true. Many of Skinner's critics would reject premise (1), and it is certainly controversial. I, however, do not reject it. More importantly, my task in this chapter will not be to establish premise (1), but to show simply why acceptance of premise (1) gives us a way to bridge the is/ought gap. That is, I will only argue that *if* (1) is true, there seems to be a viable way to derive a moral-ought from a psychological-is. (But this is the task of part II.) However, I am inclined to think that premise (2) is false, and in showing why I also hope to identify more generally the problem underlying Skinner's approach to ethics. But first I must digress about the practicality of reason. I argue as follows: first, reason is practical; second, the practicality of reason is compatible with premise (1); and third, the practicality of reason implies that premise (2) is false.

Kant also spoke of the practicality of reason, but his conditions for saying that reason is practical were more stringent than mine. Reason is practical if (1) what we do or think is sometimes determined by reasons and (2) we are able to discriminate between good and bad reasons. (Kant would also require that reason be autonomous, but I shall argue that this is not necessary.) I have no doubt that reason is practical in my sense, for any denial that it is self-stultifying.

Let us call anyone who denies that reason is practical (in my sense) the sceptic. First of all, it is clear that if the sceptic were right, all argument would be impossible or at least pointless; since no one could ever convince anyone of anything. Nor could anyone ever discriminate between good and bad arguments if the sceptic is right. That would be the end of all philosophy and science as we know it. But matters are worse than that for the sceptic. If anyone were ever convinced by the sceptic's arguments (including the sceptic), then the sceptic's denial that reasons can determine what we think would necessarily be false. Furthermore, if the sceptic admits that his arguments are good reasons for saying no one can discriminate between good and bad reasons, then he is necessarily contradicting himself. Finally, if he denies that he has given us good reasons for his conclusion, then we would by all means be well advised not to regard his

argument as a *good* one (which is to say we ought not accept it). So let the sceptic turn as he will, he can never give us any good reasons for his scepticism. We, of course, have every reason to assume the opposite, namely that reason is (in my sense) practical.

The practicality of reason in my sense is entirely compatible with Skinner's basic principles. If it were not, his basic principles would have to be modified or rejected. The fact is, however, that Skinner neither needs to nor does he deny the practicality of reason in my sense. He agrees that reasons sometimes determine what we do, for they are, on his analysis, among the contingencies of reinforcement. In particular, reasons are verbal responses (having special properties) and as such may serve as discriminative stimuli leading to other responses (verbal or non-verbal). Thus if someone says, 'It's raining', this may lead another to remark, 'The weatherman was wrong' (since the weatherman predicted sunshine) or to reach for a raincoat. If so, then the response, 'It is raining', is a reason (or discriminative stimulus) and is responsible for the respective verbal and non-verbal responses that follow it. Moreover, if it happens to be true that it is raining, then this is a good reason for the respective verbal and non-verbal responses it evokes; while if it is false, then it is a bad reason for these things. Moreover, Skinner has a nice account of how we can discriminate between true and false statements. I see no reason, therefore, why Skinner would or needs to deny the practicality of reason as I have explained it.

If we grant the practicality of reason as well as its compatibility with Skinner's basic principles, we must then consider its implications concerning our ability to adopt norms or their opposites. This immediately implies our ability to discriminate between valid and invalid norms since I mean by a *valid* norm simply one I have good reasons to follow and by an *invalid* norm one I have good reasons not to follow (or at least no good reasons to follow). Thus, for me the imperative, 'Stay away from caffeine if you want to sleep well', is a valid one, since I have a good reason to follow it; while the imperative, 'Eat a lot if you want to think clearly', is an invalid norm, since I have good reasons not to follow it. In both cases these good reasons consist of certain observations I have made concerning the respective effects of caffeine and heavy eating on me.

We must distinguish between the *validity* and the *effectiveness* of a norm. An imperative may be valid without being effective and it may also be effective without being valid. Consider the problem drinker. Drink is destroying his life. Hence, the imperative, 'Don't drink if you want to be happy', is valid for him, but it is not effective. That is, he has good reason to follow that norm (so it is valid), but (due to a failure to recognize its validity or to competing contingencies) he fails to follow the rule. Hence, it is ineffective. Conversely, someone might follow the rule, 'Eat a lot of sugar if you want to stay healthy', because they have been misguided by someone they respect. In that case the rule is effective but not valid.

We are now ready to consider what is involved in the adoption of a norm. When reason is at its best, it works something like this: the individual considers all the alternative options open to him, including not only a host of norms and their opposites but also the possibility of not adopting any norm. In this process he considers all the reasons (arguments) advanced pro and con all the various norms. He may even construct some norms and pro and con arguments of his own. There is no theoretical limit on this, though one may even have good reasons to set limits on how far to carry on in this way. Eventually, some

alternative will appear to have the strongest reasons in its favor. If he is very good at this sort of thing (if he has been exposed to the right sort of verbal communities), he stands a reasonable chance of arriving at a valid norm to follow. If so, he has completed the first step in adopting a norm which is to determine which one is valid.

In some cases step one suffices: the recognition that the rule is valid may by itself lead him to follow it quite faithfully. Adopting a norm or rule to follow in formal logic is often this simple. But in other cases, although the rule is valid, it may not be immediately effective just because the person recognizes its validity. In this case, if he has read Skinner, he knows how to make the rule that is valid also effective. He must look to the competing contingencies interfering with adoption of the rule.

Skinner's analysis is problematic precisely because he has not clearly distinguished between these two very different aspects of adopting a rule, norm or policy. If he had, he would see that Popper (and the defenders of the is/ought distinction in general) are focusing on the first and not the second step in adopting a norm. That is, they are concerned with the process of determining the *validity* of a norm and not with making it *effective*. The argument Popper presents, sometimes called the open-question argument, may be restated as follows:

> You may load your premises with all of the is-type statements (sociological facts or anything else) you want. If you confine yourself exclusively to is-type statements (without smuggling in any hidden oughts), then, no matter what moral-ought-statement you place in your conclusion, I can always *reasonably* ask: But why should I obey such a moral imperative? (That is, I can always reasonably deny that your is-type statements offer sufficiently good reasons for adopting the moral-ought in your conclusion. Hence, I can always deny the *validity* of your ought-statement.)

I do not think this argument is entirely correct. But I also do not think that what Skinner says in reply to Popper shows it is not correct. All that this argument presupposes is the practicality of reason in my sense. And this we have seen is not at all incompatible with Skinner's principles — nor in particular with his claim that we are not autonomous.

Although I do not agree with those upholding the open-question argument that we can *never* get an ought from an is, this much is right about the argument: most (possibly all) attempts to derive an ought from an is have so far failed. There is, therefore, some reasonably good inductive evidence for their contention, especially if it is true that no one has succeeded yet. But we ought not be overly impressed, for the inductive evidence runs the other way, too: every *first* in human history (from the Wright brothers to the splitting of the atom) was improbable, if one focused only on past failures. (Is not a science of morals at least as important as flying or as splitting the atom? But why, then, give up the project so easily?) Before saying why I think Skinner's principles give us good cause for hope, I want to show that, so far, Skinner has not yet derived a moral ought from his principles. I will do this by focusing on three different kinds of statements he makes about values.

Some of Skinner's statements, although *about* values, are *purely* descriptive and not normative at all. That is, they are statements which, even if true, do not *by themselves* provide us with good reasons for carrying out some sort of moral act. An example is his claim, 'Good things are positive reinforcers.'[5] This state-

ment by itself does not in the least tell me what to do, for example, whether to live only for my own reinforcement or for the reinforcement of others as well. Most of the things Skinner says regarding values are of this sort.

A second class of statements Skinner makes might well be action guiding if believed. They are genuine oughts of sorts, but not moral-oughts. An example is what is implied by the following statements: 'The use of science in designing a culture is commonly opposed.... The effect could be lethal. In spite of remarkable advantages, our culture may prove to have a fatal flaw.'[6] The implication is a central theme running throughout *Beyond Freedom and Dignity*, which may be stated as follows: 'If you want to preserve this culture, you ought to stop resisting a science of human behavior.' This statement could be true and it does follow in part from his principles. Finally, it is an ought statement. But it is not a moral-ought. Moreover, this sort of ought can be derived from *any* science whatever: 'If you want to avoid cancer, you ought to stop smoking' and 'If you want to find the distance an object has traveled, multiply the time by the speed', are examples. To get this sort of an 'ought' from a science is commonplace and not what is needed. This is simply science showing us the *means*, which as Einstein (and many others) have observed it certainly can do.

Finally, Skinner makes or implies a third sort of claim, which could qualify as a moral imperative. One of these is the following: 'You ought to work for the good of the culture.' But these sorts of statements are not adequately grounded by the other sorts of principles or statements Skinner provides. That is, it is not at all clear either that or how one might derive this third sort of statement from the other two kinds of statements. One can, therefore, apply the open question argument to Skinner's injunction to work for the good of the culture as follows: 'I accept everything you say about human behavior and human values. So I accept all of your is-type statements as well as your hypothetical imperatives. Still *I* (unlike you) simply do not find these to be good reasons to work for the good of the culture, since I find it much more reinforcing to live selfishly (for myself, my family and friends only). Nothing you have said has given me a *good reason* to do otherwise.'

What could Skinner reply to this? He can't say, 'But wait, I have given you good reasons to work for the culture. You have not read me with sufficient care.' Indeed, Skinner knows this and is courageous and honest enough to admit it. He explicitly states that he cannot give you a good reason for working for the culture. In the end all he is able to say is: 'If your culture hasn't convinced you to work for it all the worse for your culture.' This is a truism, but it will not move anyone who does not already have an antecedent concern for his culture. Thus, Skinner has admitted in effect that the open-question argument applies to his own analysis. That is, he has admitted that one can accept all his psychological-is statements (including those about values) and yet *reasonably* reject all his moral-ought statements. But if this is the case, then Skinner has not bridged the is/ought gap. All the same I am persuaded that Skinner, like a hound on the heels of a fox, has led us to the general vicinity of our quarry (the moral-ought) — even though he has temporarily lost sight of it himself. In the second part of this chapter, I offer some justification for my confidence that this is so, by picking up our quarry's trail anew, employing a somewhat different (though certainly related) approach to the problem.

II.   We must begin with the observation that if Skinner's basic principles of psychology are correct, then all value and all worth must be analyzable in terms of reinforcement. From this it follows that nothing has any worth except things that are reinforcing and creatures that are reinforced. Thus, if we consider a world in which there are just deer and vegetation, both the deer and the vegetation have worth. Only the two have a worth in different ways. The deer have a worth both as *things that are reinforcing* (to deer) and as *creatures that are reinforced* (by both deer and certain forms of vegetable life). So deer are not only a means (to reinforcement) but an end in themselves (a creature that receives reinforcement). However, vegetables in such a world have a worth *only as things* that are reinforcing to the deer and, therefore, only so far as and only to the extent that they are reinforcing to the deer. So vegetable life has a worth only as a *means* (to reinforcement). It follows that in a world of only deer, deer would still have a worth: while in a world of only vegetable life, *nothing* would have a worth. This all follows in a rigorous way if you accept Skinner's basic principles.

From the viewpoint of reinforcement theory conflicts of interest arise between individuals because the reinforcement of the one is incompatible with the reinforcement of the other. Organisms acquire a repertoire of behavior for coping with such conflicts. Stag deer, for example, fight over doe. But only humans (as far as is known) can reason and, therefore, resolve their conflicts by appeals to reason. With significant modifications Kant's classification of imperatives will provide a helpful means of discussing appeals to reason that are useful in resolving conflicts. Thus, I shall speak of imperatives of skill, of happiness and of morality.

An *imperative of skill* is an imperative that can be *technically valid*. Moreover, an imperative is technically valid just in case following it would secure some specific ends of the agent. Suppose A and B want the thermostat at different temperatures, say at 65° and 72° respectively. A might argue as follows: 'You will save money if you stay warm by wearing more clothing rather than by raising the thermostat to 72°. *So, if you want to save money, then you ought to stay warm by wearing more clothing rather than by raising the thermostat to 72°*.' This imperative of skill will be valid for B only if (1) lowering the temperature to 65° really is likely to save money and (2) B wants to save money. If the first condition fails, then the specified end is not really likely to be secured by following the imperative; while if the second condition fails, then the specified end is not really an end of B (that is, of the agent). So if either condition fails, the imperative fails to offer B a *good reason* for compliance. Imperatives of skill can only be valid (or good reasons for action) and so useful in resolving conflicts of interest in those cases where we can presuppose some specific ends on the part of one of the conflicting parties.

An *imperative of happiness* is an imperative that can be *prudentially valid*. An imperative, moreover, is prudentially valid if following it tends to promote the happiness of the agent. Happiness is not a specific end, but rather the quality of one's life as a whole. However much Kant and others may talk about the difficulties in defining happiness, it is undoubtedly real enough for all of us, for every one of us undoubtedly makes many decisions in our lives and adopts principles and policies because we believe they will increase our chances for happiness, i.e., for a better life as a whole. Such imperatives of happiness are particularly useful in helping to resolve conflicts of interest, for they remind

people to have a regard for the larger picture (for the consequences of doing this or that for their life as a whole). Suppose, for example, *A* wants *B*'s job and could secure it by making certain personal information available to *B*'s boss. *B* or another or *A* themselves might in such circumstances remind *A*, 'If you want to be a happy person, you ought to be kind to people.' This imperative will be valid for *A* just in case (1) being kind to people really would tend to promote *A*'s happiness and (2) *A* wants to be happy. Since everyone wants to be happy, condition (2) can never be in question. So it is always a matter of whether or not condition (1) holds. Kant rightly observes that we all have different conceptions of happiness. But it scarcely follows from this that the *basics* of human happiness vary. It is probable that in *detail* they do vary, e.g., a profession bringing happiness to one person may be a source of great misery to another. At the same time there may be certain conditions (e.g., kindness, close relationships with others) that are *universally* essential for a happy life. Nonetheless, I shall argue, that Kant is right in maintaining that moral imperatives cannot simply be a special class of imperatives of happiness.

Moral imperatives must be *categorically valid*. That is, an imperative to be moral must be *valid* (or provide a good reason for doing something) *for every agent* even when what is required is incompatible with some specific end of the agent or with the agent's happiness itself. I hold (in agreement with Kant) that this follows from the very conception of morality itself. For in telling someone that what they are doing (or are about to do) is immoral, I am giving them a reason (for not doing that thing) which we all recognize as *necessarily overriding all other considerations*, including any specific end of the agent or even their own happiness. It follows that no imperative of skill or of happiness can possibly serve as a moral imperative.

But how, then, is a moral imperative possible? Kant thought that in order for such an imperative to be possible it must be *absolutely unconditional*, but which he meant *absolutely independent of any end whatever*. This left him with no alternative but to say it is *the act itself* that is the good reason for the act, and so to argue that reason can only be (morally) practical if it is entirely *apriori*. This ultimately led him to the conclusion that reason must be self-legislating or *autonomous*. I cannot agree with Kant in this line of argument, since I wish to derive the moral imperative from Skinner's principles, which clearly implies that morality can be *empirically* grounded and that we are *not autonomous*. I wish, therefore, to argue that it is quite sufficient if the moral imperative is *relatively unconditional*. That is, all that need be assumed is that the *validity* of a moral imperative is *independent* of any end that is *uniquely the agent's*. How can this be possible?

It is possible because there is an end that each of us has which is not unique to us, but is entirely common to us all; that is, there is *a single end that all agents have at all times* and this end is the good culture or community. As creatures that are reinforced, each of us is an end in ourselves, for we are a source of value in the world and, as such, want to be treated as an end in itself. That is, we want others to treat us in ways that are reinforcing to us and not simply as a thing that is reinforcing to them. Each of us would, therefore, like to live in a world that would always treat us as an end. To the extent that this is so, each of us would choose such a community (which I will call the good community) over a community where we were treated as a means (to others' reinforcement) only. So the good

community is in this sense at least an end for everyone at all times. And a moral imperative is one that is valid because what it tells us to do will tend to promote the good culture or community we all desire. It is a good reason for action for all of us, therefore, for we all have that end at all times.

This does not mean that everyone has formulated or verbalized such an end, but only that it is logically entailed by the fact that we are the sort of creatures we are — rational creatures seeking reinforcement. Nor is it to say that even when formulated and believed to be valid (i.e., believed to be a good reason for overriding self-interests), the moral imperative is necessarily *effective*. The other contingencies with which morality may conflict are sometimes too powerful. Yet, by utilizing Skinner's principles, we can arrange additional contingencies to strengthen our own and others' moral behavior, once our reason has convinced us that this is what we ought to do.

Nor am I claiming that everyone who understands what is morally right will automatically prefer the good community over every other community. To the contrary, many might prefer a community where they, but not all others, were always treated as an end. People living in favored positions in a corrupt world might well prefer it to the good community. (Reinforcement theory would lead us to predict this as a likelihood.) Still two facts remain undeniable. (1) Even they would prefer the good community to their corrupt world *if they were the ones treated only as a means* in such a world. (2) The good community is the *only one* that *everyone* could possibly agree on *over every other*. Hence, it is the only possible end that can serve as the basis of a *moral* imperative. For a moral imperative must (as I have already argued) equally apply to and, therefore, be at once *valid for everyone*, i.e., offer everyone a good reason to comply.

But I have yet to state fully and clearly the moral imperative itself. One way of stating it is as follows: *you ought only do what can reasonably be willed by every agent, i.e., an act must be universalizable.* Since the only end that can be reasonably willed by every agent is the good community (in the sense recently explained), this means acting in a manner consistent with such an ideal community. This entails the alternative formula: *always treat others as an end and never as a means only*. Since no rational creature that seeks reinforcement can reasonably will to be treated as a mere means to another's reinforcement, the universalizability of an action also entails that others be treated as an end as well (i.e., that what is reinforcing and aversive to them is taken into equal consideration as well). Since reinforcement is the only source of value (according to reinforcement theory), logically speaking one person's reinforcement is just as important as the reinforcement of anyone else. Hence, equal consideration is logically required, for to say, 'My reinforcement is more important *objectively speaking*,' is absurd from the view of reinforcement theory. That we treat others as ends is essentially what the golden rule tells us to do: 'Do unto others as you would have them do unto you.'

This ends my brief sketch of how one might go from the *is* of Skinner's principles to the *ought* of morality. If it is possible to do this, as I am inclined to believe, then Skinner was essentially right in his claim that it would be a mistake for the behavioral scientist to agree that the is/ought gap cannot be bridged.

Finally, Skinner emphasized the good of the culture as an important end to work for. But it may be asked: for which (among competing cultures) shall I work? Skinner would agree, I believe, it is for the morally good culture that one

should work. Only what he says suggests that *the more survival potential a culture has, the more moral it is*. This seems to stand morality on its head, for it implies that we must first determine which culture has the most survival potential and then we will know which is the moral one. Accordingly, I would like to get morality back on its feet. I have argued that the morally good culture is the one where the principle underlying all social practices is that of treating everyone as an end (a rational creature seeking reinforcement.) If this is right, then we can determine which is the morally good culture independently of knowing its survival potential. Nonetheless, as it turns out, there is reason to think Skinner is close to the truth here too. After all, the morally good culture is the only one *everyone* has a *good reason* to promote and maintain, since it is the only one where everyone is regarded as an end. This gives us some grounds for being optimistic about the survival potential of such a morally good culture, should it ever evolve. We might be justified, therefore, in turning Skinner's notion around: *the more moral a culture is, the more survival potential it has*.

NOTES

1 Although David Hume is generally given credit for first noting the gap between the *is* and the *ought* (in Book III, Part I, Section 1 of his *Treatise*), G.E. Moore brought this notion into prominence in the twentieth century in *Principia Ethica*.
2 In 'Science and Religion' (which may be found in a collection of his work entitled *Ideas and Opinions*, published by Crown Publishers), Einstein adds that judgments about what ultimately ought to be are a matter for religious faith rather than scientific reason to determine.
3 See *Beyond Freedom and Dignity*, p. 108 (paperback edition).
4 *Ibid.*
5 *Ibid.*, p. 98.
6 *Ibid.*, p. 174.

Interchange

ZURIFF REPLIES TO GARRETT

I find myself in the somewhat awkward position of needing to formulate a rebuttal to a chapter which draws essentially the same conclusion as mine with respect to the main focus of this chapter — Skinner's naturalist ethics. Garrett and I (and possibly Skinner) agree that Skinner has not succeeded in logically deriving a system of ought-statements from his behavioral science of is-statements. We converge on this conclusion through different although parallel routes, and it is instructive to analyze the similarities.

Garrett speaks of three different kinds of Skinnerian statements which, although relevant to ethics, are not true derivations of moral imperatives from empirical statements. First, Garrett notes Skinner's purely descriptive but not normative statements such as, 'Good things are positive reinforcers.' In my analysis this kind of statement corresponds to what I refer to as empirical observations of verbal behavior. In agreement with Garrett I argue that Skinner has not logically derived ethical statements from this class of descriptive statement.

Garrett's second class consists of statements of means such as, 'If you want to preserve this culture, you ought to stop resisting a science of human behavior.' These correspond in my discussion to statements of consequences for various courses of action. I argue that these are matters of fact over which conflicting value communities can agree although they disagree over the desirability of the stated consequences. Therefore, as Garrett also concludes, such statements, involving means only, cannot serve as moral imperatives.

The third of Garrett's classes does qualify as moral. For example, the Skinnerian imperative, 'You ought to work for the good of your culture', is an ought-statement in the fullest sense. However, as Garrett and I both maintain, statements of this third class are not logically derivable from the empirical statements of Skinner's behavioral system. Each of us also notes that at various points in his writings Skinner seems to acknowledge that the gap between science and ethics has not been bridged.

However, as I suggest in my discussion, Skinner does provide a more modest connection between his behavioral science and ethics. Based on his principles of behavior, he offers a *prediction* concerning what will eventually become the ethical principles of future societies. It is this prediction, I believe, Skinner has in mind when he replies to Popper, and in this regard Garrett and I differ in our understanding of Skinner's response to Popper. My view is that Skinner ignores validity and refers, instead, to his prediction. Skinner can derive a prediction of future behavior only if there are natural laws governing behavior, i.e., only if humans are not autonomous beings. Skinner takes Popper's statement that it is

'possible to adopt a norm or its opposite' as an assertion of human free will and therefore contrary to his (predictive) connection between science and ethics. Hence, his response to Popper is a rejection of free will and thus an implicit reassertion of his derivation of a prediction about norms from statements of fact.

Following our respective analyses of Skinner's ethics, Garrett and I both offer our own ideas about how Skinner's insights can be explicated and extended. I offer a behavioral analysis of moral statements while he sketches a science of morals. Garrett argues for the derivation of a moral imperative, telling us to do only those acts which are universalizable, or equivalently to treat others as ends and never as a means only. Although I commend Garrett's attempt to provide us with a moral system derived from Skinner's principles, I find several problems with the endeavor.

My main difficulty is in discovering how the moral imperatives Garrett suggests are derived from Skinnerian principles. First of all, one of Garrett's key premises — that creatures subject to the laws of reinforcement have worth as ends in themselves — is not Skinnerian. As far as I can tell, Skinner limits the good to things that are either reinforcers or contribute to the survival of a culture.

Second, Garrett assumes, without supporting argument, Kant's definition of a moral imperative. However, this definition is not clearly consistent with Skinner's analysis of the verbal behavior involved in a moral imperative. For Skinner not all ethical statements are relatively unconditional in Garrett's sense. Some are maintained in strength because of the reinforcement ultimately derived by members of special groups and institutions within society. Given that Garrett adopts Kant's definition of a moral imperative, it is not surprising that the moral imperatives he derives are identical to Kant's categorical imperative. The connection to Skinner is tenuous.

Indeed, it is not clear that anything Skinnerian is necessary for Garrett's derivation. Given Kant's definition of the moral imperative and the fact that all of us would prefer to be treated well (as ends) rather than poorly (as means), Garrett's argument seems to follow. Reinforcement theory appears to be an unnecessary and gratuitous appendage to the derivation.

In addition to failing to show how his conclusions derive from reinforcement principles, Garrett's moral system is open to another objection on its own terms. As I discussed in my chapter, given the appropriate contingencies of social reinforcement, nearly anything can become a reinforcement for people. Under the right circumstances people can universally find self-sacrifice on behalf of a cause, a state, or a religion to be reinforcing. Furthermore, the self-sacrifice can take nearly any form. Conscripting young men into an army to march off to injury and death can, under the proper conditions, be universally reinforcing to them. Thus, nearly *any* way of treating people can conceivably function as a reinforcement for them. Therefore, Garrett's categorical imperative, couched in reinforcement language, fails to tell us what to do because *anything* we do can potentially conform to it.

Rather than end on a negative note, let me add one final parallel between Garrett's Kantian treatment and mine. For Garrett a moral imperative is one that is valid independent of any end that is unique to the agent. In my analysis an ethical ought-statement is one that establishes a contingency relatively independent of the listener's momentary drive states or idiosyncratic reinforcement history. Thus, for both of us universality is a key element in ethics.

GARRETT REPLIES TO ZURIFF

I shall confine my comments to clarifying the differences and similarities between Zuriff and myself, focusing first on the interpretation of Skinner and then on the possibility of a science of morals.

I. *Interpretation of Skinner.* As I read Skinner, he is proposing the norm that we place the good of the culture above everything else *because*, he predicts, our survival depends upon this. This strategy of Skinner's requires the following conditions: (a) the acceptance of his prediction; (b) that people in fact value survival above all else; and (c) that granted (a) and (b) you cannot but accept Skinner's proposal. Condition (c) is just what Skinner is proposing to establish in his attack on Karl Popper's argument. Popper concludes (it may be recalled) that you cannot get a proposal or norm from a fact or facts. Skinner seeks to undermine this argument by holding that we do not have a free will (are not autonomous) and that this implies *we cannot adopt a norm or its opposite* which is a key premise in Popper's argument. In my chapter I have tried to show why Skinner's reply fails and so why his entire strategy fails.

On Zuriff's reading Skinner has a dual strategy. One part Zuriff calls Skinner's 'naturalistic deduction', which Zuriff correctly shows to be an unsound argument. There are, however, problems with ascribing this argument to Skinner. For one there is absolutely no textual evidence given in support of it. For another it is too obviously unsound, e.g., its conclusion entails that we morally ought to do whatever reinforces us, which means that the Manson family morally ought to have brutally murdered the people they murdered since apparently this reinforced them. The textual evidence, moreover, runs the other way, e.g., Skinner often tells us we must sacrifice what reinforces us for the good of the culture.

A second argument Zuriff appears to ascribe to Skinner runs as follows: 'The society that puts the culture first is most likely to survive. Therefore, the principle "Put the culture first" is likely to be the morality of the future.' Zuriff rightly notes that this conclusion is not itself a norm but a *prediction* about a norm, and that the norm itself remains without any support. Zuriff seems to be suggesting that Skinner is confusing the two: the *norm* (or proposal) and the *prediction* about the norm. This gives us what Zuriff refers to as Skinner's 'paradox': either Skinner must be talking about the norm, in which case there is *no support*, or he must be talking about the prediction, in which case there is *no norm*. This seems a more plausible argument to ascribe to Skinner than the naturalistic deduction. However, it seems to be more compatible with my own interpretation than with the 'naturalistic deduction' Zuriff ascribes to Skinner.

No matter which of the above interpretations is correct, my diagnosis of Skinner's failure remains just as valid: in the end it is Skinner's failure to deal with Popper's argument (the open question argument) that underlies his failure. No matter how one reads Skinner, his analysis fails because he has not shown us how to deduce a norm (an ought) from a fact (an is). Moreover, he has ultimately failed to do so because (as I have argued in part I of my paper) he mistakenly thinks that adopting a norm presupposes free will (i.e., autonomy). Hence, he mistakenly thinks certain facts (i.e., predictions about the future) will *somehow*

yield commitment to a norm (his proposal). Skinner underestimates the practicality of reason — our capacity to discriminate between good and bad reasons and to be moved only by good reasons. As a result, he fails to see that *the kind of facts* that are needed to support a moral norm are those that would constitute *universally good reasons* for adopting that norm.

II.   *Attitude towards the Possibility of a Science of Morals.* Although Zuriff and I agree that Skinner has not bridged the is/ought gap, we seem to differ over the future possibility of doing so. I think we can, Zuriff thinks we cannot. Zuriff believes that a *moral psychology* is *all* that is possible. That is, he believes that *all we can do* is to describe under what conditions people will *call* things moral, etc., as well as the contingencies that are responsible for people behaving in ways that are *called* moral. If Zuriff is right about this, then we can do no more than predict what norms will be *effective* and when. We cannot determine which ones are *valid*, i.e., we cannot discriminate between norms or proposals that are moral and those that are immoral. This means, for example, that moral psychology cannot establish that Hitler's imperative, 'Eliminate the Jews', is any less moral than the Judeo-Christian imperative, 'Be kind of others.' Yet Zuriff has not given us any argument in support of his view that this is all we can do.

In contrast with a mere moral psychology is what I have referred to as a *science of morals or ethics.* Such a science might be founded in part upon a moral psychology, but it would go further by enabling us to determine which norms or actions are the moral ones, i.e., the universally valid ones. I believe such a science is crucial. In societies where power is more distributed (e.g., in democracies) a moral psychology alone would be *ineffective* because no one will agree on what is moral. In societies where power is highly centralized (e.g., fascism or communism) it would be *oppressive* for what is moral will be arbitrarily defined by a ruling elite. Hence, without a science of morals to tell us what is moral, moral psychology is likely to be either ineffective or oppressive.

Nor does Skinner's proposed criterion of the good of the culture or survivability by itself solve the problem. The inadequacy of this proposal is easily revealed by contemplating the following life boat situation. Suppose there are too many people for the one available life boat so that if you try to save all you will save none. Survivability by itself cannot help. It can tell you that it is better for some than for none to survive, a truism on which all can agree. And it tells us that those essential to the survival of all (e.g., crew members) must survive. But beyond that, who is to survive and who is to perish? That is the question. I hold that the only moral resolution is *the resolution that every rational person can accept.* In this circumstance this means most likely some random means of selection (e.g., drawing straws), since this alone is the only resolution that *all* rational persons are likely to find acceptable. In general, therefore, *the moral solution* is the one that all rational persons can accept, i.e., the one that is *universalizable.* To treat someone as an *end* is simply to treat them in a way that is universalizable. Hence, Skinner's principle of survivability is itself only valid and useful so far as it conforms to the higher principle of universalizability.

This way of construing the categorical imperative has, I believe, two advantages. First, it lends itself to an empirical interpretation such that it can be deduced from a psychology such as Skinner's. In my chapter I have tried to

indicate (in a suggestive not in a definitive way) how this might be done. Second, it means that, unlike Kantian ethics which is applied in a mechanical and rigid way, it lends itself to constant refinement and elaboration as human knowledge and sensitivity and, therefore, human rationality deepen and expand.

If there is something to this, then one could expect a curiously symbiotic relationship between Skinner's psychology and a science of morals: to the extent that Skinner's psychology were upheld by future research, this would lend strength to the deduced moral principle. To the extent that such a morality squared with people's moral intuitions, it would remove the greatest source of resistance to Skinnerian psychology, namely its apparently immoral consequences. Furthermore, as psychology grows as a science, our moral understanding should become more refined, while new moral situations, dilemmas and sensitivities should in turn provoke a deeper psychological analysis. Hence the two systems would be mutually supporting and mutually stimulating as well.

Part XV: Afterword: Some Concluding Remarks

27. In the Yellow Wood

ROBERT EPSTEIN

As one might have expected, there is little consensus and a great deal of controversy in this volume. Perhaps it needs a new title. On only one matter — which, unfortunately, is given little treatment — is there universal agreement and, indeed, praise: Skinner has made significant contributions to the scientific understanding of behavior. His first book, *The Behavior of Organisms* (1938), is singled out repeatedly as a *tour de force*. Skinner as researcher and methodologist is untouchable; consider the matter closed.

Other matters, mainly 'meta' or 'ismic' in nature, rouse the critics to ire. Skinner has given us 'dogmas'. His positions on various issues are 'superficial', 'scanty', 'confused', 'paltry', 'uninspired', 'restrictive', 'inherently incomplete', 'constraining', and 'naive'. Praise and damnation. Quick consensus and prolonged, perhaps unending, controversy. Why?

The history of psychology sheds some light. 'Psychology' is derived from the Greek 'psyche', which originally meant 'breath' and came to mean 'soul' or 'mind'. A concern with the nature of mind can be traced back at least as far as Aristotle's *Peri Psyches*; advances in a variety of scientific disciplines in the nineteenth century led, finally, to the application of scientific methods to the study of mind. By the end of the century a new science had taken shape, defined by the *Oxford English Dictionary* as 'the science of the nature, functions, and phenomena of the human soul or mind'. 'From the most ancient subject', said Ebbinghaus, 'we shall produce the newest science.'

But in 1905 something peculiar happened. William McDougall, in his *Primer of Physiological Psychology*, defined psychology as 'the study of behavior'. He had no particular complaints against the old subject matter, but he thought that behavior, too, deserved attention (Watson and McDougall, 1928). In 1913 Watson went a step further. Psychology should study behavior, he said, and mind, the traditional subject matter, is now *forbidden*. The assertion was absurd; proclaiming someone else's field yours does not make it so. But Watson was charismatic,

and he promised many applications. Moreover, the possibility of a science of behavior was in the air; Charles Mercier, J.S. Mill, and others had suggested that it be established as an independent field. Had their suggestions been followed, the science of behavior would now very likely be one of the most effective and respected disciplines in the world. But Watson set the new science on a steep and thorny way — as the belligerent footman of psychology.

The movement for reform had, appropriately, an ism in its name: *behaviorism*. And the ism carried with it many untested and untestable assertions, philosophical in character: unobservables are off limits; behavior is determined; thought is laryngeal movement; nurture conquers nature. All extra baggage, really, since the mission of the crusade was simply to make behavior the subject matter of a science. The movement was destined to fail. Even during the three decades when behaviorism was conspicuous in psychology, the traditional subject matter held its own. With the advent of computers and the alliances that were formed among psychologists, computer scientists, and linguists, the study of mind eventually flourished as it never had before. Today, less than 2 per cent of the membership of the American Psychological Association identifies itself openly with the behavioristic tradition.

The movement died, but its legacy is clear: it created a fanatical concern for objectivity in psychology proper. It led to the development of a school of philosophy, which today is the proper referent of the word 'behaviorism'. And, perhaps most important, it convinced many people that the behavior of organisms is a legitimate subject matter in its own right. The study of behavior, which some now call 'praxics' (from the Greek '*praxis*', for 'behavior'), may yet become an independent and important science (Epstein, 1984, 1985).

Skinner is both praised and damned because he is both praxist and behaviorist and — even though he recognizes the difference (Skinner, 1974) — because the lines of separation are not always clear. As praxist, Skinner single-handedly advanced the science as no one has done before or since. As behaviorist, Skinner greatly elaborated and refined Watson's naive philosophical views. But the overlap has caused trouble. Almost all the complaints against Skinner in this volume and elsewhere have to do with the mixing of the science and the philosophy. The 'conceptual imperatives' Skinner is said to have imposed on the science are, with few exceptions, the imperatives of the ism. Skinner's 'interpretations' are extrapolations from the science, constrained by, or at least consistent with, the ism.

Philosophy has no limits, but no science should be constrained by a philosophy. It is the subject matter of behavior that is important, not any particular methodology or set of variables. No one should be denied a place in the behavioral laboratory because he or she is not a behaviorist. Moreover, the science of behavior cannot flourish in psychology's shadow. The squabbling has only been destructive to both disciplines — especially to the intruder.

The future is clear. The science of behavior will go free of the ism that helped bring it to life, just as other natural sciences have broken free of their own philosophical forebears (consider Hopkins, 1934). With the ism left behind, Mercier's proposal may finally be realized: the new science may finally emerge as an independent field.

Skinner's contributions will be similarly partitioned, also with good effect. He will be recognized in various disciplines in different ways, just as Descartes is revered in mathematics for different reasons than he is remembered in philoso-

phy. The landscape is not yet right. We cannot yet get a dispassionate view. But we are in the yellow wood. For the good of the science — and, indeed, if Skinner is right, for the good of humanity — behaviorism and the science of behavior must go their separate ways.

REFERENCES

Epstein, R. (1984) 'The case for praxics', *The Behavior Analyst*, 7, pp. 101–19.

Epstein, R. (1985) 'Animal cognition as the praxist views it', *Neuroscience and Biobehavioral Reviews*, 9, pp. 623–30.

Hopkins, A.J. (1934) *Alchemy: Child of Greek Philosophy*, New York, Columbia University Press.

McDougall, W. (1905) *Primer of Physiological Psychology*, London, J.M. Dent.

Skinner, B.F. (1938) *The Behavior of Organisms: An Experimental Analysis*, Englewood Cliffs, N.J., Prentice-Hall.

Skinner, B.F. (1974) *About Behaviorism*, New York, Alfred A. Knopf.

Watson, J.B. (1913) 'Psychology as the behaviorist views it', *Psychological Review*, 20, pp. 158–77.

Watson, J.B. and McDougall, W. (1928) *The Battle of Behaviorism: An Exposition and an Exposure*, London, Kegan Paul, Trench, Trubner and Co.

28. The Limits of Behaviorism

W. MILLER BROWN

Unlike my colleague, Robert Epstein, I detect as much consensus as controversy in these articles, at least at one significant level. From the diversity of these papers emerges the seemingly undisputed view that Skinner pioneered in developing the sparse, minimalist doctrines of behaviorism and persisted in sustaining his vision during many long years while psychology has flourished in other and fruitful directions: psycholinguistics, cognitive psychology, revolutionary developments in artificial intelligence and the new conglomeration of cognitive science. There was always, of course, the aura of ideology, excusable, perhaps, in a pioneer struggling against indigenous doctrines and competing explorers eager to stake claims on the same territory.

Yet there is an undertone in many of the articles, both those against, and, as I shall argue, even in those for Skinner's position, that suggests an impatience to get into new and conceptually richer fields. Skinner's techniques, and even some of his cautionary outlook, are not to be rejected or revised so much as absorbed into new and more powerful systems (Brown, 1972). What was always absent in Skinner's writing, deliberately though with often confusing and conflicting justifications, was recourse to theory. And it is a concern with theory that runs like a new independent variable throughout many of this volume's contributions.

Several of the contributors (Bethlehem, Hall, and Wessels, for example) make this concern explicit. Familiar with the literature of philosophy of science and clearly acquainted with the history of other sciences, these psychologists (not, I note, philosophers) are all struck by the apparent conceptual poverty of the Skinnerian program. They view behavorism as 'excessively restrictive' (Wessels); the 'narrowness of approach' (Hall) of its central doctrines as articulated by Skinner has led to its theoretical 'shortcomings' (Bethlehem). These shortcomings are often acknowledged by the staunchest supporters of Skinner's work. Even Hayes and Brownstein, in a closely reasoned and reasonable defense of Skinner's views, close their chapter with reference to these lacks, a successful behavioral account of a variety of 'complex human behaviors'.

Still, for the most part, clarity about theory at this point is in short supply.

There is much talk of 'inner' or 'private' processes, states and events, but not much on what these are or how they might contribute to theory. The exceptions are interesting because they are contributions of Skinner's followers (Schnaitter, and Hayes and Brownstein, for example). Borrowing from Schnaitter's admirably lucid chapter, perhaps I can schematically suggest where the issues lie.

In much of the recent work of philosophers and like-minded psychologists, the metaphor of choice in these matters has been the high-speed digital computer. (See Searle, 1980, for an instructive dissenting view and replies to it.) At least since Turing, but with accelerating frequency, human cognition and behavior have been discussed and modelled with computer analogies. Moreover, many are seeking in more direct ways to simulate cognitive behavior with increasingly sophisticated computer programs. (Their modest success may be a glass half full or half empty, as one is inclined.) But in its most general terms the comparison involves supposing an interaction between machine and its immediate environ-ment: information is provided to the data processor whose pre-set program effects a variety of transformations which are then manifested by the machine in a variety of ways. In the jargon of the trade input is processed as output. Nowadays the obvious analogue of an environment, an affected organism, and its behavior scarcely needs mention. The model looks something like this:

$$\text{input} \quad \rightarrow \text{machine} \rightarrow \text{output}$$
$$\text{environment} \rightarrow \text{organism} \rightarrow \text{behavior}$$

Too close to stimulus-response theories, the model clearly needs modifying. In fact such modification owes much to Skinner's development of the concept of the operant and his stress on the interaction of organism and environment making possible a functional analysis of behavior. (See Malone's succinct discussion of Skinner's contribution.) The model needs to provide for the looping effect as the consequences of behavior, mediated by the organism's internal states, tend to modify future behavior.

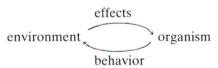

Debate about theory focuses on the need to account for the internal states of the organism as mediating the interaction of environment and behavior. Theorists can take comfort in Schnaitter's emphatic, 'Behaviorism presupposes inner states, and is inconceivable without them.' Surely he is right, too, in stressing that no part of this complex interaction can be neglected. (So much even Hayes and Brownstein may accept, urging only that the last term in a complete explanation is always the environment, never the organism's internal states.) Skinner, of course, allowed for genetic predisposition in organisms, a record of evolutionary adapta-tion (see the chapters by Richelle and Plotkin). Debate here supposes a further record, and more, internal to the organism, of its own individual history. The 'more' is the internal states and processes of the organism, a complex of the inborn and environmentally induced 'records', that function to modify behavior.

So the first part of the debate is whether there is a need for such an account of internal states to provide an explanation of behavior. (Hall's is a challenging affirmative stance.) The debate is reflected in a round-about way in the arid

dispute over what counts as 'explanation' (Bethlehem, Hayes and Brownstein, Rachlin, and others). Moreover, if there are such states, and if they may function profitably in psychological accounts of behavior, we are still left with questions concerning their nature and what we can know and say about them. Philosophers divide here, some arguing for brain states, others (Dennett, 1978, for example) for a 'functional' identification only, allowing that the physical exemplification of such theoretically characterized states may differ in different species, or even among more radically different systems, artificial or natural.

Here we encounter for the first time the echoes of ancient philosophical disputes over mind and body, and determinism and free will. No doubt Skinner sought not only to avoid but also to deny the relevance of such matters to psychology. Nowadays psychologists and most philosophers are inclined to agree, though there are important residues which are part of hard-fought battles in contemporary philosophy of psychology. (The interested reader will find a useful anthology of recent articles on this topic in Block, 1980.) These spill over into psychology in interesting ways, as indicated by the articles of Place, Dennett, Rachlin, and Lacey and Schwartz. The issue here is the language of theory, whether it must capture the intentional character of ordinary idiom, or needs only the extentional character of the first-order predicate calculus; whether dispositional explanations can be tolerated; and whether the categories of goal-directedness are essential to full accounts of human behavior. (The problems of rule-directed behavior may be relevant here; see the articles by Vaughan and Parrott.) It remains, too, to square such talk with the rapidly evolving results of the brain sciences.

In this regard controversy, not consensus, reigns. In and out of psychology theorists each seek to make chaos cosmic (to borrow a pun from Max Beerbohm). Skinner, we may imagine, aware but weary of such debate, may smugly disdain involvement. But these chapters, both pro and con, make clear that the debate may be avoided only on peril of neglect of much of the richness of current psychological science. We have surely passed the time when the ideology of behaviorism need give anyone a second thought.

REFERENCES

Block, N. (1980) *Readings in Philosophy of Psychology*, 2 vols, Cambridge, Mass., Harvard University Press.

Brown, W.M. (1972) 'Ratting on Skinner' and 'Beyond functions and deprivations', in Brown, W.M. *et al.*, *Is a Science of Man Possible?* Hartford, Conn., Trinity College.

Dennett, D.C. (1978) *Brainstorms*, Montgomery, Vt., Bradford Books.

Searle, J. (1980) 'Minds, brains and programs', *The Behavioral and Brain Sciences*, 3, pp. 417–57.

Part XVI: Tabulated Summary

29. Summary of Chapters and Interchanges

SOHAN AND CELIA MODGIL

RADICAL BEHAVIOURISM

Negative Orientation	Positive Response to Negative Orientation	Positive Orientation	Negative Response to Positive Orientation

— two major claims have been made for Skinner's radical behaviourism: first that it has generated an effective science of behaviour based on experimental work with non-human animals; second that this science can be used to predict, control, and interpret the everyday behaviour of our own species
 	
— a critical examination of these claims reveals grounds for scepticism
 	
— with respect to the first, it is argued that Skinner's notion of operant conditioning is much less powerful than might be supposed in that it ignores or undervalues the importance of other determinants of behaviour:
 	
— properly applied reinforcement procedures have sometimes failed to work
 	
— Pavlovian principles may be more important than acknowledged
 	
— schedules are not a 'given', since 'neither men nor animals are found in nature
	— Day argues that Hall has two complaints to make in regard to Skinner's stance as leader and public defender of the scientific study of behavior. One: it is wrong of Skinner to give the impression that the major achievement of the experimental investigation of behavior is the analysis of operant behavior in terms of the well-known three term contingency of discriminative stimulus, response, and reinforcing stimulus.
	
	— Second: it is misleading of Skinner to create the impression that the practical achievements of 'applied behavior analysis' constitute the bona fide application to human affairs of behavior principles determined experimentally in the laboratory; instead, what Skinner is really doing is no more than giving a 'reinterpretation of known facts in the terminology of determinism and anti-mentalism'.
	
	— Hall's first charge is that it involves contention with a straw man. Hall's man of straw consists of the conception that Skinner's science of behavior is restricted to analysis of operant behavior in terms of the three-term contingency, thus rendering it 'incomplete' and 'inadequate'. Day asserts that Skinner's systematic views have
		— an answer to the question 'What is Radical Behaviorism?' is approached by looking at examples of professional writing in which the expression 'radical behaviorism' is used. Day examines three examples of professional philosophical usage.
		
		— professional psychological usage was sampled by the following method: subject-matter indexes for *Psychological Abstracts* were searched for topic descriptions actually containing 'radical behaviorism'. In this way 28 publications were identified and it was their usage of 'radical behaviorism' that Day illustrates here.
		
		— a classification of seven non-mutually-exclusive categories was devised. These categories involved conceptions of radical behaviorism as:
		
		  (i) basically a theory of learning;
		
		  (ii) bearing similarities to phenomenology;
		
		  (iii) an original formulation derived from earlier work;
			— Hall maintains that far from wishing to reject Day's analysis, he can make use of it in justifying his own. It is Hall's contention not to deal explicitly with all of Day's seven categories of psychological usage, as there is some overlap among them, and that Day will also allow that the categories he discusses are not all of the same general type. Hall elaborates on Day's analysis and argues that to attempt to *define* radical behaviorism as that version of behaviorism that generates socially useful consequences would be an insult to the work of psychologists like Eysenck and Miller, who have attempted to derive useful applications from a version of behaviorism that is avowedly not of the radical variety.
			
			— Hall continues that it is 'a comfort to discover how readily most of the varied usages by Day can be derived from my own attempt to summarize the essence of Skinner's thought. If we accept the assertion of the

"central doctrine" that what an organism does can be explained solely in terms of what happens to it, then the notion that we can control behavior and change it in ways that will be socially beneficial follows directly. And if we further argue that what an organism does *should* be explained in this way then several things follow ... this doctrine leads naturally to the use of a certain set of experimental techniques ... it generates a particular sort of learning theory: one that finds no place for entities, processes, or events other than descriptions of behavior and of controlling environmental variables ... it implies an outright rejection of mentalism and leads to a philosophy of psychological science that takes this rejection as its foundation stone'.

— Day's conclusion that radical behaviorism allows the possibility of creating its own productive phenomenology is not supported by Hall's formulation of the central doctrine of radical behaviorism.

Hall replies to Day

(iv) encompassing an analysis of private events;

(v) intrinsically connected with the experimental analysis of behaviour;

(vi) manifesting the applied aspects of Skinner's work;

(vii) the philosophical dimensions of Skinner's thought.

Day

responding repeatedly in an unchanging environment for occasional reinforcement'

— it is not disputed that certain cues immediately follow reinforcement; what is at issue is the assertion that these cues play a critical part in producing the pattern of behaviour observed

— with respect to the second claim it is argued that Skinner's analysis of human behaviour consists, for the most part, not of the application of science as it is usually understood, but in the reinterpretation of known facts in the terminology of determinism and anti-mentalism

— the case for such a reinterpretation is weakened by the extent to which it relies upon the inadequate science of operant behaviour

Hall

always included room for organismic variables: *The Behavior of Organisms* (Skinner, 1938) and *About Behaviorism* (Skinner, 1974).

— with respect to Hall's second objection, that a variety of other forms of learning exist besides simple operant conditioning, and these other types of learning are highly relevant to considering how principles of learning are best applied in solving concrete human problems. Day argues that Hall's mistake is to look at operant conditioning as primarily a *type of learning*. The operant analysis of behavior is not a theory about the nature of the learning process: it is an analysis of *behavior*, an analysis of a certain type of relation that may exist between the environment and behavior.

— Day concludes that 'the force of Hall's paper is diminished, rather than advanced, by his speculations that radical behaviorists show a "surprising lack of confidence" (*sic*) and "a narrowness of vision" (*sic*) in wanting to restrict research to the study of behavior as a subject matter in its own right, and that they cannot "trust themselves (*sic*) to make use of the methodology of their conceptual rivals .... without fear of ceasing to be radical."'

Day replies to Hall

THE EPISTEMOLOGY OF RADICAL BEHAVIOURISM

Negative Orientation	Positive Response to Negative Orientation	Positive Orientation	Negative Response to Positive Orientation
— classically three different sorts of criticisms have been levelled against B.F. Skinner's position	— 'what we have here is an argument to the effect that American practical values are inferior to Continental intellectualistic values, and as Skinner's position is a product of these inferior values, it too is inferior'	— Skinner's naturalistic psychology focuses on the adaptation of organisms to their world	— if understood correctly, Schnaitter recognized in his chapter:
— these criticisms miss the point of Skinner's epistemology	— 'to a considerable extent the chapter speaks for itself and requires no critique beyond *caveat emptor*'	— according to such a view, knowledge consists of the capacities of the knowing organism to act with regard to the world	'knowledge as action; the epistemology of radical behaviourism':
— the criticism formulated in this chapter is of a strictly epistemological nature relying on logic and sociology	— however, cataloguing a selection of its more egregious errors cannot be resisted:	— furthermore, actions themselves are categories whose most basic feature is a relation between the external effects of what the acting organism does and certain reciprocal causal consequences of these external effects on the actor	— that knowledge rests on acts — that radical behaviourism does not explain inner acts or thoughts — that Skinner's goal is the description, control and prediction of behaviour instead of its explanation
— Skinner's system represents the most rigorous and consistent application of operationism to psychology, with all the difficulties involved in such an undertaking	— Skinner's 'criterion for the evaluation of knowledge' has to do with one's effectiveness at getting along in that aspect of the world reflected in some putative domain of knowledge	— if these premises of Skinner's are correct, then knowledge must consist, not of certain internal mental possessions of the knower, but of a set of causal interrelationships through which the knower stands to its world	— the position raises questions: — how do physical actions get truth values attached to themselves once they become thoughts or arguments in a discussion?
— according to Skinner, operationism deals with observations; computational and manipulative procedures entailed by observations and the logical and mathematical steps taken from thereon	— contrary to Vonèche's claim, Skinner does not replace causality with correlation	— in another sense, however, the inner states of the knower are fundamental to the behavioural analysis of knowledge, for such inner states provide the material means of sustaining any causal relationship in which the organism stands	— can we still apply the term 'psychology' to a science that does not explain or describe inner life?
— such a form of operationism presents several difficulties: (1) it does not give a criterion for the validation of knowledge, but a technique for the construction of concepts with a given empirical meaning; therefore it denies any validity to the logical analysis of scientific discourse in favour of a psychological one (2) the requirement for the validity of any psychological theory that it predict and control behaviour; indeed Skinner	— that scientific laws must be 'unlimited and universal' is 'an old chestnut'; all a valid generalization must do is generalize over its own domain		— how does Skinner draw the line separating description, control and prediction from explanation, from a logical point of view? — by systematically refusing one of the two terms of such dialectical

distinctions as objective and subjective meanings, facts and values, or internal and external acts, Skinner, instead of founding a truly 'scientific' and 'objective' science, replicates the ideology of Puritanism

Vonèche Replies to Schnaiter

Schnaiter

— Vonèche quite uncontroversially asserts that descriptive propositions can be evaluated only in a context, and claims that this truism is inconsistent with Skinner's epistemology — no reasons are given, indeed none can be given — such a conclusion is spurious
— Vonèche's discussion of automata theory is correct, but in consequence of misinterpreting Skinner's position, his conclusions are incorrect
— Skinner does not attempt to explain all behaviour through learning — he makes reference to phylogenetic contributions
— Skinner does not rely heavily on reflexes in accounting for learning
— Skinner is not opposed to 'interpretive discourse' and explicitly engages in it; the book *About Behaviourism* is almost exclusively interpretive

Schnaiter Replies to Vonèche

defines his system as positivistic and limited to the description rather than to the explanation behaviour
(3) the replacement of causality by the relation between the modification of an independent variable (the 'cause') and the modification of a dependent variable (the 'effect')
— another form of the logical argument can be concerned with the proof that a behaviourist explanation of external behaviour is impossible
— the epistemology of radical behaviourism is self-contradictory in at least three ways:
(1) it attempts to explain behaviour only by learning, relying heavily on reflexes
(2) learning is defined as a modification of behaviour due to experience and not as the development of competences in dealing with new issues
(3) there is a more basic contradiction in the system; reflexes, stimuli, responses are concepts
— another form of contradiction appears in the very language used by Skinner in his theorizing; it is self-contradictory to refuse interpretive discourse and to use words as interpretive as 'reinforcements' or 'contingencies'
— with reference to the sociological argument, the success of Skinner's views in spite of all their logical pitfalls is the adherence to a set of American values exported by the government of the USA along with merchandise

Vonèche

Negative Orientation	Positive Response to Negative Orientation	Positive Orientation	Negative Response to Positive Orientation

A PSYCHOLOGICAL ANALYSIS: POLITICAL, SOCIAL AND MORAL IMPLICATIONS

Negative Orientation	Positive Response to Negative Orientation	Positive Orientation	Negative Response to Positive Orientation

— Skinner has made important contributions to scientific psychology in the research and thought that went into his work on operant conditioning and schedules of reinforcement
 	
— he has always been superficial philosophically and that shortcoming somewhat limits the value of his scientific contribution and, with his lack of artistic insight, almost entirely vitiates his extensive writings on politics, ethics, philosophy and art
 	
— Skinner has a limited view of science:
  — there is the unstated assumption underlying his work that natural science is equivalent to 'radical behaviourism'
  — little attention to individual differences, behaviour genetics and developmental psychology is apparent
  — statistical sampling theory and its application in mental testing are ignored
  — there is a naivety regarding *cause*
 	
— Skinner has made no attempt to come to grips with epistemology and provides no foundation for his
	— Wright finds his colleague's comments puzzling and welcomes the opportunity to try to set the record straight
	
	— the substance of Skinner's ideas are insufficiently examined, if at all
	
	— there are misrepresentations of a particularly disconcerting nature and inaccurate pictures regarding the basic tenets of radical behaviourism
	
	— the author of the respondent/operant distinction as well as papers on phylogenetic/ontogenetic contingencies would not be guilty of claiming 'that contingencies of reinforcement can explain virtually all behaviour'; what he does claim is that much can be gained in developing a science of behaviour by investigating behaviour directly in the context of environmental contingencies
	
	— the discussion of reinforcement reveals a failure to understand Skinner's emphasis on carrying out an empirical functional analysis
	
	— the distinction between methodological behaviourism and radical behaviourism is not confronted critically; there are at
		— from a sparse but uncompromising empirically-based laboratory science, Skinner had advocated an all-embracing behavioural technology that has relevance to all aspects of our everyday existence
		
		— by eschewing a reductionist philosophy, Skinner has been able to encourage and contribute to legitimizing the study of behaviour at its own level — the proper study of behaviour is *behaviour*
		
		— the value of the insistence on this course is fully appreciated when we consider the current pervasiveness of applied operant work
		
		— as Skinner's ideas and philosophy become more widely known, his overall system receives more intense scrutiny, especially in terms of ethical and socio-political ramifications
		
		— 'the behavioural issues germane to this area of larger concern are reviewed in this chapter and the patient is found to be vigorous and of good health.'
			— the clarity of Wright's defence of Skinner's work brings out the shortcomings in the philosophizing
			
			— the value of Skinner's researches into operant conditioning and schedules of reinforcement is stretched to infiltrate areas quite beyond its powers to strengthen
			
			— the 'commitment to materialist determinism' to which Wright refers is essential to a thoroughgoing scientist in the scientific role, but it is important to stand apart from that role or the role itself becomes meaningless
			
			— 'antimentalism' cannot be adhered to wholeheartedly when dealing with truth and ethics, because the concepts themselves have no meaning outside a mentalistic framework
			
			— these points take us outside the walled domain of science — it is certain that Skinner and Wright are aware of them but it is the reflective examination that is absent from Skinner's writings
			
			Bethlehem Replies to Wright

Wright

radical behaviourism
— even the simple questions of what the radical behaviourist is to take for his data are dealt with superficially
— knowledge is a repertoire of behaviour
— if Skinner understands little of the philosophy of science, he understands less of political and ethical philosophy
— there is little awareness of the libertarian view
— democracy is dismissed
— there is no serious discussion of justice
— his views on art and life are banal
— his most prominent dogma is that contingencies in reinforcement can explain virtually all behaviour and anything that is not behaviour or a reinforcement schedule is irrelevant

Bethlehem

least two crucial distinctions — the first distinction is that not only does radical behaviorism attach scientific significance to private as well as to public events; it further assumes that the two classes of events achieve their effects through similar psychological processes. Bethlehem is unprepared for the second distinction, *viz.*, a radical behaviouristic perspective embraces the behaviour of the behavioural scientist within its theoretical domain — which, taken together, provide radical behaviourism a unique ontological status amongst the experimental sciences: that of being able to account for the behaviour of the scientist within the deterministic system that he (the scientist) espouses

Wright Replies to Bethlehem

Negative Orientation	Positive Response to Negative Orientation	Positive Orientation	Negative Response to Positive Orientation

PHILOSOPHY OF SCIENCE AND PSYCHOLOGY

Negative Orientation	Positive Response to Negative Orientation	Positive Orientation	Negative Response to Positive Orientation
— Skinner's philosophy of science consists of conceptual imperatives regarding the proper way to analyze behaviour; while he advocates the functional analysis of the external variables that control behaviour, he rejects mentalistic theories, statistical analysis, hypothesis-testing and inferred theoretical constructs — his philosophy also views philosophical and scientific verbal behaviour as phenomena to be explained via functional analysis of verbal behaviour — unfortunately, Skinner's functional analysis of verbal behaviour lacks the extensive empirical base required for his sweeping revision of philosophy — further, his psychological analysis of philosophy stands on philosophical assumptions regarding explanation which cannot be justified from within his system — being highly pragmatic, he overemphasizes the study of accessible variables, and this leads him to confuse explanation with	— Wessells' article is admirably researched and penetrating but the assessment of Skinner's philosophy of science is inadequate in some ways and mistaken in others — Wessells claims that 'the capacities and the inner workings of a system may be analyzed on a conceptual level as well as on a physical one'; the conceptual analysis of which he speaks takes the form of speculative explanation in non-physical terms: hence, it is not an analysis of the inner workings of a physical system — with respect to Skinner relegating physiology to a secondary status, Skinner's point is that in the division of labour for the study of behaviour it is the psychologist who isolates the terms between which the physiologist seeks the connections; but physiology is no less important: laws and tools developed by physiologists would enrich the resources available to the behaviourist but that would not mean that the laws of physiology had superseded the laws of behaviour	— Skinner insists that the study of the nature of science should be empirical rather than conceptual — our most adequate understanding of the nature of science will be achieved by studying the behaviour distinctive of scientists and identifying the reinforcers that bring it about — the most distinctive reinforcer of scientific behaviour is the newly discovered causal relation — because the larger community depends so heavily on scientific activity for its welfare, it seeks to identify those individuals who are most responsive to newly discovered causal relations, to strengthen and shape their behaviour toward making such discoveries, and to monitor the integrity and safety of their behaviour — this understanding of science provides an illuminating framework within which to expound the nature of explanation, theory, interpretation, technology and the laboratory	— the two descriptions of Skinner's views on science are in agreement, but there is extensive disagreement on the validity of Skinner's views particularly those regarding theory and explanation — like Skinner, Creel rejects non-physical accounts because they are difficult to confirm or to falsify by observation and manipulation and because they discourage the development of physicalist accounts; this does not apply to cognitive psychology, within which mentalistic theories are being developed — cognitive theorists assume that mental processes are physical in nature and they analyze physical systems conceptually in terms of capacities and processes; thus mentalism does not entail dualism, yet it may be pursued fruitfully on a non-physical level — the issue here is not whether the system is physical but how best to construct scientific theories about it. — scientific theories should be judged

prediction and control and to reject inferred processes, which have played an important explanatory role in other sciences

— while Skinner has helped to put psychology on a scientific footing, he has simultaneously opposed the kinds of practices that have been productive in other sciences

Wessells

— Wessells argues that the behaviourist account of a learning episode is incomplete; Skinner would agree that it is incomplete because it does not include a physiological account of the causal connections that mediate input and output

— Wessells believes that in science we can get at something more than functional relations that are utlimately opaque — Creel does not believe it possible

— Wessells states that Skinner confuses explanation with prediction and control; the emphasis on prediction and control in experimentation, however, is strictly for the sake of understanding, not application

Creel Replies to Wessells

— it should not be surprising that the scientific approach to explanation has strengthened so dramatically over the last several centuries while alternative forms of explanation have weakened; the alternatives have not provided us with effective, growing control over our situation, whereas science has

— further, science will continue to prosper because those societies that are reinforced by it will have a survival advantage over those that are not, and those that do it more effectively will have an advantage over those that do it less effectively

— because science is increasing our control over the world, its control over us is increasing

Creel

according to the usual criteria of empirical confirmation, generality, testability, internal consistency, parsimony, etc.

— some cognitive theories fare well by these criteria and they explain many phenomena that are beyond the range of Skinner's theory

— the two chapters differ in conceptions of the role of theory and of the relation between observation and theory: Creel implies that observations are the more objective and are free of theory; the problem is that observation, theory and meta-theory are tightly interwoven.

Wessells Replies to Creel

Negative Orientation	Positive Response to Negative Orientation	Positive Orientation	Negative Response to Positive Orientation
			— Richelle asks whether Skinner *was* biologically naive and, if so, how naïve
			— Plotkin's view is that Skinner *was* biologically naive, together with being unscholarly and isolated
			— he showed deficient understanding of specific and central issues in evolutionary biology; e.g., the notion of homology; the interpretation of Waddington's work on genetic assimilation; and further, there is no known instance of his referring to the use of the evolutionary analogy in the writings of others
			— Richelle is right to emphasize the potential empirical and theoretical payoff of studies on variation during learning; in doing so, he shows a keener appreciation of the uses to which the evolutionary analogy can be put than did Skinner whose references to the analogy tended to focus on selection
			— Richelle's assessment of Skinner's use of the evolutionary analogy as being praiseworthy is

VARIATION AND SELECTION

Negative Orientation	Positive Response to Negative Orientation	Positive Orientation	Negative Response to Positive Orientation
— Skinner is one of a distinguished line of psychologists who have used what is known of the process of evolution as a model to guide thinking about the problems of learning	— Plotkin's summary of the history of the evolutionary analogy as applied to learning processes could have served as an introduction to Richelle's contribution	— many aspects of Skinner's thinking have been persistently misinterpreted by his opponents	
— however, his radical behaviourism was always an obstacle to its adequate implementation	— the chapters differ on one fundamental point: Plotkin points as Richelle does to the fact that Skinner has not really used the evolutionary analogy in empirical research that would have demonstrated its heuristic value within his theory; Richelle has argued that the reasons for that were historical and methodological; Plotkin contends that the main reason is to be found in the behaviourist approach itself, which is of an ideological rather than rational nature	— misrepresentations of Skinner's position toward biology are expressed as the 'black-box' psychology, the extreme environmentalism and the neglect of species-specific behaviour	
— Skinner never achieved what Lorenz, Piaget or Campbell achieved with the evolutionary analogy because the latter had no conceptual scruples about thinking about unobservables; few scientists do		— Skinner simply insisted that there is an important place for a study of behaviour and that the progress of brain physiology itself is tied to progress in the study of behaviour	
— however, radical behaviourism is not rational in this respect, it is ideological and that is no way to do science; the very fact that Skinner never refers to the use of the analogy by others shows the extent to which his own work was forced to an isolationism born of an ideological stance	— Plotkin does not state clearly how he defines the behaviourist ideological stand	— environmentalism has nothing to do with a denial of genetic endowment: the role of the environment is crucial both in selecting particular genic structures and in shaping particular combinations of behaviour units	
— however, concentrated reading of Skinner's work for the writing of this chapter leads to a much greater respect for his work: 'if	— further, the conflict seems to be between some sort of cognitivism and some sort of behaviourism and 'it would take more than 800 words to clarify it'	— Skinner was initially interested in the nature of learning mechanisms not in the evolution of learning capacities; after the interaction between the behaviourist tradition and ethology, Skinner devoted much thought to the relation between phylogenetic and ontogenetic mechanisms accounting for behavioural repertoires	
		— it is argued that reference to Darwin in Skinner's work is crucial both in suggesting an alternative to intentionality in explaining behaviour and in offering a	

Skinner had been able to wed his exposition of the operant to a more tolerant, dare I repeat, rational, view of internal processes, then his application of the evolutionary analogy might have yielded quite profound success'

Plotkin

— Richelle's divergence from Plotkin might be reducible to a difference in the respective ways of looking at and judging Skinner's contribution to science: Plotkin takes it as a closed system, based on some *a priori* ideology (radical behaviourism) that has doomed to sterility the most promising intuitions throughout a whole intellectual career and has 'forced' Skinner to isolationism

— Richelle considers that, evaluated by such criteria, many great scientists should be suspected of the same sin

— Richelle thinks of Skinner's work as an open and dynamic system: parts of it that might look imperfectly worked out in some respects might become stimulating for future research

Richelle Replies to Plotkin

model of individual behavioural changes in terms of variation and selection.

— the nature and sources of variation have been given only occasional attention; it would seem that dealing with variation in its own right is a risk that few scientists will take as long as they can move on without it; biologists have found it more appropriate to concentrate on selection first, it is no wonder that psychologists have followed the same action; further, it seemed important to demonstrate the lawfulness of operant control so that variation within an individual's behaviour was usually overlooked

— however, there has been increasing attention on the variation aspect of the operant model: Stadden and Simmelhag (1971), giving credit to Skinner for the original idea, have worked out the evolutionary analogy, together with other contributions along the same lines; however, there is much to be done before the nature and the sources of behavioural variation are understood

— the relevance of Skinner's model to the evolution of learning capacities is compared with the relevance of other views and some convergences are noted between Skinner on one hand and Piaget and Lorenz on the other

Richelle

rejected: it is precisely because of Skinner's biological naïvety that his exposition on the analogy is one of the more trivial in the literature; it does not compare with the depth that Lorenz, Piaget and Campbell brought to their use of the analogy

— contrary to Richelle's assertion (referring to Plotkin and Odling-Smee, 1982), Plotkin does believe that a general theory of learning is possible; what he does not believe is that the associationist framework into which most of general process theory is cast is adequate

— something like the evolutionary analogy operating via different mechanisms at different levels in a hierarchy of knowledge-gaining processes is what Plotkin considers to be the appropriate conceptual scheme for a general theory of learning

— Skinner may have had that kind of vision but he has not been able to implement it in a coherent analysis or theory

Plotkin Replies to Richelle

Negative Orientation	Positive Response to Negative Orientation	Positive Orientation	Negative Response to Positive Orientation
	THE EXPLANATORY POWER OF SKINNERIAN PRINCIPLES		

THE EXPLANATORY POWER OF SKINNERIAN PRINCIPLES

Negative Orientation

— the chapter is principally concerned with evaluating the comprehensiveness of the explanatory power of radical behaviourist principles

— Skinner has maintained that his commitment to comprehensiveness is required if one adopts a scientific stance towards human beings

— it is not being asked whether behaviour principles currently are comprehensive, rather, whether behaviour principles are *in principle* comprehensive: it must be shown that there are behaviours that principles consistent with the constraints of the research programme cannot explain

— a serious argument for the inherently restricted explanatory power of the radical behaviourist research programme can be expected to spring not from a formal proof that behaviourist principles must be inconsistent with certain data, but from the positive achievements of an alternative scheme

— the demonstration of a list of achievements by an alternative scheme to behaviourism shows that

Positive Response to Negative Orientation

— mentalistic reasoning attempts to get behind the surface of behaviour to the underlying mental state while behaviourist reasoning attempts to get behind the surface of mental state to the underlying contingencies of reinforcement

— the mentalist infers current internal mental events (perceptions, beliefs, expectancies) as the causal focus of current behaviour and the behaviourist infers past external behaviour-environment interactions (stimuli, responses, reinforcers, punishers) as the causal focus of current behaviour (including current perceptions, beliefs and expectancies)

— the critical difference between the mentalist and the behaviourist lies in the point where explanations may stop: for a mentalist explanations of a behaviour may stop when they have been traced to a current internal cause; for a behaviourist explanations of behaviour (or mental states) may stop only

Positive Orientation

— as judged against three other psychological viewpoints, mentalism, cognitivism and physiologism, Skinner's radical behaviourism has great explanatory power:
  — it is internally coherent
  — especially in its recent development it is expressible in quantitative terms

— it has a firm laboratory base in which its principles clearly apply

— it is not grossly implausible

— most importantly, it has meaningful application both in relatively simple real-world situations (such as prisons, factories and armies) where control of human behaviour has been largely unidirectional

— and in relatively complex real-world situations (such as families) where control of human behaviour has been multidirectional

— in both simple and complex real-world situations the explanatory power of radical behaviourism is much greater

Negative Response to Positive Orientation

— Rachlin identifies practical application, the achievement of control, as the pre-eminent criterion for assessing the explanatory power of a theory

— the weakness lies in the difficulty and ambiguity of specifying the 'relevant domain' over which the explanatory scheme is meant to operate

— however, Lacey and Schwartz have argued that the controls (successful applications) engendered by radical behaviourism have occurred only in 'closed settings'

— on this argument the regularities expressed in radical behaviourist theories are just the laws of behaviour in closed settings

— however, what Lacey and Schwartz's argument makes clear is that the mere fact of successful control in itself tells us nothing about the extent of the explanatory power of the principles that underlie this power to control: that the principles enable control of behaviour in closed settings implies nothing about whether or not they are salient principles for explaining behaviour in general

— their explanatory scope will depend upon the relative frequency of closed and open settings in the environments in which people typically find themselves — another empirical issue

— accepting teleology in broad outline implies interacting with other human beings differently from the way implied by the behaviourist outline: emphasizing relations of dialogue rather than control

— Rachlin seems to offer two responses to this argument: first that there are clear instances of the application of operant principles in open settings, e.g., procedures of self-control and the treatment of pain; second, that mentalistic terms can be translated into behaviourist terms though complex and cumbersome

— it is suggested that self-control and pain cannot properly be regarded as exemplifications of operant principles and make sense only in terms of teleological categories; mentalistic translations into behaviourist terms are impossible

*Lacey and Schwartz
Reply to Rachlin*

than the other three viewpoints

Rachlin

behaviourism is incomplete

— a suitable alternative to behaviourism could come from either of two sources: from cognitive psychology or from an explanatory scheme whose origins lie in practical life rather than experimental research, such as that of teleological explanation

— it is concluded that there is no evidence that behavioural principles are exemplified outside closed settings, and that in open settings radical behaviourism offers neither explanations nor illuminating descriptions

— in contrast, teleological categories (goal, expectancy plan, reason, intention, etc.) are routinely successful in capturing order in human action, and in expressing the detail, sequence, novelty and significant variation that human behaviour displays

— it can be shown how this argument is associated with a coherent account of the nature of the human person which conflicts with that which is at the foundation of the radical behaviourist research programme

Lacey and Schwartz

when they have been traced to a previous external cause

— Lacey and Schwartz claim that, although it may capture behaviour-environment *regularities*, the behaviourist vocabulary is insufficient to capture behaviour-environment *irregularities* (i.e., novelty and variability)

— this argument assumes that there exist human behaviours (aside from simple reflexes) that cannot 'in principle' be traced to underlying contingencies of reinforcement

— it would seem, from the success of current applications of behaviourism to everyday life, especially to situations involving self-control, that interpretation in open settings is worthwhile and that human life, in all its richness, may be more regular than Lacey and Schwartz suspect

*Rachlin Replies to
Lacey and Schwartz*

SKINNER AND THE UNIT OF BEHAVIOUR

Negative Orientation	Positive Response to Negative Orientation	Positive Orientation	Negative Response to Positive Orientation
— Skinner provided a promising alternative to associationist and cognitive theories in his analysis of the behavioural unit, published in the thirties — yet, he seemed to fail to grasp the important aspects of his own analysis and, paradoxically, he emphasized molecular interpretations over many years — this was incompatible with his early analysis and with the defining characteristics of the research programme that has developed under his guidance — one consequence has been the tendency of recent critics, including those expert in the field, to see no difference of substance between his views and those of S-R associationism — several crucial considerations suggest that the basic terminology used in the analysis of behaviour may contribute to this misunderstanding — despite obvious dangers, the use of behavioural terms other than those used in basic conditioning research could have great advantages	— in general it is believed that Malone's arguments strengthen Hinson's — the most important points are summarized and the agreements and disagreements noted — many psychologists and philosophers have a difficult time understanding radical behaviourism; part of the confusion may occur because of the normal distinction drawn between methodological and radical behaviourism, as though they were two varieties of the same general line of thought — modern cognitive psychologists who are uniformly critical of Skinner also contribute to the misunderstanding of radical behaviourism: while the specific types of association mechanisms employed by cognitive psychologists are more complex and subtle, the form of explanation is the same as that of classic associationism — while it is believed by Hinson that Malone would agree with the foregoing statements, he would also add that Skinner has contributed to the confusion, primarily by reliance on the explanatory principle of temporal contiguity	— Skinner's operant theory is often mistakenly identified as the commonsense application of the principles of reward and punishment to the study of behaviour — also Skinner's philosophy of radical behaviourism is generally either dismissed or believed to be irrelevant to the application of the technical innovations of operant conditioning — in reality Skinner's operant theory follows directly from his philosophy of radical behaviourism — this philosophy has helped Skinner to avoid the conceptual errors of the alternative theories of his predecessors and contemporaries — the best illustration of Skinner's conceptual analysis is in his treatment of the problem of determining behavioural units of analysis, which appeared in the early works laying the foundation for modern operant theory — comparison of Skinner's position with the once dominant position of Hull shows why operant theory, based on radical behaviourism, ultimately achieved superiority — by accepting the potential complexity of behaviour, and by resisting the	— Malone illustrates further the confusion surrounding radical behaviourism — he comments that Hinson describes a wise and consistent Skinner, who seems to have spent half a century vainly arguing for radical behaviourism; Hinson provides citations to support his rendition of Skinner's career, knowing that those citations are hard to come by; it is far easier to find citations that stress molecularism, devices such as conditioned reinforcers and chains, and things that we 'find reinforcing' — Malone considers that Skinner has received credit enough so is not worried when he says that Hinson is too kind to him — Skinner gave us a version of radical behaviourism more sophisticated than the one Watson provided in 1919, and for that we should be grateful; but he also gave us a particular conditioning theory and a vocabulary which should long since have been abandoned *Malone Replies to Hinson*

— chief among these would be the decreased likelihood that the analysis of behaviour will be confused with discredited S-R theory

— furthermore, Malone would argue that a restricted set of explanatory or integrative concepts, such as discriminative stimulus, reinforcer, conditioned reinforcer, has hindered rather than aided the analysis of behaviour: what has been given is a redefinition of terms; it is difficult to disagree with this point

Malone

— despite broad agreement with Malone's criticisms, Hinson maintains that Skinner's approach to the analysis of behavioural units is cogent; many of his specific inquiries are of questionable value, such as his summary dismissal of the existence of behavioural contrast, his odd reliance on temporal contiguity and his promiscuous employment of conditioned reinforcers; on the other hand, his conceptual approach to the problems of psychology still provides the best available alternative for the analysis of behaviour

Hinson Replies to Malone

temptation to reduce behaviour to associations between simple physical events, Skinner avoided a number of problems encountered by Hull

— strangely, many of the criticisms of the operant approach seem to be addressed to limitations of the approach typified by Hull

— many cognitive theories, which are supposed to go beyond the limitations of behaviourism, posit underlying mechanisms, different in degree, but similar in function to those employed in Hull's theory

— 'While Skinner's inductive approach has often been criticized for its lack of theoretical structure, honest poverty is always preferable to suspicious wealth'

Hinson

Negative Orientation	Positive Response to Negative Orientation	Positive Orientation	Negative Response to Positive Orientation
	SKINNER'S POSITION AGAINST THEORY AND AGAINST MENTALISM		
— the chapter examines Skinner's objections to mentalism	— discussing radical behaviourism in contrast to emergent behaviourism involves comparison of a proposal for a science of behaviour and some products of this proposal with only a proposal	— Skinner has consistently claimed that prediction and control are the end products of science	— the arguments made by Hayes and Brownstein form an excellent basis for a technology of behaviour but are inadequate for a science of behaviour
— it is concluded that his only valid objections concern the 'specious explanations' that mentalism might afford — explanations that are incomplete, circular or faulty in other ways	— it can only be guessed how the products of emergent behaviourism will measure up; the aspirations are consistent in large part with those of radical behaviourism	— it seems only fair to evaluate radical behaviourism against the goals it sets for itself; other purposes might be well served by different scientific practices and beliefs	— science is about understanding, and employs prediction and control as tests of adequate understanding; understanding is intrinsically metaphorical — 'as Einstein said, it involves reducing a phenomenon to models that we already have intuitions about'
— unfortunately, the mere adoption of behaviourist terminology does not solve that problem	— the proposed approach appears to be more permissive than radical behaviourism, but Killeen intends this flexibility to be tempered by evaluating scientific activities relative to their intended functions; if this actually worked, who could disagree with such a proposal? not radical behaviourists, since for them the issue is not the form of science but its function	— Skinner believes that a scientific analysis of behaviour must assume that a person's behaviour is controlled by his genetic and environmental histories rather than by the person himself as an initiating, creative agent: '(we assume that) human behaviour as a whole is fully determined'	— hypothetical constructs may be manipulated as directly as behaviour, however directly that may be
— it camouflages the nature of 'private events', while providing no protection from specious explanations		— Skinner is quite clear that his concern over mentalism is primarily the limited type of science it allows; he has elaborated that 'in its search for internal explanations, supported by the false sense of cause associated with feelings and introspective observations, mentalism has obscured the environmental antecedents which would have led to a much more effective analysis'	— Skinner does not share the authors' reluctance to view behaviour as a cause of behaviour
— it is argued that covert states and events *are* causally effective, and may be sufficiently different in their nature to deserve a name other than 'behaviour'	— Killeen is offering a return to a more theoretical venture with inclusion of mental events, superimposing the criterion of pragmatic value; Skinner's objection to certain types of theories is largely that these types seem to become ends in themselves — when this happens, they are no longer	— Skinner further believes that an improperly placed concern over	— although one may object to 'mind' because some people associate it with non-physical 'stuff', one need not so reify the construct
— to call such events 'mental' does not force a dualistic metaphysics; such a distinction can be easily assimilated by an 'emergent behaviourism'			— we must go inside our system and not forget where are or what we study, we might call
— emergent behaviourism would make explicit use of theories; it would be inductive and pragmatic and would evaluate			

hypothetical constructs in terms of their utility in identifying and solving the outstanding problems of the discipline

Killeen

pragmatically useful; his objections to mentalism are based on the same concerns and Hayes and Brownstein believe, with good reason

— 'perhaps Killeen is right that an emergent behaviourism could have its mentalistic cake and eat it pragmatically too, but we doubt that this would be so. As we tried to show in our chapter, allowing behavioural causes (made seemingly less incomplete by calling them 'mental') ultimately tends to stop causal analysis before the point at which effective action is possible. We see nothing in Killeen's proposal that would deal with this problem'

— all of this is not to say that Killeen is incorrect to insist we get on with the important tasks at hand; it is feared that his proposal is the wrong solution made for the right reasons: there will be more long-term value in a fresh look at radical behaviourism than in 'seeking excitement . . . at the back door of cognitivism'

Hayes and Brownstein
Reply to Killeen

private causes, behavioural causes, or any 'cause' that is in principle non-manipulable will slow our progress because it diverts our efforts toward necessarily incomplete analyses

— much of the criticism of the behavioural approach arises from a failure to recognize its goals

— another, and perhaps more legitimate, criticism of the behavioural approach has been its apparent lack of experimental involvement with behaviours of special significance for understanding human interaction; much of the frustration with a behavioural position has arisen from this apparent lack and it has often been falsely attributed to the fundamentals of Skinner's view on scientific explanation and private events

— to the contrary, it is believed that as radical behaviourists become more involved with complex human behaviours (as they should) they must not inappropriately relinquish the framework of a behavioural approach and its advantages

Hayes and Brownstein

phenomena there by a different name: 'if "mental states" has too chequered a history, let us coin new terms, such as "mentate"'

— however we call them, let us not solve the spectrum of challenges we face by placing them under a single wavelength and then asserting that all is green

Killeen Replies to
Hayes and Brownstein

Negative Orientation	Positive Response to Negative Orientation	Positive Orientation	Negative Response to Positive Orientation

SKINNER AND THE 'VIRTUS DORMITIVA' ARGUMENT

Negative Orientation	Positive Response to Negative Orientation	Positive Orientation	Negative Response to Positive Orientation
— Dennett's main contribution is in the form of a reply to Place's chapter	— while it is clear from Dennett's reply that there is substantial agreement about what is wrong with Skinner's reasons, both explicit and implicit, for repudiating mentalism, Place and Dennett are still far apart on the nature of mentalism and on the question of whether there are any circumstances under which the use of mentalistic explanations needs to be repudiated for the purposes of science and, if so, what those circumstances are	— in 'Skinner Skinned', Dennett (1978, Ch. 4) discusses two arguments, the *virtus dormitiva* and intentionality arguments, which he sees as the only solid ground underlying the various arguments which Skinner gives for repudiating the use of mentalistic explanations in a scientific psychology; of these he endorses only the intentionality argument	— as there has been some misinterpretation, Dennett attempts to set out more straightforwardly what he takes the issues to be as they arise in Place's chapter
	— this is an important issue because, if Place is right, Skinner's analysis of behaviour survives more or less intact; it is only the reasons he gives for adopting that analysis which are threatened; whereas if Dennett is right, there is no room for analysis either	— Place argues (1) that what Skinner finds objectionable in mentalistic idioms is their dispositional character, (2) that both the *virtus dormitiva* and intentionality arguments are arguments against the use of dispositional property ascriptions and (3) that, since dispositional property ascriptions are essential to any causal explanation, Dennett has failed to provide any good reason for endorsing Skinner's repudiation of mentalism	— Place and Dennett agree that Skinner has not given a good reason to shun dispositional properties, not even dispositional properties of the organism
	— Place responds to Dennett's detailed criticisms in the same order	— it is suggested that mentalism is objectionable only insofar as it involves the use of idioms which	— Dennett gathers that both would agree that even the *virtus dormitiva* of opium could be cited non-vacuously to help explain *something* — if not its capacity to put people to sleep, then perhaps its capacity to anaesthetize or impair performance on memory tests: 'there are other ways of achieving anaesthesia aside from putting to sleep: opium, like novocain, might be said to anaesthetize thanks to its *virtus dormitiva*'
	— overall, Place concludes: since, for Dennett, Skinner's project has no intrinsic merit to recommend it, it stands or falls for him on the cogency of the reasons given for adopting it; that is a view that cannot be shared		— there is agreement that mentalistic explanations, even if they cannot be reduced to formulations in the first-order predicate calculus, can have their place in science; that is not so much a disagreement with Skinner as with Quine

— that mentalistic explanations presuppose rationality and that this is what creates the problems about their status in psychology, receives superficial agreement; Dennett attributed this insight to Skinner as well, but not in the version Place accepts

— Dennett considers that the question for Skinner is 'of all the criticisms he has levelled against "mentalism" which strikes him as most important . . .?'; is it that mentalistic explanations:

(1) are dualistic (imply non-physical processes)

(2) imply a non-existent privacy

(3) invoke inferred as opposed to observable entities (intervening variables)

(4) invoke internal as opposed to external dispositional properties

(5) are vacuous in the fashion of the *virtus dormitiva*

(6) presuppose rationality and hence are circular in psychology

(7) simply are dispositional?

Dennett Replies to Place

presuppose what Skinner (1969) calls 'rule-governed' behaviour to explain behaviour that is 'contingency-shaped'

Place

— the value of Skinner's project has already been amply demonstrated by the results achieved from its application; as is predicted by the theory that mentalistic explanations presuppose verbal control of the behaviour to be explained, these results are most impressive in areas such as animal behaviour and the behaviour of the mentally handicapped where the behaviour is either entirely or predominantly 'contingency-shaped' and thus uncomplicated by the superimposition of verbal control

— once the defects of Skinner's (1957) initial attempt have been put right, behaviour analysis will provide us for the first time with a fully integrated theory of language which incorporates phenomena at the pragmatic as well as the semantic and syntactic levels of analysis, linguistic performance as well as linguistic competence

— since Place's evaluation of Skinner's project does not depend on the reasons he gives for adopting it, Place has no wish to join Dennett in urging Skinner to settle for one of the various alternative reasons for repudiating mentalism

Place Replies to Dennett

Negative Orientation	Positive Response to Negative Orientation	Positive Orientation	Negative Response to Positive Orientation
		RULE-GOVERNED BEHAVIOUR	

Negative Response to Positive Orientation

— rule governance involves processes of stimulus function transfer whereby the control exerted by verbal stimuli comes to be exerted by other verbal and non-verbal events

— Vaughan makes no serious attempt to analyze these processes, accounting for the occurrence of rule governance by appeal to an amorphous 'complex conditioning history'

— little understanding of rule governance is accomplished by this means and, as a result, little contribution is made to the understanding of higher mental processes

— in short, Vaughan's analysis, like Skinner's, is only nominally functional

— a genuinely functional analysis is more than a description of temporal relations among stimuli and responses observed in a given episode of their occurrence

— it is an analysis of stimulation with respect to responding — an analysis of functions — and

Positive Orientation

— rule-governed behaviour was first alluded to by Skinner in 1947 when he gave the distinguished William James Lectures at Harvard University

— at this time he talked about such behaviour in terms of conditioning the behaviour of the listener — to explain the behaviour of the speaker

— it was not until 1965 that Skinner first referred to such behaviour as rule-governed; in doing so, he opened up a new area of investigation

— now twenty years later rule-governed behaviour is emerging as a critical class of behaviour in analyzing complex human behaviour; the descriptive power of the concept is especially appealing when analyzing instances of human activity often referred to as problem-solving or rational behaviour

— as a result, much of the behaviour studied by cognitive psychologists as higher mental activity is brought within the realm of a science of behaviour, subject to measurement in physical dimensions

— therefore, aspects of cognition or everyday intellectual behaviour are

Positive Response to Negative Orientation

— Parrott finds Skinner's (1966) distinction between behavior which is directly shaped by contingencies of reinforcement and behavior which occurs as a function of a description of such contingencies, the latter case being rule-governed — as 'spurious' and 'trivial'. However, Vaughan asserts that Parrott's solution to the situation she finds wanting, is doomed from the start. 'She must slip something inside the organism to explain behavior on the outside, but once in she can never get back out; she is forced to answer an endless regress of questions related to private events.'

— Parrott, in answering the question: how does a rule evoke not only the behavior of hearing the rule, but also the behavior of following the rule with respect to the stimulus conditions specified? formulates a three-phase process — listening, understanding, and mediating. Vaughan argues that, 'The heart, and downfall, of Parrott's is summarized in these two sentences: "It is this orientation of the listener with respect to the things spoken of that is implied by the concept of

Negative Orientation

— in order to account for the control exerted by rules, rule-governed behaviour must be conceptualized as contingency-shaped behaviour

— as such, the only distinction between rule-governed and contingency-shaped behaviour is that the antecedent stimuli in the former case are always verbal

— the significance of this distinction is not fully appreciated by Skinner, however, owing to problems in his analysis of verbal behaviour

— specifically, while verbal episodes are not assumed to exemplify relations of reference, a referential interpretation of rules is made, despite the fact that rules are simply products of verbal behaviour

— one result of this confusion is the absence of a satisfactory account of rule-following activity

— this contradiction may be resolved by adopting a non-mentalistic concept of reference applicable to both verbal

behaviour and rule governance
— by this means an important
distinction between rule-
governed and contingency-
shaped behaviour may be
sustained, and the events of rule-
following may be explained

Parrott

reference. A referential response of
the verbal type is one which produces
reactions on the part of a listener with
respect to stimuli other than the
stimulus products of verbal
responding — it produces reactions to
the things spoken of." But these
"reactions" do not explain anything;
they are representations inside the
head, historical summaries of
contingencies of reinforcement. They
only evoke further questions ... what
is the origin of such reactions? Parrott
suggests that they are a function of a
history of reinforcement and
respondent conditioning. But then
why cannot the rule that evokes the
representations (perceptual reactions)
directly evoke the behavior described
in the rule? ... how does the
organism know which response to
engage in given the perceptual
reactions? Do the perceptual
reactions include "seeing" the
behavior described in the rule? How
does the organism know that it knows
...:

Vaughan Replies to Parrott

interpreted in behavioural terms
— the emphasis has been on verbal
behaviour with special attention to
rule-governed behaviour; most
cognitive research and theory has
completely neglected the role of
verbal behaviour in facilitating
intellectual activity; further, much of
the research in cognitive psychology is
research on verbal behaviour and the
verbal contingencies which shape and
maintain it
— cognitive psychologists have been
studying cognitive activity for some
time; unfortunately, they have not
acknowledged the role of verbal
behaviour, and the contingencies of
which it is a function, in their research
— as a consequence, they have cast their
analysis in terms of unmeasurable
processes out of reach in a science of
behaviour

Vaughan

functions can only be understood
by way of an explicit and specific
account of their historical
development

Parrott Replies to Vaughan

SKINNER'S ANALYSIS OF PERCEPTION/COGNITION

Negative Orientation	Positive Response to Negative Orientation	Positive Orientation	Negative Response to Positive Orientation
— operant and cognitive psychologists have been operating in their individual arenas for too long	— the role which Robertson wishes to make for perception is a broad one and is not limited to the 'problems of perception' but rather results in a 'perceptual psychology'	— Skinner's analysis of perceptual processes and the problems of perception has been, unlike his many other contributions, largely ignored by the psychology community	— there is no question that reinforcement histories influence behaviour, that the way one perceives the world influences behaviour
— cognitive psychology could benefit from operant psychology by addressing the question of how cognitive mechanisms may change as a function of a subject's history	— her case is better understood as a set of arguments for a particular form of representationalism; it is difficult to distinguish this from the earlier cases made in psychology for intervening variables or hypothetical constructs	— Skinner has published relevant papers and research on both visual and auditory perception', has articulated a critical analysis of a widely accepted theory of perception, and has offered an analysis of perception as stimulus control through differential reinforcement of discriminative responding	— however, it is not sufficient to attribute perception to stimulus control: perception functions not only on the antecedent side of contingencies but also on the consequence side; something must detect an antecedent as potential for reinforcement and register the change in environmental energy as a result of behaving
— evidence from the studies of contingency perception suggests that the very use of a particular cognitive process depends on environmental contingencies in the past	— whatever the ultimate fate of radical behaviourism, it probably has benefited by its isolation from mainstream psychology	— moreover, he has suggested an analysis of 'seeing' as behaviour, and traced the implications of respondent and operant conditioning when applied to seeing as a response	— whether or not one calls this detection 'perception', it is reasonable to assume that there is some internal mechanism which mediates antecedents and consequences; some data have supported a perceptual role in the effectiveness of contingency control
— the process of relation formation is examined and it is argued that operant psychologists should consider such a mechanism in discussing how something like 'insight in pigeons' takes place	— Skinner and co-workers have given one kind of reasonable answer to how two or more repertoires of behaviour are integrated, by discovering the necessary and sufficient conditions to produce the 'integration' that is the novel behaviour	*Knapp*	— regarding the issue of internal representation, Skinner's infinite regress argument may have been relevant for earlier views of representationalism but is inadequate for recent theories
— this process does not need to be described at a neurophysiological level in order to understand how it works any more than overt behaviour needs to be described at a neurophysiological level to understand how it works	— another kind of answer may be provided by a neurophysiologist		— a cognitive representation is nothing
	— how does a behind-the-scenes story add to either of these kinds of answers?		
	— wondering how an organism 'perceives' a contingency is not far		

— the level at which one operates depends critically on the question one wishes to address and the type of phenomenon that one is studying

Robertson

from wondering how a species 'perceives' evolution: the environment selects

— an organism can come under the discriminative control of a visual stimulus and presumably under the discriminative control of a 'relation' or 'contingency'

— do organisms form relationships, or are the relationships formed as arrangements in the environment?; it is the old matter of locating the associations where they occur, rather than have the organism 'make' the associations

— Skinner has discussed the problem of knowledge and the difficulties arising from knowledge conceived as a possession

— if any possibility of common agreement exists between radical behaviourists and cognitivists, it may be the manner in which some cognitivists have now come to perform what behaviour analysts term task analysis — in some respects this necessarily leads the cognitivist back to the environment and to the responses of the organism

Knapp Replies to Robertson

more than a set of computations that are related to each other in some way that mimics the relationships between structures in the world

— we are not looking at copies of what we see: we are looking at the world but make sense of it through a computational system

— when Skinner is pushed to address issues of cognition, he often resorts to arguments concerning value or importance

— once the role of something like perception is even considered in contingency effectiveness, its possible importance must be included in all of Skinner's examples of value: is it the environment or the perception of the environment that is important?

—arguments based on bias or utopian ideals are not appropriate bases from which to argue for scientific omission or revision

Robertson Replies to Knapp

Negative Orientation	Positive Response to Negative Orientation	Positive Orientation	Negative Response to Positive Orientation

NATURALISTIC ETHICS

— the chapter defends Skinner's contention that his principles of psychology permit the bridging of the is/ought gap; it seeks to show how it is possible to legitimately reason from the psychological – is of Skinner's principles to the moral-ought of practical reason	— Garrett's chapter draws essentially the same conclusion as Zuriff's with respect to Skinner's naturalist ethics: they (and possibly Skinner) agree that Skinner has not succeeded in logically deriving a system of ought-statements from his behavioural science of is-statements	— Skinner provides a behavioural interpretation of the behaviour of making ethical judgments; it consists of a number of plausible empirical hypotheses based on an extrapolation from behavioural laws discovered through the Skinnerian experimental analysis of behaviour	— Garrett confines his comments to clarifying the differences and similarities between Zuriff and himself, focusing first on the interpretation of Skinner and then on the possibility of a science of morals
— it is first necessary to show that Skinner has not done this; the first part of the chapter argues that Skinner has not disarmed Karl Popper's version of what is sometimes called the 'open-question argument' and that the open-question argument, when turned on Skinner's own analysis, really does expose an inadequate grounding of his genuinely moral claims	— they converge on this conclusion through different although parallel routes and it is instructive to analyze the similarities	— Skinner offers a prediction, also extrapolated from his experimental analysis, as to what will come to be the values of the society in future	— Garrett has tried to show why the reply of Skinner to Popper fails and so why his entire strategy fails
— the second part argues that Skinner's confidence in the use of his principles as a means of bridging the is/ought gap is nonetheless warranted	— however, Zuriff has suggested that Skinner does provide a more modest connection between his behavioural science and ethics: based on his principles of behaviour, he offers a *prediction* concerning what will eventually become the ethical principles of future societies	— Skinner makes recommendations about what ought to be our culture's current values; these recommendations as opposed to his predictions are not derived from the science of behaviour and are, therefore, not a naturalistic ethics in the strong sense	— there is no textual evidence given in support of what Zuriff calls Skinner's 'naturalistic deduction'; it is too obviously unsound, Skinner often tells us we must sacrifice what reinforces us for the good of the culture
— in particular it is argued that his psychological principles, if true, offer us excellent reasons for saying that the moral act, norm or culture (or community) is the	— it is this prediction that Zuriff believes Skinner has in mind when he replies to Popper; in this regard Garrett and Zuriff differ in their understanding of Skinner's response to Popper: Zuriff's view is that Skinner	— only if his recommendations were to be adopted would we have an ethics in which ethical questions can be answered by the objective and empirical methods of science	— Zuriff seems to be suggesting that Skinner is confusing the *norm* (or proposal) vs the *prediction* about the norm: either Skinner must be talking about the norm, in which case there is *no support*, or he must be talking about the prediction, in which case there is *no norm*
		— currently his ethics are a 'redefinitional naturalism' in which a precise naturalist system is suggested as a replacement for our present vague one	— this seems a more plausible argument to ascribe to Skinner than the naturalistic deduction;
		— although Skinner's ethical recommendations are not a logical deduction from the behavioural science, they perhaps are related to that science in another way	

one that regards everyone as an ends and which, therefore, everyone has a reason to support (viz. is universalizable)

— these are approximations to Kant's principles which no one doubts are genuine moral-oughts

— but if so, then to the extent that such principles can be derived from Skinner's psychology, Skinner is right in thinking the is/ought gap can be bridged by his psychology after all

Garrett

ignores validity and refers to his prediction

— Skinner can derive a prediction of future behaviour only if there are natural laws governing behaviour, i.e., only if humans are not autonomous beings; Skinner takes Popper's statement that it is 'possible to adopt a norm or its opposite' as an assertion of human free will and therefore contrary to his (predictive) connection between science and ethics; hence his response to Popper is a rejection of free will and thus an implicit reassertion of this derivation of a prediction about norms from statements of fact

— both Garrett and Zuriff offer their own ideas about how Skinner's insights can be explicated and extended: Zuriff offers a behavioural analysis of moral statements while Garrett sketches a science of morals

— Zuriff's main difficulty is in discovering how the moral imperatives Garrett suggests are derived from Skinnerian principles; the connection to Skinner is tenuous

Zuriff Replies to Garrett

— in a behavioural interpretation science is seen as the behaviour, verbal and non-verbal, of scientists

— these scientists form a community, both a verbal community and a value community

— it is possible that exposure to the contingencies of reinforcement prevailing in this community leads one to espouse the values Skinner proposes

— this shaping of value judgments might come about partly as a result of the contingencies of social reinforcement practised by scientists

— however, these social contingencies are only secondary, and are, of course, themselves in need of explanation

— perhaps the more basic contingencies arise in the very study of behaviour itself: scientists may come to value the survival of their culture and their species when they discover the beauty, the adaptiveness and the potential of human behaviour

Zuriff

however, it seems to Garrett to be more compatible with his own interpretation than with the 'naturalistic deduction' Zuriff ascribes to Skinner

— no matter which of the above interpretations is correct, Garrett's diagnosis of Skinner's failure remains just as valid; that is, it is Skinner's failure to deal with Popper's argument (the open-question argument) that underlies his failure; no matter how one reads Skinner, his analysis fails because he has not shown how to deduce a norm (an ought) from a fact (an is), because he mistakenly thinks that adopting a norm presupposes a free will (i.e., autonomy); Skinner underestimates the practicality of reason — our capacity to discriminate between good and bad reasons and to be moved only by good reasons

— Zuriff and Garrett differ over the future possibility of bridging the is/ought gap: Garrett thinks it is possible, Zuriff thinks not possible

Garrett Replies to Zuriff

Author Index

Abelson, R.P., 224, 233
Anau, Z.
   see Vogel and Anau
Anderson, J.R., 117, 120, 121
Anderson, S.J. and Saeger, W., 31, 34, 38
Antonitis, J.J., 133, 136
Aristotle, 246, 333
Arnold, W.J., 39
Aronson, J.L., 34, 36, 38
Ashby, E., 141
Audi, R., 224, 233
Ayer, A.J., 255, 256

Bach, K. and Harnish, R., 62, 67
Bachrack, A.J., 293
Bacon, F., 186
Baldwin, J.M., 140–1, 148
Balsam, P.
   see Gibbon and Balsam
Bandura, A., 194, 196, 210, 210, 217, 259, 261, 264
Barrett, J.E. and Stanley, J.A., 197, 201
Bateson, P.P.G. and Hinde, R.A., 233
Bateson, P.P.G. and Klopfer, P.H., 148
Bealer, G., 76
Beerbohm, M., 339
Begelman, D.A., 316, 317
Behavioral and Brain Sciences, 10
Bem, D.J., 86, 201, 226, 233
Bethlehem, D., 4–5, 89–97, 98–102, 337, 339, 346–7
Bevan, W., 293, 293n2
Binswanger, L., 246, 248
Blake, R.
   see Sekuler and Blake
Blanshard, B. and Skinner, B.F., 219, 233
Block, N., 230, 233, 339
Blough, D.S., 285, 293
Blough, D.S. and Blough, P., 285, 293
Bolles, A.C., 232n1, 233
Boren, J.J. *et al.*, 133, 136
Boring, E.G., 16, 19, 38, 285, 293, 293n3
Boring, E.C. and Lindzey, C., 97, 111

Boswell, J., 89, 97
Boulanger, B., 133, 136
Bovet, P., 134, 136
Bower, G.H., 164, 176
Branch, M.N., 31, 38, 212, 217, 229, 233
Breland, K. and Breland, M., 130, 136, 230, 233
Brentano, F., 63, 64, 244, 248
Brewer, W.R., 117, 121
Bridgman, P., 16, 38, 74n2
Broadbent, D.E., 41, 50
Brodbeck
   see Feigl and Brodbeck
Broughton, J.M. and Freeman-Moir, D.J., 74n1
Brown, S.C., 100
Brown, W.M., 10, 337–9
Brown, W.M. *et al.*, 339
Brownstein, A.J.
   see Hayes and Brownstein
Bunge, M., 129, 136, 230–1, 233
Burnheim, J., 244, 247n1, 248, 251, 254, 256
Bussod, N.
   see Jacobson and Bussod

Campbell, D.T., 141–2, 148
Carbone, V.J., 29, 34, 38
Carlson, E.A., 119, 121
Carpenter, F., 99, 100
Carroll, L., 251
Catania, A.C., 1, 10, 31, 52, 197, 202, 229, 233, 262, 264, 293, 293n6
Catania, A.C. *et al.*, 230, 233, 263, 264
Changeux, J.P., 128, 136
Chisholm, R.M., 240, 244, 248
Chomsky, N., 21, 116, 121, 127, 136, 170, 176, 194, 261, 264
Cialdini, R.B. *et al.*, 226, 233
Clare, A., 93, 97
Clark, F.C. and Smith, J.B., 197, 202
Cohen, D., 48, 50
Cole, J.K., 233
Combs, A.W.
   see Snygg and Combs
Commons, M.L. and Nevin, J.A., 233

Subject Index

Falmer International Master-Minds Challenged

Psychology Series Editors: Drs Sohan and Celia Modgil

B.F. SKINNER

Consensus and Controversy

Essays in Honour of B.F. Skinner

D0203126